WRITING LIFE

A Canadian Student's Guide to Thinking, Writing, and Researching

John Van Rys
Redeemer University College

Randall VanderMey
Westmont College

Verne Meyer
Dordt College

Patrick Sebranek
University of Wisconsin-Whitewater

1914–2014
Nelson Education celebrates 100 years of Canadian publishing

NELSON EDUCATION

CELEBRATE LIFELONG LEARNING

NELSON EDUCATION

Writing Life: A Canadian Student's Guide to Thinking, Writing, and Researching
by John Van Rys, Randall VanderMey, Verne Meyer, and Patrick Sebranek

Vice President, Editorial Higher Education:
Anne Williams

Executive Editor:
Laura Macleod

Executive Marketing Manager:
Amanda Henry

Developmental Editor:
Jacquelyn Busby

Photo Researcher/Permissions Coordinator:
Sandra Mark

Senior Production Project Manager:
Imoinda Romain

Production Service:
Cenveo Publisher Services

Copy Editor:
Mariko Obokata

Proofreader:
Pushpa V Giri

Indexer:
BIM Publishing Services

Design Director:
Ken Phipps

Managing Designer:
Franca Amore

Interior Design:
Sebranek, Inc.

Cover Design:
Trinh Truong

Cover Image:
Ryan Lane/Getty Images

Compositor:
Cenveo Publisher Services

Library and Archives Canada Cataloguing in Publication

Van Rys, John C. (John Cornell), author

Writing life : a Canadian student's guide to thinking, writing, researching / John Van Rys, Randall VanderMey, Verne Meyer, Patrick Sebranek.

Includes index.
Previous title: The college writer.
ISBN 978-0-17-653159-1 (pbk.)

1. English language—Rhetoric— Textbooks. 2. Report writing— Textbooks. I. Title.

PE1408.R97 2014
808'.042   C2014-900800-7

ISBN-13: 978-0-17-653159-1
ISBN-10: 0-17-653159-9

Brief Contents

Contents

Analytical Writing

Persuasive Writing

III. Research and Writing

IV. Handbook

Thematic Table of Contents for Readings

Campus Life

Canada and the World

Character and Conscience

Culture and Society

Disease and Death

Diversity and Equity

Environments Natural and Made

Ethics and Ideology

Ethnicity and Identity

Family, Friends, Love

Gender and Integrity

Human Nature

Terror and Our Time

Work and Play

Preface

What is the relevance of writing in an age such as ours—an age of high youth unemployment, 140-character tweets, and a Web full of information? In a world characterized by serious gridlock (both in traffic and in politics), what productive role can writing play?

Writing Life is a textbook built on the belief that good writing matters. For students, many of these reasons are practical: deepening thinking skills, improving communication skills, engaging the content in a field of study, preparing for a profession, and landing an internship or a job. Beyond the classroom, however, good writing (and good reading) can be essential to work life, home life, and civic engagement. In fact, such writing and reading are part of living a larger life; life can be immeasurably enriched by productive writing and thoughtful reading.

It is this belief that lies behind *Writing Life: A Canadian Student's Guide to Thinking, Writing, and Researching*. The text is divided into four parts: (1) a rhetoric that introduces the writing process; (2) a reader comprising a wealth of sample essays and instruction in a range of writing forms; (3) a guide to doing quality research in the Internet age; and (4) a handbook offering practical guidance in grammar, punctuation, usage, and mechanics. Taken together, these four sections offer students comprehensive guidance for the writing required in postsecondary work and beyond. In other words, *Writing Life* is the only writing textbook that Canadian students need. How so? It offers students the following features.

Canadian Content in Global Context

Rooted in the lead author's specialization in Canadian literature and the Canadian essay, *Writing Life* addresses Canadian concerns in a global context.

- **Sample Essays by Canadian Authors and Authors with Strong Canadian Connections:** The sample essays have been written by professional writers, including such well-known authors as Margaret Atwood, Will Ferguson, Thomas King, June Callwood, Lawrence Hill, Adam Gopnik, Malcolm Gladwell, and David Suzuki, as well as young writers such as Emma Teitel. In addition, Canadian students are well represented in the student essays, with 17 essays by students at seven different Canadian postsecondary institutions.

- **A Rich Range of Topics:** As shown in the alternative thematic table of contents, *Writing Life* contains student and professional essays on a wide range of topics that concern Canadian students and instructors in the 21st century. A few examples: green employment, the ascetic philosophy of hipsters and hobos, the appropriation of the Aboriginal in North American culture, hockey understood through game theory, Facebook's development of Timeline, social action in the social media age, the science of the knuckleball, an ecocritical understanding of *Charlotte's Web*, WikiLeaks and democracy, building a better ketchup bottle, changes to Calgary's cultural landscape, and a critique of Fair Trade. From light to serious, the sample essays are rich in thought and illustrate writing strategies that students can emulate.

- **Writing Conventions and Practices:** In its treatment of grammar, punctuation, mechanics, and usage, *Writing Life* presents the most current Canadian practices.

Practical and Engaging Writing Instruction

Writing Life takes a can-do approach to writing. From the design of instruction to the examples and illustrations, the text divides the writing process into a series of doable tasks. Key features include the following:

- **Accessible, Concise Instruction:** The "at-a-glance" visual format presents concepts in manageable "chunks" formatted as one- or two-page spreads. Numbering, bullets, colour, and other features make the instruction easy to access and use.

- **Attention to the Writing Process:** Part I of *Writing Life* offers complete instruction on the writing process, including elements that often challenge students, such as rhetorical analysis, prewriting strategies, and revising. Writing-process instruction is then reinforced in the Part II chapters on forms of writing and in Part III, on research writing.

- **Helpful Examples and Illustrations:** In addition to the engaging samples of student and professional essays, *Writing Life* instructs by example from the first page to the end. Specific sentences, paragraphs, images, and diagrams illustrate virtually all writing concepts.

- **Coaching Tone:** As authors, our approach is to speak directly to students. We draw from our own experiences and our love of writing to encourage students to improve their own writing.

- **Learning Objectives:** To check student progress in writing improvement, each chapter begins with a list of learning objectives and ends with a learning-objectives checklist—allowing students a degree of self-assessment.

- **Visual Appeal:** In addition to the textbook's accessible design, *Writing Life* offers attention to the marriage of words and images in contemporary writing practice. This material includes the image and "visually speaking" prompt at the beginning of chapters, attention to critical viewing in the first chapter, the use of graphic organizers in the writing process, and integration of graphics into some student essays.

- **A Comprehensive Grammar Handbook:** Part IV of *Writing Life* gives students the complete instruction that they need in grammar, punctuation, mechanics, and usage—all in a ready reference format that will help students revise, edit, and proofread their own writing, and enable instructors to key their feedback on student writing to specific instruction.

- **Thoughtful Activities:** Each chapter in Parts I to III ends with activities that encourage students to reflect on their own writing practices, to apply what they have learned in the chapter, and to consider specific writing projects.

Critical Thinking Linked with Academic Writing

To help students succeed in their postsecondary studies (in any field of study), *Writing Life* integrates instruction in critical thinking with a focus on academic writing.

- **A Range of Writing Forms:** While offering instruction in personal essays, the text focuses extensively on academic modes—from a range of analytical writing strategies (e.g., definition, classification, comparison-contrast) to a variety of argumentative forms (e.g., position papers, proposals for solving problems). Moreover, one chapter explores reading literature as a case study in analysis, and online bonus chapters focus on writing in the sciences, workplace writing, and writing for the Web.

- **Critical-Thinking Elements:** From the first chapter, with its emphasis on critical thinking through reading, viewing, and writing, *Writing Life* encourages students to strengthen the thinking–writing relationship. This first-chapter instruction is reinforced throughout the text by attention to rhetorical analysis. The end-of-chapter activities include attention to critical thinking, particularly through the use of a thought-provoking quotation. In a similar way, each sample essay is followed by "reading for better writing" questions.

- **Common Traits of Academic Writing:** Introduced in Chapter 2 are common traits of academic writing—ideas, organization, voice, sentence style, word choice, correctness, and design. This introduction is then followed by integrated attention to these traits elsewhere in the text.

- **Research in the Internet Age:** Given the significant changes to the information landscape over the past two decades, *Writing Life* gives students what they need to conduct quality research today: an introduction to the wired library, guidance for using scholarly databases, in-depth treatment of source evaluation, and discussions of information giants such as Google and Wikipedia.

- **Academic Form and Style:** This textbook encourages students to absorb a mature understanding of the essay—to take a leap beyond the five-paragraph essay (the safe, familiar high-school hamburger). *Writing Life* introduces students to richer writing strategies, more distinctive levels of style, and more complex thesis thinking.

- **Attention to Academic Integrity:** In Part I of the text, students are reminded about "Working with Sources"; however, in Part III especially, students are instructed in building credibility, avoiding plagiarism, and documenting sources effectively. *Writing Life* offers full treatment of both MLA and APA referencing systems.

About the Nelson Education Teaching Advantage (NETA)

The **Nelson Education Teaching Advantage (NETA)** program delivers research-based instructor resources that promote student engagement and higher-order thinking to enable the success of Canadian students and educators. To ensure the high quality of these materials, all Nelson ancillaries have been professionally copy-edited.

Be sure to visit Nelson Education's **Inspired Instruction** website at http://www.nelson.com/inspired/ to find out more about NETA. Don't miss the testimonials of instructors who have used NETA supplements and seen student engagement increase!

Planning Your Course: *NETA Engagement* presents materials that help instructors deliver engaging content and activities to their classes. **NETA Instructor's Manuals** not only identify the topics that cause students the most difficulty, but also describe techniques and resources to help students master these concepts. Dr. Roger Fisher's *Instructor's Guide to Classroom Engagement* accompanies every Instructor's Manual.

Teaching Your Students: *NETA Presentation* has been developed to help instructors make the best use of Microsoft® PowerPoint® in their classrooms. With a clean and uncluttered design developed by Maureen Stone of StoneSoup Consulting, **NETA PowerPoints** features slides with improved readability, more multi-media and graphic materials, activities to use in class, and tips for instructors on the Notes page. A copy of *NETA Guidelines for Classroom Presentations* by Maureen Stone is included with each set of PowerPoint slides.

Technology in Teaching: *NETA Digital* is a framework based on Arthur Chickering and Zelda Gamson's seminal work "Seven Principles of Good Practice in Undergraduate Education" (AAHE Bulletin, 1987) and the follow-up work by Chickering and Stephen C. Ehrmann, "Implementing the Seven Principles: Technology as Lever"(AAHE Bulletin, 1996). This aspect of the NETA program guides the writing and development of our **digital products** to ensure that they appropriately reflect the core goals of contact, collaboration, multimodal learning, time on task, prompt feedback, active learning, and high expectations. The resulting focus on pedagogical utility, rather than technological wizardry, ensures that all of our technology supports better outcomes for students.

Instructor's Resources

All NETA and other key instructor ancillaries are provided on the Instructor Companion Site at www.nelson.com/site/writinglife, giving instructors the ultimate tool for customizing lectures and presentations.

NETA PowerPoint: Microsoft® PowerPoint® lecture slides for every chapter have been created and many feature key figures, tables, and photographs from *Writing Life*. NETA principles of clear design and engaging content have been incorporated throughout, making it simple for instructors to customize the deck for their courses.

NETA Instructor's Manual: This resource is organized according to the textbook chapters and addresses key educational concerns, such as typical stumbling blocks student face and how to address them.

DayOne: Day One—Prof InClass is a PowerPoint presentation that instructors can customize to orient students to the class and their text at the beginning of the course.

Student Ancillaries

Nelson à la Carte

Using Nelson à la Carte, students can test their knowledge by completing a series of exercises. They can work through numerous exercises, covering all the major topics in the book. For each chapter, students are encouraged to first take the pre-test for each topic. The pre-tests assess the students' initial grasp of the subject content before they encounter the material in class and highlight the areas students should review. Following the pre-test, students can focus on their areas of weakness by completing an array of exercises, including fill-in-the-blank, short-answer, true/false, multiple-choice, and other types of questions. Other student resources include Model Student Papers, bonus online chapters, videos and video exercises. Nelson à la Carte features a grade book so instructors can easily monitor and track students' progress.

Visit NELSONbrain.com to start using Nelson à la Carte for *Writing Life*. Enter the Online Access Code from the card included with your text. If a code card is not provided, you can purchase instant access at NELSONbrain.com.

Acknowledgments

As authors, we are grateful to a long list of people who have made *Writing Life* a reality.

First, we thank the many students who have shared their writing with us for this project. It is for student writers like you that we have written this text.

Second, thank you to the many colleagues who encouraged their students to share their writing with us: David Anonby, Ashley Barkman, Darren Brouwer, Katharine Bubel, Lydia Forssander-Song, Gene Haas, Jamie Hall, Tim Heath, Jim Payton, Sara Pearson, Doug Sikkema, Jitse Van Der Meer, and Helen Vreugdenhil. We appreciate the good work that you are doing in nurturing writers, whatever their field of study.

Third, thank you to the many reviewers who were instrumental in the development of this text. This list includes those who helped in the writing of five editions of the U.S. edition, but in particular we thank the following reviewers for their input into the Canadian edition:

Robyn Buchan, Lambton College
John Carroll, University of the Fraser Valley
Shannon Catherine MacRae, Niagara College Canada
Karen B. McLaren, Canadore College
Lance Semak, Lethbridge College
Gabriele Spaulding, Selkirk College

Lastly, we extend a special thanks to the Nelson team for their enthusiastic collaboration on *Writing Life*: Laura Macleod (Executive Editor), Jacquelyn Busby (Developmental Editor), Imoinda Romain (Senior Production Project Manager), Mariko Obokata (Copy Editor), Sandra Mark and Lynn Mcleod (Permissions), Rajachitra S. (Project Manager), and Amanda Henry (Executive Marketing Manager).

I. Rhetoric:
A Student's Guide to Writing

Chapter 1

Critical Thinking Through Reading, Viewing, and Writing

Writing life: the theme of this book is that writing and life are connected in practical, thoughtful, and imaginative ways. Our school lives involve learning to write and writing to learn. We write to get things done in life. And sometimes we even write our lives.

Moreover, we encounter words and images every day— we are readers and viewers, as well as writers. Exchanging these messages constitutes communication, a complex process that involves several variables. In your classes, such communication—whether in reading articles, viewing films, or writing essays—requires critical thinking, which puts ideas in context, makes connections between them, and tests their meaning. This chapter provides strategies for thinking critically as you read, view, and write.

Visually Speaking   Figure 1.1 shows people viewing art in a museum. What thinking practices does such viewing involve? Consider, as well, other types of images. What viewing do you do, for what reasons, and using what brain power?

Learning **Objectives**

By working through this chapter, you will be able to

- actively read different written texts.
- produce personal responses to texts.
- objectively summarize texts.
- actively view, analyze, and critique visual images.
- implement strategies to think critically about topics.
- practise modes of thinking through writing.

© Tetra Images/Getty Images

fig. 1.1

Reading Actively

Critical thinking begins with active reading that engages texts in a kind of mental dialogue. To initiate this dialogue, use strategies such as engaging, mapping, outlining, evaluating, responding to, and summarizing the text.

Engage the Text

Many of the complex texts that you read for your classes require a level of attentiveness and engagement beyond the everyday reading you might do. Use these techniques:

- **Remove distractions.** Engaged reading requires that you disengage from all distractions such as your cellphone, Facebook, or TV.
- **Take your time.** Read in stretches of about forty-five minutes, followed by short breaks. And when you break, think about what you have read.
- **Assess the rhetorical situation.** Where and when was this text written and published? Who is the author, and why did he or she write the piece?
- **Preview, read, review.** Start by previewing the text: scan the title, opening and closing paragraphs, headings, topic sentences, and graphics. Next, read the text carefully, asking questions such as "What does this mean?" Finally, review what you have learned.
- **Write while reading.** Take notes, and annotate the text by highlighting main points, writing a "?" beside puzzling parts, or jotting key insights in the margin.

Sample Text

The following article was written by Kate Lunau and first published in *Maclean's* on March 25, 2013. Read the essay, using the tips for engaged reading listed above and answering questions like these: What is the article's central idea? How is that idea elaborated? In what ways does the article impact your own thoughts about careers?

Good Clean Work

For Chris Rogers, owner of Corporate Chemicals and Equipment in St. Catharines, Ontario, the wake-up call came when his father Cecil was diagnosed with lymphatic cancer in 2000. Cecil, who owned the business before Chris took over, had worked in the industry since he was 18. "He opened my eyes to what he thought was the cause," Rogers says: the vats of chemicals that surrounded Cecil through his working life. "I started to rethink things." The company, which makes and sells sanitation supplies, started going green—a philosophy that's affected everything from products to marketing and, of course, its employees. "The green chemistry of today is the everyday chemistry of tomorrow," he says. The same could be true of green jobs. [1]

Canada's green economy is growing fast. Our clean-technology sector, made up of more than 700 companies, saw an 11 per cent jump in employment between 2008 and 2010, according to a January report from the Pembina Institute, a non-profit environmental think tank. Once considered a niche, the green-jobs sector is now [2]

Kate Lunau, "Good Clean Work", *Maclean's*, 25 March 2013. Reproduced by permission of *Maclean's Magazine*.

comparable to the booming oil and gas extraction sector, and has exceeded the aerospace industry, says a 2012 report from Analytica Advisors, an Ottawa-based consulting firm that specializes in clean energy.

Canada's "green-collar jobs" aren't just found at clean-technology firms. More than 12 per cent of the Canadian workforce "has some sort of environmental initiatives within its work," says Grant Trump, CEO of the non-profit ECO Canada. Another four per cent of the workforce spends more than 50 per cent of its time on environmental activities, he says. And 17 per cent of Canadian companies—318,000 in total—employ one or more environmental professional.

3

The trend is relatively new. "When I was young, there were no environmental jobs. The closest you could get was cleaning up spills," says Tom Heintzman, co-founder of Bullfrog Power, a green-energy provider. "The notion of the environment as an economic driver didn't exist." One idea pushing the green economy forward is that environmental and economic goals don't have to be at odds with each other—that it can be good business to go green, and the two often go hand-in-hand.

4

The definition of environmental employment can encompass all sorts of professions, notes a 2012 ECO Canada study on the Canadian labour force and the green economy. These include jobs that demand environmental skills, such as an air-quality engineer or an architect who creates sustainable designs; and those that don't, such as agricultural workers on organic farms. After analyzing 835 online job ads from March through May 2012, the ECO study, which focused on jobs that require environmental expertise, estimated that positions linked to the green economy account for at least one per cent of recent vacancies, probably more. "It's grown tremendously," Trump says. The largest number of vacancies was in environmental protection, resource conservation, renewable energy, green services and sustainable planning or urban design.

5

Growth in environmental jobs is unlikely to slow as the green-energy industry expands, with more investment in wind and solar power as a key driver. Oil giant Royal Dutch Shell recently predicted that solar power could become the world's biggest source of energy in the next 50 years.

6

As companies place increasing emphasis on environmental practices, the skills required in the workplace are bound to change. Nearly half of job openings linked to the green economy require between five and 10 years' work experience, the ECO Canada report notes, and the vast majority (98 per cent) demand some post-secondary education. "Two-thirds of my sales reps have a university degree, but had no concept of green until they got here," says Rogers, who has 15 full-time employees. (Manufacturers provide ongoing training about the products they sell.) The type of worker Rogers looks for is changing: "people who are open-minded, who have the ability to self-educate. That's a big thing."

7

Corporate Chemicals traces its roots back to the 1930s, when Maurice Rogers, Chris's grandfather, sold sanitation supplies. "Niagara was, up until the early 2000s, a very industrial area. For us as a company, that was a key focus," says Rogers, who took the company reins from his father in 2005. (Cecil has been cancer-free for 11 years.) The region's shift toward a greener economy is reflected in changes at Corporate Chemicals and countless other local businesses. If Rogers and others are right, more will come on board, and as the green economy continues to grow, green jobs will follow.

8

Map the Text

One way to understand a text is by mapping it through "clustering." Start by naming the main topic in an oval at the centre of the page. Then branch out using lines and "balloons," where each balloon contains a word or phrase for one major subtopic. Branch out in further layers of balloons to show even more subpoints, as in Figure 1.2.

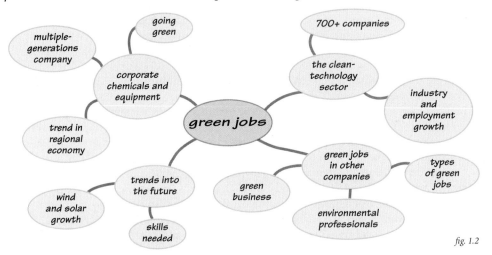

fig. 1.2

Outline the Text

Outlining is the traditional way of showing all the major parts, points, and subpoints in a text by stating those points in parallel structure. See pages 49–52 for more on outlines.

Sample Outline for "Good Clean Work"

Introduction: Chris Rogers of Corporate Chemicals and Equipment turned his company green.

1. Canada's green economy is growing fast.
   a. The clean-technology sector has seen an 11 percent employment increase between 2008 and 2010.
   b. Mainstream companies are adding "green-collar jobs".
   c. Economic and environmental goals no longer have to be in opposition.
2. Environmental employment can refer to many different professions.
3. The trend in growth of environmental jobs is expected to continue.
   a. One key driver of growth is wind and solar power investment.
   b. The growth trend likely means that the necessary workplace skills will likely change.

Conclusion: Corporate Chemicals and Equipment is participating in a regional shift toward a greener economy.

Evaluate the Text

Critical reading does not mean disproving the text or disapproving of it. It means thoughtfully inspecting, weighing, and evaluating the writer's ideas. To strengthen your reading skills, learn to evaluate texts using the criteria below.

1. **Judge the reading's credibility.** Where was it published? How reliable is the author? How current is the information? How accurate and complete does it seem to be? In addition, consider the author's tone of voice, attitude, and apparent biases.

   > *Discussion:* Kate Lunau, the author of "Good Clean Work," has a journalism diploma from Concordia University and writes on science, health, and justice for *Maclean's*, Canada's best known news magazine. How do the credentials of the publisher and author affect your reading of the article? How does the article itself build or break credibility?

2. **Put the reading in a larger context.** How do the text's ideas match what you know from other sources? Which details of background, history, and social context help you understand this text's perspective? How have things changed or remained the same since the text's publication?

   > *Discussion:* How does "Good Clean Work" relate to trends in environmentalism and in economics (e.g., recent developments in pipelines and climate change, the continuing effects of the 2008 Great Recession)? How does this article relate to trends in employment (e.g., youth employment)?

3. **Evaluate the reasoning and support.** Is the reasoning clear and logical? Are the examples and other supporting details appropriate and enlightening? Are inferences (what the text implies) consistent with the tone and message? (Look especially for hidden logic and irony that undercut what is said explicitly.)

   > *Discussion:* Lunau begins and ends with the story of Corporate Chemicals and Equipment in St. Catharines. How effective is this example? How well does it relate to the discussion in the middle of the article? The middle of the article contains many summaries of reports and statistical analysis. How logical is the analysis? Do the conclusions that follow from the statistics appear to be sound?

4. **Reflect on how the reading challenges you.** Which of your beliefs and values does the reading call into question? What discomfort does it create? Does your own perspective skew your evaluation?

   > *Discussion:* Do you see environmentalism and business as opposites or as possible partners? Do your own job interests lie in the sector explored by the article, or elsewhere? How do your interests and attitudes impact your thoughts and feelings about Lunau's article?

 For additional help evaluating texts, see pages 418–421. For information on detecting logical fallacies, which weaken writers' arguments, see pages 317–320.

Responding to a Text

In a sense, when you read a text, you enter into a dialogue with it. Your response expresses your turn in the dialogue. Such a response can take varied forms, from a journal entry to a blog to a posting in an online-comments forum.

Follow These Guidelines for Response Writing

On the surface, responding to a text seems perfectly natural—just let it happen. But it can be a bit more complicated. A written response typically is not the same as a private diary entry but is instead shared with other readers, who may be in your class or someone else. To develop a fitting response, keep in mind common expectations for this kind of writing, as well as your instructor's requirements, if the response is for a course:

1. **Be honest.** Although you want to remain sensitive to the context in which you will share your response, be bold enough to be honest about your reaction to the text— what it makes you think, feel, and question. To that end, a response usually allows you to express yourself directly using the pronoun "I."

2. **Be fluid.** Let the flow of your thoughts guide you in what you write. Don't stop to worry about grammar, punctuation, mechanics, and spelling. These can be quickly cleaned up before you share or submit your response.

3. **Be reflective.** Generally, the goal of a response is to offer thoughtful reflection as opposed to knee-jerk reaction. Show, then, that you are engaging the text's ideas, relating them to your own experience, looking both inward and outward. Avoid a shallow reaction that comes from skimming the text or misreading it.

4. **Be selective.** By nature, a response must limit its focus; it cannot exhaust all your reactions to the text. So zero in on one or two elements of your response, and run with those to see where they take you in your dialogue with the text.

Sample Response

Here is part of a student's response to Kate Lunau's "Good Clean Work" on pages 4–5. Note the informality and the exploratory tone.

> Lunau's article on green jobs and the green economy makes me think about job trends, especially as I'm trying to sort out what to study and what job choices might be there when I graduate—especially given all the doom and gloom about unemployment for people my age. I'd like to be idealistic and work for a green company, or at least one that follows sustainable practices, but sometimes being practical takes over. I may need to take what I can get, or maybe when I get a job I should be thinking about ways of making the job and the company "greener"? I sometimes wonder, though, about what the "green economy" really means and whether it's real? Is the Corporate Chemicals company in the article really "green"? Is "green" all about marketing and good PR, or is there some genuine change at work?

Summarizing a Text

Writing a summary disciplines you by making you pull only essentials from a reading—the main points, the thread of the argument. By doing so, you create a brief record of the text's contents and exercise your ability to comprehend, analyze, and synthesize.

Use These Guidelines for Summary Writing

Writing a summary requires sifting out the least important points, sorting the essential ones to show their relationships, and stating those points in your own words. Follow these guidelines:

1. **Skim first; then read closely.** First, get a sense of the whole, including the main idea and strategies for support. Then read carefully, taking notes as you do.

2. **Capture the text's argument.** Review your notes and annotations, looking for main points and clear connections. State these briefly and clearly, in your own words. Include only what is essential, excluding most examples and details. Don't say simply that the text talks about its subject; tell what it says about that subject.

3. **Test your summary.** Aim to objectively provide the heart of the text; avoid interjecting your own opinions and presence as a writer. Don't confuse an objective summary of a text with a response to it (shown on the previous page). Check your summary against the original text for accuracy and consistency.

Sample Summary

Below is a student's summary of Kate Lunau's "Good Clean Work" on pages 4–5. Note how the summary writer includes only main points and phrases them in her own words. She departs from the precise order of details, but records them accurately.

> If the example of Corporate Chemicals and Equipment is a sign, Canada's economy is going green at an increasing rate. The clean-technology sector itself has seen healthy growth, shown by an 11 percent increase in employment between 2008 and 2010. Even mainstream companies are contributing by adding "green-collar jobs" through environmental programs at work. Taken together, these trends suggest that business and environmental concerns do not have to be in conflict. As a result, the trend in environmental employment (which includes many professions that require environmental skills and many that do not) is expected to show continued growth. In particular, wind and solar power investment is one key force behind this expected growth. With such growth, workplace skills will likely need to change.

INSIGHT Writing formal summaries—whether as part of literature reviews or as abstracts—is an important skill, especially in the social and natural sciences. For help, go to www.nelson.com/writinglife.

Thinking Through Viewing

Images are created to communicate, just as words are. Most images in everyday life are made to communicate very quickly—magazine covers, ads, signs, movie trailers, and so forth. Other images require contemplation, such as the *Mona Lisa*. When you view an image, view actively and critically.

Actively View Images

Survey the image. See the image as a whole so that you can absorb its overall idea. Look for the image's focal point—what your eye is drawn to. Also consider the relationship between the image's foreground and background, its left content and right content, and its various colours.

Inspect the image. Let your sight touch every part of the image, as if you were reading Braille. Hints of its meaning may lurk in the tiny details as well as in the relationship between the image's parts.

Question the image. Think in terms of each part of the rhetorical situation.
- **Designer:** Who created the image? Why did the person create it?
- **Message:** What is the subject of the image? What is the purpose?
- **Medium:** How was the image originally shown? How is it currently shown?
- **Viewer:** Who is the intended viewer? Why are you viewing the image?
- **Context:** When and where did the image first appear? When and where does it appear now? How does the image relate to its context?

Understand the purpose. Different images have different purposes. Ask yourself, "What is this image meant to do?" and then decide on an appropriate response:
- **Arouse curiosity?** Open your imagination, but stay on guard.
- **Entertain?** Look for the pleasure or the joke, but be wary of excess or of ethically questionable material in the image.
- **Inform or educate?** Search for key instruction, noting what's left out.
- **Illustrate?** Relate the image to the words or concept being illustrated: Does the image clarify or distort the meaning?
- **Persuade?** Examine how the image appeals to the viewer's needs, from safety and satisfaction to self-worth. Are the appeals manipulative, clichéd, or fallacious? Do they play on emotions to bypass reason?
- **Summarize?** Look for the essential message in the image: Does that main idea correspond with the written text?

catwalker/Shutterstock.com

MOLDOVA 3L

View an Image

The use of *minors* as *miners* is no *minor* problem.

fig. 1.3

From VANDERMEY/VANDERMEY. The College Writer, 3E. © 2009 Wadsworth, a part of Cengage Learning, Inc.
Reproduced by permission. www.cengage.com/permissions

Discussion ▼

Figure 1.3 by Chris Krenzke and the caption by Verne Meyer effectively combine humour with instruction. Originally published in a high-school writing handbook, the image's aim is to teach students about a specific word-usage problem while also entertaining them. The image is line art in the "comic" genre, using a humorous scene to convey a serious message. Here are some thoughts on how you might actively view this image:

1. **Survey.** The image tells a story of heavily burdened children working under the demanding supervision of an authoritarian male. That story moves from left to right, from breaking rocks to loading rocks to carrying rocks toward a likely distant destination, the destination pointed to by the man. The black-and-white medium accentuates the starkness.

2. **Inspect.** In terms of the illustration's details, each figure is striking. The individual children share a thinness in their bodies and a strain in their faces. The four children in the line are pictured as beasts of burden bent over by bags that dwarf them. The repetition of figures emphasizes the trudging repetition of their work, and each child in line is pressed farther toward the ground. As for the man, his back is straight and his posture tall. His enormous chin, large nose, overly long but skinny arm, and sharply pointed finger suggest a negative authority. His stubbly face and his caveman clothing add to this figure's prehistoric character.

3. **Question.** Who is the artist Chris Krenzke? When did he first create this image? In what book was it published? When? Why did Krenzke use this caveman style? Who or what do "minors," "miners," and "minor" refer to in the illustration?

4. **Relate.** The connection between the sentence and the image becomes clear when the viewer realizes that "minors" are children not of a legal age to work, "miners" refers to an occupation, and "minor" means insignificant. But the image prompts other connections: the history of horrific child-labour practices during the Industrial Revolution as well as continuing child-labour issues in today's global economy. With these allusions, Krenzke succeeds in deepening the instruction offered by his art.

Interpreting an Image

Interpreting an image follows naturally from viewing or "reading" the image. Interpreting means figuring out what the image or design is meant to do, say, or show. Interpreting requires you to think more deeply about each element of the rhetorical situation shown in Figure 1.4, and complications with each element.

fig. 1.4

- **Designer:** Who created the image—a photographer, a painter, a Web designer, an eyewitness using a smartphone? Why did the person create it? What other people might have been involved—editors, patrons?

  Complications: The designer might be unknown or a group.

- **Message:** What is the subject of the image? How is the subject portrayed? What is the main purpose of the image—to entertain, inform, persuade, entice, or shock?

  Complications: The message might be mixed, implied, ironic, unwelcome, or distorted. The subject might be vague, unfamiliar, complex, or disturbing.

- **Medium:** What is the image—a painting, a cartoon panel, a photo? How might the image have been modified over time? What visual language has the sender used?

  Complications: The medium might be unusual or unfamiliar, or more than one medium may be involved. The visual languages might be literal, stylized, numeric, symbolic, and so on.

- **Viewer:** Whom was the image made for? Are you part of the intended audience? What is your relationship with the designer? Do you agree with the message? How comfortable are you with the medium? What is your overall response to the image?

  Complications: You might be uninterested in, unfamiliar with, or biased toward the message.

- **Context:** What was the context in which the image was first presented? What context surrounds the image now? Does the image fit its context or fight it?

  Complications: The context might be disconnected, ironic, changing, or multilayered.

INSIGHT Like words, visuals can be clichés—trite, misleading, or worn-out expressions of concepts or ideas. For example, TV ads for weight-loss drugs commonly picture scantily clad, fit young people, deceptively linking use of the drug to beauty, youth, and sex.

Interpret an Image

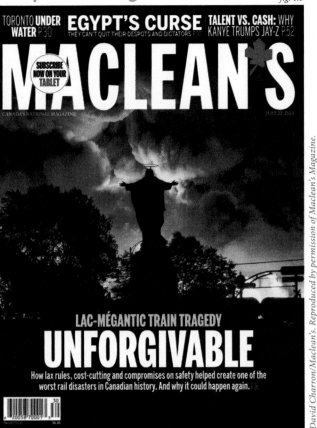

fig. 1.5

TORONTO **UNDER WATER** P.30 **EGYPT'S CURSE** THEY CAN'T QUIT THEIR DESPOTS AND DICTATORS P.36 **TALENT VS. CASH:** WHY KANYE TRUMPS JAY-Z P.52

MACLEAN'S

CANADA'S NATIONAL MAGAZINE   JULY 22 2013

SUBSCRIBE NOW ON YOUR TABLET

LAC-MÉGANTIC TRAIN TRAGEDY

UNFORGIVABLE

How lax rules, cost-cutting and compromises on safety helped create one of the worst rail disasters in Canadian history. And why it could happen again.

David Charron/Maclean's. Reproduced by permission of Maclean's Magazine.

Designer: Photographer David Charron; cover designers for *Maclean's*

Message: The cover reads "Unforgiveable" in big, bold letters. The message is that the train derailment, explosions, and fire that killed dozens of people and destroyed the centre of Lac Mégantic on July 6, 2013, represent a moral failure, not just an accidental disaster.

Medium: Digital colour photograph

Viewer: The intended viewer is anyone interested in the tragedy, meaning that the image serves a persuasive purpose along with its message.

Context: As part of the cover, this photograph serves as the magazine's first statement about the disaster.

Discussion ▼

This vivid colour photograph captures a moment in the unfolding disaster that took place in Lac Mégantic. On July 6, 2013, a train derailed in the centre of this small Quebec town, resulting in the deaths of 47 people.

The power of this image is found in both the sharp contrasts and the suggestive symbolism. In the background, the bright yellows and reds of the exploding tanker cars flare up into the sky, throwing everything in the foreground into dark relief. The result is an image that captures something of the destructive force of the night-time explosions. The religious symbolism, too, is clear and vivid. The explosions, hellish and deadly in nature and appearance, outline sharply the religious statue. Likely a figure of Christ, the statue—haloed and arms outstretched to suggest welcome, love, and care—offers both a contrast to the violence behind it and a commentary on the moral failure represented by the tragedy. In a way, the image elevates the events to the level of enduring spiritual concerns about human caring and human destructiveness at war with each other.

Evaluating an Image

As a critical thinker, you must do more than understand and interpret an image you encounter: You must assess its quality, truthfulness, and value. In other words, you must evaluate it. When you have done that well, you can fairly say you have thought it through. The following questions will guide your assessment.

Consider the Purpose

What purpose does the visual image best seem to serve?

- **Ornamentation:** Makes the page more pleasing to the eye
- **Illustration:** Supports points made in the accompanying text
- **Revelation:** Gives an inside look at something or presents new data
- **Explanation:** Uses imagery or graphics to clarify a complex subject
- **Instruction:** Guides the viewer through a complex process
- **Persuasion:** Influences feelings or beliefs
- **Entertainment:** Amuses the viewer

Evaluate the Quality

Essentially, how good is the image?

- Is the image done with skill? A map, for example, should be accurately and attractively drawn, should use colour effectively, and should be complete enough to serve its purpose.
- Does the image measure up to standards of quality?
- Is it backed by authority? Does the designer have a good reputation? Does the publication or institution have good credentials?
- How does the image compare to other images like it? Are clearer or more accurate images available?
- What are its shortcomings? Are there gaps in its coverage? Does it twist the evidence? Does it convey clichéd or fallacious information? (See pages 317–320 for a discussion of logical fallacies.)
- Could you think of a better way to approach the image's subject? If you were to produce the visual, what might you improve?

Determine the Value

What is the image's tangible and intangible worth? Its benefits and drawbacks?

- Is the visual worth viewing? Does it enrich the document by clarifying or otherwise enhancing its message?
- Does the visual appeal to you? Listen to authorities and peers, but also consider your own perspective.

Evaluate an Image

Discussion ▼

Evaluating an image such as the WWII poster in Figure 1.6 aimed at U.S. servicemen reveals its strong stereotypes of both men and women, stereotypes related to the historical period and cultural attitudes of that time. As with all images, evaluation begins with understanding and interpreting the poster.

In the poster's centre is a woman in evening dress, her hair done up, wearing jewels and a corsage. She is seated, at ease, looking at us. Perhaps she represents beauty, both sensual attractiveness and sophistication. The colours used to present her are pale and muted, except for her blue eyes and red lips.

Surrounding the woman are three men, individually dressed in the uniforms of the U.S. Army, Air Force, and Navy. Drinking and smoking, the men seem to be competing for her attention.

The poster implies that all U.S. service personnel were male, which was not true even in WWII, when WACs and WAVEs served in the armed forces. It cautions that these male members of the armed forces should be wary in seemingly innocent social situations, since even a beautiful woman, whom popular stereotypes of the day characterized as "dumb," might not be what she appears. Such a woman might, in fact, be a spy—an idea perhaps inspired by the famous case of WWI spy Mata Hari. The statement that "careless talk costs lives" is a version of another common phrase from the period: "Loose lips sink ships."

Evaluating this poster involves considering its original context while assessing it from our current perspective. In the heat of WWII, this poster could be considered a fair piece of military persuasion. Today, however, what is striking are the gender stereotypes at work in both image and words. Not only are U.S. service personnel today both male and female, in every branch of the armed forces, but they fulfill the same roles, including combat positions. With respect to the men, the image implies that in social situations (which are assumed to include smoking and drinking), they are untrustworthy and apt to boast or compete in the presence of an attractive woman. With respect to women, the image both denounces and warns, implying that women, especially attractive women, are cunning and dangerous. Today, such stereotypes press us to question the quality, truthfulness, and value of the image.

The National Archives of the UK, ref. INF3/229

fig. 1.6

Writing as Thinking

In school, your writing often must show your ability to think critically about topics and issues by analyzing complex processes, synthesizing distinct concepts, weighing the value of opposing perspectives, and practising new applications of existing principles. The following tips can help you.

Develop Sound Critical-Thinking Habits

Like everything worthwhile, improving your critical-thinking skills takes time and practice. But cultivating the habits below will pay off in sound, thoughtful writing.

1. **Be curious.** Ask "Why?" Cultivate your ability to wonder; question what you see, hear, and read—both inside and outside the classroom.

2. **Be creative.** Don't settle for obvious answers. Look at things in a fresh way, asking "what-if" questions such as "What if Ophelia didn't die in *Hamlet*?"

3. **Be open to new ideas.** Approach thinking as you would approach a road trip— looking for the unexpected and musing over mysteries.

4. **Value others' points of view.** Look at issues from another person's perspective and weigh that against your own. Honestly examine how the core of her or his perspective compares to the core of your perspective, and how each basis for thought might lead to different conclusions.

5. **Get involved.** Read books, journals, and newspapers. Watch documentaries. Join book clubs and film clubs. Participate in political and social-action events.

6. **Focus.** Sharpen your concentration, looking for details that distinguish a topic and reveal key questions related to its nature, function, and impact.

7. **Be rational.** Choose logical thinking patterns like those discussed in this chapter, and then work through the steps to deepen your understanding of a topic.

8. **Make connections.** Use writing to explore how and why topics or issues are related. Use comparisons to identify and name these relationships.

9. **Tolerate ambiguity.** Respectfully analyze issues not readily resolved—and acknowledge when your position requires further research or thought.

10. **Test the evidence.** Be properly skeptical about all claims (see pages 312–313). Look for corroboration (or verification) in other sources.

11. **Develop research-based conclusions.** Focus on understanding issues, assessing their history, development, function, and impact. During the process, gather evidence that leads to and supports a reasonable conclusion.

12. **Assess results.** Consider each paper to be a benchmark that reflects your progress in developing your thinking and writing skills. Save your papers for periodic analyses of your progress and revision of the writing.

Ask Probing Questions

Every field uses questions to trigger critical thinking. For example, scientific questions generate hypotheses, sociological questions lead to studies, mathematical questions call for proofs, and literary criticism questions call for interpretations. A good question opens up a problem and guides you all the way to its solution. But not all questions are created equal. Consider the differences:

- **Rhetorical questions** aren't meant to be answered. They're asked for effect.
    Example: Who would want to be caught in an earthquake?
- **Closed questions** seek a limited response and can be answered with "yes," "no," or a simple fact.
    Example: Would I feel an earthquake measuring 3.0 on the Richter scale?
- **Open questions** invite brainstorming and discussion.
    Example: How might a major earthquake affect this urban area?
- **Theoretical questions** call for organization and explanation of an entire field of knowledge.
    Example: What might cause a sudden fracturing of Earth's crust along fault lines?

To improve the critical thinking in your writing, ask better questions. The strategies below will help you think freely, respond to reading, study for a test, or collect your thoughts for an essay.

☑ **Ask open questions.** Closed questions sometimes choke off thinking. Use open questions to trigger a flow of ideas.

☑ **Ask "educated" questions.** Compare these questions: (A) What's wrong with television? (B) Does the 16.3 percent rise in televised acts of violence during the past three years signal a rising tolerance for violence in the viewing audience? You have a better chance of expanding the "educated" question—question B—into an essay because the question is clearer and suggests debatable issues.

☑ **Keep a question journal.** Divide a blank notebook page or split a computer screen. On one side, write down any questions that come to mind regarding the topic that you want to explore. On the other side, write down answers and any thoughts that flow from them.

☑ **Write Q & A drafts.** To write a thoughtful first draft, write quickly, then look it over. Turn the main idea into a question and write again, answering your question. For example, if your main idea is that TV viewers watch far more violence than they did ten years ago, ask *Which viewers? Why?* and *What's the result?* Go on that way until you find a key idea to serve as the main point of your next draft.

 For more help with critical thinking skills such as making and supporting claims, recognizing logical fallacies, and dealing with opposition, see "Strategies for Argumentation and Persuasion," pages 309–324.

Practise Inductive and Deductive Logic

Questions invite thinking; reasoning responds to that challenge in an organized way. Will the organization of your thoughts be inductive or deductive? Inductive logic reasons from specific information toward general conclusions. Deductive logic reasons from general principles toward specific applications. Notice in Figure 1.7 that inductive reasoning starts with specific details or observations (as shown at the base) and then moves "up" to broader ideas and eventually to a concluding generalization. In contrast, deduction starts with general principles at the top and works down, applying the principles to explain particular instances.

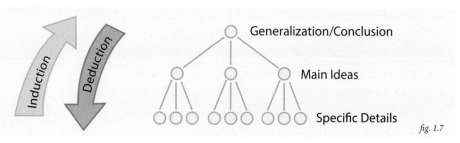

fig. 1.7

Sentences, paragraphs, and entire essays can be organized either inductively or deductively. Use induction when you want to postpone your conclusions. Use deduction for logical clarity, directness, and strength, or to apply what is already agreed on to what is still under dispute.

Example: Read through the paragraphs below from the student essay "A Fear Born of Sorrow" by Anita Brinkman. (The complete essay is on pages 232–234.) The first paragraph works inductively, the second paragraph deductively. Notice how the idea at the end of the first paragraph (the inductive conclusion) leads naturally into the contrasting idea (a deductive principle) at the beginning of the second paragraph.

Induction: specific details to generalization

More than 100 people were killed in the tragic bombing of the Oklahoma Federal Building in 1995. About 6,000 die in Africa each day of AIDS. Between 8,000 and 10,000 people worldwide die of starvation daily. Tragedies occur all around us, and we accept them out of necessity as a part of life.

Deduction: generalization to specific details

But sometimes the horror of a tragedy affects us in a new way: it overwhelms a nation and stuns the international community. This is what happened last week when two hijacked planes hit the Twin Towers of the World Trade Center, and their resulting collapse killed thousands of people from several countries. News of the tragedy flashed around the globe. Everywhere, it seemed, people in uncomprehending horror listened to reports on their radios or watched endless replays on their televisions. Several countries declared days of mourning and scheduled services of remembrance. Now, one week after the attack, tokens of grief and letters of condolence still flood U.S. embassies and government offices worldwide. But why is the outpouring of grief so much deeper for this tragedy than for others? Why isn't the attack considered just a large-scale repeat of the Oklahoma bombing? Could it be that our grief is more than sorrow, and that our loss is much more than what lies in the rubble?

Practising Modes of Thinking in Your Writing

In your various writing assignments, you will need to practise specific modes of thinking. The table below maps out these modes (from elementary to complex) and the tasks each requires. The more complex modes are then fleshed out on the following pages.

When you are asked to . . .

Know

define	memorize
identify	name
list	recall
match	recognize

Understand

comprehend	interpret
connect	restate
explain	summarize
grasp	

Analyze

characterize	contrast
classify	divide
compare	examine

Synthesize

assemble	imagine
combine	invent
construct	link
formulate	

Evaluate

assess	measure
check	monitor
critique	rank
judge	rate

Apply

anticipate	propose
choose	select
generate	

be ready to . . .

Call to mind what you have learned

- Recall information
- List details
- Define key terms
- Identify main points

Show what you have learned

- Connect related examples
- Summarize important details
- Explain how something works
- Interpret what something means

Break down information

- Divide a whole into its parts
- Group things into categories
- Analyze causes and effects
- Examine similarities and differences

Shape information into a new form

- Bring together a body of evidence
- Blend the old with the new
- Predict or hypothesize
- Construct a new way of looking at something

Determine the worth of information

- Point out a subject's strengths and weaknesses
- Evaluate its clarity, accuracy, logic, value, and so on
- Convince others of its value/worth

Use what you have learned

- Propose a better way of doing something
- Generate a plan of action
- Offer solutions to a problem

Think by Using Analysis

The word *analyze* literally means "to loosen or undo." When you analyze something, you break it down into parts and examine each part separately. You classify information, compare objects, trace a process, or explain causes.

As you analyze, think about the questions listed below. Note that each type of thinking answers certain kinds of questions. Remember, too, that thinking tasks often require two or more kinds of analysis that support one another.

Composition:	What elements does it contain? What is not part of it?
Categories:	How are things grouped, divided, or classified?
Structures:	What are the parts or elements? How are they related?
Comparisons/ contrasts:	How are things similar? How are they different?
Causes/effects:	Why did this happen? What are the results?
Processes:	How does it work or happen? What are the stages?

Example: Read through the passage below, from "Wayward Cells." In the full essay on pages 212–213, student writer Kerri Mertz explains the process by which healthy body cells become cancerous cells. Note how in this excerpt, the writer develops an overall analysis based on a process but also uses compare-contrast and cause-effect thinking within that structure, as well as informal definition.

The writer explains a cellular process and contrasts healthy and cancerous versions.

Most healthy cells reproduce rather quickly, but their reproduction rate is controlled. For example, your blood cells completely die off and replace themselves within a matter of weeks, but existing cells make only as many new cells as the body needs. The DNA codes in healthy cells tell them how many new cells to produce. However, cancer cells don't have this control, so they reproduce quickly with no stopping point, a characteristic called "autonomy" (Braun 3). What's more, all their "offspring" have the same qualities as their messed-up parent, and the resulting overpopulation produces growths called tumors.

The writer explains the three harmful effects of tumour cells (the cause).

Examples illustrate the analysis.

Tumor cells can hurt the body in a number of ways. First, a tumor can grow so big that it takes up space needed by other organs. Second, some cells may detach from the original tumor and spread throughout the body, creating new tumors elsewhere. This happens with lymphatic cancer—a cancer that's hard to control because it spreads so quickly. A third way that tumor cells can hurt the body is by doing work not called for in their DNA. For example, a gland cell's DNA code may tell the cell to produce a necessary hormone in the endocrine system. However, if cancer damages or distorts that code, sick cells may produce more of the hormone than the body can use—or even tolerate (Braun 4). Cancer cells seem to have minds of their own, and this is why cancer is such a serious disease.

Think by Using Synthesis

Synthesis is the opposite of analysis. Where analysis breaks things down into parts, synthesis combines elements into a new whole. In your writing, when you pull together things that are normally separate, you are synthesizing. Common ways of synthesizing include predicting, inventing, redesigning, and imagining a whole new way of looking at something.

Working with synthesis involves both reason and imagination. Start by looking closely at two or more items that you want to synthesize, and then think of fresh ways they can be related. Don't be afraid to see your subjects in a new way. In other words, think "sideways" rather than straight ahead. Ask the following questions:

Applying: What can I do with both? What will be the outcome?

Bridging: How can I build a connection between the two?

Combining: How can I connect, associate, or blend the two?

Conflicting: Which is good, better, or best? What strength does each offer the other?

Inventing: What parts could these two play in a drama?

Proposing: What do I suggest doing with both?

Sequencing: Which comes first? Is one an extension of the other?

Projecting: Based on current information, what is the best forecast for what will happen in the near future or the long term?

Example: The passage below is from Adam Gopnik's Massey lecture, "Recreational Winter," excerpted on pages 200–205. Leading up to this paragraph, Gopnik explains game theory as it applies to games such as chess (an open-information game) and five-card draw poker (a closed-information game). He then explores how game theory helps us understand sports such as basketball and football, arriving at the paragraph below that synthesizes game theory and hockey.

> Rejecting the idea that hockey is an open-information sport, the writer likens it to Texas hold-'em poker—synthesizing the sport and the game.
>
> Now, hockey looks, when you watch it with an unpractised eye, like an open-information sport. It looks like wild improvisation with no strategic plan underneath—a series of instinctive reactions to bouncing pucks and sliding players. (When people say they can't see the puck, I think what they really mean is that they can see it but they just can't see its point, its purpose in travelling. The game appears to be simply a brutal series of random collisions in which the invisible puck somehow sporadically ends up in the net.) But the more closely you observe the game, the more you see that it's kind of the Texas hold-'em of the world's spectator sports: there's a great deal that's open, but crucial elements are buried or cloaked and are revealed only afterwards to the eye of experience and deeper knowledge. There are hole cards in hockey, and some of the fun of being a fan is learning to look for them.   *1*

Think by Using Evaluation

Movies, proposals, arguments—anything can be evaluated. Evaluation measures the value or worth of things. For example, when you express your judgment about an issue or discuss the weak and strong points of what someone else has said, you are evaluating. Many kinds of writing are evaluative.

To evaluate a topic, start by learning as much about it as possible. Then consider which criteria or standards are appropriate. Next, judge how the topic measures up based on those criteria. Support your judgment with concrete details, examples, illustrations, and comparisons. Ask questions like these:

Aspects:	What elements of the topic will I evaluate?
Vantage point:	What are my experience and my point of view?
Criteria:	On which standards will I base my judgment?
Assessment:	How does the topic measure up by those standards?
Comparison:	How does it compare to and contrast with similar things?
Recommendation:	Based on my evaluation, what do I advise?

Example: The passage below is taken from Malcolm Gladwell's "Small Change," on pages 241–251. In the full essay, Gladwell contrasts traditional social activism (high-risk, strong-tie, and strategic) with social-media activism (low-risk, weak-tie, and unstructured). In the passage below, he evaluates both the strengths and weaknesses of the networked nature of social-media activism.

> The writer contrasts hierarchies and networks.

This is the second crucial distinction between traditional activism and its online variant: social media are not about this kind of hierarchical organization. Facebook and the like are tools for building *networks*, which are the opposite, in structure and character, of hierarchies. Unlike hierarchies, with their rules and procedures, networks aren't controlled by a single central authority. Decisions are made through consensus, and the ties that bind people to the group are loose.   1

> After evaluating the strengths of networks, he critiques their usefulness in situations requiring leadership.

This structure makes networks enormously resilient and adaptable in low-risk situations. Wikipedia is a perfect example. It doesn't have an editor, sitting in New York, who directs and corrects each entry. The effort of putting together each entry is self-organized. If every entry in Wikipedia were to be erased tomorrow, the content would swiftly be restored, because that's what happens when a network of thousands spontaneously devote their time to a task.   2

There are many things, though, that networks don't do well. Car companies sensibly use a network to organize their hundreds of suppliers, but not to design their cars. No one believes that the articulation of a coherent design philosophy is best handled by a sprawling, leaderless organizational system. Because networks don't have a centralized leadership structure and clear lines of authority, they have real difficulty reaching consensus and setting goals. They can't think strategically; they are chronically prone to conflict and error. How do you make difficult choices about tactics or strategy or philosophical direction when everyone has an equal say?   3

Think by Using Application

Thinking by using application defines the practical implications of something. It involves using what you know to demonstrate, show, relate, or extend ideas in view of their outcomes. For example, using what you have learned about the ecology of forest fires to examine the effects of a particular fire—that's application in action.

Applying involves moving from ideas to possible action. First, understand the information you have. Second, relate this information to a given situation. Third, select those facts and details that clarify and support the application. Fourth, test the application to see whether it has been reasonable.

When applying ideas, let questions like these guide your writing:

Purpose: What is something designed to be or do?
Benefits: What would this idea make clearer, better, or more complete?
Solutions: What problems are solved by application of this idea?
Outcomes: What results can be expected? Where could we go from there?

Example: The paragraphs below come from Nick Saul's "The Hunger Game" (pages 355–357), an essay in which Saul claims that food banks are not solving the problem of hunger in Canada. In the passage below, he argues that we must solve the problem by addressing poverty, and he then applies this thinking by describing concrete steps and programs that change people's relationship with food.

Identifying poverty as the true problem, the writer explains the practical steps that must be taken to resolve it.

We not only can do better, we must do better. We need to stop cheering on an approach that has already failed, and instead focus on the root of the problem: people are hungry because they are poor. They do not have enough money for food because of inadequate income supports, minimum wages that do not cover the bills, and the lack of affordable housing and child care. Instead of further entrenching food banks that let governments—and all of us—off the hook, we need to build organizations that foster the political will to tackle poverty and establish social programs, employment strategies, and supports that give all Canadians access to affordable, healthy meals. In the end, the costs of inequality and poor health are borne by all of us, straining our health care system, and compromising the safety of our neighbourhoods and the productivity of our nation.

The writer explains the practical application of this different approach to poverty in food-related programs.

Food can be a powerful tool, and in the past decade we have seen a surge in school gardens, farmers' markets, and community supported agriculture. At the Stop, we have utilized this new energy and thinking to help establish programs where low-income people are offered more than mere handouts; rather, they are given opportunities to grow, cook, eat, and learn about the healthy food we all need. Such programs build hope, skills, and self-worth among our community members, who may then become powerful advocates for change—to both the food system and the political one. This model has radically altered our neighbourhood and generated enough interest to galvanize a network of Community Food Centres across the country.

Critical-Thinking and Writing Activities

As directed by your instructor, complete the following critical-thinking and writing activities by yourself or with classmates:

1. Northrop Frye has argued that "[n]obody is capable of free speech unless he [or she] knows how to use language, and such knowledge is not a gift: It has to be learned and worked at." How does Frye's claim relate to the discussions of critical reading, viewing, and writing in this chapter?

2. What thinking, reading, viewing, and writing skills are required in your field of study? Reflect on those possibilities.

3. Choose a subject you know something about. Practise thinking about that subject both inductively and deductively. Then write two paragraphs—one developed inductively and the other developed deductively.

4. Select a sample essay from the "Strategies and Models" section. Read the piece carefully and identify where and how the writer uses different thinking modes. Do the same analysis on a recent sample of your own writing, rating your analysis, synthesis, evaluation, and application.

Learning-Objectives Checklist ✓

Have you achieved this chapter's learning objectives? Check your progress with the items below, revisiting topics in the chapter as needed. *I have* . . .

____ read texts actively by assessing their rhetorical situation (writer, message, medium, reader, context), and practising techniques such as preview, read, review (4–5).

____ read texts actively through note-taking, annotating, mapping, and outlining (6–9).

____ responded to written texts in an honest, fluid, reflective, and selective way (8).

____ objectively summarized texts in my own words, distinguishing main arguments and key supporting points from secondary content (9).

____ viewed images actively by surveying and inspecting them (10–11).

____ carefully interpreted images by deeply analyzing the rhetorical situation and its complications—designer, message, medium, viewer, and context (12–13).

____ critiqued visual images by assessing their purpose, value, and quality (14–15).

____ thought critically about topics by practising sound thinking habits, asking probing questions, and using inductive and deductive patterns strategically (16–18).

____ produced writing that practises modes of thinking such as analysis, synthesis, evaluation, and application (19–23).

Chapter 2

Beginning the Writing Process

The blank page or screen can be daunting for any writer. That's because writing doesn't go from nothing to a masterpiece in one step. Writing is a process, much like painting.

The aim of the writing process is discovery—along the way and in the finished text, both for the writer and for the reader. As Peter Stillman argues, "Writing is the most powerful means of discovery available to all of us throughout life." Discovery happens when you give ample time to each step, and when you follow strategies that encourage your thinking to deepen and your writing to sharpen.

This chapter introduces the writing process and then focuses on getting started on any writing project through prewriting strategies. As with many things in life, putting the first step right sets you up to succeed on the whole journey.

Visually Speaking Painting is the process of converting infinite possibilities into a single image. How is writing similar? How is it different? What is the starting point for painting? For writing? Consider these questions as you examine Figure 2.1.

Learning **Objectives**

By working through this chapter, you will be able to

- outline the writing process and decide how to follow it for different projects.
- analyze the rhetorical situation behind writing tasks.
- summarize seven traits of strong, academic writing.
- interpret the nature and requirements of specific writing assignments.
- generate and choose topics for writing projects.
- collect, track, and examine information for writing projects.

© Jose Luis Pelaez, Inc./CORBIS

fig. 2.1

The Writing Process: From Start to Finish

It's easy to feel overwhelmed by a writing project—especially if the form of writing is new to you, the topic is complex, or the paper must be long. However, using the writing process will relieve some of that pressure by breaking down the task into manageable steps. An overview of those steps is shown below, and key principles are addressed on the next page.

Consider the Writing Process

Figure 2.2 maps out the basic steps in the writing process. As you work on your writing project, periodically review this diagram to keep yourself on task.

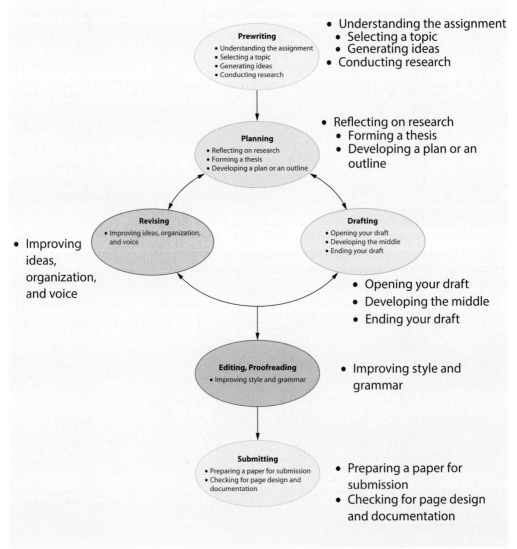

Prewriting
- Understanding the assignment
- Selecting a topic
- Generating ideas
- Conducting research

- Understanding the assignment
- Selecting a topic
- Generating ideas
- Conducting research

Planning
- Reflecting on research
- Forming a thesis
- Developing a plan or an outline

- Reflecting on research
- Forming a thesis
- Developing a plan or an outline

Revising
- Improving ideas, organization, and voice

Drafting
- Opening your draft
- Developing the middle
- Ending your draft

- Improving ideas, organization, and voice

- Opening your draft
- Developing the middle
- Ending your draft

Editing, Proofreading
- Improving style and grammar

- Improving style and grammar

Submitting
- Preparing a paper for submission
- Checking for page design and documentation

- Preparing a paper for submission
- Checking for page design and documentation

fig. 2.2

Adapt the Process to Your Project

The writing process shown on the previous page is flexible, not rigid. As a writer, you need to adapt the process to your situation and assignment. To do so, consider these essential principles.

- **Writing tends not to follow a straight path.** While writing begins with an assignment or a need and ends with a reader, the journey in between is often indirect. The steps in the flowchart show that when you write, you sometimes move back and forth between steps, meaning that the process is recursive. For example, during the revision phase, you may discover that you need to draft a new paragraph or do more research.

- **Each assignment presents distinct challenges.** A personal essay may develop best through clustering or freewriting; a literary analysis through close reading of a story; a lab report through the experimental method; and a position paper through reading of books and journal articles, as well as through careful and balanced reasoning. Moreover, an assignment may or may not involve extensive research and working with sources.

- **Writing can involve collaboration.** From using your roommate as a sounding board for your topic choice to working with a group to produce a major report, academic writing is not solitary writing. In fact, many universities and colleges have a writing centre to help you refine your writing assignments. (See pages 89–91 for more.)

- **Each writer works differently.** Some writers do extensive prewriting before drafting, while others do not. You might develop a detailed outline, whereas someone else might draft a brief list of topics. Experiment with the strategies introduced in Chapters 2–7, adopting those that help you.

- **Good writing can't be rushed.** Although some students regard pulling an all-nighter as a badge of honour, good writing takes time. A steady, disciplined approach will generally produce the best results. For example, by brainstorming or reading early in a project, you stimulate your subconscious mind to mull over issues, identify problems, and project solutions—even while your conscious mind is working on other things. Similarly, completing a first draft early enough gives you time to revise objectively.

- **Different steps call for attention to different writing issues.** As you use the writing process, at each stage keep your focus where it belongs:
    1. While getting started, planning, and drafting, focus on global issues: ideas, structure, voice, format, and design.
    2. During revising, fix big content problems by cutting, adding, and thoroughly reworking material. (Our experience is that students benefit the most from revising—but spend the least time doing it!)
    3. While editing and proofreading, pay attention to small, local issues— word choice, sentence smoothness, and grammatical correctness. Worrying about these issues early in the writing process interrupts the flow of drafting and wastes time on material that may later be deleted.

Analyzing the Rhetorical Situation

Rhetoric is the art of using language effectively. As Aristotle, Quintilian, and others have explained, your language is effective when all aspects of your message fit the rhetorical situation (Figure 2.3). For any writing project, then, prewriting can begin with analyzing the rhetorical situation that lies behind the project. By doing so, you get the project in focus. The diagram and discussion below explain what is involved in such rhetorical analysis.

Rhetorical Situation

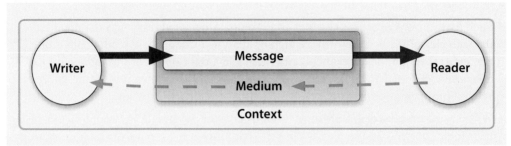

fig. 2.3

Think of Your Role as the Writer

Are you writing as a concerned citizen, as a student in a class, as a friend relating a story, as a reporter providing news, as a blogger giving an opinion? Your role in writing and otherwise communicating affects the level of language you use, the voice you use, the types of details you include, the evidence you cite to support a claim, and so on.

Understand Your Subject

To truly understand your subject, you need to gather and assimilate all relevant details about it, including its history, makeup, function, and impact on people and culture. Knowing those details will help you narrow your focus to a specific thesis and develop it well.

> **Working with Sources** | As you search for information, think about which types of sources are recommended or expected for the assignment. Which should be avoided?

Understand Your Purpose

Key words in an assignment—such as *analyze, explain, defend,* or *describe*—tell you what the purpose of the writing is supposed to be. Understanding why you are writing helps you choose an organizational strategy, such as classification, definition, or process. (See pages 62–66.)

> **Working with Sources** | Think of the sources that will most help you achieve your purpose, whether to entertain, compare, inspire, enlighten, and so on.

Sashkin/Shutterstock.com

Understand Your Audience

For any writing task, you must understand your audience in order to develop writing that meets their needs. To assess your audience, answer questions like these:

- Who are my readers: instructor? classmates? Web users?
- What do they know about my topic, and what do they need to know?
- How well do they understand the terminology involved?
- What are their attitudes toward the topic and toward me?
- How well do they read written English—or visuals such as graphs and charts?
- How will they use my writing (as entertainment or to complete a task)?

Note: Answers to such questions will help you develop meaningful sentences (pages 95–101), choose appropriate words (pages 102–108), and select relevant visuals (pages 388–389).

Working with Sources ▌ Ask yourself what sources your reader will best understand and most respect. What sources will add to your credibility and authority?

Understand the Medium (Form)

Many communication options are available for every message. Academic forms include essays, analyses, reports, proposals, research papers, reviews, and so on. It is important to understand the form of the assignment. What works well in a narrative about a past experience would not work as well in a lab report. Also, each of these forms can contain multiple media: written elements, graphics, photos, drawings, videos, audios, links, and so on. Understanding the overall medium and the media within it will help you succeed.

Working with Sources ▌ Make sure you understand the way that sources are to be cited in the form of communication you are using. (See 493–564 for MLA and APA styles.)

Think about the Context

Think about how this assignment relates to others in the course. Consider these issues:

- **Weight:** Is this an everyday assignment, a weekly or biweekly one, or the big one?
- **Assessment:** Find out how the assignment will be graded. What traits will your instructor look for? Will your writing be assessed with a rubric? (See page 30.)
- **Intent:** Make certain that you understand the goals of the assignment and understand what your instructor wants you to get out of it.

Note: If the writing you are doing is not in response to an assignment, think about the environment in which the message will be read. What is the history of this issue? What is the current climate like? What might the future be?

Working with Sources ▌ If you are writing material that will be reviewed and debated by others in your field, think about what sources you would most want your writing to appear in. Make certain you understand the submission guidelines for the source.

Aiming for Writing Excellence

What makes your writing strong enough to engage and enlighten readers? As already suggested on pages 28–29, that depends in part on the rhetorical situation: what your purpose is, who your readers are, and so on. Writing excellence can be measured by the depth of what you learn through writing, as well as by what your reader gains through reading. However, while the world of writing is so diverse that no formula or prescription can state definitively what makes for strong writing, we can point to common traits that describe such writing. Consider the relevance of these traits at the beginning of any writing project.

Common Traits of Academic Writing

Quality writing shows strengths in the traits below, which range from global issues to local, sentence-level issues.

- **Strong ideas** are what you discover and develop through your writing. They are what make your content substantial and meaningful. These elements include a clear, sharp thesis or theme; strong and balanced reasoning; and accurate, supportive information that is properly credited.

- **Logical organization** creates the structure and flow of your writing. Through organization, reasoning is delivered through a clear chain of ideas, a unified whole. Typically, an engaging opening focuses discussion, the middle effectively develops the main idea, and a closing offers conclusions and points forward—all in paragraphs that are well developed (unified, coherent, and complete).

- **Engaging voice** refers to how your writing "sounds" to readers—the attitude, pacing, and personality that come through. An engaging voice sounds authentic and natural, engaged with the topic. Moreover, the tone—whether serious, playful, or sarcastic—is confident but also sincere and measured, fitting the writing occasion.

- **Clear word choice** carries your meaning. In your writing, the vocabulary should fit the topic, purpose, and audience. Phrasing should be clear throughout—language that readers will understand, precise terminology, and plain English whenever possible.

- **Smooth sentences** express complete thoughts in a good blend of sentence lengths (short and punchy, long and thoughtful) and patterns (loose, balanced, and periodic). Such sentences use phrases and clauses in logical and expressive ways—energetically, economically, gracefully.

- **Correct writing** follows the conventions of language (grammar, punctuation, mechanics, usage, and spelling), as well as standards of citation and documentation (e.g., MLA, APA).

- **Professional document design** refers to the appearance of your writing on the page, the screen, and so on. Such design includes the document's format (e.g., essay, lab report, presentation, website), its page layout (e.g., margins, headings, bullets, white space), its typography (typefaces, type sizes, and type styles), and its use of tables and visuals.

Common Traits in Action

What do these common traits look like in a typical piece of academic writing such as the process essay below? Study this essay that explains how hair grows and falls out, exploring how it represents strong writing at the first-year level.

Hair Today, Gone Tomorrow

Ideas
Clear focus, engaging thesis, and precise content (including visual)

Imagine a field of grass covered with two layers of soil: first a layer of clay, and on top of that a layer of rich, black dirt. Then imagine that 100,000 little holes have been poked through the black dirt and into the clay, and at the bottom of each hole lies one grass seed. [1]

Slowly each seed produces a stem that grows up through the clay, out of the dirt, and up toward the sky. Now and then every stem stops for a while, rests, and then starts growing again. At any time about 90 percent of the stems are growing and the others are resting. Because the field gets shaggy, sometimes a gardener comes along and cuts the grass. [2]

Organization
Lively opening, well-structured middle, and thoughtful closing

Your skull is like that field of grass, and your scalp (common skin) is like the two layers of soil. The top layer of the scalp is the epidermis, and the bottom layer is the dermis. About 100,000 tiny holes (called follicles) extend through the epidermis into the dermis. [3]

Voice
Informed and engaging tone

At the base of each follicle lies a seed-like thing called a papilla. At the bottom of the papilla, a small blood vessel drops like a root into the dermis. This vessel carries food through the dermis into the papilla, which works like a little factory using the food to build hair cells. As the papilla makes cells, a hair strand grows up through the dermis past an oil gland. The oil gland greases the strand with a coating that keeps the hair soft and moist. [4]

Words
Precise, lively, clear phrasing

Sentences
Smooth, varied, and graceful constructions

Correctness
Error-free prose

Design
Attractive format, page layout, and typography

Shaft of hair
Scalp
Follicle
Epidermis
Dermis
Oil glands
Papilla
Blood vessel

Most of the hairs on your scalp grow about one-half inch each month. If a strand stays healthy, doesn't break off, and no barber snips it, the hair will grow about 25 inches in four years. At that point hair strands turn brittle and fall out. Every day between 25 and 250 hairs fall out of your follicles, but nearly every follicle grows a new one. [5]

Around the clock, day after day, this process goes on . . . unless your papillae decide to retire. In that case you reach the stage in your life—let's call it "maturity"—that others call "baldness." [6]

Understanding the Assignment

Each of your instructors likely has ways of personalizing a writing assignment, but most assignments will spell out (1) the objective, (2) the task, (3) the formal requirements, and (4) suggested approaches and topics. Your first step, therefore, is to read the assignment carefully, noting the options and restrictions that are part of it. The suggestions below will help you do that. (Also see pages 114–117 for one writer's approach.)

Read the Assignment

Certain words in the assignment explain what main action you must perform. Here are some words that signal what you are to do:

Keywords

Analyze:	Break down a topic into subparts, showing how those parts relate.
Argue:	Defend a claim with logical arguments.
Classify:	Divide a large group into well-defined subgroups.
Compare/contrast:	Point out similarities and/or differences.
Define:	Give a clear, thoughtful definition or meaning of something.
Describe:	Show in detail what something is like.
Evaluate:	Weigh the truth, quality, or usefulness of something.
Explain:	Give reasons, list steps, or discuss the causes of something.
Interpret:	Tell in your own words what something means.
Reflect:	Share your well-considered thoughts about a subject.
Summarize:	Restate someone else's ideas very briefly in your own words.
Synthesize:	Connect facts or ideas to create something new.

Options and Restrictions

The assignment often gives you some choice of your topic or approach but may restrict your options to suit the instructor's purpose. Note the options and restrictions in the following short sample assignment:

Reflect on the way a natural disaster or major historical event has altered your understanding of the past, the present, or the future.

Options:	(1) You may choose any natural disaster or historical event.
	(2) You may focus on the past, present, or future.
	(3) You may examine any kind of alteration.
Restrictions:	(1) You must reflect on a change in your understanding.
	(2) The disaster must be natural.
	(3) The historical event must be major.

Relate the Assignment to the Goals of the Course

1. How much value does the instructor give the assignment? (The value is often expressed as a percentage of the course grade.)
2. What benefit does your instructor want you to receive?
   - Strengthen your comprehension?
   - Improve your research skills?
   - Deepen your ability to explain, prove, or persuade?
   - Expand your style?
   - Increase your creativity?
3. How will this assignment contribute to your overall performance in the course? What course goals (often listed in the syllabus) does it address?

Relate the Assignment to Other Assignments

1. Does it build on previous assignments?
2. Does it prepare you for the next assignment?

Relate the Assignment to Your Own Interests

1. Does it connect with a topic that already interests you?
2. Does it connect with work in your other courses?
3. Does it connect with the work you may do in your chosen field?
4. Does it connect with life outside school?

Reflect on the Assignment

1. **First impulses:** How did you feel when you first read the assignment?
2. **Approaches:** What's the usual approach for an assignment like this? What's a better way of tackling it?
3. **Quality of performance:** What would it take to produce an excellent piece of writing?
4. **Benefits:** What are the benefits to your education? To you personally? To the class? To society?
5. **Features:** Reflect further on four key features of any writing assignment.
   - **Purpose:** What is the overall purpose of the assignment—to inform, to explain, to analyze, to entertain? What is the desired outcome?
   - **Readers:** Should you address your instructor? Your classmates? A general reader? How much does the reader already know about the topic? What type of language should you use?
   - **Form:** What are the requirements concerning length, format, and due date?
   - **Assessment:** How will the assignment be evaluated? Which of the traits discussed on pages 30–31 are important to this assignment? How can you be sure that you are completing the assignment correctly?

Developing a Topic

For some assignments, finding a suitable topic may require little thinking on your part. If an instructor asks you to summarize an article in a scholarly journal, you know what you will write about—the article in question. But suppose the instructor asks you to analyze a feature of popular culture in terms of its impact on society. You won't be sure of a specific writing topic until you explore the possibilities. Keep the following points in mind when you conduct a topic search. Your topic must . . .

- meet the requirements of the assignment.
- be limited in scope.
- seem reasonable (that is, be within your means to research).
- genuinely interest you.

Limit the Subject Area

Many of your writing assignments may relate to general subject areas you are currently studying. Your task, then, is to select a specific topic related to the general area of study—a topic limited enough that you can treat it with sufficient depth in the number of pages and preparation time allowed for the assignment. The following examples show the difference between general subjects and limited topics:

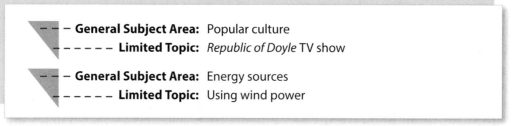

General Subject Area: Popular culture
Limited Topic: *Republic of Doyle* TV show

General Subject Area: Energy sources
Limited Topic: Using wind power

Conduct Your Search

Finding a writing idea that meets the requirements of the assignment should not be difficult, if you know how and where to look. Follow these steps:

1. **Check your class notes and handouts** for ideas related to the assignment.
2. **Search the Internet** Type in a keyword or phrase (the general subject stated in the assignment) and see what you can find. You could also follow a subject tree to narrow a subject. (See page 454.)
3. **Consult indexes, guides, and other library references** Subscription databases such as EBSCOhost, for example, list current articles published on specific topics and where to find them. (See pages 446–451.)
4. **Discuss the assignment** with your instructor or an information specialist.
5. **Use one or more of the prewriting strategies** described on the following pages to generate possible writing ideas.

Explore Possible Topics

You can generate topic possibilities by using the following strategies. These same strategies can be used when you've chosen a topic and want to develop it further.

Journal Writing

Write in a journal on a regular basis. Reflect on your personal feelings, develop your thoughts, and record the happenings of each day. Periodically go back and underline ideas that you would like to explore in writing assignments. In the following journal-writing sample, the writer came up with an idea for a writing assignment about the societal impacts of popular culture.

> I read a really disturbing news story this morning. I've been thinking about it all day. In California a little girl was killed when she was struck by a car driven by a man distracted by a billboard ad for lingerie featuring a scantily clothed woman. Not only is it a horrifying thing to happen, but it also seems to me all too symbolic of the way that sexually charged images in the media are putting children, and especially girls, in danger. That reminds me of another news story I read this week about preteen girls wanting to wear the kinds of revealing outfits that they see in music videos, TV shows, and magazines aimed at teenagers. Too many of today's media images give young people the impression that sexuality should begin at an early age. This is definitely a dangerous message.

Listing

Freely list ideas as they come to mind, beginning with a key concept related to the assignment. (Brainstorming—listing ideas in conjunction with members of a group—is often an effective way to extend your lists.) The following is an example of a student's list of ideas for possible topics on the subject of news reporting:

Aspect of popular culture: News reporting

Sensationalism
Sound bites rather than in-depth analysis
Focus on the negative
Shock radio
Shouting matches pretending to be debates
Press leaks that damage national security, etc.
Lack of observation of people's privacy
Bias
Contradictory health news confusing to readers
Little focus on "unappealing" issues like poverty
Celebration of "celebrity"

Clustering

To begin the clustering process, write a key word or phrase related to the assignment in the centre of your paper. Circle it, and then cluster ideas around it. Circle each idea as you record it, and draw a line connecting it to the closest related idea. Keep going until you run out of ideas and connections. Figure 2.4 is a student's cluster on the subject of sports:

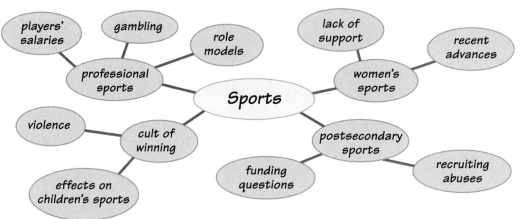

fig. 2.4

 After four or five minutes of listing or clustering, scan your work for an idea to explore in a freewriting. A writing idea should begin to emerge during this freewriting session. (See below.)

Freewrite to Discover and Develop a Topic

Freewriting is the writing you do without having a specific outcome in mind. You simply write down whatever pops into your head as you explore your topic. Freewriting can serve as a starting point for your writing, or it can be combined with any of the other prewriting strategies to help you select, explore, focus, or organize your writing. If you get stuck at any point during the composing process, you can return to freewriting as a way of generating new ideas.

Reminders

- **Freewriting helps you get your thoughts down on paper.**
  (Thoughts are constantly passing through your mind.)
- **Freewriting helps you develop and organize these thoughts.**
- **Freewriting helps you make sense out of things that you may be studying or researching.**
- **Freewriting may seem awkward at times, but just stick with it.**

The Process

- **Write nonstop and record whatever comes into your mind.** Follow your thoughts instead of trying to direct them.
- **If you have a particular topic or assignment to complete, use it as a starting point.** Otherwise, begin with anything that comes to mind.
- **Don't stop to judge, edit, or correct your writing;** that will come later.
- **Keep writing even when you think you have exhausted all of your ideas.** Switch to another angle or voice, but keep writing.
- **Watch for a promising writing idea to emerge.** Learn to recognize the beginnings of a good idea, and then expand that idea by recording as many specific details as possible.

The Result

- **Review your writing and underline the ideas you like.** These ideas will often serve as the basis for future writings.
- **Determine exactly what you need to write about.** Once you've figured out what you are required to do, you may then decide to do a second freewriting exercise.
- **Listen to and read the freewriting of others;** learn from your peers.

Freewriting

Write nonstop for ten minutes or longer to discover possible writing ideas. Use a key concept related to the assignment as a starting point. You'll soon discover potential writing ideas that might otherwise have never entered your mind. Note in the following example that the writer doesn't stop writing even when he can't think of anything to say. Note also that he doesn't stop to correct typos and other mistakes.

> Popular culture. What does that include? Television obviously but that's a pretty boring subject. What else? Movies, pop music, video games. Is there a connection between playing violent video games and acting out violent behaviour? Most video players I know would say no but sometimes news reports suggest a connection. Is this something I'd want to write about? Not really. What then? Maybe I could think about this a different way and focus on the positive effects of playing video games. They release tension for one thing and they can really be challenging. Other benefits? They help to kill time, that's for sure, but maybe that's not such a good thing. I would definitely read more if it weren't for video games, TV, etc. Maybe I could write about how all the electronic entertainment that surrounds us today is creating a generation of nonreaders. Or maybe I could focus on whether people aren't getting much physical exercise because of the time they spend with electronic media. Maybe both. At least I have some possibilities to work with.

Researching Your Topic

Writer and instructor Donald Murray said that "writers write with information. If there is no information, there will be no effective writing." How true! Before you can develop a thoughtful piece of writing, you must gain a thorough understanding of your topic; to do so, you must carry out the necessary reading, reflecting, and researching. Writing becomes a satisfying experience once you can speak with authority about your topic. Use the following guidelines when you start collecting information. (Also see "Research and Writing" in this book.)

- Determine what you already know about your topic. (Use the strategies below this bulleted list.)
- Consider listing questions you would like to answer during your research. (See page 39.)
- Identify and explore possible sources of information. (See page 40.)
- Carry out your research following a logical plan. (See pages 49–55.)

Find Out What You Already Know

Use one or more of the following strategies to determine what you already know about a writing topic.

1. **Focused freewriting:** At this point, you can focus your freewriting by (1) exploring your limited topic from different angles or (2) approaching your freewriting as if it were a quick draft of the actual paper. A quick version will tell you how much you know about your topic and what you need to find out.
2. **Clustering:** Try clustering with your topic serving as the nucleus word. Your clustering should focus on what you already know. (See page 36.)
3. **Five Ws of writing:** Answer the five Ws—Who? What? When? Where? and Why?—to identify basic information on your subject. Add How? to the list for better coverage.
4. **Directed writing:** Write whatever comes to mind about your topic, using one of the modes listed below. (Repeat the process as often as you need to, selecting a different mode each time.)

> **Describe it:** What do you see, hear, feel, smell, and taste?
> **Compare it:** What is it similar to? What is it different from?
> **Associate it:** What connections between this topic and others come to mind?
> **Analyze it:** What parts does it have? How do they work together?
> **Argue it:** What do you like about the topic? What do you not like about it? What are its strengths and weaknesses?
> **Apply it:** What can you do with it? How can you use it?

Ask Questions

To guide your collecting and researching, you may find it helpful to list questions about your topic that you would like to answer. Alternatively, you can use the questions below to guide your research.

	Description	Function	History	Value
PROBLEMS	• What is the problem? • What type of problem is it? • What are its parts? • What are the signs of the problem?	• Who or what is affected by it? • What new problems might it cause in the future?	• What is the current status of the problem? • What or who caused it? • What or who contributed to it?	• What is its significance? Why? • Why is it more (or less) important than other problems? • What does it symbolize or illustrate?
POLICIES	• What is the policy? • How broad is it? • What are its parts? • What are its most important features?	• What is the policy designed to do? • What is needed to make it work? • What are or will be its effects?	• What brought about this policy? • What are the alternatives?	• Is the policy workable? • What are its advantages and disadvantages? • Is it practical? • Is it a good policy? Why or why not?
CONCEPTS	• What is the concept? • What are its parts? • What is its main feature? • Whom or what is it related to?	• Who has been influenced by this concept? • Why is it important? • How does it work?	• When did it originate? • How has it changed over the years? • How might it change in the future?	• What practical value does it have? • Why is it superior (or inferior) to similar concepts? • What is its social worth?

TrotzOlga/Shutterstock.com

Identify Possible Sources

Finding meaningful sources is one of the most important steps you will take as you prepare to write. (That's why Part 3 of this text is dedicated to research instruction. See especially Chapters 21–23.) Listed below are tips that will help you identify good sources:

1. **Give yourself enough time.** Finding good sources of information may be time-consuming. Books and periodicals you need may be checked out, your computer service may be down, and so on.

2. **Be aware of the limits of your resources.** Print material may be out-of-date. Online information may be more current, but it may not always be reliable. (See pages 418–421 for ways to help you evaluate information.)

3. **Use your existing resources to find additional sources of information.** Pay attention to books, articles, and individuals mentioned in reliable initial sources of information.

4. **Ask for help.** The specialists in your school library can help you find information that is reliable and relevant. These people are trained to find information; don't hesitate to ask for their help.

5. **Bookmark useful websites.** Include reference works and academic resources related to your major.

Explore Different Sources of Information

Of course, books and websites are not the only possible sources of information. Primary sources such as interviews, observations, and surveys may lead you to a more thorough and meaningful understanding of a topic. (See pages 433–464.)

Primary Sources	Secondary Sources
Interviews	Articles
Observations	Reference book entries
Participation	Books
Surveys	Websites

Carry Out Your Research

As you conduct your research, try to use a variety of reliable sources. It's also a good idea to choose an efficient note-taking method before you start. You will want to take good notes on the information you find and record all the publishing details necessary for citing your sources. (See pages 424–427.)

Reserve a special part of a notebook or file on your computer to question, evaluate, and reflect on your research as it develops. Reflection helps you make sense of new ideas, refocus your thinking, and evaluate your progress.

Track Sources

Follow these strategies for tracking sources and taking notes.

- **Track resources in a working bibliography.** Once you find a useful book, journal article, news story, or Web page, record identifying information for the source. For more help, see pages 422–423.

- **Use a note-taking system that respects sources.** Essentially, your note-taking system should help you keep an accurate record of useful information and ideas from sources while also allowing you to engage those sources with your own thinking. For a discussion of possible systems, see pages 424–427.

- **Distinguish summaries, paraphrases, and quotations.** As you read sources, you will find material that answers your questions and helps you achieve your writing purpose. At that point, decide whether to summarize, paraphrase, or quote the material:
  - **A summary** pulls just the main points out of a passage and puts them in your own words: Summarize source material when it contains relevant ideas and information that you can boil down.
  - **A paraphrase** rewrites a passage point by point in your own words: Paraphrase source material when all the information is important but the actual phrasing isn't especially important or memorable.
  - **A quotation** records a passage from the source word for word: Quote when the source states something crucial and says it well. Note: In your notes, always identify quoted material by putting quotation marks around it.

Summarizing, paraphrasing, and quoting are treated more fully on pages 428–430. Here is a brief example, with the original passage coming from Coral Ann Howells' *Alice Munro*, published in 1998 by Manchester University Press as part of its Contemporary World Writers series.

Original: "To read Munro's stories is to discover the delights of seeing two worlds at once: an ordinary everyday world and the shadowy map of another imaginary or secret world laid over the real one, so that in reading we slip from one world into the other in an unassuming domestic sort of way."

Summary: Munro's fiction moves readers from recognizable reality into a hidden world.

Paraphrase: Reading Munro's fiction gives readers the enjoyment of experiencing a double world: day-to-day reality and on top of that a more mysterious, fantastic world, with the result that readers move smoothly between the worlds in a seamless, ordinary way.

Quotation: Munro's fiction takes us into "the shadowy map of another imaginary or secret world laid over the real one."

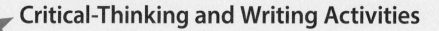

Critical-Thinking and Writing Activities

As directed by your instructor, complete the following critical-thinking and writing activities by yourself or with classmates.

1. Writer Ralph Fletcher shares, "When I write, I am always struck at how magical and unexpected the process turns out to be." Would you describe the writing process you follow as "magical" and "unexpected"? Why or why not?

2. Reread one of your recent essays. Does the writing show that you thoroughly understood your subject, met the needs of your readers, and achieved your purpose? How does it measure against the traits of strong writing? What traits in your writing are strong? Which need work? Where in this book can you find help on these traits?

3. Below is a list of general subject areas. Select one that interests you and do the following: Using the strategies on pages 34–37, brainstorm possible topics and select one. Then use the strategies on pages 38–40 to explore what you know about that topic and what you need to learn.

   Arts/music   Environment   Health/medicine   Work/occupation

Learning-Objectives Checklist ✓

Have you achieved this chapter's learning objectives? Check your progress with the items below, revisiting topics in the chapter as needed. *I have* . . .

_____ outlined the writing process, from getting started to submitting (26).

_____ adapted the writing process to a specific writing project, taking into account the assignment challenges and my own writing habits (27).

_____ analyzed the rhetorical situation for a specific writing project (including my role as writer, the subject, my purpose, the audience, the form, and the context) so as to make good decisions about my approach, tone, and content (28–29).

_____ differentiated seven traits of strong, academic writing and assessed my relative strengths and weaknesses with respect to these traits (30–31).

_____ carefully identified a writing assignment's key words, options, and restrictions, and have related the assignment to course goals, other assignments, and my own interests (32–33).

_____ developed and chosen a strong topic for a writing project by limiting the subject, conducting an exploratory search, and using techniques such as journal writing, listing, clustering, and freewriting (34–37).

_____ identified what I already know about the topic, generated questions to research, formulated a list of possible resources, and worked with those sources, while carefully tracking my use of these sources (38–41).

Chapter 3

Planning

Some of us are meticulous planners. We organize our lives in advance and formulate strategies for completing every task. Others of us live more in the moment, believing that whatever needs to get done will get done, with or without a plan.

In writing, author and instructor Ken Macrorie calls for a blend of these two approaches: "Good writing," says Macrorie, "is formed partly through plan and partly through accident." In other words, too much early planning can get in the way of the discovery aspect of writing, while not enough planning can harm the focus and coherence of your writing.

Visually Speaking   Consider the image below. What does it suggest about the nature and importance of planning? How do such ideas relate to planning a piece of writing?

Learning **Objectives**

By working through this chapter, you will be able to

- re-examine the rhetorical situation with an eye to planning your writing.
- generate a focused, thoughtful working thesis.
- determine the pattern of development suggested by your thesis.
- produce a plan or outline for your writing.

Corepics VOF/Shutterstock.com

fig. 3.1

Revisit the Rhetorical Situation

Use the following planning checklist to help you decide whether to move ahead with your planning or reconsider your topic.

Rhetorical Checklist

Writer

____ Am I interested in this topic?

____ How much do I know about this topic, and how much do I need to learn?

Subject

____ Does the topic fit with the subject requirements of the assignment?

____ Is the topic the right size—not too general or too specific—for the assignment?

____ What sources have I found so far, and how helpful have they been at deepening my understanding of the subject?

Purpose

____ What are the specific goals of the assignment?

____ Am I writing to entertain, inform, explain, analyze, persuade, reflect?

Form

____ What form should I create: essay, proposal, report, review?

Audience

____ Will my readers be interested in this topic? How can I interest them?

____ What do they know and need to know about it? What opinions do they have?

Context

____ What weight does this assignment have in terms of my grade?

____ How will the assignment be assessed?

Working with Sources | For projects that involve research, consider how the rhetorical situation can guide your use of sources:

1. **For your subject**, which sources offer reliable information and analysis that has shaped your thinking and pointed toward a working thesis?

2. **To achieve your purpose** (to entertain, inform, analyze, and/or persuade), which resources/sources should be featured in your writing?

3. **Given your audience,** which resources will help you create credibility with the audience and clarify the topic for them?

Forming Your Thesis Statement

After you have completed enough research and collecting, you may begin to develop a more focused interest in your topic. If all goes well, this narrowed focus will give rise to a thesis for your writing. A thesis statement identifies your central idea. It usually highlights a special condition or feature of the topic, expresses a specific claim about it, or takes a stand.

State your thesis in a sentence that effectively expresses what you want to explore or explain in your essay. Sometimes a thesis statement develops early and easily; at other times, the true focus of your writing emerges only after you've written your first draft.

Find a Focus

A general subject area is typically built into your writing assignments. Your task, then, is to find a limited writing topic and examine it from a particular angle or perspective. (You will use this focus to form your thesis statement.) Figure 3.2 shows this process.

General Subject

Alternative energy sources

Limited Topic

Wind power

Specific Focus

Wind power as a viable energy source in certain settings

fig. 3.2

Draft your Thesis

You can use the formula in Figure 3.3 to draft a thesis statement for your essay. A thesis statement sets the tone and direction for your writing. Keep in mind that at this point you're writing a *working thesis statement*—a statement in progress, so to speak. You may change it as your thinking on the topic evolves.

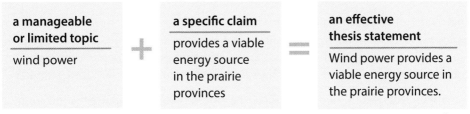

a manageable or limited topic

wind power

+

a specific claim

provides a viable energy source in the prairie provinces

=

an effective thesis statement

Wind power provides a viable energy source in the prairie provinces.

fig. 3.3

Working with Sources | Sometimes your writing can take direction specifically from your sources. You may consider making your thesis a response to a specific source. For example, if one source is especially strong or especially contrary to your own thinking, you could shape your thesis as an affirmation of the strong source's authority or as a rebuttal to the contrary source's claims.

Refine Your Thesis

Once you have drafted your working thesis, you can move on to thinking about organizing your essay. However, it may be helpful to pause, consider why the thesis is so important, and find ways to strengthen your working thesis before moving forward. Consider the following:

Why is the thesis so important for your writing? The thesis is the controlling idea of your essay—the main point or assertion about the topic. As such, the thesis is central to your essay. It sets a direction for your writing and represents your contribution to the larger "conversation" on the topic. Without a solid thesis, an essay lacks direction, purpose, and pressure; it too easily falls into traps of slackness and disorganization. With a good thesis, an essay takes on purpose, becomes naturally organized, and takes the reader on a journey.

How can you discover, develop, and refine your thesis? You can improve your chances of developing a strong thesis by doing the following:

- *Reflect on your findings.* Prewriting strategies and research should generate ideas and information for your writing. Both during and after these activities, reflect on all this material. What patterns and connections come to the surface? These connections might hold the key idea that you are looking for. (See page 407 for more on working with research findings to discover a thesis.)
- *Ask the right questions.* The thesis can be thought of as an answer to a question. But not all questions are the same, nor are all questions equal. What are the most meaningful questions about your topic?
- *Apply concepts from the field.* Some writing calls for a practical, concrete thesis. Example: the steps that should be followed to create an attractive and informative Web page. However, most essay writing centres on concepts and principles. Example: the key principles of Web design. What are the central concepts at the heart of your topic? What principles are common in the field of knowledge to which the topic belongs? Can you apply concepts from other fields of knowledge to your topic?

What is the difference between a weak and a strong thesis? A strong thesis is narrowly focused rather than broad, making it manageable for the assignment. It is challenging rather than simplistic—rarely a simple summary, a straightforward statement of fact, or a pure opinion (a taste or preference that cannot really be argued). Here are three examples:

Weak thesis: lacks depth, functions as a cliché, offers a broad or vague generalization
    Example: "Writing is an important skill."

Good thesis: demonstrates some higher level thinking, such as analysis and argument
    Example: "Reading and writing function symbiotically: strengthening one skill improves the other."

Strong thesis: shows some intellectual complexity, tension, or even risk (surprise, challenge, paradox)
    Example: "In university, writing needs to become much more than an academic exercise: it must function as part of an authentic internal and communal dialogue on issues of life-altering importance."

Using a Thesis to Pattern Your Writing

An organizing pattern for your essay may be built into your assignment. For example, you may be asked to develop an argument or to write a process paper. When a pattern is not apparent, one may still evolve naturally during the research and information-collecting steps. If this doesn't happen, take a careful look at your thesis statement.

Let Your Thesis Guide You

An effective thesis will often suggest an organizing pattern. Notice how the thesis statements below direct and shape the writing to follow. (Also see page 19.)

Thesis (Focus) for a Personal Narrative

Writers of personal narratives do not always state a thesis directly, but they will generally have in mind an implied theme or main idea that governs the way they develop their writing. In the thesis below, which comes near the end of the essay "Mzee Owitti" by Jacqui Nyangi Owitti, the writer focuses on the meaning of the experience that she has narrated: the funeral rites for her grandfather. (To read the essay, see pages 148–150.)

> Until this point, the whole has been a drama played out before my stunned, wide-eyed gaze. Rich in ancestry and tradition, its very nature and continuity are a celebration of life rather than death, fostering in me a keen sense of identity and a strong desire to keep the ancestral torch burning brightly, fiercely, and with pride. Now, however, Grandpa is dead.

Thesis for a Cause-and-Effect Essay

A cause-and-effect essay usually begins with one or more causes followed by an explanation of the effects, or with a primary effect followed by an explanation of the causes. In the thesis below, from the essay "How Canadian Newspaperwomen Won the Vote" by Megan Cécile Radford, the writer explains how female journalists contributed to the battle to win the vote for women in Canada. (See the full essay on pages 263–268.)

> Through the press, what was considered a women's issue was plunged into the general discourse, helping to usher in a new era of democracy. This is how Canadian suffrage was won through the women of the media.

Thesis for an Essay of Comparison

Some comparisons treat one subject before the other (subject by subject), others discuss the subjects point by point, and some treat similarities and then differences. The thesis below comes from an essay written by a Canadian student in the week following the 9/11 attacks. In the thesis of "A Fear Born of Sorrow" by Anita Brinkman, the writer explores the differences between these attacks and other tragedies. (For the full essay, see pages 232–234.)

> But why is the outpouring of grief so much deeper for this tragedy than for others? Why isn't the attack considered just a large-scale repeat of the Oklahoma bombing? Could it be that our grief is more than sorrow, and that our loss is much more than what lies in the rubble?

Thesis for an Essay of Classification

An essay of classification identifies the main parts or categories of a topic and then examines each one. In the thesis below from "Why We Lift," the writer, Hillary Gammons, identifies categories of weightlifters, classified according to their motivation for lifting. (See the essay on pages 192–194.)

> As I looked around, it became obvious that people work out for quite different reasons. Health enthusiasts, toning devotees, athletes, and bodybuilders seem to be the main categories of those lifting weights.

Thesis for a Process Essay

Process essays are organized chronologically. In the thesis below, from "Chasing the Stoke" by Tim Zekveld, the writer indicates that he will trace the evolution of surfing culture, all the while showing how it has remained true to its roots in *aloha*. (See the full essay on pages 214–217.)

> Throughout all the changes to surfing and its culture, the stoke—or heartfelt excitement and reverence to each and every wave's curl—remains evident.

Thesis for a Position Essay

A position paper first introduces a topic and then states a position in its thesis. The thesis statement below, from "Nuclear Is Not the Answer" by Alyssa Woudstra, identifies the writer's position on nuclear energy. (To read the essay, see pages 333–335.)

> However, the risks of nuclear power far outweigh its benefits, making fossil fuels the safer and more environmentally responsible option.

Thesis for an Essay of Definition

An essay of definition explores the denotation, connotation, and history of a term. In the following thesis of "The Gullible Family" by Mary Bruins, the writer identifies the word she will explore in an extended definition, and she signals the essential theme that she will develop. (To read the full essay, see pages 170–171.)

> The word *gullible* connects people and birds, relating them to each other by their willingness to "swallow."

Thesis for an Essay Proposing a Solution

A problem-solution essay usually begins with a discussion of the problem and its causes and then examines possible solutions. In the following thesis of "'It's a Girl!'—Could Be a Death Sentence" by Dr. Rajendra Kale, the writer follows up his identification of female feticide (selectively aborting female fetuses) as a problem in some Canadian communities, and proposes a solution. (To read the full essay, see pages 377–379.)

> This evil devalues women. How can it be curbed? The solution is to postpone the disclosure of medically irrelevant information to women until after about thirty weeks of pregnancy.

Developing a Plan or an Outline

Prior to drafting, it makes sense to develop a working plan for the structure of your writing. Your approach to planning may differ from one type of writing to another. For a short personal essay, a few brief points may be all you need to get started on a narrative; by contrast, for a major research project, you may want to develop a full, formal outline. Whatever choices you make, planning gives you a map to get started—a helpful tool for preventing writer's block and keeping you on course. To do effective planning, consider these strategies:

Discovering organization in your thesis. As discussed on the previous pages, a working thesis sets direction for your writing. With this principle in mind, your goal is to shape the essay as a unified whole around the thesis. To find that unity, ask questions like these:

- **What support is implied in the phrasing of my working thesis?** Examine the key terms and phrases for hints of where your writing needs to go. Try turning those elements into questions that need to be answered, and order the questions in a logical sequence.
- **Does my thesis naturally suggest a specific method of development?** For example, in terms of your assignment, you may have drafted a working thesis that calls for support in a problem-solution, cause-effect, or compare-contrast pattern. Not only is this concept shown on the previous two pages, but it is also explored more fully in Part 2 of this text, the forms of writing.
- **Where should I place my thesis in relation to the overall structure of my writing?** Traditionally, the thesis is placed at the end of the introduction, paving the way for elaboration and support. However, in some writing, the thesis might come toward the middle (e.g., problem-solution writing) or the end (e.g., some position papers). In fact, in some writing, such as the personal essay, the thesis might be only implied, not stated.

Looking to your prewriting. What organizational hints are in your notes? Explore how your notes suggest a way of proceeding. See how points "clump" under key ideas.

Structuring writing for the development of ideas. A strong essay is much more than a static list of points in support of a thesis, each point standing alone and equal in weight. You may recognize this approach as the five-paragraph high-school hamburger: introduction (top bun), three supporting points (meat), and conclusion (bottom bun). If this is the type of essay that you are used to cooking up, it's time to take your cooking skills to the next level. A more mature essay is about *idea development*, with each idea building upon or deepening the previous one. To be forward-looking in your planning, ask these questions:

- **What do I need to provide so the reader understands my thinking?** To carry your reader into a deeper understanding of the topic, you need to structure your thinking for your reader, not for yourself. You might, for example, need to begin by explaining the historical or social context of your topic, by supplying definitions of key terms for your analysis, or by reviewing the commonly held positions on the issue. Only then can you proceed.

- *How can I build sections that move from the known to the new?* Consider how you might "scaffold" your essay by building each new point on the previous one, now understood by the reader. This strategy is the known-new pattern, which you can apply in your writing from paragraph to paragraph, but also from section to section.

Experimenting with mapping methods. You may be comfortable with using one strategy to organize all your essays—traditional outlining, for example. However, trying other methods may unlock creative possibilities you had not imagined. Below is a list of five mapping strategies, each of which is elaborated on the pages that follow.

- **Quick List:** A brief listing of main points (See Figure 3.4.)
- **Topic Outline:** A more formal plan, including main points and essential details (See Figure 3.5.)
- **Sentence Outline:** A formal plan, including main points and essential details, written as complete sentences (See Figure 3.6.)
- **Writing Blueprints:** Basic organizational strategies preferred for different forms of writing (See Figures 3.7–3.10.)
- **Graphic Organizer:** An arrangement of main points and essential details in an appropriate chart or diagram (See Figures 3.11–3.17.)

Quick Lists

Though listing is the simplest of all the methods of organization, it can help you take stock of your main ideas and get a sense of what further research or planning needs to be done. There is no right or wrong way to go about listing. The key is to come up with a system that works best for you. Here are two examples that you may consider: **the basic bulleted list,** which briefly lists the main points you will discuss, and a **T Chart,** which lists the main points on one side and a supporting detail on the other side.

Sample Basic List

Topic: Different ways to discuss literature ——————— Topic
- Focus on the text itself
- Focus on the text and the reader
- Focus on the author of the text ——————— Main Points
- Focus on ideas outside of literature

Sample T Chart

Topic: Different ways to discuss literature ——————— Topic

Approach	Emphasis
Text-centred approach	Structure and rules
Audience-centred approach	Relationship between reader and text
Author-centred approach	The writer's life
Idea-centred approach	Interpretation via specific ideology or field of knowledge

fig. 3.4

Topic Outline

If you have a good deal of information to sort and arrange, you may want to use a **topic outline** for your planning. In a topic outline, you state each main point and essential detail as a word or phrase. Before you start constructing your outline, write your working thesis statement at the top of your paper to help keep you focused on the subject. (Do not attempt to outline your opening and closing paragraphs unless you are specifically asked to do so.)

An effective topic outline is parallel in structure, meaning the main points (I, II, III) and essential details (A, B, C) are stated in the same way. Notice how the sample outline below uses a parallel structure, making it easy to follow.

Sample Topic Outline

Thesis: There are four main perspectives, or approaches, ———— Topic
that readers can use to converse about literature.

I. Text-centred approaches ————————— Main Points
   a. Also called formalist criticism
   b. Emphasis on structure of text and rules of genre ——— Supporting
   c. Importance placed on key literary elements   Details

II. Audience-centred approaches
   a. Also called rhetorical or reader-response criticism
   b. Emphasis on interaction between reader and text

III. Author-centred approaches
   a. Emphasis on writer's life
   b. Importance placed on historical perspective
   c. Connections made between texts

IV. Ideological approaches
   a. Psychological analysis of text
   b. Myth or archetype criticism
   c. Moral criticism
   d. Ecocriticism
   e. Sociological analysis

Maxx-Studio/Shutterstock.com

fig. 3.5

INSIGHT Planning is adaptable. Some writers prefer to generate an outline before they begin writing, while others prefer to make a more detailed outline after having written a draft. In the latter strategy, an outline can serve as a tool for evaluating the logic and completeness of the paper's organization.

Sentence Outline

A **sentence outline** uses complete sentences to explain the main points and essential details in the order that they will be covered in the main part of your essay. Such an outline can help you develop your ideas when writing the paper.

Sample Sentence Outline

Thesis: There are four main perspectives, or approaches, that readers ——— Thesis
can use to converse about literature.

I. A text-centred approach focuses on the literary piece itself. ——— Main Points
  a. This approach is often called formalist criticism.
  b. This method of criticism examines text structure and the
     rules of the genre.   ⎱— Supporting
  c. A formalist critic determines how key literary elements   Details
     reinforce meaning.

II. An audience-centred approach focuses on the "transaction" between text
    and reader.
  a. This approach is often called rhetorical or reader-response criticism.
  b. A rhetorical critic sees the text as an activity that is different for each reader.

III. An author-centred approach focuses on the origin of a text.
  a. An author-centred critic examines the writer's life.
  b. This method of criticism may include a historical look at a text.
  c. Connections may be made between the text and related works.

IV. The ideological approach applies ideas outside of literature.
  a. Some critics apply psychological theories to a literary work.
  b. Myth or archetype criticism applies anthropology and classical studies
     to a text.
  c. Moral criticism explores the moral dilemmas in literature.
  d. Ecocriticism examines the environmental implications of a text.
  e. Sociological approaches include Marxist, feminist, and minority criticism.

fig. 3.6

Working with Sources | When your writing project involves sources, the planning phase will include a great deal of sorting through material. Outlining can help you organize your primary and secondary sources to best support your thesis. As you organize your research in your outline, ask these questions:

- Where and how should I work with primary sources—interviews, surveys, analyses, observations, experiments, and other data I have collected?
- Where and how should I bring in secondary sources—scholarly books, journal articles, and the like?

Writing Blueprints

The writing blueprints in Figures 3.7–3.10 lay out basic organizational strategies for different forms of writing. The blueprints may help you arrange the details of your essay or even find holes in your research.

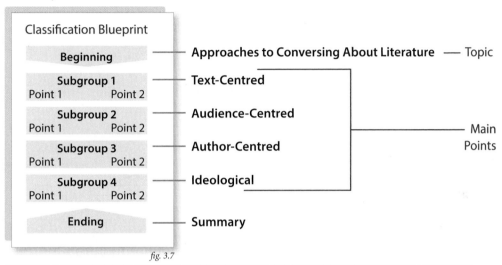

Classification Blueprint

Beginning	—— Approaches to Conversing About Literature —— Topic
Subgroup 1 Point 1 Point 2	—— Text-Centred
Subgroup 2 Point 1 Point 2	—— Audience-Centred
Subgroup 3 Point 1 Point 2	—— Author-Centred
Subgroup 4 Point 1 Point 2	—— Ideological
Ending	—— Summary

Main Points

fig. 3.7

Comparison – Contrast Blueprint

Point by Point	*Subject by Subject*	*Similarities-Differences*
Beginning	Beginning	Beginning
Point A Subject 1 Subject 2	Subject 1	Similarities
Point B Subject 1 Subject 2	Subject 2	Differences
Ending	Ending	Ending

fig. 3.8

Cause – Effect Blueprint

Cause-Focused	*Effect-Focused*
Beginning	Beginning
Cause	Effect
Cause	Effect
Cause	Effect
Effect(s)	Cause(s)
Ending	Ending

fig. 3.9

Problem-Solution Blueprint

| Problem(s) |
| Solution(s) |
| Objection(s) |
| Rebuttal(s) |

fig. 3.10

Graphic Organizers

If you are a visual person, you might prefer a graphic organizer when it comes to arranging your ideas for an essay or a report. Graphic organizers can help you map out ideas and illustrate relationships among them. The organizers in Figures 3.11–3.17 are related to the methods of development discussed on pages 47–48. Each will help you collect and organize your information. Adapt the organizers as necessary to fit your particular needs or personal style.

▼ Note how the line diagram breaks out the topic, main ideas, and supporting details for use in building an essay of classification.

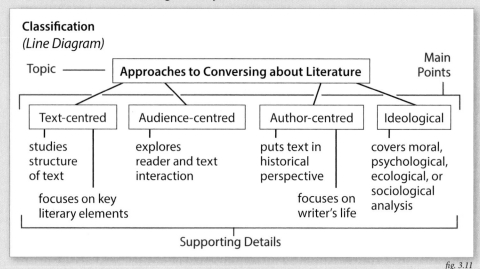

fig. 3.11

Cause/Effect
(T Chart)

Subject:

Causes	Effects
(Because of . . .)	(. . . these conditions resulted)
•	•
•	•
•	•

fig. 3.12

Comparison/Contrast
(Venn Diagram)

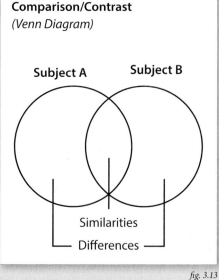

fig. 3.13

Comparison

Qualities	Subject A	Subject B

fig. 3.14

Process Analysis

Subject: _____

(Chronological Order)

Step 1

↓

Step 2

↓

Step 3

fig. 3.15

Problem/Solution

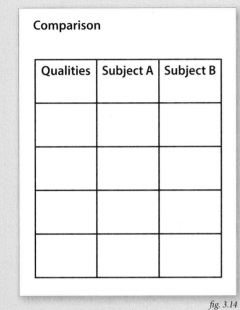

Cause of the Problem

Parts of the Problem

Problem

Future Implication

Possible Solutions

fig. 3.16

Definition

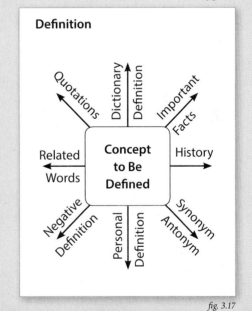

Quotations

Dictionary Definition

Important Facts

Related Words

Concept to Be Defined

History

Negative Definition

Personal Definition

Synonym Antonym

fig. 3.17

Denis Nata/Shutterstock.com

Critical-Thinking and Writing Activities

As directed by your instructor, complete the following activities.

1. Author Ken Macrorie claims that "good writing is formed partly through plan and partly through accident." Do you agree? Why or why not? Relate Macrorie's idea to your own writing experiences. How carefully do you plan? How much do you leave to accident?

2. A number of organizational patterns are discussed on pages 47–48. Choose one of these patterns and select a model essay from Chapters 11–20 that follows the pattern. Read the essay, note the thesis, and explain how the writer develops it.

3. This chapter offers instruction on developing a strong working thesis and an effective plan for your writing. Using what you have learned, do the following:
   • Examine an essay that your wrote recently, assessing the strength of the thesis and the effectiveness of the organization. What would you change, if anything?
   • Find a scholarly article on the same or a closely related topic. Read the essay, identifying the thesis and mapping out the structure of the support. How would you characterize the pattern of thinking in the article?

Learning-Objectives Checklist ✓

Have you achieved this chapter's learning objectives? Check your progress with the items below, revisiting topics in the chapter as needed. *I have . . .*

____ re-examined the rhetorical situation of my writing project (my role as writer, the subject, my purpose, the form, my readers, and the context) so that I can confidently move forward with planning my writing (44).

____ formulated a focused, insightful working thesis for my writing (45–46).

____ analyzed my working thesis so as to determine what pattern of organization it suggests (47–48).

____ generated a plan for my writing, whether a quick list, a topic outline, a formal sentence outline, a blueprint, or a graphic organizer (49–55).

Cross-Curricular Connections

In most disciplines, it is common practice early in the paper to "survey the literature" on the topic. In a literary analysis, you might survey common interpretations of a key issue in the literary work before you relay your view. In the social or natural sciences, you might write a report called a literature review—a report that surveys, summarizes, and synthesizes the studies on a specific topic. To plan a literature review, follow these steps:

1. Identify the studies that should be included in the review.
2. Categorize studies by approach or arrange them chronologically.
3. Summarize and synthesize the studies.

Chapter 4

Drafting

French novelist Anatole France once said that one of his first drafts could have been written by a schoolboy, his next draft by a bright college student, his third draft by a superior graduate, and his final draft "only by Anatole France." Think in those terms as you write your first draft. Your main objective is to get ideas down; you'll have a chance later to improve your writing.

This chapter provides instruction for drafting an academic essay. You'll find specific advice for creating the three main parts and arranging information—the writing moves that enable you to develop your thinking and impact readers.

Visually Speaking   How is drafting like sketching? Note the blurred hand with the pencil in Figure 4.1. What does it suggest about the process of drafting? Then again, are there important differences between sketching and drafting?

Learning **Objectives**

By working through this chapter, you will be able to

- re-examine the rhetorical situation as preparation for drafting.
- describe and explain the parts or "major moves" of essays.
- compose an effective opening for your writing.
- generate a substantial middle to follow the opening.
- produce a closing that effectively ends your draft.
- effectively integrate source material into your draft.

© plainpicture/Astrid Doerenbruch

fig. 4.1

Reconsider the Rhetorical Situation

As you prepare to write, think about the parts of the rhetorical situation:

Think about Your Role

Are you writing as a student, a citizen, a friend, or a member of a scholarly community or discipline? Use a voice that represents you well.

Focus on Your Subject

As you develop your first draft, these strategies can help you keep your subject in focus.

- **Use your outline; writing plan; or any charts, lists, or diagrams you've produced** as a general guide, but don't feel absolutely bound by them. Try to develop your main points, but allow new ideas to emerge naturally.
- **Write freely** without being too concerned about neatness and correctness. Concentrate on developing your ideas, not on producing a final copy.
- **Include as much detail as possible**, continuing until you reach a logical stopping point.
- **Complete your first draft** in one or two sittings.
- **Use the most natural voice you can** so that the writing will flow smoothly. If your voice is too formal during drafting, you'll be tempted to stop and edit your words.
- **Quote sources accurately** by using your word-processing program's copy-and-paste features or by handwriting or typing quotations carefully.

Reconsider Your Purpose

Briefly review (1) what you want your writing to do (your task), (2) what you want it to say (your thesis), and (3) how you want to say it (list of ideas or outline). If helpful, write that purpose or thesis on a file card and keep it nearby as you draft.

Reconsider Your Audience

Review who your readers are, including their knowledge of and attitude toward your topic. For some assignments, you may want to approach drafting as talking to your reader, person to person. This approach makes sense for argumentative essays. For other writing, you may want to forget about the reader while drafting—keeping the focus on your own thinking through of the topic (e.g., an analytical essay).

Review the Form and Context

Make sure you understand the type of writing you should do, the weight of the assignment, and any assessment issues.

Working with Sources | Use sources that aid your purpose and connect to your audience. Also, make sure your sources do not crowd out your own reasoning and thinking—your role in the assignment.

Basic Essay Structure: Major Moves

The chart in Figure 4.2 lists the main writing moves that occur during the development of a piece of writing. Use it as a general guide that you adapt as needed for all of your drafting. Remember to keep your purpose and audience in mind throughout the drafting process.

Opening

Engage your reader.
Stimulate and direct the reader's attention.

Establish your direction.
Identify the topic and put it in perspective.

Get to the point.
Narrow your focus and state your thesis.

Middle

Advance your thesis.
Provide background information and cover your main points.

Test your ideas.
Raise questions and consider alternatives.

Support your main points.
Add substance and build interest.

Build a coherent structure.
Start new paragraphs and arrange the support.

Use different levels of detail.
Clarify and complete each main point.

Ending

Reassert the main point.
Remind the reader of the purpose and rephrase the thesis.

Urge the reader.
Gain the reader's acceptance and look ahead.

fig. 4.2

Opening Your Draft

The opening paragraph is one of the most important elements in any composition. It should accomplish at least three essential things: (1) engage the reader; (2) establish your direction, tone, and level of language; and (3) introduce your line of thought.

Advice:
- The conventional way of approaching the first paragraph is to view it as a kind of "funnel" that draws a reader in and narrows to a main point. In some situations, the final sentence explicitly states your thesis.

Cautions:
- Don't feel bound by the conventional pattern, which may sound stale if not handled well.
- Don't let the importance of the first paragraph paralyze you. Relax and write.

The information on the next two pages will help you develop your opening. For additional ideas, you can refer to the sample essays in Part 2 of this text, the Reader. (See page 131.)

Engage Your Reader

Your reader will be preoccupied with other thoughts until you seize, stimulate, and direct his or her attention. Here are some effective ways to "hook" the reader:

- **Mention little-known facts about the topic.**

  Beads may have been what separated human ancestors from their Neanderthal cousins. Yes, beads.

- **Pose a challenging question.**

  Why would human ancestors spend days carving something as frivolous as beads while Neanderthals spent days hunting mammoths?

- **Offer a thought-provoking quotation.**

  "The key thing in human evolution is when people start devoting just ridiculous amounts of time to making these [beads]," says archeologist John Shea of Stony Brook University.

- **Tell a brief, illuminating story.**

  When I walked into the room, I had only to show my hand to be accepted in the group of strangers there. The Phi Delta Kappa ring on my finger—and on all of our fingers—bound us across space and time as a group. Our ancestors discovered the power of such ornamentation forty thousand years ago.

Establish Your Direction

The direction of your line of thought should become clear in the opening part of your writing. Here are some moves you might make to set the right course:

- **Identify the topic (issue).** Show a problem, a need, or an opportunity.
- **Deepen the issue.** Connect the topic, showing its importance.
- **Acknowledge other views.** Tell what others say or think about the topic.

Get to the Point

You may choose to state your main point up front, or you may wait until later to introduce your thesis. For example, you could work inductively by establishing an issue, a problem, or a question in your opening and then build toward the answer—your thesis—in your conclusion. (See page 18 for more on inductive reasoning.) Sometimes, in fact, your thesis may simply be implied. In any case, the opening should at least hint at the central issue, theme, or thesis of your paper. Here are three ways to get to the point:

1. **Narrow your focus.** Point to what interests you about the topic.
2. **Raise a question.** Answer the question in the rest of the essay.
3. **State your thesis.** If appropriate, craft a sentence that boils down your thinking to a central claim. You can use the thesis sentence as a "map" for the organization of the rest of the essay. (See pages 45–48, 114–117, and 406–407.)

Weak Opening

Although the opening below introduces the topic, the writing lacks interesting details and establishes no clear focus for the essay.

> I would like to tell you about the TV show *The Simpsons*. It's about this weird family of five people who look kind of strange and act even stranger. In fact, the characters aren't even real—they're just cartoons.

Strong Opening

In the essay opener below, the writer uses his first paragraph to get his readers' attention and describe his subject. He uses the second paragraph to raise a question that leads him to a statement of his thesis (underlined).

> *The Simpsons,* stars of the TV show by the same name, are a typical American family, or at least a parody of one. Homer, Marge, Bart, Lisa, and Maggie Simpson live in Springfield, U.S.A. Homer, the father, is a boorish, obese oaf who works in a nuclear power plant. Marge is an overprotective, nagging mother with an outrageous blue hairdo. Ten-year-old Bart is an obnoxious, "spiky-haired demon." Lisa is eight and a prodigy on the tenor saxophone and in class. The infant Maggie never speaks but only sucks on her pacifier.
>
> What is the attraction of this yellow-skinned family that stars on a show in which all of the characters have pronounced overbites and only four fingers on each hand? Viewers see a little bit of themselves in everything the Simpsons do. <u>The world of Springfield is a parody of the viewer's world, and even after more than 500 episodes, fans can't get enough of it.</u> Viewers experience this parody in the show's explanations of family, education, workplace, and politics.

INSIGHT   After stating the thesis, the writer forecasts the method of supporting that thesis.

Developing the Middle

The middle of an essay is where you do the "heavy lifting." In this part you develop the main points that support your thesis statement.

Advice: • As you write, you will likely make choices that were unforeseen when you began. Use "scratch outlines" (temporary jottings) along the way to show where your new ideas may take you.

Cautions: • Writing that lacks effective detail gives only a vague image of the writer's intent.
  • Writing that wanders loses its hold on the essay's purpose.

For both of these reasons, always keep your thesis in mind when you develop the main part of your writing. Refer to the guidelines on the next two pages for help. You can refer to the sample essays in this book for ideas.

Advance Your Thesis

If you stated a thesis in the opening, you can advance it in the middle paragraphs by covering your main points and supporting them in these ways.

Explain: Provide important facts, details, and examples.
Narrate: Share a brief story or re-create an experience to illustrate an idea.
Describe: Tell in detail how someone appears or how something works.
Define: Identify or clarify the meaning of a specific term or idea.
Analyze: Examine the parts of something to better understand the whole.
Compare: Provide examples to show how two things are alike or different.
Argue: Use logic and evidence to prove that something is true.
Reflect: Express your thoughts or feelings about something.
Cite authorities: Add expert analysis or personal commentary.

Test Your Ideas

When you write a first draft, you're testing your initial thinking about your topic. You're determining whether your thesis is valid and whether you have enough compelling information to support it. Here are ways to test your line of thinking as you write:

- **Raise questions.** Try to anticipate your readers' questions.
- **Consider alternatives.** Look at your ideas from different angles; weigh various options; reevaluate your thesis.
- **Answer objections.** Directly or indirectly deal with possible problems that a skeptical reader might point out.

Build a Coherent Structure

Design paragraphs as units of thought that develop and advance your thesis clearly and logically. For example, look at the brief essay below, noting how each body paragraph presents ideas with supporting details that build on and deepen the main idea.

Seeing the Light

The writer introduces the topic and states his thesis.

All lightbulbs make light, so they're all the same, right? Not quite. You have many choices regarding how to light up your life. Two types of bulbs are the traditional incandescent and the newer, more compact fluorescent. <u>By checking out how they're different, you can better choose which one to buy.</u>

The writer starts with a basic explanation of how the two types of lightbulbs function differently.

While either incandescent or compact fluorescent bulbs can help you read or find the bathroom at night, each bulb makes light differently. In an incandescent bulb, electricity heats up a tungsten filament (thin wire) to 450 degrees, causing it to glow with a warm, yellow light. A compact fluorescent is a glass tube filled with mercury vapor and argon gas. Electricity causes the mercury to give off ultraviolet radiation. That radiation then causes phosphors coating the inside of the tube to give off light.

The writer shifts his attention to weaknesses of compact bulbs.

Both types of bulbs come in many shapes, sizes, and brightnesses, but compacts have some restrictions. Because of their odd shape, compacts may not fit in a lamp well. Compacts also may not work well in very cold temperatures, and they can't be used with a dimmer switch.

He next explains the strengths of compacts.

On the other hand, while compact fluorescents are less flexible than incandescents, compacts are four times more efficient. For example, a 15-watt compact produces as many lumens of light as a 60-watt incandescent! Why? Incandescents turn only about 5 percent of electricity into light and give off the other 95 percent as heat.

He acknowledges that compacts cost more, but he justifies the cost.

But are compacts less expensive than incandescents? In the short run, no. Whereas a 60-watt incandescent costs about one dollar, a comparable compact can cost about $5.00. However, because compacts burn less electricity—and last 7 to 10 times longer—in the long run, compacts are less expensive.

The writer rephrases his thesis as a challenge.

Now that you're no longer in the dark about lightbulbs, take a look at the lamp you're using to read this essay. Think about the watts (electricity used), lumens (light produced), efficiency, purchase price, and lamplife. Then decide how to light up your life in the future.

Make Writing Moves

Drafting the body of your essay can involve drawing on a range of writing moves, from paragraph to paragraph or section to section. Many of these moves are addressed in Part 2 of this text, where rhetorical modes such as narrating, defining and classifying are presented. What follows, however, are some other common writing moves.

Developing an Analogy or Comparison

An analogy is a comparison that a writer uses to explain a complex or unfamiliar phenomenon. For example, in the following paragraph, the writer describes a mall security system in order to explain the human immune system.

> The human body is like a mall, and the immune system is like mall security. Because the mall has hundreds of employees and thousands of customers, security guards must rely on photo IDs, name tags, and uniforms to decide who should be allowed to open cash registers and who should have access to the vault. In the same way, white blood cells and antibodies need to use DNA cues to recognize which cells belong in a body and which do not. Occasionally security guards make mistakes, wrestling Kookie the Klown to the ground while DVD players "walk" out of the service entrance, but these problems amount only to allergic reactions or little infections. If security guards become hypervigilant, detaining every customer and employee, the situation is akin to leukemia, in which white blood cells attack healthy cells. If security guards become corrupt, letting thieves take a "five-finger discount," the situation is akin to AIDS. Both systems—mall security and human immunity—work by correctly differentiating friend from foe.
> —Rob King

Courtesy of The Write Source.

Developing an Example or Illustration

Providing an example or illustration allows you to flesh out an idea by providing an instance of that point. Well developed examples match up with the idea by clarifying its various facets. In the passage below from "Dead Indians" (pages 181–185), Thomas King provides three examples to illustrate what he means by the phrase "Dead Indians."

> You can find Dead Indians everywhere. Rodeos, powwows, movies, television commercials. At the 1973 Academy Awards, when Sacheen Littlefeather (Yaqui-Apache-Pueblo) refused the Best Actor award on behalf of Marlon Brando, she did so dressed as a Dead Indian. When U.S. Senator Benjamin Nighthorse Campbell (Northern Cheyenne) and W. Richard West, Jr. (Cheyenne-Arapaho), the director of the American Indian Museum in New York, showed up for the 2004 opening ceremonies of the museum, they took the podium in Dead Indian leathers and feathered headdresses. Phil Fontaine (Ojibway) was attired in the same manner when he stood on the floor of the House of Commons in 2008 to receive the Canadian government's apology for the abuses of residential schools.

Presenting and Interpreting Evidence

You may be familiar with the phrase "marshalling evidence," which suggests that this writing move is something of a military campaign. When you pull together, present, and analyze a range of evidence (e.g., statistics, historical records, and expert testimony), you advance your ideas by building a foundation on which your reasoning can stand. In the following paragraph from "Chasing the Stoke" (pages 214–217), Tim Zekveld explains the origins of *aloha* by presenting historical evidence.

> In Hawaii, surfing began as a joyous thanksgiving to the ocean for its providence and sustenance. Dating as far back as 800 AD, surfing was commonplace in Hawaiian society. Men, women, and children of every social status—from the commoner to the king—would surf regularly as a means of leisure and a form of ritual. When the ocean had provided food for their clan or had affected the people in a catastrophic way, Hawaiians would, while surfing the face of a wave, turn around and bow, wetting their head in the curl (Peralta). This ritual was a physical act meant to pay homage to the ocean, showing immense humility and reverence to their life force. Surfing on carved wooden boards measuring sixteen feet or longer and weighing well over a hundred pounds, the ancient Hawaiians would paddle into waves varying from three to thirty feet (Young 11). Captain James Cook, on viewing a Hawaiian surf in 1777, wrote, "I could not help concluding that this man felt the most supreme pleasure while he was being driven on so fast and so smoothly by the sea" (qtd. in Peralta). The joy that Captain Cook had witnessed, paired with the unfathomable respect that Hawaiians had for the ocean, fused into one term: *aloha*.

Applying a Concept

A lot of academic writing involves explaining and applying concepts—the key ideas that make sense of subjects. For example, an environmental science student might analyze corn production using the concept of sustainability, or an English student might explain a character's fate through the concept of *hubris*. In the following passage from "Pitch Perfect" (pages 269–270), Jay Ingram looks at the science of the knuckleball pitch by applying the concept "tricks of perception."

> This could be another example of batters' perceptions being fooled, not unlike the so-called rising fastball, which doesn't rise at all. It just doesn't drop as fast as batters assume it will. This surprising finding prompted Nathan to suggest that the apparent fluttering and zigzagging may be a trick of perception. As the pitch rotates extremely slowly, the orientation of the seams is actually visible to the batter, instead of being the usual blur. It may be that the seams' movement is confused with that of the ball. "Knuckleballs," he ventures, "are more like bullets than butterflies." Only further experiments will tell us for sure. In the meantime, we can be certain of one thing: that the knuckler is the most beautifully bizarre phenomenon in all of baseball.

Stretching an Idea

When you stretch an idea, you are making a writing move that explores the boundaries and portability of the idea. Can it be stretched to include elements and dimensions not normally associated with it? Might it be transported from one field of knowledge to another? Should you shift the direction of discussion by turning the idea upside down? In the paragraph below from "Recreational Winter" (pages 200–205), Adam Gopnik begins the process of transporting game theory from mathematics into the arena of sports—a stretching of the idea that goes on for several paragraphs.

> The funny thing about game theory is that, though it has been used to explain everything from economics to nuclear warfare, it's very rarely used to explain *games*—or at least not sports. And yet when you think about it, part of the pleasure we take in sports has everything to do with game theory, which has exactly to do with questions of how much we know, how much our opponents know, how much they know of what we know, and so on.

Exploring a Tension

This writing move to the gaps, disagreements, dualisms, and elements of confusion within your topic. Such tensions are often big and obvious, but they may also be small and subtle. Both kinds are worthy of your attention. Such a move may call out the tension, explore its meaning, and possibly seek to resolve it. The paragraph below comes from "Emma Tietel's commentary on Israeil Apartheid Week, "It's 'Apartheid' Time Again. Pick Your Villain." (see pages 336–337). Just before this excerpt, she asks why the 2012 IAW differs from previous ones. Notice how she brings into tension the reality of Syria with the protest against Israel.

Note: For an in-depth treatment of these and other writing moves as thinking moves, see *Think About It*, by John Mauk, Jayme Stayer, and Karen Mauk.

> The answer is just northeast of Israel, in Syria. In the past 11 months, almost 9,000 civilian protesters and nearly 3,000 anti-government rebels have been murdered by Syrian President Bashar al-Assad's Ba'ath party dictatorship. Approximately 400 children have been imprisoned and tortured. Meanwhile, Assad's government claims that 89.4 per cent of Syrians had approved a new constitution that could keep Bashar in power for another 16 years, along with the 12 years he's already ruled, and the 29 years his father Hafez held power before him. You'd think that anyone committed to the cause of justice in the Middle East would put the atrocities in Syria at the top of their to-do list. But the Canadian organizers of Israeli Apartheid Week—loudly devoted to ending oppression and achieving social justice for all—won't be talking about Syria this year. Instead, they'll spend March 5–9 railing exclusively against the "Zionist regime" at a university campus near you. Events will include slam poetry renditions, hip-hop shows, and an apartheid poster contest with a top prize of $400.

Ending Your Draft

Closing paragraphs can be important for tying up loose ends, clarifying key points, or signing off with the reader. In a sense, the entire essay is a preparation for an effective ending; the ending helps the reader look back over the essay with new understanding and appreciation. Many endings leave the reader with fresh food for thought.

Advice:
- Because the ending can be so important, draft a variety of possible endings. Choose the one that flows best from a sense of the whole.

Cautions:
- If your thesis is weak or unclear, you will have a difficult time writing a satisfactory ending. To strengthen the ending, strengthen the thesis.
- You may have heard this formula for writing an essay: "Say what you're going to say, say it, then say what you've just said." Remember, though, if you need to "say what you've just said," say it in new words.

The information on the next two pages will help you develop your ending. For ideas, you can refer to the sample essays elsewhere in this book.

Reassert the Main Point

If an essay is complicated, the reader may need reclarification at the end. Show that you are fully addressing the issues that you forecast earlier in the essay.
- **Remind the reader.** Recall what you first set out to do; check off the key points you've covered; or answer any questions left unanswered.
- **Rephrase the thesis.** Restate your thesis in light of the most important support you've given. Deepen and expand your original thesis.

Urge the Reader

Your reader may still be reluctant to accept your ideas or argument. The ending is your last chance to gain the reader's acceptance. Here are some possible strategies:
- **Show the implications.** Follow further possibilities raised by your train of thought; be reasonable and convincing.
- **Look ahead.** Suggest other possible connections.
- **List the benefits.** Show the reader the benefits of accepting or applying the things you've said.

INSIGHT When your writing comes to an effective stopping point, conclude the essay. Don't tack on another idea.

Complete and Unify Your Message

Your final paragraphs are your last opportunity to refocus, unify, and otherwise reinforce your message. Draft the closing carefully, not merely to finish the essay but to further advance your purpose and thesis.

Weak Ending

The ending below does not focus on and show commitment to the essay's main idea. Rather than reinforcing this idea, the writing leads off in a new direction.

> I realize I've got to catch my bus. I've spent too much time talking to this woman whose life is a wreck. I give her some spare change and then head off. She doesn't follow me. It's kind of a relief. Toronto is a great city, but sometimes you have weird experiences there. Once a street vendor gave me a free falafel. I didn't want to eat it because maybe something was wrong with it. What a weird city!

Strong Endings

Below are final paragraphs from two essays in this book : "Spare Change" by Teresa Zsuffa and "Latin American Music: A Diverse and Unifying Force" by Kathleen Kropp. Listen to their tone, watch how they reconsider the essay's ideas, and note how they offer further food for thought. (The first example is a revision of the weak paragraph above.)

> I tell her I need to get going. She should go, too, or she'll be late for the hearing. Before getting up, I reach into my wallet and give her two TTC passes and some spare change. I walk her to the street and point her toward Old City Hall. She never thanks me, only looks at me one last time with immense vulnerability and helplessness. Then she walks away.
>
> I wonder as I hurry towards the station if she'll be okay, if her boyfriend really will get out of jail, and if her grandmother will ever take her back. Either way, I think as I cross Bay Street, what more can I do? I have a bus to catch.
>
> (See the full essay on pages 151–153.)

> Passion and power permeate all of Latin America's music. The four major types of music—indigenous, Iberian and Mestizo folk, Afro-American, and popular urban—are as diverse as the people of Latin America, and each style serves a valued need or function in Latinos' everyday lives. As a result, those listening to Latin American music—whether it is a Peruvian Indian's chant, a Venezuelan farmer's whistled tune, a Cuban mambo drummer's vivacious beat, or the Bogotá rock concert's compelling rhythms—are hearing much more than music. They are hearing the passion and power of the Latin American people.
>
> (See the full essay on pages 195–197.)

Working with Sources

If you are using sources, take care not to overwhelm your draft with source material. Keep the focus on your own ideas:

- Avoid strings of references and chunks of source material with no discussion, explanation, or interpretation on your part in between.
- Don't offer entire paragraphs of material from a source (whether paraphrased or quoted) with a single in-text citation at the end. When you do so, your thinking disappears.
- Be careful not to overload your draft with complex information and dense data lacking explanation.
- Resist the urge to simply copy and paste big chunks from sources. Even if you document the sources, your paper will quickly become a patchwork of source material with a few weak stitches (your contribution) holding it together.
- Note the careful use of source material in the following paragraph.

Sample Paragraph Showing Integration of Source Material

Topic sentence: idea elaborating and supporting thesis

Development of idea through reasoning

Support of idea through reference to source material

Concluding statement of idea

Antibiotics are effective only against infections caused by bacteria and should never be used against infections caused by viruses. Using an antibiotic against a viral infection is like throwing water on a grease fire—water may normally put out fires but will only worsen the situation for a grease fire. In the same way, antibiotics fight infections, but they cause the body harm only when they are used to fight infections caused by viruses. Viruses cause the common cold, the flu, and most sore throats, sinus infections, coughs, and bronchitis. Yet antibiotics are commonly prescribed for these viral infections. *The New England Journal of Medicine* reports that 22.7 million kilograms (25,000 tons) of antibiotics is prescribed each year in the United States alone (Wenzel and Edmond, 1962). Meanwhile, the CDC reports that approximately 50 percent of those prescriptions are completely unnecessary ("Antibiotic Overuse" 25). "Every year, tens of millions of prescriptions for antibiotics are written to treat viral illnesses for which these antibiotics offer no benefits," says the CDC's antimicrobial resistance director David Bell, M.D. (qtd. in Bren 30). Such mis-prescribing is simply bad medical practice that contributes to the problem of growing bacterial infection.

Critical-Thinking and Writing Activities

As directed by your instructor, complete the following critical-thinking and writing activities by yourself or with classmates.

1. Patricia T. O'Connor says, "All writing begins life as a first draft, and first drafts are never any good. They're not supposed to be." Is this claim true? Why or why not? What do you hope to accomplish with a first draft?

2. Study the chart on page 59 and the "writing moves" on pages 64–66. Based on other material you have read or written, add another writing move for each of the three main parts of the essay: opening, middle, and ending. Name the move, explain it, and tell what types of writing it might appear in.

3. Read the final paragraphs of any three essays included in this book. Write a brief analysis of each ending based on the information on pages 68–69.

4. Imagine that you are a journalist who has been asked to write an article about a wedding, a funeral, or another significant event you have experienced. Choose an event and sketch out a plan for your article. Include the main writing moves and the type of information at each stage of your writing.

Learning-Objectives Checklist ✓

Have you achieved this chapter's learning objectives? Check your progress with the items below, revisiting topics in the chapter as needed. *I have* . . .

____ re-examined the rhetorical situation of my writing project (my role as writer, my subject, my purpose, the audience, the form, and the context) to be better prepared for drafting (58).

____ identified and explained the parts or "major moves" of an essay, including strategies for openings, middles, and closings (59).

____ composed an opening that effectively engages my readers; establishes my direction, tone, and diction level; and introduces my line of thought through a thesis or a theme (60–61).

____ generated a substantial middle that advances my thesis, tests out my ideas, builds a coherent structure, implements effective writing moves, and provides a fitting level of detail (62–66).

____ produced a closing that reasserts my main point in a fresh way, connects with readers, and unifies my writing (67–68).

____ integrated source material so that it supports my thinking rather than encumbers my ideas (69).

Chapter 5

Revising

The word revising means "taking another look," so revising is best done after a brief break. Set aside your writing and return to it later with fresh eyes. Also, enlist the fresh eyes of another reader, whether a roommate, a classmate, or someone at the writing centre. Revising is all about getting perspective.

Of course, once you have perspective, you need to figure out how to make improvements. This chapter provides numerous strategies for focusing on the global traits of your writing—ideas, organization, and voice. The changes you make should improve the work significantly, perhaps even reshaping it.

Visually Speaking To effectively revise your draft, you need to first "recharge your writing batteries" (Figure 5.1). Practically speaking, what might this idea mean for your own writing?

Learning **Objectives**

By working through this chapter, you will be able to

- assess the overall approach that you have taken in your draft.

- critique and improve the ideas, organization, and voice of your draft.

- test and strengthen your paragraphs for unity, coherence, and completeness.

- give and receive helpful feedback by collaborating with classmates.

- explain the role of the writing centre and use it to improve your own writing.

Alison Hancock/Shutterstock.com

fig. 5.1

Consider Whole-Paper Issues

When revising, first look at the big picture. Take it all in. Determine whether your content is interesting, informative, and worth sharing. Note any gaps or soft spots in your line of thinking. Ask yourself how you can improve what you have done so far. The information that follows will help you address whole-paper issues such as these.

Revisit the Rhetorical Situation

Just as the rhetorical situation helped you to set your direction in writing, it can help you make course corrections. Think about each part of the rhetorical situation.

- **Consider your role.** How are you coming across in this draft? Do you sound authoritative, engaged, knowledgeable, confident? How do you want to come across?
- **Think about your subject.** Have you stated a clear focus? Have you supported it with a variety of details? Have you explored the subject fully?
- **Remember your purpose.** Are you trying to analyze, describe, explain, propose? Does the writing succeed? Do the ideas promote your purpose? Does your organization support the purpose? Is your writing voice helpful in achieving your purpose?
- **Check the form.** Have you created writing that matches the form that your instructor requested? Have you taken best advantage of the form, including graphics or other media, if appropriate?
- **Consider your readers.** Have you captured their attention and interest? Have you provided them the information they need to understand your writing? Have you considered their values, needs, and opinions, and used them to connect?
- **Think about the context.** Is this piece of writing the correct length and level of seriousness for the assignment? Is it on schedule? How does it match up to what others are doing?

Working with Sources | Make sure that your sources work well for each part of the rhetorical situation. Verify that the sources you have used do the following:

- reflect well on you, showing that you understand and care about the topic.
- illuminate the subject with accurate, precise, substantial information.
- help you achieve your purpose, whether to inform, persuade, or reflect.
- work well within the form and can be appropriately credited.
- are seen as authoritative by readers.
- are timely and credible in the context.

Consider Your Overall Approach

Sometimes it's better to start fresh if your writing contains stretches of uninspired ideas. Consider a fresh start if your first draft shows one of these problems:

- **The topic is worn out.** An essay titled "Lead Poisoning" may not sound very interesting. Unless you can approach it with a new twist ("Get the Lead Out!"), consider cutting your losses and finding a fresh topic.
- **The approach is stale.** If you've been writing primarily to get a good grade, finish the assignment, or sound cool, start again. Try writing to learn something, prompt real thinking in readers, or touch a chord.
- **Your voice is predictable or fake.** Avoid the bland "A good time was had by all" or the phony academic "When one studies this significant problem in considerable depth . . . " Be real. Be honest.
- **The draft sounds boring.** Maybe it's boring because you pay an equal amount of attention to everything and hence stress nothing. Try condensing less important material and expanding what's important.
- **The essay is formulaic.** In other words, it follows the "five-paragraph" format. This handy organizing frame may prevent you from doing justice to your topic and thinking. If your draft is dragged down by rigid adherence to a formula, try a more original approach.

Working with Sources ▌ Test the balance of reasoning and sources. Make sure your draft is not thin on source material, but also make sure that the source material does not dominate the conversation. Use these tips for balancing reasoning and sources:

1. Before diving into source material within a paragraph or section of your paper, flesh out your thinking more fully. Offer reasoning that elaborates the claim and effectively leads into the evidence.

2. As you present evidence from source material, build on it by explaining what it means. Evidence doesn't typically speak for itself: through analysis, synthesis, illustration, contrast, and other means, you need to show how or why your sources advance your thesis.

3. After you have presented evidence that elaborates on and supports your idea, extend your thoughts by addressing the reader's "So what?" or "Why does this matter?" skepticism.

Asya Alexandrova/Shutterstock.com

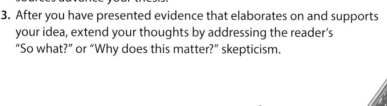

Revising Your First Draft

Revising helps you turn your first draft into a more complete, thoughtful piece of writing. The following information will help you do that.

Prepare to Revise

Once you've finished a first draft, set it aside (ideally for a few days) until you can look at the draft objectively and make needed changes. If you drafted on paper, photocopy the draft. If you drafted on a computer, print your paper (double-spaced). Then make changes with a good pencil or coloured pen. If you prefer revising on the computer, consider using your software editing program. In all cases, save your first draft for reference.

Think Globally

When revising, focus on the big picture—the overall strength of the ideas, organization, and voice.

Ideas: Check your thesis, focus, or theme. Has your thinking on your topic changed? Also think about your readers' most pressing questions concerning this topic. Have you answered these questions? Finally, consider your reasoning and support. Are both complete and sound? Now is the time to address any gaps, weaknesses, or errors in your thinking.

Organization: Check the overall design of your writing, making sure that ideas move smoothly and logically from one point to the next. Does your essay effectively elaborate the thesis in a series of sections and paragraphs that deepen understanding and take the reader on a thoughtful journey? Do you shift directions cleanly? Fix structural problems in one of these ways:

- **Reorder** material to improve the sequence.
- **Cut** information that doesn't support the thesis.
- **Add** details where the draft is thin.
- **Rewrite** parts that seem unclear.
- **Improve** links between points by using transitions.

Voice: Voice is your personal presence on the page, the tone and attitude that others hear when reading your work. In other words, voice is the between-the-lines message your readers get (whether you want them to or not). When revising, make sure that the tone of your message matches your purpose, whether it is serious, playful, or satiric.

INSIGHT Don't pay undue attention to spelling, grammar, and punctuation at this early stage in the process. Otherwise, you may become distracted from the task at hand: improving the content of your writing. Editing and proofreading come later.

Revising for Ideas and Organization

As you review your draft for content, make sure the ideas are fully developed and the organization is clear. From your main claim or thesis to your reasoning and your evidence, strengthen your thinking and sequencing.

Examine Your Ideas

Review the ideas in your writing, making sure that each point is logical, complete, and clear. To test the logic in your writing, see pages 317–320.

Complete Thinking

Have you answered readers' basic questions? Have you supported the thesis? The original passage below is too general; the revision is clearly more complete.

> **Original Passage** (Too general)
> As soon as you receive a minor cut, the body's healing process begins to work. Blood from tiny vessels fills the wound and begins to clot. In less than 24 hours, a scab forms.

> **Revised Version** (More specific)
> As soon as you receive a minor cut, the body's healing process begins to work. In a simple wound, the first and second layers of skin are severed along with tiny blood vessels called capillaries. As these vessels bleed into the wound, minute structures called platelets help stop the bleeding by sticking to the edges of the cut and to one another, forming a plug. The platelets then release chemicals that react with certain proteins in the blood to form a clot. The blood clot, with its fibre network, begins to join the edges of the wound together. As the clot dries out, a scab forms, usually in less than 24 hours.

Clear Thesis

Make sure that your writing centres on one main issue or thesis. Although this next original passage lacks a thesis, the revision has a clear one.

> **Original Passage** (Lacks a thesis)
> Teen magazines are popular with young girls. These magazines contain a lot of how-to articles about self-image, fashion, and boy–girl relationships. Girls read them to get advice on how to act and how to look. Girls who don't really know what they want are the most eager readers.

> **Revised Version** (Identifies a specific thesis statement)
> Adolescent girls often see teen magazines as handbooks on how to be teenagers. These magazines influence the ways they act and the ways they look. For girls who are unsure of themselves, these magazines can exert an enormous amount of influence. Unfortunately, the advice these magazines give about self-image, fashion, and boys may do more harm than good.

Examine Your Organization

Good writing has structure. It leads readers logically and clearly from one point to the next. When revising for organization, consider four areas: the overall plan, the opening, the flow of ideas, and the closing.

Overall Plan

Look closely at the sequence of ideas or events that you share. Does that sequence advance your thesis? Do the points build effectively? Are there gaps in the support or points that stray from your original purpose? If you find such problems, consider the following actions:

- **Refine the focus or emphasis** by rearranging material within the text.
- **Fill in the gaps with new material.** Go back to your planning notes.
- **Delete material that wanders** away from your purpose.
- **Use an additional (or different) method of organization.** For example, if you are comparing two subjects, add depth to your analysis by contrasting them as well. If you are describing a complex subject, show the subject more clearly and fully by distinguishing and classifying its parts. (See pages 64–68 for more on organizational methods.)

INSIGHT   What is the best method of organization for your essay? The writing you are doing will usually determine the choice. As you know, a personal narrative is often organized by time. Typically, however, you combine and customize methods to develop a writing idea. For example, within a comparison essay you may do some describing or classifying. See pages 47–48 and 117 for more on the common methods of development.

Opening Ideas

Reread your opening paragraph(s). Is the opening organized effectively? Does it engage readers, establish a direction for your writing, and express your thesis or focus? The original opening below doesn't build to a compelling thesis statement, but the revised version engages the reader and leads to the thesis.

Original Opening (Lacks interest and direction)

> The lack of student motivation is a common subject in the news. Educators want to know how to get students to learn. Today's higher standards mean that students will be expected to learn even more. Another problem in urban areas is that large numbers of students are dropping out. How to interest students is a challenge.

Revised Version (Effectively leads readers into the essay)

> How can we motivate students to learn? How can we get them to meet today's rising standards of excellence? How can we, in fact, keep students in school long enough to learn? The answer to these problems is quite simple. Give them money. Pay students to study and learn and stay in school.

Flow of Ideas

Look closely at the beginnings and endings of each paragraph. Have you connected your thoughts clearly? (See page 86 for a list of transition words.) The original opening words of the paragraph sequence below, from an essay of description, offer no links for readers. The revised versions use strong transitions indicating spatial organization (order by location).

Original First Words in the Four Middle Paragraphs

There was a huge, steep hill ...
Buffalo Creek ran ...
A dense "jungle" covering ...
Within walking distance from my house ...

Revised Versions (Words and phrases connect ideas)

Behind the house, there was a huge, steep hill ...
Across the road from the house, Buffalo Creek ran ...
On the far side of the creek bank was a dense "jungle" covering ...
Up the road, within walking distance from my house ...

INSIGHT   Review "Supporting Your Claims" (pages 314–316) and use those strategies to strengthen weak or unconvincing passages.

Closing Ideas

Reread your closing paragraph(s). Do you offer an effective summary, reassert your main point in a fresh way, and provide readers with food for thought as they leave your writing? Or is your ending abrupt, repetitive, or directionless? The original ending below is uninspiring; it adds little to the main part of the writing. The revision summarizes the main points in the essay and then urges the reader to think again about the overall point of writing.

Original Ending (Sketchy and flat)

Native Son deals with a young man's struggle against racism. It shows the effects of prejudice. Everyone should read this book.

Revised Version (Effectively ends the writing)

Native Son deals with a young man's struggle in a racist society, but also with so much more. It shows how prejudice affects people, how it closes in on them, and what some people will do to find a way out. Anyone who wants to better understand racism should read this book.

Tip: To generate fresh ideas for your closing, freewrite answers to questions like these: Why is the topic important to me? What should my readers have learned? Why should this issue matter to readers? What evidence or appeal (pages 322–323) will help readers remember my message and act on it? How does the topic relate to broader issues in society, history, or life?

Revising for Voice and Style

Generally, readers more fully trust writing that speaks in an informed voice and a clear, natural style. To develop an informed voice, make sure that your details are correct and complete; to develop a clear style, make sure that your writing is well organized and unpretentious. Check the issues below. (For a definition of voice, see page 74.)

Check the Level of Commitment

Consider how and to what degree your writing shows that you care about the topic and reader. For example, note how the original passage below lacks a personal voice, revealing nothing about the writer's connection to—or interest in—the topic. In contrast, the revision shows that the writer cares about the topic.

> **Original Passage** (Lacks voice)
> Cemeteries can teach us a lot about history. They make history seem more real. There is an old grave from a veteran of the War of 1812 in the Lundy's Lane Cemetery. . . .

> **Revised Version** (Personal, sincere voice)
> I've always had a special feeling for cemeteries. It's hard to explain any further than that, except to say history never seems quite as real as it does when I walk among many old gravestones. One day I discovered the grave of a veteran of the War of 1812. . . .

Check the Intensity of Your Writing

All writing—including academic writing—is enriched by an appropriate level of intensity, or even passion. In the original passage below, the writer's concern for the topic is unclear because the piece sounds neutral. In contrast, the revised version exudes energy.

> **Original Passage** (Lacks feeling and energy)
> The fact that children are being marketed to is something to be concerned about. Purchasing patterns reveal that a lot of money is spent on children. Juliet Schor notes that adults spent $670 billion on children in 2004.

> **Revised Passage** (Expresses real feelings)
> Knowing that children are the targets of aggressive mass marketing is all the more serious when the scope of the situation is considered. Much research has been done on purchasing patterns, and while the fact that North Americans spend large amounts of money on goods may not be surprising, when children are added to the equation the picture changes. Expert on consumerism, economics, and family studies Juliet Schor has done a considerable amount of convincing research in this area. She comments on the purchasing influence of children and notes that children aged four to twelve influenced an estimated $670 billion of adult purchasing in 2004.

Develop an Academic Style

Most writing in your courses requires an academic style. Such a style isn't stuffy; you're not trying to impress readers with ten-dollar words. Rather, you are using language that facilitates a thoughtful, engaged discussion of the topic. To choose the best words for such a conversation, consider the issues that follow.

Personal Pronouns

In some academic writing, personal pronouns are acceptable. Such is the case in informal writing, such as reading responses, personal essays involving narration, description, and reflection, and opinion-editorial essays written for a broad audience. In addition, *I* is correctly used in academic writing rooted in personal research, sometimes called an I-search paper.

Generally, however, avoid using *I, we,* and *you* in traditional academic writing. The concept, instead, is to focus on the topic itself and let your attitude be revealed indirectly. As E. B. White puts it, "To achieve style, begin by affecting none—that is, begin by placing yourself in the background."

> **No:** I really think that the problem of the homeless in Vancouver is serious, given the number of people who are dying, as I know from my experience where I grew up.
>
> **Yes:** Homelessness in Vancouver often leads to death. This fact demands the attention of more than lawmakers and social workers; all citizens must address the problems of their suffering neighbours.

Tip: Use the pronoun *one* carefully in academic prose. When it means "a person," *one* can lead to a stilted style if overused. In addition, the pronoun *their* (a plural pronoun) should not be used with *one* (a singular pronoun).

Technical Terms and Jargon

Technical terms and jargon—"insider" words—can be the specialized vocabulary of a subject, a discipline, a profession, or a social group. As such, jargon can be difficult to read for "outsiders." Follow these guidelines:

- **Use technical terms** as a kind of shorthand to communicate with people within the profession or discipline. However, be careful that such jargon doesn't devolve into meaningless buzzwords and catchphrases.
- **Avoid jargon** when writing for readers outside the profession or discipline. Use simpler terms and define technical terms that must be used.

> **Technical:** Bin's Douser power washer delivers 15 168 kPa p.r., runs off standard AC lines, comes with 30.5 m h.d. synthetic-rubber tubing, and features variable pulsation options through three adjustable s.s. tips.
>
> **Simple:** Bin's Douser power washer has a pressure rating of 15 168 kPa (kilopascals), runs off a common 200-volt electrical circuit, comes with 30.5 m of hose, and includes three nozzles.

Level of Formality

Most academic writing (especially research papers, literary analyses, lab reports, and argumentative essays) should meet the standards of formal English. Formal English is characterized by a serious tone; careful attention to word choice; longer and more complex sentences reflecting complex thinking; strict adherence to traditional conventions of grammar, mechanics, and punctuation; and avoidance of contractions.

You may write other papers (personal essays, commentaries, journals, and reviews) in which informal English is appropriate. Informal English is characterized by a personal tone, the occasional use of popular expressions, shorter sentences with slightly looser syntax, contractions, and personal references (I, we, you), but it still adheres to basic conventions.

Formal
> Formal English, modelled in this sentence, is worded correctly and carefully so that it can withstand repeated readings without seeming tiresome, sloppy, or cute.

Informal
> Informal English sounds like one person talking to another person (in a somewhat relaxed setting). It's the type of language that you're reading now. It sounds comfortable and real, not affected or breezy.

Tip: In academic writing, generally avoid slang—words considered outside standard English because they are faddish, familiar to few people, and sometimes insulting.

Unnecessary Qualifiers

Using qualifiers (such as *mostly, often, likely,* or *tends to*) is an appropriate strategy for developing defendable claims in argumentative writing. (See pages 296–297.) However, when you "overqualify" your ideas or add intensifiers (*really, truly*), the result is insecurity—the impression that you lack confidence in your ideas. The cure? Say what you mean, and mean what you say.

> **Insecure:** I totally and completely agree with the new security measures at sporting events, but that's only my opinion.
>
> **Secure:** I agree with the new security measures at sporting events.

fyi   Each academic discipline has its own vocabulary and its own vocabulary resources. Such resources include dictionaries, glossaries, or handbooks. Check your library for the vocabulary resources in your discipline. Use them regularly to deepen your grasp of that vocabulary.

Know When to Use the Passive Voice

Most verbs can be in either the active or the passive voice. When a verb is active, the sentence's subject performs the action. When the verb is passive, the subject is acted upon.

Active: Given the global connections between national economies, when U.S. consumers *stopped buying* automobiles, Japanese carmakers *shared* in the rapid economic downturn.

Passive: Given the global connections between national economies, when automobiles *were* no longer *being bought* by U.S. consumers, the rapid economic downturn *was shared* by Japanese carmakers.

Weaknesses of Passive Voice

The passive voice tends to be wordy and sluggish because the verb's action is directed backward, not ahead. In addition, passive constructions tend to be impersonal, making people disappear.

Passive: As a sign of a deepening recession, 600,000 job losses *were experienced* in January 2009.

Active: As a sign of a deepening recession, 600,000 workers *lost* their jobs in January 2009.

Strengths of Passive Voice

Using the passive voice isn't wrong. In fact, the passive voice has some important uses: (1) when you need to be tactful (say, in a bad-news letter), (2) if you wish to stress the object or person acted upon, and (3) if the actual actor is understood, unknown, or unimportant.

Active: The U.S. and Canadian federal governments *bailed out* both GM and Chrysler, two struggling automakers.

Passive: Both GM and Chrysler, two struggling automakers, *were bailed out* by the U.S. and Canadian governments. (stress on receiver of action)

Active: As part of the study, participants *drove* hybrids for six months.

Passive: As part of the study, hybrids *were driven* for six months. (emphasis on receiver; actor understood)

Tip: Avoid using the passive voice unethically to hide responsibility. For example, an instructor who says, "Your assignments could not be graded because of scheduling difficulties," might be trying to evade the truth: "I did not finish grading your assignments because I was watching *Murdoch Mysteries.*"

Working with Sources ▌ Academic writing must be free of plagiarism. Check that you have clearly indicated which material in your draft is summarized, paraphrased, or quoted from another source. (For more help, see pages 428–430.)

Addressing Paragraph Issues

While drafting, you may have constructed paragraphs that are loosely held together, poorly developed, or unclear. When you revise, take a close look at your paragraphs for focus, unity, and coherence (pages 83–85).

Remember the Basics

A paragraph should be a concise unit of thought. Revise a paragraph until it . . .

- is organized around a controlling idea—often stated in a topic sentence.
- consists of supporting sentences that develop the controlling idea by reasoning about it or offering concrete evidence related to it.
- concludes with a sentence that summarizes the main point and prepares readers for the next paragraph or main point.
- serves a specific function in a piece of writing—opening, supporting, developing, illustrating, countering, describing, or closing.

Sample Paragraph

Topic sentence

Supporting sentences

Closing sentence

Tumour cells can hurt the body in a number of ways. First, a tumour can grow so big that it takes up space needed by other organs. Second, some cells may detach from the original tumour and spread throughout the body, creating new tumours elsewhere. This happens with lymphatic cancer—a cancer that's hard to control because it spreads so quickly. A third way that tumour cells can hurt the body is by doing work not called for in their DNA. For example, a gland cell's DNA code may tell the cell to produce a necessary hormone in the endocrine system. However, if cancer damages or distorts that code, sick cells may produce more of the hormone than the body can use—or even tolerate (Braun 4). Cancer cells seem to have minds of their own, and this is why cancer is such a serious disease.

Keep the Purpose in Mind

Use these questions to evaluate the purpose and function of each paragraph:

- What function does the paragraph fulfill? How does it add to your line of reasoning or the development of your thesis?
- Would the paragraph work better if it were divided in two—or combined with another paragraph?
- Does the paragraph flow smoothly from the previous paragraph, and does it lead effectively into the next one?

Check for Unity

A unified paragraph is one in which all the details help to develop a single main topic or achieve a single main effect. Test for unity by following these guidelines.

Topic Sentence

Very often the topic of a paragraph is stated in a single sentence called a "topic sentence." Check whether your paragraph needs a topic sentence. If the paragraph has a topic sentence, determine whether it is clear, specific, and well focused. Figure 5.2 presents a formula for writing good topic sentences:

Formula:	A Limited Topic	+	Specific Feeling or Thought	=	Topic Sentence
Example:	The pride that Canada's Olympic medallists feel		is expressed most fully when they drape themselves in the flag		The pride that Canada's Olympic medallists feel is expressed most fully when they drape themselves in the flag.

fig. 5.2

Placement of the Topic Sentence

Normally the topic sentence is the first sentence in the paragraph. However, it can appear elsewhere in a paragraph.

Middle Placement: Place a topic sentence in the middle when you want to build up to and then lead away from the key idea.

During the making of *Apocalypse Now,* Eleanor Coppola created a documentary about the filming called *Hearts of Darkness: A Filmmaker's Apocalypse.* In the first film, the insane Colonel Kurtz has disappeared into the Cambodian jungle. As Captain Willard searches for Kurtz, the screen fills with horror. **However, as *Hearts of Darkness* relates, the horror portrayed in the fictional movie was being lived out by the production company.** For example, in the documentary, actor Larry Fishburne shockingly says, "War is fun. . . . Vietnam must have been so much fun." Then toward the end of the filming, actor Martin Sheen suffered a heart attack. When an assistant informed investors, the director exploded, "He's not dead unless I say he's dead."

End Placement: Place a topic sentence at the end when you want to build to a climax, as in a passage of narration or persuasion.

When sportsmen stop to reflect on why they find fishing so enjoyable, most realize that what they love is the feel of a fish on the end of the line, not necessarily the weight of the fillets in their coolers. Fishing has undergone a slow evolution over the last century. While fishing used to be a way of putting food on the table, most of today's fishermen do so only for the relaxation that it provides. The barbed hook was invented to increase the quantity of fish a man could land so that he could better feed his family. **This need no longer exists, so barbed hooks are no longer necessary.**

Supporting Sentences

All the sentences in the body of a paragraph should support the topic sentence. The closing sentence, for instance, will often summarize the paragraph's main point or emphasize a key detail. If any sentences shift the focus away from the topic, revise the paragraph in one of the following ways:

- **Delete the material** from the paragraph.
- **Rewrite the material** so that it clearly supports the topic sentence.
- **Create a separate paragraph** based on the odd-man-out material.
- **Revise the topic sentence** so that it relates more closely to the support.

Consistent Focus

Examine the following paragraph about fishing hooks. The original topic sentence focuses on the point that some anglers prefer smooth hooks. However, the writer leaves this initial idea unfinished and turns to the issue of the cost of new hooks. In the revised version, unity is restored: The first paragraph completes the point about anglers who prefer smooth hooks; the second paragraph addresses the issue of replacement costs.

Original Paragraph (Lacks unity)

According to some anglers who do use smooth hooks, their lures perform better than barbed lures as long as they maintain a constant tension on the line. Smooth hooks can bite deeper than barbed hooks, actually providing a stronger hold on the fish. Some people have argued that replacing all of the barbed hooks in their tackle would be a costly operation.

Revised Version (Unified)

According to some anglers who do use smooth hooks, their lures perform better than barbed lures as long as the anglers maintain a constant tension on the line. Smooth hooks can bite deeper than barbed hooks, actually providing a stronger hold on the fish. These anglers testify that switching from barbed hooks has not noticeably reduced the number of fish that they are able to land. In their experience, and in my own, enjoyment of the sport is actually heightened by adding another challenge to playing the fish (maintaining line tension).

Some people have argued that replacing all of the barbed hooks in their tackle would be a costly operation. While this is certainly a concern, barbed hooks do not necessarily require replacement. With a simple set of pliers, the barbs on most conventional hooks can be bent down, providing a cost-free method of modifying one's existing tackle. . . .

 Paragraphs that contain unrelated ideas lack unity and are hard to follow. As you review each paragraph for unity, ask yourself these questions: Is the topic of the paragraph clear? Does each sentence relate to the topic? Are the sentences organized in the best possible order?

Check for Coherence

When a paragraph is coherent, the parts stay together. A coherent paragraph flows smoothly because each sentence is connected to others by patterns in the language such as repetition and transitions. To strengthen the coherence in your paragraphs, check for the issues discussed below.

Effective Repetition

To achieve coherence in your paragraphs, consider using repetition—repeating words or synonyms where necessary to remind readers of what you have already said. You can also use parallelism—repeating phrase or sentence structures to show the relationships among ideas. At the same time, you will add a unifying rhythm to your writing.

> **Ineffective:** The floor was littered with discarded pop cans, newspapers that were crumpled, and wrinkled clothes.
>
> **Effective:** The floor was littered with discarded pop cans, crumpled newspapers, and wrinkled clothes. (Three parallel phrases are used.)
>
> **Ineffective:** Reading the book was enjoyable; to write the critique was difficult.
>
> **Effective:** Reading the book was enjoyable; writing the critique was difficult. (Two similar structures are repeated.)

Clear Transitions

Linking words and phrases like "next," "on the other hand," and "in addition" connect ideas by showing the relationship among them. There are transitions that show location and time, compare and contrast things, emphasize a point, conclude or summarize, and add or clarify information. (See page 86 for a list of linking words and phrases.) Note the use of transitions in the following examples:

> **The transition is used to emphasize a point.**
> The paradox of Scotland is that violence had long been the norm in this now-peaceful land. In fact, the country was born, bred, and came of age in war.
>
> **The transition is used to show time or order.**
> The production of cement is a complicated process. First, the mixture of lime, silica, alumina, and gypsum is ground into very fine particles.

INSIGHT Another way to achieve coherence in your paragraphs is to use pronouns effectively. A pronoun forms a link to the noun it replaces and ties that noun (idea) to the ideas that follow. As always, don't overuse pronouns or rely too heavily on them in establishing coherence in your paragraphs.

Transitions and Linking Words

The words and phrases below can help you tie together words, phrases, sentences, and paragraphs.

Words used to show location:

above	behind	down	on top of
across	below	in back of	onto
against	beneath	in front of	outside
along	beside	inside	over
among	between	into	throughout
around	beyond	near	to the right
away from	by	off	under

Words used to show time:

about	during	next	today
after	finally	next week	tomorrow
afterward	first	second	until
as soon as	immediately	soon	when
at	later	then	yesterday
before	meanwhile	third	

Words used to compare things (show similarities):

also	in the same way	likewise
as	like	similarly

Words used to contrast things (show differences):

although	even though	on the other hand	still
but	however	otherwise	

Words used to emphasize a point:

again	for this reason	particularly	to repeat
even	in fact	to emphasize	truly

Words used to conclude or summarize:

all in all	finally	in summary	therefore
as a result	in conclusion	last	to sum up

Words used to add information:

additionally	and	equally important	in addition
again	another	finally	likewise
along with	as well	for example	next
also	besides	for instance	second

Words used to clarify:

for instance	in other words	put another way	that is

fig. 5.3

Note: Use transitions to link, expand, or intensify an idea, but don't add elements carelessly, creating run-on or rambling sentences.

Check for Completeness

The sentences in a paragraph should support and expand on the main point. If your paragraph does not seem complete, you will need to add information.

Supporting Details

If some of your paragraphs are incomplete, they may lack details. There are numerous kinds of details, including the following:

facts	paraphrases	explanations	definitions
anecdotes	statistics	comparisons	summaries
analyses	quotations	examples	analogies

Add details based on the type of writing you are engaged in.

Describing: Add details that help readers see, smell, taste, touch, or hear it.

Narrating: Add details that help readers understand the events and actions.

Explaining: Add details that help readers understand what it means, how it works, or what it does.

Persuading: Add details that strengthen the logic of your argument.

Specific Details

The original paragraph below fails to answer fully the question posed by the topic sentence. In the revised paragraph, the writer uses an anecdote to answer the question.

Original Paragraph (Lacks completeness)

So what is stress? Actually, the physiological characteristics of stress are some of the body's potentially good self-defence mechanisms. People experience stress when they are in danger. In fact, stress can be healthy.

Revised Version (Full development)

So what is stress? Actually, the physiological characteristics of stress are some of the body's potentially good self-defence mechanisms. Take, for example, a man who is crossing a busy intersection when he spots an oncoming car. Immediately his brain releases a flood of adrenaline into his bloodstream. As a result, his muscles contract, his eyes dilate, his heart pounds faster, his breathing quickens, and his blood clots more readily. Each one of these responses helps the man leap out of the car's path. His muscles contract to give him exceptional strength. His eyes dilate so that he can see more clearly. His heart pumps more blood and his lungs exchange more air—both to increase his metabolism. If the man were injured, his blood would clot faster, ensuring a smaller amount of blood loss. In this situation and many more like it, stress symptoms are good (Curtis 25–26).

INSIGHT If a paragraph is getting long, divide it at a natural stopping point. The topic sentence can then function as the thesis for that part of your essay or paper.

Working with Sources

Test your evidence to make certain that it provides the support you need, support that meets the criteria below.

- **Accurate:** The information is all correct.
- **Precise:** The data are concrete and specific, not vague and general.
- **Substantial:** The amount of evidence reaches a critical mass—enough to convey the idea and convince readers of its validity.
- **Authoritative:** The evidence comes from a reliable source. Moreover, the information is as close to the origin as possible; it is not a report conveying third-hand information.
- **Representative:** The information fairly represents the range of data on the issue. Your presentation of evidence is balanced.
- **Fitting:** Given your purpose, the topic, and your reader, the evidence is appropriate and relevant for the question or issue you are discussing.

Example: The resources below come from the works-cited list for Paige Louter's essay, "Why the World Deserves Better Than Fair Trade," on pages 525–533. While we would have to go to the sources themselves to test their reliability and Paige's use of them in her essay, we can tell a number of things simply from the source details provided. First, the sources are scholarly—published in respected field-of-study journals and by an academic book publisher. Even the Web resource used is the official site of a recognizable nonprofit organization. The articles come from academic databases, and a quick Google search shows that the authors are recognized and respected experts. Furthermore, page spans indicate that the sources are fairly lengthy. Finally, the titles indicate that the sources, though likely coming from a specific argumentative perspective, are likely balanced and thoughtful. In other words, these sources promise to provide information that is accurate and precise (possibly primary data and certainly data that is properly credited), that is substantial and authoritative (given length and authorship), and that is representative and fitting (showing the range of perspectives on the specific issue Paige is exploring).

Fair Trade   12

Works Cited

Booth, Philip, and Linda Whetstone. "Half a Cheer for Fair Trade." *Economic Affairs* 27.2 (2007): 29-36. *Business Source Elite*. Web. 19 Jan. 2012.

Hutchens, Anna. "Empowering Women Through Fair Trade? Lessons from Asia." *Third World Quarterly* 31.3 (2010): 449-67. *Academic Search Premier*. Web. 18 Jan. 2012.

Nichols, Alex, and Charlotte Opal. *Fair Trade: Market-Driven Ethical Consumption.* London: Sage, 2004. Print.

Walton, Andrew. "What Is Fair Trade?" *Third World Quarterly* 31.3 (2010): 431-47. *Academic Search Premier*. Web. 19 Jan. 2012.

"What is [sic] Fairtrade?" *Fairtrade International.* Fairtrade Labelling Organizations International, n.d. Web. 10 Feb. 2012.

Revising Collaboratively

Every writer can benefit from feedback given by an interested audience, especially one that offers constructive and honest advice during a writing project. Members of an existing writing group already know how valuable it is for writers to share their work. Others might want to start a writing group to experience the benefits. Your group might collaborate online or in person. In either case, the information on the next two pages will help you get started.

Know Your Role

Writers and reviewers should know their roles and fulfill their responsibilities during revising sessions. Essentially, the writer should briefly introduce the draft and solicit honest responses. Reviewers should make constructive comments in response to the writing.

Provide Appropriate Feedback

Feedback can take many forms, including the three approaches described here.

- **Basic Description:** In this simple response, the reviewer listens or reads attentively and then simply describes what she or he hears or sees happening in the piece. The reviewer offers no criticism of the writing.

  > **Ineffective:** "That was interesting. The piece was informative."
  >
  > **Effective:** First, the essay introduced the challenge of your birth defect and how you have had to cope with it. Then in the next part you . . ."

- **Summary Evaluation:** Here the reviewer reads or listens to the piece and then provides a specific evaluation of the draft.

  > **Ineffective:** "Gee, I really liked it!" or "It was boring."
  >
  > **Effective:** "Your story at the beginning really pulled me in, and the middle explained the issue strongly, but the ending felt a bit flat."

- **Thorough Critique:** The reviewer assesses the ideas, organization, and voice in the writing. Feedback should be detailed and constructive. Such a critique may also be completed with the aid of a review sheet or checklist. As a reviewer, be prepared to share specific responses, suggestions, and questions. But also be sure to focus your comments on the writing, rather than the writer.

  > **Ineffective:** "You really need to fix that opening! What were you thinking?"
  >
  > **Effective:** "Let's look closely at the opening. Could you rewrite the first sentence so it grabs the reader's attention? Also, I'm somewhat confused about the thesis statement. Could you rephrase it so it states your position more clearly?"

Respond According to a Plan

Using a specific plan or scheme like the following will help you give clear, helpful, and complete feedback.

- **OAQS Method:** Use this simple four-step scheme—**Observe, Appreciate, Question,** and **Suggest**—to respond to your peers' writing.

  1. **Observe** means to notice what another person's essay is designed to do and say something about its design or purpose. For example, you might say, "Even though you are writing about your boyfriend, it appears that you are trying to get a message across to your parents."

  2. **Appreciate** means to praise something in the writing that impresses or pleases you. You can find something to appreciate in any piece of writing. For example, you might say, "You make a very convincing point" or "With your description, I can actually see his broken tooth."

  3. **Question** means to ask whatever you want to know after you've read the essay. You might ask for background information, a definition, an interpretation, or an explanation. For example, you might say, "Can you tell us what happened when you got to the emergency room?"

  4. **Suggest** means to give helpful advice about possible changes. For example, you might say, "With a little more physical detail—especially more sounds and smells—your third paragraph could be the highlight of the whole essay. What do you think?"

Asking the Writer Questions

Reviewers should ask the following types of questions while reviewing a piece of writing:

- **To help writers reflect on their purpose and audience . . .**
  Why are you writing this?
  Who will read this, and what do they need to know?

- **To help writers focus their thoughts . . .**
  What message are you trying to get across?
  Do you have more than one main point?
  What are the most important examples?

- **To help writers think about their information . . .**
  What do you know about the subject?
  Does this part say enough?
  Does your writing cover all of the basics? (*Who? What? Where? When? Why?* and *How?*)

- **To help writers with their openings and closings . . .**
  What are you trying to say in the opening?
  How else could you start your writing?
  How do you want your readers to feel at the end?

Using the Writing Centre

A writing centre or lab is a place where a trained adviser will help you develop and strengthen a piece of writing. You can expect the writing centre adviser to do certain things; other things only you can do. For quick reference, refer to the chart below.

Adviser's Job	Your Job
Make you feel at home	Be respectful
Discuss your needs	Be ready to work
Help you choose a topic	Decide on a topic
Discuss your purpose and audience	Know your purpose and audience
Help you generate ideas	Embrace the best ideas
Help you develop your logic	Consider other points of view; stretch your own perspective
Help you understand how to research your material	Do the research
Read your draft	Share your writing
Identify problems in organization, logic, expression, and format	Recognize and fix problems
Teach ways to correct weaknesses	Learn important principles
Help you with grammar, usage, diction, vocabulary, and mechanics	Correct all errors

Tips for getting the most out of the writing centre
- Visit the centre at least several days before your paper is due.
- Take your assignment sheet with you to each advising session.
- Read your work aloud, slowly.
- Expect to rethink your writing from scratch.
- Do not defend your wording—if it needs defence, it needs revision.
- Ask questions. (No question is "too dumb.")
- Request clarification of anything you don't understand.
- Ask for examples or illustrations of important points.
- Write down all practical suggestions.
- Ask the adviser to summarize his or her remarks.
- Rewrite as soon as possible after—or even during—the advising session.
- Return to the writing centre for a response to your revisions.

Critical-Thinking and Writing Activities

As directed by your instructor, complete the following critical-thinking and writing activities by yourself or with classmates.

1. Doris Lessing has stated that when it comes to writing, "The more a thing cooks, the better." In what sense is revision a crucial stage in that cooking process? Using Lessing's cooking metaphor as a starting point, explore how revision should function in your own writing.

2. Review the opening and closing paragraphs of one of your essays. Then come up with fresh and different approaches for those paragraphs using the information on pages 76–77 as a guide.

3. For your current writing assignment, ask a peer to provide detailed feedback using the information in this chapter as a guide. Then take a fresh copy of your paper to the writing centre and work through your draft with an adviser. Revise the draft as needed.

Learning-Objectives Checklist ✓

Have you achieved this chapter's learning objectives? Check your progress with the items below, revisiting topics in the chapter as needed. *I have . . .*

_____ re-examined the rhetorical situation of my writing project (my role as writer, my subject, my purpose, the audience, the form, and the context) to be better prepared to revise my draft (72).

_____ assessed my overall approach to see if it is stale, predicable, boring, or formulaic (73).

_____ examined my ideas for a clear thesis and complete development, making necessary improvements (75).

_____ evaluated the overall organization of my draft, including whether the opening engages readers and sets a direction, the middle clearly traces a line of reasoning, and the closing effectively ends the draft (76–77).

_____ examined and improved the voice in my draft, addressing issues of commitment, intensity, academic style, and active vs. passive voice (78–81).

_____ examined each paragraph to ensure that it is an effective unit of thought, unified in its topic or effect, coherent through transitions, and complete in its details (82–88).

_____ given and received helpful feedback on a draft by collaborating with classmates through techniques such as the OAQS method (89–90).

_____ described the role of the writing centre in improving my writing, including my responsibilities and those of the centre's tutors (91).

Chapter 6

Editing, Proofreading, and Submitting

Editing and proofreading allow you to fine-tune your writing, making it ready to submit. When you edit, look first for words, phrases, and sentences that sound awkward, uninteresting, or unclear. When you proofread, check your writing for spelling, mechanics, usage, and grammar errors. Ask one of your writing peers to help you.

The guidelines and strategies given in this chapter will help you edit your writing for style and clarity, proofread it for errors, and format it effectively. In the end, you will be ready to share your polished writing, making it public.

Visually Speaking   Piano tuning requires special skills and specialized tools (Figure 6.1). What skills and tools do you need to effectively edit and proofread your writing? How are tuning a piano and polishing your writing similar and different?

Learning **Objectives**

By working through this chapter, you will be able to

- assess the overall style of your revised draft.
- combine short, simplistic sentences into more substantial ones.
- expand sparse sentences with meaningful details.
- transform stylistically weak sentences through various techniques.
- replace vague, weak, and biased words.
- identify and correct errors in grammar, punctuation, mechanics, usage, and spelling.
- design the format and layout of your writing.
- choose an appropriate submission method.

PhotoHouse/Shutterstock.com

fig. 6.1

Strategies for Polishing Your Writing

When you have thoroughly revised your writing, you need to edit it so that the style is clear, concise, energetic, and varied. A closely related task is proofreading, which involves polishing your prose for correct grammar, punctuation, mechanics, usage, and spelling. To effectively edit and proofread, start with the strategies below.

Review the Overall Style of Your Writing

How does your writing sound? Test it for the following:

1. **Check that your style fits the rhetorical situation.** Does your writing sound as if you wrote it with a clear **goal** in mind? Will your writing sound mature, thoughtful, and direct to **readers**? Does your writing suit the **subject** and your treatment of it?

2. **Check that your style carries the right authority.** Nineteenth-century British author Matthew Arnold puts it this way: "Have something to say and say it as clearly as you can. That is the only secret of style." Does your writing communicate a clear message with a fitting confidence?

3. **Check your sentence style and word choice.** At its heart, your style is about the sentences you craft and the words crafted into those sentences. For that reason, this chapter focuses to a large degree on strengthening sentences through combining, expanding, and varying structures (pages 95–101), as well as on avoiding wordiness and make effective word choices (pages 102–108).

Use Tools and Methods That Work

Here are three tips that will help you edit and proofread effectively:

1. **Do it at the right time, and give yourself the time.** Leave time between revising and editing your paper, at least 24 hours. In addition, don't rush through editing, as doing it well takes patience and concentration.

2. **Review your draft from multiple points of view.** On-screen editing offers you tremendous power and flexibility. Then again, at some point in your editing, you need to see your words in print on a page. Finally, consider reading your paper aloud or having a classmate do so: hearing your words will help you sense where your writing needs work.

3. **Use software editing tools as an aid.** Without relying on them exclusively, use wisely such tools as spell check, grammar check, find-and-replace functions, track-changes tools, and so on. For example, spell check will not catch usage errors such as *it's* versus *its*. In the end, you need to manage the editing process, including your writing tools.

Combining Sentences

Effective sentences often contain several basic ideas that work together to show relationships and make connections. Here are five basic ideas followed by seven examples of how the ideas can be combined into effective sentences.

1. The longest and largest construction project in history is the Great Wall of China.

2. The project took 1,700 years to complete.

3. The Great Wall of China is 2,250 km long.

4. It is between 5.5 and 9 m high.

5. It is up to 9.7 m wide.

Edit Short, Simplistic Sentences

A series of short, simplistic sentences creates a choppy effect called primer style. Combine your short, simplistic sentences into longer, more detailed sentences. Sentence combining is generally carried out in the following ways:

- Use a **series** to combine three or more similar ideas.

  > The Great Wall of China is **2,250 km long,** between **5.5 and 9 m high,** and up to **9.7 m wide**.

- Use a **relative pronoun** (*who, whose, that, which*) to introduce subordinate (less important) ideas.

  > The Great Wall of China, **which is 2,250 km long and between 5.5 and 9 m high,** took 1,700 years to complete.

- Use an **introductory phrase** or **clause**.

  > **Having taken 1,700 years to complete,** the Great Wall of China is the longest construction project in history.

- Use a **semicolon** (and a conjunctive adverb if appropriate).

  > The Great Wall took 1,700 years to complete; it is 2,250 km long and up to 9 m high and 9.7 m wide.

- Repeat a **key word** or phrase to emphasize an idea.

  > The Great Wall of China is the longest construction **project** in history, a **project** that took 1,700 years to complete.

- Use **correlative conjunctions** (*either, or; not only, but also*) to compare or contrast two ideas in a sentence.

  > The Great Wall of China is **not only** up to 9 m high and 9.7 m wide, **but also** 2,250 km long.

- Use an **appositive** (a word or phrase that renames) to emphasize an idea.

  > The Great Wall of China—**the largest construction project in history**—is 2,250 km long, 9.7 m wide, and up to 9 m high.

Expanding Sentences

When you edit, expand sentences so as to connect related ideas and make room for new information. Length has no value in and of itself: The best sentence is still the shortest one that says all it has to say. An expanded sentence, however, is capable of saying more—and saying it more expressively.

Use Cumulative Sentences

Modern writers often use an expressive sentence form called the cumulative sentence. A cumulative sentence is made of a general "base clause" that is expanded by adding modifying words, phrases, or clauses. In such a sentence, details are added before and after the main clause, creating an image-rich thought. Here's an example of a cumulative sentence, with the base clause or main idea in boldface:

> In preparation for her French exam, **Julie was studying at the kitchen table,** completely focused, memorizing a list of vocabulary words.

Discussion: Notice how each new modifier adds to the richness of the final sentence. Also notice that each of these modifying phrases is set off by a comma. Here's another sample sentence:

> With his hands on his face, **Tony was laughing half-heartedly,** looking puzzled and embarrassed.

Discussion: Such a cumulative sentence provides a way to write description that is rich in detail, without rambling. Notice how each modifier changes the flow or rhythm of the sentence.

Expand with details

Here are seven basic ways to expand a main idea:

1. with **adjectives and adverbs:** *half-heartedly, once again*
2. with **prepositional phrases:** *with his hands on his face*
3. with **absolute phrases:** *his head tilted to one side*
4. with **participial (-ing or -ed) phrases:** *looking puzzled*
5. with **infinitive phrases:** *to hide his embarrassment*
6. with **subordinate clauses:** *while his friend talks*
7. with **relative clauses:** *who isn't laughing at all*

INSIGHT To edit sentences for more expressive style, it is best to (1) know your grammar and punctuation (especially commas); (2) practise tightening, combining, and expanding sentences using the guidelines in this chapter; and (3) read good writing carefully, looking for models of well-constructed sentences.

Checking for Sentence Style

Writer E. B. White advised young writers to approach style "by way of simplicity, plainness, orderliness, and sincerity." That's good advice from a writer steeped in style. It's also important to know what to look for when editing your sentences. The information on this page and the following four pages will help you edit your sentences for style and correctness.

Avoid These Sentence Problems

Always check for and correct the following types of sentence problems. When attempting to fix problems in your sentences, turn to the pages listed below for guidelines and examples.

Short, Choppy Sentences: Combine or expand any short, choppy sentences (called primer style); use the examples and guidelines on page 95.

Flat, Predictable Sentences: Rewrite any sentences that sound predictable and uninteresting by varying their structures and expanding them with modifying words, phrases, and clauses. (See pages 98–101.)

Incorrect Sentences: Look carefully for fragments, run-ons, and comma splices. Correct them as needed. (See pages 599–600.)

Unclear Sentences: Edit any sentences that contain unclear wording, misplaced modifiers, dangling modifiers, or incomplete comparisons.

Unacceptable Sentences: Change sentences that include nonstandard language, double negatives, or unparallel constructions.

Unnatural Sentences: Rewrite sentences that contain jargon, clichés, or flowery language. (See page 104.)

Review Your Writing for Sentence Variety

Use the following strategy to review your writing for variety in terms of sentence beginnings, lengths, and types.

- In one column on a piece of paper, list the opening words in each of your sentences. Then decide if you need to vary some of your sentence beginnings.
- In another column, identify the number of words in each sentence. Then decide if you need to change the lengths of some of your sentences.
- In a third column, list the kinds of sentences used (exclamatory, declarative, interrogative, and so on). Then, based on your analysis, use the instructions on the next two pages to edit your sentences as needed.

Working with Sources ▍ When you integrate a quotation into a text, make sure that the quotation works with the material around it. Either make the quotation a grammatical part of the sentence, or introduce the quotation with a complete sentence followed by a colon.

Vary Sentence Structures

To energize your sentences, vary their structures using one or more of the methods shown on this page and the next.

1. **Vary sentence openings.** If a series of sentences begin the same way, create variety by moving modifying words, phrases, or clauses to the front of some sentences.

> **Unvaried:** The problem is not just about wasteful irrigation, though. The problem is also about resistance to change. The problem is that many people have fought against restrictions.
>
> **Varied:** However, the problem is not just about wasteful irrigation. It's about resistance to change. When governments have tried to pass regulations, many people have fought against restrictions.

2. **Vary sentence lengths.** Short sentences (ten words or fewer) are ideal for making points crisply. Medium sentences (ten to twenty words) should carry the bulk of your thinking. When well crafted, occasional long sentences (more than twenty words) can develop and expand your ideas.

> **Short:** Museum exhibitions have become increasingly commercial.
>
> **Medium:** To the extent that "access" adequately measures museum performance, art as entertainment "has proven a resounding triumph."
>
> **Long:** Shows featuring motorcycles, automobiles, the treasures of King Tutankhamen, and the works of Van Gogh not only have proven immensely popular but have also offered the promise of corporate underwriting and ample commercial tie-ins.

3. **Vary sentence kinds.** The most common sentence is declarative—it states a point. For variety, try exclamatory, imperative, interrogative, and conditional statements.

> **Declarative:** Historical records indicate that the lost colonists of Roanoke may have been harbouring a dangerous virus: influenza.
>
> **Conditional:** If the influenza virus was not present in the New World, then the lost colonists of Roanoke likely served as vectors for the disease.
>
> **Interrogative:** That being said, we must now turn to a different question: What happened to those lost colonists?
>
> **Imperative:** Let us take steps to ensure that the Lumbee people do not share the fate of the colonists who disappeared from Roanoke.
>
> **Exclamatory:** Just as John White discovered over 400 years ago, something is terribly wrong! (Note: generally avoid exclamatory sentences in academic writing.)

4. **Vary sentence arrangements.** Where do you want to place the main point of your sentence? You make that choice by arranging sentence parts into loose, periodic, balanced, or cumulative patterns. Each pattern creates a specific effect.

Loose Sentence

Men are frequently mystified by women, with their unfamiliar rituals and emotional vitality—issues often addressed in romantic comedies.

Analysis: This pattern is direct. It states the main point immediately (bold), and then tacks on extra information.

Periodic Sentence

While Western culture celebrates romantic love, seen powerfully in its films and romance novels, **in the end, such attraction between a man and a woman fails to sustain a relationship for a lifetime.**

Analysis: This pattern postpones the main point (bold) until the end. The sentence builds to the point, creating an indirect, dramatic effect.

Balanced Sentence

The modern romantic comedy often portrays male characters as resistant to or clueless about love; however, **in Jane Austen's narratives, men's behaviour is further complicated by traditional codes of honour that have now largely vanished.**

Analysis: This pattern gives equal weight to complementary or contrasting points (bold); the balance is often signalled by a comma and a conjunction *(and, but)* or by a semicolon. Often a conjunctive adverb *(however, nevertheless)* or a transitional phrase *(in addition, even so)* will follow the semicolon to further clarify the relationship.

Cumulative Sentence

In spite of his initially limiting pride, **Mr. Darcy**, now properly proud, **emerges** finally **as the consummate romantic hero**, the anonymous saviour of Elizabeth's family, a true gentleman.

Analysis: This pattern puts the main idea (bold) in the middle of the sentence, surrounding it with modifying words, phrases, and clauses.

5. **Use positive repetition.** Although you should avoid needless repetition, you might use emphatic repetition to repeat a key word to stress a point.

Needlessly Repetitive Sentence

Each year, thousands of young people who read poorly leave high school unable to read well, functionally illiterate.

Emphatic Sentence

Each year, thousands of young people leave high school functionally illiterate, so **illiterate** that they can't read daily newspapers, job ads, or safety instructions.

Use Parallel Structure

Coordinated sentence elements should be parallel—that is, they should be written in the same grammatical forms. Parallel structures save words, clarify relationships, and present the information in the correct sequence. Follow these guidelines.

1. **For words, phrases, or clauses in a series,** keep elements consistent.

> **Not parallel:** I have tutored students in Biology 101, also Chemistry 102, not to mention my familiarity with Physics 200.
> **Parallel:** I have tutored students in *Biology 101, Chemistry 102,* and *Physics 200.*

> **Not parallel:** I have volunteered as a hospital receptionist, have been a hospice volunteer, and as an emergency medical technician.
> **Parallel:** I have done volunteer work as *a hospital receptionist, a hospice counsellor,* and *an emergency medical technician.*

2. **Use both parts of correlative conjunctions** (*either, or; neither, nor; not only, but also; as, so; whether, so; both, and*) so that both segments of the sentence are balanced.

> **Not parallel:** *Not only* did Blake College turn 20 this year. Its enrollment grew by 16 percent.
> **Parallel:** *Not only* did Blake College turn 20 this year *but* its enrollment *also* grew by 16 percent.

3. **Place a modifier correctly** so that it clearly indicates the word or words to which it refers.

> **Confusing:** MADD promotes *severely* punishing and eliminating drunk driving because this offence leads to a *great number* of deaths and sorrow.
> **Parallel:** MADD promotes eliminating and *severely* punishing drunk driving because this offence leads to *many* deaths and *untold* sorrow.

4. **Place contrasting details in parallel structures** (words, phrases, or clauses) to stress a contrast.

> **Weak contrast:** The average child watches 24 hours of television a week and reads for 36 minutes.
> **Strong contrast:** Each week, the average child *watches television for 24 hours but reads for only about half an hour.*

Working with Sources | When using sources, smoothly integrate text references to those sources. (For guidelines, see pages 493–534 for MLA and pages 535–564 for APA.)

Avoid Weak Constructions

Avoid constructions (like those below) that weaken your writing.

Nominal Constructions

The nominal construction is both sluggish and wordy. Avoid it by changing the noun form of a verb *(description or instructions)* to a verb *(describe or instruct)*. At the same time, delete the weak verb that preceded the noun.

Nominal Constructions (noun form underlined):	Strong Verbs:
Engineer Tim McAllister *gives a description* . . .	McAllister *describes* . . .
Scholar Lydia Balm *provides an explanation* . . .	Balm *explains* . . .

Sluggish: In her study of Austen film adaptations, Lydia Balm *provides an explanation* for the narrative power of dance scenes. Dances *offer a symbolization and visualization* of characters in situations of mutual attraction but *nonverbalization.*

Energetic: In her study of Austen film adaptations, Lydia Balm *explains* the narrative power of dance scenes. Dances *symbolize visually* the attraction characters feel for each other but cannot *verbalize.*

Expletives

Expletives such as "it is" and "there is" are fillers that serve no purpose in most sentences—except to make them wordy and unnatural.

Sluggish: *It is* believed by some people that childhood vaccinations can cause autism. *There are* several websites that promote this point of view quite forcefully. In fact, *it is* also the case that some celebrities advocate this cause.

Energetic: Some people believe that childhood vaccinations can cause autism. Some celebrities and several websites forcefully promote this point of view.

Negative Constructions

Sentences constructed upon the negatives *no, not, neither/nor* can be wordy and difficult to understand. It's simpler to state what *is* the case.

Negative: Hybrid vehicles *are not* completely different from traditional cars, as hybrids *cannot* run without gas and cannot rely only on battery power that has *not been created* by the gasoline engine.

Positive: Hybrid vehicles are similar to traditional cars, as hybrids do require gas in order to power an internal-combustion engine that in turn powers batteries.

Eliminating Wordiness

Wordy writing taxes the reader's attention. To tighten your writing, cut the types of wordiness described below.

Deadwood

Deadwood is filler material—verbal "lumber" that you can remove without harming the sentence. Look for irrelevant information and obvious statements.

Deadwood: BlackBerry *must undergo a thorough retooling process if it is to be competitive in the rapidly changing world of today's* global marketplace.
Concise: BlackBerry must change to meet global challenges.

Redundancy

Redundancy refers to unnecessary repetition. Check your sentences for words and phrases that say the same thing, doubling up the meaning. Examples: combine together, new beginner, connect up, green in colour, round in shape, plan ahead, descend down.

Redundant: Avoid the construction site, and *be sure to pick a different route* if you want to avoid riding over nails and *risking a flat tire.*
Concise: If you want to avoid a flat tire, don't drive through the construction site.

Unnecessary Modifiers

Adjectives and adverbs typically clarify nouns and verbs; however, excessive modifiers make prose dense. Use precise nouns and verbs to avoid the need for modifiers, and avoid intensifying adverbs (*very, extremely, intensely, awfully, especially*).

Wordy: To ensure *very healthy, properly growing* trees, whether *deciduous* or *coniferous*, hire a *licensed, professional* tree surgeon.
Concise: To ensure healthy trees, hire a professional tree surgeon.

Long Phrases and Clauses

Often, a long phrase or clause can be replaced by a shorter phrase or even a single word. Locate prepositional phrases (*at the beginning of the project*) and relative clauses (*who, which, that* clauses) and replace them when possible with simpler words.

Wordy: Among a variety of different devices that could possibly perform the task of preventing the wastage of water, an interesting one is LEPA, also known by many as low-energy precision application, hence the acronym.
Concise: A second device that prevents water waste is LEPA, or low-energy precision application.

Avoiding Vague, Weak, and Biased Words

As you edit your writing, check your choice of words carefully. The information on the next six pages will help you edit for word choice.

Substitute Specific Words

Replace vague nouns and verbs with words that generate clarity and energy.

Specific Nouns

Make it a habit to use specific nouns for subjects. General nouns *(woman, school)* give the reader a vague, uninteresting picture. More specific nouns *(actress, university)* give the reader a better picture. Finally, very specific nouns *(Sarah Polley, Dalhousie)* are the type that can make your writing clear and colourful.

General to Specific Nouns

Person	Place	Thing	Idea
woman	school	book	theory
actor	university	novel	scientific theory
Sarah Polley	Dalhousie	*Pride and Prejudice*	relativity

Vivid Verbs

Like nouns, verbs can be too general to create a vivid word picture. For example, the verb *looked* does not say the same thing as *stared, glared, glanced,* or *peeked.*

- Whenever possible, use a verb that is strong enough to stand alone without the help of an adverb.

  Verb and adverb: John fell down in the student lounge.
  Vivid verb: John collapsed in the student lounge.

- Avoid overusing the "be" verbs *(is, are, was, were)* and helping verbs. Often a main verb can be made from another word in the same sentence.

  A "be" verb: Cole is someone who follows international news.
  A stronger verb: Cole follows international news.

- Use active rather than passive verbs. (Use passive verbs only if you want to downplay who is performing the action in a sentence. See page 81.)

  Passive verb: Another provocative essay was submitted by Kim.
  Active verb: Kim submitted another provocative essay.

- Use verbs that show rather than tell.

  A verb that tells: Dr. Lewis is very thorough.
  A verb that shows: Dr. Lewis prepares detailed, interactive lectures.

Replace Jargon and Clichés

Replace language that is overly technical or difficult to understand. Also replace overused, worn-out words.

Understandable Language

Jargon is language used in a certain profession or by a particular group of people. It may be acceptable to use if your audience is that group of people, but to most ears jargon will sound technical and unnatural.

> **Jargon:** I'm having conceptual difficulty with these academic queries.
> **Clear:** I don't understand these review questions.

Fresh and Original Writing

Clichés are overused words or phrases. They give the reader no fresh view and no concrete picture. Because clichés spring quickly to mind (for both the writer and the reader), they are easy to write and often fail to convey a precise meaning.

an axe to grind	piece of cake
between a rock and a hard place	stick your neck out
easy as pie	throwing your weight around

While clichés fill your writing with tired expressions, using flowery phrases leads to language that is overblown. Such wording is unnecessarily fancy and often sentimental. This type of writing draws attention to itself, interfering with direct communication.

> **Flowery:** The gorgeous beauty of the Great Barrier Reef is fantastically on display in coral formations of all the colours of the rainbow and in its wondrous variety of delightful tropical fish that soar like eagles through the azure liquid.
> **Fresh:** The beauty of the Great Barrier Reef is displayed in rainbow-coloured coral formations and in a rich variety of tropical fish.

Unpretentious Language

Pretentious language aims to sound intelligent but comes off sounding phony. Such language calls attention to itself rather than its meaning; in fact, pretentious words can be so high-blown that meaning is obscured altogether.

> **Pretentious:** Liquid precipitation in the Iberian Peninsula's nation-state of most prominent size experiences altitudinal descent as a matter of course primarily in the region characterized by minimal topographical variation.
> **Plain:** The rain in Spain falls mainly on the plain.

Strive for Plain English

In many ways, plain English is the product of the principles discussed on the previous pages: avoiding jargon, technical language, clichés, flowery phrasing, and pretentious wording. However, plain English also counters these ethically questionable uses of language:

Obfuscation

When writing includes fuzzy terms, such as *throughput* and *downlink*, which muddy the issue, the result is obfuscation. These words may make simple ideas sound more profound than they really are, or they may make false ideas sound true.

> *Example:* Through the fully functional developmental process of a streamlined target-refractory system, the military will successfully reprioritize its data throughputs. (*Objection:* What does this mean?)

Ambiguity

Especially when deliberate, ambiguity makes a statement open to two or more interpretations. While desirable in some forms of writing (such as poetry and fiction), ambiguity is usually disruptive in academic writing because it obscures the meaning of the words.

> *Example:* Many women need to work to support their children through school, but they would be better off at home. (*Objection:* Does *they* refer to *children* or *women*? What does *better off* mean? These words and phrases are unclear.)

Euphemisms

A euphemism is an indirect expression that avoids stating an uncomfortable truth. In your academic writing, choose neutral, tactful phrasing, but avoid euphemisms.

> *Example:* This economically challenged neighbourhood faces some issues concerning mind-enhancing substances and scuffles between youths. (*Translation:* This impoverished neighbourhood is being destroyed by drugs and gangs.)

Doublespeak

When phrasing deliberately seeks either to hide the truth from readers or to understate the situation, the result is often doublespeak. Such slippery language is especially a temptation when the writer wields authority, power, or privilege in a negative situation (e.g., a hospital administrator writing a report, as shown in the sentence below). Avoid such verbal misdirection; be clearly honest by choosing precise, transparent phrasing.

> *Example:* The doctor executed a nonfacile manipulation of newborn. (*Translation:* The doctor dropped the baby during delivery.)

Change Biased Words

When depicting individuals or groups according to their differences, use language that implies equal value and respect for all people.

Words Referring to Language and Ethnicity

Acceptable General Terms	Acceptable Specific Terms
First Nations, Aboriginal	**Mohawk people, Inuit people,** and so forth
Asian Canadians (not Orientals)	**Chinese Canadians, Japanese Canadians,** and so forth
Latinos, Latinas, Hispanics	**Mexican Canadians, Cuban Canadians,** and so forth

Black, African Canadian, African American: "African Canadian" is widely accepted in Canada, though the term "black" is preferred by some individuals. The same is true of "African American" and "black" in the United States.

Canadians, English Canadians, Anglophones, French Canadians, Francophones: Use these terms to refer to citizens and to specify their primary language in relation to both official languages. Where appropriate, use more specific terms designating provinces, such as "Quebeckers" or "Quebecois," "Albertans," and "Nova Scotians."

Not Recommended	Preferred
Eurasian, mulatto	**person of mixed ancestry**
nonwhite	**person of colour**
Caucasian	**white**

fig. 6.2

Words Referring to Age

Age Group	Acceptable Terms
up to age 13 or 14	**boys, girls**
between 13 and 19	**youth, young people, young men, young women**
late teens and 20s	**young adults, young women, young men**
30s to age 60	**adults, men, women**
60 and older	**older adults, older people** (not elderly)
65 and older	**seniors** (senior citizens also acceptable)

fig. 6.3

Words Referring to Disabilities or Impairments

In the recent past, some writers were choosing alternatives to the term *disabled*, including *physically challenged, exceptional,* or *special*. However, it is not generally held that these new terms are precise enough to serve those who live with disabilities. Of course, degrading labels such as *crippled, invalid,* and *maimed,* as well as overly negative terminology, must be avoided.

Not Recommended	Preferred
handicap	disability
birth defect	congenital disability
stutter, stammer, lisp	speech impairment
an AIDS victim	person with AIDS
suffering from cancer	person who has cancer
mechanical foot	prosthetic foot
false teeth	dentures

Words Referring to Conditions

People with various disabilities and conditions have sometimes been referred to as though they were their condition (quadriplegics, depressives, epileptics) instead of people who happen to have a particular disability. As much as possible, remember to refer to the person first, the disability second.

Not Recommended	Preferred
the disabled	people with disabilities
cripples	people who have difficulty walking
the retarded	people with a developmental disability
dyslexics	students with dyslexia
neurotics	patients with neuroses
subjects, cases	participants, patients
quadriplegics	people who are quadriplegic
wheelchair users	people who use wheelchairs

Additional Terms

Make sure you understand the following terms that address specific impairments:

hearing impairment	=	partial hearing loss, hard of hearing (not deaf, which is total loss of hearing)
visual impairment	=	partially sighted (not blind, which is total loss of vision)
communicative disorder	=	speech, hearing, and learning disabilities affecting communication

Words Referring to Gender

- Use parallel language for both genders:

  | The **men** and the **women** rebuilt the school together.
  | **Hank** and **Marie**
  | **Mr. Robert Gumble**, **Mrs. Joy Gumble**

  Note: The courtesy titles *Mr.*, *Ms.*, *Mrs.*, and *Miss* ought to be used according to the person's preference.

- Use nonsexist alternatives to words with masculine connotations:

  | **humanity** (not *mankind*)   **synthetic** (not *man-made*)
  | **artisan** (not *craftsman*)

- Do not use masculine-only or feminine-only pronouns *(he, she, his, her)* when you want to refer to a human being in general:

  | A politician can kiss privacy goodbye when **he** runs for office.
  | (not recommended)

  Instead, use *he or she*, change the sentence to plural, or eliminate the pronoun:

  | A politician can kiss privacy goodbye when **he** or **she** runs for office.
  | Politicians can kiss privacy goodbye when **they** run for office.
  | A politician can kiss privacy goodbye when running for office.

- Do not use gender-specific references in the salutation of a business letter when you don't know the person's name:

  | Dear Sir: Dear Gentlemen: (neither is recommended)

  Instead, address a position:

  | Dear Personnel Officer:
  | Dear Members of the Economic Committee:

Occupational Issues

Not Recommended	Preferred
chairman	chair, presiding officer, moderator
salesman	sales representative, salesperson
clergyman	minister, priest, rabbi
male/female nurse	nurse
male/female doctor	doctor, physician
mailman	mail carrier, postal worker, letter carrier
insurance man	insurance agent
fireman	firefighter
businessman	executive, manager, businessperson
steward, stewardess	flight attendant
policeman, policewoman	police officer

Proofreading Your Writing

The following guidelines will help you check your revised writing for spelling, mechanics, usage, grammar, and form. For additional help, see the Handlook section of this text (pages 567–677).

Review Punctuation and Mechanics

1. **Check for proper use of commas** before coordinating conjunctions in compound sentences, after introductory clauses and long introductory phrases, between items in a series, and so on.
2. **Look for apostrophes** in contractions, plurals, and possessive nouns.
3. **Examine quotation marks** in quoted information, titles, or dialogue.
4. **Watch for proper use of capital letters** for first words in written conversation and for proper names of people, places, and things.

Look for Usage and Grammar Errors

1. **Look for words that writers commonly misuse:** *there/their/they're; accept/except.*
2. **Check for verb use.** Subjects and verbs should agree in number: Singular subjects go with singular verbs; plural subjects go with plural verbs. Verb tenses should be consistent throughout.
3. **Review for pronoun/antecedent agreement problems.** A pronoun and its antecedent must agree in number.

Check for Spelling Errors

1. **Use a spell checker.** Your spell checker will catch most errors.
2. **Check each spelling you are unsure of.** Especially check those proper names and other special words your spell checker won't know.
3. **Consult a handbook.** Refer to a list of commonly misspelled words, as well as an up-to-date dictionary.

Check the Writing for Form and Presentation

1. **Note the title.** A title should be appropriate and lead into the writing.
2. **Examine any quoted or cited material.** Are all sources of information properly presented and documented? (See pages 493–534 and 535–564.)
3. **Look over the finished copy of your writing.** Does it meet the requirements for a final manuscript?

Pixssooz/Shutterstock.com

Formatting Your Writing

A good page design makes your writing clear and easy to follow. Keep that in mind when you produce a final copy of your writing.

Strive for Clarity in Page Design

Examine the following design elements, making sure that each is appropriate and clear in your project and in your writing.

Format and Documentation

- **Keep the design clear and uncluttered.** Aim for a sharp, polished look in all your assigned writing.
- **Use the designated documentation form.** Follow all the requirements outlined in the MLA (pages 493–534) or APA (pages 535–564) style guides.

Typography

- **Use an easy-to-read serif font for the main text.** Serif type, **like this**, has "tails" at the tops and bottoms of the letters. For most writing, use a 10- or 12-point type size.
- **Consider using a sans serif font for the title and headings.** In traditional academic writing, typeface and type size should remain consistent throughout (e.g., 12-point Times New Roman.) For other documents, however, consider sans serif type and different sizes for headings. Sans serif type, **like this**, does not have "tails." Use larger, perhaps 18-point, type for your title and 14-point type for any headings. You can also use boldface for headings if they seem to get lost on the page. (Follow your instructor's formatting guidelines.)

  > Because most people find a sans serif font easier to read on screen, consider a sans serif font for the body and a serif font for the titles and headings in any writing you publish online.

Spacing

- **Follow all requirements for indents and margins.** This usually means indenting the first line of each paragraph five spaces, maintaining a one-inch margin around each page, and double-spacing throughout the paper.
- **Avoid widows and orphans.** Avoid leaving headings, hyphenated words, or the first line of a paragraph alone at the bottom of a page (an orphan). Also avoid carrying over the short last line of a paragraph to the top of a new page (a widow).

Graphic Devices

- **Create bulleted or numbered lists to highlight individual items in a list.** But be selective, using traditional paragraphs when they help you more effectively communicate your message. Writing should not include too many lists.
- **Include charts or other graphics.** Graphics should be neither so small that they get lost on the page, nor so large that they overpower the page.

Submitting Your Writing

Once you have formatted and proofread your final draft, you should be ready to share your writing. For your course assignments, you will often simply turn in your paper to your instructor. However, you should also think about sharing your writing with other audiences, including those who will want to see your writing portfolio.

Consider Potential Audiences

You could receive helpful feedback by taking any of the following steps:

- Share your writing with peers or family members.
- Submit your work to a local publication or an online journal.
- Post your writing on an appropriate website, including your own.
- Turn in your writing to your instructor.

Select Appropriate Submission Methods

There are two basic methods for submitting your work.

- **Paper submission:** Print an error-free copy on quality paper.
- **Electronic submission:** If allowed, send your writing as an email attachment.

Use a Writing Portfolio

There are two basic types of writing portfolios: (1) *a working portfolio* in which you store documents at various stages of development, and (2) *a showcase portfolio* with which you share appropriate finished work. For example, you could submit a portfolio to complete course requirements or to apply for a scholarship, graduate program, or job. The documents below are commonly included in a showcase portfolio:

- A table of contents listing the pieces included in your portfolio
- An opening essay or letter detailing the story behind your portfolio (how you compiled it and why it features the qualities expected by the intended reader)
- A specified number of—and types of—finished pieces
- A cover sheet attached to each piece of writing, discussing the reason for its selection, the amount of work that went into it, and so on
- Evaluation sheets or checklists charting the progress or experience you want to show related to issues of interest to the reader

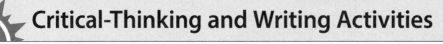

Critical-Thinking and Writing Activities

As directed by your instructor, complete the following activities.

1. Catherine Drinker Bowen has argued the following: "Writing is not apart from living. Writing is a kind of double living." Does this claim ring true for you? How do you understand the relationship between writing and living?

2. Choose a writing assignment that you have recently completed. Edit the sentences in this writing for style and correctness using pages 95–101 as a guide. Then use pages 102–108 in this chapter to edit the piece of writing for vague words, jargon, clichés, and biased language. Lastly, use page 110 to assess the quality of your formatting and page design, reformatting the paper as needed.

Learning-Objectives Checklist ✓

Have you achieved this chapter's learning objectives? Check your progress with the items below, revisiting topics in the chapter as needed. *I have . . .*

___ re-examined the overall style of my revised draft, including how well that style fits the rhetorical situation (94).

___ combined short, simplistic sentences through techniques of coordination and subordination (95).

___ expanded sparse sentences by making them cumulative, building them up with meaningful and rich details (96).

___ transformed weak sentences by varying sentence openings, lengths, types, and arrangements (98–99).

___ re-formulated sentences to strengthen parallel structure of coordinating elements (100).

___ rewritten sentences weakened by nominalizations, expletives, and negative constructions (101).

___ eliminated wordiness within sentences (102), and replaced vague terms with precise nouns and vivid verbs (103).

___ replaced jargon with understandable language and clichés with fresh, phrasing (104).

___ replaced any terms showing bias with respect to ethnicity, age, disabilities, health conditions, gender, and occupations (106–108).

___ produced a clear, reader-friendly page design by developing an overall format that fits the writing assignment and form, following the requirements of a specific style such as MLA or APA, making typographical choices that enhance readability, creating white space as needed, and effectively designing and integrating graphics (110).

___ chosen a submission method, whether paper or digital, that meets readers' needs and the assignment expectations (111).

___ integrated my writing into a portfolio, whether a working or showcase portfolio, so as to track and demonstrate my growth as a writer (111).

Chapter 7

One Writer's Process

An essay is an attempt to understand a topic more deeply and clearly. That's one of the reasons this basic form of writing is essential in many courses. It's a tool for both discovering and communicating.

How do you move from an assignment to a finished, polished essay? The best strategy is to take matters one step at a time, from understanding the assignment to submitting the final draft. Don't try to churn out the essay the night before it's due.

This chapter shows how student writer Angela Franco followed the writing process outlined in Chapters 2 through 6.

Visually Speaking   A rotary or roundabout (Figure 7.1) effectively controls the flow of traffic. How might writing be thought of as involving a flow of traffic? In what ways does the writing process involve rotaries?

Learning **Objectives**

By working through this chapter, you will be able to

- explain how one writer worked through the writing process to complete an assignment.

- compare this student's process with your own.

- assess how the writing process might help you complete your assignments.

fig. 7.1

Angela's Assignment and Response

In this chapter, you will follow student Angela Franco as she writes an assigned essay for her Environmental Policies class. Start by carefully reading the assignment and discussion below, noting how she thinks through the rhetorical situation.

Angela Examined the Assignment

Angela carefully read her assignment and responded with the notes below.

"Explain in a two- to three-page essay how a local environmental issue is relevant to the world community. Using *Writing Life* as your guide, format the paper and document sources in MLA style. You may seek revising help from a classmate or from the writing centre."

Role
- I'm writing as a student in Environmental Policies, and as a resident of Ontario.

Subject
- The subject is a local environmental issue.

Purpose
- My purpose is to explain how the issue is relevant to all people. That means I must show how this issue affects my audience—both positively and negatively.

Form
- I need to write a two- to three-page essay—that sounds formal.
- I'll need to include a thesis statement, as well as references to my sources using MLA style.

Audience
- My audience will be people like me—neighbours, classmates, and community members.
- I'll need to keep in mind what they already know and what they need to know.

Context
- I'll use the guidelines and checklists in *Writing Life* to evaluate and revise my writing.
- I'll get editing feedback from Jeannie and from the writing centre.

 For each step in the writing process, choose strategies that fit your writing situation. For example, a personal essay in an English class might require significant time getting started, whereas a lab report in a chemistry class might require little or none.

Angela Explored and Narrowed Her Assignment

Angela explored her assignment and narrowed its focus by clustering and freewriting.

Angela's Cluster

When she considered environmental issues, Angela first thought of water pollution as a possible topic for her essay. After writing the phrase in the centre of her page, she drew from memories, experiences, and readings to list related ideas and details. Notice how she used three different-coloured inks to distinguish the topic (blue) from ideas (red) and details (green) (Figure 7.2).

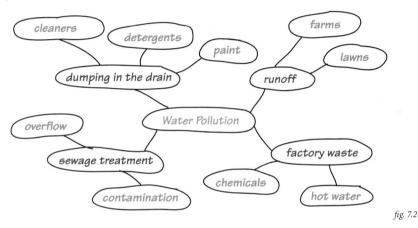

fig. 7.2

Angela's Freewriting

Angela decided to freewrite about the water pollution caused about a decade earlier by improper sewage treatment in a small Ontario town.

> I remember reading an article about problems in Walkerton, a small Ontario town. People actually died. The water they drank was contaminated. This is becoming a problem in developed countries like ours. I thought for a long time this was a problem only in developing countries. So who is responsible for sewage treatment? Who guarantees the safety of our drinking water? How does water get contaminated? Are there solutions for every kind of contamination: mercury, PCBs, sewage?

Angela's Narrowed Assignment

Based on her freewriting, Angela rephrased her assignment to narrow its focus.

> Explain in a two- to three-page essay how a local water pollution problem in a small Ontario town is relevant to the world community.

Angela's Planning

Angela reviewed her narrowed assignment and reassessed her topic.

Narrowed Writing Assignment

Explain in a two- to three-page essay how a recent water pollution problem in a small Ontario town is relevant to the world community.

Angela Focused Her Topic

To focus her topic, Angela answered the journalistic questions (five Ws and H).

Topic: Water pollution in a small Ontario town

Who?	- Farm operators, wastewater officials, Walkerton residents
What?	- Water supply contaminated
	- Spread bacteria (E. coli)
	- Caused disease
	- Clean, fresh water depleted
Where?	- Walkerton, Ontario
When?	- May 2000
Why?	- Improper regulation; human error
How?	- Groundwater from irrigation, untreated sewage, and runoff

Angela Researched the Topic

Angela then did some research to check her information and collect more details for her paper. She recorded all the essential data on each source following MLA format and then listed the specific details related to her topic. Here's one source:

"Inside Walkerton: Canada's worst ever E. coli contamination." CBC News. 17 May 2010. Web. 13 September 2013.
- May 15—water sampled
- May 17—first patients with flu-like symptoms
- May 18—Lab confirms E. coli contamination in water, but Public Utilities Commission (PUC) does not report information.
- May 19—Medical Health Office (MHO) discovers E. coli outbreak, but is assured by the PUC that the water is safe.
- May 20—At least 40 people treated at hospital with bloody diarrhea, but PUC says twice that water is safe.
- May 21—MHO tells people not to drink water, runs their own test.
- May 23—MHO finds E. coli, learns of May 18 memo, and that chlorinator not working for some time.
- May 24—Three adults and a baby die of E. coli.

Angela Decided How to Organize Her Writing

With a focus selected, Angela used the three guidelines below to choose the best organizational pattern for her writing.

Guidelines

1. **Review your assignment** and record your response.

   Assignment:
   Explain in a two- to three-page essay how a recent environmental issue is relevant to the world community.

   Response:
   My assignment clearly states that I need to explain my topic, so I have a general idea of how my paper will be organized.

2. **Decide on your thesis statement** and think about your essay's possible content and organization.

   Thesis Statement:
   The water pollution incident in Walkerton, Ontario, had a devastating effect that every town should learn from.

   Reflection:
   After reading my thesis statement, it's obvious that I'm going to be writing about a problem and its causes.

3. **Choose an overall method** and reflect on its potential effectiveness.

   Reflection:
   Looking at the list of methods, I see that I can use cause/effect or problem/solution. After making two quick lists of my main points using both approaches, I decided to use a problem/ solution approach. I will still talk about causes and effects in my essay—they just won't be front and centre.

   With problem/solution, I need to first present the problem clearly so that readers can fully understand it and see why it's important. Then I need to explore solutions to the problem—maybe what they did in Walkerton and what we all need to do to make water safe.

 Many essays you write will be organized according to one basic method or approach. However, within that basic structure you may want to include other methods. For example while developing a comparison essay you may do some describing or classifying. In other words, you should choose methods of development that (1) help you understand the topic and (2) help your reader understand your message.

Andreas Berheide/Shutterstock.com

Angela's First Draft

After composing her opening, middle, and closing paragraphs, Angela put together her first draft. She then added a working title.

Water Woes

The writer uses a series of images to get the reader's attention.

It's a hot day. Several people just finished mowing their lawns. A group of   *1*
bicyclists—more than 3,000—have been passing through your picturesque town
all afternoon. Dozens of children are running up and down the soccer pitch. What
do all these people have in common? They all drinks lots of tap water, especially on
hot summer days. They also take for granted that the water is clean and safe. But
in reality, the water they drink could be contaminated and pose a serious health

The thesis statement (boldfaced) introduces the subject.

risk. **That's just what happened in Walkerton, Ontario, where a water pollution
incident had a devastating effect that every town can learn from.**

The writer describes the cause of the problem.

What happened in Walkerton? Heavy rains fell on May 12. It wasn't until   *2*
May 21 that the townspeople were advised to boil their drinking water. The rains
washed cattle manure into the town well. The manure contained E coli, a type of
bacteria. E coli is harmless to cattle. It can make people sick. Seven days after the
heavy rains, people began calling public health officials. The warning came too late.
Two people had already died (Wickens).

The writer indicates some of her source material with a citation.

Once Walkerton's problem was identified, the solutions were known. The   *3*
government acted quickly to help the community and to clean the water supply.
One Canadian newspaper reported that a $100,000 emergency fund was set up to
help families with expenses. Bottled water for drinking and containers of bleach for
sanitizing and cleaning were donated by local businesses.

So what messed up Walkerton? Basically, people screwed up! According to one   *4*
news story, a flaw in the water treatment system allowed the bacteria-infested water
to enter the well. The manure washed into the well, but the chlorine should have
killed the deadly bacteria. In Walkerton, the PUC group fell asleep at the wheel.

> **The writer covers the solutions that were used to resolve the problem.**

At last, the Provincial Clean Water Agency restored the main water and sewage systems by flushing out all of the town's pipes and wells. The ban on drinking Walkerton's water was finally lifted seven months after the water became contaminated.

5

> **The concluding paragraph stresses the importance of public awareness.**

Could any good come from Walkerton's tragedy? Does it have a silver lining? It is possible that more people are aware that water may be contaminated. Today people are beginning to take responsibility for the purity of the water they and their families drink. In the end, more and more people will know about the dangers of contaminated water—without learning it the hard way.

6

Angela Kept a Working Bibliography

As she researched her topic, Angela kept a working bibliography—a list of resources that she thought might offer information helpful to her essay. From the start, she formatted the entries in MLA style. During the writing process, she deleted some resources, added others, and edited the document that became the works-cited list on page 128.

Working Bibliography

Blackwell, Thomas. "Walkerton Doctor Defends Response." *The Edmonton Journal.* 9 Jan. 2001. Web. 13 Sept. 2013.

"Inside Walkerton: Canada's Worst Ever E.coli Contamination." *CBC News.* 17 May 2010. Web. 13 Sept. 2013.

Johnson, Alex. Personal interview. 14 Sept. 2013.

Angela's First Revision

After finishing the first draft, Angela set it aside. When she was ready to revise it, she looked carefully at global issues—ideas, organization, and voice. She wrote notes to herself to help keep her thoughts together.

Angela's comments

> I need to give my opening more energy.

> Does my thesis still fit the paper?— Yes.

> Using time sequence, put this paragraph in better order.

> Move this paragraph — it interrupts the discussion of causes.

> My voice here is too informal.

Water Woes

1   It's a hot ~~day.~~ *an unusually* Several people just finished mowing their lawns. A group of bicyclists —more than 3,000— *Saturday afternoon* ~~have been passing through your picturesque town all afternoon.~~ *pedal up the street* Dozens of children are running up and down the soccer pitch. What do all these people have in common? They all drinks lots of tap water, especially on hot summer days. They also take for granted that the water is clean and safe. But in reality, the water they drink could be contaminated and pose a serious health risk. **That's just what happened in Walkerton, Ontario, where a water pollution incident had a devastating effect that every town can learn from.**

2   What happened in Walkerton? Heavy rains fell on May 12. It wasn't until May 21 that the townspeople were advised to boil their drinking water. The rains washed cattle manure into the town well. The manure contained E coli, a type of bacteria. E coli is harmless to cattle. It can make people sick. Seven days after the heavy rains, people began calling public health officials. The warning came too late. Two people had already died (Wickens).

3   Once Walkerton's problem was identified, the solutions were known. The government acted quickly to help the community and to clean the water supply. One Canadian newspaper reported that a $100,000 emergency fund was set up to help families with expenses. Bottled water for drinking and containers of bleach for basic sanitizing and cleaning were donated by local businesses.

4   So what ~~messed up~~ *went wrong in* Walkerton? ~~Basically, people screwed up!~~ *Human error was a critical factor. First,* According to one news story, a flaw in the water treatment system allowed the bacteria-infested water to enter the well. *Even after* The manure washed into the well, ~~but~~ the chlorine should have killed the deadly bacteria. In Walkerton, the ~~PUC group fell asleep at the wheel.~~

Explain "fell asleep." Move paragraph three here and combine.

In addition
~~At last,~~ the Provincial Clean Water Agency restored the main water and 5
sewage systems by flushing out all of the town's pipes and wells. The ban on
drinking Walkerton's water was finally lifted seven months after the water became
contaminated.

Cut the clichés.

Could any good come from Walkerton's tragedy? ~~Does it have a silver lining?~~ 6
It is possible that more people are aware that water may be contaminated. Today
people are beginning to take responsibility for the purity of the water they and their
families drink. In the end, more and more people will know about the dangers of
contaminated water—without learning it the hard way.

the Public Utilities Commission was responsible for overseeing the
testing and treating of the town's water, but it failed to monitor
it properly. Apparently, shortcuts were taken when tracking the
water's chlorine level, and as a result, some of the water samples were
mislabelled. There was also a significant delay between the time that
the contamination was identified and the time it was reported.

alexmat46/Shutterstock.com

Angela's Second Revision

Angela revised her draft, taking into account the questions and suggestions she received from a peer. His comments are in the margin, and Angela's changes, including a new opening and closing, are in red.

Reviewer's comments	**Angela's Changes**

Water Woes

Could you make the opening more relevant and urgent?

WARNING: City tap water is polluted with animal waste. Using the water for drinking, cooking, or bathing could cause sickness or death.   *1*

According to the Seirra Club, run-off pollutants from farm cites are   *2* steadily seeping into our streams, lakes, reservoirs and wells. Because much of our drinking water comes from these resources, warnings like the one above are already posted in a number of U.S. and Canadian communities, and many more

Could you clarify your focus on the topic?

postings will be needed ("Water Sentinels"). As the Seirra Club argues, the pollution and related warnings are serious, and failure to take them seriously could be deadly. For example, a few years ago the citizens of Walkerton Ontario learned that the water that they believed to be clean was actually poisoned.

The events   began   , 2000, when heavy rains
~~What happened~~ in Walkerton? ~~Heavy rains fell~~ on May 12. ~~The rains~~   *3* washed cattle manure into the town well. The manure contained E coli, a type of

Add the year and other specific details.

bacteria. E coli is harmless to cattle. It can make people sick. Seven days after the
                                to complain of nausea and diarrhea ⊙
heavy rains, people began calling public health officials⌃It wasn't until May 21 that the townspeople were advised to boil their drinking water. The warning came too
                          , and more than 2,000 were ill
late. Two people had already died⌃(Wickens).

Make sure you document all source material— you have just one citation in your draft.

Several factors contributed to the terrible tragedy in Walkerton, including human error.
      ⌃ ~~So what went wrong in Walkerton? Human error was a critical factor.~~ First,
         The Edmonton Journal
according to ~~one news story,~~ a flaw in the water treatment system allowed the
                              (Blackwell)
bacteria-infested water to enter the well. Even after the manure washed into the well, the chlorine should have killed the deadly bacteria. In Walkerton, the Public Utilities Commission was responsible for overseeing the testing and treating of the town's water, but it failed to monitor it properly. Apparently, shortcuts were taken when tracking the water's chlorine level, and as a result, some of the water samples   *4*

were mislabelled. There was also a significant delay between the time that the contamination was identified and the time it was reported.

> Once Walkerton's problem was identified, ~~the solutions were known.~~ The   5
> government acted quickly to help the community~~, and to clean the water supply.~~
> *The Edmonton Journal*
> ~~One Canadian newspaper~~ reported that a $100,000 emergency fund was set up to help
> *Local businesses donated*
> families with expenses. Bottled water for drinking and containers of bleach for basic
> sanitizing and cleaning ~~were donated by local businesses.~~ In addition, the Provincial
> Clean Water Agency restored the main water and sewage systems by flushing out
> all of the town's pipes and wells. The ban on drinking Walkerton's water was finally
> lifted seven months after the water became contaminated.

> As the Sierra Club warned and the citizens of Walkerton learned,   6
> water purity is a life-and-death issue. Fortunately, governments have been
> addressing the problem. For example, since 2001, most provinces have
> tightened their clean-water standards, more communities have begun
> monitoring their water quality, and more individuals have been using water-
> filtration systems, bottled water, or boiled tap water. However, a tragedy like
> that in Walkerton could happen again. To avoid such horror, all of us must get
> involved by demanding clean tap water in our communities and by promoting the
> polices and procedures needed to achieve that goal.

Use active voice.

Consider adding details— maybe an entire paragraph— calling readers to action, and stating your thesis clearly.

Angela's Edited Draft

When Angela began editing, she read each of her sentences aloud to check for clarity and smoothness. **The first page of Angela's edited copy is shown below.**

The writer revises the title.

                                                            in Walkerton
                              Water Woes ∧

> **Warning: City tap water is polluted with animal waste. Using the water for drinking, cooking, or bathing could cause sickness or death.**   *1*

According to the Seirra Club, run-off pollutants from farm cites are steadily seeping into our streams, lakes, reservoirs, and wells. Because much of our drinking   *2*

She qualifies her statement, replacing "will" with "might."

water comes from these resources, warnings like the one above are already posted
                                                                    might
in a number of U.S. and Canadian communities, and many more postings will be
            in the future
needed∧ ("Water Sentinels). As the Seirra Club argues, the pollution and related warnings are serious, and failure to take them seriously could be deadly. For example, a few years ago the citizens of Walkerton Ontario learned that the water
                            tragically
that they believed to be clean was ~~actually~~ poisoned.

The events in Walkerton began on May 12, 2000, when heavy rains washed   *3*
                                                        commonly called
cattle manure into the town well. The manure contained ~~E coli~~ a bacteria, E coli,

She rewrites and combines several choppy sentences.

While E coli
∧ is harmless to cattle. It can make people sick. Seven days after the heavy rains, people began calling public health officials to complain of nausea and diarrhea. It wasn't until May 21 that the townspeople were advised to boil their drinking water. The warning came too late. Two people had already died, and more than 2,000 were ill (Wickens).

Several factors contributed to the ~~terrible~~ tragedy in Walkerton, including   *4*

Angela deletes unnecessary words.

human error. First, according to *The Edmonton Journal,* a flaw in the water treatment system allowed the ~~bacteria~~ infested water to enter the well (Blackwell). Even after the manure washed into the well, the chlorine should have . . .

Angela's Proofread Draft

Angela reviewed her edited copy for punctuation, agreement issues, and spelling. **The first page of Angela's proofread essay is shown below.**

Water Woes in Walkerton

> **Warning: City tap water is polluted with animal waste. Using the water for drinking, cooking, or bathing could cause sickness or death.**

1

The writer corrects errors that the spell checker did not pick up.

According to the Sierra Club, run-off pollutants from farm sites are steadily seeping into our streams, lakes, reservoirs, and wells. Because much of our drinking water comes from these resources, warnings like the one above are already posted in a number of U.S. and Canadian communities, and many more postings might be needed in the future ("Water Sentinels"). As the Sierra Club argues, the pollution and related warnings are serious, and failure to take them seriously could be deadly.

2

She adds a comma between the city and province.

For example, a few years ago the citizens of Walkerton, Ontario, learned that the water that they believed to be clean was tragically poisoned.

She adds periods and italicizes "E. coli" to show that it is a scientific term.

The events in Walkerton began on May 12, 2000, when heavy rains washed cattle manure into the town well. The manure contained bacteria commonly called *E. coli*. While *E. coli* is harmless to cattle, it can make people sick. Seven days after the heavy rains, people began calling public health officials to complain of nausea and diarrhea. It wasn't until May 21 that the townspeople were advised to boil their drinking water. The warning came too late. Two people had already died, and more than 2,000 were ill (Wickens).

3

She adds a word for clarity.

Several factors contributed to the tragedy in Walkerton, including human error. First, according to *The Edmonton Journal,* a flaw in the water treatment system allowed the infested water to enter Walkerton's well (Blackwell). Even after the manure washed into Walkerton's well, the chlorine should have . . .

4

Angela's Finished Essay

After proofreading and formatting her essay, Angela added a heading and page numbers. She also added more documentation and a works-cited list at the end.

Franco 1

Angela Franco

Professor Kim Van Es

English 101

18 October 2013

Clean Water Is Everyone's Business

| **The writer revises the title.** |

Warning: City tap water is polluted with animal waste.

Using the water for drinking, cooking, or bathing

could cause sickness or death.

| **The warning is emphasized with red print.** |

| **An appropriate font and type size are used.** |

According to the Sierra Club, run-off pollutants from farm sites are steadily seeping into our streams, lakes, reservoirs, and wells. Because much of our drinking water comes from these resources, warnings like the one above are already posted in a number of U.S. and Canadian communities, and many more postings might be needed in the future ("Water Sentinels"). As the Sierra Club argues, the pollution and related warnings are serious, and failure to take them seriously could be deadly. For example, a few years ago the citizens of Walkerton, Ontario, learned that the water that they believed to be clean was tragically poisoned.

The events in Walkerton began on May 12, 2000, when heavy rains washed cattle manure into the town well. The manure contained the bacteria commonly called *E. coli*. While *E. coli* is harmless to cattle, it can make people sick. Seven days after the heavy rains, people began calling public health officials to complain of nausea and diarrhea. It wasn't until May 21 that the townspeople were advised to

Franco 2

The writer's last name and the page number are cited on each page.

boil their drinking water. The warning came too late. Two people had already died, and more than 2,000 were ill (Wickens).

Several factors contributed to the tragedy in Walkerton, including human   3
error. First, according to *The Edmonton Journal,* a flaw in the water treatment system allowed the infested water to enter Walkerton's well (Blackwell). Even after the manure washed into Walkerton's well, the chlorine should have killed the deadly bacteria. In Walkerton, the Public Utilities Commission was responsible for overseeing the testing and treating of the town's water, but it failed to monitor the procedure properly ("Walkerton's Water-Safety"). Apparently, shortcuts were taken when tracking the water's chlorine level, and as a result, some of the water samples were mislabelled. There was also a significant delay between the time that the contamination was identified and the time it was reported.

Each claim or supporting point is backed up with reasoning and evidence.

Once Walkerton's problem was identified, the government acted quickly to help   4
the community. In its December 7, 2000, edition, *The Edmonton Journal* reported that a $100,000 emergency fund was set up to help families with expenses. Local businesses donated bottled water for drinking and containers of bleach for basic sanitizing and cleaning. In addition, the Provincial Clean Water Agency restored the main water and sewage systems by flushing out all of the town's pipes and wells. Seven months after the water became contaminated, the ban on drinking Walkerton's water was finally lifted.

The writer continues to give credit throughout the essay.

As the Sierra Club warns and the citizens of Walkerton learned, water purity is   5
a life-and-death issue. Fortunately, governments have been addressing the problem.

Franco 3

For example, since 2001, most provinces have tightened their clean-water standards, more communities have been monitoring their water quality, and more individuals have been using water-filtration systems, bottled water, or boiled tap water. However, a tragedy like that in Walkerton could happen again. To avoid such horror, all of us must get involved by demanding clean tap water in our communities and by promoting the policies and procedures needed to achieve that goal.

The writer restates her thesis in the last sentence.

Franco 4

Works Cited

Blackwell, Thomas. "Walkerton Doctor Defends Response." *The Edmonton Journal.* 9 Jan. 2001. Web. 13 Sept. 2013.

"Walkerton's Water-Safety Tests Falsified Regularly, Utility Official Admits." *The Edmonton Journal.* 7 Dec. 2000. Web. 13 Sept. 2013.

"Water Sentinels: Keeping It Clean around the U.S.A." Sierraclub.org. *Sierra Club.* n.d. Web. 15 Sept. 2013.

Wickens, Barbara. "Tragedy in Walkerton." *Maclean's* 5 June 2000. Web. 14 Sept. 2013.

Sources used are listed correctly, in alphabetical order.

Each entry follows MLA rules for content, format, and punctuation.

Critical-Thinking and Writing Activities

Complete these activities by yourself or with classmates.

1. Scott Russell Sanders suggests that "essays are experiments in making sense of things." Does Sanders' statement ring true? What makes such experiments flop or succeed? What kinds of "sense" do essays create? Reflect on these questions in light of Angela's essay on clean water, as well as by considering an essay that you wrote recently.

2. Review Angela's writing process. How does it compare with your own writing process on a recent assignment?

3. Review the peer-editing instructions in "Revising Collaboratively" (pages 89–90). Then reread the reviewer's comments in the margins of Angela's second revision (pages 122–123). Do the comments reflect the instructions? Explain.

Learning-Objectives Checklist ✓

Have you achieved this chapter's learning objectives? Check your progress with the items below, revisiting topics in the chapter as needed. *I have* . . .

___ analyzed how Angela Franco worked through the writing process:
  - examining the assignment (114)
  - narrowing the topic (115)
  - researching her topic and organizing her thoughts (116–117)
  - completing her first draft (118–119)
  - revising the draft by herself and then through peer review (120–123)
  - and editing and proofreading her essay (124–125).

___ compared Angela's process with the process that I normally follow, considering strengths and weaknesses of my own approach.

___ assessed how I might tailor the writing process shown by Angela and outlined in Chapters 2–7 to my own writing habits and my writing assignments.

Cross-Curricular Connections

Angela used MLA style, which is standard for English and some other humanities. By contrast, APA is standard for the social sciences: psychology, sociology, political science, and education. Make sure to find out what documentation style your instructor requires.

Traits of Academic Writing: A Checklist

Early in Chapter 2, you learned about the common traits of excellent academic writing (pages 30–31). The following checklist is a reminder of those traits. You can use it to check any of your finished writing assignments.

Stimulating Ideas   *The writing . . .*

____ presents interesting ideas and important information.

____ maintains a clear focus or purpose—centred on a thesis, theme, concern, or question.

____ develops the focus through a line of thought or reasoning elaborated with sufficient details or evidence.

____ holds the reader's attention (and answers her or his questions).

Logical Organization

____ includes a clear beginning, middle, and ending.

____ contains specific details, arranged in an order that builds understanding with readers.

____ uses transitions to link sentences and paragraphs.

Engaging Voice

____ speaks in a sincere, natural way that fits the writing situation.

____ shows that the writer really cares about the subject.

Appropriate Word Choice

____ contains specific, clear words.

____ uses a level of language appropriate for the type of writing and the audience.

Overall Sentence Fluency

____ flows smoothly from sentence to sentence.

____ displays varied sentence beginnings and lengths.

____ follows a style that fits the situation (e.g., familiar versus academic).

Correct, Accurate Copy

____ adheres to the rules of grammar, spelling, punctuation, and mechanics.

____ follows established documentation guidelines.

Reader-Friendly Design

____ exhibits a polished, professional design in terms of overall format, page layout, and typographical choices.

____ makes the document attractive and easy to read.

____ is formatted correctly in MLA or APA style.

II. Reader:
Strategies and Samples

Chapter 8

Forms of Academic Writing

Professors in nearly all fields give writing assignments. Why? Because they know that writing helps you learn course material today and use that knowledge in subsequent courses and in the workplace. Similarly, academic writing develops the thinking skills needed in a field of study and a profession.

This chapter begins by showing the big picture of college writing: the three divisions into which most college curricula are divided, and the academic departments that constitute each division. The chapter then offers instruction in the methods of inquiry and forms of writing typical to each division's disciplines. Finally, the chapter provides an overview of the rhetorical modes—the typical thinking patterns that characterize academic writing and that organize this part of *Writing Life*.

Visually Speaking Consider the analogy suggested by Figure 9.1: different forms of writing are like different modes of transportation. How far can you push the comparison?

Learning **Objectives**

By working through this chapter, you will be able to

- identify and classify fields of study in the college curriculum.
- differentiate and explain writing in the humanities, the social sciences, and the natural and applied sciences.
- distinguish the rhetorical modes at work in academic writing.
- analyze the nature of writing in your own field of study or a major that interests you.

Artens/Shutterstock.com

fig. 8.1

Three Curricular Divisions

Based on each department's field of study, the academic curriculum is generally divided into three groups: humanities, social sciences, and natural and applied sciences. These groups are then subdivided into specific departments, such as biology, chemistry, and physics. Below you will find an explanation of each division, along with its common departments.

Humanities

Scholars and students within this division study human culture, both past and present. They examine topics such as the history of civilization, cultural institutions and trends, religious beliefs and practices, languages and their use, and artwork and performance skills. Some departments in this division include the following:

Archaeology	Ethnic Studies	Modern Languages	Theatre Arts
Asian Studies	Film Studies	Music	Theology
Dance	Graphic Design	Philosophy	Visual Arts
English	History	Religion	Women's Studies

Social Sciences

Scholars and students in this division study human behaviour and societies using research strategies adapted from the natural sciences. For example, a researcher may develop a hypothesis regarding a topic or phenomenon, and then devise an experiment to test that hypothesis. Students study economic systems, correctional programs, and personality disorders. Departments in this division include the following:

Anthropology	Economics	Geophysics	Psychology
Business	Education	Government	Social Work
Communications	Genetics	Health & Phys. Ed.	Sociology
Criminology	Geography	Political Science	Urban Planning

Natural and Applied Sciences

The natural sciences (such as biology, zoology, and chemistry) focus on specific aspects of nature, such as animal life, plant life, and molecular structures. In contrast, the applied sciences (such as mathematics, computer science, and engineering) consider how to use science-based information to understand concepts and develop artifacts. Here are some of the departments in this division:

Agriculture	Biology	Environment	Physics
Agronomy	Botany	Forestry	Physiology
Anatomy	Chemistry	Mathematics	Public Health
Architecture	Computer Science	Nutrition	Space Science
Astronomy	Engineering	Oceanography	Zoology

Writing in the Humanities

In a humanities class (e.g., English, history, and theatre arts), your study and writing likely focus on various types of texts, broadly understood: primary texts, such as poems, novels, historical records, and philosophical essays, as well as secondary sources (books and periodical articles). Such study is largely concerned with the world of ideas, whether creative, historical, or theoretical. Your writing will likely have the character described below.

The Purpose of Inquiry

Humanities study aims to understand more deeply some aspect of human experience and humanity's place in the world, whether that aspect of experience relates to the artistic and imaginative, the historical, the spiritual, the linguistic, or the world of ethics. As a result, writing in the humanities tends to be thesis-driven, focused on a central idea that is explored through coherent analysis and argument.

Forms of Humanities Writing

In humanities courses, you will likely write essays and research papers of this sort: interpretive analyses and arguments on a specific topic, theoretical studies of key concepts in the discipline, and book reviews or broader bibliographic surveys. Here are typical forms:

- **Analysis of a Text or Artwork:** Such a study closely examines a specific work in order to understand more fully what it means, how it communicates, and so on.
- **A Review of the Literature on a Topic:** This form of research writing identifies and synthesizes the studies that have been published on a specific issue or question.
- **A Book, Film, Music, or Performance Review:** Applying general criteria for excellence, reviews evaluate the quality, impact, strengths, and weaknesses of a specific text or artwork.

Examples: "Latin American Music: A Diverse and Unifying Force" (pages 195–197), "Other Worlds" (pages 271–273), and "E.B. White's Ethic of Humility: An Ecocritical Engagement with *Charlotte's Web*" (pages 295–301).

Humanities Research Methods

As the forms of writing above suggest, the humanities involve the careful "reading" of primary texts, artifacts, and events. In addition, humanities projects involve a careful investigation of past scholarship on a topic so that the writer can add his or her voice to the ongoing discussion or dialogue. With their focus on "reading," the humanities value skills of interpretation—sensitivity to the primary text, thoughtful use of evidence from the text, attention to the textual context, awareness of theoretical frameworks for understanding texts, insightful theses about texts, and the rhetorical skills involved in analysis and argument. In such research, the following resources may be especially helpful:

- "Analyzing Texts, Documents, Records, and Artifacts" (pages 438–439)
- MLA Documentation (Chapter 28, pages 493–534, and www.mla.org)

Writing in the Social Sciences

In a social sciences class (e.g., psychology, sociology, business, education), your writing will likely explore some dimension of the way that people behave, individually or within groups, whether the group is just two people or an entire society. Your writing will likely have the character described below.

The Purpose of Inquiry

Broadly, the social sciences aim to understand through using an adapted version of the natural-science experimental method, the rules and conventions that govern human behaviour and societies. As such, social-sciences thinking tends to be hypothesis-driven, seeking not only to describe behaviour but also to predict it. To that end, the social sciences involve observing, measuring, and testing various forms of behaviour.

Forms of Social-Science Writing

With their focus on behaviour and social laws, social scientists typically write reports, often as teams of researchers. Here are specific types of writing that you might do:

- **A Literature Review:** This form of research writing identifies and synthesizes the studies that have been published on a specific behavioural or social issue.
- **An Experiment Report:** Such a report describes a specific experiment designed to test a hypothesis about behaviour, and then share and analyze the results.
- **A Field Report:** Whether based on observations, interviews, or surveys, such a report shares insights gathered through such contact with human subjects.
- **A Case Study:** Such a study describes and examines actual individuals and situations so as to understand them more deeply.

Examples: "Why We Lift" (pages 193–194), "Small Change" (pages 241–251), "It's 'Apartheid' Time Again. Pick Your Villain." (pages 336–337), and APA research paper (pages 554–563).

Social-Science Research Methods

Like scholars in the natural sciences, social scientists tend to use the experimental method to test out observation-based hypotheses. Some social-science research, however, is more subjective, involving a speculative approach to the mysteries of human consciousness, emotions, and the like. Because much social-science research is observation-based, much of the thinking is rooted in mathematics, particularly statistical analysis. Focused on testing hypotheses, such research pays careful attention to variables, controls, experiment replication, and case studies. Objective analysis of all the data is valued. The following resources may be especially helpful:

- "Conducting Surveys" (pages 436–437), "Conducting Interviews" (pages 440–441), and "Making Observations" (page 442)
- APA Documentation (Chapter 29, pages 535–564, and www.apa.org)

Writing in the Natural and Applied Sciences

In a natural- or applied-science class (e.g., botany, chemistry, engineering, and oceanography), your writing will explore some aspect of the physical, natural world. Such writing seeks to explore and explain the nature of the world that we inhabit and are part of, as well as the natural laws that govern that world. If your major is in the natural or applied sciences, your writing will likely have the character described below.

The Purpose of Inquiry

Broadly, natural science aims to explain observations in the light of current theories, observations that are typically not now explicable. The goal of the scientist—or more likely team of scientists—is to arrive at an explanation, stimulate discussion, and prompt further research. As such, scientific thinking tends to be hypothesis driven: it begins with a possible explanation rooted in current knowledge, makes an experiment-related prediction, observes and measures results, and then accepts, rejects, or modifies the possible explanation.

Forms of Natural-Science Writing

With their focus on natural phenomena, natural scientists typically write research reports. Here are types of writing that you might do:

- **Lab or Field Reports:** Sometimes called IMRAD reports (introduction, method, results, and discussion), such reports share the results of experiments and measured observations.
- **Literature Reviews:** These reports summarize and synthesize all the current research on a specific topic, perhaps also examining the theories that underlie the topic.
- **Technical Reports:** Applied research might involve writing technical reports aimed at proposing practical solutions to a specific problem or challenge.

Examples: "Wayward Cells" (pages 212–213), "Nuclear Is Not the Answer" (pages 333–335), and "Pitch Perfect: Why the Knuckleball Confounds Even Scientists" (pages 269–270).

Natural-Science Research Methods

Natural scientists practise two predominant research methods: laboratory experiments and field work. Both rooted in objective attention to phenomena, laboratory research follows the strict procedures of the experimental method while field work relies on careful, often quantifiable observation. Both forms for research value insightful hypothesizing, carefully collecting and analyzing data (typically in a lab notebook or a field journal), and thoughtfully relating the results to past research and current theories. The following resources might be helpful:

- "Making Observations" (page 442)
- Council of Science Editors (councilscienceeditors.org)

The Rhetorical Modes

The chapters in this part of *Writing Life* are largely organized by the type of writing: personal essay, analytical essay, and argumentative essay. However, this division also features the rhetorical modes—thinking patterns that characterize writing in part or in whole. These thinking patterns are at work in your academic writing, so learning them and practising them creates a foundation for all your assignments.

The Modes as Thinking Framework

Each rhetorical mode involves a thinking move that allows you to deepen your understanding of a topic, to explore it, and to make claims about it.

Personal-writing modes focus on experience, especially the writer's experience—whether of places, people, or events—with the goal of vividly sharing that experience with readers.

- **Narration** tells a story, whether in the form of a brief anecdote, a personal essay, a short story, or a book-length novel. (See pages 142–143.)
- **Description** evokes material reality (e.g., birds outside a window) through appealing to the senses (sight, hearing, touch, taste, and smell). (See pages 143–144.)
- **Reflection** involves rumination—a kind of speculation that extends narration and description into the territory of personal and universal meaning. (See page 145.)

Analytical modes involve mentally "breaking down" a topic in an effort to reveal structures and logical relationships that hold it together.

- **Definition** seeks to clarify the meaning of a term (e.g., gullibility, asceticism, "Dead Indians"). (See Chapter 10, pages 167–188.)
- **Classification** organizes into categories large or complex sets of things: weightlifters and their motivations, musical genres popular in Latin America, positions on climate change, or sports in relation to game theory. (See Chapter 11, pages 189–208.)
- **Process** analysis explains how a specific phenomenon unfolds in time—stage by stage, step by step. The phenomenon might be natural (the development of cancer), historical (the government's relationship with Aboriginal peoples), or cultural (the growing popularity of surfing). (See Chapter 12, pages 209–228.)
- **Comparison-contrast** analysis examines the similarities and/or differences between two or more topics in order to illuminate their distinctiveness and/or their commonalities, whether the topics are characters in a play, English and French as official languages, or social actions past and present. (See Chapter 13, pages 229–254.)
- **Cause-effect** analysis examines the forces that bring about specific results—focusing on the forces at work (causes), the results (effects), or both. As such, cause-effect reasoning explores "how" and "why" questions about a wide range of topics, for example, how a knuckleball works or why humans feel the urge to imagine other worlds through science fiction. (See Chapter 14, pages 255–276.)

Argumentative modes are persuasive in nature, aiming to convince readers to accept claims about topics that are typically controversial or at least problematic.

- **Position papers** take a stand on a topic (e.g., nuclear power, WikiLeaks, Israeli Apartheid protests), either arguing for a specific claim or arguing against a claim with which the writer disagrees. (See Chapter 17, pages 325–344.)
- **Call-to-action essays** move beyond taking a position on a controversial topic to pressing readers to take a step in response to that position—a concrete action or a general change in behaviour. (See Chapter 18, pages 345–364.)
- **Problem-solution** analysis proposes specific change to address a specific challenge. This mode thus presses readers to care about a problem, embrace the recommended solution, and (sometimes) even implement the solution. (See Chapter 19, pages 365–386.)

The Modes at Work

In academic writing, a specific rhetorical mode might dominate a piece of writing, giving the essay structure and direction from start to finish, such as in an essay offering an extended definition of *gullible* (pages 170–171). However, the rhetorical modes are more often seamlessly combined in your writing, all put to service in your specific mental work with your topic. For example, your main purpose might be to explain how a knuckleball works (cause-effect), but in doing so you also walk through a typical pitch delivery (process) and describe the distinctly different ball movement of other pitches (contrast). Indeed, it is fair to say that the rhetorical modes build and rely on each other: analytical writing can contain narrative, descriptive, and reflective elements; argumentative writing, in turn, depends upon effective analytical moves to bolster its claims.

Example: The paragraph below comes from Adam Gopnik's Massey lecture, "Recreational Winter" (pages 200–205). Notice how Gopnik begins with an *argumentative* claim about hockey, *compares* it with other sports, characterizes the *cause-effect* nature of goals, shares a personal *narrative*, and summarizes the historical development (*process*) of the game.

> Hockey approaches a more perfect balance between planning and reading, idea and improvisation, than any other sport. Runs in baseball are information; in basketball, baskets are events; in soccer, goals are exclamations. But goals in hockey are *punctuation*— they end sentences that can be traced through phrases to make long chains of meaning. And so great goals, like great aphorisms, repay any amount of after-the-fact analysis. How did so much get packed into one phrase, or play? Ice hockey looks like a reflex, rapture sport but is really a rational, reasoned one. Spotting patterns amid the quick plunges is part of the fun. I often go to sleep at night running through great goals I have seen—there is a weighting towards the seventies Habs, but only because they were the greatest team of all time, not because I was a teenager then—and what astonishes me is that, no matter how often you rewind them, they still play back beautifully, and in your mind's eye (or on the YouTube screen) you always see more. Hockey offers drama at first viewing, meaning on the second, and learning on the third and fourth, even forty years on. The tradition that began a hundred years ago in Montreal, of a game that combined the collisions of rugby with the beauty of ice-skating, has, if only for a moment, been realized, and it lingers in your head.

Critical-Thinking and Writing Activities

As directed by your instructor, complete the following critical-thinking and writing activities by yourself or with classmates.

1. Using its online or print catalogue, review your school's curriculum—its organization into divisions, disciplines, and courses. What does that big picture reveal about knowledge, inquiry, and learning in your school?

2. Using what you have learned about inquiry in the humanities, social sciences, and natural sciences, browse through Chapters 9–19, identifying essays and other forms of writing that relate to the different divisions and disciplines. Read closely an essay that interests you, analyzing the thinking and writing strategies the author uses. How does this piece relate to the forms of writing described in this chapter? What rhetorical modes do you see at work in the essay?

3. Consider the major you have chosen, or select a program that interests you. To research the thinking and writing skills practised in this field, do the following:

   - **In the catalogue, study the programs and courses in the department.** What do these reveal about the structure of knowledge, the major issues, and writing practices in the field?

   - **Using library and digital resources, find and study scholarly writing in this field.** What does this writing reveal about the thinking strategies valued, as well as the writing forms used?

   - **How is knowledge from this field presented in writing to the broader culture?** Explore this question by researching an issue in the field as it is discussed in the popular print and digital media.

4. Anne Lamott explains that "[b]ecoming a writer is about becoming conscious. When you're conscious and writing from a place of insight and simplicity and real caring about the truth, you have the ability to throw the lights on for your reader." Explore how Lamott's statement applies to the world of writing described in this chapter.

Learning-Objectives Checklist ✓

Have you achieved this chapter's learning objectives? Check your progress with the items below, revisiting topics in the chapter as needed. *I have* . . .

_____ identified the three traditional curricular divisions of the humanities, the social sciences, and the natural and applied sciences (134).

_____ differentiated and explained the purpose of inquiry, the forms of writing, and the research methods in each curricular division (135–137).

_____ identified and distinguished the rhetorical modes as thinking moves used singly and together by writers to deepen understanding of a topic (138–139).

_____ analyzed how writing works in my field of study or a major that interests me, including in the program itself, in scholarly writing, in popular writing, and in related professions.

Chapter 9

Narration, Description, and Reflection

Personal essays often tell stories—not ones that the writers made up, but ones that they lived. Whatever the topics, the stories should help readers see, hear, touch, and taste those details that make the experiences come alive. To do that, writers must carefully describe key aspects of the experience. But they might also reflect on why the experiences are important—exploring their personal and shared meanings.

When reading such personal essays, do so with an open mind—seeking to go where writers guide you, to experience what they carefully describe, and to analyze how they craft their work. As you prepare to write your own story, get ready to relive it yourself—to reexperience all that you felt, thought, or sensed during the event. In addition, be ready to learn something new about the experience, about others, and even about yourself.

Visually Speaking   In what sense do images and words both tell stories? Reflect on this question by studying the photograph below and imagining elements of narration, description, and reflection attaching to the image.

Learning **Objectives**

By working through this chapter, you will be able to

- critique and create the elements of narrative writing.
- analyze and effectively utilize strategies for descriptive writing.
- evaluate and use reflective-writing strategies such as natural observation and meaningful thesis thinking.
- create and integrate enriching anecdotes in personal and academic writing.
- develop a well-organized personal essay that includes narration, description, and/or reflection.

Igor Stevanovic/Shutterstock.com

fig. 9.1

Strategies for Personal Essays

Personal essays typically present and explore some dimension of the writer's experience by blending **narration, description,** and **reflection.** This blending often follows a **fluid organization.** Whether you are reading or writing a personal narrative, start with the **rhetorical situation** and then consider the strategies that follow.

The Rhetorical Situation

To put a personal essay in context, consider the rhetorical situation that gives rise to it:

- **Purpose:** The goal is to explore topics with which writers have a personal connection. A writer's aim is to deepen his or her own insight while sharing it with readers.
- **Readers:** Most personal essays are written for a general audience, though they may be directed to a specific segment of society. The writer hopes that his or her personal experience will speak universally—that readers will empathize and connect with it.
- **Topic:** Writers address any topic that they find meaningful and worth exploring through the lens of personal experience and reflection—often events, people, and places from their own lives.

Example: In "At L'Anse aux Meadows" (pages 158–163), Will Ferguson focuses on a **topic** related to his own experiences of travelling and meaningful to his sense of Canadian history—his visit to the site of a Viking settlement. His **purpose** is to gain and share historical perspective on this Newfoundland and Labrador site, both seriously and comically. His **readership** would rightly be described as the general public, but especially Canadians interested in their country's geography and history seen through a personal lens.

Principles of Narration

Personal essays often centre on engaging narratives—stories that focus on meaningful events and people. That's the case, for example, with "Spare Change" (pages 151–153). The following elements are central to a well-crafted narrative:

Action: This refers to the unfolding sequence of events shaped into a meaningful whole, a force that drives narrative forward. Consider these strategies:

- **Handling chronology:** Narrative is time-sensitive, so a good narrative handles time effectively through clear temporal markers, verb tenses, and time transitions. Moreover, the narrative manages temporal pacing by focusing in on key events and compressing or summarizing less significant action. Finally, the narrative may "escape" strict chronology by beginning in the middle of the action before going back to the beginning, as well as by using flashbacks and foreshadowing.
- **Clarifying action:** Narratives move forward energetically when writers use precise, engaging, and suggestive verbs. Example: "The captain **reverses** the engine, bringing us to an abrupt stop, and we **bob** on the waves as he **grabs** a long snare-net and **darts** to one side of the ship. He **is scooping** up 10,000-year-old ice cubes: the crumbling

debris of icebergs, to be used by restaurants to chill the drinks of tourists. He **rinses** the salt water off a fist of smooth ice and **tosses** it over to me."

- **Shaping a plot:** A narrative's overall pattern may take many forms, but the traditional structure builds tension and complication toward a climactic moment of decision or discovery, followed by aftermath and resolution.

Character: Frequently the narrative's focus is character—what the events reveal about people. Characters need to be well-developed and engaging in order to reveal things about life and human nature. Narrative shows people feeling, thinking, acting, and interacting.

Dialogue: Conversations are used in narrative to reveal character, advance the action, and embody the conflict. Typically chosen for significant moments in the action, such dialogue should be natural in word choice, voice, and sentence rhythms (reflecting dialects if needed), with speakers clearly demarcated.

Narrative Perspective: In a personal narrative, the writer is typically the narrator—the voice telling the story. However, the narrative voice might be in the foreground (participating in the action) or the background (observing the action).

Setting: Action happens and people live within specific places and times—the narrative's setting. Settings put events and characters in physical, historical, and cultural context.

Sample Narrative Paragraph

Taken from "Mzee Owitti" by Jacqui Nyangi Owitti (pages 148–150), the paragraph below narrates the grieving some women express for the writer's dead grandfather.

> Out of seemingly nowhere, wailing answers my mother's cry. Other women appear at a run, heading for my mother, hands fluttering from the tops of their heads, to their waists, to their feet. Their heads are thrown back and from side to side in restless anguish. Their bodies are half-bent forward, and their feet are in constant motion even though no distance is covered. My aunts and close female relatives weep, letting loose high-pitched, ululating moaning in support of my mother. As the wife of the first child and only son, she commands a high place, and she must not grieve alone.

Principles of Description

Effective descriptive passages (of places, people, and objects) offer precise, evocative details that help readers thoughtfully experience the essay's topic. Such description may aim for fidelity—objectivity through accurate and complete details, including measurements and so on. Or the description may aim to create a dominant impression, a sense of the person, place, or object that is rooted in carefully selected details that work through imagination, association, and symbolism. For example, "Dryden's Backyard" (pages 154–157) is filled with vivid descriptions of places and people. Such strong description draws attention to different strategies: naming, detailing, ordering, and comparing.

Naming: At its base, description identifies things, and the beginning of such identification is naming—among available terms, choosing words that precisely or suggestively clarify the nature of what is being described.

Detailing: Description appeals to the senses through concrete details, details that may be precise but also rich in connotations and associations. Details that appeal to sight create a mental picture for readers; sounds and smells tend to evoke feelings and memories; taste and touch generate a sense of intimacy.

Ordering: While they may involve a single detail, descriptions are often much fuller. In that case, writers may need to (1) establish a vantage point from which readers will see the object, (2) orient the object in space, and (3) lead readers systematically through the description (e.g., left to right, top to bottom, back to front).

Comparing: Descriptions may be clarified and deepened through comparisons. Here are three common options:

- **Simile** is a comparison of two things in which *like* or *as* is used. Example: "There was one team in the big end, another in the small; third and fourth teams sat like birds on a telephone wire, waiting their turn on the wall that separated the big end from Carpenters' backyard." (page 156)

- **Metaphor** is a comparison in which one thing is said to be another, establishing an identity. (Neither *like* nor *as is* used.) Example: "[Moose] are the inbred Habsburg monarchs of the animal kingdom, combining regal deportment with huge, misshapen noses." (page 158)

- **Personification** is a device in which the author speaks of or describes an animal, object, or idea as if it were a person. Example: "Time itself seems to mourn, and even the wind is still." (page 148)

Sample Descriptive Paragraph

The paragraph below is the opening paragraph in Teresa Zsuffa's "Spare Change" (pages 151–153). Note how in describing the urban setting she appeals to multiple senses, offers precise details, evokes a feeling of unease, and ends with a metaphor ("starry distance").

> This grime is infectious. The smell of old cigarettes and expired perfume is constricting my throat and turning my stomach. But here I am again on the underground subway platform, changing trains at Bloor-Yonge in Toronto, the weight of my backpack thrusting me forward with the Friday morning rush hour crowd. When the subway doors open I hurry inside and look around frantically, as usual. There is an empty seat to my left, but everyone is keeping a safe four-foot distance, as if the seat will suck them in and destroy them if they sit down. Or at least destroy the facade put on with a Ralph Lauren suit, a Coach handbag, or a pair of authentic Gucci sunglasses. Not like the fake five-dollar ones I picked up from a Chinatown vendor just yesterday. The others keep their starry distance; when I sit down, I see why.

Principles of Reflection

In a personal essay, strong reflective passages—from single sentences to entire paragraphs—relay the writer's observations and insights regarding the nature, impact, and value of the experience. In some personal essays, such reflection is minimal (e.g., essays that are primarily narrative in nature, such as "Spare Change"). However, some essays are rich in reflection, particularly when the writer's purpose is to explore psychological and cultural complexity, as in "Mzee Owitti" (pages 148–150) and "At L'Anse aux Meadows" (pages 158–163). Consider these reflection strategies:

Natural Observation: Reflection within a personal essay should have an organic feel—arising naturally out of the material presented, out of the narration and description. That reflection can be thematically implied or openly stated, depending on the writer's purpose. Essentially, however, the reflection should be honest, meaningful, and thought-provoking for readers, pressing them to connect with and universalize the experience. For that reason, reflection is often stated using the pronoun *I*, but a connection to other people is stated or implied, perhaps through comparison-contrast.

Thesis Thinking: The key idea of a personal essay typically grows out of the writer's questions about the meaning of the experience. Rather than offering a simple statement of fact or a clichéd opinion, the thesis should follow these guidelines:

- **The thesis expresses some complexity about the experience**—mixed feelings (ambivalence), tensions, or paradox. The thesis is rarely a blunt, simplistic "This is the moral of the story" statement, as it doesn't do justice to the fullness of the experience or the complications of the narrative. Example: *Many marriages demonstrate the notion that opposites attract—with painful consequences for everyone involved.*
- **The thesis may be stated openly or simply implied.** If stated, it can be positioned a variety of places in the essay, though toward the middle or end seems best: action and description build inductively toward insight.

Sample Reflective Paragraph

In the passage below, from "L'Anse aux Meadows" (pages 158–163), Will Ferguson reflects on the meaning of the history he has narrated. Note how he both personalizes and extends the reflection.

> These tales converge in me, and this is not unusual. From the last Vikings to the shattered displacement of the First Nations, from resistance to revival, from New France to the New West, from dreams of utopia to dreams of prosperity, from Loyalist boat people to modern-day refugees, Canada is more than just a country: it is a sum of its stories. We are all orphans, are all survivors of shipwrecks, and we carry these stories of exile and renewal within us, whether we are aware of it or not.

Principles of Organization

If a personal essay centres on a narrative, the organization will largely be determined by chronology, arranged according to the logic of the plot. (See, for example, the outline for "Mzee Owitti" on page 148.) Generally, the structure of a personal essay tends to be fluid—flowing more freely than a traditional academic essay. Consider these strategies:

Opening: The opening seeks to get readers' attention, usher them into the world of the essay, and orient them to the topic through techniques like these: a memory, an image, an idea, a conflict, a puzzle, a moment from the middle or near the end of the story. Remember that personal essays don't always need to open at the beginning of the story; they can start from the middle or end of the action.

Middle: The body of the essay may weave together elements of narration, description, and reflection to deepen interest, and possibly to build toward a climax—a moment of discovery or decision. This process may involve

- bringing together "strands" of the past and the present
- introducing tensions, complications, and conflicts
- focusing on key moments, episodes, and encounters (including dialogue)
- foreshadowing what is to come or creating a puzzle to be solved
- comparing events, settings, or characters
- moving from a broad view to a narrow focus or vice versa

Closing: Traditional narratives follow the climax with the fallout and resolution (revealing the results of conflict, the outcome). Other narratives, however, aim to be more open-ended. The ending might also focus on authentic reflection (without trite moralism) that leaves readers with food for thought. Finally, it might supply a surprise, a dramatic turn of events, or it might return to the opening in some way.

Reading Personal Writing

On the following pages, you will find personal essays written by both students and professional authors. As you read, consider these questions:

1. Does the essay centre on narrative? How is that narrative developed through action, character, dialogue, narrative perspective, and setting? Do you find the narrative engaging?
2. What roles does description play in the essay, and what descriptive techniques are used? Are there descriptions that really jump out at you? Why?
3. What ideas or themes evolve from the story? Is reflection stated or implied? Can you locate a thesis, or is it implied? Can you put it in your own words? Why does the writer care about this topic, and how do you feel about it in the end? What have you learned?
4. How does the essay unfold? How are narrative, description, and reflection blended?

Brief Narratives: Anecdotes

A common form of narrative used in any writing is the anecdote—a brief story that enlivens the writing either by introducing a topic or illustrating an idea.

An Anecdote Introducing a Topic: Regan Burles begins his essay on media filter bubbles with the following anecdote about a journalist.

> On July 7th, 2011 journalist Kai Nagata quit his job as CTV's Quebec City Bureau Chief. His departure, and the article in which he explained the reasons for it, drew significant media attention across Canada. The essay garnered over 100,000 views in a month, and by that time over a thousand online comments had been made on the piece (Michaels).
>
> In the essay, posted to his blog the day after he quit, Nagata details the various shortcomings he encountered at CTV, which by now are quite familiar. Essentially, the main problem he identifies is the conflict between the private interests of corporate-owned media and the public good of high-quality journalism. In his opinion, there was too much of the former, and not enough of the latter. Despite the various regulatory bodies that police the journalistic community, he argues, "information is a commodity, and private TV networks need to make money" (Nagata). Profits, more often than not, trump meaningful news stories.
>
> From "'Filter Bubbles': Public Discourse in an Age of Citizen Journalism," page 369

Anecdote Illustrating an Idea: In the anecdote below, Malcolm Gladwell recounts a story of online social activism in order to analyze what it reveals about activism today.

> The bible of the social-media movement is Clay Shirky's *Here Comes Everybody*. Shirky, who teaches at New York University, sets out to demonstrate the organizing power of the Internet, and he begins with the story of Evan, who worked on Wall Street, and his friend Ivanna, after she left her smart phone, an expensive Sidekick, on the back seat of a New York City taxicab. The telephone company transferred the data on Ivanna's lost phone to a new phone, whereupon she and Evan discovered that the Sidekick was now in the hands of a teen-ager from Queens, who was using it to take photographs of herself and her friends.
>
> When Evan e-mailed the teen-ager, Sasha, asking for the phone back, she replied that his "white ass" didn't deserve to have it back. Miffed, he set up a Web page with her picture and a description of what had happened. He forwarded the link to his friends, and they forwarded it to their friends. Someone found the MySpace page of Sasha's boyfriend, and a link to it found its way onto the site. Someone found her address online and took a video of her home while driving by; Evan posted the video on the site. The story was picked up by the news filter Digg. Evan was now up to ten e-mails a minute. He created a bulletin board for his readers to share their stories, but it crashed under the weight of responses. Evan and Ivanna went to the police, but the police filed the report under "lost," rather than "stolen," which essentially closed the case. "By this point millions of readers were watching," Shirky writes, "and dozens of mainstream news outlets had covered the story." Bowing to the pressure, the N.Y.P.D. reclassified the item as "stolen." Sasha was arrested, and Evan got his friend's Sidekick back.
>
> Shirky's argument is that this is the kind of thing . . . .
>
> From "Small Change," page 250

Sample Personal Essays

Personal essays can focus on a wide range of topics as writers narrate, describe, and reflect upon their experiences. The essays that follow suggest that range as they explore a death in the family, an urban encounter, a childhood experience, and an historical site.

Narrating a Family Experience

In this essay, student writer Jacqui Nyangi Owitti recalls an important personal experience in her life that taught her the pain of loss. Note how the detailed description and narration helps you visualize places, people, and events.

Essay Outline

Introduction: rural Kenya setting, family members, theme of grieving
1. The narrator and her family arrive at her grandparents' home.
2. The narrator's mother and other women express grief through wailing.
3. A couple of days later, the funeral and procession take place.
4. A bull is brought to pay final respects.
5. The narrator views her grandfather in his casket.

Closing: funeral ceremony, connecting to both personal grief and ancestral tradition

Mzee Owitti

The opening establishes the scene and provides background.

I am about 12 years old. We are en route from Nairobi, the capital city, to the rural area of Kisumu on the eastern shores of Lake Victoria in western Kenya, where my grandparents live. My five brothers and I are traveling with Mum on the overnight train. I am not particularly sad, though I know what has happened. I base my reactions on my mother's, and since she appears to be handling the whole thing well, I am determined to do the same. You see, my grandfather has died. My dad's dad.

We reach the town of my ancestry just as dawn lazily turns into early morning. We buy snacks and hire a car for the last leg of the journey. We then meander through a bewildering maze of mud huts, sisal scrub, and sandy clay grassland, until we come within sight of my grandfather's land, the place where my father grew up.

The narrator describes what she sees and how she feels.

The first thing I notice is a crude "tent" made by sticking four poles in the ground, crisscrossing the top with long branches, and covering that with thatch. Despite the early hour, the place is filled with dignitaries, guests, and people like my mother's parents, who have traveled far to honour our family. I am struck by the stillness and all-pervading silence. Everything seems frozen. Time itself seems to mourn, and even the wind is still. The car stops a short distance from the property, and we sit motionless and quiet.

I turn to my mother, questioning. But she has drawn a handkerchief from somewhere and is climbing out of the car. Almost as an actor on the stage, she releases a sound I have never heard before. It is a moan, a scream, and a sob that

1

2

3

4

Verbs in the present tense convey the action.

is deep-throated, guttural, and high-pitched all at the same time. This sudden transformation from a calm, chipper person to a stricken stranger strikes in me a fear that I will long remember. Holding her handkerchief to her face, she breaks into a shuffling run. I sit in the car petrified, watching the drama unfold.

Out of seemingly nowhere, wailing answers my mother's cry. Other women 5
appear at a run, heading for my mother, hands fluttering from the tops of their heads, to their waists, to their feet. Their heads are thrown back and from side to side in restless anguish. Their bodies are half-bent forward, and their feet are in constant motion even though no distance is covered. My aunts and close female relatives weep, letting loose high-pitched, ululating moaning in support of my mother. As the wife of the first child and only son, she commands a high place, and she must not grieve alone.

The last sentence explains the women's actions.

In the confusion, one lady is knocked down, and she seems to rock with her 6
legs separated in a way that in other circumstances would be inappropriate and humiliating. Oddly, the people in the tent, mostly male, appear to have seen and heard nothing. They continue silent and still. The whole scene seems unreal. Seeing my fear and confusion, the driver talks soothingly, explaining what is going on.

The wailing and mourning continue intermittently for a couple of days. Then the 7
time comes for my grandfather to be taken from the mortuary in Kisumu to his final resting place. We all travel to the mortuary. He is dressed in his best suit and then taken to church, where his soul is committed to God. Afterward, the procession starts for home. On the way we are met by the other mourners, who, according to tradition, will accompany the hearse on foot, driving along the cows that are a symbol of wealth in life and a testament to a good life, respectability, and honour in death. Being city kids unable to jog for an hour with the mourners and cows, we ride in a car.

The narrator describes one phase of the ceremony.

Finally, we are back at the homestead. My grandfather is put in the house where 8
he spent the latter part of his life. The crying and mourning are now nearly at a feverish pitch, and the sense of loss is palpable. However, before people may enter the house to pay their last respects, one—they call him "Ratego"—must lead the way to say his good-byes. Suddenly, there is a commotion, and I stare in disbelief as a big bull, taller than my tall-for-my-age twelve-year-old height and wider than the doorway, is led toward my grandfather's house. Long, thick horns stick out of the colossal head. The body, pungent with an ammonia-laced, grassy smell, is a mosaic of black and brown—an odorous, pulsing mountain.

A transition word indicates a shift.

Vivid words describe sights and smells.

The bull's wild, staring eyes seem fixed on me. An old, barefoot man, dressed 9
in a worn, too-short jacket and dusty black pants, leads this bull with a frayed rope. He waves his rod, yelling and leaping in syncopation with the bull's snorting and pawing. Dust puffs dance around their feet. The bull is a symbol of high honour for my grandfather, and only the largest bull in the land can embody this deep respect. Although I do not fully comprehend its significance, I know that it is the biggest animal I have ever seen. I step back as people try to get the bull into the house to pay its respects to my grandfather. After much yelling, shoving, and cries of pain from those whose feet the bull steps on, the effort is abandoned. Ratego is much too big.

The narrative approaches its climax.

As the bull is led away into the boma, people enter the room that has been emptied of furniture. I squeeze through the heaving, weeping mass, almost suffocating in the process. The room is surprisingly cool and dim, unlike the hot and bright sun outside. I approach curiously and cautiously, not knowing what to expect. At last I stand before the casket and look at my grandfather. He does not look dead. In fact, he is smiling! He looks like the person I remember, who always had a smile and an unshared secret lurking in the depths of his eyes.   *10*

A flashback adds depth to the present moment.

I peer into his face, recalling a time when I was four and he caught me doing something that deserved a reprimand. I had thought no one had seen me. However, my grandfather, on one of his rare visits to the city, had seen. Standing in front of his casket, I again hear him laugh. I remember how his kind, brown eyes had twinkled, and his white mustache, white teeth, and rich bitter-chocolate face had broken into an all-knowing, but-you-can-trust-me smile. I remember how the deep love that radiated from him assured me that I was his no matter what. And I remember how I had responded to his love by laughing happily and then skipping away, his answering laugh reverberating in my ears.   *11*

The narrator describes a pivotal moment.

That is my grandfather. Death cannot possibly touch him! Then I look closer and realize that the white streak breaking up his face is not the white teeth I remember. It is, instead, cotton stuffed into his mouth, as white as his teeth had been, making a mockery of my memories. At that moment, my granddaddy dies.   *12*

The last sentence offers a memorable image.

Until this point, the whole has been a drama played out before my stunned, wide-eyed gaze. Rich in ancestry and tradition, its very nature and continuity are a celebration of life rather than death, fostering in me a keen sense of identity and a strong desire to keep the ancestral torch burning brightly, fiercely, and with pride. Now, however, Grandpa is dead. It is now that I cry. I am grieving. My granddaddy is gone, and the weighted arrow of sorrow pierces home. The pain is personal, unrelenting, and merciless. I stare at him and cannot tear myself away. I weep, saying over and over that he is smiling, he is smiling. My heartbreak and tears echo the refrain. He is smiling—a radiant, unforgettable smile.   *13*

Reading for Better Writing

Working by yourself or with a group, answer these questions:

1. The writer uses verbs in the present tense to tell her story. What are some of the specific effects of this choice?

2. Choose a paragraph containing a particularly vivid description. How do the language and style choices affect your ability to sense the action?

3. In a conversation with one of this book's authors, Jacqui Nyangi Owitti described her love for her grandfather and her pride in her heritage. Does the story reflect that love and pride? Explain.

4. Jacqui's essay offers a glimpse into an experience of grieving that is both unsettling and comforting. Have you experienced such grief in your own life? What did this essay contribute to your feelings about death and dying?

Narrating an Encounter

"Spare Change" is the first part of student writer Teresa Zsuffa's "A Diary of Chance Encounters," an essay that explores her experiences of living in Toronto. The piece below recounts a challenging encounter with the face of poverty. For Teresa's full essay, go to the website for *Writing Life*.

"Spare Change"

> The writer describes an urban setting and a common situation.

This grime is infectious. The smell of old cigarettes and expired perfume is constricting my throat and turning my stomach. But here I am again on the underground subway platform, changing trains at Bloor-Yonge in Toronto, the weight of my backpack thrusting me forward with the Friday morning rush hour crowd. When the subway doors open I hurry inside and look around frantically, as usual. There is an empty seat to my left, but everyone is keeping a safe four-foot distance, as if the seat will suck them in and destroy them if they sit down. Or at least destroy the facade put on with a Ralph Lauren suit, a Coach handbag, or a pair of authentic Gucci sunglasses. Not like the fake five-dollar ones I picked up from a Chinatown vendor just yesterday. The others keep their starry distance; when I sit down, I see why.   1

> She introduces the central person through concrete details, her words, and the reactions of others (including the writer's own mixed feelings).

She must be about twenty-nine. Her orange track-pants are worn and faded, her T-shirt is far too big, and her powder blue sweatshirt is tied around her waist. Her face and teeth are stained, hair greasy and unkempt. A part of me feels sorry for her. Another part follows the crowd and is careful not to make eye contact.   2

"Excuse me," she says, perching on the edge of her seat, leaning forward and clasping the metal pole with two hands. No one turns. "Excuse me, which stop do I take to the Old City Hall?" One man shrugs and shakes his head while pretending to check his phone. I feel guilt, but it's easily subdued. After all, she wasn't asking me.   3

I am deeply engrossed in my Nicholas Sparks novel by the time the driver announces "Dundas Station." As I stuff the book back into my purse and make my way towards the doorway, I'm irritated to see that she also stands up—one stop early for Old City Hall. Doesn't she know she should stay on until Queen? Oh well, she'll figure it out, I reason. The Toronto Transit Commission officers can help her.   4

> The writer narrates the events and dialogue that lead her to offer help.

I let her off the subway before me. Finally I'm free.   5

But then she stops on the platform and turns her head, like a puppy making sure her owner is following close behind. No eye contact, I remind myself, and try to walk past but she falls into step with me.   6

"Can I help you carry your bag?"   7

I may look like a tourist, but I'm smarter. "No, thanks," I reply.   8

"Well it just looks pretty heavy." We reach the escalator and the staircase and I take the left side, where I can climb the steps and go up twice as fast as those just standing there on the right and enjoying the ride. But it doesn't work; the woman is still at my heels.   9

Details describe the urban setting and the writer's acclimation to it.

"Are you going somewhere?" she asks.   *10*

"Yeah, I have to get to the Greyhound station, I'm going out of town."   *11*

"Oh." Now we are standing in front of the underground entrance to the Eaton   *12*
Center. The Atrium on Bay is to my right, on the other side of which is the bus
station and my ticket out of this alien city that is now my home. The woman stands
frozen and looks around trying to get her bearings. I start to walk away but hesitate.
Looking back, I see her blinking and flinching as people shove past her. She reminds
me of a small child lost at a summer carnival.

She refers to the city's cultural "rules."

I check my watch—quarter past eight. I just missed an express shuttle, and   *13*
the next bus to Niagara Falls, where my father lives, won't be leaving for another
forty-five minutes. Something pulls me back to the woman, and against all sworn
Torontonian rules, I ask if she needs help.

Her dull brown eyes light up. "I need to find the Old City Hall."   *14*

"Okay," I nod. "I'll take you." I lead her through the glass doors into the city's   *15*
busiest mall. It's the fastest way from Dundas to Queen Street, and from there she
will need to walk only a few blocks west. As we're walking, I'm aware of the stares
I'm getting from people I'll never see again.

The writer uses dialogue to describe the woman's life and her journey.

"So where are you from?" I ask.   *16*

"Sudbury." And I'm instantly speechless. What is this woman doing so far from   *17*
home? How did she get here? I ask why she's in the city.

"My boyfriend. He's in jail, and they're letting him go today. I came to take him   *18*
back home with me after his hearing."

While we walk past Mexx, Aritzia, and Abercrombie, I learn that she had   *19*
taken a bus from Sudbury the day before and spent the night on a park bench. Her
boyfriend is forty-two years old and has been in jail for the past ten months. I don't
ask why. She proudly tells me she was a crack addict and that she's been clean for
three months.

Short quotes create a sharp rhythm.

"I just got out of rehab," she says. "Now maybe my grandma will take me back   *20*
in."

"Back in?"   *21*

"Yeah, she kicked me out. She told me I wasn't allowed to be a hooker anymore,   *22*
but I got caught bringing someone home once."

The writer describes her confusion, sympathy, and guilt.

I have no idea how to talk to a prostitute, never mind one who is so open about   *23*
everything she's done, but this woman seems to like me and trust me. The next thing
I know, I'm offering to buy her breakfast before she meets up with her boyfriend.

There's a McDonald's at the southernmost side of the Eaton Centre, overlooking   *24*
the Queen Street entrance. I tell her she can have anything she wants. An Egg
McMuffin? Fruit and yogurt? But all she wants is Coke and a hash-brown. I order
her two.

A dash accents the irony of this unlikely pair sharing personal time and stories.

We sit down at a freshly wiped table by the window. Beside us, two men in   *25*
grey suits sip coffee over an array of files and spreadsheets. They pause in their
conversation to stare at us—the student traveler and the bedraggled prostitute. I tell

the woman a little about my life, and ask more about hers and her grandmother. She says that they used to go to church together, when she was little, but she hasn't been since. She takes another bite of her hash-brown and tells me she's now twenty-one. Only twenty-one, and her boyfriend is forty-two. She talks about the drugs and the providence of God.

| The writer acknowledges her own inexperience and confusion. |

"I know that he helped me stop," she says. "I've been clean for three months, can   26
you believe that? That's a miracle! It has to be a miracle."

At this point all I can do is smile.   27

"I wish I could get my boyfriend to quit," she says, staring off. Then she   28
suddenly leans forward and asks, "Do you know how hard it is? Have you ever done crack?"

"No."   29

"Pot, at least?"   30

"No. Sorry." I'm not sure why I'm apologizing for never having tried drugs, but   31
the way her face drops and she shifts her eyes makes me feel guilty. As though I can never fully understand her because I've never experienced the things she has.

"Well you should try it," she urges. "It's really good."   32

"Maybe one day." I glance at my watch. It's now quarter-to, and I still need to   33
stand in line to buy my ticket and get to the right platform. I wonder why I'm not panicking yet.

| The writer offers spare change, a gift that is cited in the title and that symbolizes the women's distanced relationship. |

I tell her I need to get going. She should go, too, or she'll be late for the hearing.   34
Before getting up, I reach into my wallet and give her two TTC passes and some spare change. I walk her to the street and point her toward Old City Hall. She never thanks me, only looks at me one last time with immense vulnerability and helplessness. Then she walks away.

I wonder as I hurry towards the station if she'll be okay, if her boyfriend really   35
will get out of jail, and if her grandmother will ever take her back. Either way, I think as I cross Bay Street, what more can I do? I have a bus to catch.

Reading for Better Writing

Working by yourself or with a group, answer these questions:

1. Teresa Zsuffa's essay focuses on an urban setting. What does she evoke about the city, and what descriptions create that feeling?

2. The central character in the essay is presented primarily through description, comparisons, and dialogue. Identify such passages, exploring what they communicate about the woman and how effectively they work.

3. One focus of the essay is the writer's experience of the city and of her encounter with the prostitute. Describe Teresa's thoughts and feelings about both. How does she communicate these? Identify and analyze specific passages, sentences, and phrases.

Exploring the Spaces of Childhood

Born in Hamilton, Ontario, in 1947, Ken Dryden made his name as a goalie with the Montreal Canadiens in the 1970s, when the Habs won six Stanley Cups. Dryden is also a lawyer, a former Member of Parliament, and author of the hockey biography *The Game*. In the excerpt below, Dryden recounts his childhood memories of playing hockey in his family's backyard.

Dryden's Backyard

Dryden opens in the present tense before turning to memories.

I get out of bed and pull back the curtains. It has snowed overnight and traces are still gently falling. For several minutes I stand there, my forehead pressed to the window, watching the snow, looking out at the backyards of the houses behind, where the Pritchards, the MacLarens, and the Carpenters lived, and down below at the winter's depth of snow, and at the backyard where I spent my childhood

He describes the backyard and suggests its importance for the neighbourhood.

"Dryden's Backyard." That's what it was called in our neighbourhood. It was more than 70 feet long, paved curiously in red asphalt, 45 feet wide at "the big end," gradually narrowing to 35 feet at the flower bed, to 25 feet at the porch—our center line—to 15 feet at "the small end." While Steve Shutt and Guy Lafleur were in Willowdale and Thurso on backyard rinks their fathers built, while Larry Robinson was on a frozen stream in Marvelville and Réjean Houle on a road in Rouyn under the only street light that his street had, I was here.

It was an extraordinary place, like the first swimming pool on the block, except there were no others like it anywhere. Kids would come from many blocks away to play, mostly "the big guys," friends of my brother, a year or two older than him, seven or eight years older than me. But that was never a problem. It was the first rule of the backyard that they had to let me play. To a friend who complained one day, Dave said simply, "If Ken doesn't play, you don't play."

The writer explains in detail the kinds of games they played.

We played "ball hockey" mostly, with a tennis ball, its bounce deadened by the cold. A few times, we got out a garden hose and flooded the backyard to use skates and pucks, but the big end was slightly lower than the small end, and the water pooled and froze unevenly. More important, we found that the more literal we tried to make our games, the less lifelike they became. We could move across the asphalt quickly and with great agility in rubber "billy" boots; we could shoot a tennis ball high and hard. But with skates on, with a puck, we were just kids. So after the first few weeks of the first year, we played only ball hockey.

Depending on the day, the time, the weather, there might be any number of kids wanting to play, so we made up games any number could play. With four and less than nine, we played regular games, the first team scoring ten goals the winner. The two best players, who seemed always to know who they were, picked the teams

1

2

3

4

5

and decided on ends. First choice of players got second choice of ends, and because the size of the big end made it more fun to play in, the small end was the choice to defend. Each team had a goalie—one with goalie pads, a catching glove, and a goalie stick; the other with only a baseball glove and a forward's stick. When we had more than eight players, we divided into three or more teams for a round-robin tournament, each game to five. With fewer than four, it was more difficult. Sometimes we attempted a regular game, often we just played "shots," each player being both shooter and goalie, standing in front of one net, shooting in turn at the other. Most often, however, we played "penalty shots."

But the backyard also meant time alone. It was usually after dinner when the "big guys" had homework to do and I would turn on the floodlights at either end of the house and on the porch, and play. It was a private game. I would stand alone in the middle of the yard, a stick in my hands, a tennis ball in front of me, silent, still, then suddenly dash ahead, stickhandling furiously, dodging invisible obstacles for a shot on net. It was Maple Leaf Gardens filled to wildly cheering capacity, a tie game, seconds remaining. I was Frank Mahovlich, or Gordie Howe, I was anyone I wanted to be, and the voice in my head was that of Leafs broadcaster Foster Hewitt: " . . . . there's ten seconds left, Mahovlich, winding up at his own line, at center, eight seconds, seven, over the blueline, six—he winds up, he shoots, he scores!" The mesh that had been tied to the bottoms of our red metal goalposts until frozen in the ice had been ripped away to hang loose from the cross-bars, whipped back like a flag in a stiff breeze. My arms and stick flew into the air, I screamed a scream inside my head, and collected my ball to do it again—many times, for many minutes, the hero of all my own games.

It was a glorious fantasy, and I always heard that voice. It was what made my fantasy seem almost real. For to us, who attended hockey games mostly on TV or radio, an NHL game, a Leafs game, was played with a voice. If I wanted to be Mahovlich or Howe, if I moved my body the way I had seen them move theirs and did nothing else, it would never quite work. But if I heard the voice that said their names while I was playing out that fantasy, I could believe it. Foster Hewitt could make me them.

My friends and I played every day after school, sometimes during lunch and after dinner, but Saturday was always the big day. I would go to bed Friday night thinking of Saturday, waking up early, with none of the fuzziness I had other days. If it had snowed overnight, Dave and I, with shovels and scrapers, and soon joined by others, would pile the snow into flower beds or high against the back of the garage. Then at 9:00 A.M. the games would begin.

Dryden describes the imaginative experience of playing alone in the backyard.

The rhythm of Saturday games is vividly recounted.

6

7

8

There was one team in the big end, another in the small; third and fourth   *9*
teams sat like birds on a telephone wire, waiting their turn on the wall that
separated the big end from Carpenter's backyard. Each team wore uniforms
identical to the other's. It was the Canadian midwinter uniform of the time—long,
heavy duffel coats in browns, grays, or blues; tuques in NHL team colors, pulled
snug over the ears under the watchful eye of mothers, here rolled up in some
distinctive personal style; leather gloves, last year's church gloves, now curling at the
wrist and separating between fingers; black rubber "billy" boots over layers of heavy
woolen socks for fit, the tops rolled down like "low cuts" for speed and style.

> *Their hockey uniforms are described in detail.*

Each game would begin with a faceoff, then wouldn't stop again. Action moved   *10*
quickly end to end, the ball bouncing and rolling, chased by a hacking, slashing
scrum of sticks. We had sticks without tops on their blades—"toothpicks"; sticks
with no blades at all—"stubs." They broke piece by heart-breaking piece, often
quickly, but still we used them. Only at the start of a season, at Christmas (Dave
and I routinely exchanged sticks until one year he gave me a stick and I gave him
a pair of socks) and once or twice more, would we get new ones. All except John
Stedelbauer. His father owned a car dealership and during the hockey season gave
away hockey sticks to his customers as a promotion. Stedelbauer got all the new
sticks he needed, fortunately, as they weren't very good. One year he broke nineteen
of them.

> *Narrating a typical game, Dryden pictures their sticks and conveys the motion, energy, and euphoria of their play.*

A goal would be scored, then another, and slowly the game would leapfrog to   *11*
five. Bodies grew warm from exertion, fingers and toes went numb; noses ran, wiped
by unconscious sleeves; coats loosened, tuques fell off; steam puffed from mouths
and streamed from tuqueless heads. Sticks hacked and slashed; tennis balls stung.
But in the euphoria of the game, the pain disappeared. Sitting on the wall that
overlooked his backyard, Rick "Foster" Carpenter, younger and not very athletic,
gave the play-by-play, but no one listened. Each of us had his own private game
playing in his head. A fourth goal, then a fifth, a cheer and the first game was over.
Quickly, four duffel coats, four tuques, four pairs of weathered gloves and rubber
"billy" boots would jump from the wall to replace the losers; and the second game
would begin. We paused at noon while some went home and others ate the lunch
that they had brought with them. At 6:00 P.M., the two or three who remained
would leave. Eighteen hours later, after church, the next game would begin.

When I think of the backyard, I think of my childhood; and when I think of my   *12*
childhood, I think of the backyard. It is the central image I have of that time, linking
as it does all of its parts: father, mother, sister, friends; hockey, baseball, and Dave—
big brother, idol, mentor, defender, and best friend. Yet it lasted only a few years.

In the closing paragraphs, Dryden reflects on the significance of the backyard for his childhood and for his later life as a professional hockey player.

Dave was already twelve when the backyard was built; I was six. He and his friends played for three or four years, then stopped; I played longer but, without them, less often. Yet until moments ago, I had never remembered that.

The backyard was not a training ground. In all the time I spent there, I don't remember ever thinking I would be an NHL goalie, or even hoping I could be one. In backyard games, I dreamed I was Sawchuk or Hall, Mahovlich or Howe; I never dreamed I would be like them. There seemed no connection between the backyard and Maple Leaf Gardens; there seemed no way to get to there from here. If we ever thought about that, it never concerned us; we just played. It was here in the backyard that we learned hockey. It was here we got close to it, we got inside it, and it got inside us. It was here that our inextricable bond with the game was made. Many years have now passed, the game has grown up and been complicated by things outside it, yet still the backyard remains—untouched, unchanged, my unseverable link to that time, and that game.

13

Reading for Better Writing

Working by yourself or with a group, answer these questions:

1. In this piece, Ken Dryden takes readers to a meaningful place from his childhood. Consider meaningful places from your own childhood. What makes such spaces memorable?

2. Why is Dryden describing his backyard? What essential point does he seem to be making, either stated or implied?

3. In what ways is Dryden's description of his childhood backyard both factual and personal? Focusing on specific passages, identify the descriptive techniques Dryden uses for naming, detailing, ordering, and comparing.

4. In what ways does memory organize this piece? How would you characterize the structure of the essay? How does the structure blend description, narration, and reflection?

Experiencing History

Will Ferguson is one of Canada's best-known humorists, author of books such as *Why I Hate Canadians* and *Beauty Tips from Moose Jaw: Travels in Search of Canada*, from which the essay below is taken. Winner of the Stephen Leacock Medal for Humour more than once, Ferguson is also a novelist whose works include *Happiness* and most recently *419*, which won the 2012 Giller Prize. In the essay below, Ferguson visits and explores the significance of the Viking settlement, Vinland. Note how he weaves together personal, historical, and national themes in this essay, the last in *Beauty Tips*.

At L'Anse aux Meadows

As you read this essay, annotate it and take notes— identifying strategies the writer uses to craft a personal essay rich in narration, description, and reflection.

I stagger awake in the darkness and crawl into my clothes. It is an hour before sunrise, in a small guest home in Hay Cove, on the upper reaches of Newfoundland's Great Northern Peninsula.   *1*

My plan is to hike down to the land's end and watch the sun break across the Atlantic on this, the first day of July. I tiptoe out, into pale moonlight, closing the door quietly behind me. Clapboard homes line the road. Clusters of wildflowers form perfect bouquets, and everything seems to glow a low blue. A wind is coming off the sea. I can hear the lap and roll of waves on the shore. There are tales of a whale in the inlet. "He's been scoopin' up the krill," I was told when I arrived last night.   *2*

The road from Hay Cove slopes up and onto asphalt, where a lone highway unrolls along boggy barrens. A congregation of shadows has gathered beside the road. Moose. Four, maybe five. They come out from the scrub on knob-kneed legs and move towards me, clip-clopping across the blacktop, so close I can hear their puffs of breath. Large. Imposingly so, when set against the stunted vegetation and shrub-like trees up here. Like moose everywhere, they carry with them a certain dignified ugliness. They are the inbred Habsburg monarchs of the animal kingdom, combining regal deportment with huge, misshapen noses. *Prehensile* noses. They clop nearer, loom larger. I think a moment. When was the last time I saw a moose up this close? Well, never. And the rutting season for moose, when exactly does that begin? I try to look uninterested in the females. I try to look big. I try to look calm. I try to look like someone who is Not Afraid, even as the moose begin to outflank me on either side. "G'wan. Go away," I say, my voice disconcertingly high.   *3*

It's no use. I am about to be mugged by a gang of moose, and the only comfort I draw from this is the knowledge that, if nothing else, this is certainly the single most *Canadian* way you could possible die. I see the headlines already: BELOVED AUTHOR TRAMPLED TO DEATH BY MOOSE. A NATION MOURNS. But then, on some unspoken cue, they lurch to one side and lope away.   *4*

Pulse pounding, chest tight, I walk back to Hay Cove at a brisk pace—so brisk it's more of a sprint than a walk, really. "Think I'll drive," I gasp aloud. And as I ease the car out of Hay Cove and onto the highway, I can't help but wonder if my CAA insurance plan would consider moose an Act of God.   *5*

Excerpted from Beauty Tips from Moose Jaw: Travels in Search of Canada by Will Ferguson. Copyright © 2004 Will Ferguson. Reprinted by permission of Knopf Canada.

I have come to L'Anse aux Meadows for Canada Day, because this is where   *6*
Canada—the *idea* of Canada—was first forged. In many ways, Newfoundland's
northern peninsula represents our nation's vanishing point, where parallel lines
converge. A geometric impossibility, perhaps, but not when it comes to the history of
who we are.

The shift from *Kanata* to Canada begins here at L'Anse aux Meadows. It starts   *7*
with a ship lost in the fog, a Viking vessel blown off course en route to Eirik the Red's
colony in Greenland. The Norsemen on board caught sight of a distant, unknown
shore, and the existence of this new land, poised at the end of the world, fired the
imagination of Leif Eiriksson, son of Eirik. On or around the year A.D. 1000, Leif set
sail with a small crew.

The end of the world was not that far away, after all. Leif and his men soon   *8*
arrived at a barren coast, which they named Helluland (Flat Stone Land, most likely
Baffin Island), and then, turning south, came upon the wooded shores of Labrador,
which they dubbed Markland (Forest Land). Continuing south for two more days,
they discovered a shallow bay surrounded by sloping grassy fields. A stream trickled
down, teeming with fish, and the hills were ripe with wineberries. They named it
Vinland (Wine Land).

Loading his ship with timber, as good as gold in treeless Greenland, Leif   *9*
Eiriksson sailed for home the following spring, and with that single voyage he
made both his fortune and his name. He would be known as "Leif the Lucky": the
first European to set foot in North America, legends of Irish monks and ancient
Phoenicians aside. And though Leif himself never went back to Vinland, others soon
followed.

His younger brother, Thorvald, led an expedition down the same coast, and in   *10*
one bay came upon a band of hunters asleep beneath skin boats. The Norse referred to
them as *skrælings*, a term of contempt meaning "wretches" or "barbarians," but from
the description of the boats and the men beneath them, it would appear they were
Inuit or possibly Innu. This encounter between Norse explorers and Native hunters
was a pivotal moment in world history. Spilling out of Africa, the human race had
pushed north into Europe and east into Asia, through Mongolia and either across
the sea or over the Bering Strait to the Americas. And now, on this windswept coast,
the two sides had once again met. Humanity had come full circle. It was as much a
reunion as it was "first contact."

Alas, as with many a family reunion, things were a little strained. The Vikings—   *11*
being Vikings—immediately attacked, killing all of the hunters but one. He managed
to escape, which was bad news for the Vikings, because he returned with a whole
armada of kayaks. A pitched battle ensued, during which Thorvald was hit by an
arrow. He made a farewell speech and then promptly died.

That first meeting set the tone for much of what would follow. A later expedition   *12*
ended in a full-scale war between the Norse colonists and the *skrælings*. During one

melee, Leif's half-sister Freydis grabbed up the sword of a fallen Norseman and, ripping open her shirt, slapped the blade against her breast. She stood her ground, ready to fight, but the Inuit attackers stopped, speechless at the sight of this. Freydis was pregnant at the time, as well, and one of the cardinal rules of combat is "Never piss off a pregnant woman when she's holding a sword." The Inuit scattered, and Freydis, bare-breasted and defiant, became a Viking legend. Never mind that another account of her voyage to Vinland paints a very different picture, with a bloody feud breaking out between competing Norse camps that ended with Freydis butchering her rivals. (When her own henchmen refused, Freydis killed the female prisoners herself. With an axe.)

Relentless *skræling* attacks, isolation and loneliness and the creeping cold of a *13* "little ice age" helped doom the Norse settlements. Vinland the Good was abandoned, fading into myth and memory of the Norse sagas. Clues about the lost colony were woven into these narratives, and in 1914, Newfoundland historian W. A. Munn was able to trace the location of Vinland to Pistolet Bay, at the northern end of the peninsula. "They went ashore at Lancey Meadows," he wrote.

Munn was only slightly off. They hadn't simply landed at "Lancey Meadows," *14* they had built their base camp there. A Finnish geographer followed the path of the sagas to northern Newfoundland, as did a Danish archaeologist, who explored the area around L'Anse aux Meadows in 1960 and just missed the site. The very next year, Norwegian explorer Helge Ingstad arrived at the northern strait between Labrador and Newfoundland, and he too came ashore at L'Anse aux Meadows. (The name seems descriptive—there are meadows here, indeed—but in fact it is probably derived from *l'anse aux méduses*, the French for "bay of jellyfish.") When he looked out at the sloping shore and curved bay, the open views and low height of land, Ingstad was struck by a sense of déjà-vu. He recognized this place. He had seen it before: in Norway, in Greenland, in other ancient Norse locations. *They would have felt at home here*, he thought. He knew, before he had turned a single sod of bog-iron peat, that he had found Vinland.

The Norwegian explorer also had the good fortune to strike up a friendship with *15* a local fisherman, a gregarious, bewhiskered, brogue-speaking, pipe-smoking old-timer by the name of George Decker. Decker took Ingstad to a series of grassy humps that Decker referred to as "the old Indian camp." The hillocks and hollows were not "Indian," however; they were Viking.

Ingstad's wife, archaeologist Anne Stine Ingstad, paced out an excavation site the *16* following year and, with a team of volunteers, began peeling back the peat. A village slowly emerged. A smelter, a bathhouse, a boat shed, firepits and living quarters. With this came a wealth of artifacts: iron nails, ship rivets, a stone anvil, a bronze cloak-pin and a spindle whorl. More than 2000 items have been recovered, but it's the last one— the spindle whorl—that was the single most momentous. A small piece of rounded soapstone used to spin wool into yarn, it is considered one of the great archaeological finds in North America. The reason? Spinning and weaving were an exclusively female occupation in Norse culture, and this stone spindle provided irrefutable evidence that the settlement at L'Anse aux Meadows was not a temporary camp. It was an attempt at establishing a permanent community. *They brought their families with them.* It calls to mind heartwarming images of Viking longboats ringing with cries of "Are we there yet?" "Mom, Olaf is kicking me!" "Am not!" "Am too!" "By the Blood of Thor, if you kids don't settle down, I'm turning this boat around right now!" True, no direct evidence of children has turned up at L'Anse aux Meadows, but the Norse sagas do tell of at least one child born in Vinland, a boy with the sleepy name of Snorri.

L'Anse aux Meadows was a Norse settlement. But was it Vinland? This is a question that continues to vex historians and archaeologists, with much of the mystery turning on the meaning of *vin*. Wild grapes are not found this far north. Perhaps the Norsemen were referring to the plump berries that grow in such abundance here, the currants, the squashberries, the bakeapples and partridgeberries. Journals from English explorers refer to "wild grapes" and "grapevines" in Newfoundland well into the 1740s, so it was an easy enough mistake to make. Helge Ingstad has suggested that the references to wine and grapes were added later, in error, and he points out that in Old Norse, vin (with a short "i" sound) refers to meadows rather than grapes, making it not "Wine Land" but "Land of Meadows."　*17*

Personally, I think we can end the entire debate about Vinland by using basic common sense. The settlement uncovered at L'Anse aux Meadows is the only authenticated Viking site in North America. And how was it discovered? Through a careful reading of the ancient Norse sagas, and the sailing times and geographical descriptions they provide. What are the odds, in following these clues, that archaeologists and historians would, by sheer coincidence, have stumbled upon a *completely different*, heretofore unknown Viking village? Pretty damn slim, I imagine.　*18*

Is this where Lief Eiriksson first landed? Of course it is.　*19*

Today, the pale blue of a U.N. flag flies above L'Anse aux Meadows, marking it as a World Heritage Site. I wander through the Interpretive Centre, peer at the spindle whorl, now on display behind glass, then follow the trail down. The archaeological excavations have been covered again with sod to protect them from the elements, leaving impressions in the grass that are somehow more evocative than the gaping, gravedigger squares of a scientific worksite. Reconstructed Norse dwellings stand to one side, sod-built and peaty, filled with the smell of woodsmoke and wet grass. A brook trickles into the bay, the curve of low beach leads towards islands anchored offshore: the Great Sacred, the Little Sacred. And behind them the coast of Labrador, forming a dark curtain along the water.　*20*

Hello! Meet Egil, the Chieftain, who is a bit flamboyant, single and in love with Halbera. Thorgerd, the town gossip, is married to Kvelduf. If you enjoy the spoken word, say hello to Lambi the *skald*, who spends his time carving as he recites passages from the Havamal, the Viking book of sayings.

Not far from the L'Anse aux Meadows historic site is the tourist village of Norstead, a full-scale replica of a Viking settlement, complete with Great Hall, sod-covered dwellings, some soggy-looking sheep, and people walking around dressed up like Vikings and speaking with Newfoundland accents. "Valhalla, and all dat," one of the Vikings is telling a group of visitors when I arrive. "Now dis yere, dis would be da mighty Viking sword, b'y." It is not incongruous in the least. Newfoundlanders make excellent Vikings. Both are of the sea, and both—I imagine—would be equally good in a fight. The tourist brochures "cast of characters"—quoted above—could, I'm sure, be as easily applied to any neighbourhood or outport in Newfoundland. *Now where's Kvelduf da Mighty goin' wit da bons dis hour of day?*

In the town of St. Anthony, I pass the Vinland Motel and the Viking Mall, and in   21
the former fishing cove of St. Lunaire a local family now takes passengers on excursions out of Noddy Bay on board the *Viking Saga*. This is a hand-built replica of a *knarr*, the type of vessel that Leif the Lucky sailed in—except that this one has a motor hidden in it. And snacks. And very little hand-to-hand combat. I board the Viking Saga for an iceberg tour, the square sail flapping furiously for dramatic effect as we putter out of port. The captain angles us towards a gloating mountain just as a slice of ice falls away, dropping into the water with a crash. "We'll hang back on this one," he says prudently.

Icebergs are not white. They are blue on blue and veined with green. Translucent   22
marble, Matterhorns on the move, they roll under the waves, grind along the bottom of bays, lurch to a dead stop, melt themselves free.

The captain reverses the engine, bringing us to an abrupt stop, and we bob on the   23
waves as he grabs a long snare-net and darts to one side of the ship. He is scooping up 10,000-year-old ice cubes: the crumbling debris of icebergs, to be used by restaurants to chill the drinks of tourists. He rinses the salt water off a fist of smooth ice and tosses it over to me. "There you go," he says. "Purest water you'll ever taste." I press it against my tongue. It numbs my mouth and makes my teeth ache with its clear, clean cold.

Against a backdrop of icebergs, a whale breaks the surface, spouting a plume   24
of fishy breath. It's a humpback, and it arcs into the water, tail sliding up and in like a hand waving goodbye. Silence. And then suddenly it reappears on the other side, having crossed below us. That something so large could disappear with such ease. . . . I think of villages that lie in stillness for a thousand years, of currents that run in a northern sea, of all those things that lie just below the surface of who we are, nine-tenths unseen.

My grandmother was of Viking stock. My grandfather, from Scotland. "And   25
Scotsmen," my grandma liked to say, "are just shipwrecked Norwegians." How did I get here? I ascended. I ascended from Cape Breton coal mines and the Barnardo orphanage of Belfast, from nomadic Czech migrations and Australian penal colonies. These tales converge in me, and this is not unusual. From the last Vikings to the shattered displacement of the First Nations, from resistance to revival, from New France to the New West, from dreams of utopia to dreams of prosperity, from Loyalist

boat people to modern-day refugees, Canada is more than just a country: it is a sum of its stories. We are all orphans, are all survivors of shipwrecks, and we carry these stories of exile and renewal within us, whether we are aware of it or not.

As the captain turns the ship back towards the grassy shores, with a harvest of ice in the hold, a stanza of poetry surfaces. It's a fragment of verse from "The Canadian Boat Song," something I once had to memorize for school. It's a song about a nineteenth-century Scottish emigrant, but it is more than that.   26

> Mountains divide us, and the waste of the seas—
> Yet still the blood is strong, the heart is Highland,
> And we in dreams behold the Hebrides:
> Fair these broad meads—these hoary woods are grand;
> But we are exiles from our fathers' land.

The broad meads, the grassy mounds. Vinland lost and Vinland found. "*We look / like a geography but / just scratch us / and we bleed / history.*" This last line is from Miriam Waddington's poem "Canadians." Scratch us and we bleed history.   27

Reading for Better Writing

Working by yourself or with a group, answer these questions:

1. Will Ferguson opens his essay with a narrative about his encounter with moose. What does this narrative accomplish in terms of establishing tone, topic, and theme?

2. In paragraph 6, Ferguson explains his purpose in coming to L'Anse aux Meadows. How does this purpose announce a larger theme for the essay? How does he use symbolism to express this theme?

3. A large portion of the essay explores the history of the Viking settlement, Vinland: the expeditions that led Vikings to L'Anse aux Meadows (paragraphs 7–9), encounters between the Vikings and Aboriginal people (paragraphs 10–12), and the abandonment of the settlement and efforts by scientists hundreds of years later to locate it (paragraphs 13–19). What strategies does Ferguson use to make this history interesting and memorable? What is the point of the history lesson?

4. In paragraphs 20–23, the writer describes modern-day L'Anse aux Meadows and shares his experiences there. What does this section of the essay accomplish?

5. Ferguson's concluding paragraphs (24–27) seek to put both his experience and the Viking history in a larger context. How does he do so, and with what results? In what ways do you connect with the closing paragraphs? Do Ferguson's thoughts about Canada resonate with your own?

Writing Guidelines

Planning

1. **Select a topic.** The most promising topics are experiences that gave you insights into yourself, and possibly into others as well. To identify such topics, consider the categories below and then list whatever experiences come to mind:
   - Times when you felt *secure, hopeful, distraught, appreciated, confident, frightened, exploited,* or *misunderstood.*
   - Times when you made a decision about *lifestyles, careers, education,* or *religion.*
   - Events that tested your *will, patience, self-concept,* or *goals.*
   - Events that changed or confirmed your assessment of *a person, a group,* or *an institution.*

   Tip: List topics in response to the following statement: *Reflect on times when you first discovered that the world was strange, wonderful, complex, frightening, small, full, or empty.* How did these experiences affect you?

2. **Get the big picture.** Once you have chosen a topic, gather your thoughts by brainstorming or freewriting in response to questions like these:
   - Where did the experience take place, and what specific sights, sounds, and smells distinguish the place?
   - Who else was involved, and what did they look like, act like, do, and say?
   - What were the key or pivotal points in your experiences and why?
   - What led to these key moments and what resulted from them?
   - How did your or others' comments or actions affect what happened?
   - What did others learn from this experience—and what did you learn?
   - Did the experience end as you had hoped? Why or why not?
   - What themes, conflicts, and insights arose from the experience?
   - How do your feelings now differ from your feelings then? Why?

   Tip: To find out more details about the event or people involved, sort through photo albums and home videos to trigger memories; talk to someone who shared your experiences; consult your journal, old letters, and saved digital communications, such as email.

3. **Probe the topic and reveal what you find.** The mind-searching aspect of writing this essay happens while asking so-why questions: *So why does this picture still make me smile? or Why does his comment still hurt? or Why did I do that when I knew better—or Did I know better?* Your readers need to experience what you experienced, so don't hide what's embarrassing or painful or still unclear.

4. **Get organized.** Review your brainstorming or freewriting, and highlight key details, quotations, or episodes. Then list the main events in chronological order, or use a cluster to help you gather details related to your experiences.

Drafting

5. **Write the first draft.** Rough out the first draft. Then test your narration and description by asking whether the quotations, details, and events are accurate and clear. Test your reflection by asking whether it explains how the experience affected you.

Revising

6. **Review the draft.** After taking a break, read your essay for truthfulness and completeness. Does it include needed details and questions?

7. **Get feedback.** Ask a classmate to read your paper and respond to it.

8. **Improve the ideas, organization, and voice.** Use your own review and peer review to address these issues:

____ **Ideas:** The essay offers readers an engaging, informative look into your life, personality, and perspective.

____ **Organization:** The essay includes (1) an inviting opening that pictures the setting, introduces the characters, and forecasts the themes; (2) a rich middle that develops a clear series of events, nuanced characters, and descriptions; and (3) a satisfying closing that completes the experience and unifies the essay's ideas.

____ **Voice:** The tone is fair, and it fits the experience. The voice is genuine and inviting.

Editing

9. **Edit and proofread your essay.** Polish your writing by addressing these items:

____ **Words:** The words in descriptive and narrative passages *show* instead of *tell about*; they are precise and rich, helping readers imagine the setting, envision the characters, and vicariously experience the action. The words in reflective passages are insightful and measured.

____ **Sentences:** The sentences in descriptive and reflective passages are clear, varied in structure, and smooth. The sentences in dialogue accurately reflect the characters' personalities, regional diction, and current idioms.

____ **Correctness:** The copy includes no errors in spelling, mechanics, punctuation, or grammar.

____ **Page Design:** The design is attractive and follows assigned guidelines.

Publishing

10. **Publish your writing** by sharing your essay with friends and family, posting it on a website, or submitting it to a journal or newspaper.

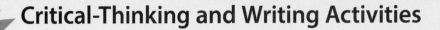

Critical-Thinking and Writing Activities

As directed by your instructor, complete the following critical-thinking and writing activities by yourself or with classmates.

1. Carol Shields writes that "Words are our life. We are human because we use language. So I think we are less human when we use less language." Explore Shields's comments in connection with the type of personal writing presented in this chapter.

2. Through vivid description and narration, "Mzee Owitti" presents an experience that is both personally and culturally meaningful for the writer. List personal experiences that carry similar cultural significance for you. Choose one and write your own narrative, using some of the same strategies used in the model.

3. In "Spare Change," Teresa Zsuffa describes her encounter with someone whose qualities, experiences, and values are different from her own. Write a personal essay in which you explore such an encounter in your life.

4. Both "Dryden's Backyard" and "At L'Anse aux Meadows" focus in part on the history (personal and beyond) of a particular location. Consider places in your home town or city that are meaningful to you; conversely, think of places that you travelled to or left behind as a child. How are such places "historied," personally or otherwise? Choose the most promising place and write an essay that draws on strategies used by Ken Dryden and Will Ferguson.

Learning-Objectives Checklist ✓

Have you achieved this chapter's learning objectives? Check your progress with the items below, revisiting topics in the chapter as needed. *I have . . .*

___ successfully identified, critiqued, and created these elements of narrative writing: setting, character, plot, dialogue, and theme (142–143).

___ developed engaging, vivid, and well-organized descriptive writing that includes precise words and sensory appeals (143–144).

___ integrated into my personal writing appropriate analytical strategies such as interesting comparisons and contrasts (145).

___ written reflective passages that include honest, relevant, and fitting observations (146).

___ blended techniques of narration, description, and reflection to craft a personal essay that enables readers to share my experience and to understand its broad significance (164–165).

___ developed a well-organized personal essay with an engaging opening, a rich and substantive middle, and a thought-provoking closing (164–165).

Chapter 10

Definition

Most forms of academic and workplace writing—from essays and reports to proposals and literature reviews—include brief (one- or two-sentence) definitions of terms, sometimes called formal definitions. Although this chapter will help you write those, its main purpose is to help you understand and write longer, essay-length pieces sometimes called extended definitions.

Such definitions clarify and deepen readers' understanding of a term—whether it refers to something concrete or abstract. When reading such essays, consider how the writers "extend" your understanding of their topics, often using examples, illustrations, comparisons, and anecdotes to do so.

Visually Speaking   Study the photograph below. What does the image suggest about our relationship to signs, symbols, and words? What image might capture something of the importance of language and meaning to you?

Learning **Objectives**

By working through this chapter, you will be able to

- investigate how writers' situations inform their definition writing.
- critically examine and critique both brief and extended definitions.
- research all elements of a word's meaning.
- compose well-researched and well-reasoned brief and extended definitions.
- produce enriching anecdotes, quotations, comparisons, and contrasts, along with smooth transitions.

© *Atlantide Phototravel/CORBIS*

fig. 10.1

Strategies for Definition Essays

Definition clarifies meaning through an equation: **term x = explanation y**. As an analyst, the writer has the task of showing that explanation y on the right amounts to the same thing as the term (or referent) x on the left. Depending on a writer's situation (purpose, readers, and topic), she or he might develop a succinct one-sentence formal definition or a six-page extended definition.

The Rhetorical Situation

To put definition writing in context, consider the situation that gives rise to it:

- **Purpose:** Writers compose definitions for many reasons—to define a misunderstood term, to plumb the meaning of a complex concept, or to entertain readers. Their writing purpose—and readers—affect what form the writing takes. For example, a writer explaining to high-school students the classical concept of *catharsis* might begin by offering a one-sentence, formal definition of the term, *tragic hero*.
- **Readers:** People who read definitions also do so for different reasons, which affect the type of definitions they seek. For example, one reader may find a term unclear but want only a brief definition. Another reader may find a term very confusing and want a lengthy analysis of it, including its etymology. A third reader may understand what the term means but want to learn how a writer might expand its meaning.
- **Topic:** For any definition, the topic is a term. But what terms do writers typically focus on, and how does the term itself affect the form and style of the definition? That again depends the writer's purpose and readers. For example, Mary Bruins defines *gullible* because she is struck by how the term may apply to her, all the while seeking to enlighten and entertain her readers. By contrast, June Callwood explores past and present understandings of forgiveness in order to convince her readers to embrace an ethic of reconciliation, while Thomas King enlightens readers about the culturally loaded concept of "Dead Indians" so as to press both Aboriginal and non-Aboriginal readers to understand the cultural landscape of North America.

Principles of Definition Writing

Definition writing depends on the principles explained on this page and the next.

Examining a term's denotative (or literal) meaning, connotative (or suggested meaning), and etymology (or historical meaning). By studying one or more of these, writers gain a foundational understanding of their topics and commonly find poignant details that lead to fresh insights. For an example, see "The Gullible Family" on pages 170–171

Seeking accurate, authoritative sources. To write accurate definitions, writers need reliable sources of information. However, not all published sources are equally reliable. For information on how to evaluate the credibility of a source, see pages 418–421.

Using anecdotes, examples, illustrations, and comparisons. Writers use strategies such as these to engage readers and help them imagine a situation, visualize details, and discern subtle connotations. For example, in "Dead Indians" (pages 181–185), Thomas King uses several illustrations of people and products representing his central concept. By doing so, King makes the idea of "Dead Indians" concrete and familiar.

Inserting transitions that lead into and out of definitions. When composing a definition within a longer piece of writing, writers typically insert a transition that introduces the definition and explains why it is relevant or needed. After the definition, writers then insert another transition that leads readers back into the discussion that follows. Look, for example, at the topic sentences for the second and third paragraphs in Adam Gopnik's "Recreational Winter" on page 200, noting how the first transitions into a definition of *game theory* and the second transitions to an application of game theory to sports.

Avoiding logical fallacies. Definitions are weakened by logical fallacies such as oversimplification (317), half-truths (319), ambiguity (320), and slanted language (320). Writers need to edit their definitions to correct any poor reasoning.

Sample Definition Paragraph

While a definition may be as short as a phrase or sentence, writers sometimes dedicate a whole paragraph to defining a key term. They often do so to establish a concept in the reader's mind or to debate a contested term before moving on to further analysis or argument. In the paragraph below, John Van Rys defines *grotesque* before moving on to further analysis of this concept's presence in literature.

> First of all, what is the grotesque—in visual art and in literature? A term originally applied to Roman cave art that distorted the normal, the grotesque presents the body and mind so that they appear abnormal—different from the bodies and minds that we think belong in our world. Both spiritual and physical, bizarre and familiar, ugly and alluring, the grotesque shocks us, and we respond with laughter and fear. We laugh because the grotesque seems bizarre enough to belong only outside our world; we fear because it feels familiar enough to be part of it. Seeing the grotesque version of life as it is portrayed in art stretches our vision of reality. As Bernard McElroy argues, "The grotesque transforms the world from what we 'know' it to be to what we fear it might be. It distorts and exaggerates the surface of reality in order to tell a qualitative truth about it."

Reading Definition Writing

As you read definition essays, consider these questions:

1. What claims are made about the term's denotative and connotative meanings?
2. Is the definition current, relevant, complete, and clear?
3. Does the definition accurately explain the term's past and current usage?
4. Do clear transitions link the definition to the writing that precedes and follows it?
5. What does the definition add to your understanding of the term?

Sample Definition Essays

This chapter includes four sample extended definitions. As you read each piece, consider how the writer's purpose, readers, and topic might have affected how she or he shaped the essay's content, voice, organization, and style.

Defining through Denotation, Connotation, and Etymology

In this essay, student writer Mary Bruins describes how she earned the nickname "Gullible." To explain what the name means, she digs into the word's etymology (its historical roots) and explores its denotations and connotations. Notice the variety of sources she uses to fully define and illustrate the meaning of the word.

Essay Outline

Introduction: anecdotes about Gullible Loris and Gullible Mary
  1. The word *gullible* is related to gulls (the birds) and swallowing.
  2. The connotations of *gullible* suggest immaturity and foolishness.
  3. Statements by Washington Irving and William Dean Howells illustrate these connotations.

Closing: possible positive connotations to gullibility—wanting to believe.

The Gullible Family

The writer uses the title and an anecdote to introduce the topic.

The other day, my friend Loris fell for the oldest trick in the book: "Hey, somebody wrote *gullible* on the ceiling!" Shortly after mocking "Gullible Loris" for looking up, I swallowed the news that Wal-Mart sells popcorn that pops into the shapes of cartoon characters. And so, as "Gullible Mary," I decided to explore what our name means, and who else belongs to our Gullible family. What I learned is that the family includes both people and birds, related to each other by our willingness to "swallow." *1*

She gives an example and the word's Germanic root.

A gullible person will swallow an idea or an argument without questioning its truth. Similarly, a gull (a long-winged, web-footed bird) will swallow just about anything thrown to it. In fact, the *gullible* comes from *gull*, and this word can be traced back to the Germanic word *gwel* (to swallow). Both *gull* and *gwel* are linked to the modern word *gulp*, which means "to swallow greedily or rapidly in large amounts." It's not surprising, then, that Loris and I, sisters in the Gullible family, both eagerly gulped (like gulls) the false statements thrown to us. *2*

She cites details from an encyclopedia.

Swallowing things this quickly isn't too bright, and *gull* (when referring to a bird or person) implies that the swallower is immature and foolish. For example, *gull* refers to an "unfledged" fowl, which the Grolier Encyclopedia describes as either "an immature bird still lacking flight feather," or something that is "inexperienced, immature, or untried." These words describe someone who is fooled easily, and that's why gull, when *3* referring to a human, means "dupe" or "simpleton." In fact, since 1550, *gullet*, which means "throat," has also meant "fooled."

| She quotes two writers. |

To illustrate this usage, the *Oxford English Dictionary* quotes two authors who use *gull* as a verb meaning to fool. "Nothing is so easy as to *gull* the public, if you only set up a prodigy," writes Washington Irving. William Dean Howells uses the word similarly when he writes, "You are perfectly safe to go on and *gull* imbeciles to the end of time, for all I care."

4

| She closes with a playful, positive spin. |

Both of these authors are pretty critical of gullible people, but does *gullible* have negative connotations? Is there no hope for Gullibles like Loris and me? C. O. Sylvester Marson's comments about *gullible* may give us some comfort. He links *gullible* to "credulous, confiding, and easily deceived." At first, these adjectives also sound negative, but credulous does mean "to follow implicitly." And the word *credit* comes from the Latin word *credo* (meaning "I believe"). So what's bad about that? In other words, isn't wanting to believe other people a good thing? Why shouldn't Loris and I be proud of at least that aspect of our gull blood? We want to be positive—and we don't want to be cynics!

5

Note: The Works-Cited page is not shown. For sample pages, see MLA (page 533) and APA (pages 562–563).

Reading for **Better Writing**

Working by yourself or with a group, answer these questions:

1. Early in her essay, Mary Bruins tells anecdotes about herself and Loris. How do these anecdotes help the writer define *gullible*? How does such personal content impact your thinking about the term?

2. Review each paragraph and explain what it adds to the extended definition.

3. The writer relies on etymological research for much of her definition. How would you describe this research? How does Mary use it in her writing?

4. Describe the writer's voice. What tone is created for this definition? Is this tone appropriate? Why or why not?

5. The writer uses "family" as a metaphor for a group that includes both birds and people. How does this metaphor work? How does it function in the larger definition?

Defining a Cultural Practice

In the following essay, student writer Paige Louter explores a modern manifestation of an ancient concept: asceticism. By doing so, she provides an extended definition that questioningly analyzes the cultural significance of the phenomenon.

Hipsters and Hobos: Asceticism for a New Generation

> **The writer introduces the concept of asceticism with an anecdote.**

In August, 1992, a young man's remains were discovered in an abandoned bus in the Alaskan wilderness. He appeared to have starved to death. Eventually, he was identified as Christopher Johnson McCandless, a graduate of Emory University, who had disappeared two years earlier with no contact to his family since. McCandless had given $25,000 in savings to a charity dedicated to eradicating world hunger just before leaving, and had spent the next years hitchhiking (after abandoning his car and most of his belongings) across the United States, eventually hiking into Alaska in April 1992. McCandless, or as he dubbed himself during his odyssey, Alexander Supertramp, left an indelible record of his life in many people he met as he journeyed, and in 1996 a writer named Jon Krakauer published a book called *Into the Wild*. In it, Krakauer details McCandless's travels and eventual death with a combination of interviews from the people the young man met, and writings from McCandless himself (a journal of sorts was discovered with his body). The book was made into a film which premiered in 2007. Beyond simply presenting a fascinating account of a fascinating individual, however, *Into the Wild* (and its subsequent success) represents an increasing interest, especially among young people, in an alternative lifestyle which, rather than being concerned with worldly possessions and experiences, is focused upon self-denial, simplicity, and ultimately some sort of transcendence. This movement, called asceticism, is not a new one: John the Baptist, medieval monastic orders, Buddhists, and Jains all practised some form of an ascetical lifestyle. But a contemporary manifestation of such a philosophy is necessarily going to look quite different from a historical manifestation. So what does a formerly well-to-do, well-educated young man like Chris McCandless have in common with a fifth-century monk, for example? Asceticism, in ways both subtle and more overt, is on the rise today, but the implications of the current cultural context may be affecting this movement in ways not immediately apparent.

> **An informal definition plus historical examples offer a starting point for understanding the term.**

1

Asceticism is a difficult concept to fully wrap one's head around. A straightforward, objective analysis might define it as the practice or lifestyle of denying oneself physical excesses, even going to Spartan extremes, in order to achieve some revelation or higher state of being. However, ascetics historically have deviated from

2

A formal definition is stated and then complicated, with the writer zeroing in on a key element of the definition.

this pattern. Some have tended towards self-flagellation, rejecting not only excessive behaviour but also physical comfort, while others do not match the end-goal of the definition above, denying any nebulous desire for enlightenment as motivation. Perhaps it is the lack of a "perfect ascetic" as a model that contributes to the difficulty of definition. There is no rulebook for asceticism, and ultimately, perhaps no fixed set of guidelines against which the aspiring can be measured. Given this uncertainty, considering the modern manifestations of asceticism—and the degree to which these manifestations conform or differ from "true asceticism"—will be difficult. However, one element of asceticism which deals less with the manifestation and more with the motivation for such behaviour, without which a lifestyle cannot be truly considered ascetic, is intentionality. If people are not intentionally (and informedly) choosing their ascetic actions, then they are ascetics in appearance only.

The writer turns to current manifestations of asceticism, categorizing them and testing them against the definition established.

Today, asceticism is explored and practised in several different forms or incarnations. The first category is that of incidental, unintentional, even completely unaware adherence; essentially, these are not truly ascetics. From the viewpoint of diet alone, most of the world could be considered ascetic, through no choice of their own. Others who choose to limit themselves from excessive purchasing, for example, without a clear idea of why they are making this choice, would also fall into this category.

The second form of contemporary asceticism is admiration, and a kind of distorted, even ironic, mimicry. Into this category would fit most members of the current hipster movement, a movement which professes to be counter-cultural but which in reality rejects societal norms in little but clothing and music choice. Breaking away from the status quo in order to live radically different, usually dramatically simplified lives has been the goal of many a counter-cultural group. However, a lack of deeper philosophical understanding on the part of the movement's members suggests that to describe the lives of these people as ascetic would be to misuse the word. Although ascetics would likely be admired by the hipster movement in general, asceticism would more properly be seen as an informed, intentional, fulfilled version of "hipsterism" (and the opposite could also be taken as true). Forrest Perry explains, in his article "Why Hipsters Aren't All that Hip," that "what unifies the diverse strategies of those who position themselves as cool, then, is the image of the nonconforming individual" (57). He goes on to argue that the materialistic focus of hipsters essentially devalues their "message," as they purchase clothes, rather than make actual lifestyle changes, to fulfill their surface-only philosophy. Other ironic forms of asceticism today include an alarming

3

4

manifestation of self-flagellation, "cutting," in which a person (usually a teen or young adult) cuts his or her skin with the intention of causing pain but not death, as well as dieting and weight loss regimens in the name of conforming to some vague societal ideal of a perfect body.

Partial intentional adherence makes up the third method of contemporary   5
exploration of asceticism. This category includes many Christians, who strive to embody the ideal of "being in the world, but not of it." Interestingly, this phrase never actually appears in the Bible—the closest match would be a paraphrase of John 17:13–16. (The phrase does, however, appear in Sufi teachings.) However, though the word-for-word quotation is absent, the concept remains and is supported throughout Scripture. In "The Ascetic Impulse in Ancient Christianity," Vincent L. Wimbush says this:

> Both in its origins as the Jesus movement in Palestine, Syria, and Egypt and in its later development into conventicles resembling (some argue) Jewish synagogues, Hellenistic mysteries, or philosophical schools—even in its turn toward the ethos of the Greco-Roman urban petit bourgeois—early Christianity generally shared the impulse toward cultural criticism or resistance. It is very difficult to account for its origins other than as a critique of resistance to different circles of establishment power and tradition. (421)

This concept of asceticism as a form of resistance against popular culture is one that is definitely present in contemporary Christianity, as well as many other counter-cultural groups. However, most Christians today do not go to the extremes of, for example, the medieval monastic orders, so while they conform to a moderate type of asceticism, they do not represent the most dedicated group of ascetics. Partial adherence is not limited to Christianity, however, or any other religious group. It is not unheard of for, as previously mentioned in the first category (unintentional adherence), a person to forgo unnecessary shopping. However, when that decision is made consciously in order to abstain from consumerism, or to live simply, that person is engaging a true, if limited, form of asceticism (whether or not the person him or herself would identify it as such).

Finally, the fourth category is that of strict, extreme adherence to an ascetic   6
lifestyle. Into this category are placed the most compelling examples: the people whose lives were unyieldingly dedicated to asceticism in one form or another. One example, arguably the most well-known in the history of asceticism, is that of Saint Simeon Stylites, a fifth-century monk who lived for more than forty years on top of a pillar. Saint Simeon's extreme self-denial, which reportedly included standing

In the third category, the writer distinguishes modern religious asceticism from historical religious practices.

for entire days and fasting for weeks on end, attracted thousands of followers and even converted the emperor to asceticism. It is also this category that contains Chris McCandless and others like him, men and women who choose to reject material belongings and easy lives in order to search for something more authentic.

Perhaps the most logical next question, however, is "why?" What would drive someone to give up comfort and ease in favour of discomfort, hardship, and even pain and death? One Internet blogger offers a potential explanation for the actions, historically, of monastic orders:

> The spirit of monasticism . . . emphasized a withdrawing from the world in order to create this community. This does not mean that monks did not care about the world, they sincerely did—but rather they believed that the only way to live out the Christian life was to depart from secular society. It was an attempt to create an alternative culture rather than reform the dominant one. It was only through this kind of asceticism and purity that the secular world could ever see what the Kingdom of God was. (Gonzaga par. 5)

This summary provides a good view of the motivation for monks, and likely other religious ascetics as well. In fact, historically, asceticism seems consistently to have been motivated by spiritual ideals. For God, in whatever form he might take, men and women have been willing to deprive themselves of sleep, starve and beat themselves, give away all their worldly possessions, and live in isolation and separation from the world. And in a historical context, this appears to make sense. But what of ascetics today? How can a seemingly barbaric and anachronistic philosophy be a relevant and powerful movement in the twenty-first century, post-modern (and increasingly secular) world?

Perhaps, as it has been historically, contemporary asceticism is mainly a reactionary philosophy. It would not be a stretch, for instance, to credit the increasingly consumerist society with motivating the anti-establishment movements in the 1950s, which in turn spawned the watered-down hipster culture of the twenty-first century. Likewise, Chris McCandless abandoned his primary identity in order to live apart from a society that he felt was excessive and cut off from the truly important aspects of life. This is not a reaction exclusive to asceticism, however; it is a common feature, in fact, of North Americans to be drawn to the unique or the exclusive, and a common conceit that goes along with this is to believe that, by bucking mainstream trends, a person is made automatically superior.

Unfortunately, it is this arrogance, as opposed to the greater-than-self awareness of the previous centuries, that best seems to characterize the

7

8

9

After looking at strict asceticism (the fourth category), the writer deepens her definition by exploring the motivation behind the practice.

She contrasts motivations of past ascetics with those of current ascetics.

contemporary manifestations of not only asceticism but also many other philosophies (and religions) as well. Armed with only a vague idea rather than a deep understanding of a philosophy like asceticism, contemporary would-be adherents cannot hope to truly experience the transcendence that would have been the ultimate goal of the historical ascetic.

Today, asceticism is clearly less grounded in intentionality and spiritual *10* meaning than it has been in the past. Because true asceticism is necessarily also intentional asceticism, the possibility even arises that asceticism in its truest form no longer exists—outside of certain religious groups. Perhaps, then, the definition of an ascetic life must be modified, or perhaps a new philosophy has arisen today that is valid in its own right. Or perhaps the longing for authenticity that dwells in many young people today will eventually drive them beyond a self-reliant, isolated philosophy to deeply engage with the true spirit of asceticism. Arguably, Chris McCandless may have been one of the first of this movement. While one respondent to McCandless's story accused him of adhering to an arrogant and "contrived asceticism" (Krakauer 72), McCandless himself did, ultimately, live out what he believed, rejecting materialism, consumerism, mainstream society, all in the name of truly living. Essentially, perhaps this is what living as an ascetic is really about.

> Bringing her extended definition to a conclusion, the writer speculates that true asceticism may no longer exist and that the definition may need to be changed.

Note: The Works-Cited page is not shown. For sample pages, see MLA (page 533) and APA (pages 562–563).

Reading for Better Writing

Working by yourself or with a group, answer these questions:

1. Paige Louter frames her essay with the story of Chris McCandless. Besides the opening, where else does she refer to McCandless? How does his story help her define asceticism?

2. Early in the essay (late in paragraph 1 and through paragraph 2), Paige is direct in her definition of asceticism. What strategies does she use? How effective are these strategies in clarifying asceticism?

3. To extend her definition, Paige analyzes different types of asceticism (paragraphs 3–6). How does she distinguish the categories, and how does her discussion of each category deepen your understanding of asceticism?

4. In the last part of her essay, Paige explores people's motivations for adopting an ascetic lifestyle. What conclusions does she draw, based on what thinking?

5. In the end, what does this essay encourage you to think and feel about asceticism? What does the essay ask of you?

Defining an Ethical Concept

June Callwood (1924–2007) was a Canadian author and broadcaster, as well as a social activist who supported the rights of women, children, gay people, and people with disabilities. In addition, she championed freedom of expression through such organizations as the Canadian Civil Liberties Association, PEN Canada, and the Writers' Union of Canada. In the extended definition below, she explores the complex moral territory of forgiveness.

Forgiveness

A small boy in an industrial city in Ontario was beaten severely many times by his father, to the extent that the boy not infrequently required a doctor to stitch up the wounds. His father, a policeman, sincerely believed that if he beat his son with chains, belts, sticks, and his fists, the boy would not grow up to be gay. That boy, now in his thirties and indelibly a gay man, says he will never forgive his father. *1*

Callwood illustrates the difficulty of forgiveness through two anecdotes.

"What he did is not forgivable," the man says with composure. "How can it ever be all right to abuse a child? But I have let it go." *2*

And a woman, raised on the Prairies in a Finnish home, married a black man and had a son. She showed the infant proudly to her mother, whose reaction was a look of naked disgust. Her mother and that son, now a charming and successful adult, have since developed an affectionate relationship, but the daughter has not forgotten or forgiven the expression on her mother's face. "The best I can do," she says, "is that I have stopped hating her." *3*

The ability to forgive is a central tenet of every major religion in the world— Christian, Judaic, Hindu, Buddhist, and Islamic. Those faiths urge followers to forgive their enemies and, indeed, even to find a way to love those who wrong them. As the twenty-first century dawns, however, the world is making a spectacular mess of such pious admonitions. Instead of goodwill, this is the age of anger, the polar opposite of forgiveness. Merciless ethnic, tribal, and religious conflicts dominate every corner of the planet, and in North America individuals live with high levels of wrath that explode as domestic brutality, road rage, vile epithets, and acts of random slaughter. *4*

The writer contrasts religion's dictates on forgiveness with contemporary attitudes.

Many people, like the gay man or the woman in a biracial marriage, find forgiveness an unreasonable dictate. Some assaults on the body or soul are unconscionable, they feel, and forgiveness is simply out of the question. It satisfies the requirements of their humanity that they gradually ease away from the primitive thoughts of revenge that once obsessed them. *5*

The moral quandary of forgiveness is outlined.

When Simon Wiesenthal, the famed Nazi hunter, was in a German concentration camp, he found himself in a strange situation. He was taken to the bedside of a dying *6*

SS officer, a youth who had killed many Jews, and the young man asked him, a Jew, for forgiveness. Wiesenthal was silent and left the room, but was haunted ever after. Thirty years later, he contacted some of the world's great thinkers and asked, what should I have done? Theologians such as Bishop Desmond Tutu and the Dalai Lama gently hinted that he should have been forgiving, for his own sake, but others, notably philosopher Herbert Marcuse, said that great evil should never be forgiven. In *The Sunflower*, a collection of fifty-three responses to Wiesenthal's question, Marcuse wrote sternly that forgiveness condones the crime.

The moral vacuum left by the pervasive disuse and misuse of religious tenets *7* has allowed a secular forgiveness industry to spring into being. People who yearn desperately to rid themselves of an obsession for vengeance will seek help in curious places. Since 1985, the University of Wisconsin–Madison has offered forgiveness studies, and an International Forgiveness Institute was founded there. Four years ago, the world's first international conference on forgiveness drew hundreds of delegates to Madison. Stanford University has a forgiveness research project and people in California, a state on the cutting edge of self-absorption, are taking part in studies on the art and science of forgiveness. Self-help shelves in bookstores abound in titles such as *Forgive Your Parents: Heal Yourself.*

Callwood describes the contemporary forgiveness industry.

An odious US daytime television show, *Forgive or Forget*, features guests who *8* say they owe someone an apology. They describe their offence, and then, *ta-dah*, the injured party appears on the appropriately tacky set and either grants or withholds forgiveness. Will the former foes embrace one another? The titillated audience can't wait.

Apologies are iffy because often they are contrived or coerced. Apologies *9* extracted by judges, mediators, and parents are thin gruel for the wronged person. One familiar genre of apology, the one which commences, "I am sorry you are feeling badly," is particularly counterproductive because there is no admission of any responsibility; it is the other person's problem for being thin-skinned. A sincere and remorseful acceptance of blame, however, can close a wound.

The issue of apologies is explored.

Psychologists are engrossed by the topic and so are theologians, philosophers, *10* psychiatrists, and—surprise—cardiologists. Unforgiving people, some studies show, are three times more likely to have heart disease as people who don't carry grudges. These findings raise the suspicion that the researchers may have the cart before the horse. Heart attacks occur more often in blow-top people who have unfortified egos, the very ones most apt to be relentlessly unforgiving. On the other hand, people who hold tolerant views of human nature and don't seem to nurse grievances unduly tend to have blood pressures in the normal range.

The writer explains what various experts say about forgiveness.

Clergy, counsellors, and people who lecture and write books about forgiveness   11
all preach reductionism as a strategy for overcoming hot resentment of someone's
nasty behaviour. They say that people who have been harmed should see the hurtful
as deeply flawed human beings working out nameless aggressions. Pitiable and
inferior, they are examples of failure to thrive. Adults still distressed by abuse, neglect,
or rejection in childhood are urged to consider what happened in their parents'
childhoods—often, bad parenting comes from being badly parented. The theory is
that understanding the reasons for their parents' limitations will enable the offspring
to acquire a measure of compassion. Maybe it works. Hillary Clinton apparently
forgave her sleazy husband because she knows he had an unhappy childhood.

Issues of empathy and responsibility are held in tension.

This technique can be applied to almost any injustice and falls within the rapists-   12
were-beaten-as-children, *poor them* school of thought, which for some skeptics veers
perilously close to non-accountability. The law and commonsense hold that adults
are responsible for what they do. While empathy may help people appreciate why
others behave badly, the exercise is somewhat patronizing. The offender is reduced
to a contemptible hive of neuroses and ungovernable aberrations, which accordingly
elevates the injured party to a morally superior person.

Demonizing the enemy is a common coping mechanism in times of adversity.   13
In military terms, it captures the high ground. Catastrophes such as divorce, job loss,
rape, robbery, infidelity, and slander are all assaults on personal dignity and self-
respect. A sense of being intact—*safe*—has been violated, and people are dismayed to
find themselves for some time emotionally crippled by anger and grief. Betrayal and
loss take big chunks out of people's confidence and leave them feeling excruciatingly
vulnerable to random harm.

Callwood explores how forgiveness might happen.

The starting place, some therapists say, is to accept that something appalling has   14
happened, and it hurts. Denial, a recourse more favoured by men than by women,
won't help. The next step they say, is to develop an off switch. When fury threatens
to make the brain reel, people should grasp for distractions. Brooding about revenge
only serves to unhinge reason. If people don't rid themselves of wrath, personal
growth stops cold. The hard part comes at the end of the process. The choices are to
enter a state of forgiveness, which is a triumph of generosity, or just to put the matter
in a box, cover it with a lid, place a brick on the lid, and move on. In healthy people, a
perverse state of mind eventually wears itself out.

In yoga, they say that it takes six years of regularly practising meditation to gain   15
spiritual insight. Forgiveness of a great wrong may take longer. The process can't even
begin until the injured person stops crying.

Some people are marvellously unbroken by great injustices. Nelson Mandela   *16*
smiled gently at his adversaries after twenty-seven years of brutal imprisonment.
A worldwide figure of wonder, he even invited his white jailer to his inauguration as
South Africa's president. In Cambodia, a pastor whose family had been wiped out by
the Khmer Rouge baptized and forgave a notorious Khmer Rouge leader known as
Duch. A university professor in Virginia had an urge to kill the intruder who beat his
mother to death, but stopped himself with the thought, "Whose heart is darker?" And
the father of a young girl casually murdered in a street encounter with a teenager she
didn't know attended the trial and sat quietly throughout the appalling testimony.
He said he would visit the youth in prison. "I do not think I can forgive him," he
explained, "but perhaps if I know him I will not hate him."

The essay ends by affirming the hard but necessary work of forgiveness.

Forgiveness is hard work. A woman, a devout Roman Catholic who forgave the   *17*
man who tortured and killed her seven-year-old daughter, said, "Anyone who says
forgiveness is for wimps hasn't tried it." The reward for giving up scalding thoughts of
reprisal is peace of mind. It is worth the candle.

Reading for Better Writing

Working by yourself or with a group, answer these questions:

1. The beginning and the ending of the essay focus on quite different illustrations or anecdotes. What do these illustrations accomplish at the start and finish of the essay?

2. June Callwood identifies several ways that people can respond to being wronged, among them denial, excusing or demonizing the wrongdoer, and distraction. Examine the paragraphs that deal with these different responses and summarize Callwood's objections to them.

3. The essay contrasts traditional religious teachings about forgiveness with contemporary culture's attitudes toward it. How does Callwood's presentation of this contrast deepen your understanding of forgiveness?

4. In paragraphs 11 and 12, Callwood describes a reductionist strategy for dealing with anger created by other people's wrongdoing. How does she present and critique this strategy?

5. Paragraph 14 describes the process of forgiveness. How does Callwood outline this process? What does she emphasize about it?

6. How does the essay's exploration of forgiveness relate to your beliefs about and experiences with this ethical dilemma?

Defining Ethnic and Racial Attitudes

Of Cherokee and Greek descent, Thomas King is an essayist, a fiction writer, and an English professor at the University of Guelph. He has authored five novels, including *Green Grass, Running Water* (1993) and *Truth and Bright Water* (1999). One of Canada's best-known Native intellectuals, King delivered the 2003 Massey Lectures, *The Truth about Stories*. His most recent book is *The Inconvenient Indian: A Curious Account of Native People in North America* (2012), from which the excerpt below is taken. "Dead Indians" comprises the opening to the third chapter, "Too Heavy to Lift." As you read, consider the strategies that King uses to confront readers with the concept of the "Dead Indian."

Dead Indians

As you read this essay, annotate it and take notes—tracing your reactions and identifying strategies the writer uses to develop an extended definition.

Indians come in all sorts of social and historical configurations. North American popular culture is littered with savage, noble, and dying Indians, while in real life we have Dead Indians, Live Indians, and Legal Indians.   1

Dead Indians are, sometimes, just that. Dead Indians. But the Dead Indians   2
I'm talking about are not the deceased sort. Nor are they all that inconvenient. They are the stereotypes and clichés that North America has conjured up out of experience and out of its collective imaginings and fears. North America has had a long association with Native people, but despite the history that the two groups have shared, North America no longer sees Indians. What it *sees* are war bonnets, beaded shirts, fringed deerskin dresses, loincloths, headbands, feathered lances, tomahawks, moccasins, face paint, and bone chokers. These bits of cultural debris—authentic and constructed—are what literary theorists like to call "signifiers," signs that create a "simulacrum," which Jean Baudrillard, the French sociologist and postmodern theorist, succinctly explained as something that "is never that which conceals the truth—it is the truth which conceals that there is none."

God, I love the French theorists. For those of us who are not French theorists   3
but who know the difference between a motor home and a single-wide trailer, a simulacrum is something that represents something that never existed. Or, in other words, the only truth of the thing is the lie itself.

Dead Indians.   4

You can find Dead Indians everywhere. Rodeos, powwows, movies, television   5
commercials. At the 1973 Academy Awards, when Sacheen Littlefeather (Yaqui-Apache-Pueblo) refused the Best Actor award on behalf of Marlon Brando, she did so dressed as a Dead Indian. When U.S. Senator Benjamin Nighthorse Campbell (Northern Cheyenne) and W. Richard West, Jr. (Cheyenne-Arapaho), the director of the American Indian Museum in New York, showed up for the 2004 opening

Excerpted from The Inconvenient Indian: a Curious Account of Native People in North America by Thomas King. Copyright © 2012 Dead Dog Café Productions Inc. Reprinted by permission of Doubleday Canada.

ceremonies of the museum, they took the podium in Dead Indian leathers and feathered headdresses. Phil Fontaine (Ojibway) was attired in the same manner when he stood on the floor of the House of Commons in 2008 to receive the Canadian government's apology for the abuses of residential schools.

I probably sound testy, and I suppose part of me is. But I shouldn't be. After all, Dead Indians are the only antiquity that North America has. Europe has Greece and Rome. China has the powerful dynasties. Russia has the Cossacks. South and Central America have the Aztecs, the Incas, and the Maya.   6

North America has Dead Indians.   7

This is why Littlefeather didn't show up in a Dior gown, and why West and Campbell and Fontaine didn't arrive at their respective events in Brioni suits, Canali dress shirts, Zegni ties, and Salvatore Ferragamo shoes. Whatever cultural significance they may have for Native peoples, full feather headdresses and beaded buckskins are, first and foremost, White North America's signifiers for Indian authenticity. Their visual value at ceremonies in Los Angeles or Ottawa is—as the credit card people say—priceless.   8

Whites have always been comfortable with Dead Indians. General Phil Sheridan, famous for inventing the scorched-earth tactics used in "Sherman's March to the Sea," is reputed to have said, "The only good Indian I ever saw was a dead one." Sheridan denied saying this, but Theodore Roosevelt filled in for him. In a speech in New York in 1886, some sixteen years before he became president of the United States, Roosevelt said, "I suppose I should be ashamed to say that I take the Western view of the Indian. I don't go so far as to think that the only good Indians are dead Indians, but I believe nine out of every ten are, and I shouldn't like to inquire too closely into the case of the tenth."   9

Which brings to mind that great scene in the 1994 film *Maverick*, in which Joseph, a Native con man played by the Oneida actor Graham Greene, spends his time pandering to the puerile whims of a rich Russian grand duke, played by Paul L. Smith. Smith is on a grand tour of the West and has become a bit bored with all the back-to-nature stuff. He has shot buffalo, lived with Indians, communed with nature, and is casting about for something new and exciting to do with his time. Greene, dressed up in standard Dead Indian garb, asks Smith if he would like to try his hand at the greatest Western thrill of all.   10

"What's the greatest Western thrill of all?" asks Smith.   11

"Kill Indians," says Greene.   12

"Kill Indians?" says Smith. "Is that legal?"   13

Sure, Greene assures him, "White man been doing it for years."   14

So Greene gets Mel Gibson to dress up like a Dead Indian, and the grand duke   *15*
gets to shoot him. The greatest Western thrill of all? You bet.

And you don't necessarily have to head west to find Dead Indians. In one of   *16*
Monty Python's skits, a gas official comes into a British household with a dead
Indian slung over his shoulder. The Indian, who isn't quite dead, turns out to be part
of the special deal the homeowner got when he bought a new stove. The free dead
Indian was "in the very small print," says the gas man, "so as not to affect the sales."

On the other hand, if you like the West and are the outdoors type, you can run   *17*
out to Wyoming and pedal your bicycle over Dead Indian Pass, spend the evening at
Dead Indian campground, and in the morning cycle across Dead Indian Meadows
on your way to Dead Indian Peak. If you happen to be in California, you can hike
Dead Indian Canyon. And if you're an angler, you can fish Dead Indian Creek in
Oregon or Dead Indian Lake in Oklahoma, though the U.S. Board on Geographic
Names recently voted to rename it Dead Warrior Lake.

Sometimes you can only watch and marvel at the ways in which the Dead   *18*
Indian has been turned into products: Red Chief Sugar, Calumet Baking Soda, the
Atlanta Braves, Big Chief Jerky, Grey Owl Wild Rice, Red Man Tobacco, the Chicago
Blackhawks, Mutual of Omaha, Winnebago Motor Homes, Big Chief Tablet, Indian
motorcycles, the Washington Redskins, American Spirit cigarettes, Jeep Cherokee,
the Cleveland Indians, and Tomahawk missiles.

Probably the most egregious example is Crazy Horse Malt Liquor, a drink that   *19*
one reviewer enthusiastically described as "smooth, slightly fruity with an extremely
clean, almost Zinfandel finish that holds together all the way to the dregs of the
bottle. Personally we think the chief should be proud." That the Hornell Brewing
Company would even think of turning the great Oglala leader into a bottle of
booze should come as no surprise. Corporate North America had already spun the
Ottawa leader Pontiac into a division of General Motors, the Apache into an attack
helicopter, and the Cherokee into a line of clothing and accessories.

I once bought a pair of Cherokee underpants that I was going to send to my   *20*
brother as a joke, but by the time I got them home and looked at them again, they
had become more embarrassing than funny.

One of my favourite Dead Indian products is Land O' Lakes butter, which   *21*
features an Indian Maiden in a buckskin dress on her knees holding a box of butter
at bosom level. The wag who designed the box arranged it so that if you fold the box
in a certain way, the Indian woman winds up *au naturel*, sporting naked breasts.
Such a clever fellow.

Of course, all of this is simply a new spin on old notions. The medicine   *22*
shows that toured the West in the eighteenth and early-nineteenth centuries used
Aboriginal iconography and invention to sell Dead Indian elixirs and liniments,
such as Kickapoo Indian Sagwa, a "blood, liver and stomach renovator," Dr. Morse's
Indian Root Pills, Dr. Pierce's Golden Medical Discovery, featuring the caption
"Used by the First Americans," White Beaver's Cough Cream, Ka-Ton-Ka, and Nez
Perce Catarrh Remedy.

All of this pales by comparison with the contemporary entrepreneurs who have   *23*
made a bull-market business out of Dead Indian culture and spirituality. Gone are
the bogus potions and rubs that marked the earlier snake oil period. They have been
replaced by books that illuminate an alternative Dead Indian reality, by workshops
that promise an authentic Dead Indian experience, by naked therapy sessions in
a sweat lodge or a tipi that guarantee to expand your consciousness and connect
you to your "inner Dead Indian." Folks such as Lynn Andrews, Mary Summer
Rains, Jamie Samms, Don Le Vie, Jr., and Mary Elizabeth Marlow, just to mention
some of the more prominent New Age spiritual CEOs, have manufactured fictional
Dead Indian entities—Agnes Whistling Elk, Ruby Plenty Chiefs, No Eyes, Iron
Thunderhorse, Barking Tree, and Max the crystal skull—who supposedly taught
them the secrets of Native spirituality. They have created Dead Indian narratives
that are an impossible mix of Taoism, Buddhism, Druidism, science fiction, and
general nonsense, tied together with Dead Indian ceremony and sinew to give their
product provenance and validity, along with a patina of exoticism.

In the late nineteenth century, Kickapoo Indian Sagwa sold for fifty cents   *24*
a bottle. Today's Indian snake oil is considerably more expensive. In her article
"Plastic Shamans and Astroturf Sun Dances: New Age Commercialization of
Native American Spirituality," Lisa Aldred makes note of someone called Singing
Pipe Woman, in Springdale, Washington, who advertises a two-week retreat with a
Husichol woman priced at $2,450. A quick trip to the Internet will turn up an outfit
offering a one-week "Canyon Quest and Spiritual Warrior Training" course for
$850 and an eight-night program called "Vision Quest," in the tradition of someone
called Stalking Wolf, "a Lipan Apache elder" who has "removed all the differences"
of the vision quest, "leaving only the simple, pure format that works for everyone."
There is no fee for this workshop, though a $300-$350 donation is recommended.
Stalking Wolf, by the way, was supposedly born in 1873, wandered the Americas in
search of spiritual truths, and finally passed all his knowledge on to Tom Brown, Jr.,
a seven-year-old White boy whom he met in New Jersey. Evidently, Tom Brown, Jr.,

or his protégés, run the workshops, having turned Stalking Wolf's teachings into a Dead Indian franchise.

From the frequency with which Dead Indians appear in advertising, in the   *25*
names of businesses, as icons for sports teams, as marketing devices for everything from cleaning products to underwear, and as stalking goats for New Age spiritual flimflam, you might think that Native people were a significant target for sales. We're not, of course. We don't buy this crap. At least not enough to support such a bustling market. But there's really no need to ask whom Dead Indians are aimed at, is there?

All of which brings us to Live Indians.   *26*

Reading for Better Writing

Working by yourself or with a group, answer these questions:

1. What is your own relationship with Aboriginal culture? How does Thomas King's exploration of "Dead Indians" complicate that relationship?

2. By the time you reached the end of King's essay, what had the phrase "Dead Indians" come to mean to you? Point to specific passages that led to that conclusion.

3. In paragraphs 1–4, King begins his exploration of "Dead Indians" by complicating the phrase: placing it beside other categories, "Live" and "Legal" Indians; offering a definition that goes beyond the literal; and introducing the concept of the simulacrum. Reread these paragraphs, and then explain how these complications work to deepen your understanding of "Dead Indians."

4. Throughout this piece, King uses anecdotes and examples to illustrate his definition of "Dead Indians." What kinds of anecdotes and examples does he use? How does he present them? What does he make of them?

5. King's style in this piece is vibrant. How would you characterize his style? Consider his tone of voice, his sentence patterns, even his paragraphing— locating specific examples. What does this style contribute to King's definition of "Dead Indians"?

Writing Guidelines

Planning

1. Select a topic. Beneath headings like these, list words that you'd like to explore:

- Words related to an art or sport
- Words that are (or should be) in the news
- Words that are overused, un-used, or abused
- Words that make you laugh or worry
- Words that do (or don't) describe you

Tip: The best topics are abstract nouns *(gullibility, forgiveness)*, complex terms *(code blue, asceticism)*, or words connected to a personal experience *(excellence, Dead Indians)*.

2. Identify what you know. To discern what you already know about the topic, write freely about the word, letting your writing go where it chooses. Explore both your personal and your academic connections with the word.

3. Gather information. To find information about the word's history, usage, and grammatical form, use strategies such as these:

- **Consult a general dictionary**, preferably an unabridged dictionary; list both denotative (literal) and connotative (associated) meanings for the word.
- **Consult specialized dictionaries** that define words from specific disciplines or occupations: music, literature, law, medicine, and so on.
- If helpful, **interview experts** on your topic.
- **Check reference resources** such as *Bartlett's Familiar Quotations* to see how famous speakers and writers have used the word.
- **Research the word's etymology and usage** by consulting appropriate Web sources such as dictionary.com, merriam-webster.com, or xrefer.com.
- **Do a general search on the Web** to see where the word pops up in titles of songs, books, or films; company names, products, and ads; nonprofit organizations' names, campaigns, and programs; and topics in the news.
- **List synonyms** (words meaning the same—or nearly the same) and antonyms (words meaning the opposite).

4. Compress what you know. Based on your freewriting and research, try writing a formal, one-sentence definition that satisfies the following equation:

Equation: Term = larger class + distinguishing characteristics

Examples: Swedish pimple = fishing lure + silver surface, tubular body, three hooks
melodrama = stage play + flat characters, contrived plot, moralistic theme
Alzheimer's = dementia + increasing loss of memory, hygiene, social skills

5. Get organized. To organize the information that you have, and to identify details that you may want to add, fill out a graphic organizer like the ones on pages 54–55.

Drafting

6. Draft the essay. Review your outline as needed to write the first draft.

- **Get the reader's attention and introduce the term.** If you are organizing the essay from general to specific, consider using an anecdote, an illustration, or a quotation to set the context. If you are organizing the essay from specific to general, consider including an interesting detail from the word's history or usage. When using a dictionary definition, avoid the dusty phrase "According to *Webster* . . . "
- **Show your readers precisely what the word means.** Build the definition in paragraphs that address distinct aspects of the word: common definitions, etymology, usage by professional writers, and so on. Link paragraphs so that the essay unfolds the word's meaning layer by layer.
- **Review your main point and close your essay.** You might, for example, conclude by encouraging readers to use—or not use—the word.

Revising

7. Improve the ideas, organization, and voice. Ask a classmate or someone from the writing centre to read your essay for the following:

____ **Ideas:** Is each facet of the definition **clear**, showing precisely what the word does and does not mean? Is the definition **complete**, telling the reader all that she or he needs to know in order to understand and use the word?

____ **Organization:** Does the **opening** identify the word and set the context for what follows? Are the **middle** paragraphs cohesive, each offering a unit of information? Does the **closing** wrap up the message and refocus on the word's core meaning?

____ **Voice:** Is the voice informed, engaging, instructive, and courteous?

Editing

8. Edit the essay by addressing these issues:

____ **Words:** The words are precise and clear to the essay's readers.

____ **Sentences:** The sentences are complete, varied in structure, and readable.

____ **Correctness:** The copy includes no errors in spelling, usage, punctuation, grammar, or mechanics.

____ **Design:** The page design is correctly formatted and attractive.

Publishing

9. Publish the essay. Share your writing with interested readers, including friends, family, and classmates. Submit the essay to your instructor.

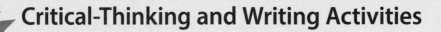

Critical-Thinking and Writing Activities

As directed by your instructor, complete the following activities.

1. Malcolm Bradbury claims that "[c]ulture is a way of coping with the world by defining it in detail." Based on your reading of the essays in this chapter, explore how Bradbury's statement makes sense of what definition does.

2. Review "The Gullible Family" and think of a word that similarly defines you. Research the word and write an essay that defines the term.

3. In "Forgiveness," June Callwood defines an abstract ethical concept with an eye to convincing readers to embrace that ethic. Consider other ethical concepts that you find significant. Choose one, research it, and write an extended definition that similarly encourages readers to follow or reject that ethic.

4. In Paige Louter's "Hipsters and Hobos: Asceticism for a New Generation" and Thomas King's "Dead Indians," the writers explore culturally significant terms, terms with a complicated present meaning and important historical roots. Think of similarly loaded terms from areas of contemporary culture with which you are familiar (e.g., gender identity, generational differences, politics, entertainment, technology), and write an essay that explores that term's contemporary meaning in historical context.

5. Consider your field of study or a field that interests you. Write an essay defining a word or phrase that is understood by people in that field but not by "outsiders." Write for the audience of outsiders.

Learning-Objectives Checklist ✓

Have you achieved this chapter's learning objectives? Check your progress with the items below, revisiting topics in the chapter as needed. *I have...*

___ carefully examined the qualities of effective brief and extended definitions (168–169).

___ investigated how writers' consideration of their situations helps them focus and refine their definitions (168–169).

___ researched and analyzed a word's roots, prefix, suffix, denotations, connotations, etymology, and usage (186–187).

___ developed well-reasoned, research-based, brief and extended definitions (186–187).

___ critiqued others' writing and my own for logical fallacies such as oversimplification, half-truths, ambiguity, and slanted language (317–320).

___ utilized enriching anecdotes, quotations, comparisons, and contrasts, along with smooth transitions leading into and out of these passages (186–187).

___ evaluated the quality of my ideas, organization, and voice, revising and editing where needed (186–187).

Chapter 11

Classification

Classification is an organizational strategy that helps writers make sense of large or complex sets of things. A writer using this strategy breaks the topic into individual items or members that can be sorted into clearly distinguishable groups or categories. For example, if writing about the types of residents who live in assisted-care facilities, a nursing student might classify them according to various physical and/or mental limitations.

By sorting residents in this way, the writer can discuss them as individuals, as representatives of a group, or as members of the body as a whole. By using an additional strategy such as comparison-contrast, she or he can show both similarities and differences between individuals within a group, or between one group and another.

Visually Speaking   Study the photograph below. What does it suggest about the challenges and benefits of classifying things?

Learning **Objectives**

By working through this chapter, you will be able to

- interpret and critique writers' use of classification reasoning.
- devise a classification plan that aligns with your writing situation.
- create a logical grouping scheme that includes clear criteria for sorting.
- utilize a classification grid to identify your topic's components and to sort them into groups.
- compose an analytical essay using primarily classification reasoning (with other analytical strategies, as needed).

Baloncici/Shutterstock.com

fig. 11.1

Strategies for Classification Essays

In writing rooted in classification, you create logical categories into which people, places, things, or concepts can be grouped. Categorization makes sense of a body of information by showing how members of the group are both related and differentiated. Classification, then, can reveal something about the overarching structure of the whole, the nature of a particular category, or the distinctive features of one member of the group.

The Rhetorical Situation

Consider the context in which writers use classification reasoning:

- **Purpose:** Writers classify a body of information to explain its order, to clarify relationships, and to "locate" specific items within a larger structure. For example, in her essay, "Latin American Music . . ." (pages 195–197), Kathleen Kropp's purpose is to explain how the many types of Latin American music reflect Latinos' cultural identity and impact social change.
- **Readers:** While readership can vary greatly, writers using classification are seeking to illuminate the deeper order of a topic, either to enhance readers' understanding or to support an argument. For example, Kropp's criteria for classifying types of Latin American music help her readers (other students) understand the history and cultural impact of Latinos' diverse forms of music.
- **Topic:** Writers typically use classification with topics that include a complex body of individual items. For example, Kropp's topic is the nature and function of Latin American music—thousands of songs. To address the topic, she sorts the songs into four categories that clarify music's diverse roles in Latino culture.

Principles of Classification Writing

Classification writing depends on the principles that follow.

Establishing clear criteria for grouping. Given his or her purpose for classifying, the writer finds a basis or standard for categorizing items. This standard becomes the "common denominator" for the ordering scheme. For example, trees could be grouped as follows:

- **Size:** types of trees grouped by height categories
- **Geography:** trees common to different areas, zones, or elevations
- **Structure or composition:** division by leaf type (deciduous vs. coniferous)
- **Purpose:** windbreak trees, shade trees, flowering trees, fruit trees, etc.

Creating a logical and orderly classification scheme. These guidelines apply:

- As they sort items into groups, writers seek . . .

  - **consistency**—applying the same sorting criterion in the same way.
  - **exclusivity**—creating groups that are distinct and do not overlap.
  - **completeness**—fitting all elements from a larger group into the subgroups with no elements left over.

- To keep the classification structure manageable, writers usually limit the number of main categories to six.
- Subcategories distinguish the elements that comprise a category. To further distinguish elements within the whole, subcategories can be broken into smaller groups. See Figure 11.2.
- When explaining the classification scheme, writers present the categories and subcategories in a logical order, selecting a sequence that will help readers digest the overall scheme and see connections and differences between categories.
- Sometimes, writers complement their discussion with graphics (tables, charts, diagrams) that help readers understand the overall scheme and individual categories.
- When classifying ideas or theoretical practices, writers might illustrate each. For example, in her classification essay on pages 195–197, Kathleen Kropp illustrates different types of Latino music by quoting from specific songs.

fig. 11.2

Sample Classification Paragraph

Writers may write a classification paragraph to organize their topic and put it in a larger context. In the paragraph below, Jessica Ten Haken uses classification to explain the theory of temperament as part of a history essay on medieval medicine.

> Medieval doctors believed that "four temperaments rule mankind wholly." According to this theory, each person has a distinctive temperament or personality (sanguine, phlegmatic, melancholy, or choleric) based on the balance of four elements in the body, a balance peculiar to the individual. The theory was built on Galen's and Hippocrates' notion of "humors," which stated that the body contains blood, phlegm, black bile, and yellow bile—four fluids that maintain the balance within the body. The sanguine person was dominated by blood, associated with fire: Blood was hot and moist, and the person was fat and prone to laughter. The phlegmatic person was dominated by phlegm (associated with earth) and was squarish and slothful—a sleepy type. The melancholy person was dominated by cold, black bile (connected with the element of water) and as a result was pensive, peevish, and solitary. The choleric person was dominated by hot, yellow bile (air) and thus was inclined to anger.

Copyright © Jessica Ten Haken.

Reading Classification Writing

As you read the essays on the following pages, consider these questions:

1. Does the writer explain the classification scheme, and is this reasoning logical, given his or her topic and purpose? Explain.
2. Are the number of categories sufficient, given the size and diversity of the topic?
3. Are the categories consistent, exclusive, and complete? Explain.
4. Are the categories presented in a clear, logical order?
5. What specific insights does the classification create?

Sample Classification Essays

Specialists in a discipline will commonly use classification—along with technical terminology—to analyze a topic for readers familiar with the discipline. However, as shown in the essays in this chapter, writers can also use classification and nontechnical language to communicate with readers.

Analyzing Weightlifters

As an analytical mode, classification can be used to make sense of human behaviour. In the following essay, student writer Hillary Gammons classifies the types of people she met while working out in a university weight room.

Essay Outline

Introduction: combatting the "freshman fifteen" by going to the weight room
1. Some students lift weights as part of an exercise program directed toward health.
2. Other students lift to tone muscles.
3. Athletes lift weights as part of training for their sports.
4. Bodybuilders lift to create muscle bulk for strength and show.

Closing: limits of the categories, but success with the "freshman fifteen"

Why We Lift

The writer provides a personal introduction to the topic, gives her criterion for classifying (why students lift), and identifies the categories.

I had heard rumors about it before I ever left for college, and once I moved into the dorm, I realized it was not just a rumor. I needed a way to combat the "freshman fifteen," that dreaded poundage resulting from a combination of late-night pizzas, care-package cookies, and cafeteria cheesecakes. So, my roommate and I headed to the university gym, where the weight-training rooms are filled with student "chain gangs" sweating and clanging their way through a serious of mechanical monsters. As I looked around, it became obvious that people work out for quite different reasons. Health enthusiasts, toning devotees, athletes, and bodybuilders seem to be the main categories of those lifting weights.

Each category of lifter is described in turn.

Some students lift weights as part of an exercise program aimed at maintaining or improving health. They have heard how strong abdominals reduce lower-back problems. They have learned that improved flexibility can help to

From Vandermey. The College Writer, IE. © 2004 Cengage Learning

reduce tension buildup and prevent headaches and other problems related to prolonged periods of sitting or studying. They know that combining weights with aerobic exercise is an efficient way to lose weight. A person who exercises can lose weight while continuing to eat well because increased muscle mass burns more calories. Typical weight-lifting routines for health enthusiasts are around 20 minutes, three times a week.

The toners' routine is different because they want smoothly defined muscles. Not surprisingly, this group includes many young women. Lifting weights can target problem spots and help shape up the body. To develop solid arms, these people use dumbbells and a bench press. Other equipment focuses on achieving toned legs, abdominals, and buttocks. Toning workouts must be done more often than three times a week. I talked to a few young women who lift weights (after aerobic activity of some kind) for about 30 minutes, five times a week.

Athletes also lift weights. Volleyball, rowing, basketball, football—all of these sports require weight training. It may seem obvious that a football player needs to be muscular and strong, but how do other athletes benefit from weight lifting? Muscles are a lot like brains: the more they are used, the more they can do. Strong muscles can increase a person's speed, flexibility, endurance, and coordination. Consider the competition required in various sports—different muscle groups matter more to different athletes. For example, while runners, especially sprinters, need bulging thighs for quick starts and speed, basketball players need powerful arms and shoulders for endless shots and passes. And while gymnasts want overall muscle strength for balance and coordination, football players develop the large muscles for strength, speed, and agility. For all members of this group, however, weight lifting is a vital part of their training.

One last group that cannot be ignored are the people who lift weights to become as big and as strong as possible. I worked out with a guy who is about 6 feet 2 inches and weighs more than 200 pounds. He bench-presses more than I weigh. In a room devoted to dumbbells and barbells (also known as free weights), bodybuilders roar bulk-boosting battle cries as they struggle to lift superheavy bars. After you spend only a short time in this grunt room, it is clear that the goal for

Paragraph topic sentences distinguish and relate the categories.

The writer explains the motivation of each group through observations, examples, and illustrations.

3

4

5

bodybuilders is not simply to be healthy, toned, or strong. These lifters want muscles for both strength and show—muscles that lift and bulge. For this reason, many participants spend little time on aerobic activity and most of their time lifting very heavy weights that build bulk and strength. My partner works out for an hour or more, five days a week.

Not everyone fits neatly into these four categories. I work out to be healthy and toned, and find that I can benefit from lifting only three times a week. Weight lifting has become more and more popular among college students who appreciate exercise as a great stress reliever. And for me, the gym proves to be the best place to combat that dreaded "freshman fifteen."

6

The conclusion, like the opening, includes a personal note.

Reading for Better Writing

Working by yourself or with a group, answer these questions:

1. Hillary Gammons opens and closes her essay by describing her own interest in weight lifting. What are the strengths and limitations of this approach?

2. The writer classifies weight lifters according to their reasons for lifting. Does this criterion effectively organize the topic? What other criteria could be used, for what purposes?

3. The essay moves from health enthusiasts to toners to athletes to bodybuilders. Is there a particular logic to this sequence? Would a different order have created a different essay?

4. Based on your own knowledge of the topic, does the essay accurately describe the people who work out in a weight room? In other words, is the classification consistent, exclusive, and complete? Explain.

Analyzing Forms of Music

In the essay below, student writer Kathleen Kropp uses classification strategies to describe the nature of Latin American music and to explain how the music both reflects and affects Latin American culture.

Title: the larger topic and the classification theme

Latin American Music: A Diverse and Unifying Force

Introduction: Latin American music's unifying power

On September 20, 2009, Latin pop, rock, and salsa rhythms danced through the air in Havana's Plaza de la Revolución as more than one million people gathered to witness Paz Sin Fronteras II (Peace Without Borders II). These benefit concerts brought together performers from Cuba, Puerto Rico, Ecuador, and Venezuela. Juanes, a popular Colombian singer who headlined the concerts, explained the event's passion and power like this: "Music becomes an excuse to send a message that we're all here together building peace, that we are here as citizens and this is what we want, and we have to be heard" (Hispanic 17). His statement demonstrates Latinos' belief that their music has the power to unify Latin American people, synthesize their cultural activities, and address their diverse needs. To understand how the music (which is as diverse as Latin America's people) can do this, it is helpful to sort the many forms of music into four major types and consider what each type contributes to Latin American society.

1 Indigenous music

One type is indigenous music, a group of musical forms that connect the human and the spiritual. Archeological evidence indicates that indigenous musical cultures of the Americas began over 30,000 years ago. Over time the first instruments, which were stone and clay sound-producing objects, evolved into wind instruments such as flutes and windpipes. An example of indigenous music connecting the human and spiritual is found among Aymara-speaking musicians in the Lake Titicaca Region of Peru. The people of this region use music to mesh pre-Columbian agricultural rites with current Catholic practices. For instance, during feasts such as the annual Fiesta de la Candelaria (Candlemas Feast), celebrants use Sicus (panpipes), pincullos (vertical duct flutes), cajas (drums), chants, dances, and costumes—in combination with Catholic symbolism—to celebrate the gift of staple crops such as corn and potatoes (Indigenous 328, 330).

2 Iberian and Mestizo (mixed) folk music

A second type, Iberian and Mestizo (mixed) folk music, enrich Latinos' everyday lives in a variety of forms, including liturgical music, working songs, and mariachi tunes. For example, whereas the traditional Catholic mass featured organ music, more recent Catholic services such as the Nicaraguan Peasant Mass use the acoustic guitar along with the colorful sounds of the marimba, maracas, and melodies from popular festivals. As a result, worshipers find the music inviting and the passionate lyrics (which can cite issues of economic or political injustice) socially relevant.

1

2

3

Another form of folk music known as tonadas (or tunes) are used as serenades *4* and working songs. For example, in Venezuela, workers might whistle or sing tonadas while milking, plowing, or fishing (Tonadas). These vocal duets, which also can be accompanied by guitar, have pleasant harmonies, two main melodies, and faster tempos ("Iberian and mestizo folk music" 338, 341).

The mariachi band, a final form of folk music, adds festivity to Mexicans' *5* many celebrations. With its six to eight violins, two trumpets, and a guitar, the band creates a vibrant, engaging sound. During birthdays or feast days, these bands commonly set up on streets and below windows where they awaken the residents above to the sounds of "Las Mañ Anitas," the traditional song for such days. Mariachis are also hired for baptisms, weddings, quinceañeras (the fifteenth birthday for a Mexican girl), patriotic holidays, and funerals (History of the Mariachi).

3 Afro-American music

Afro-American music, the third type of Latin American music, infuses *6* passion and power in its percussion-driven dances and complex rhythm structures. These songs and dances, performed throughout the Caribbean, function as an entertaining, unifying force among Latin people ("Afro-American" 345-6). The energy of Afro-American music is clear in genres such as the mambo and the rumba dances. The rumba, an Afro-Caribbean dance, is highly improvisational and exciting. The quinto (a high-pitched drum) establishes a dialogue with a solo voice and challenges the male dancer, while the tumbadora and palitos (sticks on woodblock) provide a contrast with regular, unchanging rhythm patterns.

The mambo, an Afro-Cuban dance, became popular in Havana, Cuba. In the *7* 1940s, nightclubs throughout Latin America caught the energy of this fast tempo song and dance. Arsenio Rodríguez' "Bruca Managuá" exemplifies this form. Because of the song's sound and lyrics, many black Cubans consider the piece to be an anthem of Afro-Cuban pride and resistance:

> I am Calabrí, black by birth/nation, *8*
> Without freedom, I can't live, *9*
> Too much abuse, the body is going to die. *10*
> (*Oxford Encyclopedia for Latinos and Latinas in the United States.* 218) *11*

4 Urban popular music

Urban popular music, the fourth type of Latin American music, combines *12* a dynamic sound with poignant appeals for social change, appeals that resonate with many listeners. The styles of this type of music include rock, heavy metal, punk, hip-hop, jazz, reggae, and R&B. During the September 20, 2009 Paz Sin Fronteras II concerts described earlier, urban popular music was common fare. As U.S. representative Jim McGovern observed, the message of the concerts was to "circumvent politics . . . using the medium of music to speak directly to young people, to change their way of thinking, and leave behind the old politics, hatred, prejudices, and national enmities that have locked too many people in patterns of conflict, violence, poverty, and despair. It is an attempt to break down barriers and ask people to join in common purpose" (Paz Sin Fronteras II). Popular urban musicians such as Juanes utilize music not only to entertain but also to unite Latinos in a universal cause.

Conclusion: passion and power of Latin American music and culture

Passion and power permeate all of Latin America's music. The four major types of music—indigenous, Iberian and Mestizo folk, Afro-American, and popular urban—are as diverse as the people of Latin America, and each style serves a valued need or function in Latinos' everyday lives. As a result, those listening to Latin American music—whether it is a Peruvian Indian's chant, a Venezuelan farmer's whistled tune, a Cuban mambo drummer's vivacious beat, or the Bogotá rock concert's compelling rhythms—are hearing much more than music. They are hearing the passion and power of the Latin American people.

13

Note: The Works-Cited page is not shown. For examples, see MLA (page 533) and APA (pages 562–563).

Reading for Better Writing

Working by yourself or with a group, answer these questions:

1. Review the opening in which Kathleen Kropp introduces her topic, thesis, and choice to sort the music into four categories. Then explain (a) why the passage is clear or unclear, (b) whether sorting forms into categories seems necessary or helpful, and (c) how Kropp's sorting scheme helps her develop her thesis.

2. Cite three strategies that Kropp uses to distinguish the four types of music and the various forms within those groups. Are the strategies effective? Why?

3. Identify language that Kropp uses to help you imagine the tone and tenor of the music. Is the word choice helpful? Why?

4. Review the instructions at the bottom of page 204 regarding the three guidelines for creating a logical classification scheme: consistency, exclusivity, and completeness. Then analyze Kropp's classification scheme and explain why it does or does not exemplify the three guidelines.

5. Review the third bulleted instruction on page 205: "[W]riters present the categories and subcategories in a logical order, selecting a sequence that will help readers digest the overall scheme and see connections and differences between categories." Then explain how Kropp's sequence for presenting categories does or does not help readers understand her argument.

6. In the last sentence, Kropp re-states—and re-phrases—her thesis. Review the sentence: Is it an effective closing? Why or why not?

7. Reflect on your own musical tastes. What types of music do you listen to, and why? How has Kropp's exploration of Latin American music impacted your music appreciation?

Analyzing Rhetorical Positions on Climate Change

Stewart Brand, author of *Whole Earth Discipline: An Ecopragmatist Manifesto,* published this essay in December 2009. In the piece, he argues that the climate-change debate is better understood as advocating four main perspectives—not two.

Four Sides to Every Story

The writer introduces his topic and thesis.

Climate talks have been going on in Copenhagen for a week now, and it appears to be a two-sided debate between alarmists and skeptics. But there are actually four different views of global warming. A taxonomy of the four:

He distinguishes the four viewpoints with descriptive names.

DENIALISTS They are loud, sure and political. Their view is that climatologists and their fellow travelers are engaged in a vast conspiracy to panic the public into following an agenda that is political and pernicious. Senator James Inhofe of Oklahoma and the columnist George Will wave the banner for the hoax-callers.

A hyperlink helps readers access the speech.

"The claim that global warming is caused by man-made emissions is simply untrue and not based on sound science," Mr. Inhofe declared in a 2003 speech to the Senate about the Kyoto accord that remains emblematic of his position. "CO_2 does not cause catastrophic disasters—actually it would be beneficial to our environment and our economy. . . . The motives for Kyoto are economic, not environmental—that is, proponents favor handicapping the American economy through carbon taxes and more regulations."

The writer names and describes the second group.

SKEPTICS This group is most interested in the limitations of climate science so far: they like to examine in detail the contradictions and shortcomings in climate data and models, and they are wary about any "consensus" in science. To the skeptics' discomfort, their arguments are frequently quoted by the denialists.

He offers examples illustrating the group's viewpoint.

In this mode, Roger Pielke, a climate scientist at the University of Colorado, argues that the scenarios presented by the United Nations Intergovernmental Panel on Climate Change are overstated and underpredictive. Another prominent skeptic is the physicist Freeman Dyson, who wrote in 2007: "I am opposing the holy brotherhood of climate model experts and the crowd of deluded citizens who believe the numbers predicted by the computer models. . . . I have studied the climate models and I know what they can do. The models solve the equations of fluid dynamics, and they do a very good job of describing the fluid motions of the atmosphere and the oceans. They do a very poor job of describing the clouds, the dust, the chemistry and the biology of fields and farms and forests."

The quotation relays the speaker's argument and tone.

WARNERS These are the climatologists who see the trends in climate headed toward planetary disaster, and they blame human production of greenhouse gases as the primary culprit. Leaders in this category are the scientists James Hansen, Stephen Schneider and James Lovelock. (This is the group that most persuades me and whose views I promote.)

The writer names and describes the third group.

"If humanity wishes to preserve a planet similar to that on which civilization developed and to which life on earth is adapted," Mr. Hansen wrote as the lead author of

1

2

3

4

5

6

7

Torian/Shutterstock.com

A hyperlink helps readers access the paper.

an influential 2008 paper, then the concentration of carbon dioxide in the atmosphere would have to be reduced from 395 parts per million to "at most 350 p.p.m."

The writer identifies the fourth group.

CALAMATISTS There are many environmentalists who believe that industrial civilization has committed crimes against nature, and retribution is coming. They quote the warners in apocalyptic terms, and they view denialists as deeply evil. The technology critic Jeremy Rifkin speaks in this manner, and the writer-turned-activist Bill McKibben is a (fairly gentle) leader in this category.

He quotes McKibben and cites the source.

In his 2006 introduction for *The End of Nature*, his famed 1989 book, Mr. McKibben wrote of climate change in religious terms: "We are no longer able to think of ourselves as a species tossed about by larger forces—now we are those larger forces. Hurricanes and thunderstorms and tornadoes become not acts of God but acts of man. That was what I meant by the 'end of nature.'"

He compares two groups and contrasts them with two others.

The calamatists and denialists are primarily political figures, with firm ideological loyalties, whereas the warners and skeptics are primarily scientists, guided by ever-changing evidence. That distinction between ideology and science not only helps clarify the strengths and weaknesses of the four stances, it can also be used to predict how they might respond to future climate developments.

The writer distinguishes the groups by projecting how they might respond to good news or bad news.

If climate change were to suddenly reverse itself (because of some yet undiscovered mechanism of balance in our climate system), my guess is that the denialists would be triumphant, the skeptics would be skeptical this time of the apparent good news, the warners would be relieved, and the calamatists would seek out some other doom to proclaim.

If climate change keeps getting worse, then I would expect denialists to grasp at stranger straws, many skeptics to become warners, the warners to start pushing geoengineering schemes like sulfur dust in the stratosphere, and the calamatists to push liberal political agendas—just as the denialists said they would.

8

9

10

11

12

Reading for Better Writing

Working by yourself or with a group, answer these questions:

1. Identify Stewart Brand's thesis. How does his classification thinking make sense of the topic?

2. Cite three strategies that he uses to distinguish the four viewpoints. Do you find these strategies effective? Why or why not?

3. Identify two of Brand's claims, describe how he supports each claim, and then explain why that support is or is not convincing (for information about claims, see pages 312–316).

4. Reflect on your own beliefs about climate change. Does Brand's classification help you position yourself?

5. Brand wrote this essay in 2009. Have recent years seen a change in the climate change debate? How would you update Brand's discussion?

Analyzing Hockey as a Sport

Adam Gopnik was born in Philadelphia but raised in Montreal, where he attended McGill University. For more than twenty-five years, he has written for *The New Yorker*. He has also published collections of essays such as *Paris to the Moon* and *The Table Comes First*, as well as two children's novels. The excerpt below comes from "Recreational Winter," one of the Massey Lectures Gopnik delivered in 2011, published as *Winter: Five Windows on the Season*. In this excerpt, he discusses sports in relation to game theory, situating hockey among other sports. Note how Gopnik puts classification at the service of an argument about the greatness of hockey.

From Recreational Winter

As you read this essay, annotate it and take notes— identifying and exploring the classification strategies that Gopnik uses to build his argument.

All sports entertain us in part because of the thrill of watching a great athlete do what we can't, even if what he or she's doing is in part a mental exercise. Our empathetic engagement—what a close female friend of mine (whose uncle is actually in the Hockey Hall of Fame) calls "pitiful vicarious identification" or "the sad armchair act of pretending you're doing what you're actually watching"—with the players is key. But sports also entertain us as forms of drama. We get engaged, even in the absence of a single great player or performance, with the way the game tells a thrilling and unpredictable narrative woven by ten or twenty players at once. A great game is a great show, and it's also a great story. What makes those stories great is when they're unpredictable but not unjust—uncharted enough that there's no certainty of the result but organized enough that the result does not seem to be pure chance.

I think by now most of us have heard, however vaguely, something about the branch of mathematics called game theory. It's a way of understanding competitions that began with the great mathematician John von Neumann at the end of the 1940s and has since spread and conquered the world, or at least many academic disciplines, particularly economics and some of the more hard-ass parts of political science. Game theory attempts to mathematically capture behaviour in strategic situations, games, in which an individual's success in making choices depends on the choices of others. Anyone who has seen the movie *A Beautiful Mind* knows about John Nash and his equilibrium, and the more general notion that you can understand many social phenomena in the world if you see them as simple games rooted in guessing and outguessing your opponent's plans.

1

2

Adam Gopnik, excerpt from "Recreational Winter," *Winter: Five Windows on the Season* (2011 CBC Massey Lectures), p. 165–173. Copyright 2011 Adam Gopnik and Canadian Broadcasting Corporation. Reprinted with permission from House of Anansi Press.

The funny thing about game theory is that, though it has been used to explain everything from economics to nuclear warfare, it's very rarely used to explain *games*—or at least not sports. And yet when you think about it, part of the pleasure we take in sports has everything to do with game theory, which has exactly to do with questions of how much we know, how much our opponents know, how much they know of what we know, and so on.

I am far too innumerate to even attempt a rigorous analysis of this sort, but I do think it can be enlightening to play with a few of its key concepts. One concept opposes open-information (or perfect-information) games against ones with closed, or imperfect, information. Chess is probably the most famous instance of an open-information game. When you're playing chess, you have all the information the other player has; nothing is concealed from you, and so there are truly never any surprises in the strategic sense. There are no hidden rooks.

On the other hand, old-fashioned five-card draw poker is a completely hidden or closed-information game. You don't know what's in your opponent's hand, so you have to guess on the basis of their behaviour and your knowledge of their past playing patterns what they might be holding in their hand right now. It's a game of deduced intention but also of inferred information. The best games—the games that people seem to enjoy most—offer some kind of equilibrium between a small sum of hidden information and a larger sum of open information held in tension. In Texas hold-'em, the most popular of poker games, there are five shared cards—a lot of open information—and a crucial two cards' worth of closed information.

Team sports, which are both athletic contests and strategic ones, can be ranked along the same dimensions. Basketball, for instance, in some ways comes closest to being an open-information sport. Plays are limited, surprises are unimportant—no one basket is so significant that it is worth over-planning to achieve it, and even if you could, it wouldn't matter that much. What matters are trends, tendencies, and small tactical victories—real strategic surprise is relatively limited. The great basketball coach Phil Jackson ran his famous triangle offence with the Lakers, and with the Bulls before them. It requires tactical discipline, but the other team always knows what he's doing; it's a question of whether they can do it more efficiently and consistently than you can defense it. (The key event in basketball, foul shooting, is purely mechanical, and a matter, not trivial, of consistency alone.)

Pro football, on the other hand, is a good example of something closer to a *7* closed-information sport: you have a series of particular strategic plans that you invent in secret and that you then spring on your opponent. That's why football rewards coaches like the great Bill Walsh, whose genius was not for tactical stability but for strategic innovation and surprise—half the playing time is actually spent watching people plan in secret. In the '82 Super Bowl, Walsh pulled a single play, designed to freeze a Bengals linebacker, from his script for a winning touchdown. That he had a script is proof of the partly closed nature of the game. And baseball is more like hold-'em poker: everything's evident except the hole card of the pitch that's about to be thrown.

Now, hockey looks, when you watch it with an unpractised eye, like an *8* open-information sport. It looks like wild improvisation with no strategic plan underneath—a series of instinctive reactions to bouncing pucks and sliding players. (When people say they can't see the puck, I think what they really mean is that they can see it but they just can't see its *point*, its purpose in travelling. The game appears to be simply a brutal series of random collisions in which the invisible puck somehow sporadically ends up in the net.) But the more closely you observe the game, the more you see that it's kind of the Texas hold-'em of the world's spectator sports: there's a great deal that's open, but crucial elements are buried or cloaked and are revealed only afterwards to the eye of experience and deeper knowledge. There are hole cards in hockey, and some of the fun of being a fan is learning to look for them.

Some of this is plain in the inordinate effect a man with a plan can have on a *9* hockey team; the defensive system that Jacques Lemaire installed with the Devils could take a mediocre team and make it into a champion. The trap, or shell, is tedious but it's wonderfully effective, and unlike the triangle offence it's hidden, in the sense that it takes place so quickly, and demands so many rapid adjustments, that I have found even experienced hockey fans have a hard time describing the way it works. The tension between the obvious givens and hidden hole cards is true as well at a more granular level of the game.

Just think about the difference between taking a penalty in soccer and the *10* shootout in hockey. The penalty in soccer is something that academic game theorists have actually looked at in detail: what's the best technique, they ask, the optimal strategy for the shooter to pursue when he's got a penalty shot to take? It's a play of minds, because the goalkeeper has to anticipate what the shooter will do, and the shooter, the goalkeeper. Shoot left? Shoot right? High? Low? And the theorists have discovered that the optimal strategy is . . . just to blast away. The goal is so big and the goalkeeper so small that the shooter is much better off just blasting to the middle rather than trying to pick a corner.

So, predictably, the optimal strategy for the goalkeeper in the soccer shootout   11
is just to stay in place, not dive to either corner—though it's very hard for a goalkeeper to summon the discipline to do that. And so you have this situation in soccer where basically any kind of strategic planning doesn't pay. In the shootout in hockey, you have exactly the same confrontation between shooter and goalkeeper, but the shooter just blasting away or the goalie staying in place is never going to work. There are just too many dimensions in play—the shot takes place in depth and in motion, not from a fixed spot—and the odds between goalie and shooter are too closely matched. The shootout in hockey puts a premium on having a hole card: an idea, a strategy, a plan in advance, unknown to the opposition. And the goalie needs to respond to that kind of strategic initiative, that kind of creativity, with aggressive anticipation. The obvious play, which benefits you in a sport such as soccer, penalizes you in hockey.

Though it may seems as if the great goals in hockey history were chance events,   12
stray moments seized by opportunistic players, the truth is that as you understand the sport more deeply you can see that there is a kind of hidden strategic reservoir, almost a morality play, a *history*, behind every great goal in the game. When I think about the great goals that have been scored in hockey, the famous goals in my own lifetime, I see an element of historical pattern and strategic consequence in each of them. I think, for instance, of probably the most famous goal in my own fanship, the goal that Guy Lafleur scored in 1979 in the famous "too many men on the ice" game, the Montreal Canadiens and the Boston Bruins in the seventh game of the Stanley Cup semifinals. What's remarkable about that goal, if you watch it now, is not only that Lafleur takes a terrific shot but also how much else is going on around it, pointing towards past and future alike. Seeing it now, we're stunned by the sheer incompetence of Gilles Gilbert, the Boston goalie, who is playing a stand-up-and-kick style that now looks antediluvian—a very old-fashioned kind of upright goaltending whose futility, so evident on this shot, would make it extinct within a decade. The shot invalidates a style, not just a moment.

But one also notices that the man actually carrying the puck is Jacques Lemaire, *13* Lafleur's centre, and that Lemaire draws the defence towards him before he makes a quiet drop-pass to set up the shot. Now, Lemaire was only promoted to the top line after an up-and-down career as a one-dimensional player, famous for his heavy shot. (He in effect won the Stanley Cup eight years before, by taking a more or less random shot from centre ice that happened to stun and delude the Chicago Blackhawks goalie, Tony Esposito.) But in this case Lemaire doesn't take the shot, and we're reminded that Lemaire was schooled for five years by Scotty Bowman, the Canadiens coach, who patiently transformed him from an offensive-minded player into a defensive-minded player, first demoting him to the second line, then eventually putting him back on the first line after he understood the virtues of an all-over game. And it's Lemaire, as we've seen, who then takes Bowman's regimen and, in his years with the dull but effective New Jersey Devils, turns it into the modern trap, an ice-clogging reactive defensive game plan that demands more self-discipline than style. So the pass, in a sense, is more potent than the goal. What Lemaire has learned matters as much as what Lafleur has done—a whole history compressed into a back pass and a shot.

Part of the joy of understanding the game is being able to read it well enough to *14* spot when those pivotal moments take place. The fine hockey writer Michael Farber has analyzed Sidney Crosby's goal in the most recent Olympics in that spirit: six seconds that subsume twenty years. One could do the same with Mario Lemieux's great goal in the '87 Canada Cup—seeing, for instance, how in that goal Gretzky identified himself as primarily a playmaker, not a scorer—but it's enough to say for now that each of these goals is the result of a plan and history unknown to or beyond the control of the opposition, shared among the players through their common spatial intelligence, each taking place at such high speed that the plan is invisible to all but the tutored eye. Each is crucially significant to the outcome of the contest but is not the only such moment in the contest, and each has long-term consequences for the way the sport evolves.

Hockey approaches a more perfect balance between planning and reading, *15* idea and improvisation, than any other sport. Runs in baseball are information; in basketball, baskets are events; in soccer, goals are exclamations. But goals in hockey are *punctuation*—they end sentences that can be traced through phrases to make long chains of meaning. And so great goals, like great aphorisms, repay any amount of after-the-fact analysis. How did so much get packed into one phrase, or play? Ice hockey looks like a reflex, rapture sport but is really a rational, reasoned one. Spotting patterns amid the quick plunges is part of the fun. I often go to sleep at night running through great goals I have seen—there is a weighting towards the seventies Habs, but only because they were the greatest team of all time, not because I was a teenager then—and what astonishes me is that, no matter how often you rewind them, they still play back beautifully, and in your mind's eye (or on the YouTube screen) you always see more. Hockey offers drama at first viewing, meaning on the second, and learning on the third and fourth, even forty years on. The tradition that began a hundred years ago in Montreal, of a game that combined the collisions of rugby with the beauty of ice-skating, has, if only for a moment, been realized, and it lingers in your head.

Reading for Better Writing

Working by yourself or with a group, answer these questions:

1. Are you a hockey fan and/or a hockey player? How does Adam Gopnik's analysis of hockey impact your thinking about and relationship with the game?
2. Gopnik frames his discussion of hockey in relation to other sports by characterizing sports as a form of drama or story. What does this discussion add to his analysis of hockey?
3. In paragraphs 2–5, Gopnik introduces game theory, categorizes different kinds of games, and explores game theory in relation to different sports. What categories does he create, and how does he explain each category? What is the point of this classification of games and sports?
4. From paragraph 8 onward, Gopnik explores where and how hockey fits into this game-theory classification scheme. What essential point or argument is he making about hockey? What strategies does he use to build that argument? How does the latter part of this discussion return to the themes of the first paragraph?
5. How would you characterize Gopnik's style in this excerpt from his Massey Lecture? What do his tone and attitude add to the analysis?

Writing Guidelines

Planning

1. **Select a topic.** Start by writing a few general headings like the academic headings below; then list two or three related topics under each heading. Finally, pick a topic that is characterized by a larger set of items or members that can best be explained by ordering them into categories.

Engineering	Biology	Social Work	Education
Machines	Whales	Child welfare	Learning styles
Bridges	Fruits	organizations	Testing methods

fig. 11.3

2. **Look at the big picture.** Do preliminary research to get an overview of your topic. Review your purpose (to explain, persuade, inform, and so on), and consider which classification criteria will help you divide the subject's content into distinct, understandable categories.

3. **Choose and test your criterion.** Choose a criterion for creating categories. Make sure it produces groups that are *consistent* (the same criterion is used throughout the sorting process), *exclusive* (groups are distinct—no member fits into more than one group), and *complete* (each member fits into a subgroup with no member left over).

4. **Gather and organize information.** Gather information from reliable sources. To organize your information, take notes, possibly using a classification grid like the one shown below or the one on page 54. Set up the grid by listing the classification criteria down the left column and listing the groups in the top row of the columns. Then fill in the grid with appropriate details. (The grid below lists the classification criterion and groups discussed in "Latin American Music . . . ," pages 195–197.)

Classification Criteria	Group #1 Indigenous music	Group #2 Iberian and Mestizo	Group #3 Afro-American music	Group #4 Urban popular music
Historical qualities/functions	• Trait #1 • Trait #2 • Trait #3	• Trait #1 • Trait #2 • Trait #3	• Trait #1 • Trait #2 • Trait #3	• Trait #1 • Trait #2 • Trait #3

fig. 11.4

Note: If you do not use a grid, consider using an outline to organize your thoughts.

5. **Draft a thesis.** Draft a working thesis (you can revise it later as needed) that states your topic and identifies your classification scheme. Include language introducing your criteria for classifying groups.

Drafting

6. Draft the essay. Write your first draft, using organization planned in step 4.

- **Opening:** Get the readers' attention, introduce the subject and thesis, and give your criteria for dividing the subject into categories.
- **Middle:** Develop the thesis by discussing each category, explaining its traits, and showing how it is distinct from the other groups. For example, in the middle section of "Why We Lift," the writer sequences weightlifting categories logically from those who exercise to toners to athletes to bodybuilders. For each category, she identifies the lifters, explains their reasons for lifting, and describes the kind of workout they do.
- **Closing:** Reflect on and tie together the classification scheme. While the opening and middle of the essay separate the subject into distinct categories, the closing may bring the groups back together. For example, in "Latin American Music" (pages 195–197), Kathleen Kropp closes by emphasizing that all their forms of music express the spirit of Latin American people.

Revising

7. Improve the ideas, organization, and voice. Ask a classmate or someone from the writing centre to read your essay, looking for the following:

___ **Ideas:** Are the classification criteria logical and clear, resulting in categories that are consistent, exclusive, and complete? Does the discussion include appropriate examples that clarify the nature and function of each group?

___ **Organization:** Does the essay include (1) an engaging opening that introduces the subject, thesis, and criteria for classification, (2) a well-organized middle that distinguishes groups, shows why each group is unique, and supports these claims with evidence, and (3) a unifying conclusion that restates the main idea and its relevance?

___ **Voice:** Is the tone informed, courteous, and rational?

Editing

8. Edit the essay. Polish your writing by addressing these issues:

___ **Words:** The words distinguishing classifications are used uniformly.

___ **Sentences:** The sentences and paragraphs are complete, varied, and clear.

___ **Correctness:** No usage, grammatical, or mechanical errors are present.

___ **Page Design:** The design follows MLA, APA, CMS, or CSE formatting rules.

Publishing

9. Publish the essay by sharing it with your instructor and classmates, publishing it on your website, or submitting it to a print or online journal.

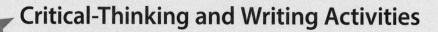

Critical-Thinking and Writing Activities

As directed by your instructor, complete the following activities.

1. Bergen Evans writes that "[w]ords are one of our chief means of adjusting to life." Reflect on this statement in relation to classification as illustrated in this chapter.

2. In "Why We Lift," Hillary Gammons categorizes students according to their motivation for weightlifting. Consider an activity that people engage and write a classification essay that makes sense of the diversity of people who do that activity.

3. In "Latin American Music: A Diverse and Unifying Force," Kathleen Kropp uses classification to analyze the nature and impact of an artform. Choose an artform that interests you, research the topic, and write an essay that uses classification to explain the artform's historical development and social impact.

4. In "Four Sides to Every Story," Steward Brand uses classification to show that the climate-change debate is more complex than a two-position argument. Select an argument that is erroneously presented as a two-option issue. Then research the topic and write a classification essay that accurately addresses the topic.

5. In his lecture "Recreational Winter," Adam Gopnik uses game theory to classify sports in order to construct an argument about the greatness of hockey. Try something similar with a topic that interests you, whether it be the greatness of a certain type of film, your appreciation for a certain piece of technology, or your preference for a certain kind of vacation. Create a classification scheme for that topic, and then put that scheme at the service of an argument.

Learning-Objectives Checklist ✓

Have you achieved this chapter's learning objectives? Check your progress with the items below, revisiting topics in the chapter as needed. *I have . . .*

_____ critically read others' classification essays, assessing their organizational schemes for consistency, exclusivity, and completeness (190–191).

_____ examined how these writers craft their analyses in accordance with their purposes, topics, and readers (190–191).

_____ evaluated my own writing situation and developed a classification framework that helped me analyze my topic as required in my writing assignment (206–207).

_____ devised a classification scheme with clear criteria for grouping (206–207).

_____ created and used a classification grid (1) to logically break down the topic into groups of components, (2) to explain why the groups are unified, complete, and distinct, and (3) to show how the groups together comprise one entity (206–207).

_____ used additional analytical strategies such as definition and compare-contrast to clarify similarities and differences between groups (206–207).

_____ drafted, revised, and edited an essay that effectively uses classification reasoning to analyze a topic and to present the analysis in clear, logical writing (206–207).

Chapter 12

Process

Process writing helps us understand our world and ourselves by answering interesting questions like these: How has surfing culture evolved over the decades? What has been the history of the Canadian government's relationship with Aboriginal peoples? How did Facebook's Timeline feature come to be, and what does it make of a person's life?

Writing that answers questions like these analyzes a process by breaking it down into steps, often grouping the steps into stages or phases. In addition to explaining the process, sometimes the writing also examines related causes and effects. Such papers are developed and formatted as essays, and the information in this chapter will help you read and write them. (Note: writing that explains how readers can complete a process typically takes the form of technical instructions.)

Visually Speaking Figure 12.1 captures a moment in a process. What is the process, and what writing strategies would you use to explain how to do the process?

Learning **Objectives**

By working through this chapter, you will be able to

- examine and assess writers' use of process reasoning.
- investigate a process so as to outline its nature and its workings.
- analyze the process, identifying its steps and related causes and effects.
- sequence the process chronologically, using transitions to link phases or steps.
- compose an analytical essay using primarily process thinking (with other analytical strategies, as needed).

Tyler Olson/Shutterstock.com

fig. 12.1

Strategies for Process Writing

Analyzing a process is an effort to explain how something happens, works, is made, or is done. The process may be natural (a phenomenon that occurs in nature, including human nature), performative (mechanical, something people do), or historical/cultural (events in time and/or within communities or groups).

The Rhetorical Situation

To put process writing in context, consider the situation that gives rise to it:

- **Purpose:** Writers write process essays in order to analyze and explain how an event or other phenomenon transpires. To that end, they first offer an overview of the process and then explain how each step leads logically to the next, and how all the steps together complete the process. (If the writer wants to help readers work through a process themselves, he or she writes instructions.)
- **Readers:** In all process writing, the text should meet the needs of all its readers, including those who know the least about the topic. To do this, writers should (1) include all the information that readers need, (2) use language that they understand, and (3) define unfamiliar or technical terms.
- **Topic:** In academic process writing, the topics are usually course-related phenomena that deepen the writer's knowledge of the field and offer readers insight into the time logic of the process. Topics addressed in professional publications should interest and educate their readers.

Example: In her essay "Wayward Cells" (pages 212–213), Kerry Mertz analyzes her **topic**: the process through which cancer cells overtake and destroy healthy cells. Her **purpose** is to help her **readers** (non-experts—other students and those without detailed technical knowledge) understand how and why the process occurs.

Principles of Process Writing

Analytical process writing should follow these principles:

Being clear and complete. Shape the analysis based on (1) how readers will use it, and (2) what they already know about it. Aim to deepen their current knowledge about how the process unfolds and what principles are at work.

Offering an overview. In order to understand individual parts of or moments in the process, readers generally need the big picture. Start, then, by explaining the process's essential principle, its goal, or its main product and/or result. That overview statement can often serve as the thesis statement. ***Example:*** *When a cell begins to function abnormally, it can initiate a process that results in cancer* (page 212).

Making the process manageable. A process essay unfolds effectively and clearly when the process is presented in manageable segments. First identify the process's major phases or stages (perhaps limiting these to three or four). Then break each stage into discrete steps or events, grouping actions in clear, logical ways.

Making the process familiar. To help readers understand the writing, use precise terms, well-chosen adjectives, and clear action verbs. Consider, as well, using comparisons for unfamiliar parts of the process, likening, for example, the growth of hair to the growth of grass (see "Hair Today, Gone Tomorrow" on page 31). Finally, design graphics such as flowcharts, time lines, or sequential drawings that display the process. (See the sample flowchart in Figure 12.2.)

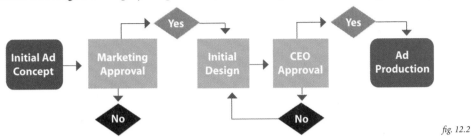

fig. 12.2

Signalling temporal relationships. Because process analysis is time related, readers need clear references to the order of events. Consider using terms such as *step, phase, stage;* transition words such as *first, second, next, finally;* or actual numbering systems (1, 2, 3).

Sample Process Paragraph

In the paragraph that follows, student writer Luke Sunukjian instructs readers in the process of entering the "tube," or "green room," while surfing. Note his attention to the clarity of the nouns and verbs that he uses.

> At this point you are slightly ahead of the barreling part of the wave, and you need to "stall," or slow yourself, to get into the tube. There are three methods of stalling used in different situations. If you are slightly ahead of the tube, you can drag your inside hand along the water to stall. If you are a couple of feet in front of the barrel, apply all your weight onto your back foot and sink the tail of the board into the water. This is known as a "tail stall" for obvious reasons, and its purpose is to decrease your board speed. If you are moving faster than the wave is breaking, you need to do what is called a "wrap-around." To accomplish this maneuver, lean back away from the wave while applying pressure on the tail. This shifts your forward momentum away from the wave and slows you down. When the wave comes, turn toward the wave and place yourself in the barrel.

Reading Process Writing

As you read process essays, consider these questions:

1. Does the essay identify the process, outline its stages, explain individual steps, and (if appropriate) discuss causes and effects?
2. Does the writer effectively state and support his or her claims?
3. Does the writer use precise language and define unfamiliar terms?
4. Are steps organized chronologically and clearly linked with transitions?
5. As a whole, what does the essay communicate about the nature and meaning of the process?

Sample Process Essays

This chapter contains four essays in which writers explain a process as part of an analysis. One author explains how cancer cells develop, another explains how surfing culture became popular, a third examines the history of government–Native relations in Canada, and the fourth examines the Timeline feature in Facebook.

Analyzing an Illness

Student writer Kerri Mertz wrote this essay to explain how cancer cells affect the body.

The title uses a metaphor for process.	**Wayward Cells**
	Imagine a room containing a large group of people all working hard toward the same goal. Each person knows his or her job, does it carefully, and cooperates with other group members. Together, they function smoothly—like a well-oiled machine.
The introduction uses a cells-workers analogy.	Then something goes wrong. One guy suddenly drops his task, steps into another person's workstation, grabs the material that she's working with, and begins something very different—he uses the material to make little reproductions of himself, thousands of them. These look-alikes imitate him—grabbing material and making reproductions of themselves. Soon the bunch gets so big that they spill into other people's workstations, getting in their way, and interrupting their work. As the number of look-alikes grows, the work group's activity slows, stutters, and finally stops.

Imagine a room containing a large group of people all working hard toward the same goal. Each person knows his or her job, does it carefully, and cooperates with other group members. Together, they function smoothly—like a well-oiled machine.   *1*

Then something goes wrong. One guy suddenly drops his task, steps into another person's workstation, grabs the material that she's working with, and begins something very different—he uses the material to make little reproductions of himself, thousands of them. These look-alikes imitate him—grabbing material and making reproductions of themselves. Soon the bunch gets so big that they spill into other people's workstations, getting in their way, and interrupting their work. As the number of look-alikes grows, the work group's activity slows, stutters, and finally stops.   *2*

A human body is like this room, and the body's cells are like these workers. If the body is healthy, each cell has a necessary job and does it correctly. For example, right now red blood cells are running throughout your body carrying oxygen to each body part. Other cells are digesting that steak sandwich that you had for lunch, and others are patching up that cut on your left hand. Each cell knows what to do because its genetic code—or DNA—tells it what to do. When a cell begins to function abnormally, it can initiate a process that results in cancer.   *3*

The problem starts when one cell "forgets" what it should do. Scientists call this "undifferentiating"—meaning that the cell loses its identity within the body (Pierce 75). Just like the guy in the group who decided to do his own thing, the cell forgets its job. Why this happens is somewhat unclear.   *4*

The problem could be caused by a defect in the cell's DNA code or by something in the environment, such as cigarette smoke or asbestos (German 21). Causes from inside the body are called genetic, whereas causes from outside the body are called carcinogens, meaning "any substance that causes cancer" (Neufeldt and Sparks 90). In either case, an undifferentiated cell can disrupt the function of healthy cells in two ways: by not doing its job as specified in its DNA and by not reproducing at the rate noted in its DNA.   *5*

Cancer starts with cell undifferentiating.

Cancer cells reproduce autonomously.

Most healthy cells reproduce rather quickly, but their reproduction rate is controlled. For example, your blood cells completely die off and replace themselves within a matter of weeks, but existing cells make only as many new cells as the body needs. The DNA codes in healthy cells tell them how many new cells to produce. However, cancer cells don't have this control, so they reproduce quickly with no stopping point, a characteristic called "autonomy" (Braun 3). What's more, all their "offspring" have the same qualities as their messed-up parent, and the resulting overpopulation produces growths called tumors.

6

Tumours damage the body.

Tumor cells can hurt the body in a number of ways. First, a tumor can grow so big that it takes up space needed by other organs. Second, some cells may detach from the original tumor and spread throughout the body, creating new tumors elsewhere. This happens with lymphatic cancer—a cancer that's hard to control because it spreads so quickly. A third way that tumor cells can hurt the body is by doing work not called for in their DNA. For example, a gland cell's DNA code may tell the cell to produce a necessary hormone in the endocrine system. However, if cancer damages or distorts that code, sick cells may produce more of the hormone than the body can use—or even tolerate (Braun 4). Cancer cells seem to have minds of their own, and this is why cancer is such a serious disease.

7

Promising treatments offer hope.

Fortunately, there is hope. Scientific research is already helping doctors do amazing things for people suffering with cancer. One treatment that has been used for some time is chemotherapy, or the use of chemicals to kill off all fast-growing cells, including cancer cells. (Unfortunately, chemotherapy can't distinguish between healthy and unhealthy cells, so it may cause negative side effects such as damaging fast-growing hair follicles, resulting in hair loss.) Another common treatment is radiation, or the use of light rays to kill cancer cells. One of the newest and most promising treatments is gene therapy—an effort to identify and treat chromosomes that carry a "wrong code" in their DNA. A treatment like gene therapy is promising because it treats the cause of cancer, not just the effect. Year by year, research is helping doctors better understand what cancer is and how to treat it.

8

The essay concludes that wayward cells are like wayward workers.

Much of life involves dealing with problems like wayward workers, broken machines, or dysfunctional organizations. Dealing with wayward cells is just another problem. While the problem is painful and deadly, there is hope. Medical specialists and other scientists are making progress, and some day they will help us win our battle against wayward cells.

9

Note: The Works-Cited page is not shown.

Reading for Better Writing

Working by yourself or with a group, answer these questions:

1. Explain why the analogy in the opening and closing is or is not effective.
2. Explain how transitions are used to lead into and out of each step.
3. Explain how the essay both describes and analyzes the process.

Analyzing a Cultural Practice

In the following essay, student writer Tim Zekveld explores surfing culture—where it started and how it has developed into a global phenomenon.

Chasing the Stoke

Surfing is much more than sliding down the face of a wave on a board. What began as a spiritual ritual in pre-modern Hawaii has transformed into a world-wide multi-billion dollar industry. This transformation has greatly affected the style of surfing and surf culture through innovation in board technology, ease of travel, and the sheer increase in the number of surfers around the globe. However, in many respects, surfing has stayed true to its Hawaiian roots through the idea of *aloha*—the concept and pursuit of a spiritual and soulful existence in relation to the ocean. Throughout all the changes to surfing and its culture, the stoke—or heartfelt excitement and reverence to each and every wave's curl—remains evident.

In Hawaii, surfing began as a joyous thanksgiving to the ocean for its providence and sustenance. Dating as far back as 800 AD, surfing was commonplace in Hawaiian society. Men, women, and children of every social status—from the commoner to the king—would surf regularly as a means of leisure and a form of ritual. When the ocean had provided food for their clan or had affected the people in a catastrophic way, Hawaiians would, while surfing the face of a wave, turn around and bow, wetting their head in the curl (Peralta). This ritual was a physical act meant to pay homage to the ocean, showing immense humility and reverence to their life force. Surfing on carved wooden boards measuring sixteen feet or longer and weighing well over a hundred pounds, the ancient Hawaiians would paddle into waves varying from three to thirty feet (Young 11). Captain James Cook, on viewing a Hawaiian surf in 1777, wrote, "I could not help concluding that this man felt the most supreme pleasure while he was being driven on so fast and so smoothly by the sea" (qtd. in Peralta). The joy that Captain Cook had witnessed, paired with the unfathomable respect that Hawaiians had for the ocean, fused into one term: *aloha*.

Aloha means much more than "hello" and "goodbye." In surfing, which is quite often a personal and introspective experience, *aloha* becomes an individual's emotional and spiritual tie to the ocean. Laird Hamilton, regarded as the world's greatest living surfer, speaks of *aloha* in his book, *Force of Nature*:

There's a depth to "aloha" that isn't easily described because it encompasses an attitude toward life. It's a spirit of grace, generosity, peace—a kind of spiritual check-list of all that's good. *Aloha's* literal meaning is "to breathe life." To have aloha means to share your life energy with others and with all that surrounds you. (175)

Aloha is a fluid concept. To have *aloha* means to live *aloha*. If surfing is a lifestyle, *aloha* underlies its virtues.

The introduction focuses on change that remains true to the roots of surf culture.

The writer traces the Hawaiian history of surfing.

A central concept is defined.

Surfing would undergo radical changes starting in the mid 1900s, though the adherence to *aloha* would remain the same. Surfing's rise in popularity was not immediate. The sport was originally brought overseas by a few Hawaiian champion swimmers in the 1920s who showed off their unique exercise to a few onlookers in California and Australia (Young 24). The spectacle enticed a handful of followers and by the early 1950s there were an estimated 5,000 surfers globally (26). However, the surfing world was about to change. Greg Noll, who began surfing in the 1940s, stated about the revolution, "Something went to hell in the late 50's. When the invention of the lightweight longboard came, something happened. It seemed that overnight, it went from 5,000 surfers, to 2 million" (qtd. in Peralta). Though advances in surfboard technology made it easier and more accessible for one to go surfing, it was the release of the Hollywood surf movie *Gidgit* in 1959 that launched surfing into mainstream America. *Gidgit* glorified the beach and surf life—honing in on Hawaiian *aloha* ideals. The media focused on the ease and relaxation that was paramount in Hawaiian culture. The widespread appearance of floral-print shirts, general beachwear, long hair for men, and surf jargon—words like radical, wipe-out, and hang-ten—were the result of the media's surf portrayal. The success of *Gidgit* was followed by an explosion of Hollywood surf films. Riding the immense popular demand, the 1960s, often referred to as the post-Gidgit era (Peralta), saw the rise of surf music, shops, movies, magazines, and clothing lines. The lifestyle that surfing appeared to encompass was pushed by the media and embraced by the public. Although the surf industry became focused on profits, the general idea of *aloha* survived.

> The writer describes the radical changes that began in the 1950s.

4

The late 1960s brought the introduction of competitive surfing, propelled by advancements in board technology. Hollywood's portrayal of short board surfing created a demand for surfboards that were shorter, more aggressive, and highly maneuverable. Previously, boards were never shorter than eight feet. By the late 1960s, the most popular boards were anywhere from six to nine feet long. The newer, smaller boards featured three fins instead of the long boards' one. The introduction of rails—exaggerated lips on the bottom edges of the board—allowed the surfer to cut into a wave. Short boards changed the style of surfing completely. Long boards were maneuverable to a certain extent, capable of wide and slow turns. Short boards, on the other hand, could be ridden straight up the face of a wave, spun around on the lip, and then made to slide back down into the curl. This maneuver was labelled a cut-back and was soon followed by a myriad of other surf moves, with this novel style of surfing later referred to as shredding, as the surfing would appear to carve lines in the face of the wave. With the development of the short board, the first structured surf contests started in the late 1960s. These contests were originally without sponsors or prizes; instead, they were a way of settling egos (ASP History). By the early 1970s, however, newly developed surf-wear clothing companies such as Billabong,

> He focuses on both technological and cultural changes through the decades.

5

Quicksilver, and Volcom began sponsoring individual surfers and contest events. Individual contest prize money exceeded $10,000 per event, completely aside from the sponsor compensation (ASP History). As the number of surfing tournaments increased, careers in professional surfing became more and more possible. In 1984, the Association of Surfing Professionals formed—a world circuit boasting twenty contests worldwide.

While the world tournament scene was erupting, a separate stream of professional surfing was also developing. Stemming from Bruce Brown's monumental surfing documentary *Endless Summer* (1966), which followed several young surfers all over the world in their quest for the perfect wave, a large market for freelance surfing began. Brown had tapped into something with *Endless Summer*, a certain aura that surrounded the surfers he had captured on film. They were selfless surfers to whom the general surf population could easily relate. Documentaries, Hollywood films, surf magazines, and surf music began to focus on the alluring notions of the perfect wave and enjoyment surfing.

The past thirty years of surfing media has been dominated by the two streams—competitive and freelance. However, evidently individual surfers are not too concerned with the implications of professional competitive surfing. R.J. Farmer, in his psychoanalysis of surfers, found that when asked to rank their motivations to surf, not one surfer listed social motivation the highest; in fact, fifty percent of all those questioned ranked social motivation the lowest. It seems that surfers have discovered instinctively the concept of *aloha* and consider social benefits bestowed by surf media as secondary. Gerry Lopez, a surfer of nearly fifty years, states that "everyone who [surfs] understands immediately how great it is. It rocks your soul. You can never leave that feeling" (qtd. in Hamilton 189). Despite the evolution of surf culture, the root Hawaiian concept remains.

Two notable surfers from different sides of the surf world are Australia's Taj Burrows and Hawaii's Laird Hamilton. Taj is the world's leading competitive surfer. His bag of tricks includes intense late-fading cutbacks, "floaters" (riding on top of the breaking curl of the wave), and jaw-dropping aerials—lifting off the lip of the wave, spinning in the air, and landing back in the curl—all strung together into lines of unimaginable proportions. Taj is commonly referred to as "the evolution of surfing" or simply "the future." Kelly Slater, six-time ASP world champion, says of Burrows' surf style and skill, "It's going to take us a long time to really catch up to Taj's level. It's going to take the ASP judges a long time to comprehend what he's actually doing out there because he's truly somebody that doesn't compare to anybody else" (qtd. in Peralta). Though pulling in over six figures annually and travelling all over the globe, Taj is purely stoked about being in the water: "After touring for weeks, the first thing I do when I get home is go to the beach and surf. I'll be addicted to the curl

Competitive surfing is contrasted with freelance.

The writer argues that both streams are linked by aloha, *and he offers two contrasting surfers as illustrations.*

6

7

8

until I die" (qtd. in Peralta). At the complete opposite end of the surfing spectrum is Laird Hamilton. Laird is regarded as the world's leading innovator in surf technology and big-wave riding. At the age of sixteen, Laird decided not to pursue the glory of competitive surfing. He has devoted his life to finding the biggest waves and being the best at surfing them. On riding big waves, Laird states, "You can't deny the spiritual world when you're staring into its eyes. I am continually humbled by the waves I surf" (Hamilton 146). In a relentless chase of the ultimate riding experience, Laird has pioneered tow-in surfing, allowing individuals to be towed by Jet-Ski into waves that were previously thought un-surfable. Laird will be search for the Nirvana of surf until the day he dies.

Anyone who has jumped in the water and surfed in some capacity knows its undeniable draw. Rob August, one of the surfers from *Endless Summer*, says, "If you've surfed for any amount of time, you can't get it out of your mind. It is peace" (qtd. in Brown). It is apparent that no matter what size or type of board you have or what your skill level, the fever of surfing will catch you, just as it did the original Hawaiian surfers thousands of years ago. As long as there are waves, there will be people stoked to surf.

> The closing connects the past and the future.

9

Note: The Works-Cited page is not shown. For sample pages, see MLA (page 533) and APA (pages 562–563).

Reading for Better Writing

Working by yourself or with a group, answer these questions:

1. Is surfing foreign or familiar to you? Did Tim Zekveld's essay deepen your understanding and appreciation of surfing? If yes, in what specific ways? If not, what was missing for you?

2. How would you characterize the tone and style of this essay? Start, for example, by considering the word "stoke" in the title. What does it mean, and why does Tim use it? Is the style fitting for the topic? Why or why not?

3. As a process essay, this piece relies upon chronology to trace the timeless yet changing nature of surfing. Scan the essay for references to time. What do they show about handling time in a process essay?

4. In addition to process analysis, the essay uses definition and comparison-contrast to analyze surfing. Review these writing moves in the essay. How do they deepen the analysis of surfing's history?

5. One strategy used in the essay is to quote frequently from surfers themselves. What do these quotations add to the analysis of surfing culture?

Analyzing a Government Policy

Daniel Francis is an editor, newspaper writer, and historian who has written extensively on Canadian history, including books such as *New Beginnings: A Social History of Canada*, *Discovery of the North*, and *Copying People: Photographing BC First Nations, 1860–1940*. In the piece below, excerpted from *The Imaginary Indian: The Image of the Indian in Canadian Culture*, Francis looks at the government's attempts to "civilize" Native peoples, showing how these efforts over time disenfranchised and diminished the Aboriginal population.

The Bureaucrat's Indian

The broad outline of Canadian Indian policy in the early twentieth century was an inheritance from the past. In the eighteenth and early nineteenth centuries, Britain needed Native people in its armed struggle for control of the continent. Accordingly, they received all the respect due to military allies. Following the War of 1812, however, when conflict with the United States ended and settlers began encroaching on the wilderness, British colonial officials who minded Canadian affairs recognized that a new relationship had to be worked out with Native people. No longer needed as military allies, the aboriginals had lost their value to the White intruders—and were now perceived to be a social and economic problem rather than a diplomatic one. Officials began to think in terms of civilizing the Indians so that they might assume a role in mainstream Canadian society. To this end, reserves were created as places where Indians would be taught to behave like Whites. Subsequent legislation codified the policy of civilization in a tangle of laws and regulations that would have the effect of erecting a prison wall of red tape around Canada's Native population.

The fundamental expression of the Official Indian became the Indian Act. First promulgated in 1876, amended often since then, the Indian Act consolidated and strengthened the control the federal government exercised over its aboriginal citizens. The aim of the Act, as of all Indian legislation, was to assimilate Native people to the Canadian mainstream.[1] Assimilation as a solution to the "Indian problem" was considered preferable to its only perceived alternative: wholesale extermination. There is nothing to indicate that extermination was ever acceptable to Canadians. Not only was it morally repugnant, it was also impractical. The American example showed how costly it was, in terms of money and lives, to wage war against the aboriginals. The last thing the Canadian government wanted to do was initiate a full-scale Indian conflict. It chose instead to go about the elimination of the Indian problem by eliminating the Indian way of life: through education and training, the Red Man would attain civilization. Most White Canadians believed that Indians were doomed to disappear anyway. Assimilation was a policy intended to preserve Indians as individuals by destroying them as a people.

The writer begins by outlining the major historical change in government–Native relations and offering a potent thesis about the outcomes.

The body of the analysis begins with an explanation of the 1876 Indian Act.

1

2

The Indian Act defined an Indian as "any male person of Indian blood reputed to belong to a particular band," his wife and children. The Act excluded certain individuals from Indian status. The most notorious exclusion was Native women who married non-Native men. These women were considered no longer to be Indians and lost any privileges under the terms of the Act, a situation which remained unchanged until 1985. Indian became a legislated concept as well as a racial one, maintained solely through political institutions to which Native people, who had no vote until 1960, had no access.

Special status—Indian status—was conceived as a stopgap measure by White legislators who expected Indians gradually to abandon their Native identity in order to enjoy the privilege of full Canadian citizenship—a process formally known as enfranchisement. As soon as Natives met certain basic requirements of literacy, education and moral character, they would be expected to apply for enfranchisement. In return for giving up legal and treaty rights, the enfranchisement would receive a portion of reserve lands and funds and cease to be an Indian, at least in law. The government expected that in time most Indians would opt for enfranchisement, which was conceived as a reward for good behaviour. In fact, the vast majority of Native people chose not to be rewarded in this way: in the sixty-three years between 1857, when enfranchisement was first legislated, and 1920, only 250 individuals took advantage of the opportunity to shed their Native identity.[2]

The Indian Act treated Native people as minors incapable of looking after their own interests and in need of the protection of the state. "The Indian is a ward of the Government still," Arthur Meighen, then minister of the interior, told Parliament in 1918. "The presumption of the law is that he has not the capacity to decide what is for his ultimate benefit in the same degree as his guardian, the Government of Canada."[3] Indians did not possess the rights and privileges of citizenship; they couldn't vote, they couldn't buy liquor, and they couldn't obtain land under the homestead system. The government expected that Indians would abuse these rights if they had them that they had to be protected from themselves and from predatory Whites who would take advantage of them. By the same token, status Indians did not have to pay federal taxes (if they were able to find employment) and were "protected from debt" (a condition that usually meant they could not secure loans from financial institutions). They were people apart from mainstream Canadian society. But the ultimate aim of Indian policy was not a system of apartheid. Segregationist, apartheid-like laws were sometimes imposed, but their purpose was tactical: they were intended to serve the long-term policy of assimilation.

If the government wanted to civilize the Indian, what constituted civilization in the official mind? There were several qualities which bureaucrats sought to impress on their Native charges. One was a respect for private property. The fact that Native people seemed to lack a sense of private ownership was widely regarded as a sign of their backwardness. Tribalism, or tribal communism as some people called it, was blamed for stifling the development of initiative and personal responsibility. In the hope of eradicating tribalism, the 1876 Act divided reserves into lots. Band members could qualify for location tickets which, after they proved themselves as farmers, gave them title (but not necessarily ownership) to their own piece of land.

A transition paragraph outlines the government's shifting attitude to the reserve system.

Meanwhile, the reserve itself was an integral part of the civilizing process. Reserves were originally intended as safe havens where Native people could live isolated from the baleful influence of their White neighbours. From the Native point of view, reserves secured a land base for their traditional lifeways. But in the nineteenth century, officials increasingly thought of reserves as social laboratories where Indians could be educated, christianized and prepared for assimilation. *7*

The writer describes what government policy attempted to do with Natives.

Agriculture was an important weapon in the war on Native culture. As game resources disappeared, farming seemed to be the only alternative way for Natives to make a living. More than that, at a time when industrialism was in its infancy, farming was seen as the profession best suited to a virtuous, civilized person: tilling the soil was an ennobling activity which fostered an orderly home life, industrious work habits and a healthy respect for private property. Farming would cause Natives to settle in one place and end the roving ways so typical of a hunting lifestyle and so detrimental to the sober, reliable routines on which White society prided itself. *8*

Another component of civilization was Christianity. Few Whites had any sympathy for or understanding of Native religious ideas, which were dismissed as pagan superstitions. Religious training was left to missionaries, but the government did its part by banning Native traditional religious and ceremonial practices—for example, the potlatch on the West Coast and the sun dance on the Prairies. *9*

Democratic self-government was also imposed on Native people. The ability to manage elected institutions was believed to be another hallmark of civilized society. Band members were required to elect chiefs and councillors who exercised limited authority over local matters. Indian Department officials retained the power to interfere in the political affairs of the band. The attempt to teach the Indians democracy was part and parcel of the assimilationist agenda. The elected councils were intended to replace traditional forms of Native government over which federal officials lacked control. *10*

A property-owning, voting, hard-working, Christian farmer, abstemious in his habits and respectful of his public duties—that was the end product of government Indian policy. "Instead of having a horde of savages in the North-West, as we had a few years ago," Clifford Sifton, the minister of the interior, told Parliament in 1902, "we shall soon have an orderly, fairly educated population, capable of sustaining themselves."[4] The message the minister intended to deliver was that the Indian had gone from painted savage to yeoman farmer in one generation. *11*

The writer traces the government's response over time to Native resistance to assimilation.

In reality it was not that simple. As time passed, officials grew impatient at the slow pace of assimilation. Native people seemed reluctant to embrace the benefits of White civilization. They resisted many of the measures the government imposed *12* on them. As the American historian Brian Dippie put it, civilization seemed to be a gift more appreciated by the donor than the recipient.[5] Officials concluded that Indians were by nature lazy, intellectually backward and resistant to change. It seemed to be the only explanation: to blame the Indian for not becoming a White man fast enough. As a result, the government passed a series of amendments to the Indian Act in an attempt to speed up the process of assimilation. Regulations became increasingly coercive. Officials received authority to spend money belonging to an Indian band without the members' permission. They could impose the elected system of government on bands, and depose elected leaders of whom they did not approve. At the end of the century, a series of industrial and residential schools removed Native children from their families so that they could be acculturated more easily. A draconian pass system was enacted by which individual Natives could not leave their reserves without the permission of an agent. A system of permits made it difficult for Native people to sell their produce on the open market. While the government said it wanted Natives to become self-sufficient farmers, it erected a series of legal obstacles which made it very difficult for aboriginal farmers to compete with their White neighbours. Frustration at the slow pace of assimilation reached its peak in 1920, when the government took upon itself the legal power to enfranchise an Indian against his or her will; in other words, Indians could be involuntarily stripped of their status. This legislation raised such opposition that it was rescinded two years later, but it was re-enacted in the 1930s. It was a sign of just how desperate the government was to rid itself of the Indian problem by ridding itself of the Indian.

> The final sentence potently captures the essence of assimilation policies and procedures.

Note: The bibliography is not shown. For sample pages, see MLA (page 533) and APA (pages 562–563).

Reading for Better Writing

Working by yourself or with a group, answer these questions:

1. While this excerpt from Daniel Francis's book does not discuss current government–Native relations and policies, what is your sense of how the history he describes is still felt today? Conversely, how have things changed?

2. What does the first paragraph of this essay accomplish? How does the opening characterize the process on which the essay focuses?

3. Paragraphs 2–7 focus on the nature and aims of the 1876 Indian Act. What key ideas does Francis present in this section? How do they deepen your understanding of the history?

4. The second half of this essay explores what government policies aimed to accomplish, how Natives resisted, and how the government reacted in turn— all over several decades. What strategies does the writer use to present the history of this relationship?

5. How would you characterize Francis's style and tone? Point to specific sentences and phrases as examples. What does this style contribute to the essay?

Analyzing a Technological Change

In the following essay first published in *The Walrus*, Ivor Tossell (a former Web programmer and a columnist for the *Globe and Mail*) examines Timeline, the Facebook feature. In a sense, this process essay is both organized by time (the evolution of Facebook) and focused on the topic of time (life as a timeline). Before you read the essay, reflect on the role (if any) Facebook has played in your life.

This Is Your Life

As you read this essay, annotate it and take notes—exploring how Tossell uses process analysis to explore Facebook and make sense of social networking.

That Facebook's new Timeline verges on outrageous was to be expected. There's 1
only one website in the world with both the gumption and the data to play back your life to you as an infographic. Introduced last December to the social network's 845 million users' home pages, Timeline arrays everything you've ever posted along one long vertical scroll, beginning in the present day and rolling off the bottom of the page with slick, magazine-style panache. (You can view your own information, while others' timelines are pruned for public consumption, according to Facebook's ever-shifting standards of who can see what.)

It comes as more of a surprise that the new format is also curiously beautiful. 2
It's the story of your life, artfully told: the friend you made in April 2011, the passing remarks you left on a pal's photos in September 2010, the website you recommended the month before, the happy banter you shared in 2008 with the partner you later left.

Yet to call the sudden regurgitation of years of photos, messages, contacts, and 3
comments disconcerting is an understatement. All along, Facebook has been tracking your data, waiting for this moment to arrive. Because it's not just your Facebook life that Timeline captures: the first date is not, as you might expect, the day you joined; it's the day you were born. A site best known for disseminating awkward party photos is now imagining itself at the foot of your mother's bed at the moment of your delivery, diligently taking notes. My timeline shows a substantial interlude between my date of birth and the day I joined Facebook. For younger users who hopped on the site in their early teens, the gap will be smaller. If Facebook is still around by the time they reach age twenty-five, more than half of their lives will have been spent in its sinuous embrace.

Since the site went live in 2004, Timeline marks the most significant overhaul of 4
how it handles the delicate question of users' biographies. It's glossy and uncomfortably personal, and its message is unmistakable: whether you knew it or not, you have put your life in our hands.

Facebook was once a creature of the eternal present. In the beginning, the network   *5*
was restricted to university students and geared specifically to their purposes. Users
had "walls" designed to emulate the whiteboards students hang on dorm room doors.
Like a wiki page, this block of text could be amended, edited, rewritten, or erased. But
friends showed deference to one another, and instead of overwriting notes they began
to post updates at the top. In response, Facebook changed the wall to a message board,
with older posts pushed down the page and eventually disappearing. The scheme
encouraged users to savour the moment, to pounce upon the latest post, photo, or
status update with a squirrel's intensity, and then let it slide into oblivion with the
happy forgetfulness of a goldfish.

Facebook continued to sharpen this immediacy with considerable ingenuity.   *6*
In 2006 (the same year the network opened its service to anyone over the age of
thirteen, welcoming a flood of teenagers and older adults), it introduced News Feed.
By collecting updates about friends' activities, this feature gave users countless
opportunities for bite-sized interactions — prompting them to chime in every time a
photo was "liked," a friendship made, a comment quipped — which made the site all
the more addictive. Since then, Facebook has still further refined this quality. Last year,
users discovered that they no longer had to click the Post button to send a message but
could simply press the Enter key, shaving off a fraction of a second and making the site
feel impossibly responsive.

This endless innovation is essential for the company. These are transitional days   *7*
for Facebook; the site announced a $5-billion initial public offering in February. But
the issue of expansion remains tricky. In North America, 65 percent of adults use social
networks, and most everyone who might want to join Facebook already has. I call this
phenomenon "peak friend," the point at which a limited number of potential users
could be recruited — and doing so takes more effort. All the while, the site is fending
off challenges from competitors like Google, as well as from its own success; familiarity
and ubiquity can breed contempt. The younger generation, eager to differentiate itself
from the mainstream, is liable to decamp. Facebook's challenge, then, is to retain
existing members and encourage them to spend more time on the site.

Enter Timeline. The feature marks a departure from the fanatical focus on   *8*
wringing the here-and-now for instant gratification. Instead, it's as if the site has re-
conjugated itself into a new tense, presenting users to one another in terms of their
entire life stories. In so doing, it has opened up a new dimension in which they can
busy themselves. You are encouraged to mark off points in your life in ever-more
personal terms: "new pet," "weight loss," "broken bone," "first kiss," "changed beliefs,"

and so on. When you make a new friend, Facebook exhorts you to "write something on his timeline." On his timeline! Facebook now has us etching items directly into one another's life stories. "Sear an item onto his soul" is not an option yet, but maybe next year.

With Timeline, the canvas of your life is literally stretched out before you and, by implication, quite a few other people. It's your achievements and aspirations, beginnings and endings, broken hearts and new romances, all collected on one page. Many websites could offer such a canvas. But only Facebook can flesh out the past seven years for you with compelling and unsettling fullness. *9*

How can Facebook animate your past so comprehensively? Well, it monitors our behaviour on the network, and tracks us as we surf other Facebook-enabled sites. Its collection of personal information allows it to target ads at exactly the eyeballs each advertiser wants to grab. Facebook has another interest in making your content public: more visible data means more interesting things to see, which means more time spent clicking through the site. In its pursuit of traffic and engagement, the company has been cavalier, to put it mildly, with users' privacy. Facebook has battled several complaints from watchdogs in Canada, the United States, and overseas. In November, it settled a series of claims with the US Federal Trade Commission, which held it to account for a series of egregious, if not illegal, manoeuvres designed to boost the amount of information its users share. In 2009, for instance, the site changed its rules so everyone's friend lists would be publicly viewable — but users weren't warned or informed of this beforehand. Later, Facebook updated its default privacy settings in a way that pushed people (neophytes, typically) into public view who never fully locked down their accounts. *10*

These schemes have generated bad press, and sporadic protests like Quit Facebook Day. Meanwhile, competitors have leaped on these concerns, as Google did by making privacy a key selling point for its rival social network. Yet while Facebook's growth shows signs of slowing in North America, which might be a function of market saturation, its global expansion continues. Facebook is not beloved (consumer satisfaction surveys put it near the bottom of the heap, alongside airlines and cable companies), but it remains, for today, very much an essential site. *11*

Over the years, its size and sway have given it enormous utilitarian value. It has replaced the phone book as a central directory of contact information, in part because phone books don't list mobile numbers (and because few people report falling in love while flipping through the white pages). More importantly, Facebook serves as a central exchange: the first place people post their baby photos, a clearing house for *12* event invitations, a thriving platform for businesses. Everyone is on Facebook because everyone is on Facebook.

Timeline effectively reminds us that personal data reflects personal moments. Even wary users like me, who have kept the site at arm's length, find themselves considering it with as much intrigue as discomfort. The scattered handfuls of posts I have made over the years, and the random collection of people from whom I have grudgingly accepted friend requests, suddenly knit together into something that seems like, well, my life. And it is undeniably affecting.   *13*

Timeline offers a glimpse of the depth of our complicated relationship with Facebook. In giving users a full accounting of what they have posted, it makes it easier for them to manage their public profiles and selectively clean them up. That's a step in the right direction. But insofar as it has turned the site from a party planning tool to a repository for life stories, it is also sending us a wake-up call.   *14*

Rather than downplaying the mountain of data it has collected, Facebook put it on display. Look, it says, look at how much we've learned about one another. We've come a long way, you and I. Look at what we've built together. You wouldn't walk away from that, now, would you?   *15*

Reading for Better Writing

Working by yourself or with a group, answer the following questions:

1. Consider the title "This Is Your Life." What does Ivor Tossell seem to imply with it?

2. In the opening four paragraphs, Tossell creates an impression of Facebook's Timeline feature. How would you describe that impression, and how does the writer create it?

3. Paragraphs 5–8 outline the evolution of Facebook toward Timeline. Review these paragraphs and outline the steps or stages. What is the point of this process analysis?

4. In paragraphs 9–12, Tossell discusses debates about Facebook and its evolution. In what ways does this discussion deepen his analysis of Facebook's development?

5. In the closing paragraphs, Tossell sums up the significance of Timeline for users and for Facebook itself. What conclusions does he seem to be offering? How would you characterize the tone of the ending?

6. How would you characterize your own relationship with Facebook? How has Tossell's analysis of Facebook impacted your understanding of and attitude toward social media?

Writing Guidelines

Planning

1. **Select a topic.** Use prompts like those below to generate a list of topics.
   - A course-related process
   - A process in nature
   - A process in the news
   - A process that helps you get a job
   - A process that would help you achieve a personal goal

2. **Review the process.** Use your knowledge of the topic to fill out an organizer like the one on the right. List the subject at the top, each of the steps in chronological order, and the outcome at the bottom. For a complex process, break it down into stages or phases first; then outline the steps or events within each phase.

   > **Process Analysis**
   > **Subject:**
   > - **Step #1**
   > - **Step #2**
   > - **Step #3**
   >
   > **Outcome:**
   >
   > *fig. 12.3*

3. **Research the process.** Find all the information that you need to fully understand the process yourself and to clearly explain it to your readers. To guide your research, you might list headings and related questions like these:
   - **Context:** When, where, how, and why does the process transpire? How is the context related to the nature of the process?
   - **Content:** What individual steps—or groups of steps—make up the process?
   - **Order:** In what order do the steps take place? Is the order important? Why?
   - **Connections:** What links steps to steps or stages to stages and how?
   - **Causes:** What causes each individual step or event—or what causes the process as a whole? How can I distinguish between false causes (page 319) and actual causes?
   - **Effects:** What is the outcome of each step or event—and what is the outcome of the whole process? What side effects are associated with the outcome?
   - **Materials:** What materials are used in the process and how do they affect it?
   - **History:** When did this process begin? How has it changed over time and why?
   - **Personnel:** Who is involved in the process? Why? How do they affect the process, and how does it affect them?
   - **Cost:** What is the financial cost? The emotional cost? The environmental cost?
   - **Impact:** How does the process affect my community, my friends, or me?

4. **Organize information.** Revise the organizer as needed. Then develop an outline, including steps listed in the organizer, as well as supporting details from your research.

Drafting

5. **Write the first draft.** Write the document using the guidelines below.
   - **Opening:** Introduce the topic and give an overview of the process, possibly forecasting its main stages. Explain why the process is important: e.g., how it affects a person, community, or country.

- **Middle:** Clearly describe each step in the process, and link steps with transitional words such as *first, second, next, finally,* and *while*. Explain the importance of each step, and how it is linked to other steps in the process. If the process is complex and has many steps, consider grouping them into 3–5 phases or stages. Describe the outcomes of steps and phases, as well as the overall outcome and relevance of the process. Depending on your purpose for writing, you might also analyze the causes and effects related to specific steps, or to the entire process.
- **Closing:** Summarize the process and restate key points as needed, such as why understanding the process has value. If appropriate, explain follow-up activity, such as how readers might learn more about the topic.

Revising

6. **Improve the ideas, organization, and voice.** Evaluate the following:

____ **Ideas:** Is the process presented as a unified phenomenon that includes a logical series of stages and steps? Are all claims clear, rational, and supported with reliable evidence? Are assertions regarding causes and effects relevant and explained fully? Does the writing include logical fallacies such as false cause (page 319), broad generalization (page 319), and false analogy (page 320)?

____ **Organization:** Does the essay include an opening that introduces the process, offers an overview, and states the thesis; a middle that describes stages and steps clearly and correctly; and a closing that unifies the essay?

____ **Voice:** Is the tone informed, concerned, and objective? Are sensitive issues well researched, addressed respectfully, and shown to be relevant?

Editing

7. **Edit the essay.** Polish your writing by addressing the following:

____ **Words:** The words are precise, clear, and correct. In particular, technical terms are correct, used uniformly, and defined.

____ **Sentences:** The sentences are smooth, varied in structure, and engaging.

____ **Correctness:** The usage, grammar, punctuation, and spelling are correct.

____ **Page Design:** The page design is attractive and features steps in the process. Essays are correctly formatted in MLA or APA style.

Publishing

8. **Publish the essay** by offering it to instructors, students, and nonprofit agencies working with the process.

Critical-Thinking and Writing Activities

As directed by your instructor, complete the following activities by yourself or in a group.

1. Sir Arthur Conan Doyle said in 1914 that "Canada is like an expanding flower—wherever you look you see some fresh petal unrolling." By contrast, in the 1999 film *South Park: Bigger, Longer & Uncut,* viewers are serenaded with the lyrics "It seems that everything's gone wrong / Since Canada came along." What do *you* think? Focusing on one element of national life, explore how Canada is a country under development.

2. Review "Wayward Cells." Then choose another natural or social science process and write an essay describing and analyzing that process. Conversely, think of a process within the arts and humanities (e.g., a historical movement).

3. "Chasing the Stoke" and "The Bureaucrat's Indian" both focus on cultural developments that have shaped the present—the enduring presence of *aloha* in surfing culture and the legacy of the Indian Act for Canada's Aboriginal peoples. Consider other cultural practices and situations. How did they come to be? Choose one such topic and explore this question.

4. In "This Is Your Life," Ivor Tossell analyzes the evolution of Facebook, especially its feature Timeline. Based on your reading of this essay, consider two possible approaches to writing your own process essay: (a) analyze one or two critical phases in the timeline of your own life development; or (b) think of another software or technology that has evolved and research that technology's development.

5. Write an essay about a time in your own life during which your understanding of—or position on—an issue, event, or other topic changed.

Learning-Objectives Checklist ✓

Have you achieved this chapter's learning objectives? Check your progress with the items below, revisiting topics in the chapter as needed. *I have . . .*

____ examined what process essays are, why they are written, and how they are used to analyze and explain phenomena (210–211).

____ analyzed the content and evaluated the quality of process essays (210–211).

____ researched a process, analyzed it, identified steps in the process, and found reliable evidence that distinguishes related causes and effects (226–227).

____ presented this information in a well-crafted essay that introduces the topic, offers an overview of the process, describes the steps clearly in chronological order, links the steps effectively, and explains the overall outcome or impact of the process (226–227).

____ revised the essay for weaknesses in organization and voice, and corrected errors in logic such as false cause, broad generalization, and false analogy (226–227).

____ edited the essay for errors in grammar, punctuation, spelling, and mechanics (226–227).

Chapter 13

Comparison and Contrast

In his plays, William Shakespeare creates characters, families, and even plot lines that mirror each other. As a result, we see Hamlet in relation to Laertes and the Montagues in relation to the Capulets. In the process, we do precisely what the writer wants us to do—we compare and contrast the subjects. The result is clarity and insight: by thinking about both subjects in relation to each other, we understand each one more clearly.

But academic and workplace writers also use comparison-contrast as an analytical strategy. To help you read and write such essays, the following pages include instructions and four model essays.

Visually Speaking As you study the photograph below, what do you see—literally and figuratively? What does the image suggest about the nature of and relationship between comparing and contrasting?

Learning **Objectives**

By working through this chapter, you will be able to

- examine and assess writers' use of compare-contrast reasoning.
- differentiate between subject-by-subject and trait-by-trait strategies for comparison-contrast.
- use transitional words and supporting details to clarify compare-contrast claims.
- establish a clear basis for comparison between two or more topics.
- choose clear elements or features for comparison.
- compose an analytical essay using primarily compare-contrast reasoning (with other analytical strategies).

Mazzzur / Shutterstock.com

fig. 13.1

Strategies for Compare-Contrast Essays

Compare-contrast writing holds two or more things, phenomena, or concepts side by side—with comparison focusing on similarities, and contrast focusing on differences. By looking at subjects side-by-side, we more clearly see their unique and shared traits.

The Rhetorical Situation

Consider the context in which writers use compare-contrast reasoning:

- **Purpose.** Writers commonly compare and contrast subjects in order to explain how, why, and to what effect their distinguishing features make the subjects similar or different. Depending on their purpose, writers may focus on the similarities between seemingly dissimilar things, or on the differences between things that seem similar.
- **Readers.** A writer using compare-contrast reasoning may have virtually any reader in mind—the instructor for a student essay or potential clients for a marketing document. Whatever the situation, the writer believes that his or her comparative analysis of the topic will enrich readers' understanding of that topic.
- **Topic.** Writers address a wide range of topics through compare-contrast: people, events, phenomena, technologies, problems, products, stories, and so on.

Example: In "English, French: Why Not Both?" Peggy Lampotang's **topic** is Canada's two official languages—the distinctive nature of each language and the relationship between the two. Because the essay was published in the "Facts and Arguments" section of the *Globe and Mail* newspaper, Lampotang's **purpose**, as an immigrant to Canada, is to encourage her **readers**, other Canadians, to appreciate both languages and Canada's marriage of the two.

Principles of Compare-Contrast Writing

Compare-contrast writing should be guided by the principles that follow:

Establishing a solid basis for comparison. Comparable items are types of the same thing (e.g., two rivers, two bodies of water, the atmosphere and oceans). Moreover, the subjects are of the same order—one cannot simply be an example of the other: e.g., all lakes and Lake Louise. Whereas such a discussion would work as an example or illustration, the topics are not truly comparable.

Developing criteria (standards, features, etc.) on which to base the comparison. For example, a comparison of two characters in a play might focus on their backgrounds, their actions in the play, their psychology, their fate, and so on. Once writers choose the criteria, those criteria must be applied consistently. For help comparing and contrasting subjects, use a Venn Diagram (Figure 13.2), listing the subjects' differences on the left or right, and their similarities in the centre.

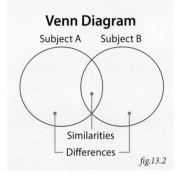

Venn Diagram

Subject A   Subject B

Similarities

Differences

fig.13.2

Considering how to use compare-contrast. For example, comparison-contrast may be
- the framework for the entire essay, offering a compare-contrast thesis and structuring the discussion around appropriate points of comparison, or
- a strategy used in a paragraph or a section of an essay, comparing and contrasting details to illuminate an idea.

Phrasing a compare-contrast thesis to clarify relationships. Consider these templates:
- **Emphasizing similarities:** Whereas [subjects A and B] appear quite different in terms of their _____, they show important similarities in that _____.
- **Emphasizing differences:** Whereas [subjects A and B] appear quite similar in terms of their _____, they are essentially different in that _____.

Organizing your comparison to clarify similarities and differences for readers.
Writers have two choices for organizing comparisons so as to illuminate the topics.
- **Whole vs. whole** discusses items separately, giving a strong overview of each. This pattern works well with short, simple comparisons.
- **Point by point** discusses items together, criterion by criterion. This pattern stresses fine distinctions, making sense for long, complex comparisons.

Sample Compare-Contrast Paragraph

Writers frequently use a compare-contrast paragraph to relate their topic to something familiar or to make surprising connections to something dissimilar. In the opening paragraph from "Pitch Perfect" (pages 269–270), Jay Ingram establishes his focus on the knuckleball by contrasting this pitch with other pitches.

> A standard baseball pitch—slider, curveball, fastball—seems to slavishly follow the laws of physics, making it possible to predict where a ball will go and how it will get there. The knuckleball is different. It appears to dip suddenly, dart to one side or the other, or—when you least expect it—to float in straight over the plate. Hitters are left flailing desperately at it. On a six-game streak last season, pitcher R. A. Dickey struck out sixty-three batters and gave up a single unearned run. And yet Dickey, who joined the Blue Jays this season, is the only active knuckler in the major leagues. When he won the National League Cy Young Award in 2012, he was the first knuckleball pitcher ever to do so.

Reading Compare-Contrast Writing

As you read the essays on the following pages, consider these questions:
1. Does the writer compare these topics to stress similarities, differences, or both?
2. What features or traits of the topics are compared? Why?
3. How does the writer present the topics and the criteria for comparison?
4. Is the essay free of logical fallacies (pages 317–320)?
5. What insights does the writer develop through compare-contrast analysis?

Sample Compare-Contrast Essays

Writers compare and contrast a wide range of topics in order to illuminate those topics' complex nature. For example, in the essays that follow, the writers compare violent attacks, clothing and character in a play, languages, and protest movements.

Analyzing a Violent Event

Canadian student Anita Brinkman wrote the following editorial one week after the September 11, 2001, attack on the World Trade Center. While the causes and consequences of the attack were still unclear at that time, she compares the attack to other significant tragedies. By holding up 9/11 "side by side" with other tragedies, Anita draws out similarities and differences.

Essay Outline

Introduction: putting 9/11 in the context of other attacks and tragedies around the globe.

1. Describing the overwhelming immediate impact of the 9/11 attack.
2. Contrasting 9/11 with the Oklahoma City bombing.
3. Identifying U.S. fear as rooted in uncertainty.
4. Contrasting 9/11 with the bombing of Pearl Harbor.

Conclusion: the possibility that the West is mourning a lost way of life.

A Fear Born of Sorrow

More than 100 people were killed in the tragic bombing of the Oklahoma Federal Building in 1995. About 6,000 die in Africa each day of AIDS. Between 8,000 and 10,000 people worldwide die of starvation daily. Tragedies occur all around us, and we accept them out of necessity as a part of life.

But sometimes the horror of a tragedy affects us in a new way: it overwhelms a nation and stuns the international community. This is what happened last week when two hijacked planes hit the Twin Towers of the World Trade Center, and their resulting collapse killed thousands of people from several countries. News of the tragedy flashed around the globe. Everywhere, it seemed, people in uncomprehending horror listened to reports on their radios or watched endless replays on their televisions. Several countries declared days of mourning and scheduled services of remembrance. Now, one week after the attack, tokens of

The writer introduces her topic with stark statistics.

1

2

grief and letters of condolence still flood U.S. embassies and government offices worldwide. But why is the outpouring of grief so much deeper for this tragedy than for others? Why isn't the attack considered just a large-scale repeat of the Oklahoma bombing? Could it be that our grief is more than sorrow, and that our loss is much more than what lies in the rubble?

She asks the central question of her essay.

The Oklahoma bombing was grievous and alarming, but localized. The bomber was soon arrested, his motives deduced, and justice served. While lives were changed and a nation was shaken, the world community remained composed. However, the September 11 attack unsettled us more, in part because the World Trade Center stood for so much more than the Oklahoma Federal Building did. The Twin Towers symbolized American domination of world finances: they were a major center for the Internet, a hub for international business, and an emblem of American life. The fall of the towers struck violently at the nation's psyche, and the manner in which they were destroyed—with America's own airplanes filled with passengers—has raised questions about America's security and future. Threatened to their core, Americans have demanded retaliation—but against whom? The terrorists' identity is not clear, and evidence seems elusive. In a sense, an unknown offender has injured Americans, and they beat the air in the dark. In such a case, terrorism is aptly named, for America's outcry expresses more than sorrow—it also expresses fear.

Two parallel events are compared and contrasted.

3

The fear that Americans feel comes partly from the uncertainty related to this attack. The attackers demonstrated technical and planning skills that have surprised Americans, making them question their safety and fear future attacks. Air travel, long considered safe, now includes security measures like armed guards, luggage searches, and bomb-sniffing dogs—all strategies to achieve safety. As Americans struggle to find answers in the shattered peace, nations are forming alliances, war seems imminent, and the whole world waits anxiously to see where it all will lead.

The word "fear" links the two paragraphs.

4

Fear and uncertainty are new to Americans living today because America has not been attacked in this way since Britain ruled her as a colony. While the bombing of Pearl Harbor awoke many to the fact that America could be targeted, the Japanese bombers hit Hawaii—then a U.S. territory, not a state, and not the mainland. Following World War II, many in the world community again thought of America

Pearl Harbor and 9/11 are compared.

5

as the invulnerable Land of Opportunity. However, this belief is now shattered, and many citizens of the global village fear that what was lost last week includes more than what lies in the rubble.

On September 11, 2001, America, along with its Western allies, lost its aura of   6
invincibility. As the whole world watched, the towers fell, and we stumbled in shock and pain. Moreover, as time passes, America may fail to identify its enemy and to understand the attack. If this happens, the oppressed people of the world—to some extent victims of Western culture—will take notice.

The closing restates her thesis.

It is now one week since the towers fell, and the world still grieves. However,   7
mingled with this grief is the fear that we may be mourning not only for the lives lost, but also for our lost way of life.

Reading for Better Writing

Working by yourself or with a group, answer the following questions:

1. What do you remember of 9/11? What direct and indirect impacts has it had on your life? In what ways does Anita Brinkman's editorial evoke a sense of that time?

2. Anita's main theme is identified in her title. Where does she directly refer to this theme in her editorial? What has the title phrase come to mean by the end?

3. The writer compares and contrasts the September 11 attack with the Oklahoma City and Pearl Harbor attacks. What does she conclude from each comparison? How do these comparisons contribute to her central point?

4. More than a decade has passed since the 9/11 attack. How well have Anita's ideas stood the test of time? How would you compare the situation of the world today with the situation one week after 9/11?

Analyzing Literary Characters

In the following essay, student writer Meaghan Delaney compares three characters in a play, focusing on the way clothing imagery and references help distinguish them. Note how she examines each character in turn and then ties together the comparisons in her conclusion.

Anything but 'Wash and Wear': Exploring the Connections between Clothing and Character in Oscar Wilde's *An Ideal Husband*

Oscar Wilde's Victorian comedy of manners *An Ideal Husband* was first performed on the London stage on 3 January 1895 (*New World Encyclopedia*). Following the malicious Mrs. Cheveley's attempts at blackmail and the surprisingly honourable Lord Goring's prowess in managing the whole situation, the spectacle also takes into account the poor hearts and romantic affairs of its characters, bringing the whole circus to a satisfying conclusion with, of course, a wedding. What is most interesting about Wilde's comedy is the manner in which he has used his considerable knowledge about the fashions of the day to enhance the audience's perception of the characters. So subtly is this done that one does not immediately recognise the significance of seemingly idle conversation. The saying "the clothes make the man" is not far amiss in *An Ideal Husband*, which portrays a society that defines respectability by the length of one's pedigree, the irreproachability of one's reputation, and the quality of one's dress. The importance of clothing to character can be seen especially in Wilde's contrasting treatment of Lord Goring, Mrs. Cheveley, and Mabel Chiltern.

Lord Goring is singularly obsessed with maintaining an appearance of youth and affected naïveté, masking his philosopher's nature beneath that of the dandy. Goring's trademark fixation is his "buttonhole," or rather, the flower that would adorn the buttonhole on his lapel. He is constantly adjusting it, or changing it for a new one that is "more trivial," lest he should look "almost in the prime of life," as he says to his butler, Phipps (Wilde 294). Yet, though afraid of age, Goring is unafraid of being if not a pioneer of Fashion, then a man confident of his own style, stating that "Fashion is what one wears oneself. What is unfashionable is what other people wear . . . just as vulgarity is simply the conduct of other people . . . and falsehoods the truths of other people" (293-294). (The capitalization of *Fashion* in the play is intended to draw attention to its importance in society.) While contemporary followers of Fashion might call this sentiment "owning it," one might more perceptively describe such a seemingly arrogant statement as simple self-confidence. Wilde uses Goring's misleading attention to the details of fashion and the idleness of his set to reveal a man more than capable of taking care of his friends' affairs with tact and sound advice.

Through his acquaintanceship with Mrs. Cheveley, Goring has formed a definite opinion of the lady—an opinion expressed again through clothing references but resulting in a quite different estimate of her character. He describes her to Sir Robert Chiltern as "one of those very modern women of our time who find

1

2

3

Meaghan offers a lively summary of the play and turns the focus to clothing and three characters.

She examines the first character by looking closely at textual references.

Transitioning to the second character, Meaghan looks at her through the first character's eyes.

a new scandal as becoming as a new bonnet and air them both in the Park every afternoon at five-thirty. I am sure she adores scandals, and the sorrow of her life is that she can't manage to have enough of them" (275). The basis Goring gives for this deduction and for the idea that Mrs. Cheveley has come to a less-than-ideal situation is that "she wore far too much rouge last night, and not quite enough clothes. That is always a sign of despair in a woman" (275). The reasons for this "despair" are hinted at in an allusion to the idea that pretty women usually "have a past" (276). He implies that Mrs. Cheveley's past has been more risqué than most by referring to it as "décolleté," softening the blow with a remark that "there is a fashion in pasts just as there is a fashion in frocks [. . . and] a slightly décolleté one [is] excessively popular nowadays" (276). According to R. Turner Wilcox, "décolleté is a French term referring to a dress with a low neckline in both front and back, usually baring the shoulders" (105-06). In this sense, a décolleté neckline functions as the perfect emblem of Mrs. Cheveley's history and character.

Towards the end of the nineteenth century, women were gradually obtaining more freedom in dress. Although still corseted within an inch of their lives, "clothes were slowly becoming simpler and more practical, emphasizing a small, hand-span waist, curved 'cello' hips and a high, rounded bosom" (Hawthorne 12). A well-tailored ensemble of rich material nearly always promised acceptance in the highest social circles (12). Is it any wonder then, with so much of society's judgement and approval resting on a garment, that Mrs. Cheveley cites her dressmaker's disapproval in declining Lord Goring's offer of a cigarette (Wilde 306)? A skilled, loyal dressmaker would have been invaluable to a nineteenth-century socialite, and Mrs. Cheveley was no exception. In her opinion, "a well-made dress has no pockets," a decree that was perhaps not entirely true of the time, but served her well in postponing the relinquishment of Robert Chiltern's letter (306). Yet, for all that she would have relied on her dressmaker to clothe her in the latest, most becoming fashions, Mrs. Cheveley refutes Lady Markby's comment that "a man on the question of dress is always ridiculous" (286). Instead, she puts forth her opinion that "men are the only authorities on dress" (286). Having had two husbands (and, implicitly, more lovers) Mrs. Cheveley has likely developed a taste in clothing defined by the response it can wrest from the male sensibility. Men were, after all, a gentlewoman's only means of livelihood.

Mrs. Cheveley asserts that one of the reasons she detests Gertrude Chiltern is her ignorance. She justifies this claim with the oblique statement that "[a] woman whose size in gloves is seven and three-quarters never knows much of anything" (309). Mrs. Cheveley's jealousy of Gertrude's small hands is not as ridiculous as the modern woman might find. Rosemary Hawthorne, a published collector of antique and vintage "costume," stresses that, in Wilde's time, "[a] lady . . . always aspired to have tiny hands" and required gloves "for every conceivable occasion, day and night: [a woman] was incorrectly dressed if her hands were not covered in public" (31). Therefore, in Hawthorne's opinion, Mrs. Cheveley's jealousy is not unjustifiable and, in fact, possibly alludes to a sense of her own self-loathing.

Of all the women portrayed in *An Ideal Husband* it is not Gertrude but Mabel   6
Chiltern who most truthfully embodies the pure spirit of the true moral sense. In
that sense, Mabel stands as the true opposite to Mrs. Cheveley—an idea revealed
once again through references to fashion. Though proposed to by Tommy Trafford
on a regular basis, Mabel knows she would never be truly content with him, and
invariably refuses, aware that she is meant to marry Lord Goring. However, she
does not push the point, and allows him to gradually discover his true feelings for
her. In Act 1, Mabel complains that her sister-in-law, Gertrude, restricts her jewelry
to pearls, a stone traditionally associated with purity, but Mabel is "thoroughly
sick of pearls [because they] make one look so plain, so good and so intellectual"
(261). Mabel would prefer to wear the diamond brooch for the dash of excitement
that those jewels offer, a departure from stuffy Puritanical ideas about unmarried
women and purity. She has a sense of wanting to control her own destiny, and chafes
at the dependence she has on her brother for social security and welfare. Yet, for all
Mabel's witty and impatient talk, she remains the only truly *good* female in the play.
Even Lady Markby is here able to make her only truly observant remark: "You will
always be as pretty as possible. That is the best fashion there is, and the only fashion
England succeeds in setting" (283).

> A third character is contrasted with others in the play.

While Lord Goring appears the picture of idleness and frivolity, his security   7
in himself and his own tastes endears him to the audience. Mrs. Cheveley, contrasting
both Goring and Mabel, appears cunning and scheming, but her own veneer of
poise decays and crumbles as the audience sees her mask stripped away and her own
clothing betray her to the observant eye, even before the final dialogue has been
spoken. Mabel Chiltern yearns to be an exotic and vibrant woman of wit, but her
attire reveals her true nature as the one truly pure woman in *An Ideal Husband*.

> The conclusion summarizes the contrasts between the characters.

Reading for Better Writing

Working by yourself or with a group, answer the following questions:

1. Put simply, in this essay Meaghan Delaney compares three characters. What
   is the purpose of that comparison? To what use does she put comparison
   strategies?

2. After her introduction, Meaghan deals with each character in turn before
   offering her conclusion. What does she do to analyze each character? Does
   she spend equal time with each character? How does she connect them? What
   is the effect of the conclusion as part of her compare-contrast approach?

3. When you watch a play or a film, what do you look for in the characters? What
   elements contribute to a sense of character and distinguish characters? How
   has Meaghan's essay impacted your thinking about character and costuming?

Follow Up: Watch the 1999 film adaptation of *An Ideal Husband*, starring Cate Blanchett,
Minnie Driver, Rupert Everett, Julianne Moore, and Jeremy Northam. Consider how the
film uses clothing to distinguish characters. Does the film version support Meaghan's
analysis?

Analyzing Languages

In the following essay, first published as an article in the "Facts and Arguments" section of the *Globe and Mail*, Peggy Lampotang compares and contrasts French and English as languages. Note how she fills her article with concrete examples and details to support her thinking.

English, French: Why Not Both?

When I came to Canada at the age of 20, I was very excited to be part of a bilingual country. I was born in Mauritius, a predominantly French-speaking island whose dialect is Creole and official language, English.   *1*

Creole is colourful but was considered a crude form of French and teachers forbade its use at school. French was the language of choice and I loved the way it flowed in my blood; I danced in it, flirted with it. When I spoke it, I felt alive.   *2*

I studied in a British system of education, and enjoyed writing in English, but speaking it was a different matter. The shock upon arriving in Toronto and discovering that French was limited to the Harbourfront Francophone Centre and the Alliance Française prompted me to take trips to Montreal.   *3*

I was fascinated by the lifestyle differences of the expressive Québécois and the reserved Torontonians. But I stayed in Toronto. I liked its industrious quality. I wanted to feel at home in English. My accent, source of much hilarity, and sometimes, romantic speculations, was frustrating, but did open doors for me.   *4*

The first lesson I learned from a boyfriend was to curl my tongue, put its tip under the upper teeth, and blow gently the feathery sound "th" so that when I said three, people knew it was number three and not tree, the wonder of nature that sprouts from the soil and grows into trunk, branches and leaves.   *5*

Soon I learned to respect the nuances in each language, pronouncing words, delivering them in ways that sharpened my awareness of fundamental cultural differences between English and French.   *6*

Ever notice how French translations are much longer than English ones?   *7*

While reading a cereal box, I realized it wasn't a problem with the translator. This concise and brief statement instills the down-to-earth, good sense of English: "It can be an important part of your family's nutritious breakfast." The French translation, however, with its lengthy enticing words, gives a frisson about how   *8*

The writer starts with personal background related to the topic—her own bilingual experience.

She begins to explore the nuances of and differences between each language, as each is spoken.

In the middle, the writer presents linguistic differences as expressions of cultural difference.

pleasurable and extreme the cereal experience: "Ces céréales irrésistibles occuperont sûrement une place de choix à votre table lors du petit déjeuner familial." (These irresistible cereals will surely occupy a place of choice on your table during the family breakfast.)

During a French conversation, I can elaborate at leisure my descriptions; the more words, the better. However, in English, I use clear exact words, with the least repetition possible.   *9*

An Anglophone finds it hard to say certain French words such as "cracher" (to spit) because there's a tendency to roll the "r" with the tongue and utter the word with a half-open mouth. As an Anglophone, if one is willing to open one's mouth wide and throw the sound from the back of the throat, one will sense the openness of French. However, as a Francophone, the challenge of speaking English is to restrain the elasticity of one's lips. One has to roll words out on one's curled tongue while decreasing the opening of one's mouth to feel the smooth fluidity of English. How else would one make Toronto sound as if it has only two syllables?   *10*

Anglophones struggle with the letter u as in "écureuil" (squirrel) because they can't keep the tongue down and form the lips into a tiny oval shape to emit the sound as if it's easing into a kiss. On the other hand, Francophones could alleviate their difficulty with silent h as in, "Ow is e?" if they are willing to make the h sound come out as a short breathy exhalation.   *11*

The economy of movement in delivering words in English, whether it's from the mouth or the rest of the body, gives a feeling of preciseness but also of control. The French language, however, with its constant shifting of the mouth opening, from the jaw-breaking "Ah" to the pouting "Oh," while the hands point, close, open, spread, or jiggle in all directions, expresses unbound passion. An Anglophone could see this openness as too dramatic, vulnerable and exposed, but a Francophone could interpret the lack of movement of the Anglophone as rigid and cold.   *12*

At the end, she turns to the pleasure that being bilingual brings to her and the richness it brings to the country.

I have lived in Toronto for almost three decades. I even dream in English.   *13*

There were times when my craving for French made me feel part of me was missing. When I enrolled my children in French Immersion, I discovered with pleasant surprise a new community of bilingual parents.   *14*

The opportunity to speak French regularly has brought a new balance in my life. I feel lucky to be among Canadians who can speak both languages.   *15*

My personality changes when I switch from one language to the other.   *16*

I feel in charge, efficient, and love the flow of English sounds rolling and   *17*
swishing from my mouth.

When I speak French, I feel sensual, demonstrative, perhaps a bit excitable,   *18*
but I relish its intensity.

Fluency in English and French brings familiarity to the quirkiness of their   *19*
inherent differences and makes it easier for me to tolerate and accept both.

My experience with these two languages makes me see the depth of Pierre   *20*
Trudeau's vision for this country when he implemented official bilingualism.

Allez-y, Canada. Let's get along. Why not both, hey?   *21*

Reading for Better Writing

Working by yourself or with a group, answer the following questions:

1. What is Peggy Lampotang's purpose in this essay? Who is her intended audience? How do you reach your conclusions on these questions?
2. Does the essay have a stated or implied thesis? If it is stated, identify it. If it is implied, put it in your own words.
3. What exactly is Lampotang comparing in her article, and how does she organize her comparison: trait by trait or subject by subject? What are her main points of comparison?
4. Lampotang extends her discussion of language into the realm of personality and culture. Do you find her conclusions compelling, stereotyped, or something else? Explain.
5. Why does Lampotang refer to Pierre Trudeau in paragraph 20? What is the effect of doing so near the end of the essay?
6. Reflect personally on Lampotang's celebration of Canada's official languages. How does her discussion relate to your own language heritage, education, and experiences?

Analyzing Social Activism

Malcolm Gladwell, author of *The Tipping Point, Blink, Outliers, What the Dog Saw,* and, most recently, *David and Goliath,* writes regularly for *The New Yorker* magazine. Gladwell was born in England, grew up in Ontario, and graduated from the University of Toronto. In the essay below, he compares incidents of social activism from the Civil Rights era and the present. Gladwell uses compare-contrast strategies to explore the distinction between high-risk and low-risk activism.

Small Change

As you read this essay, annotate it and take notes—exploring how Gladwell compares and contrasts the past and present of social activism. Reflect as well on your own participation in social change.

At four-thirty in the afternoon on Monday, February 1, 1960, four college students sat down at the lunch counter at the Woolworth's in downtown Greensboro, North Carolina. They were freshmen at North Carolina A. & T., a black college a mile or so away.   *1*

"I'd like a cup of coffee, please," one of the four, Ezell Blair, said to the waitress.   *2*

"We don't serve Negroes here," she replied.   *3*

The Woolworth's lunch counter was a long L-shaped bar that could seat sixty-six people, with a standup snack bar at one end. The seats were for whites. The snack bar was for blacks. Another employee, a black woman who worked at the steam table, approached the students and tried to warn them away. "You're acting stupid, ignorant!" she said. They didn't move. Around five-thirty, the front doors to the store were locked. The four still didn't move. Finally, they left by a side door. Outside, a small crowd had gathered, including a photographer from the Greensboro *Record*. "I'll be back tomorrow with A. & T. College," one of the students said.   *4*

By next morning, the protest had grown to twenty-seven men and four women, most from the same dormitory as the original four. The men were dressed in suits and ties. The students had brought their schoolwork, and studied as they sat at the counter. On Wednesday, students from Greensboro's "Negro" secondary school, Dudley High, joined in, and the number of protesters swelled to eighty. By Thursday, the protesters numbered three hundred, including three white women, from the Greensboro campus of the University of North Carolina. By Saturday, the sit-in had reached six hundred. People spilled out onto the street. White teen-agers waved Confederate flags. Someone threw a firecracker. At noon, the A. & T. football team arrived. "Here comes the wrecking crew," one of the white students shouted.   *5*

By the following Monday, sit-ins had spread to Winston-Salem, twenty-five miles away, and Durham, fifty miles away. The day after that, students at Fayetteville   *6*

State Teachers College and at Johnson C. Smith College, in Charlotte, joined in, followed on Wednesday by students at St. Augustine's College and Shaw University, in Raleigh. On Thursday and Friday, the protest crossed state lines, surfacing in Hampton and Portsmouth, Virginia, in Rock Hill, South Carolina, and in Chattanooga, Tennessee. By the end of the month, there were sit-ins throughout the South, as far west as Texas. "I asked every student I met what the first day of the sitdowns had been like on his campus," the political theorist Michael Walzer wrote in *Dissent*. "The answer was always the same: 'It was like a fever. Everyone wanted to go.' " Some seventy thousand students eventually took part. Thousands were arrested and untold thousands more radicalized. These events in the early sixties became a civil-rights war that engulfed the South for the rest of the decade—and it happened without e-mail, texting, Facebook, or Twitter.

The world, we are told, is in the midst of a revolution. The new tools of social media have reinvented social activism. With Facebook and Twitter and the like, the traditional relationship between political authority and popular will has been upended, making it easier for the powerless to collaborate, coördinate, and give voice to their concerns. When ten thousand protesters took to the streets in Moldova in the spring of 2009 to protest against their country's Communist government, the action was dubbed the Twitter Revolution, because of the means by which the demonstrators had been brought together. A few months after that, when student protests rocked Tehran, the State Department took the unusual step of asking Twitter to suspend scheduled maintenance of its Web site, because the Administration didn't want such a critical organizing tool out of service at the height of the demonstrations. "Without Twitter the people of Iran would not have felt empowered and confident to stand up for freedom and democracy," Mark Pfeifle, a former national-security adviser, later wrote, calling for Twitter to be nominated for the Nobel Peace Prize. Where activists were once defined by their causes, they are now defined by their tools. Facebook warriors go online to push for change. "You are the best hope for us all," James K. Glassman, a former senior State Department official, told a crowd of cyber activists at a recent conference sponsored by Facebook, A. T. & T., Howcast, MTV, and Google. Sites like Facebook, Glassman said, "give the U.S. a significant competitive advantage over terrorists. Some time ago, I said that Al Qaeda was 'eating our lunch on the Internet.' That is no longer the case. Al Qaeda is stuck in Web 1.0. The Internet is now about interactivity and conversation."

7

These are strong, and puzzling, claims. Why does it matter who is eating whose *8*
lunch on the Internet? Are people who log on to their Facebook page really the best
hope for us all? As for Moldova's so-called Twitter Revolution, Evgeny Morozov, a
scholar at Stanford who has been the most persistent of digital evangelism's critics,
points out that Twitter had scant internal significance in Moldova, a country where
very few Twitter accounts exist. Nor does it seem to have been a revolution, not least
because the protests—as Anne Applebaum suggested in the Washington Post—
may well have been a bit of stagecraft cooked up by the government. (In a country
paranoid about Romanian revanchism, the protesters flew a Romanian flag over the
Parliament building.) In the Iranian case, meanwhile, the people tweeting about the
demonstrations were almost all in the West. "It is time to get Twitter's role in the
events in Iran right," Golnaz Esfandiari wrote, this past summer, in *Foreign Policy*.
"Simply put: There was no Twitter Revolution inside Iran." The cadre of prominent
bloggers, like Andrew Sullivan, who championed the role of social media in Iran,
Esfandiari continued, misunderstood the situation. "Western journalists who
couldn't reach—or didn't bother reaching?—people on the ground in Iran simply
scrolled through the English-language tweets post with tag #iranelection," she
wrote. "Through it all, no one seemed to wonder why people trying to coordinate
protests in Iran would be writing in any language other than Farsi."

Some of this grandiosity is to be expected. Innovators tend to be solipsists. They *9*
often want to cram every stray fact and experience into their new model. As the
historian Robert Darnton has written, "The marvels of communication technology
in the present have produced a false consciousness about the past—even a sense that
communication has no history, or had nothing of importance to consider before the
days of television and the Internet." But there is something else at work here, in the
outsized enthusiasm for social media. Fifty years after one of the most extraordinary
episodes of social upheaval in American history, we seem to have forgotten what
activism is.

Greensboro in the early nineteen-sixties was the kind of place where racial *10*
insubordination was routinely met with violence. The four students who first sat
down at the lunch counter were terrified. "I suppose if anyone had come up behind
me and yelled 'Boo,' I think I would have fallen off my seat," one of them said later.
On the first day, the store manager notified the police chief, who immediately
sent two officers to the store. On the third day, a gang of white toughs showed up

at the lunch counter and stood ostentatiously behind the protesters, ominously muttering epithets such as "burr-head nigger." A local Ku Klux Klan leader made an appearance. On Saturday, as tensions grew, someone called in a bomb threat, and the entire store had to be evacuated.

The dangers were even clearer in the Mississippi Freedom Summer Project of 1964, another of the sentinel campaigns of the civil-rights movement. The Student Nonviolent Coordinating Committee recruited hundreds of Northern, largely white unpaid volunteers to run Freedom Schools, register black voters, and raise civil-rights awareness in the Deep South. "No one should go *anywhere* alone, but certainly not in an automobile and certainly not at night," they were instructed. Within days of arriving in Mississippi, three volunteers—Michael Schwerner, James Chaney, and Andrew Goodman—were kidnapped and killed, and, during the rest of the summer, thirty-seven black churches were set on fire and dozens of safe houses were bombed; volunteers were beaten, shot at, arrested, and trailed by pickup trucks full of armed men. A quarter of those in the program dropped out. Activism that challenges the status quo—that attacks deeply rooted problems—is not for the faint of heart.

What makes people capable of this kind of activism? The Stanford sociologist Doug McAdam compared the Freedom Summer dropouts with the participants who stayed, and discovered that the key difference wasn't, as might be expected, ideological fervor. "*All* of the applicants—participants and withdrawals alike—emerge as highly committed, articulate supporters of the goals and values of the summer program," he concluded. What mattered more was an applicant's degree of personal connection to the civil-rights movement. All the volunteers were required to provide a list of personal contacts—the people they wanted kept apprised of their activities—and participants were far more likely than dropouts to have close friends who were also going to Mississippi. High-risk activism, McAdam concluded, is a "strong-tie" phenomenon.

This pattern shows up again and again. One study of the Red Brigades, the Italian terrorist group of the nineteen-seventies, found that seventy per cent of recruits had at least one good friend already in the organization. The same is true of the men who joined the mujahideen in Afghanistan. Even revolutionary actions that look spontaneous, like the demonstrations in East Germany that led to the fall of the Berlin Wall, are, at core, strong-tie phenomena. The opposition movement in East

11

12

13

Germany consisted of several hundred groups, each with roughly a dozen members. Each group was in limited contact with the others: at the time, only thirteen per cent of East Germans even had a phone. All they knew was that on Monday nights, outside St. Nicholas Church in downtown Leipzig, people gathered to voice their anger at the state. And the primary determinant of who showed up was "critical friends"—the more friends you had who were critical of the regime the more likely you were to join the protest.

[14] So one crucial fact about the four freshmen at the Greensboro lunch counter—David Richmond, Franklin McCain, Ezell Blair, and Joseph McNeil— was their relationship with one another. McNeil was a roommate of Blair's in A. & T.'s Scott Hall dormitory. Richmond roomed with McCain one floor up, and Blair, Richmond, and McCain had all gone to Dudley High School. The four would smuggle beer into the dorm and talk late into the night in Blair and McNeil's room. They would all have remembered the murder of Emmett Till in 1955, the Montgomery bus boycott that same year, and the showdown in Little Rock in 1957. It was McNeil who brought up the idea of a sit-in at Woolworth's. They'd discussed it for nearly a month. Then McNeil came into the dorm room and asked the others if they were ready. There was a pause, and McCain said, in a way that works only with people who talk late into the night with one another, "Are you guys chicken or not?" Ezell Blair worked up the courage the next day to ask for a cup of coffee because he was flanked by his roommate and two good friends from high school.

The kind of activism associated with social media isn't like this at all. The platforms of social media are built around weak ties. Twitter is a way of following (or being followed by) people you may never have met. Facebook is a tool for efficiently managing your acquaintances, for keeping up with the people you would not otherwise be able to stay in touch with. That's why you can have a thousand "friends" on Facebook, as you never could in real life.

This is in many ways a wonderful thing. There is strength in weak ties, as the sociologist Mark Granovetter has observed. Our acquaintances—not our friends— are our greatest source of new ideas and information. The Internet lets us exploit the power of these kinds of distant connections with marvellous efficiency. It's terrific at the diffusion of innovation, interdisciplinary collaboration, seamlessly matching up buyers and sellers, and the logistical functions of the dating world. But weak ties seldom lead to high-risk activism.

14

15

16

In a new book called "The Dragonfly Effect: Quick, Effective, and Powerful   *17*
Ways to Use Social Media to Drive Social Change," the business consultant Andy
Smith and the Stanford Business School professor Jennifer Aaker tell the story of
Sameer Bhatia, a young Silicon Valley entrepreneur who came down with acute
myelogenous leukemia. It's a perfect illustration of social media's strengths. Bhatia
needed a bone-marrow transplant, but he could not find a match among his relatives
and friends. The odds were best with a donor of his ethnicity, and there were few
South Asians in the national bone-marrow database. So Bhatia's business partner
sent out an e-mail explaining Bhatia's plight to more than four hundred of their
acquaintances, who forwarded the e-mail to their personal contacts; Facebook pages
and YouTube videos were devoted to the Help Sameer campaign. Eventually, nearly
twenty-five thousand new people were registered in the bone-marrow database, and
Bhatia found a match.

[18] But how did the campaign get so many people to sign up? By not asking   *18*
too much of them. That's the only way you can get someone you don't really know
to do something on your behalf. You can get thousands of people to sign up for a
donor registry, because doing so is pretty easy. You have to send in a cheek swab
and—in the highly unlikely event that your bone marrow is a good match for
someone in need—spend a few hours at the hospital. Donating bone marrow isn't
a trivial matter. But it doesn't involve financial or personal risk; it doesn't mean
spending a summer being chased by armed men in pickup trucks. It doesn't require
that you confront socially entrenched norms and practices. In fact, it's the kind of
commitment that will bring only social acknowledgment and praise.

The evangelists of social media don't understand this distinction; they seem   *19*
to believe that a Facebook friend is the same as a real friend and that signing up for
a donor registry in Silicon Valley today is activism in the same sense as sitting at a
segregated lunch counter in Greensboro in 1960. "Social networks are particularly
effective at increasing motivation," Aaker and Smith write. But that's not true.
Social networks are effective at increasing *participation*—by lessening the level
of motivation that participation requires. The Facebook page of the Save Darfur
Coalition has 1,282,339 members, who have donated an average of nine cents
apiece. The next biggest Darfur charity on Facebook has 22,073 members, who have
donated an average of thirty-five cents. Help Save Darfur has 2,797 members, who
have given, on average, fifteen cents. A spokesperson for the Save Darfur Coalition

told *Newsweek*, "We wouldn't necessarily gauge someone's value to the advocacy movement based on what they've given. This is a powerful mechanism to engage this critical population. They inform their community, attend events, volunteer. It's not something you can measure by looking at a ledger." In other words, Facebook activism succeeds not by motivating people to make a real sacrifice but by motivating them to do the things that people do when they are not motivated enough to make a real sacrifice. We are a long way from the lunch counters of Greensboro.

The students who joined the sit-ins across the South during the winter of 1960 described the movement as a "fever." But the civil-rights movement was more like a military campaign than like a contagion. In the late nineteen-fifties, there had been sixteen sit-ins in various cities throughout the South, fifteen of which were formally organized by civil-rights organizations like the N.A.A.C.P. and CORE. Possible locations for activism were scouted. Plans were drawn up. Movement activists held training sessions and retreats for would-be protesters. The Greensboro Four were a product of this groundwork: all were members of the N.A.A.C.P. Youth Council. They had close ties with the head of the local N.A.A.C.P. chapter. They had been briefed on the earlier wave of sit-ins in Durham, and had been part of a series of movement meetings in activist churches. When the sit-in movement spread from Greensboro throughout the South, it did not spread indiscriminately. It spread to those cities which had preëxisting "movement centers"—a core of dedicated and trained activists ready to turn the "fever" into action. *20*

The civil-rights movement was high-risk activism. It was also, crucially, strategic activism: a challenge to the establishment mounted with precision and discipline. The N.A.A.C.P. was a centralized organization, run from New York according to highly formalized operating procedures. At the Southern Christian Leadership Conference, Martin Luther King, Jr., was the unquestioned authority. At the center of the movement was the black church, which had, as Aldon D. Morris points out in his superb 1984 study, "The Origins of the Civil Rights Movement," a carefully demarcated division of labor, with various standing committees and disciplined groups. "Each group was task-oriented and coordinated its activities through authority structures," Morris writes. "Individuals were held accountable for their assigned duties, and important conflicts were resolved by the minister, who usually exercised ultimate authority over the congregation." *21*

This is the second crucial distinction between traditional activism and its   *22*
online variant: social media are not about this kind of hierarchical organization.
Facebook and the like are tools for building *networks*, which are the opposite, in
structure and character, of hierarchies. Unlike hierarchies, with their rules and
procedures, networks aren't controlled by a single central authority. Decisions are
made through consensus, and the ties that bind people to the group are loose.

This structure makes networks enormously resilient and adaptable in low-   *23*
risk situations. Wikipedia is a perfect example. It doesn't have an editor, sitting in
New York, who directs and corrects each entry. The effort of putting together each
entry is self-organized. If every entry in Wikipedia were to be erased tomorrow, the
content would swiftly be restored, because that's what happens when a network of
thousands spontaneously devote their time to a task.

There are many things, though, that networks don't do well. Car companies   *24*
sensibly use a network to organize their hundreds of suppliers, but not to design
their cars. No one believes that the articulation of a coherent design philosophy is
best handled by a sprawling, leaderless organizational system. Because networks
don't have a centralized leadership structure and clear lines of authority, they have
real difficulty reaching consensus and setting goals. They can't think strategically;
they are chronically prone to conflict and error. How do you make difficult choices
about tactics or strategy or philosophical direction when everyone has an equal say?

The Palestine Liberation Organization originated as a network, and the   *25*
international-relations scholars Mette Eilstrup-Sangiovanni and Calvert Jones argue
in a recent essay in *International Security* that this is why it ran into such trouble as
it grew: "Structural features typical of networks—the absence of central authority,
the unchecked autonomy of rival groups, and the inability to arbitrate quarrels
through formal mechanisms—made the P.L.O. excessively vulnerable to outside
manipulation and internal strife."

In Germany in the nineteen-seventies, they go on, "the far more unified and   *26*
successful left-wing terrorists tended to organize hierarchically, with professional
management and clear divisions of labor. They were concentrated geographically in
universities, where they could establish central leadership, trust, and camaraderie
through regular, face-to-face meetings." They seldom betrayed their comrades in
arms during police interrogations. Their counterparts on the right were organized
as decentralized networks, and had no such discipline. These groups were regularly

infiltrated, and members, once arrested, easily gave up their comrades. Similarly, Al Qaeda was most dangerous when it was a unified hierarchy. Now that it has dissipated into a network, it has proved far less effective.

The drawbacks of networks scarcely matter if the network isn't interested in 27 systemic change—if it just wants to frighten or humiliate or make a splash—or if it doesn't need to think strategically. But if you're taking on a powerful and organized establishment you have to be a hierarchy. The Montgomery bus boycott required the participation of tens of thousands of people who depended on public transit to get to and from work each day. It lasted a *year*. In order to persuade those people to stay true to the cause, the boycott's organizers tasked each local black church with maintaining morale, and put together a free alternative private carpool service, with forty-eight dispatchers and forty-two pickup stations. Even the White Citizens Council, King later said, conceded that the carpool system moved with "military precision." By the time King came to Birmingham, for the climactic showdown with Police Commissioner Eugene (Bull) Connor, he had a budget of a million dollars, and a hundred full-time staff members on the ground, divided into operational units. The operation itself was divided into steadily escalating phases, mapped out in advance. Support was maintained through consecutive mass meetings rotating from church to church around the city

Boycotts and sit-ins and nonviolent confrontations—which were the weapons 28 of choice for the civil-rights movement—are high-risk strategies. They leave little room for conflict and error. The moment even one protester deviates from the script and responds to provocation, the moral legitimacy of the entire protest is compromised. Enthusiasts for social media would no doubt have us believe that King's task in Birmingham would have been made infinitely easier had he been able to communicate with his followers through Facebook, and contented himself with tweets from a Birmingham jail. But networks are messy: think of the ceaseless pattern of correction and revision, amendment and debate, that characterizes Wikipedia. If Martin Luther King, Jr., had tried to do a wiki-boycott in Montgomery, he would have been steamrollered by the white power structure. And of what use would a digital communication tool be in a town where ninety-eight per cent of the black community could be reached every Sunday morning at church? The things that King needed in Birmingham—discipline and strategy—were things that online social media cannot provide.

The bible of the social-media movement is Clay Shirky's *Here Comes Everybody*.   *29*
Shirky, who teaches at New York University, sets out to demonstrate the organizing
power of the Internet, and he begins with the story of Evan, who worked on Wall
Street, and his friend Ivanna, after she left her smart phone, an expensive Sidekick,
on the back seat of a New York City taxicab. The telephone company transferred the
data on Ivanna's lost phone to a new phone, whereupon she and Evan discovered
that the Sidekick was now in the hands of a teen-ager from Queens, who was using it
to take photographs of herself and her friends.

When Evan e-mailed the teen-ager, Sasha, asking for the phone back, she   *30*
replied that his "white ass" didn't deserve to have it back. Miffed, he set up a Web
page with her picture and a description of what had happened. He forwarded
the link to his friends, and they forwarded it to their friends. Someone found the
MySpace page of Sasha's boyfriend, and a link to it found its way onto the site.
Someone found her address online and took a video of her home while driving by;
Evan posted the video on the site. The story was picked up by the news filter Digg.
Evan was now up to ten e-mails a minute. He created a bulletin board for his readers
to share their stories, but it crashed under the weight of responses. Evan and Ivanna
went to the police, but the police filed the report under "lost," rather than "stolen,"
which essentially closed the case. "By this point millions of readers were watching,"
Shirky writes, "and dozens of mainstream news outlets had covered the story."
Bowing to the pressure, the N.Y.P.D. reclassified the item as "stolen." Sasha was
arrested, and Evan got his friend's Sidekick back.

Shirky's argument is that this is the kind of thing that could never have   *31*
happened in the pre-Internet age—and he's right. Evan could never have tracked
down Sasha. The story of the Sidekick would never have been publicized. An army of
people could never have been assembled to wage this fight. The police wouldn't have
bowed to the pressure of a lone person who had misplaced something as trivial as a
cell phone. The story, to Shirky, illustrates "the ease and speed with which a group
can be mobilized for the right kind of cause" in the Internet age.

Shirky considers this model of activism an upgrade. But it is simply a form of   *32*
organizing which favors the weak-tie connections that give us access to information
over the strong-tie connections that help us persevere in the face of danger. It shifts
our energies from organizations that promote strategic and disciplined activity
and toward those which promote resilience and adaptability. It makes it easier for

activists to express themselves, and harder for that expression to have any impact. The instruments of social media are well suited to making the existing social order more efficient. They are not a natural enemy of the status quo. If you are of the opinion that all the world needs is a little buffing around the edges, this should not trouble you. But if you think that there are still lunch counters out there that need integrating it ought to give you pause.

Shirky ends the story of the lost Sidekick by asking, portentously, "What happens next?"—no doubt imagining future waves of digital protesters. But he has already answered the question. What happens next is more of the same. A networked, weak-tie world is good at things like helping Wall Streeters get phones back from teen-age girls. *Viva la revolución.*

33

Reading for Better Writing

Working by yourself or with a group, answer the following questions:

1. Malcolm Gladwell opens with the story of the 1960 lunch-counter protest in Greensboro, North Carolina, an event that "happened without e-mail, texting, Facebook, or Twitter" (end of paragraph 6). Why is this story so important to Gladwell, so important that he repeatedly comes back to it?

2. Gladwell ends his essay with a contrasting narrative about a lost cellphone (paragraphs 29–33). What are the key points of contrast that he establishes or implies? Through the contrast of this story with the Greensboro story, what is Gladwell pressing readers to think about?

3. Consider Gladwell's use of illustrations and examples more broadly. How does he integrate and work with examples to deepen his analysis of social activism?

4. Examine the two main points of comparison that Gladwell makes: strong-tie activism vs. weak-tie activism (paragraphs 12–19) and hierarchical, structured organizations vs. loose networks (paragraphs 20–28). How does each comparison unfold? What argument does each comparison make?

5. Reflect on what social action means for you. Volunteering? Supporting a cause? Joining a march or demonstration? Making a career choice? Consider, as well, recent protest movements, such as the Occupy Wall Street movement and the Idle No More movement. How has Gladwell's essay informed your thinking on social action and your understanding of recent movements?

Writing Guidelines

Planning

1. **Select a topic.** List subjects that are similar and/or different in ways that you find interesting, perplexing, disgusting, infuriating, charming, or informing. Then choose two subjects whose comparison and/or contrast gives the reader some insight into who or what they are. *Note:* Make sure that the items have a solid *basis* for comparison. Comparable items are types of the same thing (e.g., two rivers, two characters, two films, two mental illnesses, two banking regulations, two search engines, two theories).

2. **Get the big picture.** Using a computer or a paper and pen, create three columns as shown below. Brainstorm a list of traits under each heading. (Also see the Venn diagram on page 54.)

Features Peculiar to Subject #1	Shared Features	Features Peculiar to Subject #2

fig. 13.3

3. **Gather information.** Review your list of features, highlighting those that could provide insight into one or both subjects. Research the subjects, using hands-on analysis when possible. Consider writing your research notes in the three-column format shown above.

4. **Draft a working thesis.** Review your expanded list of features and eliminate those that now seem unimportant. Write a sentence stating the core of what you learned about the subjects: what essential insight have you reached about the similarities and/ or differences between the topics? If you're stuck, try completing the sentence below. (Switch around the terms "similar" and "different" and replace "differences" with "similarities" if you wish to stress similarities.)

   Whereas _____ and _____ seem similar, they are different in several ways, and the differences are important because _____.

5. **Get organized.** Decide how to organize your essay. Generally, *subject by subject* works better for short, simple comparisons. *Trait by trait* works better for longer, more complex comparisons, in that you hold up the topics side by side, trait by trait. Consider, as well, the order in which you will discuss the topics and arrange the traits, choices that depend on what you want to feature and how you want to build and deepen the comparison.

Subject by Subject:	Trait by Trait:
Introduction	Introduction
Subject #1	Trait A
• Trait A	• Subject #1
• Trait B	• Subject #2
Subject #2	Trait B
• Trait A	• Subject #1
• Trait B	• Subject #2

fig. 13.4

Drafting

6. **Write your first draft.** Review your outline and draft the paper.

   Subject-by-subject pattern:
   - **Opening:** get readers' attention, introduce the subjects, and offer a thesis.
   - **Middle:** discuss the first subject, then analyze the second subject, discussing traits parallel to those you addressed with the first subject.
   - **Conclusion:** summarize similarities, differences, and implications.

   Trait-by-trait pattern:
   - **Opening:** get readers' attention, introduce the subjects, and offer a thesis.
   - **Middle:** compare and/or contrast the two subjects trait by trait; include transitions that help readers look back and forth between the two subjects.
   - **Conclusion:** summarize the key relationships and note their significance.

Revising

7. **Get feedback.** Ask someone to read your paper, looking for a clear thesis, an engaging introduction, a middle that compares and/or contrasts parallel traits in a logical order, and a unifying closing.

8. **Rework your draft.** Based on feedback, revise for the following issues:

   ____ **Ideas:** The points made and conclusions drawn from comparing and contrasting provide insight into both subjects.

   ____ **Organization:** The structure, whether subject by subject or trait by trait, helps readers grasp the similarities and differences between the subjects.

   ____ **Voice:** The tone is informed, involved, and genuine.

Editing

9. **Carefully edit your essay.** Look for the following issues:

   ____ **Words** are precise, clear, and defined as needed.

   ____ **Sentences** are clear, well reasoned, varied in structure, and smooth.

   ____ **Correctness:** The writing is clean and properly formatted.

   ____ **Page design** is attractive and follows MLA or APA guidelines.

Publishing

10. **Publish your essay.** Share your writing by submitting it to your instructor, posting it on a website, sharing it with friends and family who might be interested in the topic, crafting a presentation or demonstration, or reshaping your comparison as a blog.

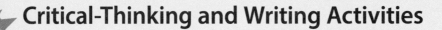

Critical-Thinking and Writing Activities

As directed by your instructor, complete the following activities.

1. According to George Santayana, "Almost every wise saying has an opposite one, no less wise, to balance it." Reflect on wisdom, opposition, and balance as concepts at the heart of compare-contrast writing.

2. Anita Brinkman's "A Fear Born of Sorrow" reflects on the 9/11 attack one week after the event. More than a decade later, can you put 9/11 in a larger historical perspective? Doing research as needed, write a compare-contrast essay in which you analyze some aspect of life pre-9/11 and post-9/11.

3. Follow up your reading of Meaghan Delaney's analysis of *An Ideal Husband* by choosing one of your favourite plays, films, or novels and performing a similar compare-contrast analysis of two or three characters.

4. Peggy Lampotang's "English, French: Why Not Both?" examines cultural differences as rooted in language. What other elements contribute to cultural difference in Canada? What elements bind Canadians together? Using compare-contrast thinking, explore one such element.

5. Using the ideas in Malcolm Gladwell's essay "Small Change" as a starting point, research a recent instance of social action (e.g., the Occupy movement, Idle No More, the Arab Spring). Narrowing your focus as needed, compare the event or movement you have chosen with the Greensboro lunch-counter protest, as described by Gladwell.

Learning-Objectives Checklist ✓

Have you achieved this chapter's learning objectives? Check your progress with the items below, revisiting topics in the chapter as needed. *I have* . . .

___ interpreted compare-contrast essays, ascertaining how the writers' purposes, readers, and topics may have shaped their patterns of reasoning (230–231).

___ examined subject-by-subject and trait-by-trait organizational patterns, identifying their similarities, differences, strengths, and weaknesses (230–231).

___ established a logical basis for a comparison claim by analyzing topics of the same order or type (230–231).

___ developed a reasonable comparison by assessing each subject using the same criteria in the same manner (230–231).

___ supported my compare-contrast reasoning with precise details, as well as with transitional words that clarify similarities and differences (253).

___ strengthened my compare-contrast writing by using effective revising and editing strategies (252–253).

___ successfully planned, drafted, revised, and polished a logical compare-contrast essay (252–253).

Chapter 14

Cause and Effect

Now, why did that happen? We ask this question every day at home, in school, and on the job in order to understand and cope with things that happen in our lives. For example, knowing why a computer crashed will help us avoid that problem, and knowing the causes and effects of a disease such as diabetes can help us control the condition. In other words, cause and effect reasoning helps us deal with everyday issues, whether large or small.

In a cause and effect essay, the writer develops the thesis through cause and effect reasoning. That is, she or he analyzes and explains the causes, the effects, or both the causes and the effects of a phenomenon. In addition, the writer may use other analytical strategies (such as definition or classification) to clarify a concept or further develop a claim. This chapter includes instructions and samples that will help you read and write cause-effect analyses.

Visually Speaking We see causes and effects everywhere around us, every day. How does the image below vividly capture the nature of causes and effects, as well as the relationship between them? How might writing create a parallel image of such cause-effect relationships?

Learning **Objectives**

By working through this chapter, you will be able to

- understand, interpret, and critique writing that utilizes cause-effect reasoning.
- analyze a phenomenon by identifying and explaining its causes and effects.
- identify and correct related logical fallacies.
- support cause-effect reasoning with detailed, reliable evidence.
- clarify cause-effect relationships through transitional words.
- draft, revise, and edit an essay that uses cause-effect reasoning in conjunction with other relevant analytical modes.

Strahil Dimitrov/Shutterstock.com

fig. 14.1

Strategies for Cause-Effect Essays

Cause-effect thinking can move in two directions. First, it can explore the effects of a particular event, action, or phenomenon—the logical results, actual or anticipated. Second, it can trace backward from a particular result to those forces that created the results—the causes. As writers think through causes and effects, their job is to establish and explain solid cause-effect links, as discussed in the strategies below.

The Rhetorical Situation

To put cause-effect writing in context, consider the situation that gives rise to it:

- **Purpose.** Writers use cause-effect analysis to deepen understanding regarding how specific forces work to bring about particular results. In academia and the workplace, cause-effect logic operates in many forms of writing—from persuasive essays and lab reports to project proposals and market analyses. In each situation, writers use cause-effect thinking to explain a phenomenon or to prove a point.
- **Readers.** The readers of cause-effect writing typically understand the topic at a basic level but want or need a deeper understanding of the forces operating within it so as to make decisions about or take positions on it.
- **Topic.** Cause-effect topics are phenomena—events, occurrences, developments, processes, problems, conditions, and so on—that need to be more fully explained in terms of their operating forces.

Example: In "Pitch Perfect" (pages 269–270), Jay Ingram's **topic** is the knuckleball pitch in baseball. His **purpose** is to explore the way that this pitch works to confound hitters so that **readers** of *The Walrus*, the magazine where the article was published, will better understand and appreciate the pitch.

Principles of Cause-Effect Writing

Cause-effect writing depends upon the logical principles explained below.

Exploring cause-effect links. Such writing tests all possible explanations for a given phenomenon's causes and effects. Consider these options:

- **Causes:** What forces can be designated primary or root causes? What forces are secondary or contributing causes? Which causes are immediate (near), and which are remote (distant)? What cause-effect "evidence" is simply coincidental? What evidence—measurements, testimony, and so on—supports or disproves the causal links? Can the links be tested?
- **Effects:** What are the primary, secondary, and ripple effects? Which are main effects and which are side effects, which immediate and which long-term? What is the seriousness or strength of each effect? What aspects of the cause led to the various effects? Do the effects themselves become causes of a different set of effects in a kind of "chain reaction"?

Establishing a cause-effect thesis. The thesis is an insight growing out of careful study of the topic, often following one of these patterns:

- **Focus on causes:** Based on a close examination of the forces at work, we can conclude that A and B are the fundamental causes of C.
- **Focus on effects:** Based on a close examination of the forces at work, we can conclude that the most important results of A have been X, Y, and Z.

Example: When people around the globe watch Hollywood blockbuster films, they absorb a distorted vision of U.S. culture that fuels misunderstanding and, in fact, undermines that government's "war on terror."

Supplying reliable cause-effect evidence. Cause-effect analysis is based on a logical interpretation of the evidence, analysis that avoids these problems: (1) relying extensively on circumstantial evidence, (2) drawing firm conclusions without adequate support, and (3) mistaking sequence for a cause-effect link (see the *false-cause fallacy*, page 319).

Organizing cause-effect analysis to feature the chain of reasoning. The phrasing of the thesis implies a certain method of developing and supporting the thesis—a way of proceeding with and handling the cause-effect evidence. Generally, writers structure their essays according to the direction of analysis (from effect to causes or from cause to effects). It is often necessary to begin by exploring background in order to situate the cause-effect analysis.

Sample Cause-Effect Paragraph:

A writer may shape a paragraph into a cause-effect pattern in order to explain the forces at work within a phenomenon. In the sample below, Laura Black explains the effects of hypothermia on the human body.

> Even a slight drop in the normal human body temperature of 37 degrees Celsius causes hypothermia. Often produced by accidental or prolonged exposure to cold, the condition forces all bodily functions to slow down. The heart rate and blood pressure decrease. Breathing becomes slower and shallower. As the body temperature drops, these effects become even more dramatic until it reaches somewhere between 30 and 27 degrees Celsius and the person lapses into unconsciousness. When the temperature reaches between 18 and 15 degrees Celsius, heart action, blood flow, and electrical brain activity stop. Normally such a condition would be fatal. However, as the body cools down, the need for oxygen also slows down. A person can survive in a deep hypothermic state for an hour or longer and be revived without serious complications.

Courtesy of The Write Source.

Reading Cause-Effect Writing

As you read the essays on the following pages, consider these questions:

1. Why is the writer exploring the cause-effect relationships of this topic?
2. Who is the intended audience, and does the essay present all the necessary information?
3. Is the topic clearly identified and explored as a phenomenon?
4. Is the thesis clear, and is the argument free of logical fallacies?
5. Are the writer's claims sufficiently limited, focused, and logical?

Sample Cause-Effect Essays

In the following essays, writers address topics as varied as the effects in Eastern Europe of the fall of Communism, the role of Canadian newspaperwomen in the suffrage movement, the dynamics of the knuckleball pitch, and the source of other worlds in science fiction.

Analyzing the Effects of Communism

In the following essay, essentially a book review of Slavenka Drakulić's *Café Europa*, student writer Jade Barsalou analyzes the long-term effects for Eastern Europeans of living under Soviet Communist rule for decades.

Essay Outline

Introduction: Drakulić's *Café Europa* as a book that explores the post-Communism struggles of Eastern Europeans

1. As a concept, "nation" fails to capture the cultural complexity of Eastern Europe, the village of Istria being a helpful example.
2. Drakulić effectively explores how the kind of poverty created by Communism impacted all areas of life, even in the post-Communist period.
3. Albania illustrates the paradox that life under Capitalism is littler better than life under Communism.
4. Drakulić repeatedly argues that Eastern Europeans need time to make a successful cultural shift.

Conclusion: the need to break down continuing barriers around Eastern Europeans.

From Communism to Capitalism: The More Things Change, the More They Remain the Same

The writer describes the book's focus, building to her thesis about Communism's lasting effects.

As much as *Café Europa* is a story about one woman's experience growing up under Communist rule, Slavenka Drakulić also offers a glimpse into the lived experiences of all Eastern Europeans who grew up in the shadows of pillboxes, border patrols, ethnic cleansing, and the concentration camp Jasenovac (18, 53, 136–37, 164, 210). For fifty years under Communism, Eastern Europeans, like Drakulić, were taught that there was no "you," "I," or "individual"; there was only "us," "the state," or the "collective" (2). Although Drakulić compellingly alternates between stories and reflections that are part of the public realm and those that are personal and private remembrances, the anecdotes she offers illustrate the myriad ways in which the personal is political. This perspective, or rather her perspective,

1

presents an instructive analysis of the ways in which Communist subjects were ostensibly enslaved by an ideology that used dictatorial politics and violence as a means to achieve obedience, assimilation, conformity, and complicity. In this respect, the effects and after-effects of the Communist period are really beyond measure, for, as Drakulić astutely points out, generations of Croatians, Serbians, Bosnians, Albanians, Romanians, Czecks, Slovenians, Bulgarians, and Hungarians have been denied a political voice, individual identities, a fully developed cultural heritage, and free-market economic participation (2–3, 50, 97, 103–04). Moreover, because these Eastern Europeans have not simply become bastions of democratic promise in the wake of Communism, they continue to find themselves encircled by borders, both real and imagined.

In 1983, Benedict Anderson published his seminal work *Imagined Communities*, where he defined the nation as "an imagined political community" (6). For our purposes, Benedict's definition of a nation is important because it underscores the fact that ideas about nations, nationhood, and nationalism, in general, are socially and politically constructed categories of belonging. Like Anderson, Drakulić observes that just because someone or something creates or imagines these categories does not mean that they are accepted or internalized by the peoples they are supposed to describe or encompass (Anderson 6; Drakulić 162–64). For example, in Istria, it seems that although national identity was, in a Marxist sense, defined from above and applied from without, this was also a concept that was being challenged from below.

In the early 1990s, after the fall of Communism, Istria was a village divided by three borders: Italian, Croatian, and Slovenian. The oddity of dividing this tiny peninsula into three separate though not necessarily equal territorial parts stems from the region's shifting population and complex history as an occupied territory (160, 166). As a result, many Istrians seem to identify with their region, or physical place, rather than with the differences between nationalities, dialects, foods, religions, or political ideologies (165, 167–68). Hence, in the census of 1991, 20 per cent of the local population identified themselves as "Istrians," and not as "Croatians" or "Others" (164). To my mind, this was not only a dramatic political declaration, but it also seems to be the type of political action, self-identification, that democracies enshrine. However, the Istrians' attempts to self-identify, or perhaps their desire to create a political community of their own imagining,

Jade begins her analysis by defining a key term and then exploring the term's complexity with a specific example.

2

3

was denounced by the Croatian government. In an effort to understand the official response from Zagreb, Drakulić astutely asks, "how can these authorities understand the meaning of Istrianism—the enlarging concept of identity, as opposed to the reducing concept of nationality?" (164). In this sense, Drakulić identifies the reductive experience of nationalism as a relic of Communism that continues to exact an enduring and powerful influence on mundane aspects of life and the newly enshrined and supposedly democratic political principles (166, 169). Thus, it seems that in the post-Communist context, the introduction of democracy and Capitalism throughout Eastern Europe did not result in the immediate acceptance, or uniform application, of these values.

Within the text, Drakulić explores the manifold and complex ways in which   4
the legacy of Communism and particularly the enduring cycle of poverty it engendered have impacted every aspect of social, political, economic, and cultural life (11). Although many Eastern European countries were impoverished before Communism, under this regime, loyal and obedient citizens, or "comrades," were promised "progress." According to the leaders of the Communist party, however, "progress" meant paved roads, electricity in homes, more factories, and a decent pair of shoes (30). Indeed, it seems that "progress" and not "prosperity" was the "compensation" the people received in exchange for their freedom, their independence and individuality, and their futures (29, 2–4, 67). That being said, it is also worth noting that under Communism, Eastern Europeans had access to a number of fairly progressive programs and services, such as medical care, pensions, maternity leave, and sick days (67). Ironically, instead of creating an "instant welfare society," the introduction of democracy and a free-market economy actually eliminated these benevolent programs (50, 67). Thus, it would seem that in many respects, Capitalism has not made life in Eastern Europe better than it was under Communism, and nowhere is this paradox more strikingly illustrated than in Albania.

The writer turns to Communism's legacy of poverty.

Upon her arrival at the airport near Tirana, Albania, Drakulić immediately   5
encountered the "pillboxes," or the 600,000 to 1 million military style compounds that Communist leader, Enver Hoxha, constructed throughout the country (54). While the sheer number and size of these structures was designed to create a physical barrier, to keep "others" out and Albanians in, they were also engineered to inspire fear, obedience, and conformity (55). Although this type of psychological

Albania serves as a specific illustration of the challenges created by Communism.

indoctrination was one of the hallmarks of Communist rule, in the shadows of the pillboxes, many Albanians seem to have internalized these values, and the result was an unusually violent rejection of collectivism. Of course, the destruction of schools, hospitals, factories, and greenhouses during the revolution of 1992 can also be linked to the televised promise that "democracy will replace the old with the new" (54–56). According to Drakulić, the mere existence, or televised representation, of democracy was not enough to teach this "nation of peasants" how to exercise their newfound rights and freedoms overnight (36, 56). What this suggests, therefore, is that while the official economic and political policies may have changed, the social and cultural experience of what it means to be a citizen in these formerly-Communist countries has not really changed all that much.

Over and over again, Drakulić reminds us that these people need time, education, and resources in order to begin the process of acclimatizing themselves to these new ways of life. For Drakulić, true democratic participation and free-market economics will likely remain theoretical constructs, to be manipulated and controlled by wolves in sheep's skin, until Eastern Europeans accept their Communist and Fascist past, until they learn to wash their hands and care for their teeth, and until they learn to recognize that Europe, or more particularly, Western Europe is not a Utopia or the Promised Land (12, 36–37, 97, 132-33, 147–49, 209). In essence, meaningful social, economic, and political change will not be possible until a widespread cultural revolution takes place among ordinary people (51). Until that time, these European "exile[s]" are ostensibly people who were forced from Feudalism to Communism to Capitalism; and as such, they have no real identity of their own (10, 31). Moreover, while citizens of former-Communist countries may now have access to democracy and a free-market economy, these people cannot claim a true European identity because they are not considered "Europeans" (14–15, 21). In this context therefore, the European community's refusal to intervene in the Balkan wars clearly demonstrates that one of the lasting and profound legacies of Communism is that Europe continues to be divided between East and West (209–10, 212, 213).

As much as this book is about breaking down barriers, the sad reality is that borders or boundaries, real or imagined, are still being constructed around these former Communist countries and their citizens. And in doing so, everyone who is complicit in this process is helping to perpetuate the sense of fear, oppression,

> The writer explores the deeper nature of the problem as traced in the book.

> The conclusion offers a reflective call to enlarge our vision.

6

7

inferiority, and insecurity born under Communism to a supposedly democratic, progressive, enlightened, and united Europe. Perhaps it was for this reason that Drakulić chose not to capitalize the word *communism* in her book, because to do so would symbolically infuse this word, this concept, this ideology with the enduring power to oppress, humiliate, and degrade. The real challenge for us all, it seems, is to learn to look beyond linguistic differences, political affiliations, and territorial borders, and recognize that peace, hope, and prosperity can only be truly achieved when we embrace our collective identity as human beings. In this sense, there is no "I" or "we," "us" or "them," "inferior" or "superior," "Communism" or "Capitalism"; there is only human dignity, a shared sense of purpose or belonging, and a future worth building together.

Note: The Works-Cited page is not shown. For sample pages, see MLA (page 533) and APA (pages 562–563).

Reading for Better Writing

Working by yourself or with a group, answer the following questions:

1. Is the world of Eastern Europe familiar or unfamiliar to you? Did Jade Barsalou's analysis of *Café Europa* bring you closer to that world? How does this essay press you to connect to this far-away world?

2. The essential point of this essay focuses on the effects and after-effects of Communism in Eastern Europe. In your own words, what is this essential point—the thesis?

3. Paragraph 2 offers a definition of *nation*. What does this extended definition add to Jade's analysis of the effects of Communism on Eastern Europe?

4. The essay uses two examples to illustrate the cause-effect analysis (Istria in paragraph 3 and Albania in paragraph 5). How do these illustrations support specific cause-effect points?

5. How does the conclusion expand upon the analysis of Eastern Europe?

Analyzing Political Change

In the following essay, student writer Megan Cécile Radford explains how the work of Canadian newspaperwomen contributed to the success of the suffrage movement, leading to women gaining the right to vote. In other words, the essay examines one contributing cause to a particular effect.

How Canadian Newspaperwomen Won the Vote

"There was a tradition among women in newspaper work not only to write the news, but to make it." Marjory Lang, *Women Who Made the News* (226)

On May 24th, 1918, they did it. After decades of petitions, demonstrations, and rallies, female citizens over the age of 21 in the Dominion of Canada won the right to vote. The girls of the newspapers put down their pens to celebrate, then sat up straighter at their desks, ready to take on another social issue. The women of the press had fought for the vote in every way available to them. Their women's pages had provided a forum for people of many social classes across the country to discuss suffrage, in all its complications. Through the press, what was considered a women's issue was plunged into the general discourse, helping to usher in a new era of democracy. This is how Canadian suffrage was won through the women of the media.

From the start, suffrage was caught up in the newspaper business because the press was one of the only places where women could voice their opinions. In the late 1890s and into the early 1900s, it was not considered appropriate for a woman of good breeding to stand at a pulpit, pound with her fist, and preach social change. A more liberal view of a "woman's place" began to evolve as the new century wore on, but more often women would take the avenue that was available to them: writing in letters or editorials in the women's pages, or under pseudonyms if they managed to break into the main pages of the paper (Rex x). According to information from a 1911 census, 25 percent of female suffrage leaders were journalists or authors, the highest-represented profession among the group (Bacchi 6).

In an interview, Carleton Journalism adjunct professor Barbara Freeman maintained that women working for newspapers in those early days were well-educated, bright, progressive and informed. They meshed well with other professionals, such as doctors, teachers, and civil servants who joined them as

The writer begins with the end of the story—the women's suffrage victory.

A discussion of women's roles in society contextualizes the cause-effect analysis.

Expert opinion, statistics, and facts add concrete depth to the discussion.

1

2

3

leaders of the suffrage movement. In 1911, almost 60 percent of female suffrage leaders were employed outside the home, compared to 14.3 percent of the general population of females over the age of ten in 1911 (Bacchi 6). They were privileged, and with that came the responsibility to represent the concern of the common woman, despite the fact that for many this consideration did not seem to encompass those outside the Anglo-Saxon race (Bacchi 104).

Freeman argues that for many female journalists, their support of suffrage was a reflection of their concern for women and their families, and later their patriotism. Many suffragettes were teetotalers, including the vivacious Nellie McClung. Their desire to ban alcohol arose from the plight of women whose husbands came home drunk and penniless, leaving their children hungry. Then, when many women took up work on the home front of the First World War, women of the media lobbied Prime Minister Borden for the right to vote for conscription. It was this fight that pushed Borden to grant women the federal vote (Freeman). Their passion and awareness served them well, both on the women's pages and in the public sphere.

The essay turns to the newspaperwomen's actual writing on suffrage.

In the corners of Canadian papers and magazines, women editors, writers and readers alike gave vent to their opinions concerning their right to vote. Early in the game, the globe-trotting Sara Jeanette Duncan sparred with readers and politicians with her characteristic wit and satire (Fiamengo 11). Marjory Lang writes that views like Duncan's were ignored in other sections of the paper (156). Indeed, it seemed as though women were carrying out a revolution under the very noses of the men who isolated them.

But it wasn't kept secret for long. In the *Grain Grower's Guide* and other newspapers, women began to circulate petitions demanding women's rights and the right to vote (Lang 225). Coverage of women's club events often discussed the issue of suffrage, and gave rise to lively debate in letters from readers. One example is from a woman named Elizabeth to the Grain Growers Guide on March 18th, 1914:

> I am a farmer's wife, or rather a homesteader's wife, nineteen miles from a town and certainly know what the farm woman has to contend with. Cheer up, sisters, better days are coming. The men are waking up and so are women. . . .

I noticed in The Guide that Premier Roblin refuses to grant suffrage to women. How can he, having a good wife, and addressed by such a splendid woman, wife and mother as Mrs. McClung, also petitioned by so many other progressive women, deny a woman's right to have a voice in the affairs of the nation? It is certainly a "mother's" right. Oh, that we could do something effective to put a stop to this awful traffic of liquor. . . .

The talented women's pagers were inspiring ordinary women to take a stand with them. And while their peers in England resorted to molotov cocktails and hunger strikes, all Canadians seemed to need were words.

Their words often earned them undesirable consequences. In 1913, during a presentation at the Alberta Legislature, Premier Sifton was reported to have said to Nellie McClung and Emily Murphy: "Did you ladies wash up your luncheon dishes before you came down here...? If you haven't you'd better go home because you're not going to get any votes from me" ("Interview"). Even the brave Kit Coleman of the *Toronto Daily Mail* held back her opinions on suffrage because of the views of her conservative paper (Freeman). It was not easy or popular to be a "progressive woman."

7

> The writer outlines the opposition women received and their courage in meeting that resistance.

But women of the press had been standing up to the insults of men since they had first entered the newsroom. Kay Rex writes that in the early 1900s the newspaper business was all but closed to the female sex because men did not want women in their "smoke-filled dens" (Rex x). Women at the turn of the century were "expected to be 'seen and not heard'" (x). Those women who did manage to become reporters did so by crashing through barriers or by setting up shop as permanent fixtures in the discourse of women's pages. They fought for their jobs, earning them on the skill of their pens and the strength of their connections in the world of women. As Isabel A.R. MacLean of the *Vancouver Province* once said, "Why shouldn't women become first-rate book reviewers and critics of music and drama?" (qtd. in Rex 19).

8

> The role of women's pages is explored.

Still, many female journalists had to content themselves with editorials in the women's section. There, at least, women were needed for economic reasons,

9

to attract advertisements from companies that sold household and fashion goods (Lang 8). The women's pages helped to finance the news, and even the stodgiest newsman could not say a thing about that.

Women's page editors would often use their columns to debate men's   *10* arguments against suffrage, or to argue with other women who were less sympathetic towards the cause. Most suffrage supporters were not shy of public speaking, but expressing their views in print allowed them to reach a wider audience. This was especially true of Camille Lessard-Bissonnette, a columnist for *Le Messager* of Maine. Lessard-Bissonnette is often overlooked as a suffrage supporter in the annals of both Canadian suffrage and Canadian women of the press, perhaps because she spent part of her life writing for the Quebec diaspora in the United States. But in those days the debate across borders was fluid, and Lessard-Bissonnette engaged with other French-Canadians as well as with Franco-Americans (Shideler 74). She offered scathing observations about the hypocritical nature of saying that women should not get involved with politics or voting because it would soil their superior virtue (Shideler 70). On February 4th, 1910, she wrote the following in the *Le Messager*:

> You say, sirs, that it is the woman who lights up your home. You compare her to a ray of sunshine. You exclaim that women must not be dragged into the mud of politics. But sirs, when a ray of sunshine falls on the mud does it dirty itself, or does it dry up and purify the mud?

It was not only men that suffrage writers had to contend with. To see the deep   *11* divisions within Canada on the issue of suffrage, you need look no further than the fact that the National Council of Women did not declare its support for the cause until 1910. Even within the Canadian Women's Press Club, consensus could not be reached. Despite being a founding member of the CWPC, Anne-Marie Gleason-Huguenin (pen name Madeleine) of La Patrie did not support the women's vote. While Lessard-Bissonnette was less harsh in disagreeing with Madeleine than with men, she stood firm in her conviction that women must support their suffragette

The writer examines the ideas of one particular newspaper-woman to illustrate the challenges.

Debates and disagreements among women themselves are explored.

"sisters," even if they did not agree with them (Shilderer 74). She bitterly rebuked women who, as Janet Shilderer writes, "maliciously characterize, generalize, and verbally assault their sisters engaged in the fight on behalf of all women" (75). Her frustration was warranted: Quebec chose not to give women the vote until April 1940, decades after most other provinces.

Women from all provinces were often recruited to write for newspapers because *12* of their work in women's clubs (Lang 222). Their connections meant that women would pay attention, and advertisers would want their wares shown alongside prominent female columns. Their social aptitude may have landed them the job, but it also helped them promote their pet cause (Lang 224). Emily Murphy is said to have "dragged the CWPC's Edmonton branch kicking and screaming into the feminist world of confrontation" (Rex 15). Journalism was a medium for change.

> The writer describes the work done by newspaperwomen to advance the cause of suffrage.

Networking was crucial to spreading the word about the need for women to *13* vote, but the women of the press went further than that. They staged rallies, and hosted prominent British suffragettes to make sure that the public heard their cries loud and clear. Flora MacDonald Denison of the Toronto Sunday *World* was a key player in bringing controversial British suffrage leader Emmeline Pankhurst to Massey Hall in Toronto in the fall of 1909 (Fiamengo 155). Denison, who was at the time the vice-president of the Canadian Suffrage Association, wrote in her column after meeting Pankhurst that "she left us crowned with the admiration of everyone who heard her" (qtd. in Fiamengo 155)

Of course, no account of the effect Canadian journalists had on suffrage would *14* be complete without mention of the famous Mock Parliament staged in Winnipeg in 1914. Nellie McClung had joined the Canadian Women's Press Club in 1910. Because of her efforts, those of agricultural reporter Cora Hind and the spirited Beynon sisters, the journalists of Winnipeg became the keepers of "the cradle of the women's suffrage movement in Canada," forming the Political Equality League (Lang 225; Rex 14). Women of the press played the key roles in the Mock Parliament held by the Political Equality League, with Nellie McClung starring as the premier, Sir Rodmond Roblin (Lang 226). Their efforts to promote equality outside of paper and

> The essay zooms in on a specific event and culture in Winnipeg.

ink were as fervent as their written words. Even after suffrage had passed, McClung, Murphy and others were not satisfied. Equality would not be achieved until women could not only vote for their representatives, but become them.

> The conclusion quotes a key suffragette and connects this history to the present.

In the May 1916 issue of *Maclean's*, one month after Alberta became the third Canadian province to allow female citizens to vote, Nellie McClung wrote, "Democracy has its faults; the people may run the country to the dogs, but they will run it back again. People, including women, will make mistakes, but in paying for them they will learn wisdom." It is because of McClung and her peers that Canadian women now have the opportunity to make those political mistakes. Whether we will "learn wisdom" from those mistakes is now a choice that is solely our own.

15

Note: The Works-Cited page is not shown. For sample pages, see MLA (page 533) and APA (pages 562–563).

Reading for Better Writing

Working by yourself or with a group, answer the following questions:

1. When you consider the right to vote, what comes to mind? What opportunities have you had to vote, and what have you done with those occasions? How does Megan Cécile Radford's essay put your own voting in historical perspective?
2. Megan begins with a quotation from Marjorie Lang (which functions as an epigraph for the essay) and with women winning the right to vote in Canada. What sense do you make of this beginning? How does it frame the essay?
3. To convince readers of the significant role of newspaperwomen, Megan creates historical context (paragraph 2) and provides background on the newspaperwomen themselves (paragraph 3). How does this information deepen the cause-effect analysis?
4. The remainder of the essay is dedicated to outlining the work of newspaperwomen and the opposition they met and overcame. Describe the strategies that Megan uses to examine this work as a cause that brought about the right to vote.
5. What does the closing paragraph accomplish in terms of the analysis?

Analyzing a Sports Technique

Jay Ingram is a science broadcaster who has hosted such shows as CBC Radio's *Quirks and Quarks* and the Discovery Channel's *Daily Planet*. Ingram is also a science writer of such books as *Theatre of the Mind*, *The Science of Everyday Life*, and, most recently, *Fatal Flaws*. A great promoter of strong science writing, Ingram is the Chair of the Science Communications Program at the Banff Centre and the co-founder of Beakerhead, an arts and engineering event. In the following essay, Ingram explores the cause-effect science behind the knuckleball pitch.

Pitch Perfect:

Why the Knuckleball Confounds Even Scientists

[1] A standard baseball pitch—slider, curveball, fastball—seems to slavishly follow the laws of physics, making it possible to predict where a ball will go and how it will get there. The knuckleball is different. It appears to dip suddenly, dart to one side or the other, or—when you least expect it—to float in straight over the plate. Hitters are left flailing desperately at it. On a six-game streak last season, pitcher R. A. Dickey struck out sixty-three batters and gave up a single unearned run. And yet Dickey, who joined the Blue Jays this season, is the only active knuckler in the major leagues. When he won the National League Cy Young Award in 2012, he was the first knuckleball pitcher ever to do so.

> The writer begins by describing the uniqueness of the knuckleball within baseball culture.

Set against the heroics of home run hitters and base stealers, even the most successful knuckleball pitchers are seen as curios. The pitch is thrown at an unimpressive velocity, seldom hitting more than seventy or eighty miles per hour, while the best fastballs can crack 100 mph (baseball is still measured in imperial). It's considered the pitch of second chances: because of that leisurely velocity, knuckleballers' arms don't wear out. Its reputation for unpredictability is both a blessing and a curse. Even Dickey doesn't know how he will perform from day to day, or what will happen after the ball leaves his grasp, and while he may have led the National League in strikeouts last season he also gave up twenty-four home runs. Only fourteen pitchers in the league gave up more.

> To prepare for his analysis of the knuckleball, the writer first explains the science of more common pitches.

To understand why the knuckleball seems so perverse, we must first consider a standard pitch and why a baseball curves when it's spinning. Imagine you're hovering over a baseball as it leaves the pitcher's hand, spinning clockwise as it makes its way to the plate. A thin layer of air, called the boundary layer, momentarily clings to the surface of the ball, then separates as the ball moves on, creating an outboard motor-like wake behind it.

On the right, the boundary layer and the air flowing past it are moving in the same direction. But on the other side, the left, things are very different. The boundary layer is turning into the oncoming air, forcing it to separate sooner than on the right. This shifts the wake over to the left side of the ball, pushing the ball to the right.

Jay Ingram, "Pitch Perfect: Why the Knuckleball Confounds Even Scientists", The Walrus, June 2013, pp. 21–22. Copyright © Jay Ingram.

So the ball we're following will curve left to right; an over spin (imagine it rolling 5 forward) will drive it down or to one side. That's the major-league curveball. Add an under spin (so the bottom moves forward and up), and you have a fastball that seems not to drop at all on its way to the plate. All predictable.

But the knuckleball doesn't spin, at least not much. In 1975, wind tunnel tests at 6 Tulane University in New Orleans showed that a very slowly rotating knuckleball—a mere quarter turn from pitcher's mound to home plate—could be pushed one way, then the other. It's all about the stitches.

The cause-effect science but also the mystery of the knuckleball are explored.

There are 216 stitches on a baseball, arranged in a figure eight, the equivalent of 7 mountain ranges on the otherwise smooth surface. Air flowing past a slowly rotating ball will suddenly encounter the stitches, and push the ball in an unpredictable direction with unpredictable speed—especially if the boundary layer happens to meet a stitch exactly where it's separating from the ball.

Yet, the more the pitch is studied, the more mysterious it seems. Physicist Alan 8 Nathan from the University of Illinois recently used a video tracking system to analyze it further. Examining data from 2011 games pitched by Dickey and retired knuckler Tim Wakefield, Nathan concluded that, contrary to the opinion of every batter who has faced a knuckleball, the ball follows a smooth trajectory. It doesn't bob and weave suddenly; it just seems to.

The essay concludes with speculation and celebration.

This could be another example of batters' perceptions being fooled, not unlike 9 the so-called rising fastball, which doesn't rise at all. It just doesn't drop as fast as batters assume it will. This surprising finding prompted Nathan to suggest that the apparent fluttering and zigzagging may be a trick of perception. As the pitch rotates extremely slowly, the orientation of the seams is actually visible to the batter, instead of being the usual blur. It may be that the seams' movement is confused with that of the ball. "Knuckleballs," he ventures, "are more like bullets than butterflies." Only further experiments will tell us for sure. In the meantime, we can be certain of one thing: that the knuckler is the most beautifully bizarre phenomenon in all of baseball.

Reading for Better Writing

Working by yourself or with a group, answer the following questions:

1. Jay Ingram's cause-effect analysis is built on clear, scientific explanations. Re-examine these explanations. What techniques does Ingram use to explain causes and effects?

2. The essay is also structured around a contrast between the knuckleball and more common pitches such as the fastball and the curveball. What does this contrast accomplish?

3. How would you characterize the tone of this essay? Where and how does that tone come through? And does such a tone fit the essay? Why or why not?

4. How would you characterize your relationship with sports? Are you a participant? A fan—specifically of baseball? How does a scientific cause-effect explanation such as Ingram's contribute to your understanding of and feelings about sports?

Analyzing a Narrative Genre

A prolific poet and novelist, Margaret Atwood is well known for what she herself calls "speculative fiction," novels such as *The Handmaid's Tale, Oryx and Crake, The Year of the Flood,* and, most recently, *MaddAddam.* In 2011, she published a collection of essays on speculative fiction, *In Other Worlds: SF and the Human Imagination.* The piece below is an excerpt from "Flying Rabbits: Denizens of Distant Planets." Here, she speculates on why humans create other worlds—the possible sources of our imaginings.

Other Worlds

As you read this essay, annotate it and take notes—considering how Atwood explores the possible causes behind the human imagining of other worlds.

Where do other worlds and alien beings come from? Why do young children so routinely fear that there is something horrible under the bed, other than their slippers? Is the under-bed monster an archetype left over from prehistory, when we were hunted by cave tigers, or is it something else? Why do young children also believe that such inanimate objects as spoons and stones—let along their stuffed teddy bears—have thoughts like theirs, and good and bad intentions toward them? Are these three questions related?

The ability to see things from the point of view of another being has been receiving a lot of attention from biologists lately, most notably Frans de Waal in his book *The Age of Empathy.* It used to be thought that only human beings could imagine life from the position of another, but not so, it seems. Elephants can, and chimpanzees, but not monkeys. Only a being with a sense of "self" can do this, it is supposed. One way of testing for this sense-of-self capacity is through mirrors. Does an animal looking at its reflection in a mirror recognize the reflection of itself? Intriguing experiments have been done in which elephants are presented with elephant-sized mirrors, having first had a visible mark painted on one side of the head and an invisible mark painted on the other side to exclude the sense of touch as a factor. If the elephant sees the mark on its reflected image and then touches the real mark on its head with its trunk, it must know that the reflection is "itself." Often, before coming to the realization that the reflection is indeed self, an elephant will look behind the mirror. So will a human child.

If you can image—or imagine—yourself, you can image—or imagine—a being not-yourself; and you can also imagine how such a being may see the world, a world that includes you. You can see yourself from outside. To the imagined being, you may look like a cherished loved one or a potential friend, or you may look like a

1

2

3

Excerpted from In Other Worlds: SF and the Human Imagination by Margaret Atwood. Copyright © 2011 O.W. Toad Ltd. Reprinted by permission of McClelland & Stewart.

tasty dinner or a bitter enemy. When a young child is imagining what's under the bed, it is also imagining what it might represent to that unseen creature: usually prey. It is possibly not a good idea to tell the little ones that they look good enough to eat. Frisky the Cat wouldn't be bothered by such a statement, lacking as she does a capacity for empathy, but Charlie the Child may well have hysterics.

One of the more brilliant innovations of H. G. Wells's *The War of the Worlds* is   4
that it so clearly sets forth what we puny human beings might look like to godlike intellects far superior to ours. From that time to this, we've been told many stories along these lines. Or, as Shakespeare put it, about gods thought of as somewhat closer to home than Mars: "As flies to wanton boys are we to th' gods, / They kill us for their sport."

. . . . .

Other worlds with strange inhabitants have been numerous in human mythologies   5
and literatures. I'd speculate that, including all the fantasylands devised by children that never see publication, there are many more imaginary locations than there are real ones. Whether they are places we go after death—good or bad—or homes of the gods or supernaturals, or lost civilizations, or planets in a galaxy far, far away, they all have this in common: they aren't here and now. They may be long ago or far away; they may be situated in that nebulous region, "the future"; they may even be given real estate in "another dimension" of the space-time we ourselves inhabit. The convention seems to be that other beings can pop into our living rooms from somewhere else, but they can't drag along the entire world from which they come. We, on the other hand, can slip through a cupboard or through a wormhole in space and find ourselves transported to their realm. Stories about encounters with other beings thus always involve travel, one way or another. Something or someone moves from "there" to "here," or we ourselves move from "here" to "there." Portals, gateways, waystations, and vehicles abound, as in—come to think of it—ancient myths, with their cave entrances and chariots of fire.

Our ability to conceive of imaginary places—somewhere that isn't immediately   6
tangible in the way that the dinnertime pork chop is tangible—appears very early in our individual lives. At first—when we're extremely young—it's a case of out of sight, out of mind: objects hidden from our view simply disappear, then appear again. It takes us a while to figure out that the rubber duck that went behind the curtain is still somewhere rather than nowhere.

Once we've decided things go to another place rather than simply ceasing to exist, we find it hard to shake that notion. Being "here," then suddenly not being here: is that where the concepts of, for instance, afterlives and teleportation originate? Does *Star Trek*'s Scotty derive his ability to beam people up from the discovery that the rubber duck in our early games of peek-a-boo was still there really? Is dead Granddad floating around in the spirit world trying to get in touch with us? And will we, too, float around in that way, since it is very hard to picture the self as being nowhere at all? Surely the dead go somewhere, other than the tomb. Once, they went to the Egyptian Afterlife to get their souls weighed, or to the Fields of Asphodel, or up into the sky to become constellations, or to a physical location called Heaven. Now, perhaps, they might go to the Planet Krypton or wherever it is that E.T. went. And are the Fields of Asphodel and the Planet Krypton more or less the same place?

7

One method of approaching Other Worlds would be to trace their literary lines of descent—from the Mesopotamian underworld to the Egyptian Afterlife to the Domain of Pluto to the Christian Hell and Heaven to the Utopia of Sir Thomas More to the Islands of the Houyhnhnms and Dr. Moreau, and finally to Planet X and Gethen and Chiron. But Other Worlds have existed in many cultures, within which they can trace many separate literary and cultural lines of descent. Could it be that the tendency to produce such worlds is an essential property of the human imagination, via the limbic system and the neocortex, just as empathy is?

8

Reading for Better Writing

Working by yourself or with a group, answer the following questions:

1. Are you a SF fan? Why or why not? What would you point to in science (or speculative) fiction and fantasy that attracts you or fails to do so? What does Margaret Atwood's piece contribute to your thinking about SF?

2. Atwood opens this excerpt with a series of questions. In what sense are these cause-effect questions? What tone do they set for the essay?

3. She follows up these questions with a discussion of empathy. In what sense does empathy begin to answer her questions? How can empathy be thought of as a cause?

4. In paragraph 5, Atwood turns specifically to connections between mythology and modern writing. What does she make of these connections? How are the connections causal?

5. Consider the final paragraph and especially the last sentence. Where does Atwood leave off (or at least pause) in her cause-effect discussion?

Writing Guidelines

Planning

1. **Select a topic.** Begin by thinking about categories such as those listed below and listing phenomena related to each. From this list, choose a topic and analyze its causes, its effects, or both.

   - **Family Life:** adult children living with parents, more stay-at-home dads, families simplifying their lifestyles, adults squeezed by needs of children and parents
   - **Politics:** fewer student voters, increasing support for green-energy production, increased interest in third-party politics, tension between political-action groups
   - **Society:** nursing shortage, doctor shortage, terrorist threats, increasing immigrant-advocacy efforts, shifting ethnic ratios, decreasing number of newspapers
   - **Environment:** common water pollutants, new water-purification technology, decreasing U.S. space exploration, increasing number of nuclear power plants

2. **Narrow and research the topic.** State your topic and below it, list related causes and effects in two columns. Next, do preliminary research to expand the list and distinguish primary causes and effects from secondary ones. Revise your topic as needed to address only primary causes and/or effects that research links to a specific phenomenon.

Cause-effect Topic: _____	
Causes (Because of)	**Effects** (this results)
1. _____	1. _____
2. _____	2. _____
3. _____	3. _____

   fig. 14.2

3. **Draft and test your thesis.** Based on your preliminary research, draft a working thesis (you may revise it later) that introduces the topic, along with the causes and/or effects you intend to discuss. Limit your argument to only those points you can prove.

4. **Gather and analyze information.** Research your topic, looking for clear evidence that links specific causes to specific effects. As you study the phenomenon, distinguish between primary and secondary causes (main and contributing), direct and indirect results, short-term and long-term effects, and so on. At the same time, test your analysis to avoid mistaking a coincidence for a cause-effect relationship. Use the list of logical fallacies (see pages 317–320) to weed out common errors in logic. For example, finding chemical pollutants in a stream running beside a chemical plant does not "prove" that the plant caused the pollutants.

5. **Get organized.** Develop an outline that lays out your thesis and argument in a clear pattern. Under each main point asserting a cause-effect connection, list details from your research that support the connection.

   Thesis: _____

Point #1	Point #2	Point #3
• Supporting details	• Supporting details	• Supporting details
• Supporting details	• Supporting details	• Supporting details

   fig. 14.3

Drafting

6. **Use your outline to draft the essay.** Try to rough out the essay's overall argument before you attempt to revise it. As you write, show how each specific cause led to each specific effect, citing examples as needed. To show those cause-effect relationships, use transitional words like the following:

- accordingly
- as a result
- because
- consequently
- for this purpose
- for this reason
- hence
- just as
- since
- so
- such as
- thereby
- therefore
- thus
- to illustrate
- whereas

Revising

7. **Get feedback.** Ask a peer reviewer or someone from the writing centre to read your essay for an engaging opening, a thoughtful cause-effect thesis, clear and convincing reasoning that links specific causes to specific effects, and a closing that deepens and extends the cause-effect analysis of the phenomenon.

8. **Revise the essay.** Whether your essay presents causes, effects, or both, use the checklist below to trace and refine your argument.

____ **Ideas:** The essay explains the causes and/or effects of the topic in a clear, well-reasoned analysis. The analysis is supported by credible information and free of logical fallacies.

____ **Organization:** The structure helps clarify the cause-effect relationships through a well traced line of thinking, and the links between the main points, supporting points, and evidence are clear.

____ **Voice:** The tone is informed, logical, and measured.

Editing

9. **Edit the essay for clarity and correctness.** Check for the following:

____ **Words:** The diction is precise and clear, and technical or scientific terms are defined. Causes are linked to effects with transitional words and phrases.

____ **Sentences:** Structures are clear, varied, and smooth.

____ **Correctness:** The grammar, punctuation, mechanics, usage, and spelling are correct.

____ **Design:** The format, layout, and typography adhere to expectation; any visuals used enhance the written analysis and clarify the paper's cause-effect reasoning.

Publishing

12. **Publish your essay.** Share your writing by submitting it to your instructor, posting it on the class's or department's website, or turning it into a presentation.

Critical-Thinking and Writing Activities

As directed by your instructor, complete the following critical-thinking and writing activities by yourself or with classmates.

1. According to Ralph Waldo Emerson, "Shallow men believe in luck. Strong men believe in cause and effect." Reflect on Emerson's judgment: how does it align with your own thinking about cause and effect, as well as with the essays in this chapter?

2. Both Jade Barsalou in "From Communism to Capitalism" and Megan Cécile Radford in "How Canadian Newspaperwomen Won the Vote" examine cause-effect relationships at work during times of political change. Consider key political changes that matter to your life (a particular bill, law, policy, cause, etc.). Then write an essay in which you explore the causes and/or effects of a specific change.

3. In "Pitch Perfect," Jay Ingram explores the science behind the knuckleball. What other actions in sports would be enlightened by a scientific explanation? More broadly, is there something in everyday life that you would like to understand better at a cause-effect level? Do the research and write the essay.

4. Margaret Atwood speculates in "Other Worlds" about the source of imagined places in SF. Consider other genres of writing and even of films that interest you— mystery novels, romances, Westerns, James Bond films, the Harry Potter series, and so on. Choose one genre and explore your attraction to it.

Learning-Objectives Checklist ✓

Have you achieved this chapter's learning objectives? Check your progress with the items below, revisiting topics in the chapter as needed. *I have . . .*

____ examined, interpreted, and critiqued arguments that utilize cause-effect reasoning (256–257).

____ analyzed a phenomenon by identifying and explaining its primary and secondary causes and effects (256–257).

____ developed a credible cause-effect thesis based on my study of the topic (274).

____ explained how and why a given cause is linked to one or more logically related effects (274–275).

____ identified and corrected logical fallacies related to cause-effect thinking (317–320).

____ supported my cause-effect reasoning with current, reliable, and detailed evidence (274–275).

____ clarified cause-effect relationships through the effective use of transitional words and phrases (275).

____ used cause-effect reasoning along with other analytical strategies to effectively plan, draft, revise, and polish a cogent, logical essay (274–275).

Chapter 15

Reading Literature:
A Case Study in Analysis

In college and university, analyzing a literary text is a critical, interpretive process. For that reason, the process must begin with a deep reading of a poem, short story, play, or other literary work. When you research and write the essay, you assume that your readers have also read the text, and your aim is to illuminate some not-fully-understood dimension of the work: the motivations of a particular character, the image patterns of a lyric, the historical context of a Renaissance play, and so on.

In this way, literary analysis is a special form of the analytical writing explained in Chapters 10–14. In this application of analysis, you interpret the literary work through strategies such as cause-effect and compare-contrast reasoning.

Visually Speaking Study the painting below. What does it depict of and about life? What does such an image suggest about the relationship between art and life? How is such visual art distinct from verbal art?

Learning **Objectives**

By working through this chapter, you will be able to

- examine and assess writers' analyses of literature and the arts.

- investigate how writers' situations inform their analyses.

- use literary terms and concepts to evaluate others' analyses and enrich your own.

- conduct primary and secondary research to analyze a literary text or other artwork.

- develop an analysis with an insightful thesis, clear reasoning, and sound evidence.

To Prince Edward Island, 1965, Colville, Alex, NGC 14954.

fig. 15.1

Strategies for Analyzing Literature and the Arts

Analyzing the arts is something that most people do (at least informally) every day, whether they're reading reviews of concerts or albums, responding to paintings or photographs in public places, or assessing the value of a film or TV drama. However, this chapter explains a more formal, research-based analysis that is carefully articulated in well-crafted writing. To understand how and why writers produce such analyses, it's helpful to examine the rhetorical situations that give rise to them and review the principles of such analysis.

The Rhetorical Situation

Consider the context in which writers analyze literature and the arts:

- **Purpose:** Most writers aim to describe the work's features, to explain how it impacts an audience, and to understand its essential qualities. However, writers reviewing (rather than only analyzing) an artwork focus more on its strengths and weaknesses.
- **Readers:** In college, the primary readers for writing about the arts are students and instructors; outside of the classroom, art news stories and reviews are written for any community members interested in art events, art-related issues, or books.
- **Topic:** The topic might be one artwork (e.g., a sculpture, novel, or film), multiple works created by the same artist (e.g., a series of poems or paintings), a group performance (e.g., a play, an opera, or a symphony), an individual performance (e.g., a pianist, an actor, or a dancer), or critical approaches to an art.

Example: In "E.B. White's Ethic of Humility: An Ecocritical Engagement with *Charlotte's Web*" (pages 295–301), Denae Dyck's primary **readers** are her professor and classmates. Her **topic** is an ecocritical understanding of the children's novel *Charlotte's Web*, and her **purpose** is to interpret the ecological importance of the word *humble* in the narrative.

Principles of Literary-Analysis Writing

Literary-analysis writing depends on the principles of reading, research, and writing that follow.

Understanding approaches to literary analysis. Literary texts can be interpreted through different critical approaches or schools. Each school, with its specific focuses and questions, offers a way of "conversing" about a text. While the critical approaches described below seem quite distinct, they actually share many traits: (1) a close attention to literary elements such as character, plot, symbolism, and metaphor; (2) an effort to interpret the text accurately and effectively; and (3) a desire to increase understanding of the text. Moreover, whatever approach you take will likely combine concerns of more than one school. The four approaches are illustrated with reference to Robert Browning's poem, "My Last Duchess," which is included for reference after the description of all four approaches.

1. **Formalist criticism** is text-centred, focusing on how the structure of a work and the rules of its genre contribute to the text's meaning. Such criticism determines how various elements (plot, character, diction, imagery, and so on) work to build

meaning, as well as how generic conventions (e.g., the rules of tragedy) function in a particular text.

Formalist Questions about "My Last Duchess": How do the main elements in the poem—irony, symbolism, and verse form—help develop the main theme (deception)? How does Browning use the dramatic monologue genre in this poem?

2. **Rhetorical criticism** is audience-centred, focused on the transaction between text and reader—the dynamic way that the reader interacts with the text. Often called reader-response criticism, these approaches see the text not as an object to be analyzed, but as an activity that differs from reader to reader.

Rhetorical Questions about "My Last Duchess": How does the reader become aware of the duke's true nature if it's never actually stated? Do men and women read the poem differently? Who were Browning's original readers?

3. **Historical criticism** is origins-centred, focused on the author and the text's historical background. For example, an author-focused interpretation might study the text in light of the author's life—showing connections, contrasts, and conflicts. Broader historical studies explore social and intellectual currents, showing links between an author's work and the ideas, events, and institutions of that period. Finally, the literary historian might make connections between the text in question and earlier and later literary works.

Historical Questions about "My Last Duchess": What were Browning's views of marriage, men and women, art, class, and wealth? As an institution, what was marriage like in Victorian England (Browning's era) or Renaissance Italy (the duke's era)? Who was the historical Duke of Ferrara?

4. **Ideological criticism** is centred on idea systems, on applying ideas outside literature to literary works. Because literature mirrors life, argues such criticism, disciplines that explore human life can help us understand literature. Here are examples:

   - *Psychological criticism* applies psychological theories (Freudian, Jungian, trauma theory, and so on) to literary works by exploring dreams, symbolic meanings, character motivations, author creativity, and mental illness.
   - *Myth or archetype* criticism uses insights from psychology, cultural anthropology, and classical studies to explore a text's universal appeal or recurring patterns.
   - *Moral criticism,* rooted in religious studies and ethics, explores the moral dilemmas literary works raise.
   - *Ecocriticism,* connecting literature and environmental studies, examines the nature–culture relationship expressed by literary texts, the importance of the natural world to them.
   - *Marxist, gender, minority, and postcolonial criticism* are sociological approaches to interpretation. While Marxist analysis examines the themes of class struggle, economic power, and social justice in texts, gender criticism explores the

treatment of human sexuality in texts, whether the just or unjust treatment of women, the theme of homosexuality, or the effects of gender on language, writing, reading, and the literary canon. Minority analysis focuses on race and ethnic identity in similar ways (e.g., African American and Aboriginal criticism), while postcolonial criticism focuses specifically on the literature of former colonies in terms of the effects of colonialism and the development of a literary culture after the end of colonial status.

Ideological Questions about "My Last Duchess": What does the poem reveal about the duke's psychological state and his personality? How does the reference to Neptune deepen the poem? What does the poem suggest about the nature of evil and injustice? In what ways are the duke's motives class-based and economic? How does the poem present the duke's power and the duchess's victimization?

Reading Browning's "My Last Duchess": Robert Browning, a British Victorian poet, first published "My Last Duchess" in 1842. The poem is a dramatic monologue, meaning that the speaker (here the Duke of Ferrara, indicated below the poem's title) is imagined as speaking to a silent listener (an agent for a count with whom the duke is attempting to negotiate another marriage after the death of his first wife). The duke speaking in the poem is believed to be the historical Alfonso Il d'Este (1533–1598), who at the age of 25 married 14-year-old Lucrezia di Cosimo de Medici, the figure in the portrait being described by the duke. It is suspected that when Lucrezia died at the age of 17, she had been poisoned by her husband, the duke.

With this background in mind, engage "My Last Duchess" by doing the following, either on your own or with classmates:

1. Read the poem aloud (more than once, if helpful), paying attention to the rhythms and sounds at work.

2. Work through the poem slowly, line by line, to sort out what the duke is saying to the agent and why he would be saying it.

3. Through freewriting, explore your response to the poem—the story that it tells, the voice and personality of the duke, the ethical puzzle that it presents, or anything else that strikes you about this dramatic monologue.

4. Use the discussion above of approaches to literary analysis, plus the instruction on literary terms and research that follow to develop a fuller interpretation of the poem.

"My Last Duchess"
Ferrara

That's my last Duchess painted on the wall,
Looking as if she were alive. I call
That piece a wonder, now: Frà Pandolf's hands
Worked busily a day, and there she stands.
Will't please you sit and look at her? I said
"Frà Pandolf" by design, for never read
Strangers like you that pictured countenance,
The depth and passion of its earnest glance,
But to myself they turned (since none puts by
The curtain I have drawn for you, but I)   10
And seemed as they would ask me, if they durst,
How such a glance came there; so, not the first
Are you to turn and ask thus. Sir, 'twas not
Her husband's presence only, called that spot
Of joy into the Duchess' cheek: perhaps
Frà Pandolf chanced to say "Her mantle laps
Over my Lady's wrist too much," or "Paint
Must never hope to reproduce the faint
Half-flush that dies along her throat": such stuff
Was courtesy, she thought, and cause enough   20
For calling up that spot of joy. She had
A heart—how shall I say?—too soon made glad,
Too easily impressed; she liked whate'er
She looked on, and her looks went everywhere.
Sir, 'twas all one! My favour at her breast,
The dropping of the daylight in the West,
The bough of cherries some officious fool
Broke in the orchard for her, the white mule
She rode with round the terrace—all and each
Would draw from her alike the approving speech,   30

Robert Browning

Or blush, at least. She thanked men,—good! but thanked

Somehow—I know not how—as if she ranked

My gift of a nine-hundred-years-old name

With anybody's gift. Who'd stoop to blame

This sort of trifling? Even had you skill

In speech—(which I have not)—to make your will

Quite clear to such an one, and say, "Just this

Or that in you disgusts me; here you miss,

Or there exceed the mark"—and if she let

Herself be lessoned so, nor plainly set   40

Her wits to yours, forsooth, and made excuse,

—E'en then would be some stooping, and I choose

Never to stoop. Oh sir, she smiled, no doubt,

Whene'er I passed her; but who passed without

Much the same smile? This grew; I gave commands;

Then all smiles stopped together. There she stands

As if alive. Will't please you rise? We'll meet

The company below, then. I repeat,

The Count your master's known munificence

Is ample warrant that no just pretence   50

Of mine for dowry will be disallowed;

Though his fair daughter's self, as I avowed

At starting, is my object. Nay, we'll go

Together down, sir. Notice Neptune, though,

Taming a sea-horse, thought a rarity,

Which Claus of Innsbruck cast in bronze for me!

Understanding literary terms that help you read and write about the arts. The terms used to address specific artforms, such as the three examples below, help writers read literature carefully and discuss their topics precisely. To refine your reading skills, learn how the literary elements that these terms identify shape or enrich a literary work. Then when reading a piece of literature, think about how these elements impact what you feel, see, and think. (For definitions of common literary terms, see pages 302–304.)

- **Poetry:** Writers might describe word sounds with terms such as *assonance, consonance,* and *alliteration*; rhythmic effects with words such as *iambic* or *trochaic metre*; and figurative language with words such as *metaphor* and *simile.*
- **Fiction:** Writers might describe diction with terms such as *archaic, colloquial,* or *slang*; narrative method with phrases such as *first person* and *third person*; or genre with terms such as *satire* or *melodrama.*
- **Plays and Films:** To describe characters, writers use terms such as *antagonist, protagonist,* or *tragic hero*; to discuss plots, they use words such as *exposition, rising action,* and *denouement*; or to describe a setting, they might use *stage picture, proscenium arch,* or *thrust stage.*

Understanding primary and secondary research. Writers' reading of a literary text—primary research—is usually the focus of their analyses. However, secondary research can serve many purposes, such as these:

- **Biographical research:** Learning about the author's life may enrich a writer's analysis by helping the person to explore sources of inspiration, personal and literary influences, and modes of thought. Such insights might be gained through learning about the author's childhood, cultural and ethnic background, education, writing apprenticeship, and relationships. Caution: Writers must be careful not to make simplistic connections between biographical details and literary texts (e.g., that the speaker of a poem or the narrator of a story is the author in a direct sense; that because the novelist grew up in the 1960s, the female characters are radical feminists; or that the author's intention must direct an interpretation of the text).
- **Research into historical and cultural context:** Such research illuminates the text by clarifying important contextual issues and historical details. These issues might be the historical realities surrounding the text's writing, its content, and its reception (past and present). Or the issues might be cultural concepts relevant to the text: class, economics, technology, religious institutions and practices, and so on.
- **Research into literary concepts:** This type of secondary research deepens the writer's understanding of literary issues and techniques. For example, he or she might read about methods and theories of irony, or might study the nature of tragedy with the aim of enriching the analysis of the text.
- **Research into theory:** Such research strengthens the writer's understanding of the philosophical and ideological underpinnings of a particular literary school or theorist. Theoretical research—whether into reader-response theory, deconstruction, feminism, or the ideas of a particular theorist such as Mikhail Bakhtin—informs and directs the writer's analysis of the literary text.

- **Research into scholarly interpretations:** In such research, writers join the critical conversation about the text, a conversation that might have been going on for a few years, a few decades, or a few centuries. Many scholarly articles and books will likely offer interpretations of the text—ways of reading, analyzing, and understanding some aspect of the work, typically from a particular point of view. Reading these sources can strengthen a writer's own interpretation in the following ways:

  - She can locate her own reading within the critical conversation, placing her interpretation in context.
  - She can refine her own reading through critical engagement, exploring why different readers interpret the text as they do (comparing their perspectives and values with her own).
  - She can create a critical survey early in her paper, one that reviews the interpretive schools on the issues addressed and makes space for her own reading.
  - Within her essay, she might use the critical comment of a scholar to (a) add expert support to her interpretive argument, (b) create a starting point for further reflection and analysis, or (c) present a claim with which she disagrees.

Focusing on Research Essentials: In a literary analysis project, a writer should use secondary sources carefully and avoid these problems:

- **Substituting his own interpretation** of the text with the readings offered by secondary sources. If he finds himself continually talking about other people's interpretations or simply parroting their interpretations, he needs to get back to his own interpretation in his own voice.
- **Limiting his secondary research** to opinions that he gathers off the free Web (including sites such as SparkNotes and CliffsNotes). Instead, he should rely on substantial sources in academic journals and scholarly books.

Reading Literary-Analysis Writing

As you read the essays on the following pages, consider these questions:

1. Does the writer understand the elements of the art form, what distinguishes a quality artwork, and how to assess those qualities?
2. Does the essay explore nuances such as ironies, motifs, symbols, and allusions?
3. Does the essay have a clear thesis and logical claims, all supported by relevant evidence?
4. Is the tone informed, respectful, and honest?
5. Does the writing sound informed regarding the foci and approaches of schools of literary criticism?
6. Does the writing use literary terms correctly and effectively? (See the list of literary terms on pages 302–304.)
7. Does the writing correctly document both primary and secondary sources?

Analyzing a Poem

In the essay on the following two pages, student writer Sherry Van Egdom analyzes the form and meaning of the poem below, "Let Evening Come," by American poet Jane Kenyon. Born in 1947 and raised on a farm near Ann Arbor, Michigan, Kenyon settled in New Hampshire at Eagle Pond Farm after she married fellow poet Donald Hall. During her life, Kenyon struggled with her faith, with depression, and with cancer. At the time of her death in 1995 from leukemia, she was the poet laureate of New Hampshire.

Before you read the student writer's analysis, read the poem aloud to enjoy its sounds, rhythm, images, diction, and comparisons. Then read the piece again to grasp more fully how the poem is structured, what it expresses, and how its ideas might relate to your life. Finally, read Van Egdom's analysis and answer the questions that follow it.

Let Evening Come

Let the light of late afternoon
shine through chinks in the barn, moving
up the bales as the sun moves down.

Let the crickets take up chafing
as a woman takes up her needles
and her yarn. Let evening come.

Let dew collect on the hoe abandoned
in long grass. Let the stars appear
and the moon disclose her silver horn.

Let the fox go back to its sandy den.
Let the wind die down. Let the shed
go black inside. Let evening come.

To the bottle in the ditch, to the scoop
in the oats, to air in the lung
let evening come.

Let it come, as it will, and don't
be afraid. God does not leave us
comfortless, so let evening come.

Jane Keynon, "Let Evening Come" from Collected Poems. Copyright © 2005 by The Estate of Jane Kenyon. Reprinted with the permission of The Permissions Company, Inc. on behalf of Graywolf Press, Minneapolis, Minnesota, www.graywolfpress.org

Analysis of Kenyon's Poem

In the essay below, student writer Sherry Van Egdom analyzes "Let Evening Come." Watch how she develops the essay by introducing the poem, describing how it unfolds, and then examining its structure, ideas, poetic devices, and theme.

"Let Evening Come": An Invitation to the Inevitable

The writer introduces the poet and her poetry.

The work of American poet Jane Kenyon is influenced primarily by the circumstances and experiences of her own life. She writes carefully crafted, deceptively simple poems that connect both to her own life and to the lives of her readers. Growing out of her rural roots and her struggles with illness, Kenyon's poetry speaks in a still voice of the ordinary things in life in order to wrestle with issues of faith and mortality (Timmerman 163). One of these poems is "Let Evening Come." In this poem, the poet takes the reader on a journey into the night, but she points to hope in the face of that darkness.

Narrowing her focus to the specific poem, the writer states her thesis.

That movement toward darkness is captured in the stanza form and in the progression of stanzas. Each three-line stanza offers a self-contained moment in the progress of transition from day to night. The first stanza positions the reader in a simple farm setting. Late afternoon fades into evening without the rumble of highways or the gleam of city lights to distract one's senses from nature, the peace emphasized by the alliteration of "l" in "Let the light of late afternoon." As the sun sinks lower on the horizon, light seeps through cracks in the barn wall, moving up the bales of hay. In the second stanza, the crickets get busy with their nighttime noises. Next, a forgotten farm hoe becomes covered with dew drops, and the silvery stars and moon appear in the sky. In the fourth stanza, complete blackness arrives as a fox returns to its empty den and the silent wind rests at close of day. The alliteration of "d" in "den" and "die down" gives a sinking, settling feeling (Timmerman 176). In the fifth stanza, a bottle and scoop keep still, untouched in their respective places, while sleep comes upon the human body. In the final stanza, Kenyon encourages readers to meet this emerging world of darkness without fear.

She begins her analysis by explaining the stanza structure and progression.

The writer shows attention to the poem's fine details and to secondary sources on the poem.

Within this stanza progression, the journey into the night is intensified by strong images, figures of speech, and symbols. The natural rhythm of work and rest on the farm is symbolized by the light that rises and falls in the first stanza (Timmerman 175). The simile comparing the crickets taking up their song to a woman picking up her knitting suggests a homespun energy and conviction. The moon revealing her "silver horn" implies that the moon does not instantly appear with brightness and beauty but rather reveals her majesty slowly as the night comes on. The den, the wind, and the shed in stanza four stress a kind of internal, hidden darkness. Then stanza five focuses on connected objects: the thoughtlessly discarded bottle resting in the ditch, oats and the scoop for feeding, human lungs and the air that fills them. Kenyon mentions the air in the lung after the bottle, ditch, scoop, and

She advances her reading of the poem by exploring images, comparisons, and symbols: the poem's "imaginative logic."

Courtesy of Sherry (Van Egdom) Mantel.

1

2

3

oats in order to picture humanity taking its position among the established natural rhythm of the farm (Harris 31).

The writer compares possible interpretations of a central, repeated statement in the poem.

The refrain, "let evening come," is a powerful part of the poem's journey toward darkness, though critics interpret the line differently. Judith Harris suggests that it symbolizes an acceptance of the inevitable: Darkness will envelop the world, and night will surely come, just as mortality will certainly take its toll in time. This acceptance, in turn, acts as a release from the confinement of one's pain and trials in life. Rather than wrestle with something that cannot be beaten or worry about things that must be left undone, Kenyon advises herself and her readers to let go (31). Night intrudes upon the work and events of the day, perhaps leaving them undone just as death might cut a life short and leave it seemingly unfinished. 4

By contrast, John Timmerman argues that "let" is used twelve times in a supplicatory, prayer-like manner (176). The final two lines, in turn, act as a benediction upon the supplications. The comfort of God is as inevitable as the evening, so cling to faith and hope and let evening come. Although the Comforter is mentioned only in the last two lines, that statement of faith encourages readers to find a spiritual comfort in spite of the coming of the night. 5

In her conclusion, the writer offers the poet's explanation of the poem's origin and then expands on the thesis.

When asked how she came to write "Let Evening Come," Jane Kenyon replied that it was a redemptive poem given to her by the Holy Ghost. When there could be nothing—a great darkness and despair, there is a great mystery of love, kindness, and beauty (Moyers 238). In the poem's calm journey into the night, Kenyon confronts darkness and suffering with a certain enduring beauty and hope (Timmerman 161). Death will come, but there remains divine comfort. "Let Evening Come" encourages readers to release their grip on the temporary and pay attention to the Comforter who reveals Himself both day and night. 6

Note: The Works-Cited page is not shown. For sample pages, see MLA (page 533) and APA (pages 562–563).

Reading for Better Writing

Working by yourself or with a group, answer these questions:

1. Review the opening and closing paragraphs of the essay. How do they create a framework for the writer's analysis of the poem?
2. On which elements of the poem does the writer focus? Does this approach make sense for her analysis? Explain.
3. In her essay, the writer refers to the poet's life and to ideas from secondary sources. Do these references work well with her analysis? Why or why not?
4. Review the approaches to literary analysis on pages 278–280. Which approach does the student writer use to analyze Kenyon's poem? Does this approach make sense? How might another approach interpret the poem differently?

Analyzing a Short Story

"A Short History of Indians in Canada" is a short story written by Thomas King. In both his fiction and his nonfiction, King focuses on Aboriginal life and experience. (See, for example, the excerpt from his book *The Inconvenient Indian* on pages 181–185.) Read the story carefully, noting how King opens the story, develops it, and brings it to a close. After reflecting on the thoughts and feelings that the story evokes, read the student essay analyzing the story.

A Short History of Indians in Canada

Can't sleep, Bob Haynie tells the doorman at the King Eddie. Can't sleep, can't sleep. *1*

First time in Toronto? says the doorman. *2*

Yes, says Bob. *3*

Businessman? *4*

Yes. *5*

Looking for excitement? *6*

Yes. *7*

Bay Street, sir, says the doorman. *8*

Bob Haynie catches a cab to Bay Street at three in the morning. He loves the smell of concrete. He loves the look of city lights. He loves the sound of skyscrapers. *9*

Bay Street. *10*

Smack! *11*

Bob looks up just in time to see a flock of Indians fly into the side of the building. *12*

Smack! Smack! *13*

Bob looks up just in time to get out of the way. *14*

Whup! *15*

An Indian hits the pavement in front of him. *16*

Whup! Whup! *17*

Two Indians hit the pavement behind him. *18*

Holy Cow! shouts Bob, and he leaps out of the way of the falling Indians. *19*

Whup! Whup! Whup! *20*

Bob throws his hands over his head and dashes into the street. And is almost hit 21
by a city truck.

Honk! 22

Two men jump out of the truck. Hi, I'm Bill. Hi, I'm Rudy. 23

Hi, I'm Bob. 24

Businessman? says Bill. 25

Yes. 26

First time in Toronto? says Rudy. 27

Yes. 28

Whup! Whup! Whup! 29

Look out! Bob shouts. There are Indians flying into the skyscrapers and falling 30
on the sidewalk.

Whup! 31

Mohawk, says Bill. 32

Whup! Whup! 33

Couple of Cree over here, says Rudy. 34

Amazing, says Bob. How can you tell? 35

By the feathers, says Bill. We got a book. 36

It's our job, says Rudy. 37

Whup! 38

Bob looks around. What's this one? he says. 39

Holy! says Bill. Holy! says Rudy. 40

Check the book, says Bill. Just to be sure. 41

Flip, flip, flip. 42

Navajo! 43

Bill and Rudy put their arms around Bob. A Navajo! Don't normally see Navajos 44
this far north. Don't normally see Navajos this far east.

Is she dead? says Bob. 45

Nope, says Bill. Just stunned. 46

Most of them are just stunned, says Rudy. 47

Some people never see this, says Bill. One of nature's mysteries. A natural 48
phenomenon.

They're nomadic, you know, says Rudy. And migratory. *49*

Toronto's in the middle of the flyway, says Bill. The lights attract them. *50*

Bob counts the bodies. Seventy-three. No Seventy-four. What can I do to help? *51*

Not much that anyone can do, says Bill. We tried turning off the lights in the *52*
buildings.

We tried broadcasting loud music from the roofs, says Rudy. *53*

Rubber owls? asks Bob. *54*

It's a real problem this time of the year, says Bill. *55*

Whup! Whup! Whup! *56*

Bill and Rudy pull green plastic bags out of their pockets and try to find the *57*
open ends.

The dead ones we bag, says Rudy. *58*

The live ones we tag, says Bill. Take them to the shelter. Nurse them back to *59*
health. Release them in the wild.

Amazing, says Bob. *60*

A few wander off dazed and injured. If we don't find them right away, they don't *61*
stand a chance.

Amazing, says Bob. *62*

You're one lucky guy, says Bill. In another couple of weeks, they'll be gone. *63*

A family from Alberta came through last week and didn't e en see an Ojibway, *64*
says Rudy.

You're first time in Toronto? says Bill. *65*

It's a great town, says Bob. You're doing a great job. *66*

Whup! *67*

Don't worry, says Rudy. By the time the commuters show up, you'll never even *68*
know the Indians were here.

Bob catches a cab back to the King Eddie and shakes the doorman's hand. I saw *69*
the Indians, he says.

Thought you'd enjoy that, sir, says the doorman. *70*

Thank you, says Bob. It was spectacular. *71*

Not like the old days. The doorman sighs and looks up into the night. In the old *72*
days, when they came through, they would black out the entire sky.

Analysis of "A Short History of Indians in Canada"

In the following essay, student writer Nicholas Jeffries explicates "A Short History of Canada" by analyzing the conflict between the urban and the natural in King's story. As you read Nicholas's essay, note how he explains the conflict by contrasting the two sides and uses evidence from the story itself to support his interpretation.

When Worlds Collide: City and Nature in "A Short History of Indians in Canada"

As a writer of mixed descent (Cherokee and German-Greek), Thomas King is well qualified to explore the relationship between different ethnic and racial worlds. In "A Short History of Indians in Canada," he does exactly that by showing (almost literally) the collisions between Aboriginal culture and the culture that has largely displaced it in North America. King presents this conflict in a highly imaginative way by pitting the city of Toronto against migratory Indians ("Indians" being the term used by King in the story). The new urban landscape, a human-made environment, erects barriers to the natural, including the Aboriginal. While King at first presents this human-natural collision in energetic and comical terms, in the end the short history of Indians in Canada turns more tragic and ironic. By closely examining these contrasting worlds of city and nature, readers become aware of this tragic turn.

> The writer introduces the story, the key conflict, and his thesis about that conflict.

King's story moves forward largely through dialogue; however, the story does contain some telling descriptions of the city. At the beginning, we learn that Bob Haynie, the main character, is staying at the "King Eddie" hotel (367). Because Bob is "[l]ooking for excitement," the hotel doorman sends Bob to Bay Street (367). Both of these details are important. "King Eddie" suggests that the city is linked with the British monarchy and hence the British Empire. The city of Toronto is one city that this empire has built. Moreover, the reference to Bay Street alludes to Canada's economic and commercial power, as Bay Street is the home of Canada's major financial institutions, including its big banks. In this way, the opening of the story associates the urban with both political and economic power.

> The interpretation unfolds by first analyzing the urban setting.

The people that we meet in this city—Bob, Bill, and Rudy—clearly love Toronto. With their ordinary names, all three come to represent urban values, experiences, and beliefs that line up with the political and economic description of the city. Bob

> The writer turns to the characters' urban connections.

1

2

3

Haynie, we learn at the beginning of the story, is a businessman visiting Toronto for the first time. In the very first sentence, Bob tells the doorman three times, "Can't sleep" (367). Perhaps his insomnia is due to excitement at being in the city, or perhaps it represents a certain urban restlessness. When Bob goes to Bay Street at 3:00 a.m., the narrator relates of Bob, "He loves the smell of concrete. He loves the look of city lights. He loves the sound of skyscrapers" (367). Bob's senses enjoy the urban landscape in a way that is normally reserved for natural landscapes. Instead of loving the smell of flowers, the sight of moon and stars, and sounds of birds and other creatures, Bob celebrates the human-made, the artificial, and the paved.

While Bill is a businessman, Bill and Rudy are city workers who come on the   *4*
scene when the Indians start hitting the skyscrapers and falling to the pavement. As representatives of the city government, Bill and Rudy are the clean-up crew who "pull green plastic bags out of their pockets" to deal with the mess (369). In a kind of chorus, Rudy explains, "The dead ones we bag," and Bill echoes, "The live ones we tag" (369). Ironically, Bill and Rudy are experts in Indians, able to identify different tribes from a book they carry with them. In this way, Bill and Rudy function almost as tour guides for the visiting Bob, with the nighttime city the scene of this remarkable collision with nature.

The collision between Indians and the city is very much the heart of this   *5*
story, and at first that collision appears to be treated comically. The parallel that King creates between Indians and migratory birds is clever in that it seems both ridiculous and fitting. It is ridiculous to imagine Aboriginal people as migratory birds flying into skyscrapers because of the confusion created by the city lights, but this image is a very fitting emblem of the Aboriginal experience of invasion and displacement. The initial comedy of these collisions is supported by the word play and the reactions of the characters. Repeatedly, we hear the sound effect, "Whup! Whup! Whup!" as Indians hit the pavement (368). Comically, Bob has to leap out of the way to avoid being clobbered, yelling "Holy cow!" (368). Bill and Rudy are also excited by what falls to the ground: they yell "Holy," identify different types of Indians "by the feathers," and assure Bob that most of the Indians are just stunned (368). For Bob, this whole event is "amazing" and "spectacular" (369).

> **Direct quotations from the story support the interpretation.**

> **The writer turns to the natural imagery, first examining its comical treatment.**

However, closer attention to the text reveals a darkness below the comedy. 6
Essentially, the parallel between migratory birds and Indians raises difficult
questions. When Bill describes this event as "One of nature's mysteries. A natural
phenomenon," and Rudy adds that "They're nomadic [. . .] and migratory" (368),
King is pressing readers to consider how the solid concrete, bright lights urban
world has displaced both the natural and the Aboriginal. Moreover, the likening of
the Indians to migratory birds makes Aboriginal people "other" and exotic rather
than fully human. They become nameless and voiceless creatures identified only
by species, a source of eco-tourism entertainment or a nuisance to be cleaned up—
bagged or tagged. As the story moves toward its conclusion, the parallels between
migratory birds and Indians become even darker. Injured Indians, says Bill, are not
just tagged: "Take them to the shelter. Nurse them back to health. Release them in
the wild" (369). These short sentences suggest a process in which Indians are cared
for and then freed, but the connotations of "shelter" and "wild" could point to the
homelessness and disorientation of some Aboriginal people. Further statements
indicate that the bird-Indian parallel refers to the possibility of extinction. Bill tells
Bob, "In another couple of weeks, they'll be gone" (369), while Rudy relates, "By
the time the commuters show up, you'll never even know that Indians were here"
(369). These statements from the city workers point toward not only the historical
displacement of Aboriginal people by urban development but also their invisibility
and possibly permanent disappearance. These ideas are driven home by the end
of the story. When Bob returns to the King Eddie and tells the doorman that the
experience of the Indians was "spectacular," the doorman sighs, looks up at the sky,
and remarks nostalgically, "Not like the old days. . . . In the old days, when they
came through, they would black out the entire sky" (369). This closing statement
clearly links the pressures on Aboriginal peoples with the decimation of bird
populations, raising the spectre of extinction.

> The tragic side of the conflict is elaborated in depth.

As a very short, short story, "A Short History of Indians in Canada" is able 7
to capture that history powerfully by establishing and elaborating this parallel
between Indians and migratory birds. In this parallel, Thomas King pits the natural
against the urban as representations of two different world views that have collided,
and flying Indians are no match for Toronto's skyscrapers and concrete. In his

> After restating his thesis, the writer expands it by discussing a key idea in King's thinking.

introduction to *All My Relations: An Anthology of Contemporary Canadian Native Fiction,* King explains that "all my relations" refers not only to family relationships and the relationships we share with all people but also to "the web of kinship extending to the animals, to the birds, to the fish, to the plants, to all the animate and inanimate forms that can be seen or imagined" (446). This kinship involves living "in a harmonious and moral manner" (446). By treating urban-natural collisions both comically and tragically, King argues in "A Short History of Indians in Canada" that the web of kinship is broken and needs to be repaired.

Note: The Works-Cited page is not shown. For sample pages, see MLA (page 533) and APA (pages 562–563).

Reading for Better Writing

Working by yourself or with a group, answer the following questions:

1. Thomas King's story and Nicholas Jeffrey's analysis of it focus on conflicts between Aboriginal and non-Aboriginal cultures in North America. What has been your experience of that conflict? How well do the story and the essay resonate with your experience?

2. Nicholas's essay focuses on collisions within the story. What collisions does he identify and how does he discuss them. Where and how does he use elements from the story itself, including quotations?

3. Nicholas argues that the collisions are treated both comically and tragically in the story. Do you agree? Why or why not?

4. Study the introduction and the conclusion to the essay. How does Nicholas frame his analysis of the story? What strategies does he use to open and close his analysis?

5. Review the approaches to literary analysis on pages 278–280. How would you characterize the approach that Nicholas has taken to interpreting King's story?

Analyzing a Novel

As with analyzing a poem or a short story, analyzing a novel requires careful attention to the text. However, because a novel typically involves an expansive narrative, analysis requires greater focus. In the following essay, student writer Denae Dyck analyzes a familiar children's novel, *Charlotte's Web,* by adopting an ecocritical perspective and focusing on the significance of the word "humble."

E.B. White's Ethic of Humility: An Ecocritical Engagement with *Charlotte's Web*

> As you read this essay, annotate it and take notes—considering how Denae engages this children's story deeply and thoughtfully.

In *Charlotte's Web*, E.B. White displays the efforts of his characters to accept and enjoy their place on earth, efforts which cause them to consider the relationship of one species to another. White puts the words that Charlotte writes on her webs into the story's centre and thus offers an opportunity to analyze their ecocritical significance. "Humble," Charlotte's very last message, warrants an especially careful reading, for it is on this note that Charlotte concludes her labours to convince the human characters of Wilbur's merit (141). When considering whether her word will suit Wilbur, Charlotte observes, "'Humble' has two meanings: it means 'not proud' and it means 'near the ground'" (140). These nuances of the word "humble" animate White's story, allowing him to subtly yet effectively counter the arrogance and ignorance of anthropocentrism, that is, of viewing human beings as the central and most significant species on the planet. White points instead towards an ethic of humility that emerges from acknowledging limitations and embracing the interconnectivity uniting all that is alive.

Charlotte's Web challenges the unproblematic speciesism that underlies anthropocentrism by exposing the complexity of the relationships between one kind of living being and another. Although Fern initiates the story's action by protesting the hierarchy her father posits—"A little girl is one thing, a little runty pig is another"—White does not ultimately dissolve or resolve differences between species (3). Michael Sims's article "The Nature of E.B. White" draws attention to this puzzle in *Charlotte's Web*. Sims notes that even though White's story generates sympathy between different types of creatures White himself remained a farmer and concludes, "White's attitude towards animals was more imaginative than sentimental . . . . The morality of farming bothered him, but didn't turn him away from it" (n.pag.). What Sims observes in White's biography also holds true for the characters in *Charlotte's Web*: they too must confront the uncomfortable yet inescapable realities of killing and eating. Wilbur initially expresses horror at Charlotte's predatory behaviour; however, as a spider born into a family of trappers,

1

2

Charlotte challenges Wilbur's squeamishness by revealing that she has no other means of survival (38-39). In response to Wilbur's dismal surmise that Charlotte has received "a miserable inheritance," Charlotte reminds him "*you* can't talk . . . . *You* have your meals brought to you in a pail. Nobody feeds me" (39). Because Charlotte's remark implicitly raises questions about where Wilbur's own food actually comes from—that is, before it is brought to him in a pail—White prompts his readers to wrestle with the fact that all are born into a similar inheritance. Every living creature thus faces the task of finding ways, despite inevitable difficulties, to live with dignity and goodness. Charlotte's web itself becomes emblematic of this quest by bringing together interspecies friendship and predation. The image of the web that opens Chapter IX allusively intertwines these two threads: "A spider's web is stronger than it looks. Although it is made of thin, delicate strands, the web is not easily broken. However, a web gets torn every day by the insects that kick around in it, and a spider must rebuilt it when it gets full of holes" (55). White does not blench from the fact that Charlotte uses her web to trap insects, yet he also lets the web represent the bond between Charlotte and Wilbur. By evoking the words of the Teacher of Ecclesiastes on friendship—"A cord of three strands is not quickly broken"—White implicitly associates Charlotte's web with the Old Testament wisdom tradition (Eccles. 4.12). In so doing, White does not prescribe a definitive way to conceptualize relationships between different species, yet his willingness to grapple with conventional and often unexamined hierarchies adumbrates a more thoughtful and reverent attitude, one based on mutual respect.

Charlotte's Web further interrogates anthropocentrism by suggesting that many of its values remain significantly flawed. In a conversation with Wilbur about performance and achievement, Charlotte offers her perspective on human ideas of success. Likening the Queensborough Bridge to a web, Charlotte characterizes people's endeavours as foolish and futile:

> "[D]o you know how long it took men to build it? Eight whole years. My goodness, I would have starved to death waiting that long. I can make a web in a single evening."
>
> "What do people catch in the Queensborough Bridge—bugs?" asked Wilbur.
>
> "No," said Charlotte. "They don't catch anything. They just keep trotting back and forth across the bridge thinking there is something better on the other side. If they'd hang head-down at the top of the thing and wait quietly, maybe something good would come along. But no—with men it's rush, rush, rush, every minute. I'm glad I'm a sedentary spider." (60)

Charlotte draws attention to the frenzied quality of human pursuits and suggests that, despite this inexplicable and manic activity, people accomplish little in the end. Later in the dialogue, Charlotte observes, "men aren't as good at it [spinning webs] as spiders, although they *think* they're pretty good," indicating that the pride humans take in their achievements remains largely groundless (60).

The human fallibility that Charlotte's words expose emerges elsewhere in *Charlotte's Web* also. At the beginning of the story, Mrs. Arable's offhand remarks about the runt pig associate greatness with physical strength, yet subsequent events contest this equation. Mrs. Arable describes Wilbur as "very small and weak" and concludes that he "will never amount to anything" (1). Near the close of the narrative, however, Charlotte tells Wilbur that the friendship he has offered her is "a tremendous thing" (164). Charlotte's statement undercuts Mrs. Arable's assessment by revealing that even small and seemingly insignificant creatures remain capable of greatness, for this quality depends not on achievement as an abstraction but on the commitment to living in a right relationship with others who are profoundly different from oneself.

White intensifies his critique of the anthropocentrism by gently but persistently mocking Mr. Zuckerman's estimation of his own success. By drawing a comical similitude between Zuckerman and Avery at the fairgrounds, White suggests that Zuckerman's idea of triumph lacks maturity and depth. Throughout the awards ceremony, Avery consistently shadows his uncle: he mimics Zuckerman in shaking hands with the judge and with Zuckerman becomes drenched by Lurvy's failed attempt to dash water over Wilbur (160-61). The unexpected shower offers an occasion for Avery to act as a clown, entertaining the onlookers with his antics (162). White's emphasis on the boy's delight in pleasing the crowd recalls his statements regarding Zuckerman earlier in the chapter: "This was the greatest moment in Zuckerman's life. It is deeply satisfying to win a prize in front of a lot of people" (160). White places Avery's clowning into apposition with Zuckerman's achievement and thus effectively undermines the notion that success consists in receiving an honour before a crowd. By concluding the chapter depicting Zuckerman's acceptance of the prize—entitled "The Hour of Triumph"—with the description of Avery's wet trousers leaving a spot on the seat of Mr. Arable's truck, White underscores the foolishness and childishness of this sense of victory (162). In the following chapter, White reveals that Charlotte conceives of her triumph in far more modest yet rich terms. Although Charlotte acknowledges her role in bringing about Wilbur's salvation, she rejoices in this victory not for her own sake but for

Wilbur's (163). Remarking, "All these sights and sounds will be yours to enjoy, Wilbur—this lovely world, these precious days," Charlotte finds the greatest value in earthly beauty rather than in public glory (164). Her unpretentious and humble attitude establishes a striking contrast to the arrogance that underlies Zuckerman's notions, and, by extension, anthropocentrism.

Throughout *Charlotte's Web*, White suggests that this sense of humility remains closely connected with accepting mortality. White repeatedly implies that the joy of being alive necessarily coexists with an awareness that life does not last forever. In the midst of the summertime, a season described as "the happiest and fairest days of the year," White notes that the sparrow's melody conveys the poignancy and brevity of life (42-43). Likewise, White interprets the crickets' August song as a refrain about the death of summer, commenting, "Even on the most beautiful days in the whole year—the days when summer is changing into fall—the crickets spread the rumors of sadness and change" (113). White's description of the craftsmanship and reception of the final word on Charlotte's web possesses a similarly diminutive note:

> By the time the Arables and the Zuckermans and Lurvy returned from the grandstand, Charlotte had finished her web. The word HUMBLE was woven neatly in the center. Nobody noticed it in the darkness. (140-41)

This message differs significantly from Charlotte's initial statement—"SOME PIG"—a sign which attracts Lurvy's immediate attention and awe (77–78). The obscurity of Charlotte's final word for Wilbur heightens Charlotte's assertion that she is, to use her own word, "languishing" (146). White draws attention to Charlotte's approaching death, yet his barnyard characters meet this inevitable reality without fear. Charlotte faces the end of her life with stoic courage, asking "After all, what's a life anyway? We're born, we live a little while, we die" (164). Charlotte's readiness to acknowledge her own finitude stands against the emphasis on progress and achievement figured in many of the human characters of *Charlotte's Web*. Moreover, Charlotte's use of the first person plural pronoun unites all living creatures in this cycle of birth and death, thus displaying the error inherent in the anthropocentric desire to surpass natural limitations.

White brings together the ordinary and the miraculous in a manner that interrogates the disproportionate emphasis on transcendence that emerges in many versions of anthropocentrism. Descriptively and conceptually, Charlotte's web amalgamates the wonderful and the commonplace. The different images of the web White provides highlight both its ethereal quality and its practical function: the web "glistened in the light and made a pattern of loveliness and mystery" but also "gets torn every day by the insects that kick around in it" (77, 55). White persistently exposes the folly of human explanations of the writing in Charlotte's web that associate these words with the working of supernatural powers. The judge who announces Zuckerman's prize asks, "Whence came this mysterious writing? Not from the spider, we can rest assured of that . . . needless to say spiders cannot write" (158). By inserting a sarcastic aside from Charlotte—"Oh, they can't, can't they?"—immediately after the judge's assertion, White underscores the ignorance of this claim and thereby hints at how little humans know about non-humans (158). Earlier in the narrative, White suggests that the minister's effort to interpret Charlotte's web reflects a similar lack of understanding: "On Sunday the church was full. The minister attempted to explain the miracle. He said that the words on the spider's web proved that human beings must always be on the watch for the coming of wonders" (85). White's unusually rigid and inelegant syntax in this passage achieves a flat cadence that mirrors the vapidity of the minister's judgment. Both the judge and the minister implicitly privilege the supernatural over the natural, an attitude which risks engendering abuse of the earth. Lynn White Jr. focuses on this danger in his essay "The Historical Roots of Our Ecological Crisis," arguing that the damaging effects of Western science and technology on the environment can be traced to Christian notions that "not only established a dualism of man and nature but also insisted that it is God's will that man exploit nature for his proper ends" (10). Although *Charlotte's Web* exhibits a less vehement tone than White Jr.'s essay, White's description of the church service draws a similar connection between Christian institutions and an asymmetrical transcendence that leads individuals to disregard the earth. In White's story, Dr. Dorian is the only human who displays a sense of wonder for the web without invoking higher powers. Dorian remarks, "When the words appeared, everyone said that they were a miracle. But nobody pointed out that the web itself is a miracle" (109). Dorian's valuation of the web not only indicates his appreciation for nature itself but also prompts him to recognize his limitations. After Mrs. Arable reveals that her inability to understand the spider's web makes her feel uncomfortable, Dorian responds, "Doctors are supposed to understand everything. But I don't understand everything, and I don't intend to let it worry me" (110). Dorian's perspective on Charlotte's web brings together the two senses of the word "humble" that Charlotte glosses: the mysterious writing leads him to admit that his understanding is not complete, and his appraisal of all spiders' webs as miraculous in their own right signals esteem for the earth and its other inhabitants.

In the barnyard scenes of *Charlotte's Web*, White allows Wilbur's position   *8*
"near the ground" to offer him a perspective of even greater insight regarding his
relationship with the rest of nature (140). White's story suggests that Wilbur's being
"humble" in this sense involves both physical proximity to and emotional kinship
with the earth. Writing that Wilbur "loved to be a part of the world on a summer
evening," White intimates that Wilbur's zest for life emanates from his desire
to be in harmony with other living things (62). This statement also emphasizes
Wilbur's utter immersion within his environment. In his analysis of White's
nature writings, Robert Root argues that White's depictions of place emphasize
dwelling within—not merely passing through—a geographical area, tracing this
tendency to White's emulation of Henry David Thoreau (n.pag.). The deep sense
of communion with the earth that Root identifies in Charlotte's Web possesses
distinctly ecocritical resonances. Neil Evernden's "Beyond Ecology: Self, Place, and
the Pathetic Fallacy" argues that the truly subversive element of ecology arises from
its emphasis on inter-relatedness, a state which Evernden defines as encompassing
not "a causal connectedness" but "a genuine *intermingling* of parts of the ecosystem"
(93). Evernden's conclusion that "[t]here is no such thing as an individual, only an
individual-in-context, an individual as a component of place, defined by place" helps
to illuminate Wilbur's position in *Charlotte's Web* (103). In the closing paragraph of
the story, Wilbur's celebratory meditation figures forth a similar coalescence of self
and environment:

> Life in the barn was very good—night and day, winter and summer, spring
> and fall, dull days and bright days. It was the best place to be, thought
> Wilbur, this warm delicious cellar, with the garrulous geese, the changing
> seasons, the heat of the sun, the passage of swallows, the nearness of rats, the
> sameness of sheep, the love of spiders, the smell of manure, and the glory of
> everything. (183)

The descriptive phrases naming the various elements that compose life in the barn
show Wilbur's complete and total delight in the barnyard place. Furthermore,
White's diction and syntax recall the Creation narrative in the first chapter of
Genesis, for his opening statement echoes the Creator's declaration after the sixth
day that what he had made was "very good" (Gen 1.31). By bringing together
the entire range of times and seasons in a pattern of merismus—"night and day,
winter and summer, spring and fall, dull days and bright days"—White evokes the
recurring refrain "and it was evening and it was morning" that closes each element

of the Genesis account (1.5-31). White thus locates Wilbur's joy at being alive in a primal sense of the earth made right, for Wilbur finds his place on earth to be one of beauty and fullness.

The word "humble" questions anthropocentrism in that it betokens meekness and, indeed, reverence. This reverence recalls White Jr.'s insistence that "[s]ince the roots of our crisis are so largely religious, the remedy must also be essentially religious, whether we call it that or not" (14). White Jr. concludes his essay by proposing St. Francis of Assisi as "a patron saint for ecologists," suggesting that Francis's Christology counters the dismissal of nature found in many versions of Christianity as it has been historically appropriated (13). White Jr. explains Francis's thought as grounded in a belief in the Creator "who, in the ultimate gesture of cosmic humility, assumed flesh, lay helpless in a manger, and hung dying on a scaffold" (13). Likewise, *Charlotte's Web* finds the basis for a renewed appreciation of earthly existence in immanence and humility. White shows anthropocentrism's emphasis on progress and transcendence to be unfounded, suggesting that the crux of the beautiful and the wonderful resides within the state of being "not proud" and "near the ground" (140).

Reading for Better Writing

Working by yourself or with a group, answer the following questions:

1. How familiar are you with *Charlotte's Web*? Is it one of your favourite stories from childhood? Or is it a gap in your reading education? If you have read this book, how does Denae Dyck's essay contribute to your feelings for the story? If you haven't read the book, does her essay make you want to read it?

2. Denae approaches her analysis of *Charlotte's Web* through the lens of ecocriticism. Examine those places where she refers to this critical approach. How does she introduce it, discuss it, and apply it?

3. In a sense, Denae's essay is all about the word *humble* and its importance to understanding the story. Her introduction and conclusion focus on this word. What analytical strategies does she use in the middle of the essay to argue for the significance of humility in the story? Can you identify strategies such as definition, classification, process, comparison-contrast, and cause-effect?

4. Like most literary analyses, this essay includes extensive quotations from the literary text, as well as some from secondary sources. Examine carefully two examples of such quotation, one from the novel and one from a secondary source. How does Denae lead up to the quotation, integrate it, and follow it up? What purpose does each quotation serve to advance her analysis?

Literary Terms

Your analysis of novels, poems, plays, and films will be deeper and more sophisticated if you understand the most common literary terms.

Allusion is a reference to a person, a place, or an event in history or literature.

Analogy is a comparison of two or more similar objects, suggesting that if they are alike in certain respects, they will probably be alike in other ways, too.

Anecdote is a short summary of an interesting or humorous, often biographical event.

Antagonist is the person or thing actively working against the protagonist, or hero.

Climax is the turning point, an intense moment characterized by a key event.

Conflict is the problem or struggle in a story that triggers the action. There are five basic types of conflict:

- **Person versus person:** One character in a story is in conflict with one or more of the other characters.
- **Person versus society:** A character is in conflict with some element of society: the school, the law, the accepted way of doing things, and so on.
- **Person versus self:** A character faces conflicting inner choices.
- **Person versus nature:** A character is in conflict with some natural happening: a snowstorm, an avalanche, the bitter cold, or any other element of nature.
- **Person versus fate:** A character must battle what seems to be an uncontrollable problem. Whenever the conflict is a strange or unbelievable coincidence, the conflict can be attributed to fate.

Denouement is the outcome of a play or story. See **Resolution**.

Diction is an author's choice of words based on their correctness or effectiveness.

- **Archaic** words are old-fashioned and no longer sound natural when used, such as "I believe thee not" for "I don't believe you."
- **Colloquialism** is an expression that is usually accepted in informal situations and certain locations, as in "He really grinds my beans."
- **Heightened language** uses vocabulary and sentence constructions unlike that of standard speech or writing, as in much poetry and poetic prose.
- **Profanity** is language that shows disrespect for someone or something regarded as holy or sacred.
- **Slang** is the everyday language used by group members among themselves.
- **Trite** expressions lack depth or originality, or are overworked or not worth mentioning in the first place.
- **Vulgarity** is language that is generally considered common, crude, gross, and, at times, offensive. It is sometimes used in fiction, plays, and films to add realism.

Exposition is the introductory section of a story or play. Typically, the setting, main characters, and themes are introduced, and the action is initiated.

Falling action is the action of a play or story that follows the climax and shows the characters dealing with the climactic event or decision.

Figure of speech is a literary device used to create a special effect or to describe something in a fresh way. The most common types are *antithesis, hyperbole, metaphor, metonymy, personification, simile,* and *understatement.*

- **Antithesis** is an opposition, or contrast, of ideas.
  "It was the best of times, it was the worst of times, it was the age of wisdom, it was the age of foolishness . . ."   — Charles Dickens, *A Tale of Two Cities*

- **Hyperbole** (hi-pur′ ba-lee) is an extreme exaggeration or overstatement.
  "I have seen this river so wide it had only one bank."
                                                          —Mark Twain, *Life on the Mississippi*

- **Metaphor** is a comparison of two unlike things in which no word of comparison (*as* or *like*) is used: "Life is a banquet."

- **Metonymy** (ma-ton′a-mee) is the substituting of one term for another that is closely related to it, but not a literal restatement.
  "Friends, Romans, countrymen, lend me your ears." (The request is for the attention of those assembled, not literally their ears.)

- **Personification** is a device in which the author speaks of or describes an animal, object, or idea as if it were a person: "The rock stubbornly refused to move."

- **Simile** is a comparison of two unlike things in which *like* or *as* is used.
  "Uncle walks jerkily as a baby on the unsure ground, his feet widespread, his arms suddenly out like a tightrope walker's when he loses his balance."
                                                          —Joy Kogawa, *Obasan*

- **Understatement** is stating an idea with restraint, often for humorous effect. Mark Twain described Aunt Polly as being "prejudiced against snakes." (Because she hated snakes, this way of saying so is *understatement.*)

Genre refers to a category or type of literature based on its style, form, and content. The mystery novel is a literary genre.

Imagery refers to words or phrases that a writer uses to appeal to the reader's senses.
  "The sky was dark and gloomy, the air was damp and raw . . . "
                                                          —Charles Dickens, *The Pickwick Papers*

Irony is a deliberate discrepancy in meaning. There are three kinds of irony:
- **Dramatic irony**, in which the reader or the audience sees a character's mistakes or misunderstandings, but the character does not.
- **Verbal irony**, in which the writer says one thing and means another ("The best substitute for experience is being sixteen").
- **Irony of situation**, in which there is a great difference between the purpose of a particular action and the result.

Mood is the feeling that a piece of literature arouses in the reader: *happiness, sadness, peacefulness, anxiety,* and so forth.

Paradox is a statement that seems contrary to common sense yet may, in fact, be true: "The coach considered this a good loss."

Plot is the action or sequence of events in a story. It is usually a series of related incidents that build upon one another as the story develops. There are five basic elements in a plot line: *exposition, rising action, climax, falling action,* and *resolution.*

Point of view is the vantage point from which the story unfolds.

> • In the **first-person** point of view, the story is told by one of the characters: "I stepped into the darkened room and felt myself go cold."
> • In the **third-person** point of view, the story is told by someone outside the story: "He stepped into the darkened room and felt himself go cold."
> • **Third-person narrations** can be *omniscient,* meaning that the narrator has access to the thoughts of all the characters, or *limited,* meaning that the narrator focuses on the inner life of one central character.

Protagonist is the main character or hero of the story.

Resolution (or denouement) is the portion of the play or story in which the problem is solved. The resolution comes after the climax and falling action and is intended to bring the story to a satisfactory end.

Rising action is the series of conflicts or struggles that build a story or play toward a fulfilling climax.

Satire is a literary tone used to ridicule or make fun of human vice or weakness, often with the intent of correcting, or changing, the subject of the satiric attack.

Setting is the time and place in which the action of a literary work occurs.

Structure is the form or organization a writer uses for her or his literary work. A great number of possible forms are used regularly in literature: parable, fable, romance, satire, farce, slapstick, and so on.

Style refers to how the author uses words, phrases, and sentences to form his or her ideas. Style is also thought of as the qualities and characteristics that distinguish one writer's work from the work of others.

Symbol is a person, a place, a thing, or an event used to represent something else. For example, the dove is a symbol of peace.

Theme is the statement about life that a particular work shares with readers. In stories written for children, the theme is often spelled out clearly at the end. In more complex literature, the theme will often be more complex and will be implied, not stated.

Tone is the overall feeling, or effect, created by a writer's use of words. This feeling may be serious, mock-serious, humorous, satiric, and so on.

Poetry Terms

Alliteration is the repetition of initial consonant sounds in words.

> "Our gang paces the pier like an old myth . . ."
>> —Anne-Marie Oomen, "Runaway Warning"

Assonance is the repetition of vowel sounds without the repetition of consonants.

> "My words like silent rain drops fell . . ."   —Paul Simon, "Sounds of Silence"

Blank verse is an unrhymed form of poetry. Each line normally consists of ten syllables in which every other syllable, beginning with the second, is stressed. As blank verse is often used in very long poems, it may depart from the strict pattern from time to time.

Consonance is the repetition of consonant sounds. Although it is very similar to alliteration, consonance is not limited to the first letters of words:

> " . . . and high school girls with clear skinned smiles . . ."   —Janis Ian, "At Seventeen"

Foot is the smallest repeated pattern of stressed and unstressed syllables in a verse (see below).

- **Iambic:** an unstressed followed by a stressed syllable (re-peat´)
- **Anapestic:** two unstressed followed by a stressed syllable (in-ter-rupt´)
- **Trochaic:** a stressed followed by an unstressed syllable (old´-er)
- **Dactylic:** a stressed followed by two unstressed syllables (o´-pen-ly)
- **Spondaic:** two stressed syllables (heart´-break´)
- **Pyrrhic:** two unstressed syllables (Pyrrhic seldom appears by itself.)

Onomatopoeia is the use of a word whose sound suggests its meaning, as in *clang or buzz*.

Refrain is the repetition of a line or phrase of a poem at regular intervals, especially at the end of each stanza. A song's refrain may be called the *chorus*.

Rhythm is the ordered or free occurrences of sound in poetry. Ordered or regular rhythm is called metre. Free occurrence of sound is called *free verse*.

Stanza is a division of poetry named for the number of lines it contains:

- **Couplet:** two-line stanza
- **Triplet:** three-line stanza
- **Quatrain:** four-line stanza
- **Quintet:** five-line stanza
- **Sestet:** six-line stanza
- **Septet:** seven-line stanza
- **Octave:** eight-line stanza

Verse is a metric line of poetry. It is named according to the kind and number of feet composing it: *iambic pentameter, anapestic tetrameter,* and so on. (See **Foot**.)

- **Monometer:** one foot
- **Dimeter:** two feet
- **Trimeter:** three feet
- **Tetrameter:** four feet
- **Pentameter:** five feet
- **Hexameter:** six feet
- **Heptameter:** seven feet
- **Octometer:** eight feet

Writing Guidelines

Planning

1. **Select a topic.** Choose a work of literature or another artwork with which you are familiar or about which you are willing to learn.

2. **Understand the work.** Read or experience it thoughtfully (two or three times, if possible), looking carefully at its content, form, and overall effect.
   - **For plays and films,** examine the plot, props, setting, characters, dialogue, lighting, costumes, sound effects, music, acting, and directing.
   - **For novels and short stories,** focus on point of view, plot, setting, characters, style, diction, symbols, and theme. (See pages 302–304.)
   - **For poems,** examine diction, tone, sound patterns, figures of speech (e.g., metaphors), symbolism, irony, structure, genre, and theme. (See page 305.)
   - **For music,** focus on harmonic and rhythmic qualities, lyrics, and interpretation.

3. **Develop a focus and approach.** Take notes on what you experience, using the list above to guide you. Seek to understand the whole work before you analyze the parts, exploring your ideas and digging deeply through freewriting and annotating. Select a dimension of the work as a focus, considering what approach to analyzing that element might work. (See the approaches to literary analysis on pages 278–280.)

4. **Organize your thoughts.** Review the notes that you took as you analyzed the work. What key insights has your analysis led you to see? Make a key insight your thesis, and then organize supporting points logically in an outline.

Drafting

5. **Write the first draft.**

   Opening: Use ideas like the following to gain your readers' attention, identify your topic, narrow the focus, and state your thesis:
   - Summarize your subject briefly. Include the title, the author or artist, and the literary form or performance.
     > *Example:* Michael Ondaatje's "The Time Around Scars," a poem written in quasi-free verse, deals with scars, the stories they tell, and the people who can and cannot share these stories.
   - Start with a quotation from the work and then comment on its importance.
   - Open with a general statement about the artist's style or aesthetic process.
     > *Example:* Flannery O'Connor's stories are filled with characters who are bizarre, freakish, devious, and sometimes even murderous.
   - Begin with a general statement about the plot or performance.
     > *Example:* In Stephen Spielberg's movie *War of the Worlds,* Ray Ferrier and his two children flee from their New Jersey home in a stolen minivan.

- Assert your thesis. State the key insight about the work that your analysis has revealed—the insight your essay will seek to support.

Middle: Develop or support your focus by following this pattern:
- State the main points, relating them clearly to the focus of your essay.
- Support each main point with specific details or direct quotations.
- Explain how these details prove your point.

Conclusion: Tie key points together and assert your thesis or evaluation in a fresh way, leaving readers with a sense of the larger significance of your analysis.

Revising

6. **Improve the ideas, organization, and voice.** Review your draft for its overall content and tone. Ask a classmate or writing-centre tutor for help, if appropriate.

_____ **Ideas:** Does the essay show clear and deep insight into specific elements of the text, artwork, or performance? Is that insight effectively developed with specific references to the work itself?

_____ **Organization:** Does the opening effectively engage the reader, introduce the text or artwork, and focus attention on an element or issue? Does the middle carefully work through a "reading" of the work? Does the conclusion reaffirm the insight into the work and expand the reader's understanding?

_____ **Voice:** Does the tone convey a controlled, measured interest in the text or artwork? Is the analytical attitude confident but reasonable?

Editing

7. **Edit and proofread the essay by checking issues like these:**

_____ **Words:** Language, especially terminology, is precise and clear.

_____ **Sentences:** Constructions flow smoothly and are varied in length and structure; quotations are effectively integrated into sentence syntax.

_____ **Correctness:** The copy includes no errors in spelling, usage, punctuation, grammar, or mechanics.

_____ **Design:** The page design is correctly formatted and attractive; references are properly documented according to the required system (e.g., MLA).

Publishing

8. **Publish your essay.** Submit your essay to your instructor, but consider other ways of sharing your insights about this work or artist—blogging, submitting a review to a periodical (print or online), or leading classmates in a discussion (e.g., book club, post-performance meeting, exhibition tour).

Critical-Thinking and Writing Activities

As directed by your instructor, complete the following activities.

1. According to Gabrielle Roy, "The main engagement of the writer is towards truthfulness; therefore he must keep his mind and his judgement free." How are the literary works and the essays in this chapter concerned with truth?

2. While Robert Browning is a British poet and Jane Kenyon an American, there are many fine Canadian poets, such as Earle Birney, Margaret Avison, Al Purdy, Leonard Cohen, Margaret Atwood, Don McKay, Lorna Crozier, and Ken Babstock. Find a short poem by one of these and write an analysis of it.

3. After reading "A Short History of Indians and Canada" and the sample analysis of this story, check out King's "Dead Indians" (pages 181–185), Daniel Francis's "The Bureaucrat's Indian" (pages 218–221), and Joanne Arnott's "Speak Out, For Example" (pages 358–361). Using these pieces as idea resources, write your own analysis of King's story. Option B: choose another story from King's collection, *A Short History of Indians in Canada*.

4. Using Denae Dyck's essay on *Charlotte's Web* as inspiration, revisit a children's story from your past. Consider the critical approaches available (pages 278–280), and write an analysis of that children's text.

5. Study the online bonus essays for this chapter: "Why Would You Do It, Lizzie?" by David Giesbrecht; "Fish Stories or Some Likeness Thereof," by Andrew Atkinson; and "Dystopia Now," by Brian Bethune. Taking inspiration from one of these essays, research an author mentioned and write your own essay about his or her work.

Learning-Objectives Checklist ✓

Have you achieved this chapter's learning objectives? Check your progress with the items below, revisiting topics in the chapter as needed. *I have . . .*

____ critically examined and assessed analyses of literature and the arts for clarity, reasoning, insight, and the writer's critical perspective (278–280).

____ assessed how each analyst's critique of an artwork might be informed by her or his purpose, readers, and topic (278–280).

____ effectively used arts-related terminology and concepts to accurately critique others' analyses and to informatively craft my own (302–305).

____ analyzed and evaluated an artwork by addressing relevant issues, including its content, form, style, and special features (306–307).

____ written an analysis that has an insightful thesis, clear reasoning, and relevant supporting evidence from and about the work (306–307).

____ examined my ideas, organization, and voice for weaknesses such as inadequate supporting evidence or misused literary terms (306–307).

Chapter 16

Strategies for Argumentation and Persuasion

"I'm not convinced." "I just don't buy it." Maybe you've said something similar while watching a political debate, viewing a TV ad, or discussing an issue in class or at work. You simply didn't find the argument logical or convincing.

Your courses offer opportunities to think through and argue out big issues. To participate in that dialogue, you must be able to read and listen to others' arguments, analyze them, and build your own.

This chapter will help you do that. It explains what argumentation is, how to identify weak arguments, and how to construct strong ones. The three ensuing chapters then explain and model three forms of written argumentation: taking a position, persuading readers to act, and proposing a solution.

Visually Speaking Study Figure 16.1. What does it suggest about the nature of argumentation and the desire to persuade other people of something?

Learning **Objectives**

By working through this chapter, you will be able to

- build a convincing evidence-based argument.
- distinguish and develop three types of claims.
- assess the nature and function of nine types of evidence.
- identify and correct logical fallacies.
- draft logical claims with reliable evidence and valid warrants.
- make needed concessions, develop rebuttals, and use appropriate appeals.

© Reuters/CORBIS

fig. 16.1

Building Persuasive Arguments

What is an argument? Formally, an *argument* is a series of statements arranged in a logical sequence, supported with sound evidence, and expressed powerfully so as to sway your reader or listener. Arguments appear in a variety of places:

- A research paper about email surveillance by CSIS.
- An analysis of "Mrs. Turner Cutting the Grass" (short story) or *The Englishman's Boy* (novel).
- A debate about the ethics of transferring copyrighted music over the Internet.

This chapter will outline a process commonly used to build arguments of all kinds. The process includes the following steps:

Step 1: Prepare your argument.

- **Identify your readers and purpose.** Who are your readers and what is your goal? Do you want to take a position, persuade readers to act, or offer a solution?
- **Generate ideas and gather solid evidence.** You can't base an argument on opinions. Find accurate, pertinent information about the issue and uncover all viewpoints on it.
- **Develop a line of reasoning.** To be effective, you need to link your ideas in a clear, logical sequence.

Step 2: Make and qualify your claim.

- **Draw reasonable conclusions from the evidence.** State your claim (a debatable idea) as the central point for which you will argue. For example, you might assert that something is true, has value, or should be done.
- **Add qualifiers.** Words such as "typically" and "sometimes" soften your claim, making it more reasonable and acceptable.

Step 3: Support your claim.

- **Support each point** in your claim with solid evidence.
- **Identify logical fallacies.** Test your thinking for errors in logic. (See pages 317–320.)

Step 4: Engage the opposition.

- **Make concessions,** if needed, by granting points to the opposition.
- **Develop rebuttals** that expose the weaknesses of the opposition's position, whenever possible.
- **Use appropriate appeals**—emotional "tugs" that ethically and logically help readers see your argument as convincing.

Preparing Your Argument

An argument is a reason or chain of reasons used to support a claim. To use argumentation well, you need to know how to draw logical conclusions from sound evidence. Preparing an effective argument involves a number of specific steps, starting with those discussed below.

Consider the Situation

- **Clearly identify your purpose and audience.** This step is essential for all writing, but especially true when building an argument. (See pages 28–29.)
- **Consider a range of ideas** to broaden your understanding of the issue and to help focus your thinking on a particular viewpoint. (See pages 44–45.)
- **Gather sound evidence** to support your viewpoint. (See pages 314–316.)

Develop a Line of Reasoning

Argumentative writing requires a clear line of reasoning with each point logically supporting your argument. Develop the line of reasoning as you study the issue, or use either of the following outlines as a guide.

Sample Argumentative Outlines

fig. 16.2

> *Outline 1:* **Present your supporting arguments, then address counterarguments, and conclude with the strongest argument.**
>
> **Introduction:** question, concern, or claim
> 1. Strong argument-supporting claim
>   - Discussion and support
> 2. Other argument-supporting claims
>   - Discussion of and support for each argument
> 3. Objections, concerns, and counterarguments
>   - Discussion, concessions, answers, and rebuttals
> 4. Strongest argument-supporting claim
>   - Discussion and support
>
> **Conclusion:** argument consolidated—claim reinforced
>
> *Outline 2:* **Address the arguments and counterarguments point by point.**
>
> **Introduction:** question, concern, or claim
> 1. Strong argument-supporting claim
>   - Discussion and support
>   - Counterarguments, concessions, and rebuttals
> 2. Other argument-supporting claims
>   - For each argument, discussion and support
>   - For each argument, counterarguments, concessions, and rebuttals
> 3. Strongest argument-supporting claim
>   - Discussion and support
>   - Counterarguments, concessions, and rebuttals
>
> **Conclusion:** argument consolidated—claim reinforced

Making and Qualifying Claims

An argument centres on a claim—a debatable statement. That claim is the thesis, or key point you wish to explain and defend so well that readers agree with it. A strong claim has the following traits:

- **It's clearly arguable**—it can be vigorously debated.
- **It's defendable**—it can be supported with sufficient arguments and evidence.
- **It's responsible**—it takes an ethically sound position.
- **It's understandable**—it uses clear terms and defines key words.
- **It's interesting**—it is challenging and worth discussing, not bland and easily accepted.

Distinguish Claims from Facts and Opinions

A claim is a conclusion drawn from logical thought and reliable evidence. A fact, in contrast, is a statement that can be checked for accuracy. An opinion is a personally held taste or attitude. A claim can be debated, but a fact or an opinion cannot.

> **Fact:** *The Fellowship of the Ring* is the first book in J.R.R. Tolkien's trilogy *The Lord of the Rings*.
>
> **Opinion:** I liked the movie almost as much as the book.
>
> **Claim:** While the film version of *The Fellowship of the Ring* does not completely follow the novel's plot, the film does faithfully capture the spirit of Tolkien's novel.

Note: While the fact's accuracy can easily be checked, the opinion statement simply offers a personal feeling. Conversely, the claim states an idea that can be supported with reasoning and evidence.

Distinguish Three Types of Claims

Truth, value, and policy—these types of claims are made in an argument. The differences among them are important because each type has a distinct goal.

- **Claims of truth** state that something is or is not the case. As a writer, you want readers to accept your claim as trustworthy.

  > The Arctic ice cap will melt completely during the summer as early as 2080.
  >
  > The cholesterol in eggs is not as dangerous as previously feared.
  >
  > **Comment:** Avoid statements that are (1) obviously true or (2) impossible to prove. Also, truth claims must be argued carefully because accepting them (or not) can have serious consequences.
  >
  > *Sample Essay:* "It's 'Apartheid' Time Again. Pick Your Villain," pages 336–337.

- **Claims of value** state that something does or does not have worth. As a writer, you want readers to accept your judgment.

  > Volunteer reading tutors provide a valuable service.
  >
  > Many music videos fail to present positive images of women.
  >
  > **Comment:** Claims of value must be supported by referring to a known standard or by establishing an agreed-upon standard. To avoid a bias, base your judgments on the known standard, not on your feelings.
  >
  > *Sample Essay:* "Our Wealth: Where Is It Taking Us?" pages 348–351.

- **Claims of policy** state that something ought or ought not to be done. As a writer, you want readers to approve your course of action.

  > Special taxes should be placed on gas-guzzling SUVs.
  >
  > The developer should not be allowed to fill in the pond where the endangered tiger salamander lives.
  >
  > **Comment:** Policy claims focus on action. To arrive at them, you must often first establish certain truths and values; thus an argument over policy may include both truth and value claims.
  >
  > *Sample Essay:* "'It's a Girl!'—Could Be a Death Sentence," pages 377–379.

Develop a Supportable Claim

An effective claim balances confidence with common sense. Follow these tips:

- **Avoid all-or-nothing, extreme claims.** Propositions using words that are overly positive or negative—such as *all, best, never,* and *worst*—may be difficult to support. Statements that leave no room for exceptions are easy to attack.

  > **Extreme:** All people charged for a DUI should never be allowed to drive again.

- **Make a truly meaningful claim.** Avoid claims that are obvious, trivial, or unsupportable. None is worth the energy needed to argue the point.

  > **Obvious:** Some people are against oil pipelines.
  >
  > **Trivial:** Oil pipelines are good at moving oil.
  >
  > **Unsupportable:** Building pipelines is immoral.

- **Use qualifiers to temper your claims.** Qualifiers are words or phrases that make claims more reasonable. Notice the difference between these two claims:

  > **Unqualified:** Big oil companies take far too many environmental shortcuts.
  >
  > **Qualified:** Some oil companies take improper environmental shortcuts.

Note: The "qualified" claim is easier to defend because it narrows the focus and leaves room for exceptions. Use qualifier words or phrases like these:

almost	if done correctly	maybe	tends to
before 2014	in one case	might	typically
frequently	likely	probably some	usually

Supporting Your Claims

A claim stands or falls on its support. It's not the popular strength of your claim that matters, but rather the strength of your reasoning and evidence. To develop strong support, consider how to select and use evidence.

Gather Evidence

Several types of evidence can support claims. To make good choices, review each type, as well as its strengths and weaknesses.

- **Observations and anecdotes** share what people (including you) have seen, heard, smelled, touched, tasted, and experienced. Such evidence offers an "eyewitness" perspective shaped by the observer's viewpoint, which can be powerful but may also prove narrow and subjective.

  > Most of us have closets full of clothes: jeans, sweaters, khakis, T-shirts, and shoes for every occasion.

- **Statistics** offer concrete numbers about a topic. Numbers don't "speak for themselves," however. They need to be interpreted and compared properly—not slanted or taken out of context. They also need to be up-to-date, relevant, and accurate.

  > In the past 11 months, almost 9,000 civilian protesters and nearly 3,000 anti-government rebels have been murdered by Syrian President Bashar al-Assad's Ba'ath party dictatorship. Approximately 400 children have been imprisoned and tortured. Meanwhile, Assad's government claims that 89.4 percent of Syrians had approved a new constitution that could keep Bashar in power for another 16 years.

- **Tests and experiments** provide hard data developed through the scientific method, data that must nevertheless be carefully studied and properly interpreted.

  > According to the two scientists, the rats with unlimited access to the functional running wheel ran each day and gradually increased the amount of running; in addition, they started to eat less.

- **Graphics** provide information in visual form—from simple tables to more complex charts, maps, drawings, and photographs. When poorly done, however, graphics can distort the truth. See the visuals used in the sample presentation on page 297.

- **Analogies** compare two things, creating clarity by drawing parallels. However, every analogy breaks down if pushed too far. (See the full text of the speech "I Have a Dream" on pages 392–395.)

  > It is obvious today that America has defaulted on this promissory note insofar as her citizens of color are concerned. Instead of honoring this sacred obligation, America has given the Negro people a bad check; a check which has come back marked "insufficient funds." But we refuse to believe that the bank of justice is bankrupt.
  >
  > —Martin Luther King, Jr.

- **Expert testimony** offers insights from an authority on the topic. Such testimony always has limits: Experts don't know it all, and they work from distinct perspectives.

  > Psychiatrist Susan Linn describes the marketing aimed at children as "precisely targeted, refined by scientific method, and honed by child psychologists" (5).

- **Illustrations, examples, and demonstrations** support general claims with specific instances, making such statements seem concrete and observable. Of course, an example may not be your best support if it isn't familiar. (See the full text of Thomas King's "Dead Indians" on pages 181–185.)

  > You can find Dead Indians everywhere. Rodeos, powwows, movies, television commercials. At the 1973 Academy Awards, when Sacheen Littlefeather (Yaqui-Apache-Pueblo) refused the Best Actor award on behalf of Marlon Brando, she did so dressed as a Dead Indian.
  >
  > —Thomas King

- **Analyses** examine parts of a topic through thought patterns—cause/effect, compare/contrast, classification, process, or definition. Such analysis helps make sense of a topic's complexity, but muddles the topic when poorly done.

  > Faceless, non-contextualized journalism cannot be rebutted or engaged in any meaningful dialogue. It comes from nowhere and has no face for healthy dialogue. From WikiLeaks we have at times seen mass frustration not simply because of the content leaked, but because there is no legitimate, fair venue for retort.

- **Predictions** offer insights into possible outcomes or consequences by forecasting what might happen under certain conditions. Like weather forecasting, predicting can be tricky. To be plausible, a prediction must be rooted in a logical analysis of present facts.

  > What will happen when no stray opinions or bits of information can any longer pierce the thick film of the bubbles we've so carefully constructed around our media-consuming selves? As the volume of discourse increases, its comprehensibility will decrease. As our access to diverse media grows, our ability to discuss it with our fellow citizens will diminish.

Use Evidence

Finding evidence is one thing; using it well is another. You want to reason with the evidence effectively, to use that evidence to advance and deepen your argument—to "thicken" it, so to speak. To marshal evidence in support of your claim, follow three guidelines:

1. **Go for quality and variety, not just quantity.** More evidence is not necessarily better. Instead, aim for sound evidence in different forms. Quality evidence is
   - **accurate:** correct and verifiable in each detail.
   - **complete:** filled with pertinent facts.
   - **concrete:** filled with specifics.
   - **relevant:** clearly related to the claim.
   - **current:** reliably up-to-date.
   - **authoritative:** backed by expertise, training, and knowledge.
   - **appealing:** able to influence readers.

2. **Use inductive and deductive patterns of logic.** Depending on your purpose, use inductive or deductive reasoning. (See page 18.)

Induction: Inductive reasoning works from the particular toward general conclusions. In a persuasive essay using induction, look at facts first, find a pattern in them, and then lead the reader to your conclusion.

> For example, in "Nuclear Is Not the Answer," Alyssa Woudstra first examines the benefits and liabilities of nuclear energy versus fossil fuels before asserting her claim that using the latter is a better choice. (See pages 333–335.)

Deduction: Deductive reasoning—the opposite of inductive reasoning—starts from accepted truths and applies them to a new situation so as to reach a conclusion about it. For deduction to be sound, be sure the starting principles or facts are true, the new situation is accurately described, and the application is logical.

> For example, examine the deductive pattern of the passage below, taken from Rajendra Kale's "'It's a Girl!'—Could Be a Death Sentence" on pages 377–379.

> A woman has the right to medical information about herself that is available to a health care professional to provide advice and treatment. The sex of the fetus is medically irrelevant information (except when managing rare sex-linked illnesses) and does not affect care. Moreover, such information could in some instances facilitate female feticide. Therefore, doctors should be allowed to disclose this information only after about 30 weeks of pregnancy—in other words, when an unquestioned abortion is all but impossible.

3. **Reason using valid warrants.** To make sense, claims and their supporting reasons must have a logical connection. That connection is called the *warrant*—the often unspoken thinking used to relate the reasoning to the claim. If warrants are good, arguments hold water; if warrants are faulty, then arguments break down. In other words, beware of faulty assumptions.

Check the short argument outlined below. Which of the warrants seem reasonable and strong, and which seem weak? Where does the argument fail?

> **Reasoning:** If current trends in water usage continue, the reservoir will be empty in two years.
>
> **Claim:** Therefore, Emeryville should immediately shut down its public swimming pools.

Unstated Warrants or Assumptions:

> It is not good for the reservoir to be empty.
>
> The swimming pools draw significant amounts of water from the reservoir.
>
> Emptying the pools would help raise the level of the reservoir.
>
> No other action would better prevent the reservoir from emptying.
>
> It is worse to have an empty reservoir than an empty swimming pool.

Identifying Logical Fallacies

Fallacies are false arguments—that is, bits of fuzzy, dishonest, or incomplete thinking. They may crop up in your own thinking, in your opposition's thinking, or in such public "arguments" as ads, political appeals, and talk shows. Because fallacies may sway an unsuspecting audience, they are dangerously persuasive. By learning to recognize fallacies, however, you may identify them in opposing arguments and eliminate them from your own writing. In this section, logical fallacies are grouped according to how they falsify an argument.

Distorting the Issue

The following fallacies falsify an argument by twisting the logical framework.

- **Bare Assertion** The most basic way to distort an issue is to deny that it exists. This fallacy claims, "That's just how it is."

   > Because the Internet is a public space, downloading music for free is perfectly acceptable. (*Objection:* The claim shuts off discussion of the nature of the Internet and of laws governing copyright.)

- **Begging the Question** Also known as circular reasoning, this fallacy arises from assuming in the basis of your argument the very point you need to prove.

   > We don't need a useless film series when students have computers and DVD players. (*Objection:* There may be uses for a public film series that private video viewing can't provide. The word "useless" begs the question.)

- **Oversimplification** This fallacy reduces complexity to simplicity. Beware of phrases like "It's a simple question of." Serious issues are rarely simple.

   > Capital punishment is a simple question of protecting society.

- **Either/Or Thinking** Also known as black-and-white or dualistic thinking this fallacy reduces all options to two extremes. Frequently, it derives from a clear bias.

   > Either this community develops light-rail transportation or the community will not grow in the future. (*Objection:* The claim ignores the possibility that growth may occur through other means.)

- **Complex Question** Sometimes by phrasing a question a certain way, a person ignores or covers up a more basic question.

   > Why can't we bring down the prices that corrupt gas stations are charging? (*Objection:* This question ignores a more basic question—"Are gas stations really corrupt?")

- **Straw Man** In this fallacy, the writer argues against a claim that is easily refuted. Typically, such a claim exaggerates or misrepresents the opponents' position.

   > Those who oppose euthanasia must believe that individuals who are terminally ill deserve to suffer.

Sabotaging the Argument

These fallacies falsify the argument by twisting it. They destroy reason and replace it with something hollow or misleading.

- **Red Herring** This strange term comes from the practice of dragging a stinky fish across a trail to throw tracking dogs off the scent. When a person puts forth a volatile idea that pulls readers away from the real issue, readers become distracted. Suppose that the argument addresses the pros and cons of drilling for oil in the Arctic Ocean, and the writer begins with this statement:

  > From the air, the Alberta oil sands stretch out like a vast strip mine filled with smoke and devastation, like Mordor in *The Lord of the Rings*. (*Objection:* Introducing the oil sands and its appearance distracts from the real issue—how drilling will impact the Arctic Ocean.)

- **Misuse of Humour** Jokes, satire, and irony can lighten the mood and highlight a truth; when humour distracts or mocks, however, it undercuts the argument. What effect would the mocking tone of this statement have in an argument about tanning beds in health clubs?

  > People who use tanning beds will just turn into wrinkled old prunes or leathery sun-dried tomatoes!

- **Appeal to Pity** This fallacy engages in a misleading tug on the heartstrings. Instead of using a measured emotional appeal, an appeal to pity seeks to manipulate the audience into agreement.

  > Affirmative action policies ruined this young man's life. Because of them, he was denied admission to Veterinary College.

- **Use of Threats** A simple but unethical way of sabotaging an argument is to threaten opponents. More often than not, a threat is merely implied: "If you don't accept my argument, you'll regret it."

  > If opponents don't get out of the way of oil sands and pipeline development, the Canadian economy will face a bleak future: your job and your home are at stake.

- **Bandwagon Mentality** Someone implies that a claim cannot be true because a majority of people are opposed to it, or it must be true because a majority support it. (History shows that people in the minority have often had the better argument.) At its worst, such an appeal manipulates people's desire to belong or be accepted.

  > It's obvious to intelligent people that cockroaches live only in the apartments of dirty people. (*Objection:* Based on popular opinion, the claim appeals to a kind of prejudice and ignores scientific evidence about cockroaches.)

- **Appeal to Popular Sentiment** This fallacy consists of associating your position with something popularly loved: the Canadian flag, hockey, maple syrup. Appeals to popular sentiment sidestep thought to play on feelings.

  > Anyone who has seen *Bambi* could never condone hunting deer.

Drawing Faulty Conclusions from the Evidence

This group of fallacies falsifies the argument by short-circuiting proper logic in favour of assumptions or faulty thinking.

- **Appeal to Ignorance** This fallacy suggests that because no one has proven a particular claim, it must be false; or, because no one has disproven a claim, it must be true. Appeals to ignorance unfairly shift the burden of proof onto someone else.

  > Flying saucers are real. No scientific explanation has ruled them out.

- **Hasty or Broad Generalization** Such a claim is based on too little evidence or allows no exceptions. In jumping to a conclusion, the writer may use intensifiers such as *all, every,* or *never.*

  > Today's voters spend too little time reading and too much time being taken in by 30-second sound bites. (*Objection:* Quite a few voters may, in fact, spend too little time reading about the issues, but it is unfair to suggest that this is true of everyone.)

- **False Cause** This well-known fallacy confuses sequence with causation: If *A* comes before *B, A* must have caused *B.* However, *A* may be one of several causes, or *A* and *B* may be only loosely related, or the connection between *A* and *B* may be entirely coincidental.

  > Since that new school opened, drug use among young people has skyrocketed. Better that the school had never been built.

- **Slippery Slope** This fallacy argues that a single step will start an unstoppable chain of events. While such a slide may occur, the prediction lacks evidence.

  > If we legalize marijuana, it's only a matter of time before hard drugs follow and Cananda becomes a nation of junkies and addicts.

Misusing Evidence

These fallacies falsify the argument by abusing or distorting the evidence.

- **Impressing with Numbers** In this case, the writer drowns readers in statistics and numbers that overwhelm them into agreement. In addition, the numbers haven't been properly interpreted.

  > At 35 ppm, CO levels factory-wide are only 10 ppm above the OSHA recommendation, which is 25 ppm. Clearly, that 10 ppm is insignificant in the big picture, and the occasional readings in some areas of between 40 and 80 ppm are aberrations that can safely be ignored. (*Objection:* The 10 ppm may be significant, and higher readings may indicate real danger.)

- **Half-Truths** A half-truth contains part of but not the whole truth. Because it leaves out "the rest of the story," it is both true and false simultaneously.

  > The new welfare bill is good because it will get people off the public dole. (*Objection:* This may be true, but the bill may also cause undue suffering for some truly needy individuals.)

- **Unreliable Testimonial** An appeal to authority has force only if the authority is qualified in the proper field. If he or she is not, the testimony is irrelevant. Note that fame is not the same thing as authority.

  > On her talk show, Alberta Magnus recently claimed that most pork sold in Canada is tainted. (*Objection:* Although Magnus may be an articulate talk show host, she is not an expert on food safety.)

- **Attack Against the Person** This fallacy, also called an "*ad hominem* attack," directs attention to a person's character, lifestyle, or beliefs rather than to the issue.

  > Would you accept the opinion of a candidate who experimented with drugs in college?

- **Hypothesis Contrary to Fact** This fallacy relies on "if only" thinking. It bases the claim on an assumption of what would have happened if something else had, or had not, happened. Being pure speculation, such a claim cannot be tested.

  > If only BlackBerry had developed its Q10 on schedule by 2011, it would have withstood challenges from the iPhone, and BlackBerry shares would still be riding high.

- **False Analogy** Sometimes a person will argue that X is good (or bad) because it is like Y. Such an analogy may be valid, but it weakens the argument if the grounds for the comparison are vague or unrelated.

  > Don't bother voting in this election; it's a stinking quagmire. (*Objection:* Comparing the election to a "stinking quagmire" is unclear and exaggerated.)

Misusing Language

Essentially, all logical fallacies misuse language. However, three fallacies falsify the argument, especially by the misleading use of words.

- **Obfuscation** This fallacy involves using fuzzy terms like *throughput* and *downlink* to muddy the issue. These words may make simple ideas sound more profound than they really are, or they may make false ideas sound true.

  > Through the fully functional developmental process of a streamlined target-refractory system, the Canadian military will successfully reprioritize its data throughputs. (*Objection:* What does this sentence mean?)

- **Ambiguity** Ambiguous statements can be interpreted in two or more opposite ways. Although ambiguity can result from unintentional careless thinking, writers sometimes use ambiguity to obscure a position.

  > Many women need to work to support their children through school, but they would be better off at home. (*Objection:* Does *they* refer to *children* or *women*? What does *better off* mean? These words and phrases can be interpreted in opposite ways.)

- **Slanted Language** By choosing words with strong positive or negative connotations, a writer can draw readers away from the true logic of the argument. Here is an example of three synonyms for the word stubborn that the philosopher Bertrand Russell once used to illustrate the bias in slanted language:

  > I am firm. You are obstinate. He is pigheaded.

Engaging the Opposition

Think of an argument as an intelligent, lively dialogue with readers. Anticipate their questions, concerns, objections, and counterarguments. Then follow these guidelines.

Make Concessions

By offering concessions—recognizing points made by the other side—you acknowledge your argument's limits and the truth of other positions. Paradoxically, such concessions strengthen your overall argument by making it seem more credible. Concede your points graciously, using words such as the following:

Admittedly	Granted	I agree that	I cannot argue with
It is true that	You're right	I accept	No doubt
Of course	I concede that	Perhaps	Certainly it's the case

Example: While it is true that foot-and-mouth disease is not dangerous to humans, other animal diseases are.

Develop Rebuttals

Even when you concede a point, you can often answer that objection by rebutting it. A good rebuttal is a small, tactful argument aimed at a weak spot in the opposing argument. Try these strategies:

1. **Point out the counterargument's limits** by putting the opposing point in a larger context. Show that the counterargument omits something important.
2. **Tell the other side of the story.** Offer an opposing interpretation of the evidence, or counter with stronger, more reliable, more convincing evidence.
3. **Address logical fallacies in the counterargument.** Check for faulty reasoning or emotional manipulation. For example, if the counterargument presents a half-truth, offer information that presents "the rest of the story."

> It is true that Chernobyl occurred more than twenty years ago, so safety measures for nuclear reactors have been greatly improved. However, that single accident is still affecting millions of people who were exposed to the radiation.

Consolidate Your Claim

After making concessions and rebutting objections, you may need to regroup. Restate your claim so carefully that the weight of your whole argument can rest on it.

> Although it is not ideal, burning fossil fuels is still a better option than nuclear power until renewable energy sources such as wind, solar, and geothermal power become more available.

Pi-Lens/Shutterstock.com

Using Appropriate Appeals

For your argument to be persuasive, it must not only be logical but also "feel right." It must treat readers as real people by appealing to their common sense, hopes, pride, and notion of right and wrong. How do you appeal to all these concerns? Do the following: (1) build credibility, (2) make logical appeals, and (3) focus on readers' needs.

Build Credibility

A persuasive argument is credible—so trustworthy that readers can change their minds painlessly. To build credibility, observe these rules:

- **Be thoroughly honest.** Demonstrate integrity toward the topic—don't falsify data, spin evidence, or ignore facts. Document your sources and cite them wherever appropriate.
- **Make realistic claims, projections, and promises.** Avoid emotionally charged statements, pie-in-the-sky forecasts, and undeliverable deals.
- **Develop and maintain trust.** From your first word to your last, develop trust—in your attitude toward the topic, your treatment of readers, and your respect for opposing viewpoints.

Make Logical Appeals

Arguments stand or fall on their logical strength, but your readers' acceptance of those arguments is often affected more by the emotional appeal of your ideas and evidence. To avoid overly emotional appeals, follow these guidelines:

- **Engage readers positively.** Appeal to their better natures—to their sense of honour, justice, social commitment, altruism, and enlightened self-interest. Avoid appeals geared toward ignorance, prejudice, selfishness, or fear.
- **Use a fitting tone.** Use a tone that is appropriate for the topic, purpose, situation, and audience.
- **Aim to motivate, not manipulate, readers.** While you do want them to accept your viewpoint, it's not a win-at-all-costs situation. Avoid bullying, guilt-tripping, name calling, and exaggerated tugs on heartstrings.
- **Don't trash-talk the opposition.** Show tact, respect, and understanding. Focus on issues, not personalities.
- **Use arguments and evidence that readers can understand and appreciate.** If readers find your thinking too complex, too simple, or too strange, you've lost them.

INSIGHT ▶ Remember the adage: The best argument is so clear and convincing that it sounds like an explanation.

Focus on Readers' Needs

Instead of playing on readers' emotions, connect your argument with readers' needs and values. Follow these guidelines:

- **Know your real readers.** Who are they—peers, professors, or other citizens? What are their allegiances, their worries, their dreams?
- **Picture readers as resistant.** Accept that your readers, including those inclined to agree with you, need convincing. Think of them as alert, cautious, and demanding—but also interested.
- **Use appeals that match needs and values.** Your argument may support or challenge readers' needs and values. To understand those needs, study the table below, which is based loosely on the thinking of psychologist Abraham Maslow. Maslow's hierarchy ranks people's needs on a scale from the most basic to the most complex. The table begins at the bottom with *having necessities* (a basic need) and ends at the top with *helping others* (a more complex need). For example, if you're writing to argue for more affordable housing for seniors, you'd argue differently to legislators (whose focus is on *helping others*) than to seniors who need the housing (whose focus is on *having necessities*). Follow these guidelines:

  - Use appeals that match the foremost needs and values of your readers.
  - If appropriate, constructively challenge those needs and values.
  - Whenever possible, phrase your appeals in positive terms.
  - After analyzing your readers' needs, choose a persuasive theme for your argument—a positive benefit, advantage, or outcome that readers can expect if they accept your claim. Use this theme to help readers to care about your claims.

Reader needs . . .	Use persuasive appeals to . . .
To make the world better by helping others	values and social obligations
To achieve by being good at something, getting recognition	self-fulfillment, status, appreciation
To belong by being part of a group	group identity, acceptance
To survive by avoiding threats, having necessities	safety, security, physical needs

fig. 16.3

Critical-Thinking and Writing Activities

As directed by your instructor, complete the following critical-thinking and writing activities by yourself or with classmates.

1. Canadian politician Tommy Douglas once wrote, "Courage, my friends; 'tis not too late to build a better world." In what ways is argumentation concerned with courageous efforts to improve the world?

2. Select an essay from Chapters 17–19. Read the essay carefully. Then describe and evaluate the essay's argumentative strategies by answering the questions below:
   - What is the essay's main claim? Is it a claim of truth, value, or policy?
   - Is the claim arguable—supportable, qualified, and effectively phrased?
   - What arguments does the writer develop in support of the claim? Are these arguments logical?
   - What types of evidence does the writer provide to support his or her discussion?
   - Is the evidence valid, sufficient, current, and accurate?
   - Does the writer effectively address questions, alternatives, objections, and counterarguments?

3. Review the essay that you read for the second activity, answering these questions:
   - Describe the writer's tone. Does it effectively engage readers?
   - Does the argument seem credible and authoritative? Explain.
   - Identify ways that the writer connects with readers' needs and values. How does he or she develop a persuasive theme that appeals to those needs and values?

Learning-Objectives Checklist ✓

Have you achieved this chapter's learning objectives? Check your progress with the items below, revisiting topics in the chapter as needed. *I have...*

____ examined the process of building an argument, starting with situation analysis, researching the topic, and developing clear and logical reasoning (311–312).

____ analyzed the logical nature and persuasive effects of three types of claims: truth, value, and policy (312–313).

____ revised arguments, correcting these weaknesses: all-or-nothing claims, obvious claims, trivial assertions, and claims lacking needed qualifiers (313).

____ analyzed the strengths and weaknesses of nine types of evidence (314–315).

____ identified and corrected logical fallacies in arguments (317–320).

____ linked claims and their supporting reasons with valid warrants (316).

____ revised and strengthened my arguments by making needed concessions, developing rebuttals, and generating appropriate appeals (321–323).

____ drafted, revised, and edited a unified, well-reasoned argument with fitting appeals, logical claims, and current, reliable evidence (322–323).

Chapter 17

Taking a Position

Sometimes you just have to take a stand. An issue comes up that upsets you or challenges your thinking, and in response, you say, "Okay, this is what I believe, and this is why I believe it."

Learning to read and write position papers enables you to do this. The reading skills help you analyze others' positions, recognize their strengths, and identify their weaknesses. The writing skills help you probe a topic, refine your own perspective on the issues, educate others about the topic, and convince them that your position has value.

This chapter will help you refine both skills. In addition, because both skills are used in virtually all disciplines and most professions, learning this chapter's writing skills and strategies will help you succeed in the classroom today and in the workplace throughout your career.

Visually Speaking   What does the image below suggest about the nature of taking a position? What is required to do so effectively, productively? Does taking a stand always involve risk and confrontation? What are the similarities and differences between taking a stand in person and through writing?

Learning **Objectives**

By working through this chapter, you will be able to

- critically examine and assess the arguments in position papers.
- identify logical fallacies that are especially a danger when taking a position.
- make concessions and rebut opposing arguments.
- develop claims with reliable evidence.
- write a logical position paper in a measured, rational voice.

© *Reuters/CORBIS*

fig. 17.1

Strategies for Position Papers

Writing that takes a position goes out on a limb. It examines a controversial or debatable issue, and then articulates and defends a stance on that issue. To understand how writers defend positions, study the principles below.

The Rhetorical Situation

Consider how position papers aim to achieve a specific purpose, affect a particular audience, and address a given topic.

- **Purpose:** Writers produce position papers to inform readers about the nature and relevance of a topic and to persuade them that the position presented in the paper is the best stance. A more limited goal might be to convince readers that the position itself is reasonable and worth of respect—a strategy especially pertinent to polarizing issues.
- **Readers:** A writer may address a variety of readers: people opposed to the writer's position, people uncertain of what position to take, people unaware that an issue exists, or even people who agree with the writer's position but are looking for sensible reasons. Good writers shape the content, organization, and tone of position essays to effectively address such intended readers.
- **Topic:** The topics addressed in meaningful position papers are debatable issues about which informed people can reasonably disagree. Therefore, as a reader, you will learn more about a paper's topic by focusing not only on the writer's position but also on the reasoning that she or he uses to develop that position, including her or his attention to alternative positions.

Example: In "It's 'Apartheid' Time Again. Pick Your Villain" (pages 336–337), Emma Teitel's **topic** is "Israeli Apartheid Week," a protest that happens annually on Canadian campuses to speak out against Israel's treatment of Palestinians. Her **purpose** is to argue against the movement's actions and position. In this commentary, she hopes to convince her **readers**—generally *Maclean's* subscribers but perhaps more specifically students—that the movement's position is, in part, wrongheaded.

Principles of Taking a Position

Effectively taking a position depends on the principles below.

1. **Researching, exploring, and respecting all available positions.** Before settling on a particular position, writers need to openly and thoroughly examine all the options—getting inside different stances, examining the reasoning and evidence objectively, weighing the pluses and minuses. Doing so helps writers better determine where to stand and prepares them to speak to all the alternatives.

2. **Making a stance reasonable and measured.** A solid position must go beyond a pure opinion that is shouted shrilly. (Whereas an opinion may be uninformed and inherited, writers *think* their way into a position.) Writers are certainly free to advance their positions forcefully, but they also need to do so thoughtfully and respectfully: conceding points, addressing objections, and softening the stance (if necessary) with

qualifiers. Essentially, writers need to determine whether to advance their positions firmly or to seek a fair and reasonable compromise. Such position statements can be phrased as affirmations or as arguments against a claim:

- *Position Statement:* Barbed fishing hooks should be banned in favour of smooth hooks in order to protect fish stocks.
- *Argument against a Claim:* Contrary to Motz's contention, Barbie play does not make girls victims of gender stereotypes.

3. **Rooting the position in sound analysis and reliable evidence.** Writers need to show how the evidence weighs in favour of their position. The evidence needs to be sound, soundly reasoned with, and complete: writers should not hide, ignore, or lightly dismiss evidence that does not support their stance. Reasoning needs to be solid in these ways:

- **Built on an analytical foundation:** For a stance to hold up, writers may need to carefully *define key* terms in the debate or even the issue itself. Similarly, they may need to position the issue historically (*process* analysis), exploring how and why the issue arose. Finally, effective *comparison-contrast* makes sense of the range of possible positions on the issue.
- **Sensitive to logical fallacies:** Writers need to be aware of specific thinking errors within the debate, address them in opposing positions, and avoid them in their own stance. Particularly problematic are either-or thinking (page 317), broad generalizations (page 319), and oversimplification (page 317).

Sample Position Paragraph

Sometimes, writers take a position on a topic almost as an aside, not as a full essay but perhaps in a single paragraph briefly gesturing toward argumentation. In the paragraph below from "At L'Anse aux Meadows" (pages 158–163), Will Ferguson takes a stand on the debate over whether a particular site is truly Vinland, the historic Viking settlement.

> Personally, I think we can end the entire debate about Vinland by using basic common sense. The settlement uncovered at L'Anse aux Meadows is the only authenticated Viking site in North America. And how was it discovered? Through a careful reading of the ancient Norse sagas, and the sailing times and geographical descriptions they provide. What are the odds, in following these clues, that archaeologists and historians would, by sheer coincidence, have stumbled upon a *completely different*, heretofore unknown Viking village? Pretty damn slim, I imagine.

Reading Position Papers

As you read the essays on the following pages, consider these questions:

1. What is the topic, and is it debatable, stated fairly, and addressed fully?
2. What stance does the writer take among the available positions on the topic?
3. What are the writer's claims, and are they supported by reliable evidence?
4. Is the overall argument clear, unified, and free of logical fallacies?
5. Is the tone measured, reasonable, and free of manipulative language?

Sample Position Papers

The essays on the following pages take a stand on a wide range of issues: nuclear energy as an option in an environmental context, the relationship between WikiLeaks and democracy, the Israeli Apartheid protests on many Canadian campuses, and plans to allow private ownership of First Nations residential land. As you read, engage these positions thoughtfully and study the strategies the writers use.

Taking a Stand on Freedom of Information

A strong position on a debatable issue is essentially a sound claim rooted in reliable evidence. Student writer Joshua Noble wrote the following essay for the Dalton Camp Award, an essay competition on the link between democracy and the media in Canada. As you read his essay, a finalist for the award in 2011, identify his position on WikiLeaks and the evidence he marshals in support of that position.

Essay Outline

Introduction: The controversies surrounding WikiLeaks point to the need for "journalism with a face."

1. The upside of WikiLeaks: the public's right to know
2. The downside of WikiLeaks: anonymity and inappropriate information disclosure
3. The stumbling block: WikiLeaks as simultaneous social good and social evil
4. Accountability in the Canadian media: context and category, responsibility and repercussion, disagreement and dialogue

Conclusion: Media with accountability as a daily dose of democracy

WikiLeaks, Canadian Media, and Democracy

WikiLeaks has proven a rich source of news, however tenuous its journalistic status. WikiLeaks certainly thinks of itself as doing the work of journalism, as evidenced in Julian Assange's comment: "It is the role of good journalism to take on powerful abusers, and when powerful abusers are taken on, there's always a bad reaction. So we see that controversy, and we believe that is a good thing to engage in." WikiLeaks' inherent structure, principally anonymity, is in fact antithetical to journalism and leaves the organization an odd blend of information leaker, newsmaker, editorializer, self-styled journalist, and general unclassified news medium.

WikiLeaks has vaulted onto the international stage to a mix of adulation and anger. The international, non-profit organization is in possession of some "1.5 million documents so far from dissident communities and anonymous sources." Since the founding of WikiLeaks in 2006, the organization has released sensitive documents

The writer quotes from the founder of WikiLeaks to create a sense of context.

1

2

of a political, legal, martial or economic nature. The releases have made shockwaves in international diplomacy, the world economy, and every level of politics. Thus, WikiLeaks has garnered both public awe and public ire. In turn, Canadian journalists and the Canadian blogosphere have buzzed with questions. "Is anonymous leaking and faceless journalism ethical?" "Does this style of reporting endanger or protect?" "Is WikiLeaks democratic or anarchistic?" If one can step back from the rhetoric that surrounds WikiLeaks, there is an opportunity for reflection on the importance of responsible journalism—what I will call in this essay "journalism with a face." Particularly, it is valuable for a democratic society to hold journalists professionally accountable for publications, to ask their media to publish in a meaningful context, and to insist that a healthy public dialogue is created through journalistic work. In short, WikiLeaks demonstrates that in the Canadian context (or in any democratic nation), a media that is accountable to the public is invaluable.

> The introduction ends with the writer's position on WikiLeaks and on journalism in Canadian democracy.

The Upside of WikiLeaks: The Public's Right to Know

The "company profile," and informal mandate, of WikiLeaks is defined as follows: "WikiLeaks is a distributed organization which publishes and analyzes information through an uncensorable approach—focusing on documents, photos, and video which have political or social significance." WikiLeaks has been awarded both the 2008 *Economist* New Media Award and the 2009 Amnesty International New Media Award. The stories that WikiLeaks has broken include politically motivated killings and disappearances in Kenya; a myriad of embarrassing stories, facts, and loose talk about politicians and diplomats; a controversial video of the allegedly unprovoked killing of innocents by U.S. soldiers in Baghdad; and details of the treatment of detainees in Guantanamo Bay. These stories have exposed government lies, human rights abuses, and private sentiments and opinions. In this way, WikiLeaks has disclosed vital information to the otherwise unwitting public.

> The writer considers both positives and negatives of WikiLeaks.

3

The Downside of WikiLeaks: Anonymity and Inappropriate Information Disclosure

WikiLeaks has also come under fire from governments such as Australia, France, Iran, and the United States for a host of reasons. Some nations, organizations, and individual citizens have called into question the validity of the information released. Others have accused WikiLeaks of editorializing "unbiased" leaks. One particularly contentious video, dubbed *Collateral Murder*, has been heavily criticized as an edit of the original "uncensored" video. Additionally, some have criticized WikiLeaks for endangering careers, relationships, and lives by its cavalier decisions to release private documents.

4

Some have argued that WikiLeaks will actually mean that people will be less likely to engage in resistance exercises that may be compromised by an anonymous leak. Still others have made the point that WikiLeaks may choose to release only whatever leaks support the agendas of insiders or may even blatantly falsify documents and "leak" them.

5

The Stumbling Block: WikiLeaks as Simultaneous Social Good and Social Evil

So we find ourselves at an impasse. There are impressive reasons for and against   6
WikiLeaks—and, more broadly speaking, anonymous, faceless journalism. Neither
the merits nor the dangers can be dismissed or trumped by the other in any de
facto manner. We love WikiLeaks, we hate WikiLeaks. Or more importantly, we
have reason to love WikiLeaks, we have reason to hate WikiLeaks. And so we find
ourselves either caught with an ambivalent attitude toward WikiLeaks or mired
in polemic side-taking and name-calling. Though I do not dream that I am able to
resolve all the ethical questions of Wikileaks, I do believe that these ethical problems
offer an opportunity for reflection on the importance of responsible media. In the
Canadian context—our context—the media plays a vital informational role that is in
danger of being distorted by the effects of anonymous journalism. For democracy to
continue to thrive in Canada, an accountable, honest media must flourish. Without
passing judgment on the complex ethical and moral questions of WikiLeaks, I hold
that there is no doubt that in daily journalism practice, democracy needs a media
with a face.

Accountability in the Canadian Media

Journalists of the Canadian media are held accountable for what they have   7
published. When journalists do not work behind the mask of anonymity, they
must be willing to put their career, principles, and reputation on the line with
every story they publish. Thus, members of the Canadian media (as individuals
or organizations) must be professionally responsible—must "own up"—to what
they have written. There is obvious value to accountability in journalism. Let us
consider three values of a professionally accountable media, the three values of
media with a face.

1. Context and Category

The published work of any journalist or news source may be evaluated and   8
reviewed in the context of a larger agenda, opinion, tone, and perspective. Though
all worthwhile journalism strives for an unbiased weighing of all sides of an
issue, there is no doubt that news outlets and individual journalists have distinct
perspectives. Therefore, an article found in one of the major national newspapers
or in a special-interest magazine or on a blog can be fairly contextualized by what
has been previously published by that organization in general and that journalist in
particular. Criticism and praise of a political party, organization, social movement,
etc. are best understood with a healthy appreciation of the underlying reasons
and history of the author's sympathies. To get a thorough understanding of these
sympathies it is imperative to evaluate both the journalist's previous publications
and any links with organizations reported on. Furthermore, having categories to
help us understand journalism is worthwhile. An article read in the opinion section
of a newspaper, in a trade journal, or a comments board online are all read in the

---

Joshua presents his conclusion about WikiLeaks and his claim about responsible journalism.

The three values of "media with a face" are distinguished and discussed.

tone of the category in which they are published. It is difficult to know what the tone in the category of anonymous journalism is because the reasons for protecting identity are diverse and potentially malicious. Where anonymous journalism and pseudo-journalism leave a trail of context-less information disclosed by people for a myriad of unknown reasons (political leanings, personal retribution, religious beliefs, etc.) responsible Canadian journalism promotes contextualized reporting.

2. Responsibility and Repercussion

    Dangerous, slanderous, inappropriate and offensive material cannot be   *9*
published without repercussions. In Section 2b of the Canadian Charter of Rights and Freedoms, the "freedom of thought, belief, opinion, and expression, including freedom of the press and other media of communication" is guaranteed. Unfortunately, some have taken freedom of the press to mean that unprofessional, reckless or slanderous writing is acceptable. This is simply untrue. Section 1 of the Charter states, "The Canadian Charter of Rights and Freedoms guarantees the rights and freedoms set out in it subject only to such reasonable limits prescribed by law as can be demonstrably justified in a free and democratic society." I am not interested in attempting to build a legal case; rather, my point is simply this: freedom of speech does not mean that all expression is accepted and valued in a democratic society. Take as an example hate speech—not protected under the Canadian Charter as a ruling of the R. v. Keegstra case. Anonymous journalism working under the guise of "freedom of the press" that engages in hate speech, constitutes slander, or endangers lives/national defense is the antithesis of democratic free speech. The structure of accountability—the imperative to self-identify, support your claims, and answer detractors—means the Canadian media does not allow the unchecked, dangerous, and destructive derivatives of free speech to run amok. In a global context where secrets that endanger national security can be published anonymously, it is clear that accountable journalism is vital to the democratic process.

3. Disagreement and Dialogue

    Journalism with a face leaves room for rebuttal, collaboration, and dialogue—   *10*
the very heart of democracy. Faceless, non-contextualized journalism cannot be rebutted or engaged in any meaningful dialogue. It comes from nowhere and has no face for healthy dialogue. From WikiLeaks we have at times seen mass frustration not simply because of the content leaked, but because there is no legitimate, fair venue for retort. In this way the faceless gain the advantage by being unseen in their accusations, whereas those who have been implicated via leaks are sometimes unfairly vaulted into the public eye without an opportunity for a contextualized conversation with an opponent. The Canadian media is essential to democracy because it takes the form of democracy—it promotes dialogue and gives a venue for disagreement. Dialogue requires that two or more equals come to the table with honesty about their convictions. Dialogue requires that people look one another

in the face and debate, argue, agree, and negotiate. Dialogue requires that people offer to one another, as a show of good faith and respect that is the backdrop for any productive conversation, their own faces. Dialogue cannot be done with the faceless, and a society without dialogue—even heated dialogue—is forever in danger of power concentrations and power vacuums that are antithetical to democracy.

Media with Accountability as a Daily Dose of Democracy

> The writer restates his position on WikiLeaks and Canada's dependence on accountable journalism.

Literary giant Mark Twain once said, "There are laws to protect the freedom of the press's speech, but none that are worth anything to protect the people from the press." Twain's words take on poignant, frightening new meaning in a context that includes anonymous journalism done from all corners of the globe. Anonymity is understandable, perhaps even courageous, in contexts of totalitarian regimes, hidden corruption, and flagrant human rights abuses. However, anonymity is indefensible, sometimes abhorrent, in various other contexts. As a daily model for journalism in a democratic society it is unreliable and unsafe. Because of the problems in the structure of anonymous journalism, the Canadian public—and Canadian democracy in general—are dependent on an accountable media. We may not always agree with what is printed in our newspapers, but the fact that we can know the identity of the writers—and disagree with the writers—means that, as far as our media is concerned, democracy is still at work.

11

Note: The Works-Cited page is not shown. For examples, see MLA (page 533) and APA (pages 562–563).

Reading for Better Writing

Working by yourself or with a group, answer the following questions:

1. In your own words, state Joshua Noble's position on WikiLeaks.
2. How do the first two paragraphs introduce WikiLeaks as a debatable topic? What strategies does the writer use to put the debate before readers?
3. In paragraphs 3–6, Joshua debates the pros and cons of WikiLeaks before offering his conclusion. Does his organization make sense? Is his reasoning compelling? Why or why not?
4. In the second half of his essay, Joshua supports his position by outlining the benefits of "media with a face." How effective is this phrase? Is each of his three claims about the benefits of accountable media well reasoned and well supported? Point to specifics in each section to support your answer.
5. Joshua begins with a quotation from Julian Assange and ends with a quotation from Mark Twain. How does Joshua use these quotations? What do they add to his essay?
6. Consider your own attitudes concerning whether information should be public or private on the Internet—starting with information about yourself. How has Joshua's essay impacted your thinking about freedom of information?

Taking a Stand on Energy and the Environment

Student writer Alyssa Woudstra wrote the following essay to take a position on an environmental issue—energy production.

Copyright © Alyssa Woudstra.

The title partly declares the position.

Alyssa starts with common ground and narrows to her position on energy production.

She examines the positives of what she actually opposes.

She turns to the disadvantages of nuclear energy: its risks and dangers.

The writer reminds readers of a historical illustration.

Nuclear Is Not the Answer

In recent years, it has become popular to be "green" in all areas of life. Celebrities and corporations constantly advertise natural cleaning products, fuel-efficient cars, and energy-efficient light bulbs. Governments offer home-improvement grants to people who renovate their homes to include low-flush toilets, weather-proof windows, and additional insulation. Due to climate change and pollution, concern for the environment is rising. One major issue centers on which type of energy production is best for the environment. Nuclear power and fossil fuels are two major methods for energy production, and nuclear power could be seen as the "greener" option. However, the risks of nuclear power far outweigh its benefits, making fossil fuels the safer and more environmentally responsible option.

As a significant method of energy production, nuclear power does offer distinct advantages. The Nuclear Energy Institute's statistics show that nuclear energy accounted for fourteen percent of the world's electricity production in 2008, and that as of September 2009, thirty countries were using nuclear power ("Around the World"). This popularity speaks to nuclear power's advantages over fossil fuels. First, nuclear power plants do not release the harmful emissions that coal-burning plants do, so nuclear power does not contribute greatly to global warming (Evans 115). Second, a single nuclear power plant can produce a large amount of energy, making nuclear an efficient source ("Pros and Cons"). In fact, according to Robert Evans, "The amount of thermal energy released from just one kilogram of U235 undergoing fission is equivalent to that obtained by burning some 2.5 million kilograms, or 2500 tonnes, of coal" (116).

Nevertheless, these advantages of nuclear power are outweighed by its disadvantages. Nuclear power plants produce radioactive waste, which is an enormous health and safety concern. The waste cannot simply be disposed of but must be carefully stored for hundreds of generations. The isotopes used in nuclear reactions have half-lives of thousands of years. For example, plutonium-239 has a half-life of around 24,000 years (American Assembly 24). This radioactive waste must be stored safely to prevent radiation poisoning, but it would be nearly impossible to do so for that long.

A further danger of nuclear power is that while every safety precaution might be in place, it is possible for terrible accidents to happen. The most famous nuclear accident took place on April 26, 1986, when reactor number four at the Chernobyl Nuclear Power Plant in the Ukraine, which was then part of the Soviet Union, exploded after a power excursion. That explosion then caused the rest of the plant

1

2

3

4

to explode (Hawks et. al. 98-102). This accident released one hundred times more radiation than the bombing of Hiroshima and Nagasaki combined ("No More Chernobyls"). Chernobyl's radiation spread all over Europe, affecting people as far away as Romania and Bulgaria, exposing more than 600,000 to the effects of radiation poisoning (Medvedev 194-216). More than twenty years after Chernobyl, people are still dying from cancer that was likely caused by the disaster.

Alyssa concedes and rebuts a concern.

Whereas it is true that Chernobyl occurred more than twenty years ago, recent   5
disasters (such as the March 2011 incident at the Fukushima Nuclear Power Plant) demonstrate that additional accidents could happen at any other nuclear power plant currently in use. In addition, it is also true that if more nuclear power plants are built, the risk of similar accidents will rise.

Beyond accidents, however, is the possibility of deliberate sabotage in the form   6
of terrorism ("Pros and Cons"). If terrorists wanted to cause mass devastation, they could attack a nuclear power plant or become employees that purposely cause errors to create an explosion. On September 11, 2001, millions of people were affected at once. If a power plant were attacked, it would also affect millions, since it would cause the loss of not only many jobs but also many lives. Moreover, the risk of terrorism also surrounds the nuclear waste left behind after the reactions. Easier to obtain than pure uranium, such waste could be used to build "dirty bombs" (Evans 133).

Beyond the risks and dangers of nuclear power, still another argument against   7
it is that it is nonrenewable. Fossil fuels are also nonrenewable, but nuclear power is not an alternative in this way. In their reactors, nuclear power plants use uranium, a rare element. It is estimated that the Earth's supply of Uranium will last only thirty to sixty years, depending on how much is actually used in reactors ("Pros and Cons").

With a question, she turns to her own position, acknowledging its problems.

But is energy from fossil fuels really better than nuclear power? The burning   8
of fossil fuels (including coal, oil, and natural gas) is the most common method of energy production. Like nuclear, fossil fuels are nonrenewable. However, burning fossil fuels, for the time being, is a better option than using nuclear energy. It is true that using fossil fuels has a negative effect on the environment. In order to obtain fossil fuels, much damage is caused to the environment by drilling for oil or mining for coal. The 2010 Deepwater Horizon oil spill (also referred to as the BP oil spill) is a prime example. Also, burning fossil fuels produces gases that can aggravate respiratory conditions like asthma and emits greenhouse gases that damage the atmosphere. Moreover, particles emitted from smokestacks collect in clouds, causing acid rain (Sweet 25). With oil, spills can contaminate groundwater and surface water, creating risks to animals, plants, and humans.

Despite the fact that using fossil fuels involves many risks, it has some   9
advantages over nuclear energy. Significantly, fossil fuels are much less expensive than uranium. Although it is still expensive to access fossil fuels, it is drastically cheaper than the cost of nuclear energy. In addition, if large deposits of coal or oil

Alyssa supports her position on fossil fuels by stressing its advantages and calling for improvements.

are found, it will not be necessary to excavate in as many places to retrieve them. Although a larger area would be disturbed, fewer sites would be affected. Also, while fossil fuels are nonrenewable, they may be used wisely, conserving them until a better energy source can be established (Heron).

However, perhaps the biggest advantage of fossil fuel energy over nuclear energy   10
lies in the possibility of progress to make current methods more environmentally friendly. At this time, burning coal for power uses only one-third of its potential energy (Heron). If scientists study more efficient uses of the coal, this waste, as well as many health and environmental concerns, could be prevented. For example, burning coal can be made cleaner through electrostatic precipitators. Also known as "smokestack scrubbers," these filters can be used in smokestacks to prevent soot particles from getting into the air. As the soot-filled air passes through the smokestack, it goes through a set of wires that negatively charge the soot particles. As the air continues through the pipe, it passes through positively charged metal plates. The negatively charged soot particles, which are made up mostly of unburned carbon, "stick" to the positively charged plates, and the particle-free air continues out the smokestack. The stuck particles are then either manually scraped or automatically shaken off by the machine itself ("Static Electricity"). If more factories used electrostatic precipitators, a large amount of air pollution would be prevented.

She restates her position and places it within a larger context of environmental changes.

Although it is not ideal, burning fossil fuels is still a better option than nuclear   11
power until renewable energy sources such as wind, solar, and geothermal power become more available. Clearly, society must continue to work toward greater conservation and use of renewable energy. As stewards of the Earth, all humans should be concerned about the environment. If people continue to use nuclear power, the risks related to accidents, sabotage, and radioactive waste will not only be their responsibility but will also impact their descendants for many generations.

Note: The Works-Cited page is not shown. For sample pages, see MLA (page 533) and APA (pages 562–563).

Reading for Better Writing

Working by yourself or with a group, answer these questions:
1. Alyssa Woudstra begins her essay by examining extensively an opposing position—support for nuclear energy. How effective is this strategy?
2. Review how Alyssa supports her position on energy from fossil fuels. How complete and compelling is this support?
3. Review Alyssa's reference to the BP oil spill (page 334). Then explain why this information does or does not strengthen her argument.
4. Consider your own energy consumption. What do you use and where does it come from? How does Alyssa's essay impact your thinking about power, the environment, and personal attitudes and behaviours?

Taking a Stand on a Political Issue

Emma Teitel writes an opinion column in *Maclean's*. In the essay below, she takes a position on Israeli Apartheid Week, a protest against Israel's treatment of Palestinians.

It's "Apartheid" Time Again. Pick Your Villain.

March is upon us, which means the Oscars have been awarded, and that other harbinger of spring is around the corner: Israeli Apartheid Week. Ordinarily, both events are masterpieces of predictability, with the Academy Awards ushering the usual suspects to the podium (Meryl Streep anyone?), and Israeli Apartheid Week featuring the usual anti-Zionist suspects on megaphones (among them the now famous IAW sub-group, Queers Against Israeli Apartheid, which I'd argue is largely composed of gay Jewish girls who didn't have fun at summer camp). This year the Oscars have come through in predictability, but Israeli Apartheid Week is shaping up quite differently. It's traditional at Passover seders for the youngest member of Jewish families to ask the "four questions," which inquire why "this night is different from all other nights." This year it might be prudent to ask a fifth: why is this Israeli Apartheid Week different from all the others?

> **The writer begins with a comparison that leads to a question.**

The answer is just northeast of Israel, in Syria. In the past 11 months, almost 9,000 civilian protesters and nearly 3,000 anti-government rebels have been murdered by Syrian President Bashar al-Assad's Ba'ath party dictatorship. Approximately 400 children have been imprisoned and tortured. Meanwhile, Assad's government claims that 89.4 per cent of Syrians had approved a new constitution that could keep Bashar in power for another 16 years, along with the 12 years he's already ruled, and the 29 years his father Hafez held power before him. You'd think that anyone committed to the cause of justice in the Middle East would put the atrocities in Syria at the top of their to-do list. But the Canadian organizers of Israeli Apartheid Week—loudly devoted to ending oppression and achieving social justice for all—won't be talking about Syria this year. Instead, they'll spend March 5–9 railing exclusively against the "Zionist regime" at a university campus near you. Events will include slam poetry renditions, hip-hop shows, and an apartheid poster contest with a top prize of $400.

> **She introduces the problem of Syria to raise questions about Israeli Apartheid Week.**

You could accurately call this tunnel vision activism. Most hopes for mainstream credibility IAW activists might have in their criticism of Israel tends to be destroyed by their singular abhorrence of the Jewish state. No country deserves a free pass because its crimes don't add up to its neighbour's, but to boycott one injustice and ignore the far bloodier one next door isn't just odd: it's a clear statement that those at the helm of Israeli Apartheid Week hate Israel more than they hate oppression itself.

This is a reality noted by even the anti-Zionist darling and American intellectual Norman Finkelstein, in an interview at Imperial College this month. Finkelstein, who has long been a supporter of the BDS movement, named for its focus on punishing Israel through boycotts, divestments, and sanctions, now claims, scathingly, that the BDS is doomed to irrelevancy by its gross "disingenuousness" on the subject of whether or not

> **An authority lends supports the writer's position.**

1

2

3

4

Emma Teitel, "It's 'Apartheid' Time Again. Pick your villain", Maclean's, 12 March 2012, Vol 125, No. 9, p.15. Reproduced by permission of Maclean's Magazine.

Israel should exist to begin with. "I support the BDS," he says, "[but] their goal has to include the recognition of Israel, or it's a non-starter." Finkelstein is right. If you want to uproot a country's policies, you should make it explicitly clear that you don't want to uproot the country itself. Unless, of course, you do.

That the folks behind Israeli Apartheid Week wouldn't mind if the country disappeared is evident in their blasé response to terrorism against Israelis. The movement's promotional video features a series of cartoon slides about the conflict, one of which reads: "When a people fight the occupier / It is not terrorism / It is resistance." But there is nothing noble or necessary about blowing up innocent civilians at a falafel stand. Such terrorism is not resistance. It's murder—something IAW leaders have accused Israel of time and time again.

The writer distinguishes two significant concepts and illustrates the difference with a personal anecdote.

Hypocrisy aside, the movement's reluctance to recognize the Jewish state's right to exist (they claim to be "agnostic" about Israel's existence), coupled with its failure to stand up for any other oppressed or occupied peoples, is an open invitation for Jews to cry anti-Semitism. Anti-Zionism is not anti-Semitism, anti-Zionists argue, but Israel's unique distinction in their ideology as the very worst place in the entire world has most Jews begging to differ. In my final year of university, a friend of mine—who we'll call Sandy Cohen—wanted to organize a non-aligned event to run alongside Israeli Apartheid Week, to educate uninformed students about the conflict from a neutral standpoint. Organizers of Israeli Apartheid Week were less than pleased with the idea— they were having a party, and she was trying to crash it. One organizer even compared her to a Nazi and claimed that, like "all Zionists," she had a knack for "twisting her words." Not once did Cohen declare herself a Zionist. The only thing her detractor knew about her was her name—which is, undeniably, Jewish.

The conclusion clarifies and deepens the writer's position.

If all people who criticized Israel were anti-Semites, I'd be an anti-Semite. But it's this kind of nastiness and hypocrisy that makes you wonder if the week isn't an indictment of so-called Israeli apartheid, but rather a morbid celebration of a problem none of the protesters really wants solved. *Haaretz* columnist Bradley Burston argues that peace isn't the product of "freedom for one people at the expense of another, but freedom and independence for both." Until the Israeli Apartheid Movement acknowledges this, it will remain nothing more than a thinly veiled anti-Semitic frosh week for the far, far left.

Reading for Better Writing

Working by yourself or with a group, answer the following questions:

1. What is Emma Teitel's essential position on Israeli Apartheid Week? Where does she most clearly state it?
2. What reasoning does she offer in support of her position, and what evidence does she rely upon? How convincing do you find Teitel's logic?
3. The Israeli-Palestinian issue has a long, complex history. What does Teitel's article contribute to your own experiences, attitude, and thinking?

Taking a Stand on Native Land

Kyle Carsten Wyatt is the managing editor of *The Walrus*, a monthly magazine publishing articles on Canadian culture. In the essay below (published in March 2013), he takes a position against legislation to allow private land ownership of First Nations land.

Losing the Land Again

As you read Wyatt's essay, take notes and make annotations exploring how he states, elaborates, and supports his position. Consider, as well, your own response to the issue.

Sometime this year, the federal government is expected to introduce legislation that will pave the way for fee-simple (read: private) land ownership on First Nations reserves. According to its champions—former Kamloops chief Manny Jules and on-again, off-again Harper adviser Tom Flanagan—the new law will generate business efficiencies, investment opportunities, and individual prosperity for the 300,000 Native people living on reserves in Canada.

Editorial boards and political affairs observers have commended the First Nations Property Ownership Initiative, a working proposal crafted by Jules and Flanagan, along with Christopher Alcantara and André Le Dressay, in their 2011 book, *Beyond the Indian Act: Restoring Aboriginal Property Rights*. Proponents, who include a handful of First Nations, dismiss the alarms raised by most of the 600-plus Native communities in Canada, as well as Native studies scholars and the Assembly of First Nations. The *Globe and Mail*'s John Ibbitson has summarized their objections thusly: "The first is that native land is traditionally communally owned. Private property is yet another assimilationist Western concept being imposed on native culture. The second is that once reserve members own their land, they can sell it to non-natives, eroding the land base."

Ibbitson rejects these concerns out of hand, arguing that "the legislation will be strictly voluntary. Only those first nations that want to embrace the concept of private property will do so." This line of reasoning presumes that communities and individuals driven to desperation can freely engage in decision making, when in fact many of them will succumb to a coercive land grab that has been 500 years in the making. He also contrasts the proposed legislation with the US General Allotment Act of 1887, better known as the Dawes Act, pointing out that it was involuntary. He is not alone in dismissing the nineteenth-century law. Backers of the First Nations

Kyle Carsten Wyatt, "Losing the Land Again", The Walrus, March 2013, pp. 17–19 Copyright © Kyle Carsten Wyatt.

Property Ownership Initiative regard its dismal legacy as a trivial aside, a laughable historical analogy: different time, different place. But as Cherokee novelist and 2003 Massey Lecturer Thomas King observes in his new book, *The Inconvenient Indian: A Curious Account of Native People in North America*, "When we look at Native–non-Native relations, there is no great difference between the past and the present."

Sponsored by Massachusetts senator Henry L. Dawes, one of many sincere reformers who sought to fix America's "Indian problem" after the Civil War, the Dawes Act empowered the president to subdivide reservations into 160-acre parcels that would be "allotted" to tribe members. The idea behind the sweeping legislation was to nullify treaty obligations and de-tribalize Indians through forced acculturation—what Teddy Roosevelt benevolently described as "a mighty pulverizing engine to break up the tribal mass." Eliminate reservations, dissolve tribes, and, voila, Indians are transformed into self-supporting citizen farmers and ranchers, integrated into the mainstream economy, and insulated from the forced removals that had previously characterized relations between Indians and the US government.

But what to do with the excess land after the president allotted a reservation? The surplus would be sold on the open market, with the government holding the revenues on behalf of the tribes. And sold it was—to white farmers and ranchers, railroads, timber companies. By the time John Collier, commissioner of Indian Affairs under Franklin Roosevelt, convinced Congress in 1934 that allotment was an unequivocal failure and a national embarrassment, tribal lands in the United States had plummeted from 55.8 million hectares to 19.4 million, half of which was arid or semi-arid desert. However noble the savage, it is no small feat to raise wheat and livestock in the desert while the federal government mismanages your royalties.

The Dawes Act, along with the supplementary Dawes Commission of 1893 and the Curtis Act of 1898, unleashed a bonanza for mining and petroleum interests, including Standard Oil and 3M. (And I would be surprised if resource extraction companies, looking to expand their operations or secure rights-of-way on reserves in Canada, were not quietly studying the unscrupulous tactics of their allotment era predecessors.) For American Indians, the Dawes Act proved to be a disaster that obliterated tribal land bases, imposed the rights and responsibilities of land ownership (taxes, foreclosures, distressed sales, the legal and financial complexities of property) on allottees who did not ask for it, and left those not formally recognized as Indians on the government rolls homeless. While Senator Dawes did not intend it, his legislative hobby horse destroyed communities; uprooted and broke apart families; sent many into abject poverty and others to bankruptcy; disrupted land-based education and traditional knowledge; and destabilized tribal political and legal systems for generations.

But as Native humorist Will Rogers once said, "If there is one thing that America does worse than any other nation, it is to try and manage somebody else's affairs." Two decades after Congress scrapped allotment in 1934, it once again attempted to convert tribal lands to fee-simple ownership, with the Indian Termination Act of 1953. This, too, was disastrous. 7

Is the 3.2 million hectares of reserve land held in trust by the Canadian government as economically productive as it could be? Likely not. But we should be cautious of productive versus non-productive talk, especially when it comes to a Native land base that, in a country of 909 million hectares, is already minuscule. Thomas King calls this dichotomy "the logical fallacy that has haunted Indian history and policy in North America since contact—to wit, that all people yearn for the individual freedom to pursue economic goals." Simple discussions of dollars and cents, mortgages and investment capital fail to consider the symbolic, religious, and cultural purchase of communal lands for the larger Native community: Status and Treaty Indians, as well as non-Status Indians; those on reserve and those off; those who can vote in band elections and those who cannot. Nor do current conversations entertain the possibility that band membership might someday expand through means other than birth—that Ottawa's punitive "two-generation cut-off clause" might be replaced with community-specific definitions of citizenship. Indeed, as Metis-Cree journalist Miles Morrisseau has pointed out, the only thing we know with any certainty about the top-down legislation "is that First Nations will have less land than before." 8

Yes, the First Nations Property Ownership Initiative is intended to be voluntary. Early drafts of the Dawes Act called for voluntary allotment, too. But it is curious how the fine print can change at the last minute—especially when it concerns 9

Native issues. In the debate over private ownership, smug dismissals of the General Allotment Act should give us pause, not because Canada will inevitably repeat America's mistakes, but because legislators and policy wonks seem so convinced that it won't.

Reading for Better Writing

Working by yourself or with a group, answer the following questions:

1. What is your understanding of and your attitude toward private property? Do you own property or hope to sometime in the future? How does Kyle Carsten Wyatt's essay complicate your understanding of land and property?

2. In the first two paragraphs, Wyatt outlines opposing stances on the issue of private ownership of First Nations reserve land. What strategies does he use to present the positions?

3. In paragraph 3, Wyatt offers his position. Does he do so overtly, or does he imply it? How does he frame his position?

4. Beginning part way through paragraph 3 and continuing through paragraph 7, Wyatt outlines historical attempts in the United States to impose private land ownership on Native peoples. What is the point of Wyatt's history lesson? How does this narrative support his position?

5. In the final paragraphs, Wyatt turns back to the Canadian situation. How does he translate the American example into the current Canadian context? How are the two brought together in the closing?

6. Peppered through the essay are quotations from a range of voices: John Ibbitson (paragraphs 2 and 3), Thomas King (paragraphs 3 and 8), Teddy Roosevelt (paragraph 4), Will Rogers (paragraph 7), and Miles Morrisseau (paragraph 8). Examine these quotations again and explore how Wyatt uses them to outline and advance his position.

Writing Guidelines

Develop a position paper by implementing the strategies for argumentation in Chapter 16 and following the steps below.

Planning

1. **Select a debatable topic.** Review the list below and add topics as needed.
   - **Current Affairs:** Explore recent trends, new laws, and emerging controversies discussed in the news media, blogs, or online discussion groups.
   - **Burning Issues:** What issues related to family, work, education, recreation, technology, the environment, or popular culture do you care about?
   - **Dividing Lines:** What issues divide your communities? Religion, gender, politics, regionalism, nationalism? Choose a topic and freewrite to clarify your position.
   - **Fresh Fare:** Avoid tired issues unless you take a fresh perspective.

2. **Take stock.** Before you dig into your topic, assess your starting point. What is your current position on the topic? Why? What evidence do you have?

3. **Get inside the issue.** To take a defensible position, study the issue carefully:
   - **Investigate all possible positions** on the issue and research as needed.
   - **Do first-hand research** that produces current, relevant information.
   - **Write your position** at the top of a page. Below it, set up "Pro" and "Con" columns. List arguments in each column.
   - **Develop reasoning** that supports your position and test it for the following:
     (a) no logical fallacies, such as either/or thinking (see pages 317–320); and
     (b) an effective range of support: statistics, observations, expert testimony, comparisons, experiences, and analysis (see pages 314–315).

4. **Refine your position.** By now, you may have sharpened or radically changed your initial position on the topic. Before you organize and draft your essay, reflect on those changes. If it helps, use this formula:

   I believe this to be true about _____.

5. **Organize your argument and support.** Now you've committed yourself to a position. Before drafting, review these organizational options:
   - **Traditional Pattern:** Introduce the issue, state your position, support it, address and refute opposition, and restate your position.
   - **Blatant Confession:** Place your position statement in the first sentence.
   - **Delayed Gratification:** Describe various positions on the topic, compare and contrast them, and then take and defend your position.
   - **Changed Mind:** If your research changed your mind, explain how and why.
   - **Winning Over:** If readers oppose your position, address their concerns by anticipating and answering each objection or question.

Drafting

6. **Write your first draft.** Using freewriting and/or your notes, draft the paper.
   - **Opening:** Seize the reader's attention, possibly with a bold title—or raise concern for the issue with a dramatic story, a pointed example, a vivid picture, a thought-provoking question, or a personal confession. Supply background information that readers need to understand the issue.
   - **Development:** Deepen, clarify, and support your position statement, using solid logic and reliable support. Address opposing views fairly as part of a clear, well-reasoned argument that helps readers understand and accept your position.
   - **Closing:** End on a lively, thoughtful note that stresses your commitment. If appropriate, make a direct or indirect plea to readers to adopt your position.

Revising

7. **Improve the ideas, organization, and voice.** Ask a classmate or someone from the writing centre to read your position paper for the following:
   - **Ideas:** Does the writing effectively establish and defend a stand on a debatable issue? Is the position clearly stated and effectively qualified and refined? Do the reasoning and support help the reader understand and appreciate the position?
   - **Organization:** Does the opening effectively raise the issue? Does the middle offer a carefully sequenced development and defence of the position? Does the closing successfully drive home the position?
   - **Voice:** Is the voice thoughtful, measured, committed, and convincing?

Editing

8. **Edit and proofread the essay by addressing these issues:**
   - **Words:** Language is precise, concrete, and lively—no jargon, clichés, or insults.
   - **Sentences:** Constructions vary in length and flow smoothly.
   - **Correctness:** The copy includes no errors in spelling, usage, punctuation, grammar, or mechanics.
   - **Design:** The page design is correctly formatted and attractive; information is properly documented according to the required system (e.g., MLA, APA).

Publishing

9. **Publish your essay.** Submit your position paper according to your instructor's requirements. In addition, seek a forum for your position—with peers in a discussion group, with relatives, or online.

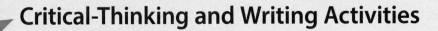

Critical-Thinking and Writing Activities

As directed by your instructor, complete the following critical-thinking and writing activities by yourself or with classmates.

1. Famously, Dr. Martin Luther King, Jr. stated that "[t]he ultimate measure of man is not where he stands in moments of comfort and convenience, but where he stands at times of challenge and controversy." How does such a claim function as a theme for the essays in this chapter, and generally for position papers?

2. Joshua Noble's essay takes a position on WikiLeaks. What media issues interest you? Write an essay arguing for a position on a media-focused topic.

3. Review Alyssa Woudstra's essay, "Nuclear Is Not the Answer." Then research this or another energy-related topic and write an essay in which you take a clear, well-reasoned position on one or more key issues.

4. Emma Teitel's and Kyle Carsten Wyatt's essays offer commentaries on controversial political issues. Browse print or digital news sources for stories on controversial issues. Choose an issue that interests you, research it, and write your own commentary.

5. Draft a position paper that addresses a controversial issue that exists within a community to which you belong (e.g., city, neighbourhood, generation, race or ethnic group, gender, consumer group, online network).

Learning-Objectives Checklist ✓

Have you achieved this chapter's learning objectives? Check your progress with the items below, revisiting topics in the chapter as needed. *I have . . .*

____ critically examined position papers for a convincing argument with well-crafted claims, reliable evidence, and valid warrants (326).

____ identified these logical fallacies in others' writing and corrected them in my own writing: oversimplification, either/or thinking, straw-man and red-herring claims, appeals to pity, and personal attacks (317–320).

____ chosen and researched a debatable topic, compared and contrasted arguments both for and against, discerned the most convincing position, and outlined the argument in a clear, logical pattern (342–343).

____ drafted, revised, and edited a well-reasoned position paper in a measured but compelling voice (342–343).

____ analyzed and strengthened my writing by answering opponents' questions, making reasonable concessions, and rebutting opposing positions (342–343).

____ scrutinized and revised my writing to clarify my claims, insert needed transitions, and achieve a strong presentation of my position (342–343).

____ corrected errors in mechanics, usage, and grammar and developed an attractive page design (343).

Chapter 18

Persuading Readers to Act

Persuading people to do something is challenging, requiring that you convince them to believe you, to rethink their own perspectives, and to take a concrete step. In the end, you need to change people's minds in order to change their actions.

Writers achieve this goal with sound logic, reliable support, and fitting appeals. Every day, persuasive writing like this appears in newsletters, editorials, marketing documents, business proposals, academic journals, white papers, and traditional essays.

Because persuasive writing is so common, you can expect to read and write versions of it in your courses and on the job. As you read the essays in this chapter, carefully analyze how writers develop convincing appeals for action. Then when you write your own essay, try these same strategies.

Visually Speaking What does the image below suggest about the motivation to act? When it comes to persuading people to act, what is the relationship between words and deeds?

Learning **Objectives**

By working through this chapter, you will be able to

- critically examine and assess the arguments in call-to-action papers.
- identify logical fallacies that are especially a danger in call-to-action writing.
- support claims with appropriate and convincing evidence.
- develop reasonable claims, especially a thesis that calls for action.
- write a compelling call-to-action paper in a mature, informed voice.

Clive Chilvers/Shutterstock.com

fig. 18.1

Strategies for Call-to-Action Writing

Change is tough, so calling others to action in writing can be especially challenging—starting with readers' possible but perfectly natural inertia. In this sense, call-to-action writing not only takes a position on an issue (encouraging readers to adopt or at least respect that position) but also presses readers to take the next logical step—translating that stance into concrete action or behavioural change. Persuading readers to such action requires attention to the rhetorical situation and a range a strategies.

The Rhetorical Situation

To put a call-to-action essay in context, consider the rhetorical situation behind it:

- **Purpose:** Whether in academics, the workplace, or public life, writers call for action because they believe change is needed. Something is not right. Something needs to be improved or fixed. The writer's goal is to convince readers to care about the issue strongly enough to take a concrete step.
- **Readers:** The intended readers are people whom the writer believes need to be pressed to act. Readers may be unaware of the issue, may feel overwhelmed by it, may have an interest in not acting, or may not care enough about the issue to actually act. The writer thus educates and urges such readers.
- **Topic:** In academics, the topics addressed might be related to a specific discipline (e.g., educational mentoring campaign, expanding an arts program), a political or social issue (e.g., shelter for abused women, Special Olympics program), or a general humanitarian concern (e.g., help for victims of an epidemic, a flood, or a war).

Example: In "The Hunger Game" (pages 355–357), Nick Saul's **topic** is the function of food banks in addressing poverty. His **purpose** is to convince his **readers**, who may never have needed to use a food bank but may have supported one through donations and volunteering, that better institutions need to be built to fight hunger by fighting poverty.

Principles for Calling Readers to Act

Persuading readers to act relies on writing principles like those below.

- **Rooting the writing in sound reasoning.** Asking readers to act must be built on a foundation of trustworthy evidence and sound reasoning. Because action is involved, writers need to get it right. Especially important is cause-effect analysis—reasoning that can sort out the forces at work in an issue and predict the consequences of action. Similarly, call-to-action writing needs to avoid logical fallacies such as half-truths, unreliable testimonials, and false analogies (pages 317–320).
- **Building credibility through an encouraging but measured voice.** A writer's aim is to motivate, not manipulate. To that end, the tone in most call-to-action writing should communicate a kind of objective urgency, though in some situations humour works well to deflate some tension and open a new perspective on the issue. Above all, the writing should never sound threatening or engage in guilt-tripping in order to

prompt action. Not only is such an approach ethically questionable but it also tends to have the opposite effect than the one desired.

- **Convincing readers to care about the issue.** Motivating readers to act begins with encouraging them to embrace the issue as their own. Writers do so by sharing compelling anecdotes and illustrations to put a human face on the issue, by correcting misunderstandings or commonly held views about the issue (often through the voices of respected experts), and by making sound appeals to shared needs and values (page 323). Through such strategies, writers change readers' view of the issue.

- **Motivating readers to undertake a doable action.** First of all, writers must imagine points of resistance for readers—those thoughts and feelings that make them reluctant to act. With these realities in mind, writers need to then determine what is a doable action, a concrete step, or general change that is within reach for readers. Can a writer expect readers to re-examine their spending habits, to stop using a word thoughtlessly, to contribute to organizations that fight poverty? That doable action then becomes the theme and thesis of the writing, what it builds toward.

Example Thesis: It's time for all consumers to learn more about where their food comes from and how it gets to their table.

Sample Call-to-Action Paragraph

Either directly or through implication, writers can call readers to act or encourage them to change in virtually any type of writing. A paragraph pressing readers to act, even as an aside to the main discussion, can energize and direct the discussion of any topic. For example, the paragraph below is the closing to June Callwood's "Forgiveness" (pages 177–180). Notice how Callwood encourages readers to cultivate habits of forgiveness, to "try it."

> Forgiveness is hard work. A woman, a devout Roman Catholic who forgave the man who tortured and killed her seven-year-old daughter, said, "Anyone who says forgiveness is for wimps hasn't tried it." The reward for giving up scalding thoughts of reprisal is peace of mind. It is worth the candle.

Reading Call-to-Action Writing

As you read the essays on the following pages, consider these questions:

1. What is the issue, and what action is requested to address it?
2. Who are the intended readers, and what capacity to act do they have?
3. Are the writer's claims accurate, compelling, and logical?
4. Is the argument's tone informed, genuine, and respectful?
5. Is the writing convincing—does it move readers to do what the writer requests?

Sample Call-to-Action Essays

The student and professional essays on the following pages call readers to a variety of actions on a range of issues: for North Americans to rethink how they use their wealth, for Canadians to rethink softening attitudes about the "N" word, for people to change the way poverty is aided through food banks, and for readers to become partners in respecting people of mixed race. As you read, consider your own reactions and study the strategies these writers use to call for action.

Calling for a Change in Spending Practices

Henry Veldboom, a student with children of his own, wrote this essay to call North American readers to reconsider what they value.

Outline

Introduction: the issue of North American wealth and its real cost

1. Modern capitalism is based on harmful consumerism.
2. Consumers must consider the results of their consumption.
3. People must examine especially how consumerism impacts children.

Conclusion: individual consumer change necessary for social change

Title: issue and central question

Introduction: North American wealth and its real cost

1 Modern capitalism is based on harmful consumerism.

Our Wealth: Where Is It Taking Us?

North America's wealth and the lifestyle it affords are known throughout the world. This knowledge has created a belief that wealth and happiness are synonymous, which in turn has perpetuated the dreams of people around the globe who hope to achieve the same successes witnessed here in the West. Is there truth to the idea that wealth and happiness coexist? Ask North Americans if they would willingly trade life here for that in a struggling country and they would likely say "No." Their wealth has made their lives quite comfortable. Most would admit to enjoying the lifestyle such wealth allows; few would want to give it up. But what is this wealth really costing North Americans—especially children?

While North American wealth grew out of the capitalism that culminated in the nineteenth-century Industrial Revolution, today's capitalism is a system largely based on consumerism—an attitude that values the incessant acquisition of goods in the belief that they are necessary and beneficial. The goal, then, of a modern capitalist economy is to produce many goods as cheaply as possible and have these goods purchased on a continual basis. The forces behind capitalism—business owners at the demand of stockholders—employ an ever-expanding array

1

2

of marketing techniques to accomplish the goal of selling products. Expert on marketing George Barna defines marketing as the process of directing "goods and services from the producer to the consumer, to satisfy the needs and desires of the consumer and the goals of the producer" (41). On the receiving end of today's capitalism are consumers whose needs are in general self-serving and based on self-actualization. Corporations promote this way of thinking and capitalize on it through marketing techniques. Social commentator Benjamin Barber describes this modern interaction in the following way: "[This thinking] serves capitalist consumerism directly by nurturing a culture of impetuous consumption necessary to selling puerile goods in a developed world that has few genuine needs" (81).

2 Consumers must consider the results of their consumption.

Admittedly, deciphering genuine needs from superfluous wants is not an easy task. However, putting debates about materialism aside, people must consider the results of their consumption. The 2008-2009 economic upheaval still lingers in people's minds despite the recent upward trend in the North American economy. When such financial turmoil happens, the typical response is to lay blame. Some people are quick to accuse corporations of causing the turmoil and governments of allowing corporations to operate as they do. Noted journalist and anti-establishment advocate Linda McQuaig comments on the shift in the 1970s that gave individuals more freedoms; in turn, corporations accommodated the lax attitudes of government to themselves and were "ensured freedom from their restraints on their profit-making" (22). McQuaig addresses this issue as well, highlighting "the power and centrality of greed in our culture" (23). She raises a word that no one wants to be labeled with—greed. When people begin discussing their financial woes in relation to individual greed, the blame rests squarely on each member of society.

Do North American corporations and governments share the responsibility to properly use wealth and direct the economy? Yes, they most certainly do. However, individuals must also examine their own fiscal responsibility.

3

3 People must examine how consumerism harms children.

The behavior that has led to the current financial crisis is not only impacting adults but also putting children at risk. Deceptive marketing tactics make use of psychological knowledge and social patterning research to convince consumers to

4

purchase particular products. Adults who possess the mental capacity to discern motives and detect subversion are being effectively manipulated by cunning advertising techniques, resulting in massive debt loads, addiction, and bankruptcy. However, the greater concern with these marketing practices is that they are being aimed at children who have less ability to defend themselves. Psychiatrist Susan Linn describes the marketing aimed at children as "precisely targeted, refined by scientific method, and honed by child psychologists . . ." (5). It isn't the case that children are getting caught in marketing traps set for adults; rather, kids are being targeted. Linn remarks that developmental psychology which was once used solely for treating children's mental health is now used to determine "weaknesses" in children's thinking in order to exploit these weaknesses (24). The weaknesses are due to children's brains not having reached full cognitive development, resulting in unstable patterns of thinking in areas such as reasoning, memory, and problem solving (Weiten 47). At such a disadvantage, children are unable to withstand the marketing ploys aimed at them.

(a) marketing manipulation

Knowing that children are the targets of aggressive mass marketing is all the more serious when the scope of the situation is considered. Much research has been done on purchasing patterns, and while the fact that North Americans spend large amounts of money on goods may not be surprising, when children are added to the equation the picture changes. Expert on consumerism, economics, and family studies Juliet Schor has done a considerable amount of convincing research in this area. She comments on the purchasing influence of children and notes that children aged four to twelve influenced an estimated $670 billion of adult purchasing in 2004 (23). Children having influence on such large amounts of money being spent catches the attention of producers who consequently aim their marketing at kids in order to sell adult products. Schor also notes the results of a Nickelodeon (an entertainment company) study that states when it comes to recognizing brands, "the average ten year old has memorized 300 to 400 brands" (25). Kids know the products and they know what they want; the dollar amount parents are spending in response to their children reflects this.

(b) influence on parental spending

5

The effects of aggressive marketing and consumerism on North American children are exhibited in a wide range of health problems.

(c) physical and mental health problems

At first glance, the relationship between consumerism and children's health may appear to be coincidental. However, much research shows a direct link

6

between marketing to children and their health. Having done her own research and examined other studies, Juliet Schor concludes that "the more [children] buy into the commercial and materialist messages, the worse they feel about themselves, the more depressed they are, and the more they are beset by anxiety, headaches, stomachaches, and boredom" (173). (On a related note, the time spent by children sitting in front of televisions and computers is an important factor in this outcome. These media are the prime vehicles for advertising and are contributing to sedentary lifestyles, which in turn cause health problems.) Materialism is having an effect not only on adults but also on youth. When children are asked what they aspire to be, the top answer is "to be rich" (37). The health of the minds and bodies of North American children is deteriorating as a result of consumerism and the new capitalism.

> **Conclusion:**
> Individual consumers must change if society is to change.

Having examined the current state of North American society in terms of the economic and personal health related to the new capitalism, one begins to see that society is in a situation that is neither beneficial nor sustainable. Changes must be made. If the response is to look for someone or something to blame, everyone must stop and take a look in the mirror. Changing habits and attitudes must start with the individual. While adopting a particular economic ideology is not the point, North Americans must take a hard look at their society and decide if this is how they want to live. If this society carries on unchanged, what future will its children have? North America has an abundance of wealth; the decision of where to go with it must be made: time is running out.

7

Note: The Works-Cited page is not shown. For sample pages, see MLA (page 533) and APA (pages 562–563).

Reading for Better Writing

Working by yourself or with a group, answer these questions:

1. In his title, Henry Veldboom identifies the issue as wealth. How does he clarify and deepen the issue in the essay's opening paragraphs?
2. While acknowledging economic and social systems, Veldboom stresses individual values and responsibilities. How effective is this emphasis?
3. What action does the essay call for? Do you find the action practical and compelling? Why or why not? Reflect on your own attitudes toward wealth and your habits with respect to it.

Calling for a Language Change

Lawrence Hill is a fiction writer, most notably of *The Book of Negroes*, a critically acclaimed and award-winning work of historical fiction that examines the nature and legacy of slavery. A writer of nonfiction as well (e.g., *Black Berry, Sweet Juice: On Being Black and White in Canada*), Hill is concerned with issues of identity and belonging, a concern he has acted upon by working with Canadian Crossroads International. Most recently, Hill delivered the 2013 Massey Lectures, published as *Blood: The Stuff of Life*. In the following essay, Hill addresses the continuing presence of the N-word in contemporary culture, pressing readers not to use it even in ways that now seem to have become acceptable.

Don't Call Me That Word

Growing up in the 1960s in the affluent, almost all-white Don Mills, Ont., I was told by my black father that education and professional achievement were the only viable options for black people in North America. He laid down three rules as if they had been received from the mouth of God: 1) I was to study like the dickens; 2) anything less than complete success in school or at work was to be regarded as failure; 3) if anybody called me "nigger," I was to beat the hell out of him.

> Hill begins with a personal anecdote related to the N-word.

This is the legacy of being black in Canada. You overcompensate for the fluke of your ancestry, and stand on guard against those who would knock you down. Over 400 years of black history here, we have had to overcome numerous challenges: the chains of slave vessels, the wrath of slave owners, the rules of segregation, the killing ways of police bullets, our own murderous infighting, and all the modern vicissitudes of polite Canadian oppression.

> The writer puts the issue of the N-word in a larger historical context of black history and experience.

Blacks in Canada, like our metaphorical brothers and sisters all over the world, have a vivid collective memory. We know what our ancestors have been through, and we know what our children still face. Most of us cringe when we hear the word "nigger." No other word in the English language distills hatred so effectively, and evokes such a long and bloody history.

These days, more people than ever are talking about the word "nigger," as a result of the publication this year of the book *Nigger: The Strange Career of a Troublesome Word*, by Randall Kennedy, a black American law professor at Harvard University. It's a fascinating read, but it raises a troublesome argument that I

> The writer identifies and disagrees with a specific claim about the word.

1

2

3

4

Adapted from Black Berry, Sweet Juice: On Being Black and White in Canada © 2001 by Lawrence Hill. Published by HarperCollins Publishers Ltd. All rights reserved.

ultimately reject: Kennedy praises "African American innovators" (by which he means comedians and hip hop stylists) for "taming, civilizing, and transmuting 'the filthiest, dirtiest, nastiest word in the English language.'"

Some misguided white people have bought into this same way of thinking. We have hit the pinnacle of absurdity when white teenagers sling their arms around black friends and ask, "Whassup my nigger?" And some white people seem to want a piece of that word, and feel the need to apply it to their own difficult experiences. The Irish have been referred to as "the niggers of Europe." In the 1970s, Québécois writer Pierre Vallières titled one of his books *White Niggers of America*. And just the other night, when I visited a drop-in centre catering mostly to black junior high and high school students in Toronto's Kensington Market area, a white teenager decked out in baggy pants and parroting what he imagined to be blackspeak complained that some kids accused him of being a "wigger"—an insulting term for whites who are trying to act black. Whatever that means.

5

As Randall Kennedy rightly asserts, the word abounds in contemporary black urban culture. True, when it crops up in hip hop lyrics, it's not intended to carry the hate of the racist. It signals an in-group, brotherly, friendly trash talk. This is well known in American culture but it has penetrated black Canadian culture, too. Choclair, a leading black Canadian hip hop artist, uses the word "nigga"—a derivation of "nigger"—frequently in his lyrics.

6

> He concedes but then carefully counters points made by the opposing argument.

Some people might say that the N-word is making a comeback. That the old-style, racist use of the word has faded into history and that it's now kosher to use the word in ordinary conversation. This argument fails on two counts. First, racists and racism haven't disappeared from the Canadian landscape. The comeback argument also fails because it suggests that reappropriating the word reflects a new linguistic trend. This is naive. As a way of playing with the English language's most hateful word, black

Black people use the word "nigger" precisely because it hurts so much that we need to dance with our own pain, in the same way that blues music dives straight into bad luck and heartbreak.

7

people—mostly young black males—have called themselves "nigger" for generations. The difference now is that these same young blacks have broadcast the word, via music and TV, to the whole world. In the middleclass black cultures I've encountered in Canada and the United States, such a young man usually gets slapped or tongue-lashed by his mother, at just about that point, and he learns that the only time it's safe to use that word is when he's chilling on the street with his buddies. This is very much part of the black North American experience: we don't run from our pain, we roll it into our art.

Using a question-answer format, Hill presses readers to rethink their attitude toward and use of the N-word.

But does that take the sting out of the word? No. And what's the proof of that? We don't use the word around our mothers, our teachers, the people we fall in love with, or our children. "Nigger" is a word that young black men use on each other. But the word still pains most black Canadians. Let me share an image of just how much the word hurts. A friend of mine—a black woman, community activist and graduate student—was dying to read Kennedy's book. She bought it last week, but couldn't bring herself to start devouring it on the subway to work until she had ripped off the cover: she wouldn't allow herself to be seen on the subway with the word "nigger" splashed on the cover of a book, so close to her face.

8

Reading for Better Writing

Working by yourself or with a group, answer these questions:

1. Where does Lawrence Hill call for action in this essay? What exactly is the action?
2. Hill begins and ends his essay with personal anecdotes. What do these contribute to his argument about the N-word?
3. How does Hill characterize the history of black people in Canada? How is this description important for his argument?
4. In paragraph 4, Hill quotes from Randall Kennedy. What purpose does this quotation serve in the essay? How does Hill's argument about the N-word flow forward from this quotation? Trace the line of reasoning that runs through the subsequent paragraphs.
5. The N-word is clearly a hateful one, if not the most hateful in the language. What has been your relationship with and experience of this word? Is there another word that has caused you significant pain or that you have used to inflict pain on others? How does Hill's essay give you pause?

Calling for Change in Addressing Hunger

Nick Saul is the president and chief executive officer (CEO) of Community Food Centres Canada. He is also the author (with Andrea Curtis) of *The Stop: How the Fight for Good Food Transformed a Community and Inspired a Movement*. In the essay below, published in the April 2013 edition of *The Walrus*, Saul encourages readers to participate in the fight against hunger by supporting poverty initiatives rather than leaving the problem to food banks.

The Hunger Game

The essay opens with a description of a food warehouse.

Picture a vast warehouse the size of a football field. Forklifts stand loaded with wooden pallets and cardboard boxes tightly secured with heavy-duty plastic wrap. In aisle upon aisle, boxes sit on metal shelves that reach all the way to the ceiling. It might be an IKEA store or any modern commodity warehouse. But this is a food bank or, more accurately, a food bank distribution warehouse. Every major Canadian city has one. The largest send out nearly 8 million kilograms of food a year to the hungry people lining up at community-based food banks. *1*

The writer contrasts what is admirable about food banks with what is depressing about them.

The scale and sophistication of these operations are impressive. There are hundreds of employees and volunteers who handle thousands of donated food items, trucks and boxes, cans and bags. There is also a large fridge and freezer section for storing all manner of perishables. *2*

Yet each time I visit such warehouses, I find myself alternating between hope and despair. Hope born of the understanding that all of this is motivated by the human urge to help others with that most basic of needs: food. Despair because this effort, and that of food banks all over Canada, has not solved the problem of hunger. On the contrary, I believe food banking makes it worse. *3*

The origins of food banks is examined.

Most Canadians assume that food banks have always been with us, but they only began to pop up across the country in the '80s, in response to the economic downturn. They were meant to be temporary. Among the first was the Stop Community Food Centre in Toronto. By the time I took over as its executive director in the late '90s, the Stop was already a tiny, broken-down place handing out donated cans and boxes of cheap, highly processed food to broken-down people. Even then, we knew we were doing little to stem the tide of hunger and poverty among the most vulnerable in our Davenport West community. But it was also clear that thousands of recipients, many of them children, relied on these handouts to survive. They had nowhere else to go. *4*

The writer explores the apparent success of food banks with the continuing reality of hunger.

Funded almost entirely by individual and corporate donations, food banks have become an unquestioned part of our social fabric, and our primary response to hunger. From the outside—hell, even from inside those warehouses—they seem to be doing a good job of it. There are walkathons and barbecues, a food drive at almost every school during the "hunger seasons" around Christmas and Easter. CBC collects hundreds of thousands of dollars and thousands of kilograms of food during its *Sounds of the Season* holiday broadcast. The big food corporations have *5* established close ties with large distribution centres, donating surplus packaged goods, making financial contributions, and getting employees to pitch in on sorting days. Churches, law firms, youth groups, and many, many committed individuals generously support the cause every day with their money, food, and time.

These people are doing such a good job that it can look as if the problem has been solved. Our elected officials feel no political heat to tackle the issue, because feeding the hungry is already checked off our collective to-do list. But even while food banks have proliferated, hunger has increased. Certainly, they can serve as a valuable support in emergencies, but too many users are forced to rely on them regularly. Nearly 900,000 Canadians (38 percent of them children) turned to food banks each month last year—a 31 percent rise overall since before the recession began in 2008. And these figures do not even take into account the hundreds of thousands who need assistance but don't seek it, in part because of the associated stigma. Many who do use food banks routinely go hungry. Furthermore, the poor—who receive mostly cheap processed items in their hampers—are disproportionately affected by such diet-related illnesses as diabetes, obesity, and heart disease.

Food banks, with all of their collecting and sorting and distributing and thanking, are meeting the needs of everyone except the people they were set up to help: the poor and hungry. This emergency handout approach divides us as citizens, breaking down our society into us and them, givers and takers. The former feel generous and kind, while the latter feel ashamed, their agency, their health, and their dignity diminished.

We not only can do better, we must do better. We need to stop cheering on an approach that has already failed, and instead focus on the root of the problem: people are hungry because they are poor. They do not have enough money for food because of inadequate income supports, minimum wages that do not cover the bills, and the lack of affordable housing and child care. Instead of further entrenching food banks that let governments—and all of us—off the hook, we need to build organizations that foster the political will to tackle poverty and establish social programs, employment strategies, and supports that give all Canadians access to affordable, healthy meals. In the end, the costs of inequality and poor health are borne by all of us, straining our health care system, and compromising the safety of our neighbourhoods and the productivity of our nation.

Food can be a powerful tool, and in the past decade we have seen a surge in school gardens, farmers' markets, and community supported agriculture. At the Stop, we have utilized this new energy and thinking to help establish programs where low-income people are offered more than mere handouts; rather, they are given opportunities to grow, cook, eat, and learn about the healthy food we all need. Such programs build hope, skills, and self-worth among our community members, who may then become powerful advocates for change—to both the food system and the political one. This model has radically altered our neighbourhood and generated enough interest to galvanize a network of Community Food Centres across the country.

Problems with the food-bank approach are analyzed.

With "we," the writer calls readers to action—adopting a new model for fighting hunger, illustrated by one food centre.

6

7

8

9

With some urgency, the conclusion repeats the call to action.

The towers of cans and boxes, the forklifts, and the volunteers in this warehouse 10 and others demonstrate the compassion we feel for one another, and the desire among Canadians to tackle hunger. But it is time to have a frank conversation about the limitations of this approach and start harnessing that caring and the engagement with food issues into a new political force. We need to ask ourselves and our elected representatives how we can make real, lasting change, and ensure that everyone finds health and dignity at our nation's table.

Reading for Better Writing

Working by yourself or with a group, answer the following questions:

1. Nick Saul opens and closes his essay with a description. What does this description accomplish?

2. What strategies does Saul use to help readers understand and accept that food banks are an imperfect solution to the hunger problem? What do you find compelling about his argument? Are there elements that you find less convincing?

3. Examine places where Saul calls for action. What precisely is he asking readers to do, and how doable is it? What kind of language and tone does he adopt when he calls for action? Do you find this approach compelling? Why or why not?

4. Reflect on your own relationship with food banks. Have you ever donated to one, volunteered at one, or used the services of one? How does Saul's essay connect with your experience and impact your thinking about hunger and poverty?

Calling for Action against Racial Stereotypes

Beyond making compelling claims about an issue and urging action, writers often spell out the required action concretely. Born in Winnipeg and now living in British Columbia, Joanne Arnott is a Métis writer of poetry and essays, as well as a facilitator of workshops on unlearning racism and on mothering. In the following essay, Arnott uses her own experience as workshop participant and facilitator to offer advice and suggest concrete action that will make readers allies in the anti-racism struggle.

Speak Out, For Example

> As you read this essay, take notes and make annotations exploring how Arnott calls readers to specific actions.

One day, I stopped by unexpected at a friend's place, knock knock. As she opened the door, she said with pretend irritation, "What do you want now?" When she saw it was me, she laughed. "Sorry. I thought it was my mutt. . . ." [1]

No dear woman, it is not your mutt. It is someone else's mutt at the front door. [2]

At the time I was too surprised, and too unsafe, to do more than focus my attention carefully on whatever had brought me to her door in the first place. But the incident has stayed with me, the sort of sting that crystallizes much into its simplicity. [3]

In 1989, I attended an Unlearning Racism workshop presented by Rikki Sherover-Marcuse, and subsequently have attended and led many such workshops. I have met a diversity of women and men with mixed/multiple heritages. I will take a few minutes, now, to talk about racism, but there is no way that I can speak for everyone. The format I will use is that of a Speak Out exercise, as taught by Rikki Sherover-Marcuse. It is used as a tool for educating people, and as a platform for people targeted for oppression to speak and be heard. I will address these three points: [4]

1. What I want you to know about me and my people [5]
2. What I never want to hear again [6]
3. What I expect of you as my allies [7]

Your job is just to listen. If you are also a mixed race person, take some time to answer the questions for yourself. Remember to leave space for your feelings, because feelings and experience are essential and need to be channelled, embraced, and cherished. If you are not a mixed-race person, please repeat whatever you remember of what I said in response to points 1 and 3, and bear 2 in mind but remember, I really don't want to hear it again. [8] [9]

1. What I want you to know about me and my people [10]

ABOUT ME: I am a person of mixed Native and European ancestry, and I know lots about my European ancestry and almost nothing about my Native heritage: this is one impact of racism. I was raised in a white community as a white working-class [11] person. When, as a child, I or my sisters or brothers attempted to talk about our relationship to or similarities with Native people, we were punished. Our parents seemed to believe in lies about our ancestry, and we were forced to believe, or pretend to believe, the same: this is one aspect of internalized racism. At the same time that this white-out policy was in effect, we were constantly being recognized by friends and strangers, by people not under the sway of the family's survivalist lies.

This combination of input created in me an attempt to sort a world of responses   12
to a Métis person through an insecure identity of whiteness. Confusion, dissonance, incongruity, self-doubt, endless inadequacy, deep shame were the results. The process of healing has been a tearing down and tearing up of almost every constituent belief that I held about myself and my world, and a recentering in the truth of bodymind, of spirit, a reawakening of my deep self and a reconstruction of my social self, my being in the world, on this new/old/original foundation.

ABOUT MY PEOPLE: People with multiple ethnic heritages are an extremely   13
diverse bunch of people. Our looks are diverse, our habits and heritages are diverse, our knowledge of ourselves, our ancestries, our traditions, our families, are diverse. To use the example of mixed Native and European heritage people, some of us are raised on reserve, in the bush, in small towns, on farms, in cities, and/or any combination of these places; as Indians, as Métis, as "breeds," as whites, Blacks, Asians; with great pride, with great shame, with full knowledge, in complete ignorance, with double and triple messages about who we are and about our place in the world. For many of us, the greatest source of racism, hurt, and shame is our own families. For many of us, our families are the cradles of safety against racist abuse and rejection from the outside world.

Big Issues: passing, and the not-Black-enough, not-Indian-enough hassles we   14
put on ourselves, collect from other people. "Where are you from?" "Are you two related?" In terms of multi-generational denial, complicities, it is important for us to acknowledge the privileges of European people, the very real dangers to our physical survival as Indians, Blacks, Asians in the context of the Americas. The decisions of family members to deny who we are do not come easy; they are meant to save lives. It is one strategy. Many of us choose other strategies, or override the decisions of our predecessors to reclaim the fullness and complexity of who we are and the histories of our families and communities. To attempt to enforce silence is soul murder. To attempt to induce identifications that are, because of racism, too threatening, is to rip a seed from its pod and is pointless: the seed will either ripen in its own time, or it will moulder and die within its protective casing.

Further layers of complexity get laid in when we are raised by people not   15
targeted for oppression in the same way we are, the situation of the black child of the white woman who affectionately called him "mutt" to her Métis girlfriend. Our worlds differ fundamentally, in how we are received and who we are received by, and there are basic truths and survival skills a person of colour must learn that white parents don't know about.

Possibly the most difficult issue for people of mixed heritage is that of *16* belonging, and a part of that is safety: constantly testing the waters to see how I am seen, and what the perceiver's response to their perceptions might be. The wide world that is laid open for people with multiple heritages is a well of potential, centred in a sometimes perilous terrain, The sliding identity that can be so difficult at first can become a very powerful tool for peacemakers.

2. What I never want to hear again: *17*

"Mutt" "Half-breed" "Heinz 57" "Wannabe" I never want to face another door *18* opened by a mother who calls the child of her own body racist names.

3. What I expect of you as my allies: *19*

Question: What is an ally? *20*

An ally can be a friend, family member, co-worker, complete stranger; but none *21* *of these is automatically an ally. Ideally, an ally is someone who is aware of their own issues of hurt and oppression, accumulated over the years, and is healing, and who is aware of the differences between us and who cherishes me, intervenes when they can to interrupt attacks against me, and supports me in my struggles against oppression and internalized oppression.* *22*

The possibility for every one of us to be allies against oppression is always present. Mistakes are made, and as allies, we commit ourselves to confronting rather than ignoring them, and doing the emotional and other kinds of work needed to correct and clean up mistakes and misunderstandings.

Notice the great pain carried by many, many, many mixed heritage people. *23* Notice our strength, our great pride. Notice us, everywhere in the world.

Stop making assumptions about the heritage of other people, thinking that if someone looks white, looks European, that they want to hear your racist jokes in a buddy-buddy fashion. Or conversely, if someone looks Indian, that they are an automatic font of deep wisdom via continuous ancient tradition.

As an ally you must never expect me to choose sides, because I am all sides. You *24* must never silence the parts of me that need to be given voice, especially when the parts of me do not agree. I need the fullness of that space to sort out the contradictions of my life experience, and to solidify a grounded and wellrounded sense of who I am, my place, and what my work in the world might be, based on that reality.

What I expect of my allies is not to divide up the world by race and caste *25* without acknowledging that every single boundary is blurred, and that these blurrings occur not only out of a conqueror mentality, but also out of love and need, and further that these blurrings have a name: we are called human beings. What I expect of my allies is to expect full pride from me, and to foster it.

We all learn the same racist crap, and we all need to stop perpetrating it *26* on ourselves, on one another, and on the young people. Participating in the diminishing of ourselves and of others is how we have learned to survive, and it takes a conscious effort, storming and weeping, and a courageous collaboration to turn things around. There are many things that each one of us can do. Actions large and small can be taken. Alone, together. Heal old wounds, demand the fullness of life. Listen carefully. Speak out, for example.

Reading for Better Writing

Working by yourself or with a group, answer the following questions:

1. Joanne Arnott begins with an anecdote. Why is this story important for understanding the subject of her essay?

2. Arnott shapes her essay in the form of a "speak out" exercise. What is such an exercise, and why do you think that she chooses this approach? Who is her audience and what does she expect from them?

3. The essay's action focuses on knowledge, language, and behaviour. In each section, for what actions and responses does Arnott call? Why is the second part so short? Why does Arnott define *ally* at the start of the third part, and then follow with verbs in the command form, such as *notice* and *stop*?

4. What would the process of "unlearning racism" involve for racial minorities, people of mixed race, and people who are white?

5. Re-read Arnott's final paragraph. What strategies does she use to connect with readers and to bring the "speak out" exercise to a close?

6. Reflect on your own relationship to the subject matter of Arnott's essay. Where do you find yourself in Canada's racial spectrum, and how has Arnott's call-to-action impacted that position?

Writing Guidelines

By implementing the strategies in Chapter 16 and following the steps below, write an essay persuading readers to act.

Planning

1. Select a topic. List issues about which you feel passionately, such as community problems, international issues, disaster-relief efforts, educational outreach programs, environmental clean-up efforts, or social or political campaigns. Then choose a related topic that is debatable, significant, current, and manageable.

Not Debatable	**Debatable**
Statistics on spending practices	The injustice of consumerism
Recyclables are dumped in landfills	Tax on paper/plastic grocery bags

2. Choose and analyze your readers. Think about who your readers are and why they might resist the change that you advocate.

3. Narrow your focus and determine your purpose. Should you focus on one aspect of the issue or all of it? What should you and can you try to change? How might you best organize your argument?.

4. Generate ideas and support. Use prewriting strategies like those below to develop your thinking and gather support:

- Set up "opposing viewpoints" columns in which you list arguments accepted by advocates of each position.
- Research the issue to find current, reliable sources from many perspectives.
- Research other calls to action on this issue, noting their appeals, supporting evidence, and success.
- Brainstorm the range of actions that might be taken in response to the issue. For each action, explore how attractive and doable it might be for your readers.
- Consider what outcomes or results you want.

5. Organize your thinking. Consider using the following strategies:

- Make a sharp claim (like those below) that points toward action:

    On the issue of _____, I believe _____.
    Therefore, we must change _____.

- Review the evidence, and develop your line of reasoning by generating an outline or using a graphic organizer. (See pages 49–55.)

    Simple Outline: Introduction: the issue and initial claim
        Describing the issue and its importance: point 1, 2, etc.
        Explaining possible actions and benefits: point 1, 2, etc.
    Conclusion: call to specific action

Drafting

6. Write your first draft. As you write, remember your goal and specific readers:

- **Opening:** Gain the readers' attention, raise the issue, help the readers care about it, and state your claim.
- **Development:** Decide where to place your most persuasive supporting argument: first or last. Anticipate readers' questions and objections, and use appropriate logical and emotional appeals to overcome their resistance to change.
- **Closing:** Restate your claim, summarize your support, and call your readers to act.
- **Title:** Develop a thoughtful, energetic working title that stresses a vision or change. (For ideas, scan the titles of the sample essays in this chapter.)

Revising

7. Improve the ideas, organization, and voice. Ask a classmate or someone from the writing centre to read your call-to-action paper for the following:

____ **Ideas:** Does the writing prompt readers to change their thinking and behaviour? Does the essay show effective reasoning, good support, and a clear call to action—without logical fallacies such as half-truths, unreliable testimonials, attacks against a person, and false analogies (see pages 317–320)?

____ **Organization:** Does the opening engagingly raise the issue? Does the middle carefully press the issue and the need for action? Does the closing successfully call for specific changes and actions?

____ **Voice:** Is the tone energetic but controlled, confident but reasonable? Does the writing inspire readers to join your cause and act?

Editing

8. Edit and proofread the essay by checking issues like these:

____ **Words:** Language is precise, concrete, and easily understood—no jargon, clichés, doublespeak, or loaded terms.

____ **Sentences:** Constructions flow smoothly and are varied in structure.

____ **Correctness:** The copy includes no errors in grammar, punctuation, usage, or spelling.

____ **Design:** The page design is correctly formatted and attractive; information is properly documented according to the required system (e.g., MLA, APA).

Publishing

9. Prepare and publish your final essay. Submit the essay to your instructor. If appropriate, solicit feedback from others—perhaps on a website or in a newspaper.

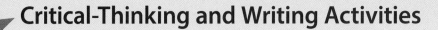

Critical-Thinking and Writing Activities

As directed by your instructor, complete the following critical-thinking and writing activities by yourself or with classmates.

1. One of Aesop's fables goes like this: "Passion is often more effectual than force." Given the essays that you read in this chapter, reflect on how this fable functions as a theme for writing that calls readers to action.

2. The four essays in this chapter address significant social and ethical issues: wealth, poverty, and race. List topics like these, choose one, narrow the focus to a specific issue, and then write an essay that persuades readers to do something related.

3. If you are a natural sciences major, consider debatable issues that are central to studying and applying the sciences—environmental, medical, biotechnical, and agricultural issues, for example. If you are a social science or humanities major, do the same brainstorming in your area. Then chose an issue where you see a need for change and write an essay in which you describe the issue and persuade readers to take the action that you recommend.

4. As a service project, visit an administrator at a local nonprofit agency (e.g., school, hospital, religious agency, employment office, YMCA) and offer to write an editorial, news article, or letter in which you describe one of the agency's needs and persuade readers to offer their help.

5. What issues have come up in your job? Contemplate issues such as pay equity, equal opportunity, management policies, and unsafe work conditions. Then write a persuasive report to a decision maker or to fellow employees.

Learning-Objectives Checklist ✓

Have you achieved this chapter's learning objectives? Check your progress with the items below, revisiting topics in the chapter as needed. *I have* . . .

___ critically examined and evaluated call-to-action papers for logical, evidence-based arguments that effectively address the writers' situations (346–347).

___ identified logical fallacies in others' writing and corrected them in my own writing (317–320).

___ strengthened my appeals with appropriate supporting evidence such as anecdotes, tests, experiments, analogies, and expert testimony (314–315).

___ developed reasonable claims, especially my call to action, rather than claims that are extreme, trivial, unqualified, or unwarranted (312–313).

___ integrated clarifying definitions and analyzed key cause-effect relationships.

___ researched and written a convincing call-to-action essay that develops its argument in a mature, informed voice (362–363).

___ edited my essay for all errors in mechanics, usage, grammar, and page design (363).

Chapter 19

Proposing a Solution

Proposals are prescriptions for change. As such, they challenge readers to care about a problem, accept a solution, and act on it. A strong proposal offers a logical, practical, and creative argument that leads toward positive change, whether it's getting ketchup out of the bottle easier, escaping the "filter bubbles" created for us by the Internet, practising environmental stewardship each day, or preventing sex-selective abortions.

Proposal writers argue for such remedies in all areas of life. In your coursework, you'll be challenged to generate solutions to many difficult problems. In your community, you may participate in policy making and civic development. In the workplace, you may write proposals that justify expenditures, sell products, or troubleshoot problems. In each situation, you'll have to clearly explain the problem, offer a solution, argue for adopting it, and possibly also explain how to implement it.

Visually Speaking   Study the photograph below, considering both its focal point and its broader context. What does the image suggest about the nature of problems and solutions? How might writing expose problems and contribute to solutions?

Learning **Objectives**

By working through this chapter, you will be able to

- critically examine and assess the arguments in problem-solution essays.

- analyze a problem's history, causes, and effects.

- analyze a solution's benefits and drawbacks.

- identify logical fallacies that are especially a danger in problem-solution writing.

- write a convincing essay that logically analyzes a problem and proposes a reasonable, reliable solution.

© *China Photos/Stringer/Getty Images News/Getty Images*

fig. 19.1

Strategies for Problem-Solution Writing

Explaining a problem flows naturally into arguing for a solution. For the problem-solution writer, the task is to convince the reader that the solution matches the problem. Doing so requires paying attention to the rhetorical situation and practising a range of strategies.

The Rhetorical Situation

To focus on problems and their potential solutions, writers start by thinking about the purpose, the readers, and the specific topic of their writing.

- **Purpose:** Problem-solution writing aims to inform: to describe a problem accurately, to present workable solutions, and to explain the strengths and weaknesses of each. However, such writing also aims to persuade: to convince readers that a problem is urgent, that one solution is better than others, and that readers should implement that solution.
- **Readers:** Potentially, writers could have four groups of readers: people responsible for the problem, decision makers with the power to adopt a solution, people affected by the problem, and a public who just want information about the problem. When reading the document, note whether it (1) offers all of its readers the information that they need and (2) communicates in language that they can understand and trust.
- **Topic:** Clearly, problem-solution writing focuses on a problem, but it can be a problem broadly conceived—perhaps as a challenge or an opportunity. Across the academic curriculum, such problems are typically discipline-related (e.g., dyslexia in Education, oil spills in Environmental Studies, agoraphobia in Psychology). In the workplace, problem-solution reasoning is used in documents such as proposals.

Example: In "'It's a Girl!'—Could Be a Death Sentence" (pages 377–379), Dr. Rajendra Kale tackles the sensitive, difficult **topic** of female feticide, the practice of aborting female fetuses. As this essay was published as an editorial in the *Canadian Medical Association Journal*, its **readers** are primarily other healthcare professionals but also policymakers and the general public. His **purpose** is to press for policy changes that will discourage female feticide.

Principles of Problem-Solution Writing

While problem-solution writing begins with a strong analysis of the rhetorical situation, it succeeds by following principles like those below.

1. **Rooting the Argument in Quality Research.** A proposal stands or falls on the quality of both the reasoning and its support. Writers convince the reader of their credibility by referring to reliable sources for quality evidence, ranging from the statistical to the historical, and by doing their homework concerning debates about the problem, its broader context, and past attempts at solutions.
2. **Thinking Creatively.** While problem-solution thinking needs to be sound, it must also be creative. Writers apply creativity by thinking outside the box of what has already been done, by considering alternative perspectives on both the problem

and possible solutions, and by importing ideas from other fields of knowledge. Proposal writing requires a willingness to challenge the status quo and a mind that is open to creative possibilities—a willingness to ask, "What's really wrong here, and how can we fix it?"

3. **Considering Ethical Issues.** Inherently, problem-solution writing involves an ethical dimension. It involves realizing that while some people may be harmed by the problem, other people may benefit from its existence. It can require seeking common ground on some of life's most enduring challenges. And it attempts to motivate readers to embrace a specific solution, a change that the writer stands behind and that might fail partly or wholly. Smart writers are aware of and speak to these ethical dimensions.

4. **Presenting Problems.** The first part of a proposal typically lays out the problem. The aim here is not only to convince readers that the problem exists but to persuade them to care about it enough to embrace a solution. Laying out the problem involves strategies like these:

   - A measured approach: Writers determine how deeply to treat and explain the problem based on what their audience needs to know and the level of seriousness inherent to the problem. The writer must go deeper into presenting the problem in all its complexity and must adopt a more serious tone in certain situations: the more unfamiliar and more serious the problem is, the more resistant readers are likely to be, the more extensive the damage caused by the problem, and the longer its history.

   - Sound analysis: Problems make sense when they are precisely defined (What is it?), vividly described (What does it look like?), explored as a narrative (What's the story?), explained as a process (When and how did it develop?), and/or probed for causes and effects (What brought about the problem? What are its consequences?).

5. **Arguing for Solutions.** When writers turn from problems to solutions, they approach the heart of their writing—their thesis about what will end the problem or at least mitigate its harmful consequences. (The thesis thus often comes partway through the essay, not at the beginning.) Arguing for a solution involves strategies like these:

   - Criteria for successful solution: Writers establish a measurement for what a solution must accomplish, what it must look like.

   - Comparison of all options: Using these criteria, writers boldly explore all possible solutions, weighing and balancing them against each other in terms of how they attack root causes and bring about real benefits. In addition, writers consider to what degree past strategies both succeeded and fell short.

- Support for the best solution (or a series of related solutions): The best solution is not a band-aid solution, one that temporarily treats surface harms. Nor is it a vague suggestion that something must be done. Instead, writers need to present a solution in precise and exact terms, addressing possible objections and explaining the positive outcomes that will result and the negative consequences that will be avoided by adopting this exact solution.
- Feasibility: Writers need to show that their solution is workable, not an unrealistic dream. They do so by considering the resources of time and money required, by mapping out step by step how the solution should be implemented, and by addressing any roadblocks to success.

Sample Problem-Solution Paragraph

In any essay, a writer might make an aside about a problem and its solution at the paragraph level. Doing so, the writer gestures toward an aspect of the topic that is not necessarily central to the essay's purpose but worthy of the reader's consideration. For example, Paige Louter's "Hipsters and Hobos" (pages 172–177) defines contemporary practices of asceticism; in her concluding paragraph, however, Paige identifies a problem with these practices and imagines a solution.

> Today, asceticism is clearly less grounded in intentionality and spiritual meaning than it has been in the past. Because true asceticism is necessarily also intentional asceticism, the possibility even arises that asceticism in its truest form no longer exists—outside of certain religious groups. Perhaps, then, the definition of an ascetic life must be modified, or perhaps a new philosophy has arisen today that is valid in its own right. Or perhaps the longing for authenticity that dwells in many young people today will eventually drive them beyond a self-reliant, isolated philosophy to deeply engage with the true spirit of asceticism. Arguably, Chris McCandless may have been one of the first of this movement. While one respondent to McCandless's story accused him of adhering to an arrogant and "contrived asceticism" (Krakauer 72), McCandless himself did, ultimately, live out what he believed, rejecting materialism, consumerism, mainstream society, all in the name of truly living. Essentially, perhaps this is what living as an ascetic is really about.

Reading Problem-Solution Writing

As you read the essays in this chapter, consider these questions:

1. What is the problem, what is its history, and why should the problem be resolved?
2. What is the solution, how does it resolve the problem, and with what side effects?
3. What action does the writer call for, and is it beneficial, realistic, and cost-effective?
4. Are persuasive statements reasonable, well-documented, and free of fallacies?

Sample Problem-Solution Essays

The student and professional essays on the following pages address a range of problems: the information "filter bubbles" created by our search habits on the Internet, the challenge of getting the last drop of ketchup out of the bottle, sex-selective abortion rooted in some cultures' valuing of male over female children, and practical steps for leading a more environmentally friendly life. As you read these essays, explore not only your own relationship to the problems discussed but also the strategies used by the writers to explain the problems and argue for specific solutions.

Addressing the Problem of the "Filter Bubble"

The first step toward solving a problem is to clearly articulate the problem. In the essay below, student writer Regan Burles carefully explores a problem with journalism in order to point toward a solution. This essay won the 2012 Dalton Camp Award for an essay on the media and democracy.

Essay Outline

Introduction: the meaning of Kai Nagata quitting his job at CTV

1. Problems in journalism: corporate profits and the public's desire for entertaining news
2. Blowing bubbles: exploring problems with a possible solution, citizen journalism

Conclusion: the need for all citizens to be aware of the "filter bubbles" that limit the knowledge and perspective they gain from the news

"Filter Bubbles": Public Discourse in an Age of Citizen Journalism

Out with the old, in with the new.   *1*

On July 7th, 2011 journalist Kai Nagata quit his job as CTV's Quebec City   *2*
Bureau Chief. His departure, and the article in which he explained the reasons for
it, drew significant media attention across Canada. The essay garnered over 100,000
views in a month, and by that time over a thousand online comments had been
made on the piece (Michaels).

In the essay, posted to his blog the day after he quit, Nagata details the various   *3*
shortcomings he encountered at CTV, which by now are quite familiar. Essentially,
the main problem he identifies is the conflict between the private interests of
corporate-owned media and the public good of high-quality journalism. In his
opinion, there was too much of the former, and not enough of the latter. Despite
the various regulatory bodies that police the journalistic community, he argues,
"information is a commodity, and private TV networks need to make money"
(Nagata). Profits, more often than not, trump meaningful news stories.

> The writer shares a problem articulated by Kai Nagata.

This wouldn't be so much of a problem if it weren't for another conflict, the conflict between peoples' desire for relevant journalism and their often competing desire for entertaining, palatable news stories. As Nagata puts it, "there is an underlying tension between 'what the people want to see' and 'the important stories we should be bringing to the people.'" Because of their primary goal of remaining profitable, news organizations will prioritize popular, if unimportant, news stories over significant, if less entertaining, journalism. These conflicts feed one another in a cycle that produces poor journalism: "people like low-nutrition TV...and that shapes the internal, self-regulated editorial culture of news" (Nagata).

4

> The problem is placed in a larger, broader context.

These problems obviously do not exist only at CTV, but extend across the entire spectrum of media organizations, from newspapers to television. Nagata identifies two significant consequences of these problems, both of which compromise the role of the media as a vital organ in a healthy democratic body.

5

First, news organizations have no incentive to produce material that is challenging or uncomfortable to its viewers: what people like, the networks are told, are "easy stories that reinforce beliefs they already hold" (Nagata). And second, there is a lack of debate and exchange of competing ideas in the public sphere: "I don't see any true debate within the media world itself, in the sense of a national, public clash of ideas" (Nagata).

6

> Citizen journalism is introduced and then analyzed as replicating the problems of traditional journalism.

Nagata—and a host of others—offer an alternative to the model of journalism described above. Whatever its particular name—new media, citizen journalism, crowd-sourcing—the new model tends to be sold as a panacea for the diseased hulk of traditional journalism. Whether it's crowd-sourced news sites like Digital Journal, social media platforms like Facebook and Twitter, or independent bloggers, "citizen journalists" are portrayed as the freer, faster answer to the problems posed by the quickly eroding monopoly that traditional media had on the flow of information. No longer needed are the organizations that set the standards for the profession and mediated its content: "what all of these experiments are pointing to," Nagata writes, "is that it's possible to do your thing, eat well, and build your audience—completely independent of existing institutions."

7

Blowing Bubbles

> Burles introduces and applies the concept of "filter bubbles" to explain the problem with citizen journalism.

Yet the rise of citizen journalism presents both an opportunity and a danger. Much ink has been spilled over the potential value of such unmediated forms of journalism and clearly they do permit experimentation that has the potential to greatly improve public discourse. However, citizen journalism is in danger of reproducing the very difficulties that exist in traditional media, and that it purports to eliminate. This point is best illustrated by a comparison with another modern phenomenon involving technology and the flow of information: filter bubbles.

8

The term was coined by Internet activist and author Eli Pariser to indicate the now pervasive activity of the "invisible, algorithmic editing of the web." Google,

9

for example, tailors its search results to individual users using fifty-seven different indicators such as their computer model, location, and browser. With these algorithms, each user receives specific search results geared to what the algorithm calculates she wants and expects. The result, Pariser explains, is filter bubbles: "your own personal, unique universe of information that you live in online."

This phenomenon is not just limited to search engines. In fact, a range of news websites have begun experimenting with personalization, including *The Huffington Post*, the *New York Times*, and *Slate* (Pariser). Readers now have total control over which authors or topics reach their eyeballs—no longer any need to bother with articles or opinions they don't care for.   *10*

The problem can be glimpsed elsewhere in the media universe too, as even traditional news providers seek to narrow their perspective in order to please a target audience. Openly partisan news outlets such as Sun TV News in Canada show that this sort of pandering to a particular set of views is becoming increasingly common. Furthermore, as independent bloggers who report on the news proliferate, it is becoming significantly easier to limit one's engagement with the news to stories and commentary that simply reinforce previously held views.   *11*

As media becomes increasingly personalized, the very problems that afflict traditional journalism that Nagata identifies are replicated in different ways. Eli Pariser anticipates the Canadian journalist's criticism of traditional media with his description of the consequences of filter bubbles: "the Internet is showing us what it thinks we want to see, but not necessarily what we need to see." This reflects almost to the word Nagata's concern over the profit-driven model of journalism he experienced at CTV. Just as corporate-owned media outlets, in a bid to remain profitable, offer easy, entertaining forms of journalism, so an increasingly differentiated and personalized media landscape offers such control and variety that avoiding challenging or controversial news stories is simply a matter of choice. We can now construct our very own media echo chambers, where the only stories and opinions presented are ones that reinforce our dearly held beliefs, and even fellow readers simply parrot back to us our own sedimented perspectives.   *12*

Yet it is not just a matter of a lowering of the journalistic bar. It also means that possibilities for meaningful public discourse are severely limited. What unreserved proponents of new media often miss is that meaningful debate is about more than just self-expression; it's more than simply yelling an opinion into the void. Rather, it requires an openness to new and opposing viewpoints and a willingness to consider novel and potentially difficult ideas—qualities that cannot be fostered in an environment designed to keep the original and the challenging at bay. Just as traditional media organizations often refrain from fostering meaningful public debate, so too do the filter bubbles induced by new media limit possibilities for genuine democratic discourse.   *13*

> The essay explores what's at stake with media filter bubbles.

Nagata is excited that journalism can now take place outside of existing media   *14*
institutions, and to a large degree that excitement is valid. The ways in which
traditional media institutions often constrain journalists in terms of what stories
they cover and how they cover them are well-documented. What institutions are
able to do, however, is act as mediators for both agreement and disagreement:
agreement on the basic presuppositions about society and the world that underlie—
and are necessary for—almost all public discourse. And disagreement about what
does—and ought to—go on within those agreed-upon parameters. The most
frightening consequence of the vast multiplicity of available media that exists today
is that we seem less and less capable of determining those crucial presuppositions
that a society must hold in common for democratic discourse to take place.

Yet even the traditional role of institutions as crafters and guardians of   *15*
agreed-upon standards appears to be eroding. In July 2011, for example, Sun Media
announced that it was pulling its chain of newspapers from the Ontario Press
Council, an organization that adjudicates complaints and acts as a watchdog for 191
different newspapers. The Council's decisions, according to its website, "represent
a consensus of a broad cross-section of Ontario society and active journalists." Sun
Media made the decision to withdraw from the group because of concerns over its
"politically correct mentality" (Jones). This is one small example of the way in which
consensus over the foundational beliefs and assumptions that make the exchange
of ideas possible is becoming more and more tenuous. This is not to say that those
assumptions and beliefs that currently exist are necessarily the best ones, or that
they should remain fixed. It is to say, however, that without such a foundation, any
hope of a public sphere in which ideas and opinions are exchanged and considered
across a broad spectrum of Canadian society is a faint one.

Admittedly, the situation may not seem so dire. Tens of millions of Canadians   *16*
still rely on traditional media for their news, whether it's on TV, in the newspaper, or
online. Furthermore, our media sources have not yet become so differentiated and
narrowly targeted that engagement between individuals and groups with competing
views has completely broken down. But what will happen when the range of media
resources available to us becomes so vast, our control over them so complete, that
we lose that most basic type of consensus that renders even the most alien viewpoint
comprehensible? What will happen when no stray opinions or bits of information
can any longer pierce the thick film of the bubbles we've so carefully constructed
around our media-consuming selves? As the volume of discourse increases, its
comprehensibility will decrease. As our access to diverse media grows, our ability
to discuss it with our fellow citizens will diminish. We'll no longer be able to talk to
one another.

Popping the Bubbles

In his essay, Nagata writes that during his time at CTV "every question [he] asked, every tweet [he] posted, and even what [he] said to other journalists and friends had to go through a filter, where [his] own opinions and values were carefully strained out." Even outside of existing institutions, though, filters abound: they are the ones we place around ourselves, aided by the ever-advancing capabilities of modern technology. If new media is to fulfill its promise, if it is to escape the constraints of traditional institutions without reproducing their failures, recognition must be given to the ways in which new forms of media are filtered to conform to our existing preferences and beliefs. Those involved in its production and reception—that is, all of us—must attempt to extricate ourselves from these moulds, to seek out new and disquieting information and opinion, and to find among ourselves the common threads that unite our varied outlooks and unique experiences in the world. If we can do that—break the bubbles that so narrowly limit the scope of our access to media—then certainly a public discourse that is genuinely democratic will be possible.

17

> Burles calls for each reader to enact a solution by resisting the filter bubbles in our lives.

Note: The Works-Cited page is not shown. For sample pages, see MLA (page 533) and APA (pages 562–563).

Reading for Better Writing

Working by yourself or with a group, answer the following questions:

1. In paragraphs 1–7, Regan Burles introduces problems with modern media journalism but referring to Kai Nagata. What strategies does Burles use to help readers understand and care about the problem? In your own words, what exactly is the problem?

2. As Regan begins to critique citizen journalism as a problem, he uses an extended analogy of "filter bubbles." Based on Regan's explanation, what do you understand a filter bubble to be? How effectively does this comparison clarify the problem?

3. Review paragraphs 13 and following. What does Regan do to encourage readers to understand the complexity and importance of the problem?

4. In his final paragraph, Regan directs readers toward a solution. What is that solution, and how well does it follow from his explanation of the problem?

5. After reading this essay, how would you characterize your own "filter bubble"? Is it a problem that needs solving?

Exploring Food Fixes

In addition to fully explaining a problem, writers of problem-solution essays often explore the nature of possible solutions. In the following essay, Chris Sorensen, who writes for *Maclean's*, explores nanotechnology as a solution for some of the most pressing problems in the food industry—like getting ketchup out of a bottle.

Ketchup Catch-Up

The humble ketchup bottle is a food-packaging icon. With its thin neck, metal cap and eight-sided body, the glass bottle developed by H.J. Heinz in the 1890s remains a cultural touchstone even though most ketchup is now sold in squat plastic containers.

> Sorensen identifies his topic and briefly spells out the problem, putting it in historical context.

But even icons have their flaws. Though initially designed to be practical—the bottle's clear glass allows consumers to see the condiment's freshness, while the thin neck helps slow oxidization—consumer preference for thicker ketchup meant the slender bottles soon became an exercise in frustration. Even constant evolutions of the bottle, including the most recent upside-down models, didn't fully solve the problem of how to easily get all the ketchup out of the bottle.

So after more than a century of consumers banging, slapping and prodding their ketchup bottles with a knife, researchers at the Massachusetts Institute of Technology think they have the answer. They unveiled a high-tech coating earlier this year called LiquiGlide that allows ketchup and other viscous condiments—from mustard and mayo to salsa and steak sauce—to slide easily out of a tipped bottle, like ice cream off a warm spoon. It's just one example of how the food-packaging industry is suddenly going through a period of rapid innovation—much of it driven by nanotechnology, which is the manipulation of matter on a molecular scale. "Food packaging research with nano-materials has exploded over the past decade," says Loong-Tak Lim, a professor in the University of Guelph's department of food science.

> The writer presents a solution under development and broadens the discussion to include the role of nanotechnology in solving other food-packaging problems.

Though its inventors claim LiquiGlide is not technically a nanotech product, the definition of which can sometimes be a bit fuzzy (it generally refers to the use of particles thinner than 100 nanometers), Lim says there are several familiar examples—like the inside of a potato-chip bag. "It looks like aluminum foil, but it's not," he says. "It's actually a plastic material that's coated with a thin layer of aluminum deposits. And that layer is about 20 to 30 nanometres thick."

Chris Sorensen, "Ketchup Catch-Up", Maclean's, 22 October 2012. Reproduced by permission of Maclean's Magazine.

Much of the nano-level research in food packaging focuses not on convenient   *5*
pouring, but on finding ways to keep food fresher, longer. And that means keeping
air out. "It's about extending the shelf life of the product, which means you can
ship it farther away," Lim says. Areas of particular interest for researchers include
embedding enzymes that can scavenge for oxygen and bacteria and the use of silver
nano-composites to kill micro-organisms.

Nano-particles can also be used as sensors to detect when food is spoiling and   *6*
change the exterior colour of a package to warn consumers. Lim pointed to a New
Zealand company that enclosed pears in nano-sensor packages. The label indicated
the fruit's ripeness. The idea, he says, was to stop shoppers from handling pears in
the store, leaving them bruised and unsellable.

Public acceptance remains an issue. As was the case with genetically   *7*
modified foods, consumers are concerned about the possible health effects of
nano-particles—a fear that's not entirely unwarranted. Lim says some substances
normally considered safe can be harmful to humans at the molecular level. The
U.S. Food and Drug Administration earlier this year issued draft guidelines that
covered the use of nanotechnology in foods, while Health Canada is evaluating new
approaches on a case-by-case basis.

Challenges to nanotechnology solutions are discussed objectively.

For its part, Heinz won't say if it's considering adopting LiquiGlide or any   *8*
other new packaging technologies, including nano-materials. "We love the idea
of making it easier to pour out Heinz ketchup from the bottle, and we're always
exploring technologies like this to help enhance the overall consumer experience,"
says Joan Patterson, a spokesperson for Heinz Canada. She adds that Heinz views
packaging as "a way to differentiate and build brand equity," but that consumer
acceptance is key.

Sorensen returns to ketchup and its packaging adaptations, past and future.

Heinz has already adopted a number of key changes to its ketchup packaging   *9*
over the years. From the plastic squeeze bottles introduced to Canadians in 1985
to the upside-down bottles that arrived in 2003, the new designs made storing
and dispensing ketchup faster and more convenient. Not surprisingly, they also
encouraged consumers to use more ketchup.

The conclusion focuses on innovation as a force behind solutions.

The latest effort, unveiled in Canada this year, may not be nanotech but it   *10*
certainly qualifies as revolutionary in the minds of consumers: single-serve "dip &
squeeze" ketchup packets. The individual tubs are three times as large as existing
packets, and allow the ketchup to be squeezed out one end, or the top peeled back for

dipping. Heinz called it "the most significant packaging innovation for the ketchup packet in more than 42 years." However, judging by the research now taking place, the next big leap forward is likely to come a whole lot quicker.

Reading for Better Writing

Working by yourself or with a group, answer the following questions:

1. How would you characterize the tone and style of Chris Sorensen's essay, starting with the title? In what ways is this style fitting for the topic and the audience?

2. Sorensen spends little time on discussing the problem itself. Why? Does his strategy work?

3. Much of the essay focuses on nanotechnology as a solution to food-packaging problems or challenges. What strategies does Sorensen use to explore and present nanotechnology?

4. The essay begins and ends with ketchup. How does this illustration work in the essay? What does it accomplish for Sorensen?

5. This essay presents innovation as a force that solves problems. What is innovation? How has your own life been impacted or even shaped by innovations?

Follow-up: If you are a lover of ketchup (and a fan of all things related to condiments), check out Malcolm Gladwell's "The Ketchup Conundrum," originally published in the September 6, 2004, edition of *The New Yorker* and available online.

Addressing an Ethical Problem

One of the crucial elements of problem-solution writing is showing that the solution fits the problem, that the fix actually solves the problem or at least effectively holds back its harmful effects. The following editorial, published in the *Canadian Medical Association Journal (CMAJ)* by the editor-in-chief, Dr. Rajendra Kale, offers a controversial solution to a controversial ethical problem: female feticide in some immigrant Canadian communities.

"It's a Girl!"—Could Be a Death Sentence

When Asians migrated to Western countries they brought welcome recipes for curries and dim sum. Sadly, a few of them also imported their preference for having sons and aborting daughters. Female feticide happens in India and China by the millions, but it also happens in North America in numbers large enough to distort the male to female ratio in some ethnic groups. Should female feticide in Canada be ignored because it is a small problem localized to minority ethnic groups? No. Small numbers cannot be ignored when the issue is about discrimination against women in its most extreme form. This evil devalues women. How can it be curbed? The solution is to postpone the disclosure of medically irrelevant information to women until after about 30 weeks of pregnancy. *1*

> **The introduction summarizes the problem and states the solution.**

A pregnant woman being told the sex of the fetus at ultra-sonography at a time when an unquestioned abortion is possible is the starting point of female feticide from a health care perspective. A woman has the right to medical information about herself that is available to a health care professional to provide advice and treatment. The sex of the fetus is medically irrelevant information (except when managing rare sex-linked illnesses) and does not affect care. Moreover, such information could in some instances facilitate female feticide. Therefore, doctors should be allowed to disclose this information only after about 30 weeks of pregnancy—in other words, when an unquestioned abortion is all but impossible. A similar proposal has been made elsewhere. Postponing the time when such information is provided is a reasonable ethical compromise. It would still allow prospective parents enough time to prepare the nursery. *2*

> **The writer argues that the solution is a reasonable ethical compromise.**

The College of Physicians and Surgeons of British Columbia states that testing to identify sex during pregnancy should not be used to accommodate societal preferences, that the termination of a pregnancy for an undesired sex is repugnant *3*

> **Current laws and codes are surveyed in the context of the solution.**

Kale, Rajendra "It's a Girl!"—Could Be a Death Sentence," CMAJ: Canadian Medical Association Journal, Vol. 184 No. 4, 2012, p. 387–388. Copyright © 2012 Canadian Medical Association. This work is protected by copyright and the making of this copy was with the permission of Access Copyright. Any alteration of its content or further copying in any form whatsoever is strictly prohibited unless otherwise permitted by law.

and that it is unethical for physicians to facilitate such action. The college in Ontario states that it is inappropriate and contrary to good medical practice to use ultrasound solely to determine the sex of the fetus. The Society of Obstetricians and Gynaecologists of Canada says that the problem of the small number of pregnant women who may consider abortion when the fetus is of unwanted sex is best addressed by the health professionals who are providing care for these women, but it does not say how this can be done effectively. These statements do little more than provide lip service to tackling female feticide and a band-aid for the souls of those who draft policy. Fortunately, the Canadian Assisted Human Reproduction Act of 2004 prohibits any action that would ensure or increase the probability that an embryo will be of a particular sex or identifies the sex of an in-vitro embryo, except to prevent, diagnose or treat a sex-linked disorder or disease—thus closing this avenue for sex selection.

The colleges need to rule that a health care professional should not reveal the   4
sex of the fetus to any woman before, say, 30 weeks of pregnancy because such information is medically irrelevant and in some instances harmful. Doing so should be deemed contrary to good medical practice. Such clear direction from regulatory bodies would be the most important step toward curbing female feticide in Canada.

Some readers might be skeptical about whether female feticide is in fact taking   5
place in Canada and the United States. Research in Canada has found the strongest evidence of sex selection at higher parities if previous children were girls among Asians—that is people from India, China, Korea, Vietnam and Philippines. What this means is that many couples who have two daughters and no son selectively get rid of female fetuses until they can ensure that their third-born child is a boy. These researchers have also documented male-biased sex ratios among US-born children of Asian parents in the 2000 US census. A small qualitative study in the US involving 65 immigrant Indian women documents the pressure they face to have sons, the process of deciding to use sex selection technologies, and the physical and emotional health implications of both son preference and sex selection. Of these women, 40% had terminated pregnancies with female fetuses and 89% of the women carrying female fetuses in their current pregnancy pursued an abortion. Results from this study could be reasonably extrapolated to Indians in Canada. We should,

The writer anticipates objections about the problem's extent and seriousness in Canada.

however, avoid painting all Asians with the same broad brush and doing injustice to those who are against sex selection.

The writer argues for his solution one last time, placing it in a global context.

The execution of a "disclose sex only after 30 weeks" policy would require the understanding and willingness of women of all ethnicities to make a temporary compromise. Postponing the transmission of such information is a small price to pay to save thousands of girls in Canada. Compared with the situation in India and China, the problem of female feticide in Canada is small, circumscribed and manageable. If Canada cannot control this repugnant practice, what hope do India and China have of saving millions of women?

6

Note: The references for this essay are not shown. For examples, see MLA (page 533) and APA (pages 562–563).

Reading for Better Writing

Working by yourself or with a group, answer the following questions:

1. How would you characterize Dr. Rajendra Kale's tone and approach in explaining the problem and arguing for his specific solution?
2. Reflect on the traditional organization of this essay. Is it effective, given the nature of the problem and the solution proposed?
3. What strategies does Kale use to argue that his proposed solution fits the problem? Are these strategies successful?
4. The topic of this essay is both highly personal and highly polarizing. What impact has reading Kale's editorial had on your own thinking? Does it speak to your own experience in particular ways? Does it press you to think about your own gender, ethnic identity, and family plans?

Arguing for Practical Environmental Solutions

As discussed with the previous essay, writers should strive to show that a solution fits the problem in question. However, good problem-solution writing also focuses on the practical—the concrete "how to" of the solution, sometimes even explaining how to implement the solution step by step. In the essay below, renowned scientist and broadcaster David Suzuki suggests some down-to-earth solutions to the environmental challenges facing the planet.

Saving the Planet One Swamp at a Time

As you read this essay, take notes and annotate it— examining especially how Suzuki presents the environmental problem and offers solutions.

Do you have a swamp? I don't mean literally. I mean a special place where, at some point, you really connected with nature—a place that made an indelible imprint on your mind, the smell, the sound, the feel of which has stayed with you forever.   *1*

Maybe yours was a family cabin at the lake. Or a special river where you canoed with your grandfather. Or a tree you climbed in your backyard. Mine actually was a swamp near my home in London, Ont. I spent hours there, looking for frogs and birds, and wading through the brackish water, searching for new life. Afterward, I would lie on my back in the tall grass, drying off, breathing the humid air, staring up at the sky, and wondering about it all. How vast it all seemed and how puny I felt in comparison.   *2*

Back then, I would never have imagined human beings could significantly alter something as huge as the planet's atmosphere. It was beyond comprehension. Sure, when I was very young, I remember smoke fogs from wood and coal burning in Vancouver, where I was born, that settled in on the city and made it difficult to see across the street. But a good wind would eventually clear the smoke. That's the way it always was. Nature took care of our waste, cleansing our air and water and making them pure again.   *3*

What I didn't know as a boy was that my swamp and the sky above me were not actually separate things at all. Our atmosphere, our oceans, our lakes, soils and all living things are intricately connected. Making a major change to any one thing in this zone of life, our biosphere, will have profound repercussions throughout the entire system. It can actually affect how our natural services function. That's why global warming is such a big deal.   *4*

David Suzuki, "Saving the Planet One Swamp at a Time" Toronto Star, 2 June 2007. Reprinted by permission of the David Suzuki Foundation.

In Canada, it's tempting to shrug off global warming as something that will   *5*
make life in our cold country more pleasant. Vineyards in Winnipeg, farms in the
Arctic. But the reality is not so simple. And decidedly less fun.

By burning vast quantities of fossil fuels like coal, oil and gas, and by cutting   *6*
down massive forested areas, humans have released enough greenhouse gases
and reduced the absorptive capacity of nature enough to fundamentally alter our
atmosphere. There is now 32 per cent more carbon dioxide, the main greenhouse
gas, in our atmosphere today than there was before the industrial revolution.

The trouble with greenhouse gases like carbon dioxide is that they trap heat,   *7*
much like a blanket, and hold it near the planet's surface. If we didn't have any
of these gases, heat from the sun would shine onto the planet and then radiate
back into space, and our planet would be either too hot or too cold. Over millions
of years, our Earth has created the perfect conditions for life, with just the right
amount of greenhouse gases to ensure that it is never too hot or too cold. Without
this stable climate, human civilization would likely never have developed to where
we are today. We depend on it.

But all the extra carbon dioxide and other gases we keep adding to the air   *8*
are disrupting the stable climate that has been so very important to us. I say
"disrupting" because it is really a more accurate description of what happens.
Adding heat to the atmosphere also means adding energy that can manifest itself in
unusual ways—more frequent or extreme storms, for example.

In other words, global warming does not equate to a modest, pleasant warming.   *9*
Rather, it means higher global temperatures overall, which translates to a host of other,
often unforeseen, problems. This year, the headlines have been full of these issues:
falling water tables, retreating lakeshores, acidification of oceans, shrinking ice caps
and glaciers, expanded ranges for invasive species, and more. Even noxious weeds like
poison ivy are expected to blossom in a carbon-dioxide enriched atmosphere.

Air quality in urban areas will also be affected. Smog is created from a   *10*
chemical interaction in the atmosphere between automobile and smokestack
pollution, and heat and sunlight. More heat and more sunlight will mean more
smog. Resulting new infrastructure needs and increasing health care costs add
up quickly. Already, the Ontario Medical Association says air pollution costs the
province more than $1 billion in hospital charges and lost workdays. That will only
get worse as our climate warms.

But enough about the risks—most people are aware of them by now. Scary 11
stories have been all over the news for the past six months. In fact, it seems
like results of yet another study are published practically every day confirming
something bad about global warming. It's getting to the point where I worry people
will be tempted to just throw up their hands and say "I give up!" Yet that would be
a huge mistake, because it's not too late to avoid what scientists call "dangerous
warming." Yes, some warming has already occurred and more will come, but we can
still avoid the brunt of a disrupted climate by taking action now.

Sir Nicholas Stern, former chief economist with the World Bank, has estimated 12
that to pay for all the changes necessary to avoid dangerous warming, it will cost the
global economy about 1 per cent of the world's annual GDP. That's not insignificant.
But what's astounding is what it will cost us if we carry on with business as usual:
up to 20 per cent of the global economy per year, which could lead to a worldwide
depression.

So taking action now is far and away the most prudent financial course. We 13
simply cannot afford to wait. A recent statement by the scientific academies of
13 countries put it this way: "The problem is not yet insoluble, but becomes more
difficult with each passing day."

Tackling the problem sufficiently will involve all sectors of society, from 14
governments to businesses and individuals. It means having firm national targets
and timelines that will spur innovation and provide certainty and a level playing
field for industry.

It means giving individuals options so they can more easily pick the most 15
sustainable choice. And it means leadership at all levels to break us away from the
status quo and put us on a new path.

Individuals can learn about reducing their own footprint at dozens of 16
environmental websites or they can take the initiative and:
- Leave the car at home and sometimes walk.
- Bike or take transit.
- Switch all their light bulbs to modern energy-efficient CFLs.
- Buy a fuel-efficient vehicles.
- Choose more local foods.
- Use a programmable thermostat.
- Buy Energy Star appliances.

• Weather-strip their homes.

• Encourage friends or political leaders to take action.

I could go on and on.   *17*

Many people are already doing these things, but to really solve global warming   *18*
we need our leaders to take it seriously, too. Because right now, Canada is still
falling behind. And our world, which once seemed so vast and limitless, is actually
far smaller and more interconnected than we could ever have imagined.

Reading for Better Writing

Working by yourself or with a group, answer the following questions:

1. In the first paragraphs, David Suzuki offers a personal anecdote and invites
   readers to consider their own stories. What purpose does this opening serve
   in the larger essay? Do you have a story about your own connection to nature?
   Conversely, do you have a story about your distance from it? How do such
   stories capture something of the relationship between nature and human
   nature?

2. Starting in paragraph 5, Suzuki explains global warming and its impacts in
   lay terms. What is the point of this explanation with respect to outlining the
   problem for readers?

3. Paragraph 11 begins "Enough about the risks," signalling a turn to solutions.
   Map out the solutions that Suzuki proposes from this point to the end of his
   essay. How does he argue that these solutions are practical?

4. What fears, anxieties, and other emotions are Suzuki's solutions meant to
   address?

Writing Guidelines

Planning

1. Select and narrow a topic. Brainstorm possibilities from this list:

- **People Problems:** Consider generations—your own or a relative's. What problems face this generation? How can they be solved?
- **Academic Problems:** List problems faced by college and university students. In your major, what problems are experts trying to solve?
- **Social Problems:** What problems do our communities and country face? Where do you see suffering, injustice, inequity, waste, or harm?
- **Workplace Problems:** What job-related problems have you experienced or might you experience?

Then test your topic:

- Is the problem real, serious, and currently—or potentially—harmful?
- Do you care about this problem and believe that it must be solved? Why?
- Can you offer a workable solution—or should you focus on part of the problem?

2. Identify and analyze your audience. You could have four audiences: people responsible for the problem, decision makers with the power to deliver change, people affected by the problem, and a public that wants to learn about it.

- What do readers know about the problem? What are their questions or concerns?
- Why might they accept or resist change? What solution might they prefer?
- What arguments and evidence would convince them to acknowledge the problem, to care about it, and to take action?

3. Probe the problem. If helpful, use the graphic organizer on page 55.

- **Define the problem.** What is it, exactly? What are its parts or dimensions?
- **Determine the problem's seriousness.** Why should it be fixed? Who is affected and how? What are its immediate, long-term, and potential effects?
- **Analyze causes.** What are its root causes and contributing factors?
- **Explore context.** What is the problem's background, history, and connection to other problems? What solutions have been tried in the past? Who, if anyone, benefits from the problem's existence?
- **Think creatively.** Look at the problem from other perspectives—other provinces, territories, and countries, both genders, different races and ethnic groups, and so on.

4. Choose the best solution. List all imaginable solutions—both modest and radical fixes. Then evaluate the alternatives:

- List criteria that any solution should meet.
- List solutions and analyze their strengths, weaknesses, costs, and so on.
- Choose the best solution and gather evidence supporting your choice.

Drafting

5. Outline your proposal and complete a first draft. Describe the problem, offer a solution, and defend it using strategies that fit your purpose and audience.

- **The problem:** Inform and/or persuade readers about the problem by using appropriate background information, cause-effect analysis, examples, analogies, parallel cases, visuals, and expert testimony.
- **The solution:** If necessary, first argue against alternative solutions. Then present your solution, stating what should happen, who should be involved, and why.
- **The support:** Show how the solution solves the problem. Use facts and analysis to argue that your solution is feasible and to address objections. If appropriate, use visuals such as photographs, drawings, or graphics to help readers grasp the nature and impact of the problem.

Revising

6. Improve the ideas, organization, and voice. Ask a classmate or someone from the writing centre to read your problem-solution paper for the following:

_____ **Ideas:** Does the solution fit the problem? Is the proposal precise, well researched, and well reasoned—free from oversimplification and obfuscation?

_____ **Organization:** Does the writing move convincingly from problem to solution, using fitting compare-contrast, cause-effect, and process structures?

_____ **Voice:** Is the tone positive, confident, objective, and sensitive to opposing viewpoints—and appropriate to the problem's seriousness?

Editing

7. Edit and proofread the essay. Look for these issues:

_____ **Words:** Words are precise, effectively defined, and clear.

_____ **Sentences:** Sentences are smooth, energetic, and varied in structure.

_____ **Correctness:** The copy has correct grammar, spelling, usage, and mechanics.

_____ **Design:** The design includes proper formatting and documentation.

Publishing

8. Prepare and share your final essay. Submit your essay to your instructor, but also consider sharing it with readers who have a stake in solving the problem.

Critical-Thinking and Writing Activities

As directed by your instructor, complete the following critical-thinking and writing activities by yourself or with classmates.

1. Albert Einstein once argued that "[t]he significant problems we face today cannot be solved at the same level of thinking we were at when we created them." Reflect on the truth of this idea, particularly in light of today's problems.

2. Chris Sorensen's essay "Ketchup Catch-Up" (pages 374–376) focuses on innovations in food packaging. Consider innovation in another area of life, and write an essay about how a specific innovation did or did not solve a particular problem or need.

3. The essays on media "filter bubbles" (Burles) and on actions to take in response to global warming (Suzuki) both focus on the public good. Consider other public problems connected with communities and groups you belong to. Then research and write a problem-solution essay that speaks to one of these problems.

4. As you can imagine, "'It's a Girl!'—Could Be a Death Sentence" generated a measure of controversy and strong response. See, for example, the response of the Society of Obstetricians and Gynaecologists of Canada (SOGC) to Dr. Kale, or some of the comments at the *CMAJ* website. Given the controversy, do additional research and offer your own solution to the problem—supporting Dr. Kale, modifying his solution, or recommending something altogether different.

Learning-Objectives Checklist ✓

Have you achieved this chapter's learning objectives? Check your progress with the items below, revisiting topics in the chapter as needed. *I have . . .*

____ critically examined and evaluated problem-solution essays for clear information, logical claims, reliable evidence, and arguments that effectively address the writers' situations (366–368).

____ analyzed a problem's history, causes, effects, and impact (384–385).

____ researched potential solutions, evaluated their strengths and weaknesses, selected the best solution, and rationally explained my choice (384–385).

____ identified and corrected logical fallacies such as obfuscation, oversimplification, false cause, and slanted language (317–320).

____ integrated needed definitions and pointed out clarifying comparisons, contrasts, and classifications.

____ produced accurate descriptions, thorough analyses, and well-organized, rational arguments (384–385).

____ written, revised, and edited a convincing essay that logically analyzes a problem, proposes a reasonable solution, and advocates its implementation (384–385).

Chapter 20

Preparing Oral Presentations

What do you fear? Heights, small spaces, spiders, zombies? Studies suggest that the number one fear for most people is public speaking. That fear can make for a panic-filled presentation that leaves the presenter breathless and the audience clueless.

If you identify with this description, the bad news is that presentations may be a common part of your work in school, in the workplace, and even in the communities to which you belong. The good news is that with some practical strategies, you can make your presentations informative and compelling.

While we can't promise that this chapter will ease all your fears, it will give the practical instruction you need to put together and deliver productive presentations.

Visually Speaking What does the photograph below communicate about the nature and power of speeches and presentations? What relationship is implied between the written and the spoken word? What other images and ideas come to mind when you consider making a presentation?

Learning **Objectives**

By working through this chapter, you will be able to

- effectively plan presentations through analysis of the rhetorical situation, selection of a format, and research.
- draft a presentation with a compelling opening, a substantial middle, and a productive closing.
- compose a presentation using presentation software.
- deliver a presentation in a clear, engaging manner.

AP/The Canadian Press

fig. 20.1

Planning Your Presentation

A strong presentation doesn't just *happen*—it requires effective planning. Such preparation includes analyzing the rhetorical situation behind the presentation and considering the format to use, the multimedia elements to include, and sound practices to follow.

Analyze the Presentation Situation

Consider the rhetorical context—the topic, your goals, your audience, and the context:

- *Topic:* What precise topic must you cover? Can you break it down into manageable parts? Should you give equal weight to each?
- *Purpose:* Are you trying to inform, teach, analyze, inspire, persuade? What exactly do you want your audience to take away from your presentation?
- *Audience:* What are your listeners' knowledge of and attitudes toward your topic? What are their ages, interests, and reasons for attending the presentation?
- *Context:* What are the possibilities and constraints for your presentation—the physical or digital setting, the time limits, the hardware and software available? How complex is the information and the reasoning you need to share? What media make sense for this presentation? What level of formality is expected? What degree of audience involvement is appropriate?

Choose a Fitting Format

Occasionally, you might be asked to speak to a topic informally and spontaneously. Generally, however, you have time to prepare your presentation according to a particular format. Three commonly used formats are the list, the outline, and the manuscript:

- *List:* Use a list for a short, informal presentation. Write the first sentence, create a summary phrase for each main point, and write your closing sentence.
- *Outline:* Use an outline for a more complex topic or formal presentation. By using an outline, you can organize material in greater detail without tying yourself to a word-for-word presentation. For example, you might write the opening statement as complete sentences, phrase all main points as complete sentences, include supporting points as phrases or clauses, write any quotations word-for-word, and state your conclusion as complete sentences. (For more on effective outlining, see pages 49–55.)
- *Manuscript:* For highly formal presentations in which your words must be carefully chosen, develop a manuscript. Make sure to double space your speech, number all pages, mark difficult words for pronunciation, mark the script for interpretation and emphasis using boldface or italics, and clearly indicate references to visual aids and other resources. (See Martin Luther King, Jr.'s speech "I Have a Dream" on pages 392–395.)

Consider Multimedia Elements

Multimedia elements need to be used effectively and wisely: they should be informative and compelling, advancing your discussion of the topic. To choose multimedia elements, ask questions like these: Given my audience, what multimedia support do they need to understand the topic? What multimedia elements will illuminate the topic, bringing it to life? What different media will help to convey my presentation's key ideas and information? With these questions in mind, you can choose among multimedia elements like these:

- **Audio clips** effectively emphasize sound information—the human voice and its tones, sounds in nature and in urban settings, the language of music, and so on.
- **Video clips** add a richness of motion, colour, sound, and even story.
- **Tables** arrange data in a grid of rows and columns to show the intersection of two factors, making it easy to categorize data for comparison.
- **Graphs** show relationships between numbers—differences, proportions, and trends. They can be formatted as line graphs, bar graphs, or pie graphs.
- **Charts** show the relationships between parts, steps, and stages, and include organizational charts and flow charts.
- **Images** such as photos, maps, and line drawings visualize places, objects, and people. By stressing certain details, these images help the audience understand ideas, see concepts concretely, and organize information.

Examples: The sample visuals on this page are taken from the poster presentation, "Sewage Contamination in the Chedoke Creek Watershed." (The full report is in the online chapter on science writing.) Note how the map and the bar graph communicate complex information clearly.

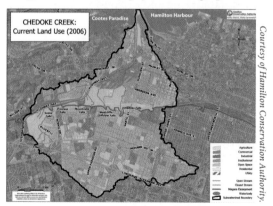

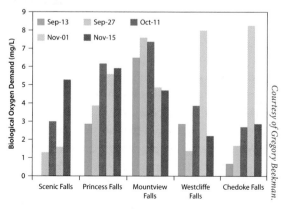

Consider Tips for an Effective Presentation

Your presentation should be a teaching-learning opportunity for you and your audience. To make it so, consider these guidelines:

1. **Make your presentation idea-driven.** Have a working thesis that provides a focus for your discussion. In other words, avoid your presentation being simply the presentation of information.

2. **Aim to offer a fairly challenging idea.** For example, offer a specific and nuanced analysis of the topic, not sweeping generalizations. Root your presentation in issues and questions that you yourself find meaningful and engaging.

3. **Build in elements that help the audience keep pace with you.** Help your audience follow your train of thought by including occasional summaries, transitions, and "checks" of understanding. Particularly helpful is providing the audience with a clearly written handout that gives them a physical reminder of your message to take away and may prompt them to apply your ideas to their own thinking on the topic.

4. **Keep things clear but substantial.** On the one hand, you don't want to overwhelm your audience with information that they cannot process effectively. On the other hand, you want your presentation to have meaningful, helpful substance. Linger over key details, analyzing and explaining them to a depth that your audience will understand and appreciate.

5. **Keep in mind these qualities of an effective presentation:**

   Content: The presentation
   - Demonstrates a thorough and deep knowledge of an effectively focused, clear, and manageable topic.
   - Offers a clear key idea, effective elaboration of the idea, and strong details and evidence.

   Organization: The presentation
   - Delivers an interesting introduction that focuses and grasps the audience's attention, as well as providing necessary background and context.
   - Maintains a clear focus and an effective sequencing of supporting points.
   - Concludes thoughtfully, pressing the audience to think further and deeper about the topic and its essential issues.

   Oral and Visual Communication: The presentation
   - Is delivered with an engaging tone, appropriate pacing, good eye contact, clear and fluid speech, fitting enthusiasm and interest.
   - Engages the audience with thought-provoking questions, dialogue, and participatory activities that deepen understanding of the topic.
   - Provides the audience with informative and engaging materials—whether handouts, visuals, or audio clips—and uses these materials well.
   - Is completed within the allotted time frame.

Drafting Your Presentation

Think about your presentation having three distinct parts: an introduction, a body, and a conclusion. The common advice here is to tell your audience what you are going to say, say it, and tell them what you've said. However, here is a bit more advice on shaping the three parts of your presentation:

Introduction

Explore possibilities for greeting your audience, identifying yourself if needed, focusing listeners' attention, clarifying your topic and its importance, framing your key question or idea, and forecasting the parts of your presentation. Consider a variety of creative strategies for opening:

- stating a little-known fact or statistic
- asking a probing question
- telling a relevant anecdote
- offering a thought-provoking quotation
- describing a problem
- projecting an engaging image on a screen
- playing a short video or audio clip
- performing a short demonstration.

Body

Shape your essential message—main points, reasoning, and evidence—so clearly that your audience will understand it after hearing it only once. To do so, consider these tips:

- Use a straightforward organizational pattern such as problem/solution, cause/effect, chronology, order of importance.
- Provide clear, emphatic transitions by using such words as *first, second, third; therefore, however, by contrast; in summary.*
- Structure your presentation around a limited number of memorable points (3–4), rather than around many smaller points.
- Avoid overwhelming listeners with complex details and dense explanations. Instead, make information clear through visuals and handouts.
- Make abstract ideas concrete by offering examples, illustrations, and anecdotes.
- Whenever possible, use plain English and a direct, vigorous sentence style rather than jargon and convoluted sentence syntax.

Conclusion

Create a bookend for your introduction by reinforcing your main idea and supporting points, re-emphasizing the importance of the ideas, and reviewing for your audience what they might take away from your presentation in terms of new understanding, changed attitudes, or possible actions. In addition, you might outline where listeners can access additional information. Finally, make sure that your conclusion also thanks the audience.

Sample Speech

Dr. Martin Luther King, Jr., was a leader in the Civil Rights Movement during the 1950s and 1960s. On August 28, 1963, he delivered this persuasive speech to a crowd of 250,000 people gathered at the Lincoln Memorial in Washington, D.C.

I Have a Dream

King starts with a tragic contrast.

Five score years ago, a great American, in whose symbolic shadow we stand, signed the Emancipation Proclamation. This momentous decree came as a great beacon light of hope to millions of Negro slaves who had been seared in the flames of withering injustice. It came as a joyous daybreak to end the long night of captivity.

He uses figurative language to describe the present situation.

But one hundred years later, we must face the tragic fact that the Negro is still not free. One hundred years later, the life of the Negro is still sadly crippled by the manacles of segregation and the chains of discrimination. One hundred years later, the Negro lives on a lonely island of poverty in the midst of a vast ocean of material prosperity. One hundred years later, the Negro is still languishing in the corners of American society and finds himself an exile in his own land. So we have come here today to dramatize an appalling condition.

An analogy clarifies the problem.

In a sense we have come to our nation's Capitol to cash a check. When the architects of our republic wrote the magnificent words of the Constitution and the Declaration of Independence, they were signing a promissory note to which every American was to fall heir. This note was a promise that all men would be guaranteed the unalienable rights of life, liberty, and the pursuit of happiness.

It is obvious today that America has defaulted on this promissory note insofar as her citizens of color are concerned. Instead of honoring this sacred obligation, America has given the Negro people a bad check; a check which has come back marked "insufficient funds." But we refuse to believe that the bank of justice is bankrupt. We refuse to believe that there are insufficient funds in the great vaults of opportunity of this nation. So we have come to cash this check—a check that will give us upon demand the riches of freedom and the security of justice. We have also come to this hallowed spot to remind America of the fierce urgency of now. This is no time to engage in the luxury of cooling off or to take the tranquilizing drug of gradualism. Now is the time to make real the promises of Democracy. Now is the time to rise from the dark and desolate valley of segregation to the sunlit path of racial justice. Now is the time to open the doors of opportunity to all of God's children. Now is the time to lift our nation from the quicksands of racial injustice to the solid rock of brotherhood.

Repeated words and phrases create urgency.

It would be fatal for the nation to overlook the urgency of the moment and   5
to underestimate the determination of the Negro. This sweltering summer of the
Negro's legitimate discontent will not pass until there is an invigorating autumn of
freedom and equality. 1963 is not an end, but a beginning. Those who hope that the
Negro needed to blow off steam and will now be content will have a rude awakening
if the nation returns to business as usual. There will be neither rest nor tranquility in
America until the Negro is granted his citizenship rights. The whirlwinds of revolt
will continue to shake the foundations of our nation until the bright day of justice
emerges.

King addresses specific audiences in turn.

But there is something I must say to my people who stand on the warm   6
threshold which leads into the palace of justice. In the process of gaining our
rightful place we must not be guilty of wrongful deeds. Let us not seek to satisfy
our thirst for freedom by drinking from the cup of bitterness and hatred. We must
forever conduct our struggle on the high plane of dignity and discipline. We must
not allow our creative protest to degenerate into physical violence. Again and again
we must rise to the majestic heights of meeting physical force with soul force. The
marvelous new militancy which has engulfed the Negro community must not lead
us to a distrust of all white people, for many of our white brothers, as evidenced by
their presence here today, have come to realize that their destiny is tied up with our
destiny and their freedom is inextricably bound to our freedom. We cannot walk
alone.

He responds to the arguments of opponents.

And as we talk, we must make the pledge that we shall march ahead. We cannot   7
turn back. There are those who are asking the devotees of civil rights, "When will
you be satisfied?" We can never be satisfied as long as the Negro is the victim of the
unspeakable horrors of police brutality. We can never be satisfied as long as our
bodies, heaving with the fatigue of travel, cannot gain lodging in the motels of the
highways and the hotels of the cities. We cannot be satisfied as long as the Negro's
basic mobility is from a smaller ghetto to a larger one. We can never be satisfied as
long as a Negro in Mississippi cannot vote and a Negro in New York believes he has
nothing for which to vote. No, no, we are not satisfied, and we will not be satisfied
until justice rolls down like waters and righteousness like a mighty stream.

Appropriate emotional appeals are used in the context of suffering.

I am not unmindful that some of you have come here out of great trials and   8
tribulations. Some of you have come fresh from narrow jail cells. Some of you have
come from areas where your quest for freedom left you battered by the storms
of persecution and staggered by the winds of police brutality. You have been the
veterans of creative suffering. Continue to work with the faith that unearned
suffering is redemptive.

Go back to Mississippi, go back to Alabama, go back to South Carolina, go back 9
to Georgia, go back to Louisiana, go back to the slums and ghettos of our northern
cities, knowing that somehow this situation can and will be changed. Let us not
wallow in the valley of despair.

I say to you today, my friends, that in spite of the difficulties and frustrations of 10
the moment I still have a dream. It is a dream deeply rooted in the American dream.

I have a dream that one day this nation will rise up and live out the true 11
meaning of its creed: "We hold these truths to be self-evident; that all men are
created equal."

I have a dream that one day on the red hills of Georgia the sons of former slaves 12
and the sons of former slaveowners will be able to sit down together at the table of
brotherhood.

> The repetition of key phrases becomes a persuasive refrain.

I have a dream that the state of Mississippi, a desert state sweltering with the 13
heat of injustice and oppression, will be transformed into an oasis of freedom and
justice.

I have a dream that my four little children will one day live in a nation 14
where they will not be judged by the color of their skin but by the content of their
character.

> King's vision offers hope and motivates readers to change society.

I have a dream today. 15

I have a dream that the state of Alabama, whose governor's lips are presently 16
dripping with the words of interposition and nullification, will be transformed into
a situation where little black boys and black girls will be able to join hands with little
white boys and girls and walk together as sisters and brothers.

I have a dream today. 17

I have a dream that one day every valley shall be exalted, every hill and 18
mountain shall be made low, the rough places will be made plain, and the crooked
places will be made straight, and the glory of the Lord shall be revealed, and all flesh
shall see it together.

This is our hope. This is the faith with which I return to the South. With this 19
faith we will be able to hew out of the mountain of despair a stone of hope. With this
faith we will be able to transform the jangling discords of our nation into a beautiful
symphony of brotherhood. With this faith we will be able to work together, to pray
together, to struggle together, to go to jail together, to stand up for freedom together,
knowing that we will be free one day.

This will be the day when all God's children will be able to sing with new 20
meaning.

He appeals to ideals and to humanity's better nature, ending with a vision of a just society.

My country 'tis of thee   21
Sweet land of liberty,
Of thee I sing,
Land where my fathers died,
Land of the pilgrims' pride,
From every mountainside
Let freedom ring.

And if America is to be a great nation this must become true. So let freedom   22
ring from the prodigious hilltops of New Hampshire. Let freedom ring from the
mighty mountains of New York. Let freedom ring from the heightening Alleghenies
of Pennsylvania!

Let freedom ring from the snow-capped Rockies of Colorado! Let freedom ring   23
from the curvaceous peaks of California!   24

But not only that; let freedom ring from Stone Mountain of Georgia!   25

Let freedom ring from Lookout Mountain of Tennessee!   26

Let freedom ring from every hill and molehill of Mississippi! From every   27
mountainside, let freedom ring.

The closing urges readers to work for a better future.

When we let freedom ring, when we let it ring from every village and every   28
hamlet, from every state and every city, we will be able to speed up that day when
all of God's children, black men and white men, Jews and Gentiles, Protestants and
Catholics, will be able to join hands and sing in the words of the old Negro spiritual,
"Free at last! Free at last! Thank God almighty, we are free at last!"

Reading for Better Writing

Working by yourself or with a group, answer these questions:

1. King is actually speaking to several audiences at the same time. Who are these different audiences? How does King address each?
2. For what specific changes does King call? What does he want his listeners to do?
3. Explore the writer's style. How does he use religious imagery, comparisons, and analogies? How does repetition function as a persuasive technique?
4. In a sense, King's speech addresses a gap between reality and an ideal. How does he present this gap?

Follow-up: Find and listen to a recording of King's speech online. What happens when the words you have read on the page are spoken by King? What lessons can you take away about the spoken word in relation to the written word?

Using Presentation Software Effectively

Presentation software can aid an effective presentation, but should not be considered a substitute for it. With the popularity of presentation software such as PowerPoint, certain bad habits have crept into presentation practices. As you consider using presentation software to develop and deliver you presentation, avoid these pitfalls:

1. Reducing your thinking to a list of bulleted points.
2. Filling your slides with small, dense text without visual relief.
3. Reading slide after slide to your audience.

Should you use presentation software for your research presentation? If yes, how should you use it? Start with the advice below.

Enhance Your Oral Presentation with Slides

An effectively developed slide show can deepen and strengthen your speaking in several ways. Use slides to do the following:

- *Feature your main points:* Slides can forecast what your presentation will cover and can highlight the main points as you proceed. Consider, for example, how your opening slide can identify your presentation, set the tone, and identify your focus and approach. Similarly, your last slide can review the territory you have covered and help your audience apply the ideas to their own situations.
- *Share complex information:* While you don't want slides to be dense with text or numbers, slides can effectively share information that might be too hard to process by only hearing it. For example, tables can illustrate comparisons, or two images can be placed side by side for a discussion of their links.
- *Control the flow of ideas:* With its slide structure and animation tools (dissolves, fades, wipes, etc.), you can focus listeners' attention on one point, gradually unfolding your points so that relationships become clear. However, make sure that the tools you use are not distracting.
- *Add multimedia impact to your ideas:* Use photos, illustrations, charts, and diagrams to visually enhance slides and provide information not communicated through your words alone. In addition, you can link to or embed audio and video files to provide illustrations, examples, and demonstrations.
- *Create a tone:* The colours, background features, and animation all create a mood for your presentation—from lighthearted and humorous to scholarly and serious.

Sample Presentation Slides

The slides on the next page come from the methods section of the student presentation, "Sewage Contamination in the Chedoke Creek Watershed." (The full report on which the presentation is based is available in the online chapter on science writing.) These slides show an effective use of presentation software's possibilities. Text is kept to a minimum as reference points for talking; visuals offer a focused form of information that complements spoken words and creates an opportunity for explanation; and the slide's design conveys a tone fitting the subject matter.

Opening Slide: The first slide in the methods section provides a clear overview and uses a visual to set the scene of the research.

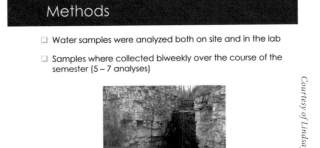

Middle Slide: A middle slide offers textual and visual information that enhances the spoken presentation.

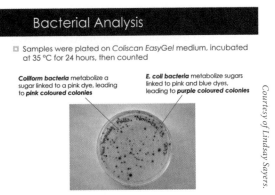

Closing Slide: The final slide identifies in summary fashion other elements of the research performed.

Other Analyses Performed

- Total Alkalinity
- Conductivity (Total dissolved solids)
- Turbidity (Suspended solids)
- Sulfate
- Ion selective electrodes (Chloride, Calcium)
- Atomic emission spectroscopy (Calcium, Sodium)

Courtesy of Lindsay Sayers.

Delivering Your Presentation

A presentation involves much more than creating a script: you need to effectively deliver that script by bringing it to life through communicating with the audience. To do so, consider the tips below.

Rehearse Your Presentation

Whatever format you choose for the script (list, outline, manuscript), carefully rehearse your presentation for clarity, emphasis, and pacing. If you are using a microphone, handouts, projections, or other visuals, include these elements in your rehearsal. When you practise, time your presentation and adjust it to fit within your allotted time. In addition, record your presentation or have a classmate or friend offer feedback on your rehearsal: doing so will give you a more objective view of your presentation's content and delivery.

Get Set Up Prior to Your Presentation

If possible, test the room and equipment prior to your presentation. Check the following:

- Are tables and chairs set up in an arrangement that will work?
- Is your equipment set up so that you can deliver your presentation comfortably (from lectern or otherwise), without blocking the audience's view of the screen?
- Is the AV hardware and software working, and are the visual elements ready to go?
- Is your script in the right order and in place?
- Do you have drinking water?

Be Professional and Engaging

As you deliver your presentation, aim to communicate in a clear and engaging manner:

- Be confident, positive, and energetic in your speaking; don't rush, mumble, or trail off. Remember the listeners at the back of the room.
- Maintain eye contact with various listeners around the room; avoid constantly looking down at your script.
- Use gestures and movement during your presentation in a natural way; maintain good posture.
- Provide for audience participation, even if in a small way (e.g., a show of hands in response to a question).
- If your audience looks confused, pause, reword, and clarify your discussion. Improvise an illustration, example, or comparison.

Demiro/Shutterstock.com

Effectively Manage Discussion and Q&A

As part of your planning, you first need to decide whether to lay out your presentation in full and then have discussion, or whether to have more of a dialogue along the way. Next, practise effective strategies for leading a discussion and answering questions in a Q&A session.

Generating and Leading Discussion: Managing discussion during a presentation is largely reliant on the art of asking good questions. Consider these strategies:

- Sometimes, move from basic questions (establishing that we are all on the same page) to more complex questions of meaning and interpretation.
- Tap the range of questions available, centring them on your purpose: who, what, when, where, why, and how (noting that the last two tend to probe more complex issues).
- If fitting, ask for alternative conclusions and perspectives to the ones being offered: create a space for alternative or opposing voices. If you can do so in a helpful manner, play "devil's advocate."
- Be flexible enough that you can ask follow-up and deeper-probing questions.
- As discussion unfolds, be alert to connections, contrasts, further evidence of the point, and contrary evidence that may lead to further questions.

Holding a Q&A Session after Your Presentation: A Q&A session is a good opportunity for the group to clarify, elaborate, and apply points from your discussion. Be prepared to pose a question or two yourself if no one asks one. Respond to questions by following these tips:

- Listen carefully, think about each part of the question, and repeat or rephrase the question for the whole group, if needed.
- Answer the question concisely, clearly, and honestly. Avoid rambling, but make your answer a kind of dialogue or exploration with the questioner and the audience. Look directly at the questioner when answering, but also look to your whole audience as your answer unfolds.

Sergey Nivens/Shutterstock.com

Critical-Thinking and Writing Activities

As directed by your instructor, complete the following activities.

1. Dale Carnegie, a well-known expert on public speaking, once said, "There is only one excuse for a speaker's asking the attention of his audience: he must have either truth or entertainment for them." Reflect on this claim: what are a public speaker's responsibilities toward his or her audience? toward the truth?

2. Select one of the sample essays, either student or professional, in this part of *Writing Life*. Read that essay with an eye to turning it into a presentation. Then transform it from a written text to a presentation outline, doing so by tapping your own creativity, conducting any additional research needed, and finding or developing appropriate multimedia elements.

3. Review an essay or report that you have written recently. Consider what it would take to build a presentation based on that written document. Then develop an engaging speech on the topic, deliver that speech to your classmates, and gather their feedback on the quality of your delivery.

Learning-Objectives Checklist ✓

Have you achieved this chapter's learning objectives? Check your progress with the items below, revisiting topics in the chapter as needed. *I have . . .*

___ planned a presentation by analyzing the situation (topic, purpose, audience, and context), choosing a fitting format (list, outline, or manuscript), selecting multimedia elements, and considering tips for an effective presentation.

___ composed a presentation with an introduction that engages the audience and quickly focuses on my topic, a body that shapes my essential message into a sequence of three or four manageable key points, and a conclusion that reinforces my main point.

___ developed slides using presentation software that enhance my oral delivery by supplying structure, featuring key and complex information, controlling the flow of ideas, adding multimedia impact, and setting a tone.

___ delivered my presentation by first rehearsing it, setting up the room effectively, being professional and engaging, and managing the discussion and Q&A well.

III. Research and Writing

Chapter 21

Getting Started: From Planning Research to Evaluating Sources

At first glance, research looks like a dry-as-dust business carried out by obsessed scholars in dim libraries and mad scientists in cluttered laboratories. Research couldn't be further from the reality of your life.

But is it? Consider car tires. Before these were mounted, scientists researched which materials would resist wear and which adhesives would keep treads on steel belts. Sloppy research could cause blowouts; good research builds safe tires.

For you, the rewards of research projects can be great—new insights into a subject that really interests you, a deepened understanding of your major or profession, reliable knowledge to share with others, and sharpened thinking skills. This chapter will help you get started on such a project.

Visually Speaking   Figure 21.1 shows one form of research in action. Study the details. What does this image suggest about research? What other images would capture other dimensions of research today?

Learning **Objectives**

By working through this chapter, you will be able to

- interpret the rhetorical situation for research.
- identify the phases of the research process.
- focus a research assignment into a manageable project.
- identify primary, secondary, and tertiary sources.
- generate a research plan.
- choose different information resources and sites.
- perform keyword searches.
- examine and evaluate print and digital resources.
- produce a working bibliography.
- choose a note-taking system.
- summarize, paraphrase, and quote source material.

kurhan/Shutterstock.com

fig. 21.1

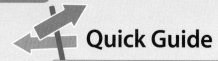

Quick Guide

Papers with Documented Research

When you work on a research project, you ask important questions, look systematically for answers, and share your conclusions with readers. The rhetorical situation for such a project centres on the writer's purpose of inquiring into a topic so as to advance understanding for him- or herself and the reader. In other words, it's all about curiosity, discovery, and dialogue.

- **Starting Point:** The assignment usually relates to a course concept, so consider what your instructor wants you to learn and how your project will be evaluated. Then take ownership of the project by looking for an angle that makes the writing relevant for you.

- **Purpose:** The project requires you to conduct research and share results. Your main goal is to discover the complex truth about a topic and clarify that discovery for others.

- **Form:** The traditional research paper is a fairly long essay (5 to 15 pages) complete with thesis, supporting paragraphs, integrated sources, and careful documentation. However, you may be asked to shape your research into a field report, a website, or a multimedia presentation.

- **Audience:** Traditionally, research writing addresses "the academic community," a group made up mainly of instructors and students. However, your actual audience may be more specific: addicted smokers, all Albertans, fellow immigrants, and so on.

- **Voice:** The tone is usually formal or semiformal, but check your instructor's expectations. In any research writing, maintain a thoughtful, confidently measured tone. After all, your research has made you somewhat of an authority on the topic.

- **Point of View:** Generally, research writers avoid the pronouns "I" and "you" in an effort to remain properly objective and academic sounding. Unfortunately, this practice can result in an overuse of both the pronoun "one" and the passive voice. Some instructors encourage students to connect research with experience, meaning that you may use the pronouns "I" and "you" occasionally. Be careful, however, to keep the focus where it belongs—on the topic. Bottom line: Follow your instructor's requirements concerning pronoun use. For more on developing a strong academic style for your research writing, see pages 79–81.

INSIGHT   The best research writing centres on your ideas—ideas you develop through thoughtful engagement with sources. In poor research papers, the sources dominate, and the writer's perspective disappears.

The Research Process: A Flowchart

The research process involves getting started, planning, conducting the research, and organizing the results. This process is flexible enough to be adapted to diverse research projects. In fact, real research is typically dynamic: You might think during the planning phase that you've nailed down your topic, only to discover a surprising topical detour while conducting research. Generally, however, the research process maps out as shown in Figure 21.2. When you get your assignment—whether to write a five-page paper on pasteurization or to develop a website on Middle Eastern political conflicts—review the process and tailor it to the task.

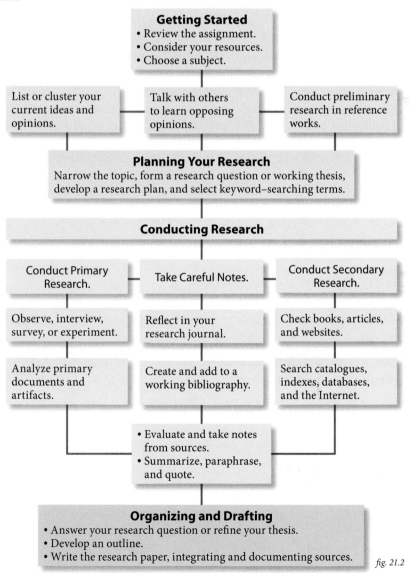

fig. 21.2

Getting Focused

Early in your project, get focused by narrowing your topic, brainstorming research questions, and developing a working thesis. For help understanding assignments and selecting topics, as well as other prewriting strategies, see pages 32–37.

Establish a Narrow, Manageable Topic

To do good research, you need an engaging, manageable topic. Once you have a broad topic, narrow your focus to a specific feature or angle that allows for in-depth research. Try these strategies:

- **Check your topic in the Library of Congress subject headings, available in your library in print.** An online version is available at classificationweb.net (a subscription service) or at authorities.loc.gov (free). Note "narrower terms" listed (see page 416).
- **Read about your topic.** By consulting specialized reference works, explore background that directs you to subtopics (see page 447).
- **Check the Internet.** For example, follow a subject directory to see where your topic leads (see pages 448–451).
- **Freewrite to discover which aspect of the topic interests you most:** a local angle, a connection with a group of people, or a personal concern.

Broad Topic	**Manageable Focus**
Homelessness	Homeless Families in Vancouver
The North-West Rebellion of 1885	The aftermath of the Rebellion for the Métis
Alternative Energy Sources	Hydrogen Fuel-Cell Vehicles

Brainstorm Research Questions

Good research questions help you find meaningful information and ideas about your topic. These questions sharpen your research goal, and the answers will become the focus of your writing. Brainstorm questions by following these guidelines:

List both simple and substantial questions. Basic questions aim for factual answers. More complex questions get at analysis, synthesis, and evaluation.

- **Question of fact:** How long did Kim Jong Il rule North Korea?
- **Question of interpretation:** How did Kim Jong Il maintain power?

List main and secondary questions. Ask a primary question about your topic—the main issue that you want to get at. Then brainstorm secondary questions that you need to research to answer your primary question.

- **Main Question:** Should consumers buy hydrogen fuel-cell cars?
- **Secondary Questions (Who, What, When, Where, Why, How):** Who has developed hydrogen fuel-cell cars? What is a hydrogen fuel-cell car? When were these cars developed? Where are hydrogen fuel-cell cars currently used? Why are they being developed? How does one work?

Testing Your Main Research Question

_____ Is the question so broad that I can't answer it in the project's time and page limits?

_____ Is the question so narrow that I won't be able to find sources?

_____ Is the question so simple that it will be too easy to answer?

_____ Will the question lead to significant sources and intellectual challenge?

_____ Am I committed to answering this question? Does it interest me?

_____ Will the question and answers interest my readers?

Develop a Working Thesis

A working thesis offers a preliminary answer to your main research question. As your initial perspective on the topic, a good working thesis keeps you focused during research, helping you decide whether to carefully read a particular book or just skim it, fully explore a website or quickly browse through it. Make your working thesis a statement that demands "Prove it!" Don't settle for a simple statement of fact about your topic; instead, choose a working thesis that seems debatable or that requires some explanation. Try this formula:

Formula:

Working Thesis = limited topic + tentative claim, statement, or hypothesis

Examples:

E-communication technologies are rewiring our brains.

Downtown revitalization in Saint John will have distinct economic, environmental, and social benefits.

The defeat of the Métis in the North-West Rebellion of 1885 led to a long-term struggle to gain their basic rights.

Working Thesis Checklist

_____ Does my working thesis focus on a single, limited topic?

_____ Is my working thesis stated in a clear, direct sentence?

_____ Does my working thesis convey my initial perspective about the topic?

_____ Do I have access to enough good information to support this working thesis?

_____ Does my working thesis direct me to write a paper that meets all assignment requirements?

INSIGHT Your working thesis is written in sand, not stone. It may change as you research the topic because sources may push you in new directions. In fact, such change shows that you are engaging your sources and growing in your thinking.

Understanding Primary, Secondary, and Tertiary Sources

Information sources for your project can be primary, secondary, or tertiary, depending on their nearness to your topic. With your course assignments, you will likely be expected to rely upon primary and secondary sources, not tertiary sources. As part of project planning, then, you need to understand the distinction between primary, secondary, and tertiary sources.

Primary Sources

A primary source is an original source, one that gives first-hand information on a topic: the source is close to the issue or question. This source (such as a log, a person, a document, or an event) informs you directly about the topic, not through another person's explanation or interpretation. Common primary sources are observations, interviews, surveys, experiments, documents, and artifacts. Frequently, you generate the primary source yourself; sometimes, that primary information is available in published form.

> *Example:* For a project on Jane Austen's *Pride and Prejudice* in fiction and film, these sources would be primary: the text of the novel itself, the 2005 film adaptation of the novel, Jane Austen's letters, and an interview with a screenwriter who adapts novels into films.
>
> **Strengths of Primary Research:** Primary sources produce information precisely tailored to your research needs, giving you direct, hands-on access to your topic. If, for example, you were researching the impact of tornadoes on communities, interviews with survivors would provide information directly tailored to your project.
>
> **Downsides of Primary Research:** Primary research can take a lot of time and many resources, as well as specialized skills (e.g., designing surveys and analyzing statistics).

Secondary Sources

Secondary sources present information one step removed from the origin: information has been collected, compiled, summarized, analyzed, synthesized, interpreted, and evaluated by someone studying primary sources and other secondary sources. Scholarly studies, journal articles, and documentaries are typical examples of such resources. Typically, you track down secondary resources in your library, through library databases, and on the free Web (see pages 443–461).

> *Example:* For a project on Jane Austen's *Pride and Prejudice* in fiction and film, these sources would be secondary: books and articles by scholars on Austen and on film, literary biographies about Austen's life, and film reviews.

Strengths of Secondary Research: Good secondary sources—especially scholarly ones that have gone through a peer review process—offer quality information in the form of expert perspectives on and analysis of your topic. As such, secondary sources can save you plenty of research labour while providing you with extensive data. In addition, secondary sources can help you see your topic from multiple angles through multiple perspectives; they can tell you the story of research done on your topic.

Downside of Secondary Research: Because secondary research isn't written solely with you and your project in mind, you may need to do some digging to find relevant data. Moreover, the information that you do find may be filtered through the researcher's bias. In fact, the original research related through the secondary source may be faulty, a point suggesting that the quality of secondary sources can vary greatly (especially on the free Web). Finally, because knowledge about your topic can grow or radically change over time, secondary sources can become dated.

Tertiary Sources

Some resources are tertiary—essentially reports of reports of research. That is, writers of tertiary sources are not reporting on the primary research they themselves have done but are compiling information based on their reading of secondary sources. Examples of tertiary sources would include some articles in popular magazines and entries in Wikipedia (see pages 458–459).

Example: For a project on Jane Austen's *Pride and Prejudice* in fiction and film, these sources would be tertiary: an online discussion group exchanging thoughts on a recent Austen biography and a Wikipedia entry on Austen.

Upside of Tertiary Research: Tertiary sources are typically easy to find, easy to access, and easy to read. Note, for example, that a free-Web search of a specific topic frequently lists a Wikipedia entry in the first ten items. Used cautiously, such tertiary sources can serve as one starting point for your research—to find basic facts that you'll likely have to verify elsewhere, some ideas for narrowing your topic, or some leads and links for further research.

Downside of Tertiary Research: The main weakness of tertiary sources is their distance from the original research and information. Because the information and ideas have been passed along in this way, the possibility of error, distortion, gaps, and over-simplification of complex issues is greater than with primary and secondary sources. Generally, tertiary sources lack the reliability and depth necessary for academic research projects.

 Whether a source is primary, secondary, or tertiary often depends on what your focused topic is. For example, if you were studying why power brown-outs happen during heat waves, a newspaper editorial on the topic would be secondary. But if you were focusing on public attitudes toward and responses to brown-outs, the editorial might prove primary. In other words, a given source is not always primary or always secondary: proximity depends on the research context.

Developing a Research Plan

It pays to plan your research, including decisions about primary, secondary, and tertiary sources. In fact, minutes spent planning research can save hours doing research. With your limited topic, main research question, and working thesis in front of you, plan your project more fully using the research tips on the next two pages.

Choose Research Methods

Consider these questions: What do you already know about the topic? What do you need to know? Which resources will help you answer your research question? Which resources does the assignment require? Based on your answers, map out a research plan that draws resources from fitting categories.

Background research: To find information about your topic's context, central concepts, and key terms, take these steps:
- Use the Library of Congress subject headings to find keywords for searching the library catalogue, periodical databases, and the Internet (see page 416).
- Conduct a preliminary search of the library catalogue, journal databases, and the Internet to confirm that good resources on your topic exist.
- Use specialized reference works to find background information, definitions, facts, and statistics (see page 447).

Field or primary research: If appropriate for your project, conduct field research:
- Use interviews (pages 440–441) or surveys (pages 436–437) to get key information from experts or others.
- Conduct observations or experiments (page 442) to obtain hard data.
- Analyze key documents or artifacts (pages 438–439).

Library research: Select important library resources:
- Use scholarly books to get in-depth, reliable material (pages 443–447).
- Use periodical articles (print or electronic) to get current, reliable information (pages 443–451). Select from news sources, popular magazines, scholarly journals, and trade journals.
- Consider other library resources, such as a documentary, recorded interview, pamphlet, marketing study, or government publication.

Free-Web research: Plan effective free-Web searches using the following:
- Search engines and subject guides: Choose tools that will lead you to quality resources (pages 454–457).
- Expert guidance: Select reputable websites that librarians or other experts recommend (page 460).
- Evaluation: Test all Web resources for reliability (pages 461–463).
- Limitations: How many Web resources are you allowed to use, if any?

Get Organized to Do Research

An organized approach to doing your research will save you time, help you work efficiently, and prevent frustration. Get organized by addressing these issues:

Establishing Priorities for Resources, Time, and Effort

- How much research material do you need?
- What range of resources will give you quality, reliable information?
- Which types of research does the assignment specify? Are you limited, for example, in the number of Internet sources you can use?
- What are the project's priorities: What must you do? Which tasks are secondary in nature?
- What weight does the project carry in the course? How should you match your time and effort with that weight?

INSIGHT   Gather more information than you could ever use in your paper. That richness gives you choices and allows you to sift for crucial information.

Selecting Research Methods and Systems

- **Given the resources and technologies available, select methods that help you do research efficiently:** signing out hard-copy library holdings or using interlibrary loan; photocopying book sections and journal articles; printing, saving, downloading, bookmarking, or emailing digital materials.
- **Develop a note-taking system.** Choose from the note-card, double-entry notebook, copy-and-annotate, and research-log methods (pages 424–427). In addition, set up a working bibliography (pages 422–423).
- **Choose and review a documentation system.** It's likely that your instructor will designate a system such as MLA (pages 493–534) or APA (pages 535–564). If he or she doesn't do so, then use a method that suits the subject matter and discipline. Review the system's basic rules and strategies.

Establishing a Schedule

The time frame for completing a research project obviously varies from one assignment to the next. What you have to work with is the time frame between getting the assignment and turning in the project at the deadline, whether that time frame is two weeks or two months, along with any intermediate deadlines set by your instructor for specific phases of the project (e.g., topic selection, project proposal, working bibliography, first draft). Generally, however, you should spend about half your time on research and half on writing. To stay on track, sketch out a preliminary schedule with tentative deadlines for completing each phase of your work.

A schedule template is available at www.nelson.com/writinglife

Writing a Research Proposal

For some research projects, you may need to submit a proposal early in the process. The proposal seeks to explain what you plan to research, why, and how. Such a proposal has several aims: (1) to show that the research is valid (makes good scholarly sense), (2) to argue that the research is valuable (will lead to significant knowledge), (3) to communicate your enthusiasm for the project, and (4) to demonstrate that your plan is workable within the constraints of the assignment—all in order to gain your instructor's feedback and approval. Note the parts modelled in the sample proposal.

Understand the Parts of a Research Proposal

1. **Introduction:** In a brief paragraph, state your research idea, explaining why the topic is important and worth researching. Provide any background information that the instructor may need.

2. **Description:** Discuss your proposed research topic by identifying the central issue or concern about the topic, indicating the main question that you want to answer through research, listing secondary questions that relate to the main question, stating a working thesis or hypothesis in response to the main question, and explaining the research outcomes that you expect from the study.

3. **Plan (methods and procedures):** Explain how you plan to answer your questions, how you plan to research your topic. Include an explanation of your primary research (the "firsthand" investigation), a description of research tools you plan to use (e.g., catalogues, reference works, lab equipment, survey software), and a working bibliography indicating your initial survey of resources.

4. **Schedule:** List deadlines that are part of the assignment and deadlines that you've set for yourself.

5. **Approval Request:** Ask for feedback and approval from your instructor.

Sample Research Proposal

The research proposal below offers a student's plan for analyzing Jane Austen's *Pride and Prejudice*, both the novel and a film adaptation.

Film Studies 201 Proposal:
Jane Austen's *Pride and Prejudice* as Fiction and Film
Gwendolyn Mackenzie

Nearly 200 years after her death, Jane Austen's novels still captivate readers, filmmakers, and filmgoers—including me. For my research paper, I will explore one aspect of this phenomenon within *Pride and Prejudice* and the 2005 film adaptation directed by Joe Wright.

Description: Specifically, I want to see how the novel and film explore gender prejudice. My main research question is, What sense do these texts make of prejudice as it relates to

---

relationships between men and women? My working thesis is that the 2005 film portrayal of gender inequality in *Pride and Prejudice* highlights and intensifies the issue of gender inequality introduced in the novel.

This study of gender prejudice will allow me (1) to appreciate the treatment of this theme in fiction and in film, (2) to understand film adaptations more fully, and (3) to explain in a small way the Jane Austen phenomenon. As part of the project, I will write a 6-8 page paper.

Plan: My primary research will involve rereading the novel and reviewing the 2005 film adaptation. In terms of secondary research, I have done an initial search of our library's catalogue and of EBSCOhost for books and articles. This is my working bibliography:

Primary Sources

Austen, Jane. *Pride and Prejudice: An Authoritative Text, Background and Sources, Criticism.* Ed. Donald J. Gray. New York: Norton, 2001. Print.

Wright, Joe, dir. *Pride and Prejudice.* Universal Pictures, 2005. Film.

Secondary Sources

Cartmell, Deborah, and Imelda Whelehan. *Adaptations: From Text to Screen, Screen to Text.* London: Routledge, 2004. Print.

Crusie, Jennifer. *Flirting with* Pride and Prejudice: *Fresh Perspectives on the Original Chick-Lit Masterpiece.* Dallas: BenBella, 2005. Print.

Grandi, Roberta. "The Passion Translated: Literary and Cinematic Rhetoric in *Pride and Prejudice* (2005)." *Literature Film Quarterly* 36.1 (2008): 45-51. Print.

McFarlane, Brian. "Something Old, Something New: 'Pride and Prejudice' on Screen." *Screen Education* (2005): 6-14. Print.

Stovel, Nora Foster. "From Page to Screen: Dancing to the Altar in Recent Film Adaptations of Jane Austen's Novels." *Persuasions: The Jane Austen Journal* (2006): 185-98. EBSCOhost. Web. 6 Nov. 2013.

Sutherland, Kathryn. *Jane Austen's Textual Lives: From Aeschylus to Bollywood.* Oxford: Oxford UP, 2007. Print.

Todd, Janet M. *The Cambridge Introduction to Jane Austen.* Cambridge: Cambridge UP, 2006. NetLibrary. Web. 6 Nov. 2013.

Schedule: Here is my schedule for completing this project:

1. Finish rereading the novel and reviewing the film: November 14.
2. Complete secondary research: November 20.
3. Develop outline for paper: November 23.
4. Finish first draft of paper: November 30.
5. Revise, edit, and proofread paper: December 4.
6. Submit paper: December 6.

Approval Request: Dr. Rajan, I would appreciate your feedback on my proposed project, as well as your approval of my plan.

Exploring Information Resources and Sites

To conduct thorough, creative, but efficient research, you need a sense of which types of resources are available for your project and where to find them. Check the tables that follow.

Consider Different Information Resources

Examine the range of resources available: Which will give you the best information for your project? While one project (for example, a sociological report on airport behaviours) might require personal, direct sources, another project (for example, the effects of the 9/11 terrorist attacks on the air transportation industry) might depend on government reports, business publications, and journal articles. Generally, a well-rounded research paper relies on a range of quality resources; in particular, it avoids relying on insubstantial Web information.

fig. 21.3

Type of Resource	Examples
Personal, direct resources	Memories, diaries, journals, logs, experiments, tests, observations, interviews, surveys
Reference works (print and electronic)	Dictionaries, thesauruses, encyclopedias, almanacs, yearbooks, atlases, directories, guides, handbooks, indexes, abstracts, catalogues, bibliographies
Books (print and electronic)	Nonfiction, how-to, biographies, fiction, trade books, scholarly and scientific studies
Periodicals and news sources	Print newspapers, magazines, and journals; broadcast news and news magazines; online magazines, news sources, and discussion groups
Audiovisual, digital, and multimedia resources	Graphics (tables, graphs, charts, maps, drawings, photos), audiotapes, CDs, videos, DVDs, Web pages, online databases
Government publications	Guides, programs, forms, legislation, regulations, reports, records, statistics
Business and nonprofit publications	Correspondence, reports, newsletters, pamphlets, brochures, ads, catalogues, instructions, handbooks, manuals, policies and procedures, seminar and training materials

Consider Different Information Sites

Where do you go to find the resources that you need? Consider the information "sites" listed below, remembering that many resources may be available in different forms in different locations. For example, a journal article may be available in library holdings or in an electronic database.

fig. 21.4

Information Location	Specific "Sites"
People	Experts (knowledge area, skill, occupation) Population segments or individuals (with representative or unusual experiences)
Libraries	General: public, school, online Specialized: legal, medical, government, business
Computer resources	Computers: software, disks Networks: Internet and other online services (email, limited-access databases, discussion, groups, MUDs, chat rooms, websites, blogs, YouTube, Twitter, image banks, wikis); intranets
Mass media	Radio (AM and FM) Television (network, public, cable, satellite, Internet) Print (newspapers, magazines, journals)
Testing, training, meeting, and observation sites	Plants, facilities, field sites, laboratories Research centres, universities, think tanks Conventions, conferences, seminars Museums, galleries, historical sites
Municipal, provincial, territorial and federal government offices	Elected city officials, members of Parliament and of provincial and territorial legislatures, Offices and agencies Government websites (e.g., www.canada.gc.ca/home.html for Canada, www.gpoaccess.gov for U.S.)
Business and nonprofit publications	Computer databases, company files Desktop reference materials Bulletin boards (physical and electronic) Company and department websites Departments and offices Associations, professional organizations Consulting, training, and business information services

Conducting Effective Keyword Searches

Keyword searching can help you find information in electronic library catalogues, online databases that index periodical articles (for example, EBSCOhost), print indexes to periodical publications (for example, *Business Periodicals Index*), Internet resources, print books, and ebooks. Learn to choose keywords and use specific search strategies.

Choose Keywords Carefully

Keywords give you "compass points" for navigating through a sea of information. That's why choosing the best keywords is crucial. Consider these tips:

1. **Brainstorm a list of possible keywords**—topics, titles, and names—based on your current knowledge and/or background reading.

2. **Consult the Library of Congress subject headings.** These headings, available in print or online at classificationweb.net (subscription) or at authorities.loc.gov (free), contain the keywords librarians use when classifying materials. For example, if you looked up *immigrants*, you would find the entry below, indicating keywords to use and tips to follow (including that the topic may subdivide geographically), along with narrower, related, and broader terms. When you are conducting subject searches of catalogues and databases, these are the terms that will get you the best results.

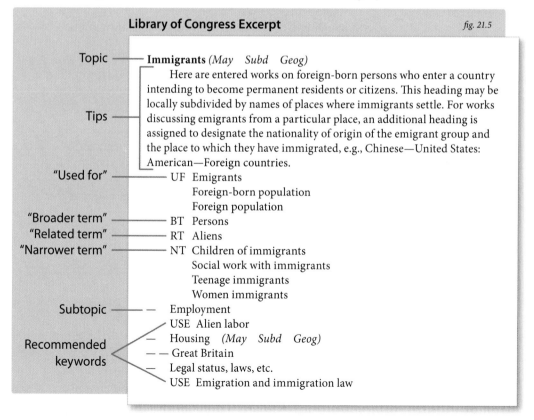

Library of Congress Excerpt   *fig. 21.5*

Topic —— **Immigrants** *(May Subd Geog)*

Tips —— Here are entered works on foreign-born persons who enter a country intending to become permanent residents or citizens. This heading may be locally subdivided by names of places where immigrants settle. For works discussing emigrants from a particular place, an additional heading is assigned to designate the nationality of origin of the emigrant group and the place to which they have immigrated, e.g., Chinese—United States: American—Foreign countries.

"Used for" —— UF Emigrants
　　　　　　　　Foreign-born population
　　　　　　　　Foreign population

"Broader term" —— BT Persons
"Related term" —— RT Aliens
"Narrower term" —— NT Children of immigrants
　　　　　　　　　　Social work with immigrants
　　　　　　　　　　Teenage immigrants
　　　　　　　　　　Women immigrants

Subtopic —— — Employment
　　　　　　　USE Alien labor
Recommended keywords —— — Housing *(May Subd Geog)*
　　　　　　　—— Great Britain
　　　　　　　— Legal status, laws, etc.
　　　　　　　USE Emigration and immigration law

Use Keyword Strategies

The goal of a keyword search is to find quality research sources. To ensure that you identify the best resources available, follow these strategies:

1. **Get to know the database.** Look for answers to these questions:
   - What material does the database contain? What time frames?
   - What are you searching—authors, titles, subjects, full text?
   - What are the search rules? How can you narrow the search?

2. **Use a shotgun approach.** Start with the most likely keyword. If you have no "hits," choose a related term. Once you get some hits, check the citations for clues regarding which words to use as you continue searching.

3. **Use Boolean operators to refine your search.** When you combine keywords with Boolean operators—such as those below—you will obtain better results.

Boolean Operators

fig. 21.6

Narrowing a Search **And, +, not, -** Use when one term gives you too many hits, especially irrelevant ones.	buffalo and bison *or* buffalo + bison buffalo not water + buffalo – water	Searches for citations containing both keywords Searches for "buffalo" but not "water," so that you eliminate material on water buffalo
Expanding a Search **Or** Combine a term providing few hits with a related word	buffalo or bison	Searches for citations containing either term
Specifying a Phrase **Quotation marks** Indicate that you wish to search for the exact phrase enclosed	"reclamation project"	Searches for the exact phrase "reclamation project"
Sequencing Operations **Parentheses** Indicate that the operation should be performed before other operations in the search string	(buffalo or bison) and ranching	Searches first for citations containing either "buffalo" or "bison" before checking the resulting citations for "ranching"
Finding Variations **Wild card symbols** Depending on the database, symbols such as $, ?, or # can find variations of a word.	ethic# ethic$	Searches for terms like *ethics* and *ethical*

Engaging and Evaluating Sources

Using reliable benchmarks, you should test all sources before you rely on them in your writing. After all, credible sources help your own credibility; sources that aren't credible destroy it. The benchmarks on the next four pages will help you test your sources' usefulness and reliability.

Engage Your Sources

Engaged reading is the opposite of passive reading—treating all sources equally, swallowing whole what's in the material, or looking only for information that supports your opinion. Full engagement involves these practices:

Test each source to see if it's worth reading. When reviewing source citations and generating a working bibliography, study titles, descriptions, lengths, and publication dates, asking these questions:

- How closely related to my topic is this source?
- Is this source too basic, overly complex, or just right?
- What could this source add to my overall balance of sources?

If you were writing about the International Space Station, for example, you might find a ten-page article in *Scientific American* more valuable and insightful than a brief news article on a specific event onboard or a *Star Trek* fan's blog on the topic.

INSIGHT Don't reject a source simply because it disagrees with your perspective. Good research engages rather than ignores opposing points of view.

Skim sources before reading in-depth. Consider marking key pages or passages with sticky notes, tabs, or a digital bookmark.

- Review the author biography, preface, and/or introduction to discover the perspective, approach, scope, and research methods.
- Using your keywords, review any outline, abstract, table of contents, index, or home page to get a sense of coverage.

Read with an open but not an empty mind. Carry on a dialogue with the source, asking questions like "Why?" and "So what?"

- Note the purpose and audience. Was the piece written to inform or persuade? Is it aimed at the public, specialists, supporters, or opponents?
- Read to understand the source: What's clear and what's confusing?
- Relate the source to your research question: How does the source affirm or challenge your ideas? Synthesize what you read with what you know.
- Record your reactions to it—what it makes you think, feel, believe.
- Consider how you might use this source in your writing—key facts, important ideas, opposing perspectives, or examples.
- Check footnotes, references, appendices, and links for leads on other sources.

Rate Source Reliability and Depth

You should judge each source on its own merit. Generally, however, types of sources can be rated for depth and reliability, as shown in the table below, based on their authorship, length, topic treatment, documentation, publication method, review process, distance from primary sources, allegiances, stability, and so on. Use the table to

1. target sources that fit your project's goals,
2. assess the approximate quality of the sources you're gathering, and
3. build a strong bibliography that readers will respect.

fig. 21.7

Deep, Reliable, Credible Sources

Scholarly Books and Scholarly Articles: largely based on careful research; written by experts for experts; address topics in depth; involve peer review and careful editing; offer stable discussion of topic

Trade Books and Articles in Quality, Specialized Magazines: largely based on careful research; written by experts for educated general audience. ***Sample periodicals:*** *The Atlantic, Canadian Geographic, Nature, Orion, The Walrus*

Government Resources: books, reports, Web pages, guides, statistics developed by experts at government agencies; provided as service to citizens; relatively objective. ***Sample sources:*** *Statistics Canada Website, Statistical Abstract of the United States*

Reviewed Official Online Documents: Internet resources posted by legitimate institutions—colleges and universities, research institutes, service organizations; although offering a particular perspective, sources tend to be balanced.

Reference Works and Textbooks: provide general and specialized information; carefully researched, reviewed, and edited; lack depth for focused research (e.g., general encyclopedia entry).

News and Topical Stories from Quality Sources: provide current affairs coverage (print and online), introduction-level articles of interest to general public; may lack depth and length. ***Sample sources:*** the *Globe and Mail,* the *New York Times; Maclean's, Psychology Today;* CBC's *The Fifth Estate*

Popular Magazine Stories: short, introductory articles often distant from primary sources and without documentation; heavy advertising. ***Sample sources:*** *Chatelaine, Seventeen, Reader's Digest*

Business and Nonprofit Publications: pamphlets, reports, news releases, brochures, manuals; range from informative to sales-focused.

List Server Discussions, Usenet Postings, Blog Articles, Talk Radio Discussions: highly open, fluid, undocumented, untested exchanges and publications; unstable resource.

Unregulated Web Material: personal sites, joke sites, chat rooms, special-interest sites, advertising and junk email (spam); no review process, little accountability, biased presentation.

Shallow, Unreliable, Not Credible Sources

Tabloid Articles (print and Web): contain exaggerated and untrue stories written to titillate and exploit. ***Sample sources:*** the *National Enquirer, Weekly World News*

Evaluate Print and Online Sources

As you work with a source, you need to test its reliability. The benchmarks that follow apply to both print and online sources; note, however, the additional tests offered for Web sources. For more on evaluating material on the Web, see pages 460–463.

Credible author An expert is an authority—someone who has mastered a subject area. Is the author an expert on this topic? What are her or his credentials, and can you confirm them? For example, an automotive engineer could be an expert on hydrogen fuel-cell technology, whereas a celebrity in a commercial would not.

> *Web test:* Is an author indicated? If so, are the author's credentials noted and contact information offered (for example, an email address)?

Reliable publication Has the source been published by a scholarly press, a peer-reviewed professional journal, a quality trade-book publisher, or a trusted news source? Did you find this resource through a reliable search tool (for example, a library catalogue or database)?

> *Web test:* Which individual or group posted this page? Is the site rated by a subject directory or library organization? How stable is the site—has it been around for a while and does material remain available, or is the site "fly-by-night"? Check the site's home page, and read "About Us" pages and mission statements, looking for evidence of the organization's perspective, history, and trustworthiness.

Unbiased discussion While all sources come from a specific perspective and represent specific commitments, a biased source may be pushing an agenda in an unfair, unbalanced, incomplete manner. Watch for bias toward a certain region, country, political party, industry, gender, race, ethnic group, or religion. Be alert to connections among authors, financial backers, and the points of view shared. For example, if an author has functioned as a consultant to or a lobbyist for a particular industry or group (oil, animal rights), his or her allegiances may lead to a biased presentation of an issue.

> *Web test:* Is the online document one-sided? Does the site originate in Canada, the United States, or elsewhere? Is the site nonprofit, governmental, commercial, or educational? Is this organization pushing a cause, product, service, or belief? How do advertising or special interests affect the site? You might suspect, for example, the scientific claims of a site sponsored by a pro-smoking organization.

MikiR/Shutterstock.com

Web Link: Beware especially of masquerade sites— those that appear to be legitimate but are joke sites or, worse, propaganda lures. Check, for example, www.dhmo.org.

Current information A five-year-old book on computers may be outdated, but a forty-year-old book on Sir Wilfrid Laurier could still be the best source. Given what you need, is this source's discussion up to date?

> **Web test:** When was the material originally posted and last updated? Are links live or dead?

Accurate information Bad research design, poor reporting, and sloppy documentation can lead to inaccurate information. Check the source for factual errors, statistical flaws, and conclusions that don't add up.

> **Web test:** Is the site information-rich or -poor? More specifically, is it filled with helpful, factual materials or fluffy with thin, unsubstantiated opinions? Can you trace and confirm sources by following links or conducting your own search?

Full, logical support Is the discussion of the topic reasonable, balanced, and complete? Are claims backed up with quality evidence? Does the source avoid faulty assumptions, twisted statistical analysis, logical fallacies, and unfair persuasion tactics? (See pages 317–320, for help.)

> **Web test:** Does the Web page offer well-supported claims and helpful links to additional information?

Quality writing and design Is the source well written? Is it free of sarcasm, derogatory terms, clichés, catchphrases, mindless slogans, grammar slips, and spelling errors? Generally, poor writing correlates with sloppy thinking.

> **Web test:** Are words neutral ("conservative perspective") or emotionally charged ("fascist agenda")? Are pages well designed—with clear rather than flashy, distracting multimedia elements? Is the site easy to navigate?

Positive relationship with other sources Does the source disagree with other sources? If yes, is the disagreement about the facts themselves or about how to interpret the facts? Which source seems more credible?

> **Web test:** Is the site's information logically consistent with print sources? Do other reputable sites offer links to this site?

INSIGHT Engage and evaluate visual resources as thoroughly as verbal materials. For example, ask yourself what tables, graphs, and photos really "say":

- Is the graphic informative or merely decorative?
- Does the graphic create a valid or manipulative central idea? For example, does the image seek to bypass logic by appealing to sexual impulses or to crude stereotypes?
- What does the graphic include and exclude in terms of information?
- Is the graphic well designed and easy to understand, or is it cluttered and distorted?
- Is a reliable source provided?

Creating a Working Bibliography

A working bibliography lists sources you have used and intend to use. It helps you track your research, develop your final bibliography, and avoid plagiarism. Here's what to do:

Select an Efficient Approach for Your Project

The following tools may be helpful for recording the sources you have used:

- **Paper note cards:** Use 7.6 x 12.7 cm cards, and record one source per card.
- **Paper notebook:** Use a small, spiral-bound book to record sources.
- **Computer program:** Record source information electronically, either by capturing citation details from online searches or by recording bibliographic information using word-processing software or research software such as TakeNote, EndNote Plus, or Bookends Pro.

Including Identifying Information for Sources

Start by giving each source its own code number or letter: Doing so will help you when drafting and documenting your paper. Then include specific details for each kind of source listed below, shown on the facing page.

- A. **Books:** author, title and subtitle, publication details (place, publisher, date)
- B. **Periodicals:** author, article title, journal name, publication information (volume, number, date), page numbers
- C. **Online sources:** author (if available), document title, site sponsor, database name, publication or posting date, access date, other publication information, URL
- D. **Primary or field research:** date conducted, name and descriptive title of person interviewed, place observed, survey conducted, document analyzed

Adding Locating Information

Because you may need to retrace your research footsteps, include details about your research path:

- A. **Books:** Include the Library of Congress or Dewey call number.
- B. **Articles:** Note where and how you accessed them (stacks, current periodicals, microfilm, database).
- C. **Web pages:** Record the complete URL, not just the broader site address.
- D. **Field research:** Include a telephone number or an email address.

> **INSIGHT** Consider recording bibliographic details in the format of the documentation system you are using—MLA (pages 493–534) or APA (pages 535–564), for example. Doing so now will save time later. In addition, some research software such as RefWorks allows you to record bibliographic information and then format it according to a specific system.

Annotate the Source

Add a note about the source's content, focus, reliability, and usefulness, as shown in Figure 21.8.

Sample Working Bibliography Entries

fig. 21.8

A. Book Source Note:

#2

Howells, Coral Ann. *Alice Munro.*

Contemporary World Writers. Manchester and New York: Manchester UP, 1998. Print.

PS 8576.U57 Z7 1998

Book provides good introduction to Alice Munro's fiction, chapters arranged by Munro's works; contains intro, conclusion, and bibliography; 1998 date means author doesn't cover Munro's recent fiction.

B. Periodical Source Note

#5

Valdes, Marcela. "Some Stories Have to Be Told by Me: A Literary History of Alice Munro." *Virginia Quarterly Review* 82.3 (Summer 2006): 82-90.

EBSCOhost Academic Search Premier http://web.ebscohost.com accessed 17 April 2014.

Article offers good introduction to Munro's life, her roots in Ontario, her writing career, and the key features of her stories.

C. Internet Source Note:

#3

"Alice Munro." Athabasca University Centre for Language and Literature: Canadian Writers. Updated 11 Oct. 2012. Accessed 17 April 2014.

canadian-writers.athabaskau.ca/english/writers/amunro/amunro.php
Site offers good introduction to Munro's writing, along with links to bibliography and other resources.

D. Interview Source Note:

#4

Thacker, Robert. Email interview. 7 March 2014.

rthacker@mdu.edu

Author of critical biography on Munro, *Alice Munro: Writing Her Lives,* offered really helpful insights into her creative process, especially useful for story "Carried Away."

Developing a Note-Taking System

Accurate, thoughtful notes create a foundation for your research writing. The trick is to practise some sensible strategies and choose an efficient method.

Develop Note-Taking Strategies

What are you trying to do when you take notes on sources? What you are not doing is (a) collecting quotations to plunk in your project, (b) piling isolated grains of data into a large stack of disconnected facts, or (c) intensively reading and taking notes on every source you find. Instead, use these strategies:

Be selective. Guided by your research questions and working thesis, focus on sources that are central to your project. From these sources, record information clearly related to your limited topic, but also take notes on what surprises or puzzles you. Be selective, avoiding notes that are either too meagre or too extensive. Suppose, for example, that you were writing a paper on the engineering problems facing the International Space Station. If you were reading an article on the history and the future of this facility, you might take careful notes on material describing the station's technical details, but not on astronauts' biographies.

Develop accurate, complete records. Your notes should . . .
- Accurately summarize, paraphrase, and quote sources (pages 428–431).
- Clearly show where you got your information.
- Cover all the research you've done—primary research (e.g., interviews, observations), books and periodical articles, and online sources.

Engage your sources. Evaluate what you are reading and develop your own responses. (See pages 4–9.) For example, with an article about the International Space Station, you might test the author's biases, credentials, and logic; and you might respond with knowledge you have gained about other space endeavours.

Take good notes on graphics in sources—tables, line graphs, photographs, maps, and so on. Such graphics are typically packed with information and powerfully convey ideas. (See "Thinking Through Viewing," pages 10–15.)

INSIGHT Different disciplines use different note-taking practices. In your major, learn these practices through courses that introduce you to the subject matter. Here are two examples:
- In literature studies, students conduct literary analyses by annotating print texts. Students may also take notes through keyword searches of ebooks (for example, a Shakespeare play) and reviews of literary criticism.
- In environmental studies, students conduct research by (a) taking notes on published research to develop literature reviews, and (b) using a standard field notebook to collect data, make drawings, and reflect on results.

Employ a Note-Taking System

A good note-taking system should help you do the following:

- Avoid unintentional plagiarism by developing accurate records, distinguishing among sources, and separating source material from your own ideas.
- Work efficiently at gathering what you need for the project.
- Work flexibly with a wide range of resources—primary and secondary, print and electronic, verbal and visual.
- Engage sources through creative and critical reflection.
- Record summaries, paraphrases, and quotations correctly.
- Be accurate and complete so that you need not reread sources.
- Efficiently develop your paper's outline and first draft.

Four note-taking systems are outlined on the pages that follow. Choose the system that works best for your project, or combine elements to develop your own.

System 1: **Paper or electronic note cards.** Using paper note cards is the traditional method of note taking; however, note-taking software is now available with most word-processing programs and special programs like TakeNote, EndNote Plus, and Bookends Pro. Here's how a note-card system works:

1. Establish one set of cards (7.6 × 12.7 cm, if paper) for your bibliography.
2. On a second set of cards (10 × 15 cm, if paper), take notes on sources:
   - Record one point from one source per card.
   - Clarify the source: List the author's last name, a shortened title, or a code from the matching bibliography card. Include a page number.
   - Provide a topic or heading: Called a slug, the topic helps you categorize and order information.
   - Label the note as a summary, paraphrase, or quotation of the original.
   - Distinguish between the source's information and your own thoughts.

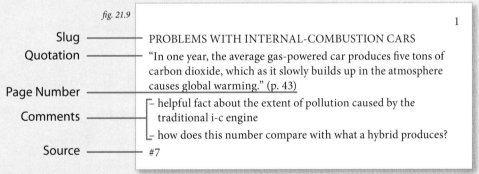

fig. 21.9

1

Slug	PROBLEMS WITH INTERNAL-COMBUSTION CARS
Quotation	"In one year, the average gas-powered car produces five tons of carbon dioxide, which as it slowly builds up in the atmosphere causes global warming." (p. 43)
Page Number	
Comments	– helpful fact about the extent of pollution caused by the traditional i-c engine
	– how does this number compare with what a hybrid produces?
Source	#7

▲ **Upside:** Note cards are highly systematic, helping you categorize material and organize it for an outline and a first draft.

▼ **Downside:** The method can be initially tedious and time-consuming.

System 2: Copy (or save) and annotate. The copy-and-annotate method involves working with photocopies, print versions, or digital texts of sources:

1. Selectively photocopy, print, and/or save important sources. Copy carefully, making sure you have full pages, including the page numbers.
2. As needed, add identifying information on the copy—author, publication details, and date. Each page should be easy to identify and trace. When working with books, simply copy the title and copyright pages and keep them with the rest of your notes.
3. As you read, mark up the copy and highlight key statements. In the margins or digital file, record your ideas:
   - Ask questions. Insert a "?" in the margin, or write out the question.
   - Make connections. Draw arrows to link ideas, or make notes like "see page 36."
   - Add asides. Record what you think and feel while reading.
   - Define terms. Note important words that you need to understand.
   - Create a marginal index. Write keywords to identify themes and main parts.

Upside: Copying, printing, and/or saving helps you record sources accurately; annotating encourages careful reading and thinking.

Downside: Organizing material for drafting is inconvenient; when done poorly, annotating and highlighting involve skimming, not engaged, critical reading.

System 3: The computer notebook or research log. The computer notebook or research log method involves taking notes on a computer or on sheets of paper. Here's how it works:

1. Establish a central location for your notes—a notebook, a file folder, a binder, or an electronic folder.
2. Take notes one source at a time, making sure to identify the source fully. Number your note pages.
3. Using your initials or some other symbol, distinguish your own thoughts from source material.
4. Use codes in your notes to identify which information in the notes relates to which topic in your outline. Then, under each topic in the outline, write the page number in your notes where that information is recorded. With a notebook or log, you may be able to rearrange your notes into an outline by using copy and paste—but don't lose source information in the process!

Upside: Taking notes feels natural without being overly systematic.

Downside: Outlining and drafting may require time-consuming paper shuffling.

System 4: The double-entry notebook. The double-entry notebook involves parallel note taking—notes from sources beside your own brainstorming, reaction, and reflection. Using a notebook or the columns feature of your word-processing program, do the following:

1. Divide pages in half vertically.
2. In the left column, record bibliographic information and take notes on sources.
3. In the right column, write your responses. Think about what the source is saying, why the point is important, whether you agree with it, and how the point relates to other ideas and other sources.

Upside: This method creates accurate source records while encouraging thoughtful responses; also, it can be done on a computer.

Downside: Organizing material for drafting may be a challenge.

fig. 21.10

Cudworth, Erika. <u>Environment and Society.</u> Routledge Introductions to Environment Series. London and New York: Routledge, 2003. Print.	
Ch. 6 "Society, 'Culture' and 'Nature'— Human Relations with Animals"	I've actually had a fair bit of personal experience with animals—the horses, ducks, dogs, and cats on our hobby farm. Will this chapter make trouble for my thinking?
chapter looks at how social scientists have understood historically the relationship between people and animals (158)	
the word <u>animal</u> is itself a problem when we remember that people too are animals but the distinction is often sharply made by people themselves (159)	Yes, what really are the connections and differences between people and animals? Is it a different level of intelligence? Is there something more basic or fundamental? Are we afraid to see ourselves as animals, as creatures?
"In everyday life, people interact with animals continually." (159)–author gives many common examples	Many examples—pets, food, TV programs, zoos—apply to me. Hadn't thought about how much my life is integrated with animal life! What does that integration look like? What does it mean for me, for the animals?

Summarizing, Paraphrasing, and Quoting Source Material

As you work with sources, you must decide what to put in your notes and how to record it—as a summary, a paraphrase, or a quotation. Use these guidelines:

- How relevant is the passage to your research question or working thesis?
- How strong and important is the information offered?
- How unique or memorable is the thinking or phrasing?

The more relevant, the stronger, and the more memorable the material is, the more likely you should note it. The passage below comes from an article on GM's development of fuel-cell technology. Review the passage; study how the researcher summarizes, paraphrases, and quotes from the source; and then practise these same strategies as you take notes on sources.

From Burns, L. D., McCormick, J. B., and Borroni-Bird, C. E. "Vehicle of Change." *Scientific American 287*(4), 64-73.

When Karl Benz rolled his Patent Motorcar out of the barn in 1886, he literally set the wheels of change in motion. The advent of the automobile led to dramatic alterations in people's way of life as well as the global economy—transformations that no one expected at the time. The ever-increasing availability of economical personal transportation remade the world into a more accessible place while spawning a complex industrial infrastructure that shaped modern society.

Now another revolution could be sparked by automotive technology: one fueled by hydrogen rather than petroleum. Fuel cells—which cleave hydrogen atoms into protons and electrons that drive electric motors while emitting nothing worse than water vapor—could make the automobile much more environmentally friendly. Not only could cars become cleaner, they could also become safer, more comfortable, more personalized—and even perhaps less expensive. Further, these fuel-cell vehicles could be instrumental in motivating a shift toward a "greener" energy economy based on hydrogen. As that occurs, energy use and production could change significantly. Thus, hydrogen fuel-cell cars and trucks could help ensure a future in which personal mobility—the freedom to travel independently—could be sustained indefinitely, without compromising the environment or depleting the earth's natural resources.

A confluence of factors makes the big change seem increasingly likely. For one, the petroleum-fueled internal-combustion engine (ICE), as highly refined, reliable and economical as it is, is finally reaching its limits. Despite steady improvements, today's ICE vehicles are only 20 to 25 percent efficient in converting the energy content of fuels into drive-wheel power. And although the U.S. auto industry has cut exhaust emissions substantially since the unregulated 1960s—hydrocarbons dropped by 99 percent, carbon monoxide by 96 percent and nitrogen oxides by 95 percent—the continued production of carbon dioxide causes concern because of its potential to change the planet's climate.

Summarize Useful Passages

Summarizing condenses in your own words the main points in a passage. Summarize when the source provides relevant ideas and information on your topic.

1. **Reread the passage,** jotting down a few keywords.
2. **State the main point in your own words.** Add key supporting points, leaving out examples, details, and long explanations. Be objective: Don't include your reactions.
3. **Check your summary against the original,** making sure that you use quotation marks around any exact phrases you borrow.

Sample Summary:

> While the introduction of the car in the late nineteenth century has led to dramatic changes in society and world economics, another dramatic change is now taking place in the shift from gas engines to hydrogen technologies. Fuel cells may make the car "greener," and perhaps even safer, cheaper, and more comfortable. These automotive changes will affect the energy industry by making it more environmentally friendly; as a result, people will continue to enjoy mobility while transportation moves to renewable energy. One factor leading to this technological shift is that the internal-combustion engine has reached the limits of its efficiency, potential, and development—while remaining problematic with respect to emissions, climate change, and health.

Paraphrase Key Passages

Paraphrasing involves putting a passage from the source into your own words—keeping the content but phrasing it in your own voice and style, so to speak. Typically, you would paraphrase a passage that contains important points, explanations, or arguments but that is not phrased memorably or clearly. The passage might be primarily factual, making direct quotation unnecessary, or the passage might be technical, dense, and complex, requiring that you put it in plainer terms. To paraphrase effectively, follow these steps:

1. **Review the passage** to make sure that you have the gist of the whole.
2. **Go through the passage carefully,** sentence by sentence, doing the following:
   - State the ideas in your own words, substituting terms and defining words as needed.
   - Rework the sentence patterns, as needed—changing syntax, combining clauses, and so on—so that the passage takes on your voice.
   - If you do borrow phrases directly, put them in quotation marks.
3. **Check your paraphrase against the original:** Is the meaning accurate and complete? Have you fairly "translated" the source into your own wording and voice?

Sample Paraphrase of the Second Paragraph in the Passage:

Automobile technology may lead to another radical economic and social change through the shift from gasoline to hydrogen fuel. By breaking hydrogen into protons and electrons so that the electrons run an electric motor with only the by-product of water vapour, fuel cells could make the car a "green" machine. But this technology could also increase the automobile's safety, comfort, personal tailoring, and affordability. Moreover, this shift to fuel-cell engines in automobiles could lead to drastic, environmentally friendly changes in the broader energy industry, one that will be now tied to hydrogen rather than fossil fuels. The result from this shift will be radical changes in the way we use and produce energy. In other words, the shift to hydrogen-powered vehicles could promise to maintain society's valued mobility, while the clean technology would preserve the environment and its natural resources.

Quote Crucial Phrases, Sentences, and Passages

Quoting records statements or phrases in the original source word for word. Quote nuggets only—statements that are well phrased or authoritative:

1. **Note the quotation's context**—how it fits in the author's discussion.
2. **Copy the passage word for word,** enclosing it in quotation marks and checking its accuracy.
3. **If you omit words, note that omission with an ellipsis.** If you change any word for grammatical reasons, put changes in brackets. (See page 485.)

Sample Quotation:

"[H]ydrogen fuel-cell cars and trucks could help ensure a future in which personal mobility . . . could be sustained indefinitely, without compromising the environment or depleting the earth's natural resources."

Note: This sentence captures the authors' main claim about the benefits and future of fuel-cell technology.

INSIGHT Whether you are summarizing, paraphrasing, or quoting, aim to be true to the source by respecting the context and spirit of the original. Avoid shifting the focus or ripping material out of its context and forcing it into your own. For example, in the sample passage the authors discuss the limits of the internal-combustion engine. If you were to claim that these authors are arguing that the internal-combustion engine was an enormous engineering and environmental mistake, you would be twisting their comments to serve your own writing agenda.

 For instruction on effectively integrating quotations, paraphrases, and summaries into your writing, see pages 482–485.

Avoiding Unintentional Plagiarism

Careful note taking helps prevent unintentional plagiarism. Plagiarism—using source material without giving credit—is treated more fully in Chapter 23; essentially, however, unintentional plagiarism happens when you accidentally use a source's ideas, phrases, or information without documenting that material. At the planning stage of your project, you can prevent this problem from happening by adhering to principles of ethical research and following some practical guidelines.

Practise the Principles of Ethical Research

Because of the nature of information and the many challenges of working with it, conducting ethical research can be very complex and involved. To start with, however, commit to these principles of ethical research:

- Do the research and write the paper yourself.
- Adhere to the research practices approved in your discipline.
- Follow school- and discipline-related guidelines for working with people, resources, and technology.
- Avoid one-sided research that ignores or conceals opposition.
- Present real, accurate data and results—not "fudged" or twisted facts.
- Treat source material fairly in your writing.

Practices That Prevent Unintentional Plagiarism

The principles of ethical research above find expression when you prevent unintentional plagiarism. Do so by following these practices:

- Maintain an accurate working bibliography (pages 422–423).
- When taking notes, distinguish source material from your own reflection by using quotation marks, codes, and/or separate columns or note cards.
- When you draft your paper, transfer source material carefully by coding material that you integrate into your discussion, using quotation marks, double-checking your typing, or using copy and paste to ensure accuracy.
- Take time to do the project right—both research and writing. Avoid pulling an all-nighter during which you can't properly work with sources.

Practices That Prevent Internet Plagiarism

An especially thorny area related to unintentional plagiarism centres on the Internet. As with traditional print sources, Internet sources must be properly credited; in other words, Web material cannot simply be transferred to your paper without acknowledgement. So treat Web sources like print sources. And if you copy and paste digital material while taking notes and drafting, always track its origins with codes, abbreviations, or separate columns.

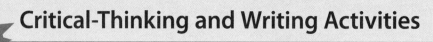

Critical-Thinking and Writing Activities

As directed by your instructor, complete the following activities.

1. Speaking metaphorically, Alexander Graham Bell once advised, "Leave the beaten track behind occasionally and dive into the woods. Every time you do you will be certain to find something you have never seen before." Reflect on how this advice might apply to doing research.

2. Using all that you have learned in this chapter, develop a research proposal that identifies a topic of interest to you, clarifies the value of the research, maps out research methods (including a working bibliography), and establishes a schedule.

3. If you have not already done so, get the resources that you listed in your research proposal's working bibliography (activity 2 above). Then do the following:

   • Identify each source as primary, secondary, or tertiary. Consider the relative value of these sources for your project.

   • Test the reliability of your sources. Refer to the scale on page 419 and the questions on pages 420–421. Are the sources credible?

   • From your bibliography, choose a short article or a passage from a longer source. Read that material carefully and do the following: (a) write a summary of the material, (b) choose a paragraph and paraphrase it, and (c) choose a key statement to quote directly, indicating why it is worthy of quotation.

Learning-Objectives Checklist ✓

Have you achieved this chapter's learning objectives? Check your progress with the items below, revisiting topics in the chapter as needed. *I have . . .*

_____ analyzed the rhetorical situation of my research project (404).

_____ identified the phases of the research process (405).

_____ focused my research project by establishing a manageable topic, brainstorming questions, and developing a working thesis (406–407).

_____ differentiated the nature and uses of primary, secondary, and tertiary sources (408–409).

_____ generated a research plan by choosing research methods and getting organized to do research, as well as composing a research proposal, if required (410–411).

_____ chosen fitting information sources from promising information sites (414–415).

_____ performed effective keyword searches by choosing productive keywords and implementing search strategies (416–417).

_____ critically engaged print and digital sources, evaluating them for depth, reliability, credibility, lack of bias, currency, and accuracy (418–421).

_____ produced and maintained an orderly, accurate working bibliography (422–423).

_____ chosen a note-taking system that allows me to keep accurate, complete records and engage my sources (424–427).

_____ accurately summarized, paraphrased, and quoted material from sources in my notes (428–431).

_____ identified principles of ethical research and implemented them in my own project (431).

Chapter 22

Conducting Research: Primary, Library, Web

Today, conducting research is both easy and difficult. It's easy because research technology is powerful and many research methods are available. It's difficult because that technology and those methods provide access to so much information—the good, the bad, and the ugly.

How do you meet this challenge and conduct quality research? First, consider whether your project would benefit from primary research—gathering information first hand by observing sites, interviewing people, and analyzing documents, for example. Second, learn how to use an expert resource—your school library. The library is your gateway to quality print and electronic materials. Third, learn to access reliable resources on the free Web.

Visually Speaking "Libraries are research centres." Think about this statement in light of Figure 22.1, and relate this idea to your own experience of research, inside and outside of libraries.

Learning **Objectives**

By working through this chapter, you will be able to

- choose, design, and conduct primary research for your project.
- identify, locate, retrieve, and work with library resources.
- implement free-Web research tools to locate and evaluate free-Web resources.

Jens Goepfert/Shutterstock.com

fig. 22.1

Planning Primary Research

As discussed on pages 408–409, resources can be primary, secondary, or tertiary. Doing primary research is particularly hands-on and requires careful planning. To do truly useful primary research, you need to choose methods that will gather information directly related to your main research question and learn the proper methods of doing such research. To start your planning, consider these factors:

- **The assignment:** Does the assignment dictate a particular form of primary research?
- **The field of study:** Does the course's subject matter point you toward particularly valued methods of primary research?
- **The topic:** How might your understanding of the topic deepen with information gathered through a particular method?
- **The timing:** How much time do you have for doing primary research?
- **The audience:** What forms of primary research will your readers expect, respect, or value?

Methods of Primary Research

After considering the factors above, review the methods below and choose those that make sense for your project. You can find instruction for each method at the page numbers indicated.

- **Surveys and Questionnaires** (pages 436–437) gather information from representative groups of people as responses you can review, tabulate, and analyze, most often statistically. Whether gathering simple facts or personal opinions, such research can give you strong insights into how the group thinks about your issue; however, it may be difficult to gather complex responses.

- **Analyses of Texts, Documents, Records, and Artifacts** (pages 438–439) involve studying original correspondence, reports, legislation, images, literary works, historical records, and so on. Such research provides a direct experience of your topic and insights into its immediate nature, products, or remnants, but the quality of research depends on how fully and effectively you analyze the "text" in question.

- **Interviews** (pages 440–441) involve consulting people through a question-and-answer dialogue. Interviewees can be either experts on your topic or people who have had a particular experience with the topic, either witnessing it or involved in some way. Interviewing experts can add authoritative input, though experts sometimes disagree. Interviewing someone with experience of your topic can give an inside perspective into its causes and effects, as well as its personal dimensions.

- **Observations** (page 442) involve systematically examining and analyzing places, spaces, scenes, equipment, work, events, and other sites or phenomena. Whether you rely simply on your five senses or use scientific techniques, observation provides a range of information—from personal impressions to precise data (e.g., measurements).

- **Experiments** (see the online chapter "Writing in the Sciences") test hypotheses—predictions about why things are as they are or happen as they do—so as to arrive at conclusions that can be tentatively accepted, related to other knowledge, and acted upon. Such testing often explains cause-effect relationships for varied natural, social, or psychological phenomena, offering a degree of scientific certainty about the forces at work in your topic.

Principles for Doing Primary Research

Whatever primary research you choose to do, you should conduct that research in a systematic, careful manner in order to generate valid, reliable primary information and ideas. Here are some principles common to doing any method of primary research:

1. **Locate a reliable source.** Make sure, in other words, that the person, place, group, document, or image is the real thing—an authoritative, representative, respected source of information. Whether you find your source in a print publication (e.g., a version of a Shakespeare play published by a scholarly press), on the Internet (e.g., a piece of legislation), in an archive or museum (e.g., a sculpture), through personal contact (e.g., a home visit), or through exploration (e.g., a ravine in your city)—make sure that the source matches your research need and has the right "weight" for your project.

2. **Aim for objectivity.** You should approach most primary research with an objective frame of mind: remain open to the evidence that arises by keeping your wishes in check; otherwise, your research will be slanted and your readers will recognize the biases in your thinking.

3. **Get ready through background research.** That is, don't go cold into your primary research. Do your homework first—learning the key concepts and perspectives on your topic, the theories debated, and the knowledge that has already been built by others. That way, your primary research will grow out of some foundational thinking and be driven by a specific purpose and specific questions.

4. **Use the right tools.** Each method of primary research requires tools—physical tools (e.g., field notebook, instruments), software (e.g., survey software, spreadsheet software), or analytical tools (e.g., the ability to sort out causes and effects). Make sure that you have reliable tools and are using them effectively.

5. **Gather and work with data carefully.** Primary information is only as good as the care with which it is gathered, interpreted, and presented. Keep accurate, complete records of your research; in some projects, you may even have to include such records and "raw data" in an appendix. Above all, work ethically with your data by avoiding errors, gaps and omissions, and by not fudging your data or doctoring graphics.

fyi If your research involves working with people, typically called "human subjects," strive to (1) do no harm, whether psychological, social, or financial, and (2) respect individual autonomy—participants' rights, dignity, and privacy, for example. Check if your school has a research-ethics committee that reviews, approves, and oversees such research by students.

Conducting Surveys

One source of primary information that you can use for research projects is a survey or questionnaire. Surveys can collect facts and opinions from a wide range of people about virtually any topic. To get valid information, follow these guidelines:

1. Find a focus.
- Limit the purpose of your survey.
- Target a specific audience.

2. Ask clear questions.
- Phrase questions so they can be easily understood.
- Use words that are objective (not biased or slanted).

3. Match your questions to your purpose.
- Closed questions give respondents easy-answer options, and the answers are easy to tabulate. Closed questions can provide two choices (*yes* or *no*, *true* or *false*), multiple choices, a rating scale (*poor 1 2 3 excellent*), or a blank to fill.
- Open-ended questions bring in a wide variety of responses and more complex information, but they take time to complete, and the answers can be difficult to summarize.

4. Organize your survey so that it's easy to complete.
- In the introduction, state who you are and why you need the information. Explain how to complete the survey and when and where to return it.
- Guide readers by providing numbers, instructions, and headings.
- Begin with basic questions and end with any complex, open-ended questions that are necessary. Move in a logical order from one topic to the next.

5. Test your survey before using it.
- Ask a friend or classmate to read your survey and help you revise it, if necessary, before printing it.
- Try out your survey with a small test group. If the test group seems to misunderstand or misinterpret a question, then revise it.

6. Conduct your survey.
- Distribute the survey to a clearly defined group that won't prejudice the sampling (random or cross section).
- Get responses from a sample of your target group (10 percent at minimum).
- Tabulate responses carefully and objectively.

Note: To develop statistically valid results, you may need expert help. Check with your instructor. In addition, consider online survey tools such as SurveyMonkey.com and LimeSurvey.org.

Sample Survey

Confidential Survey

The introduction includes the essential information about the survey.

My name is Cho Lang, and I'm conducting research about the use of training supplements. I'd like to hear from you, Alfred University's athletes. Please answer the questions below by circling or writing out your responses. Return your survey to me, care of the Dept. of Psychology, through campus mail by Friday, April 5. Your responses will remain confidential.

The survey begins with clear, basic questions.

1. Circle your gender. **Male   Female**

2. Circle your year.
   First year   Second year   Third year   Fourth year

3. List the sports that you play.

4. Are you presently using a training supplement?
   Yes   No

   Note: If you circled "no," you may turn in your survey at this point.

The survey asks an open-ended question.

5. Describe your supplement use (type, amount, and frequency).

6. Who supervises your use of this training supplement?
   Coach   Trainer   Self   Others

7. How long have you used it?
   Less than 1 month   1–12 months   12+ months

The survey covers the topic thoroughly.

8. How many kilograms have you gained while using this supplement?

9. How much has your athletic performance improved?
   None   1   2   3   4   5   Greatly

10. Circle any side effects you've experienced.
    Dehydration   Nausea   Diarrhea

Analyzing Texts, Documents, Records, and Artifacts

An original document or record is one that relates directly to the event, issue, object, or phenomenon you are researching. Examining original documents and artifacts can involve studying letters, email exchanges, case notes, literary texts, sales records, legislation, and material objects such as tools, sculptures, buildings, and tombs. As you analyze such documents and records, you examine evidence in an effort to understand a topic, arrive at a coherent conclusion about it, and support that judgment. How do you work with such diverse documents, records, and artifacts? Here are some guidelines:

Choose Evidence Close to Your Topic

Which texts, documents, records, and artifacts originated from or grew out of the topic you are researching? The closer to the topic, the more primary the source. Select materials that are directly related to your research questions and/or working thesis.

> *Example:* If you were studying English labour riots of the 1830s, you could investigate these primary sources:
> - To identify the rioters, names from police reports or union membership lists
> - To understand what rioters were demanding, copies of speeches given at demonstrations
> - To learn the political response to the riots, political speeches or legislation
> - To get at the attitudes of people from that time, newspaper reports, works of art, or novels from the period
> - To find people's personal stories and private opinions related to the riots, personal letters, diaries, family albums, gravestones, and funeral eulogies

Put the Document or Artifact in Context

So that the material takes on meaning, clarify its external and internal natures. First, consider its external context—the five Ws and H: What exactly is it? Who made it, when, where, why, and how? Second, consider its internal nature—what the document means, based on what it can and cannot show you: What does the language mean or refer to? What is the document's structure? What are the artifact's composition and style?

> *Example:* If you were examining Susanna Moodie's *Roughing It in the Bush* in a literature or women's studies course, you would consider the following:
> - **External Context:** who Susanna Moodie was; when and why she wrote *Roughing It* and under what conditions; for whom she wrote it and their response; the type of document it is
> - **Internal Context:** Moodie's narratives and their themes; the nature of her views, their relationship to her times, and their relevance today

Frame Your Examination with Questions

To make sense of the text, document, record, or artifact, understand what you are looking for and why. List the secondary questions that you want to answer in relation to the main question behind your research project.

> *Example:* To study how U.S. legislation contributed to the development of cleaner cars, such as the hybrid-fuel vehicle, you could access various documents on the Clean Air Act of 1990 (for example, *The Plain English Guide to the Clean Air Act*, an Environmental Protection Agency publication). As you study this legislation, you could frame your reading with these additional questions:
> - What are the requirements of the Clean Air Act?
> - Specifically, how do those requirements affect automotive technology?
> - What research projects likely grew out of these requirements?
> - Are schedules for change or deadlines written into the Clean Air Act?

Draw Coherent Conclusions about Meaning

Make sense of the source in relation to your research questions. What connections does it reveal? What important developments? What cause/effect relationships? What themes?

> *Example:* A study of the Clean Air Act might lead you to conclusions regarding how environmental legislation relates to the development of hybrid technology—for example, that the United States must produce cleaner cars if it hopes to gain improved air quality.

INSIGHT Studying primary documents and artifacts is central to many disciplines—history, literature, theology, philosophy, political studies, and archaeology, for example. Good analysis depends on asking research questions appropriate for the discipline. With the English labour riots of the 1830s again as an example, here's what three disciplines might ask:

- **Political science:** What role did political theories, structures, and processes play in the riots—both in causing and in responding to them?
- **Art:** How were the concerns of the rioters embodied in the new "realist" style of the mid-1800s? Did artists sympathize with and address an alienated working-class audience? How did art comment on the social structures of the time?
- **Sociology:** What type and quality of education did most workers have in the 1830s? How did that education affect their economic status and employment opportunities? Did issues related to the riots prompt changes in the English educational system? What changes and why?

With these examples in mind, consider your own major: What questions would this discipline ask of the English labour riots, of Susanna Moodie's *Roughing It in the Bush,* or of the Clean Air Act of 1990?

Conducting Interviews

The purpose of an interview is simple: To get information, you talk with someone who has significant experience or someone who is an expert on your topic. Use the guidelines below whenever you conduct an interview.

1. **Before the interview,** research the topic and the person you are planning to interview.
   - Arrange the interview in a thoughtful way. Explain to the interviewee your purpose and the topics to be covered.
   - Think about the specific ideas you want to cover in the interview and write questions for each. Addressing the 5 Ws and H (*Who? What? Where? When? Why?* and *How?*) is important for good coverage.
   - Organize your questions in a logical order so the interview moves smoothly from one subject to the next.
   - Write the questions on the left side of a page. Leave room for quotations, information, and impressions on the right side.

2. **During the interview,** try to relax so that your conversation is natural and sincere.
   - Provide some background information about yourself, your project, and your plans for using the interview information.
   - Use recording equipment only with the interviewee's permission.
   - Jot down key facts and quotations.
   - Listen actively. Show that you're listening through your body language—eye contact, nods, smiles. Pay attention not only to what the person says but also to how he or she says it.
   - Be flexible. If the person looks puzzled by a question, rephrase it. If the discussion gets off track, redirect it. Based on the interviewee's responses, ask follow-up questions, and don't limit yourself to your planned questions only.
   - End positively. Conclude by asking if the person wants to add, clarify, or emphasize anything. (Note: important points may come up late in the interview.) Thank the person, gather your notes and equipment, and part with a handshake.

3. **After the interview,** do the appropriate follow-up work.
   - As soon as possible, review your notes. Fill in responses you remember but couldn't record at the time.
   - Analyze the results. Study the information, insights, and quotations you gathered. What do they reveal about the topic? How does the interview confirm, complement, or contradict other sources on the topic? What has the interview added to your understanding?
   - Thank the interviewee with a note, an email, or a phone call.
   - If necessary, ask the interviewee to check whether your information and quotations are accurate.
   - Offer to send the interviewee a copy of your writing.

Sample Interview Note-Taking Sheet

Below, note how the researcher sets up questions for an interview with an automotive engineer regarding hybrid technology. The interviewer begins with identifying information for future reference, and then moves from a basic "connecting" question into the technology's principles, strengths, challenges, and future. On the right, he would leave room (approximately half the sheet) for taking notes.

Interview with Jessica Madison, automotive engineer for Future Fuel Corporation (email jmadison@futurefuel.ca; phone 555-555-5555) January 22, 2014: 2:30 p.m.

Notes, quotations, observations:

Preliminaries: thanks/appreciation; introduction of myself; background, purpose, hoped-for outcome of research (report on hybrids' environmental potential)

Initial Question
1. Please tell me about your research into hybrid technology. When and how did you become interested? What discoveries have you made?

Hybrid Technology: Principles
2. How does hybrid technology actually work? What's the principle behind the hybrid vehicle?
3. How is the hybrid engine different from the traditional internal-combustion engine?

Strengths and Challenges
4. What are the strengths of hybrid vehicles?
5. What are some of the challenges of hybrids? Some of the weaknesses?

The Future/Viability
6. Where is hybrid technology going? What's the next generation of clean-car technology?
7. What are the benefits or drawbacks of society investing in hybrids? Why should the average person care about hybrid technologies?
8. Would you like to add or clarify anything about hybrid technologies?

Closing: thank for taking time, offering insights

Making Observations

Observation places you at a site directly related to your topic. Whether you are examining people's behaviour, natural phenomena, or a location's features, observation can gather subjective impressions, sensory data, various recordings, or concrete measurements.

Prepare to Observe

1. **Know your goal.** Do you need to understand a place or a process? Solve a problem? Answer a question? What kind of information do you want to gather?
2. **Consider possible perspectives and vantage points.** Should you observe the site passively or interact with it? Should you simply record data or also include impressions? Should you observe from one position or several?
3. **Plan your observation.** Preparation involves both academic and practical issues: doing sufficient background research; listing questions to answers; seeking permission to observe, if needed; taking safety precautions; considering timing issues; and gathering observation tools.

Conduct Your Observations

1. **Be flexible but focused.** Follow your plan, but be open to surprises. Pay attention to the big picture (the context, time frame, and surroundings), but focus on your observational goal by filtering out unnecessary details.
2. **Identify your position.** Where are you in the site? What is your angle? More broadly, what is your personal and/or cultural stance here?
3. **Take notes on specific details and impressions.** While being careful not to miss too much, jot down data for later review—conditions, appearances, actions, events, and so on. If appropriate, focus on your five senses: sight, sound, smell, touch, and taste.
4. **Gather other forms of evidence.** Take measurements, record images and sound, gather samples, interview people, study event programs, get brochures.

Make Sense of Your Observations

1. **Complete and review your notes and evidence.** As soon as possible, flesh out your notes a bit more fully—while your memory is still good. Then examine closely everything that you have written, recorded, and collected, looking for patterns and themes.
2. **List your conclusions.** Describe what has been clarified about your topic through the observation.
3. **Relate your observations to your other research.** Explore how your observations confirm, contradict, complement, or build on other sources of information.

Becoming Familiar with the Library

The library door is your gateway to information. Inside, the library holds a wide range of research resources, from books to periodicals, from reference librarians to electronic databases.

To improve your ability to succeed at all your research assignments, become familiar with your school's library system. Take advantage of tours and orientation sessions to learn its physical layout, resources, and services. Check your library's website for policies, tutorials, and research tools. As shown below, the library offers a variety of resources for your research projects.

Librarians: Librarians are information experts:
- Librarians manage the library's materials and guide you to resources.
- They help you perform online searches.

Collections: The library collects and houses a variety of materials:
- **Books and electronic materials**—CDs and DVDs
- **Periodicals**—journals, magazines, and newspapers (print or microform)
- **Reference materials**—directories, indexes, handbooks, encyclopedias, and almanacs
- **Special collections**—government publications, historical documents, and original artifacts

Research tools: The library contains many tools that direct you to materials:
- The online catalogue allows you to search everything in the library.
- Print indexes and subscription databases (Lexis-Nexis, EBSCOhost, ProQuest Direct) point you to abstracts and full-text articles.
- Internet access connects you with other library catalogues and online references.

Special services: Special services may also help you to complete research:
- Interlibrary loan allows you to obtain books and articles not available in your library.
- "Hold" allows you to request a book that is currently signed out.
- "Reserve" materials give you access to materials recommended by your instructors or heavily in demand.
- The reference desk can help you find information quickly, point you to the right resources, and help you with a search.
- Photocopiers, scanners, and presentation software help you perform and share your research.

Cross-Curricular Connection: As you advance in your field of study, become especially familiar with the reference holdings, journals, book stacks, and Web resources related to your major.

Searching the Catalogue

Library materials are catalogued so they are easy to find. In most libraries, books, videos, and other holdings are catalogued in an electronic database. To find material, use book titles, author names, and related keyword searching. (See also pages 416–417.)

Sample Electronic Catalogue

fig. 22.2

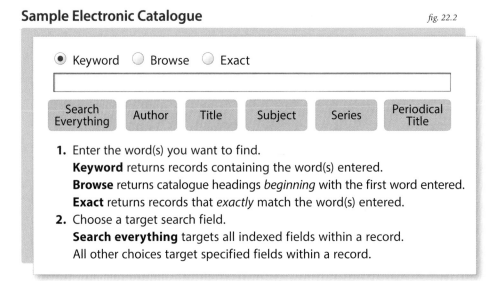

● Keyword ○ Browse ○ Exact

| Search Everything | Author | Title | Subject | Series | Periodical Title |

1. Enter the word(s) you want to find.
   Keyword returns records containing the word(s) entered.
   Browse returns catalogue headings *beginning* with the first word entered.
   Exact returns records that *exactly* match the word(s) entered.
2. Choose a target search field.
   Search everything targets all indexed fields within a record.
   All other choices target specified fields within a record.

When you find a citation for a book or other resource, the result will provide some or all of the following information. Use that information to determine whether the resource is worth exploring further and to figure out other avenues of research. Note that a number of items appearing in blue, underlined type provide links to related books and other resources in the catalogue.

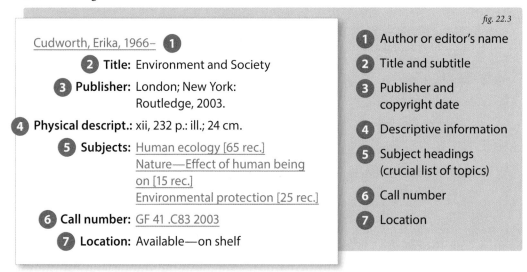

fig. 22.3

Cudworth, Erika, 1966– **1**

2 Title: Environment and Society

3 Publisher: London; New York: Routledge, 2003.

4 Physical descript.: xii, 232 p.: ill.; 24 cm.

5 Subjects: Human ecology [65 rec.]
Nature—Effect of human being on [15 rec.]
Environmental protection [25 rec.]

6 Call number: GF 41 .C83 2003

7 Location: Available—on shelf

1 Author or editor's name
2 Title and subtitle
3 Publisher and copyright date
4 Descriptive information
5 Subject headings (crucial list of topics)
6 Call number
7 Location

Locating Resources by Call Numbers

Library of Congress (LC) call numbers combine letters and numbers to specify a resource's broad subject area, topic, and authorship or title. Finding a book, DVD, or other item involves combining both the alphabetical and the numerical order. Here is a sample call number for *Arctic Refuge: A Vanishing Wilderness?*:

VIDEO QH84.1.A72 1990

subject area (**QH**) topic number (**84**) subtopic number (**1**) cutter number (**A72**)

To find this resource in the library, first note the tab VIDEO. Although not part of the call number, this locator may send you to a specific area of the library. Once there, follow the parts of the call number one at a time:

1. Find the library section on natural history containing videos with the "QH" designation.
2. Follow the numbers until you reach "84."
3. Within the "84" items, find those with the subtopic "1."
4. Use the cutter "A72" to locate the resource alphabetically with "A," and numerically with "72."

Note: In the LC system, pay careful attention to the arrangement of subject area letters, topic numbers, and subtopic numbers: Q98 comes before QH84; QH84 before QH8245; QH84. A72 before QH84.1.A72.

Classification Systems

The LC classification system combines letters and numbers. The Dewey decimal system, which is used in some libraries, uses numbers only. Here is a list of the subject classes for both the LC and Dewey systems.

The Library of Congress and Dewey Decimal Systems

fig. 22.4

LC Category		Dewey Decimal	LC Category		Dewey Decimal
A	General Works	000–999	K	Law	340–349
B	Philosophy	100–199	L	Education	370–379
	Psychology	150–159	M	Music	780–789
	Religion	200–299	N	Fine Arts	700–799
C	History: Auxiliary		P	Language	800–899
	Sciences	910–929		Literature	400–499
D	History: General and		Q	Science	500–599
	Old World	930–999	R	Medicine	610–619
E–F	History of the Americas	970–979	S	Agriculture	630–639
G	Geography	910–919	T	Technology	600–699
	Anthropology	571–573	U	Military Science	355–359, 623
	Recreation	700–799	V	Naval Science	359, 623
H	Social Sciences	300–399	Z	Bibliography	010–019
J	Political Science	320–329		Library Science	020–029

Using Books in Research

Your school library contains a whole range of books for you to use. Unfortunately, for many research projects you simply don't have time to read an entire book, and rarely do the entire contents relate to your topic. Instead, use the strategies outlined below.

Approach the Book Systematically

1. **Identify the book type.** Trade books are typically written for a broad public and published by for-profit presses. Often written by experts, such books can be filled with reliable, useful information for a lay audience, though quality, depth, and reliability can vary. Example: *Flirting with* Pride & Prejudice: *Fresh Perspectives on the Original Chick-Lit Masterpiece*. By comparison, scholarly books are typically written for a specialized audience and for students in college and university. Published by university presses and other respected scholarly presses, such studies typically provide advanced research findings. Example: *Jane Austen on Screen* (Cambridge University Press).

2. **Check out front and back information.** The title and copyright pages give the book's full title and subtitle; the author's name; and publication information, including publication date and Library of Congress subject headings. The back may contain a note on the author's credentials and other publications.

3. **Scan the table of contents.** Examine the contents page to see what the book covers and how it is organized. Ask yourself which chapters are relevant to your project.

4. **Using keywords, search the index.** Check the index for coverage and page locations of the topics most closely related to your project. Are there plenty of pages, or just a few? A scattered mention of keywords likely represents more superficial coverage than concentrated, in-depth coverage.

5. **Skim the preface, foreword, or introduction.** The opening materials will often indicate the book's perspective, explain its origin, and preview its contents.

6. **Check appendices, glossaries, or bibliographies.** These special sections may be a good source of tables, graphics, definitions, statistics, and clues for further research.

7. **Carefully read appropriate chapters and sections.** Think through the material you've read and take good notes. (See pages 424–427.) Follow references to authors and other works to do further research on the topic. Study footnotes and endnotes for insights and leads.

Consider these options for working productively with books:
- When you find a helpful book, browse nearby shelves for more books.
- To confirm a book's quality, check the Internet or a periodical database for a review.
- If your library subscribes to an ebook service such as NetLibrary, you have access to thousands of books in electronic form. You can conduct electronic searches, browse or check out promising books, and read them online.

Using Reference Resources

Reference works, whether print or digital, are information-rich resources that can give you an overview of your topic, supply basic facts, share common knowledge about your topic, and offer ideas for focusing and furthering your research. While some reference resources are available on the free Web (see, for example, the discussion of Wikipedia on pages 458–459), your library offers you excellent access to reference resources in both print and digital formats. Consider options like those below.

Check Reference Works That Supply Information

- **Encyclopedias** supply facts and overviews for topics arranged alphabetically. General encyclopedias cover many fields of knowledge: *Encyclopedia Britannica* (online version). Specialized encyclopedias focus on a single topic: *The Canadian Encyclopedia* (online) and the *Encyclopedia of American Film Comedy* (print).
- **Almanacs, yearbooks, and statistical resources,** normally published annually, contain diverse facts. For example, the Statistics Canada website (www.statscan. gc.ca) provides data on population, geography, politics, employment, business, science, and industry.
- **Vocabulary resources** supply information on languages. General dictionaries, such as *The Canadian Oxford Dictionary,* supply definitions and histories for a whole range of words. Specialized dictionaries define words common to a field, topic, or group: *The New Harvard Dictionary of Music.* Bilingual dictionaries translate words from one language to another.
- **Biographical resources** supply information about people. General biographies cover a broad range of people. Other biographies focus on people from a specific group. ***Examples:*** *Dictionary of Canadian Biography, World Artists 1980–1990.*
- **Directories** supply contact information for people, groups, and organizations. ***Examples:*** *Canada Post–Find a Postal Code* (online), *Members of Parliament Directory*

Check Reference Works That are Research Tools

- **Guides and handbooks** help readers explore specific topics: *The Handbook of North American Indians, A Guide to Prairie Fauna.*
- **Indexes** point you to useful resources. Whether general or specialized, such indexes are available online in databases your library subscribes to. (See pages 448–451.)
- **Bibliographies** list resources on a specific topic. A good, current bibliography can be used as an example when you compile your own bibliography on a topic.
- **Abstracts**, like indexes, direct you to articles on a particular topic. But abstracts also summarize those materials so you learn whether a resource is relevant before you invest time in locating and reading it. Such abstracts are typically incorporated into many online subscription databases.

Finding Articles Via Databases

Periodicals are publications or broadcasts produced at regular intervals (daily, weekly, monthly, quarterly). Although some periodicals are broad in their subject matter and audience, as a rule they focus on a narrow range of topics geared toward a particular audience.

- **Daily newspapers and newscasts** provide up-to-date information on current events, opinions, and trends—from politics to natural disasters *(The Globe and Mail, The Chronicle Herald* [Halifax], CBC's *The National).*
- **Weekly and monthly magazines** generally provide more in-depth information on a wide range of topics *(Maclean's, The Walrus, The Fifth Estate).*
- **Journals**, generally published quarterly, provide specialized scholarly information for a narrowly focused audience *(The Journal of the Canadian Historical Association).*

With thousands of periodicals available, how do you find helpful articles? Learn (a) which search tools your library offers, (b) which periodicals it has available in which forms, and (c) how to gain access to those periodicals.

Search Online Databases

If your library subscribes to EBSCOhost, Lexis-Nexis, or another database service, use keyword searching (see pages 416–417) to find citations on your topic. You might start with the general version of such databases, such as EBSCOhost's Academic Search Premier, which provides access to more than 4,100 scholarly publications covering all disciplines.

- **Basic Search:** Figure 22.5 shows an EBSCOhost search screen for a search on hybrid electric cars. Notice how limiters, expanders, and other advanced features help you find the highest-quality materials.

fig. 22.5

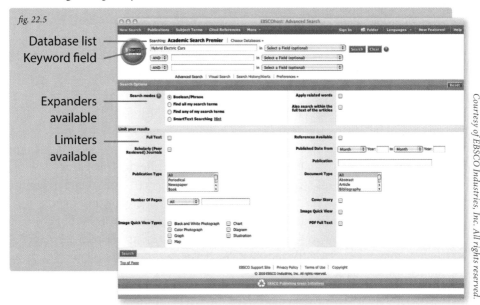

Database list
Keyword field
Expanders available
Limiters available

- **Advanced Search:** A more focused research strategy would involve turning to specialized databases, which are available for virtually every discipline and are often an option within search services such as EBSCOhost (for example, Business Source Elite, PsycINFO, ERIC) and Lexis-Nexis (for example, Legal, Medical, and Business databases). If a basic search turns up little, turn to specialized databases, seeking help from a librarian if necessary. For a list of specialized databases, see page 451.

 Particularly if you need articles published before 1985, you may need to go to the *Readers' Guide to Periodical Literature* or another print index. While databases are converting pre-1985 articles to digital form (for example, the JSTOR database), many excellent periodical articles are available only in print. To use the *Reader's Guide,* consult a librarian.

Generate Citation Lists of Promising Articles

Your database search should generate lists of citations, brief descriptions of articles that were flagged through keywords in titles, subject terms, abstracts, and so on. For example, a search focused on hybrid electric cars leads to the results shown in Figure 22.6. At this point, study the results and do the following:

- Refine the search by narrowing or expanding it.
- Mark specific citations for "capture" or further study.
- Re-sort the results.
- Follow links in a specific citation to further information.

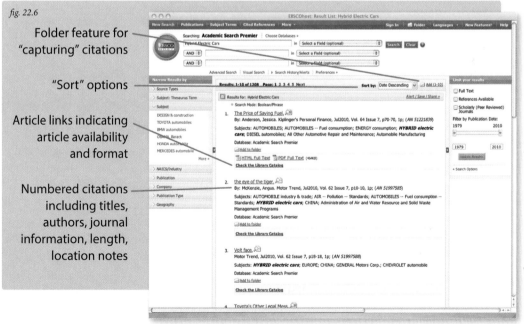

fig. 22.6

Folder feature for "capturing" citations

"Sort" options

Article links indicating article availability and format

Numbered citations including titles, authors, journal information, length, location notes

Study Citations and Capture Identifying Information

By studying citations (especially abstracts), you can determine three things:

- Is this article relevant to your research?
- Is an electronic, full-text version available?
- If not, does the library have this periodical?

To develop your working bibliography (see pages 422–423), you should also "capture" the article's identifying details by using the save, print, or email function, or by recording the periodical's title, the issue and date, and the article's title and page numbers. These functions are shown in the EBSCOhost citation in Figure 22.7.

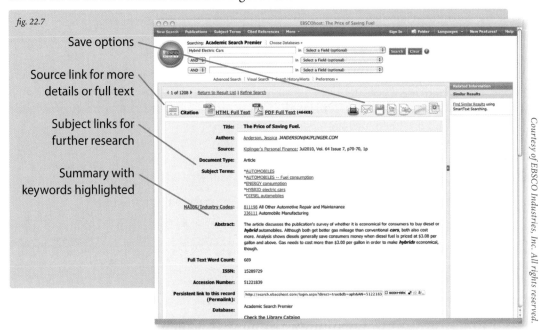

fig. 22.7

Save options

Source link for more details or full text

Subject links for further research

Summary with keywords highlighted

Find and Retrieve the Full Text of the Article

When citations indicate that you have promising articles, access those articles efficiently, preferably through a direct link in the citation to an electronic copy. From there you can print, save, or email the article. If the article is not available electronically, track down a print version:

- Check the online citation to see if your library has the article. If necessary, check your library's inventory of periodicals held; this list should be available online and/or in print. Examine especially closely the issues and dates available, the form (print or microfilm), and the location (bound or current shelves).
- To get the article, follow your library's procedure. You may have to submit a request slip so that a librarian can get the periodical, or you may be able to get it yourself in the current, bound, or microfilm collection. If the article is not available online or in your library, use interlibrary loan.

Databases for Disciplines

Most libraries offer access to databases from a wide range of disciplines. Check your library's website for access to databases like these:

- **Agricola** offers citations from the National Agricultural Library group—with materials focused on issues from animal science to food and nutrition.
- **ARTbibliographies Modern** provides abstracts of articles, books, catalogues, and other resources on modern and contemporary art.
- **CAIRSS for Music** offers bibliographic citations for articles on music-related topics, from music education to music therapy.
- **Canadian Periodical Index Quarterly (CPI.Q)** covers a broad range of subjects related to Canada by indexing approximately 1,200 Canadian periodicals, both English and French, and offering full-text articles for about 500 periodicals.
- **Communication & Mass Media Complete** offers access to resources on topics like public speaking and TV broadcasting.
- **Engineering E-journal Search Engine** offers free, full-text access to more than 150 online engineering journals.
- **ERIC** offers citations, abstracts, and digests for more than 980 journals in the education field.
- **First Search**, a fee-based information service, offers access to more than 30 scholarly databases in a range of disciplines.
- **GPO**, the Government Printing Office, offers access to records for U.S. government documents (e.g., reports, hearings, judicial rules, addresses, and so on).
- **Health Source** offers access to abstracts, indexing, and full-text material on health-related topics, from nutrition to sports medicine.
- **JSTOR** offers full-text access to scholarly articles in a full range of disciplines, articles once available only in print.
- **Math Database** offers article citations for international mathematics research.
- **MEDLINE** offers access to journals in medicine and medicine-related disciplines through references, citations, and abstracts.
- **MLA Bibliography** provides bibliographic citations for articles addressing a range of modern-language and literature-related topics.
- **PsycINFO** offers access to materials in psychology and psychology-related fields (for example, social work, criminology, organizational behaviour).
- **Scirus** indexes science resources, citing article titles and authors, source publication information, and lines of text indicating the article's content.
- **Vocation and Career Collection** offers full-text access to more than 400 trade- and industry-related periodicals.
- **Worldwide Political Science Abstracts** offers bibliographic citations in politics-related fields, from public policy to international law.

Understanding Internet Basics

Did you know that the World Wide Web and the Internet are not the same? Do you know what the *deep Web* is? Can you identify the parts of a Web page? These two pages provide basic definitions and explanations of the digital world.

- The **Internet** is a vast array of interconnected computers and computer networks. It began in 1969 with the ARPANET, a connection of U.S. government computers. Since then, the Internet has expanded into a worldwide system. Email, cellphones, and satellites all access and use the Internet, as do people on the World Wide Web.

- The **World Wide Web** is a huge collection of websites and pages on the Internet, accessible through the hypertext transfer protocol (HTTP). Put simply, this protocol is a set of rules that allow computers to trade information. The World Wide Web was begun in 1989 by a British engineer named Tim Berners-Lee.

- A **uniform resource locator (URL)** is the Web address for each page available on the World Wide Web. Just as every home and business has a specific street address, every website has a specific Web address that allows other computers to find and access it.

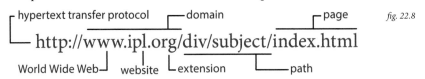

fig. 22.8

- A **domain name** is the website address, often beginning with www and ending with an extension that indicates the origin of the site or its type. Generally, the domain name for websites of Canadian organizations (government, business, educational, and so on) is **.ca**, sometimes with the province abbreviation preceding the .ca (e.g., .on.ca for Ontario). Similarly, websites originating in other nations have parallel domain names, such as **.uk** (United Kingdom) for British sites. Such national domain names help you understand where the site originated and where, in a sense, it is coming from. However, with U.S. websites, the situation is different. Because the Internet originated in the United States, a national domain abbreviation has never been used; instead, domain names indicate the type of organization that created the site and give you clues about the site's goals or purpose—to educate, inform, persuade, sell, and so on. Here are the typical domain names used by U.S. sites:

  .com a commercial or business site
  .gov a U.S. government site, for federal, state, or local government
  .edu an educational site
  .org a site for a nonprofit organization
  .net a site for an organization that belongs to the Internet's infrastructure
  .mil a U.S. military site
  .biz a business site
  .info an information site

- A **Web browser** is a program on your computer that provides access to the Web. Common browsers include Chrome, Internet Explorer, and Safari.

- A **Web page** is a specific grouping of information on the Web (Figure 22.9). Web pages often include text, graphics, photographs, videos, and hyperlinks—which are words or graphics that can be clicked to take the user to different Web pages.

- A **search engine** is a specialized Web page that allows you to find specific terms on sites throughout the Web. Here are some popular search engines:

Google http://www.google.ca
Bing http://www.bing.com
Yahoo http://www.ca.yahoo.com

- A **metasearch engine** is a Web page that searches several other search engines at once, compiling the information. Here are some popular metasearch engines:

Ask http://www.ask.com
Dog Pile http://www.dogpile.com
Ixquick http://www.ixquick.com

- A **deep-Web** tool is an Internet search engine or database that can access materials not available to basic search engines, materials found on what is called the *deep Web*.

Complete Planet http://www.completeplanet.com

Common Web Page Elements

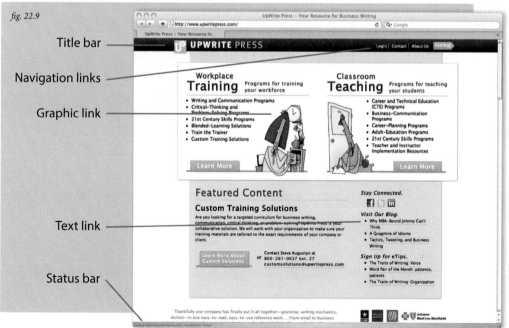

fig. 22.9

Title bar

Navigation links

Graphic link

Text link

Status bar

Image courtesy of UpWrite Press

Using a Subject Guide/Directory

A subject tree, sometimes called a *subject guide* or *directory*, lists websites that have been organized into categories by experts who have reviewed those sites. As such, a subject tree includes sites selected for reliability and quality.

1. **Search out the subject trees available to you.** Check whether your library subscribes to a service such as NetFirst, a database in which subject experts have catalogued Internet resources by topic. Here are some other common subject directories:

   WWW Virtual Library http://vlib.org/Overview.html
   lpl2 http://www.ipl.org/
   LookSmart http://looksmart.com

2. **Follow categories from broad to specific.** A subject tree is arranged from general to specific, so you will need to begin by clicking on a broad category to see a more selective list. Clicking on subcategories will take you to progressively more focused lists. Read the name of a site, review the information beneath the name, check out the domain and extension, and decide if the site is worth exploring. If so, click on it. If not, go back and continue your search. Figure 22.10 illustrates common subject guide elements.

Common Subject Guide Elements

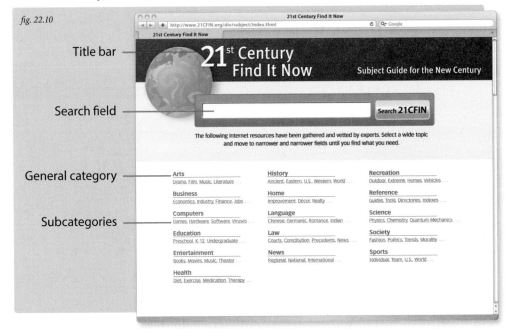

fig. 22.10

Title bar —
Search field —
General category —
Subcategories —

Using Search and Metasearch

Search and metasearch engines provide quick and powerful access to much of the content of the Web. They are invaluable tools for researchers. This page gives tips for getting the most out of your searches, and the next two pages look at search in depth.

1. **Select effective keywords:** Keywords are words or phrases that the search engine looks for across the Web. The more specific a keyword or phrase is, the more tightly a search will be focused. Here are a set of keywords for the research topic of "games used to simulate real-world scenarios":

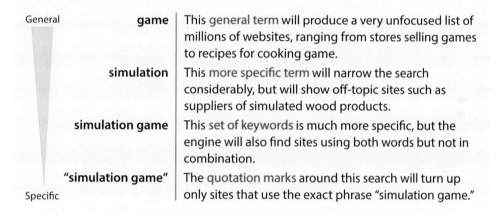

General ... Specific		
game	This general term will produce a very unfocused list of millions of websites, ranging from stores selling games to recipes for cooking game.
simulation	This more specific term will narrow the search considerably, but will show off-topic sites such as suppliers of simulated wood products.
simulation game	This set of keywords is much more specific, but the engine will also find sites using both words but not in combination.
"simulation game"	The quotation marks around this search will turn up only sites that use the exact phrase "simulation game."

2. **Use Boolean operators:** In addition to using quotation marks, you can use words and symbols to make your search specific. (See also page 417.)

game and **war**	*and* indicates sites with both terms
game + **war**	+ indicates sites with both terms
game not **war**	*not* indicates sites with the first term but not the second
game – **war**	– indicates sites with the first term but not the second
game or **simulation**	*or* indicates sites with either term

3. **Act on search results:** Once a search engine has generated a list of possible sites, you need to survey the results and act on them.
   - Read the name of the site and determine how the term is used.
   - Review the domain and extension to decide if you will click it.
   - Look for information and links.

Using Search Engines as Research Tools

Like millions of people, you probably "Google it" when you have a question. But how should you use search engines for academic research projects? A search engine is a program that automatically scours a large amount of Web material using keywords and commands that you submit. In that respect, the search is only as productive as the terms you use, the quality of the search program, and the amount and areas of the Web that the engine searches. When you use search engines, be aware of the issues below, and use the tips on the following page to work around the limitations discussed.

- **Web Coverage:** Even though the largest search engines search billions of Web resources, those pages represent just a portion of the Web—as little as 20 percent. The point to keep in mind is that any given search engine is not searching the entire Web for you and may be focusing on particular kinds of pages and documents. Moreover, a given engine may not be searching each resource in its entirety but only certain portions (e.g., citations) or up to a certain size of the document.

- **Resource Ranking:** A search engine returns results in a ranking of resources based on complex mathematical algorithms—a weighing of a variety of criteria that differ from one engine to the next. One criterion used is the number of times your keywords appear in a given resource. A second criterion might be the number and type of links to a given page—a measure, in other words, of the site's importance or popularity on the Web. A third criterion relates to your search history: given sites that you have looked at in the past, what types of sites do you prefer? Algorithms answer this question by *personalizing* your search, potentially creating what Eli Pariser calls a "filter bubble"—results restricted to your interests and biases. One more point: organizations on the Web work very hard to make sure that their pages get ranked near the top of searches; some companies hire consultants to help achieve this result or even try to fool the programs. In other words, what you are getting in your search is not necessarily an objective listing of the most relevant and reliable resources for an academic research project.

- **Search Habits:** Using search engines is complicated not just by algorithms but by the habits of users themselves. Studies suggest, for example, that very few users look past the first three hits returned by a search, in fact, that only one percent of searchers go past the first ten hits. (You can understand, then, why some organizations work so hard to get into that top-ten list for specific keyword searches.) Moreover, very few users go on to refine their search after the initial results, supposedly satisfied with what they have found, although studies also suggest that few users can effectively evaluate the returned resources in terms of their quality, authority, objectivity, and timeliness (currency of information). The implications for your research projects are clear: such search habits rarely lead to quality resources that you can use in an academic project.

Use Search Engines Well

Given how search engines work, what practices should you follow in using them for an academic research project? Obviously, start by following the assignment's restrictions about using free-Web resources. But here are four additional guidelines:

1. **Restrict search-engine use to specific purposes.** Generally, a search engine is useful for academic research projects in these circumstances:
   - You have a very narrow topic in mind or an exact question you need answered.
   - You have a highly specific word or phrase to use in your search.
   - You want a large number of results.
   - You are looking for a specific type of Internet file.
   - You have the time to sort the material for reliability.

2. **Learn to do advanced searches.** Basic searches tend to lead to basic results. Most search engines actually allow you to do quite complex searches through advanced-search screens. With these, you can employ Boolean logic to a degree, use limiters and expanders, and refine your results in other ways. Study the search engine's help pages for instructions on how to benefit from these advanced-searching techniques.

3. **Approach results with suspicion.** Given the wide-ranging quality and reliability of material on the free Web, it is imperative that you evaluate resources that you find through search engines. See "Evaluating Online Sources" on pages 460–461.

4. **Use search engines that seem to give you more quality results.** Try out a variety of search engines using the same search, and compare the results. While you generally want to choose search engines that cover a large portion of the Web, offer quality indexing, and give you high-powered search capabilities, you also want to consider a search engine's information focus: try out search engines whose goals seem more obviously focused on academics.
   - **Internet Public Library:** http://www.ipl.org Offering access to electronic reference resources, to ebooks and electronic articles, and to special collections, this site's chief resource is its subject collections of Web resources.
   - **Infomine:** http://infomine.ucr.edu Subtitled Scholarly Internet Resource Collections, this librarian-built site is designed for college and university faculty and students; the site offers researchers access to databases, electronic journals and books, and more, including government information.
   - **LookSmart Find Articles.com:** http://findarticles.com This commercial site can give you citations for articles on your topic, although getting full-text access may involve fees.
   - **Google Scholar:** http://scholar.google.com While it indexes just a small portion of all published articles, Google Scholar can help you build citations from a variety of sources, citations you can then find in your library's subscription databases. Moreover, it ranks articles by weighing the full text, the author, the publication, and frequency of citation in other sources.

Understanding the Uses and Limits of Wikipedia

You likely recognize Figure 22.11—an article from Wikipedia. From Wikipedia's beginning in 2001 to today, a large population of volunteer writers and editors has made it a top-ten Internet-traffic site. But is Wikipedia acceptable for academic research? Put simply, Wikipedia is a controversial resource for such projects.

fig. 22.11

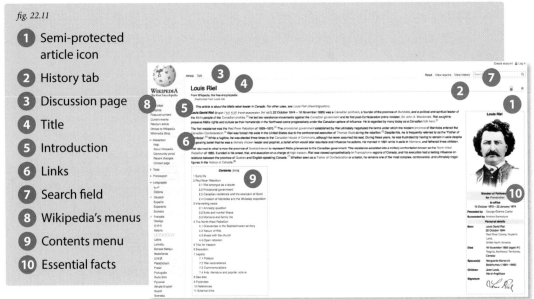

1 Semi-protected article icon
2 History tab
3 Discussion page
4 Title
5 Introduction
6 Links
7 Search field
8 Wikipedia's menus
9 Contents menu
10 Essential facts

Know Wikipedia's Strengths

Because of its wiki nature, Wikipedia offers researchers a number of advantages.

- **Consensus Model of Knowledge:** Articles represent a collaborative agreement about a topic—a topical knowledge base that is fair and fairly comprehensive. Generally, articles improve over time, offering "open-source" knowledge.
- **Currency of Information:** Because they are Web-based, articles are regularly monitored and updated—a distinct advantage over print encyclopedias.
- **Breadth of Information:** With its size and global community, Wikipedia offers articles on a wide range of topics—especially strong in pop culture, current events, computer, and science topics.
- **Links:** Articles are linked throughout so that readers can pursue associated topics, sources, recommended reading, and related categories.

Understand Wikipedia's Standards for Truth

Wikipedia applies a different standard of truth than more traditional sources of information. In his revealing article, "Wikipedia and the Meaning of *Truth*," Simson L. Garfinkle explains this standard of truth. (This article can be found online with a search using the title or author.)

Know Wikipedia's Weaknesses

In some ways, Wikipedia's strengths are closely related to its weaknesses for academic research. Consider these issues:

- **Popularity Model of Knowledge:** The dynamics of popularity can lead to bias, imbalance, and errors. In some ways, this approach minimizes the value of training, education, and expertise while promoting a kind of democracy of knowledge.
- **Anonymity of Authorship:** Wikipedia allows contributors to remain anonymous. Researchers thus have little way of checking credentials and credibility.
- **Variable Quality of Content:** While many well-established articles are quite stable, balanced, and comprehensive, other articles can be partial, driven by a biased perspective, erroneous, and poorly sourced.
- **Variable Coverage:** Wikipedia's strength in some content areas is matched by gaps and incompleteness in other content areas.
- **Vulnerability to Vandalism:** Wikipedia has a number of processes in place to limit people from harming articles with misinformation, with the result that most vandalism is corrected within hours, but some errors have persisted for months.
- **Tertiary Nature of Information:** For most research projects, Wikipedia articles function as tertiary sources—reports of reports of research. As such, Wikipedia articles are not substantial enough for academic projects.

Use Wikipedia Cautiously

Based on Wikipedia's strengths and weaknesses, follow these guidelines:

1. **Respect your assignment.** Instructors may give you varied instruction about using Wikipedia. Respect their guidelines.
2. **Verify Wikipedia information.** If you use information from Wikipedia, also use other more traditional sources to verify that information.
3. **Use Wikipedia as a semi-authoritative reference source.** Generally, the more academic your research assignment, the less you should rely on Wikipedia articles, which are essentially sources of basic and background information.
4. **Use Wikipedia as one starting point.** From a Wikipedia article, you can learn what is considered "open-source" knowledge on your topic, gather ideas for developing a topic, find links to related topics and other resources, and begin to build a bibliography.
5. **Study individual articles to get a sense of their reliability.** When you find a Wikipedia article relevant to your research project, check the article for quality and stability. Use the evaluation criteria on the following pages, but also check the article's history, its discussion page, any tags or icons indicating the article's state, and the "what links here" link in the toolbox at the left of the screen.

Evaluating Online Sources

The Internet contains a wealth of information, but much of it is not suitable for academic research writing. The information may be incorrect, biased, outdated, plagiarized, or otherwise unreliable. These pages discuss issues to watch for.

Assignment Restrictions

Before engaging any Web resources, carefully review your assignment and note any restrictions on what type of sources may be used. If Web resources are allowed, abide by the number or percentage indicated in the assignment.

Author/Organization

When using Web resources, make sure the sites are sponsored by legitimate, recognizable organizations: government agencies, nonprofit groups, and educational institutions. For most projects, avoid relying on personal or special-interest sites, as well as chat rooms, blogs, news groups, or wikis. (These sources may help you explore a topic, but they do not provide scholarly material suitable for most research writing.)

Balance or Bias

Be aware of the purpose of a site or an article. Editorials and reviews, for example, express the point of view of a given author but are not sources for unbiased information. Unless your purpose is to show the author's point of view or point out two sides of an argument, avoid sources that show a bias toward or against a specific region, country, political party, industry, gender, race, ethnic group, or religion. Also, avoid sites that promote a specific cause, product, service, or belief.

Quality of Information

Test the quality of information on a site. Note whether the information is current (when was it posted/updated last) and check it against other sources for corroboration. Also, favour sites with a depth of information and those that show they truly engage their topic rather than treating it superficially.

Quality of Writing and Design

Avoid sites that show sloppy editing and poor design. These surface flaws can reveal a lack of scholarly rigour or serious commitment on the part of the site's creators. At the same time, don't be fooled by flashy sites where the design masks problems with the content.

Evaluation Checklist

Use this checklist to assess the reliability of Web sources. The more items you check off, the more reliable the source is.

Assignment Restrictions

____ **1.** Does the source fit with the type and number allowed in the assignment?

Author/Organization

____ **2.** Is the person or organization behind the site reliable?

____ **3.** Is contact information for the person or organization provided?

____ **4.** Is the site well known and well connected in the field?

____ **5.** Does the site have a clear "About Us" page and mission statement?

Balance or Bias

____ **6.** Is the material on the site balanced and unbiased?

____ **7.** Does the site avoid unfair and inflammatory language?

____ **8.** Does the site avoid pushing a particular product, cause, service, or belief?

____ **9.** Does the site provide ample support for its claims?

____ **10.** Does the site avoid logical fallacies and twisted statistics? (See pages 317–320.)

Quality of Information

____ **11.** Is the material current?

____ **12.** Is the website often updated?

____ **13.** Is the website information-rich?

____ **14.** Is the information backed up by other reputable print and online sources?

Quality of Writing and Design

____ **15.** Is the text free of errors in punctuation, spelling, and grammar?

____ **16.** Is the site effectively and clearly designed?

Gts/Shutterstock.com

Sample Evaluations

Assignment Restrictions	• The site shown in Figure 22.12 would be appropriate for most assignments about the life and work of the American fiction writer William Faulkner, as long as free-Web sources are allowed.
Author/ Organization	• This site is sponsored by the University of Mississippi, a scholarly source for information, and the article's author, Dr. John B. Padgett, is an authority on Faulkner.
Balance or Bias	• The site clearly extols Faulkner as a great writer but does not shy from showing his shortcomings. The claims are fair and amply supported, without logical fallacies.
Quality of Information	• The website is current, often updated, and information-rich. It is also connected to many other Faulkner resources available on the Web.
Quality of Writing and Design	• The site is well designed, with easy navigation, readable text, informative headings, helpful photos, and strong links. The text is well written and well edited.

fig. 22.12

MWP: William Faulkner (1897–1962)

http://www.olemiss.edu/mwp/dir/faulkner_william/

▶ Publications
▶ Other Features
▶ Writer Listings

Go to
▶ Gallery
▶ Publications
▶ Bibliography
▶ Media Adaptations
▶ Internet Resources

See also:
▶ Book Info:

Faulkner in the Twenty-first Century (February 2003)

William Faulkner: Six Decades of Criticism (October 2002)

Absalom, Absalom! (September 2002)

Faulkner and the Politics of Reading, by Karl Zender (August 2002)

Faulkner and Postmodernism, edited by John Duvall and Ann Abadie (July 2002)

New Orleans Sketches (June 2002)

The Unvanquished (Large Print edition)

William Faulkner
© The Cofield Collection

William Faulkner

The man himself never stood taller than five feet, six inches tall, but in the realm of American literature, William Faulkner is a giant. More than simply a renowned Mississippi writer, the Nobel Prize-winning novelist and short story writer is acclaimed throughout the world as one of the twentieth century's greatest writers, one who transformed his "postage stamp" of native soil into an apocryphal setting in which he explored, articulated, and challenged "the old verities and truths of the heart." During what is generally considered his period of greatest artistic achievement, from *The Sound and the Fury* in 1929 to *Go Down, Moses* in 1942, Faulkner accomplished in a little over a decade more artistically than most writers accomplish over a lifetime of writing. It is one of the more remarkable feats of American literature, how a young man who never graduated from high school, never received a college degree, living in a small town in the poorest state in the nation, all the while balancing a growing family of dependents and impending financial ruin, could during the Great Depression write a series of novels all set in the same small Southern county — novels that include *As I Lay Dying*, *Light in August*, and above all, *Absalom, Absalom!* — that would one day be recognized as among the greatest novels ever written by an American.

The Early Years

William Cuthbert Falkner (as his name was then spelled) was born on September 25, 1897, in New Albany, Mississippi, the first of four sons born to Murry and Maud Butler Falkner. He was named after his great-grandfather, William Clark Falkner, the "Old Colonel," who had been killed eight years earlier in a duel with his former business partner in the streets of Ripley, Mississippi. A lawyer, politician, planter, businessman, Civil War colonel, railroad financier, and finally a best-selling writer (of the novel *The White Rose of Memphis*), the Old Colonel, even in death, loomed as a larger-than-life model of personal and professional success for his male descendants.

A few days before William's fifth birthday, the Falkners moved to Oxford, Mississippi, at the urging of Murry's father, John Wesley Thompson Falkner. Called the "Young Colonel" out of homage to his father rather than to actual military service, the younger Falkner had abruptly decided to sell the railroad begun by his father. Disappointed that he would not inherit the railroad, Murry took a series of jobs in Oxford, most of them with the

Related Links & Info

William Clark Falkner
© The Cofield Collection

Courtesy of Dr. John B. Padgett.

NEL

- As a blog, the site shown in Figure 22.13 would not be appropriate for an assignment about the life and work of William Faulkner. A site such as this should be recognized as reflective only of the writer's opinion, not of reliable information or fact.
- There is no author or organization listed for this website. The domain name—myviewsonliterature.wordpress.com—shows that this is a personal opinion blog. Its lack of connection to other websites shows it represents an isolated opinion.
- This blog post shows a strong bias against William Faulkner. The few facts cited inadequately support the writer's main point, and logical fallacies are apparent. The tone of the post is unscholarly, with inflammatory language.
- Though this website is frequently updated, the blog post does not represent current scholarship about William Faulkner. The website is information-poor and is not backed up by any reputable print or online sources.
- The site has an amateurish design and numerous errors, including the persistent misspelling of William Faulkner's name. The writing is slipshod, and the editing is poor.

fig. 22.13

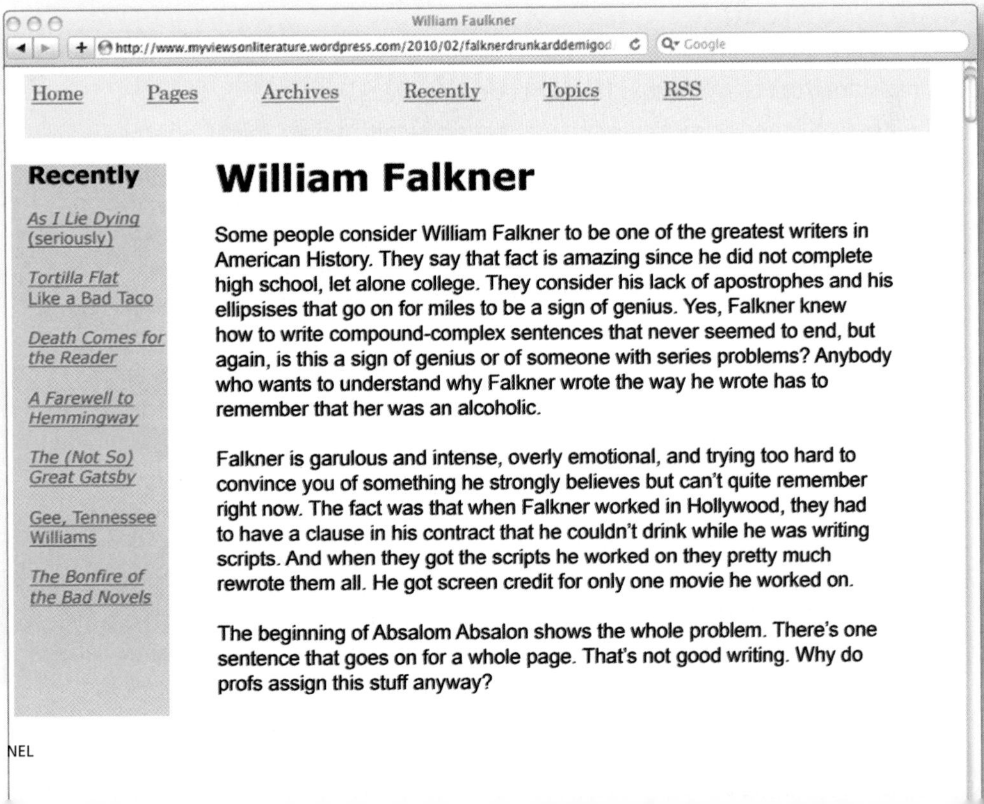
William Faulkner
http://www.myviewsonliterature.wordpress.com/2010/02/falknerdrunkarddemigod
Google
Home
Pages
Archives
Recently
Topics
RSS
Recently
As I Lie Dying (seriously)
Tortilla Flat Like a Bad Taco
Death Comes for the Reader
A Farewell to Hemmingway
The (Not So) Great Gatsby
Gee, Tennessee Williams
The Bonfire of the Bad Novels
William Falkner
Some people consider William Falkner to be one of the greatest writers in American History. They say that fact is amazing since he did not complete high school, let alone college. They consider his lack of apostrophes and his ellipsises that go on for miles to be a sign of genius. Yes, Falkner knew how to write compound-complex sentences that never seemed to end, but again, is this a sign of genius or of someone with series problems? Anybody who wants to understand why Falkner wrote the way he wrote has to remember that her was an alcoholic.
Falkner is garulous and intense, overly emotional, and trying too hard to convince you of something he strongly believes but can't quite remember right now. The fact was that when Falkner worked in Hollywood, they had to have a clause in his contract that he couldn't drink while he was writing scripts. And when they got the scripts he worked on they pretty much rewrote them all. He got screen credit for only one movie he worked on.
The beginning of Absalom Absalon shows the whole problem. There's one sentence that goes on for a whole page. That's not good writing. Why do profs assign this stuff anyway?

Courtesy of Dr. John B. Padgett.

Critical-Thinking and Writing Activities

As directed by your instructor, complete the following activities.

1. Wernher von Braun once said, "Basic research is what I am doing when I don't know what I am doing." In what sense does all research involve figuring out what you are doing?

2. Think about a research project that you have done or are doing now. How might primary research and library research (scholarly books and journals) strengthen your writing? Why not do all your research on the free Web?

3. Working with your library's website and its orientation tools, identify where you can physically and/or electronically locate books, reference resources, and journals.

4. Explore your library's handouts and website for information about Internet research. What services, support, and access does the library provide?

5. Brainstorm issues related to food production, consumption, or culture. Choosing one issue, use your library's catalogue and database tools to track down and evaluate print books and periodical articles. Then do a free-Web search of the topic, comparing the results.

6. Using the variety of methods outlined in this chapter, work with some classmates to search the Internet for information on a controversial topic, event, person, or place. Carefully analyze and evaluate the range of Web information you find.

Learning-Objectives Checklist ✓

Have you achieved this chapter's learning objectives? Check your progress with the items below, revisiting topics in the chapter as needed. *I have . . .*

____ effectively planned primary research, if needed for my project, following sound principles and practices (434–435).

____ performed primary research successfully, whether conducting a survey, analyzing documents or artifacts, doing an interview, or making observations (436–442).

____ familiarized myself with the library and its research tools (443).

____ performed keyword searches of the catalogue, locating through call numbers relevant books and other resources for my project (444–445).

____ approached books systematically in order to work with them productively (446).

____ located and mined reference works relevant to my topic (447).

____ searched library databases to generate citations of periodical articles, studied those citations, and retrieved promising articles (448–451).

____ differentiated elements of the Internet related to research, including the distinction between the free Web and the deep Web (452–453).

____ effectively searched the Web using subject directories and search engines, aware of the strengths and limits of such tools and such resources as Wikipedia (454–459).

____ carefully evaluated free-Web resources in terms of authorship or sponsorship, balance, quality of information, and quality of writing and design (460–463).

Chapter 23

Building Credibility: Avoiding Plagiarism

"That's incredible!" is normally a positive exclamation of amazement. But maybe it's an exclamation that you do not want to hear about your research writing, if "incredible" means "unbelievable." If your paper is unbelievable, your credibility as a researcher and a writer is seriously damaged.

Obviously, you want to draft a strong, well-documented paper—a credible discussion of your carefully researched topic. While the next chapter focuses on drafting such a paper, this chapter prepares you for drafting by explaining how to build and maintain credibility. It starts with these principles:

1. Write the paper yourself. Take ownership of your thinking, research, and writing.
2. Be honest, accurate, and measured.
3. Show respect to your reader, the topic, and opposing viewpoints.
4. Establish your credentials by showing that you have done careful research.

Visually Speaking Copying—what's wrong with it? Using Figure 23.1 as a starting point, reflect on the nature of copying as an issue in life and in research.

Learning **Objectives**

By working through this chapter, you will be able to

- differentiate between poor and effective uses of sources in your writing.
- define and recognize plagiarism.
- explain why plagiarism is a serious academic offence.
- prevent plagiarism within your own writing.
- distinguish other source abuses and avoid them in your writing.

Jason Benz Bennee/Shutterstock.com

fig. 23.1

Developing Credibility through Source Use

Your credibility—how fully readers trust and believe you—is partly rooted in how well you treat your sources. While abuses such as distorting a source's ideas damage your credibility, good practices enhance it. Contrast the passages below and on the next page.

Writing with Poor Use of Sources

A poor paper might read like a recitation of unconnected facts, unsupported opinions, or undigested quotations. It may contain contradictory information or illogical conclusions. A source's ideas may be distorted or taken out of context. At its worst, poor source use involves plagiarism.

The writing offers weak generalizations in several spots.

It goes without saying that cell phone usage has really increased a lot, from the beginning of the cell phone's history until now. How many people still don't have a cell—basically, no one! The advantages of cell phones are obvious, but has anyone really thought about the downside of this technological innovation? For example, there's "rinxiety," where people believe that their cell phones are ringing but they're not. Two-thirds of cell users have reported this feeling, which some experts believe to be a rewiring of the nervous system similar to phantom limb pain, while other experts thinks it's about the pitch of cell rings. It's not good.

Material from sources is clearly borrowed but not referenced through in-text citation.

But the most serious problem with cell phones is without a doubt driving while talking or texting. Due to the increasing complexity of mobile phones—often more like mobile computers in their available uses—it has introduced additional difficulties for law enforcement officials in being able to tell one usage from another as drivers use their devices. This is more apparent in those countries who ban both hand-held and hands-free usage, rather than those who have banned hand-held use only, as officials cannot easily tell which function of the mobile phone is being used simply by visually looking at the driver. This can mean that drivers may be stopped for using their device illegally on a phone call, when in fact they were not; instead using the device for a legal purpose such as the phones' incorporated controls for car stereo or satnav usage—either as part of the cars' own device or directly on the mobile phone itself.

A passage from an online source is copied and pasted into the paper without credit.

The writer uses a visual without indicating the source or effectively discussing its meaning.

The question arises, is the cell phone even being used as a phone? And are these other uses legitimate or just gimmicks? This chart makes the point.

Cell Phone Usage

- Text Messaging
- Making Phone Calls
- Checking the Time

1

2

3

Writing with Strong Use of Sources

A strong paper centres on the writer's ideas—ideas advanced through thoughtful engagement with and crediting of sources. It offers logical analysis or a persuasive argument built on reliable information from quality sources that have been treated with intellectual respect. Note these features at work in the excerpt below from student writer Brandon Jorritsma's essay on cellphone dependency.

Facts and ideas are credited through in-text citations, which are linked to full source information on a works-cited page.

The writer builds on and reasons with source material.

This dependency on cells is reflected in the phenomenon that has come to be termed "rinxiety." Frequent cell phone users are reporting numerous instances of either hearing their phones ring or feeling them vibrate, even if their phones are not around. Two thirds of cell phone users in a recent survey report having experienced this ("Phantom Ringing"), which is thought by some to be a rewiring of the nervous system similar to phantom limb pain (Lynch). Others theorize that it is a result of the pitch of typical cell rings being similar to elements of commonplace sounds, such as running water, music, traffic, and television (Lynch, Goodman). Regardless of the particular explanation, the experience of rinxiety is more common among young, frequent users of cell phones, which seems to indicate a constant expectation of calls ("Phantom Ringing"). This expectation is damaging to relationships because someone expecting a phone call or email to arrive at any moment is not mentally present in other interactions he or she may be involved in. We've all experienced being around someone who was waiting on a phone call. How much more distracted would that person be if he or she were subconsciously expecting a phone call every hour of the day?

Direct quotations from sources are indicated with quotation marks.

A case study from a source makes a concept concrete through cause-effect reasoning.

The corollary of constantly expecting incoming cell communication is the constant impulse to send out messages. Fifty-two percent of respondents to an informal survey at CSU, Fresno, admitted to being "preoccupied with the next time they could text message," and forty-six percent of students "reported irritability when unable to use their cell phones" (Lui). In a study of an international sample of cell phone users, some respondents recounted how they felt anxiety if they forgot to take their phone out of the house with them (Jarvenpaa 12). Even when the phone was not anywhere near them, they couldn't escape its demands on their attention. The phone has moved from being an object of utility to being one of psychological necessity, which constantly demands attention from its user regardless of its proximity or restrictions on its use. Lauren Hawn, a student at Pennsylvania State University, reports that when she is near her cell, she does the following: "I seem to look at it a lot and check the time [on the phone's digital display] even when I don't need to" (qtd. in Lynch). Hawn does not consciously think that there is a phone call or text message . . . .

Recognizing Plagiarism

The road to plagiarism may be paved with the best intentions—or the worst. Either way, the result is still a serious academic offence. As you write your research paper, do everything you can to stay off that road! Start by studying your school's and your instructor's guidelines on plagiarism and other academic offences. Then study the following pages.

What Is Plagiarism?

Plagiarism is using someone else's words, ideas, or images (what's called intellectual property) so they appear to be your own. When you plagiarize, you use source material—whether published in print or online—without acknowledging the source. In this sense, plagiarism refers to a range of thefts:

- Submitting a paper you didn't write yourself
- Pasting large chunks of a source into your paper and passing it off as your own work
- Using summaries, paraphrases, or quotations without documentation
- Using the exact phrasing of a source without quotation marks
- Mixing up source material and your own ideas—failing to distinguish between the two

 Plagiarism refers to more than "word theft." Because plagiarism is really about failing to credit ideas and information, the rules also apply to visual images, tables, graphs, charts, maps, music, videos, and so on.

What Does Plagiarism Look Like?

Plagiarism refers to a range of source abuses. What exactly do these violations look like? Read the passage below, and then review the five types of plagiarism that follow, noting how each example misuses the source.

> **The passage below is from page 87 of "Some Stories Have to Be Told by Me: A Literary History of Alice Munro," by Marcela Valdes, published in the *Virginia Quarterly Review* 82.3 (2006).**
>
> What makes Munro's characters so enthralling is their inconsistency; like real people, at one moment they declare they will cover the house in new siding, at the next, they vomit on their way to the hospital. They fight against and seek refuge in the people they love. The technique that Munro has forged to get at such contradictions is a sort of pointillism, the setting of one bright scene against another, with little regard for chronology.

Sielan/Shutterstock.com

Marcela Valdes, "Some Stories Have to be Told by Me: A Literary History of Alice Munro", Virginia Quarterly Review, Vol. 82 No. 3, 2006.

NEL

Using Copy and Paste

It is unethical to take chunks of material from another source and splice them into your paper without acknowledgment. In the example below, the writer pastes in a sentence from the original article (boldfaced) without using quotation marks or a citation. Even if the writer changed some words, it would still be plagiarism.

> Life typically unfolds mysteriously for Munro's characters, with unexplained events and choices. **Like real people, at one moment they declare they will cover the house in new siding, at the next, they vomit on their way to the hospital.**

Failing to Cite a Source

Borrowed material must be documented. Even if you use information accurately and fairly, don't neglect to cite the source. Below, the writer correctly summarizes the passage's idea but offers no citation.

> For the reader, the characters in Munro's stories are interesting because they are so changeable. Munro shows these changes by using a method of placing scenes side by side for contrast, without worrying about the chronological connections.

Neglecting Necessary Quotation Marks

Whether it's a paragraph or a phrase, if you use the exact wording of a source, that material must be enclosed in quotation marks. In the example below, the writer cites the source but doesn't use quotation marks around a phrase taken from the original (boldfaced).

> What makes Munro's characters so typically human is that they **fight against and seek refuge in the people they love (Valdes 87).**

Confusing Borrowed Material with Your Own Ideas

Through carelessness (often in note taking), you may confuse source material with your own thinking. Below, the writer indicates that he borrowed material in the first sentence, but fails to indicate that he also borrowed the next sentence.

> As Marcela Valdes explains, "[w]hat makes Munro's characters so enthralling is their inconsistency" (87). **To achieve this sense of inconsistency, Munro places brightly lit scenes beside each other in a kind of pointillist technique.**

Submitting Another Writer's Paper

The most blatant plagiarism is taking an entire piece of writing and claiming it as your own work. Examples:

- Downloading, reformatting, and submitting an article as your own work
- Buying a paper from a "paper mill" or taking a "free" paper off the Internet
- Turning in another student's work as your own (see "Falstaffing" on page 473)

 Just as it's easy to plagiarize using the Internet, it's easy for your professors to recognize and track down plagiarism using Internet tools.

Understanding Why Plagiarism Is Serious

Perhaps the answer is obvious. But some people operate with the notion that material on the Internet is "free" and, therefore, fair game for research writing. After all, a lot of stuff on the Web doesn't even list an author, so what's the harm? Here's some food for thought:

Academic Dishonesty

At its heart, plagiarism is cheating—stealing intellectual property and passing it off as one's own work. Colleges and universities take such dishonesty seriously. Plagiarism, whether intentional or unintentional, will likely be punished in one or more ways:

- A failing grade for the assignment
- A failing grade for the course
- A note on your academic transcript (often seen by potential employers) that failure resulted from academic dishonesty
- Expulsion from your school

Theft from the Academic Community

The research paper represents your dialogue with other members of the academic community—classmates, the instructor, others in your major, others who have researched the topics, and so on. When you plagiarize, you short-circuit the dialogue:

- You gain an unfair advantage over your classmates who follow the rules and earn their grades.
- You disrespect other writers, researchers, and scholars.
- You disrespect your readers by passing off others' ideas as your own.
- You insult your instructor, a person whose respect you need.
- You harm your school by risking its reputation and its academic integrity.

Present and Future Harm

Because research projects help you master course-related concepts and writing skills, plagiarism robs you of an opportunity to learn. Moreover, you rob yourself of your integrity and reputation. After all, as a student you are seeking to build your credibility within the broader academic community, your major, and your future profession.

In addition, research projects often train you for your future work in terms of research, thinking, and writing skills—skills that you will need to succeed in the workplace. If you do not learn the skills now, you will enter the workplace without them—a situation that your employer will, at some point, find out.

 One tool to deter plagiarism is Turnitin.com. Students submit their papers for comparison against millions of Web pages and other student papers. Students and instructors get reports about originality and matching text.

Avoiding Plagiarism

Preventing plagiarism begins the moment you get an assignment. Essentially, prevention requires your commitment and diligence throughout the project. Follow these tips:

1. **Resist temptation.** With the Internet, plagiarism is a mouse click away. Avoid last-minute all-nighters that make you desperate; start research projects early. Note: It's better to ask for an extension or to accept a penalty for lateness than to plagiarize.

2. **Play by the rules.** Become familiar with your school's definition, guidelines, and policies regarding plagiarism so that you don't unknowingly violate them. When in doubt, ask your instructor for clarification.

3. **Take orderly, accurate notes.** From the start, carefully keep track of source material and distinguish it from your own thinking. Specifically, do the following:
   - Maintain an accurate working bibliography (pages 422–423).
   - Adopt a decent note-taking system (pages 424–427).
   - Accurately summarize, paraphrase, and quote sources (pages 428–431).

4. **Document borrowed material.** Credit information that you have summarized, paraphrased, or quoted from any source, whether that information is statistics, facts, graphics, phrases, or ideas. Readers can then see what's borrowed and what's yours, understand your support, and do their own follow-up research.

   > **Common Knowledge Exception:** Common knowledge is information—a basic fact, for instance—that is generally known to readers or easily found in several sources, particularly reference works. Such knowledge need not be cited. However, when you go beyond common knowledge into research findings, interpretations of the facts, theories, explanations, claims, arguments, and graphics, you must document the source. Study the examples below, but whenever you are in doubt, document.

   > *Examples:*
   > - The fact that automakers are developing hybrid-electric cars is common knowledge, whereas the details of GM's AUTOnomy project are not.
   > - The fact that Shakespeare wrote *Hamlet* is common knowledge, whereas the details of his sources are not.

5. **Work carefully with source material in your paper.** See pages 482–485 for more on integrating and documenting sources, but here, briefly, are your responsibilities:
   - Distinguish borrowed material from your own thinking by signalling where source material begins and ends.
   - Indicate the source's origin with an attributive phrase and a citation (parenthetical reference or footnote).
   - Provide full source information in a works-cited or references page.

Avoiding Other Source Abuses

Plagiarism, though the most serious offence, is not the only source abuse to avoid when writing a paper with documented research. Consider these pitfalls, which refer again to the sample passage on page 468.

Using Sources Inaccurately

When you get a quotation wrong, botch a summary, paraphrase poorly, or misstate a statistic, you misrepresent the original. In this quotation, the writer carelessly uses several wrong words that change the meaning, as well as adding two words that are not in the original.

> As Marcela Valdes explains, "[w]hat makes Munro's characters so appalling is their consistency. . . . They fight against and seek refuse in the people they say they love" (87).

Using Source Material Out of Context

By ripping a statement out of its context and forcing it into yours, you can make a source seem to say something that it didn't really say. This writer uses part of a statement to say the opposite of the original.

> According to Marcela Valdes, while Munro's characters are interesting, Munro's weakness as a fiction writer is that she shows "little regard for chronology" (87).

Overusing Source Material

When your paper reads like a string of references, especially quotations, your own thinking disappears. The writer below takes the source passage, chops it up, and splices it together.

> Anyone who has read her stories knows that "[w]hat makes Munro's characters so enthralling is their inconsistency." That is to say, "like real people, at one moment they declare they will cover the house in new siding, at the next, they vomit on their way to the hospital." Moreover, "[t]hey fight against and seek refuge in the people they love." This method "that Munro has forged to get at such contradictions is a sort of pointillism," meaning "the setting of one bright scene against another, with little regard for chronology" (Valdes 87)

"Plunking" Quotations

When you "plunk" quotations into your paper by failing to prepare the reader for them and follow them up, the discussion becomes choppy and disconnected. The writer below interrupts the flow of ideas with a quotation "out of the blue." In addition, the quotation hangs at the end of a paragraph with no follow-up.

> Typically, characters such as Del Jordan, Louisa Doud, and Almeda Roth experience a crisis through contact with particular men. "They fight against and seek refuge in the people they love" (Valdes 87).

Using "Blanket" Citations

Your reader shouldn't have to guess where borrowed material begins and ends. For example, if you place a parenthetical citation at the end of a paragraph, does that citation cover the whole paragraph or just the final sentence?

Relying Heavily on One Source

If your writing is dominated by one source, readers may doubt the depth and integrity of your research. Instead, your writing should show your reliance on a balanced diversity of sources.

Failing to Match In-Text Citations to Bibliographic Entries

All in-text citations must clearly refer to accurate entries in the works-cited, references, or endnotes page. Mismatching occurs in the following circumstances:

- An in-text citation refers to a source that is not listed in the bibliography.
- A bibliographic resource is never actually referenced anywhere in the paper.

Related Academic Offences

Beyond plagiarism and related source abuses, steer clear of these academic offences:

Double-dipping: When you submit one paper in two different classes or otherwise turn in a paper you have turned in before without permission from both instructors, you take double credit for one project.

Falstaffing: This practice refers to a particular type of plagiarism in which one student submits another student's work. Know that you are guilty of Falstaffing if you let another student submit your paper.

Copyright violations: When you copy, distribute, and/or post in whole or in part any intellectual property without permission from or payment to the copyright holder, you commit a copyright infringement, especially when you profit from this use. To avoid copyright violations in your research projects, do the following:

- **Observe fair use guidelines:** Quote small portions of a document for limited purposes, such as education or research. Avoid copying large portions for your own gain.
- **Understand what's in the public domain:** You need not obtain permission to copy and use public domain materials—this includes most very old documents (where the author has been dead over fifty years), some documents created by the government, and some material posted on the Internet as part of the "copy left" movement.
- **Observe intellectual property and copyright laws:** First, know your school's policies on copying documents. Second, realize that copyright protects the expression of ideas in a range of materials—writings, videos, songs, photographs, drawings, computer software, and so on. Always obtain permission to copy and distribute copyrighted materials.
- **Avoid changing a source** (e.g., a photo) without permission of the creator or copyright holder.

Critical-Thinking and Writing Activities

As directed by your instructor, complete the following critical-thinking and writing activities by yourself or with classmates.

1. Gabrielle Roy has suggested that "[t]he main engagement of the writer is towards truthfulness; therefore he must keep his mind and his judgement free." How does this claim relate to the general issue of a research writer's credibility, as well as to the more specific issue of a writer's treatment of sources?

2. Find three articles on the same topic, articles from different media (e.g., newspaper, magazine, website). Explore how each writer attempts to establish and build credibility. How well does each succeed?

3. With some classmates, debate the seriousness of plagiarism and the use of tools such as Turnitin.com.

4. Research your school's academic-integrity policies. How does your school define plagiarism, and how does it address it in its policies and procedures?

5. Compare and contrast the writing samples on pages 466–467 showing poor and strong use of sources. Then examine a research paper that you wrote recently. Is your writing closer to the poor or strong model? What improvements do you need to make in your working with sources?

6. Review the list of source abuses on pages 472–473. Which of these abuses is most common in research writing? Which abuse is most serious? Write a paragraph focusing on one type of source abuse and explaining its effect on scholarship.

Learning-Objectives Checklist ✓

Have you achieved this chapter's learning objectives? Check your progress with the items below, revisiting topics in the chapter as needed. *I have* . . .

____ differentiated between writing that uses sources poorly and writing that uses sources effectively (466–467).

____ defined plagiarism and distinguished the various forms that it might take (468–469).

____ explained the seriousness of plagiarism as a form of academic dishonesty that harms the academic community, as well as my own integrity now and in the future (470).

____ prevented plagiarism in my own writing, following strategies that include knowing the difference between material that must be credited and material that is common knowledge (471).

____ distinguished other source abuses, from inaccurate use of a source to mismatched in-text citations and bibliographic entries, and avoided these abuses in my writing (472–473).

____ identified and avoided academic offences such as double dipping, falstaffing, and copyright violations (473).

Chapter 24

Drafting Papers with Documented Research

When you write a research paper, you enter a larger conversation about your topic. Because you are seeking to add your voice to the conversation, the paper should centre on your own ideas while thoughtfully engaging with the ideas of others. Crediting sources ensures that each voice in the conversation is fairly represented.

This chapter explains how to make the shift from researching your topic to writing about it, focuses on effective and conscientious use of sources in your writing, and helps you write a first draft of your paper. The chapter then shows you good research-writing practices at work in a sample essay on the changing cultural landscape of Calgary.

Visually Speaking   Scales like the one shown in Figure 24.1 are all about weighing and balancing. In what ways does drafting research-based writing involve mental versions of these activities?

Learning **Objectives**

By working through this chapter, you will be able to

- examine your research findings so as to deepen your thinking on a topic.
- assess and strengthen your working thesis.
- organize your writing with your research findings in mind.
- draft your essay so as to respect, smoothly integrate, and effectively document source material.
- compare and contrast research-writing practices in a sample essay with your own practices.

Vicente Barcelo Varona/Shutterstock.com

fig. 24.1

Reviewing Your Findings

With every research project, the time comes when you must transition from exploring your topic to sharing discoveries, from research to writing. To start this transition, take time to review your findings—to go over your notes as many times as necessary, using them to stimulate your thinking and planning. Try these strategies, in particular:

Conduct Q & A

Early in your project, you may have generated a set of research questions (see page 406). Now that you have completed the bulk of your research, you might do the following Q & A activity to clarify how your research has impacted your thinking:

- **Review your primary research question:** What answers has your research produced? Are the answers affirming, engaging, or unsettling?
- **Review your secondary research questions:** What information have you found to answer these questions? How do the answers enhance your thinking?

Deepen Your Thinking on the Topic

During note-taking, you focused on making sense of what individual sources said about your topic. Now, take these steps to deepen and expand your thinking:

- **Identify key discoveries.** What central ideas and new facts have you learned through research? What conclusions have you reached, and why?
- **Identify connections between sources.** How are your sources related to each other? Do they share similar points of view and similar conclusions? Do some sources build on other sources? Which one was published first, second, third, etc.?
- **Identify differences between sources.** In what ways and on what issues do sources disagree? Why? What sense do you make of the differences?
- **Identify limits and gaps.** What issues do your sources not cover? For what questions have you not found answers? How are these gaps important for your project?

Imagine Your Paper

As you review your findings, you can also prepare to write your paper by imagining what it might include. Consider these strategies:

1. **Look for organizational clues.** How do your sources organize their discussions of your topic? Are there particular patterns that make sense of the issues?
2. **Anticipate how you might use source material.** As you study your notes, imagine how different points could be used in your writing. Here are possibilities:
   - background, historical context, and definitions—foundational information
   - principles and theories—idea "tools" for exploring your topic
   - expert reasoning—the thinking of those most knowledgeable about the topic
   - examples and case studies—illustrations that vivify an idea
   - concrete evidence—the facts that support your claims

Sharpening Your Working Thesis

As you prepare to draft your research paper, you might refine your focus by revisiting and revising your working thesis (page 407).

Deepen Your Thesis

Review your working thesis. Given the research that you have completed, does this thesis stand up? It is possible, of course, that your research has led you to a conclusion quite different from your original working thesis. If so, rewrite your thesis accordingly. However, you might also retain your original thesis but strengthen it by using these strategies:

1. **Use richer, clearer terms.** Test your working thesis for vague, broad, or inappropriate terms or concepts. Replace them with terms that have rich meanings, are respected in discussions of your topic, and refine your original thinking.
2. **Introduce qualifying terms where needed.** With qualifying terms such as "normally," "often," and "usually," as well as with phrases that limit the reach of your thesis, you are paradoxically strengthening your thesis by making it more reasonable.
3. **Stress your idea through opposition.** You can deepen your working thesis by adding an opposing thought (usually phrased in a dependent clause).

> **Original Working Thesis:** In Alice Munro's "An Ounce of Cure," infatuation messes with the narrator's head so her life gets turned upside down.
>
> **Revised Working Thesis:** While Alice Munro's "An Ounce of Cure" tells a simple story of infatuation leading to confusion and trouble, the story is more importantly about the "plots of life"—the ways in which the narrator experiences life as a competing set of stories (romance, fairy tale, farce), none of which does justice to the complexity of real life.

Question Your Thesis

You can also sharpen your working thesis by questioning it—viewing it from your readers' point of view. What questions might readers have, given the phrasing of your thesis? Here, for example, are questions about the revised working thesis above:

- In what ways is the story primarily about infatuation? What kinds of trouble flow from the infatuation? What confusions?
- What do you mean by the phrase "plots of life" and where does it come from?
- What is the nature of the types of stories listed? In what ways are they "competing"?
- How is real life more complex than these fictional stories? Does the narrator experience real life? If so, where and how?

Probing your thesis in this way can help you (1) decide which questions you want to answer in your paper, and (2) imagine a question-answer structure for your paper.

Considering Methods of Organization

Before drafting, explore which methods of organization would work well for your paper. For help, see Chapter 3, "Planning." The discussion on this page and the next will help you make choices, but start by avoiding these simplistic patterns:

- The five-paragraph essay: Popularly known as the high-school hamburger, this structure is too basic and limiting for most academic research projects.
- Information regurgitation: Generally, academic research requires analytical thinking about information, not just the presentation of data.
- A series of source summaries: Your paper should not be structured simply as a summary of one source after another.

Organizational Practices That Consider Sources

Because the writing you are doing is research based, you want to factor your sources into your thinking about organization. Here are some ideas that may work with your project.

Consider where to position primary and secondary sources. Different writing projects require different approaches to using, balancing, and integrating primary and secondary sources (pages 408–409). Where and how should you work in primary sources—interview material, survey data, textual and artifact analysis, observation results? Where and how should you bring in secondary sources—scholarly books, journal articles, and the like? *Example:* In a literary analysis, you might rely on primary textual analysis of a novel throughout your paper but support—or establish the context for—that analysis with secondary-source information from biographical research placed early in your paper.

Order your writing around key sources. While you shouldn't organize your whole paper as a series of source summaries, sometimes your writing can take direction specifically from the sources that you have researched. Consider these options:

- **Make one of your key points a response to a specific source.** Did a particular source stand out as especially supportive of or especially contrary to your own thinking? Shape part of your paper as an affirmation or rebuttal of the source.
- **Structure your paper around a dialogue with sources.** Do your sources offer multiple, divergent, even contradictory perspectives on your topic? If they do, consider organizing your paper around a dialogue with these sources.

Map out relationships between sources and ideas. Having reviewed your findings and sharpened your working thesis, consider how your sources support that thesis. To visualize your options, create a diagram, map, or flowchart that shows where particular sources speak to particular points.

Put your discussion in context. Often, the early part of your paper will involve establishing a context for exploring your topic. Consider, then, tapping your sources to present necessary background, explain key terms, describe the big picture, set out key principles, or establish a theoretical framework for your discussion.

Traditional Organizational Patterns

As shown in the "writing moves" chart on page 64, organizing your paper into an opening, middle, and closing can involve a variety of strategies. The traditional patterns below offer sound methods for developing your thinking. Each choice offers a basic structure for your paper, but several patterns may be useful within your paper's body. As indicated, full instruction for many of these patterns can be found elsewhere in this book.

- **Analysis** clarifies how something works by breaking the object or phenomenon into parts or phases and then showing how they work together. See pages 277–308.

- **Argumentation** asserts and supports a main claim with supporting claims, logical reasoning about each claim, and concrete evidence to back up the reasoning. This pattern also includes acknowledging and countering any opposition, as well as reasserting the main claim (perhaps in a modified form). See pages 309–324.

- **Cause-effect** can (1) explore the factors that led to an event or phenomenon, (2) explore the consequences of an event or phenomenon, or (3) do both. See pages 255–276.

- **Chronological order** arranges items in a temporal sequence (order of events, steps in a process). See pages 209–228.

- **Classification** places items within categories. Each category is characterized by what the items share with each other and by what makes them different from items in the other categories. See pages 189–208.

- **Comparison-contrast** examines two or more items for similarities, differences, or both. Such a study typically holds the items side by side, comparing or contrasting traits point by point. See pages 229–254.

- **Definition** clarifies a term's meaning through appropriate strategies: explaining the term's origin and history, offering examples and illustrations, elaborating key concepts at the heart of the term, and so on. See pages 167–188.

- **Description** orders details in terms of spatial relationships, sounds, components, colour, form, texture, and so on. See pages 143–144.

- **Evaluation** measures the strength or quality of something against particular standards, standards that are already accepted or that are established prior to the evaluation.

- **Order of importance** arranges items from most to least important, or least to most.

- **Partitioning** breaks down an object, a space, or a location into ordered parts, or a process into steps or phases.

- **Problem-solution** describes a problem, explores its causes and effects, surveys possible solutions, proposes the best one, and defends it as desirable and doable. This pattern may also involve explaining how to implement the solution. See pages 365–386.

- **Question-answer** moves back and forth from questions to answers in a sequence that logically clarifies a topic.

Considering Drafting Strategies

With research writing, developing the first draft involves exploring your own thinking in relation to the ideas and information that you have discovered through research. Your goal is to develop and support your ideas—referring to and properly crediting sources, but not being dominated by them. Such drafting requires both creativity and care: the creativity to see connections and to trace lines of thinking, and the care to respect ideas and information that you are borrowing from sources. Consider the tips below.

Choose a Drafting Method

Before starting your draft, choose a drafting method that makes sense for your project (its complexity, formality, etc.) and your writing style. Here are two options:

Writing Systematically

1. Develop a detailed outline, including supporting evidence, such as the formal sentence outline on page 52.
2. Arrange all your research notes in the precise order of your outline.
3. Write methodically, following your thesis, outline, and notes. However, be open to taking your writing in an interesting direction and modifying your outline as you write.
4. Cite sources as you draft.

Writing Freely

1. Review your working thesis and notes. Then set them aside.
2. If you need to, jot down a brief outline (see the basic list on page 50).
3. Write away—get all your research-based thinking down without stressing about details and flow.
4. Going back to your notes, develop your draft further and carefully integrate and cite research material.

Respect Your Sources While Drafting

Research writing involves handling your sources with care, including during the first draft. While drafting, try to have source material at your fingertips so that you can integrate summaries, paraphrases, and quotations without disrupting the flow and energy of your drafting. Moreover, take care not to overwhelm your draft with source material. As you draft, keep the focus on your own ideas:

- **Avoid strings of references and chunks of source material** without your discussion, explanation, or interpretation in between.
- **Don't offer entire paragraphs of material from a source** (whether paraphrased or quoted) with a single in-text citation at the end: when you do so, your thinking disappears.
- **Be careful not to overload your draft with complex information** and dense data lacking explanation.
- **Resist the urge to copy and paste big chunks from sources.** Even if you document the sources, your paper will quickly become a patchwork of source material with a few stitches (your slim contribution) holding the paper together.

Reason with the Evidence

Your paper presents the weight of your research findings in the light of your best thinking. Here you support your thesis with a line of reasoning that is carefully thought out and backed up by evidence. That line of reasoning is typically carried by well-developed paragraphs. A typical body paragraph starts with a topic sentence that makes a point in support of your thesis, then elaborates that point with careful reasoning and detailed evidence, and finishes with a concluding sentence that reiterates and advances the idea.

Sample Body Paragraph Showing Reasoning with Evidence

Topic Sentence: idea elaborating and supporting thesis

Development of idea through reasoning

Support of idea through reference to evidence from source material

Concluding statement of idea

Finally, Fairtrade consumers can misjudge producers. Whereas Fairtrade has been rightly criticized for inadvertently spreading a sort of neo-colonial attitude, consider, for instance, the problem of quality control that was explored earlier: that Fairtrade does not press producers to develop high-quality products. "Companies such as Green & Black's," on the other hand, "say they aid farmers more by helping them to improve quality and go organic rather than just guaranteeing a price" (Beattie 34). The Fairtrade model ensures that producers will never be able to grow beyond the need for a fixed minimum, while alternate models seek to empower producers. It is not hard to see which paradigm is rife with paternalistic, colonialist implications. Getting consumers in the right frame of mind is not an irrelevant need. As Ian Hussey puts it, "decolonization is not just a material process, but also a mental one" (17). Fair trade, he says, "serves to reinforce racist and colonial distinctions between the poor Global South farmer and the benevolent Global North consumer" (15). In the long run, this mindset is destructive in that it denigrates Fairtrade producers as charity cases rather than potential partners.

As your writing unfolds, make sure that your thinking is sound. To that end, consider these points:

- **Supporting Ideas:** Your topic sentence is essentially a claim—an idea that explains or argues a point. Clearly and logically tie your claim to your thesis.
- **Reasons:** These sentences develop and deepen the claim in the topic sentence. However, reasoning also functions to explain the evidence when you present it. Just remember that the evidence does not generally speak for itself: you will likely have to introduce it to your reader, who is seeing it for the first time.
- **Evidence:** This material is foundational to your thinking—the facts, statistics, quotations, artifacts, illustrations, case studies, and more that you have gathered through research. Always choose evidence that clarifies and convinces, and aim for providing a level of detail that makes your discussion concrete, clear, and convincing.

Using Source Material in Your Writing

After you've found good sources and taken good notes on them, you want to use that research effectively in your writing. Specifically, you want to show (1) what information you are borrowing and (2) where you got it. By doing so, you create credibility. This section shows you how to develop credibility by integrating and documenting sources so as to avoid plagiarism and other abuses (see Chapter 23). *Note:* For a full treatment of documentation, see Chapter 25 (MLA) and Chapter 26 (APA).

Integrate Source Material Carefully

Source material—whether a summary, a paraphrase, or a quotation—should be integrated smoothly into your discussion. Follow these strategies:

The Right Reasons

Focus on what you want to say, not on all the source material you've collected. Use sources to do the following:

- **Deepen and develop your point** with the reasoning offered by a source.
- **Support your point and your thinking** about it with evidence—with facts, statistics, details, and so on.
- **Give credibility to your point** with an expert's supporting statement.
- **Bring your point to life** with an example, an observation, a case study, an anecdote, or an illustration.
- **Address a counterargument** or an alternative.

Quotation Restraint

In most research documents, restrict your quoting to nuggets:

- **Key statements by authorities** (e.g., the main point that a respected Shakespeare scholar makes about the role of Ophelia in *Hamlet*)
- **Well-phrased claims and conclusions** (e.g., a powerful conclusion by an ethicist about the problem with the media's coverage of cloning debates and technological developments)
- **Passages where careful word-by-word analysis and interpretation** are important to your argument (e.g., an excerpt from a speech made by a politician about the International Space Station—a passage that requires a careful analysis for the between-the-lines message)

Quotations, especially long ones, must pull their weight, so generally paraphrase or summarize source material instead.

> **Primary Document Exception:** When a primary text (a novel, a piece of legislation, a speech) is a key piece of evidence or the actual focus of your project, careful analysis of quoted excerpts is required. See pages 438–439 for more.

Smooth Integration

When you use quotations, work them into your writing as smoothly as possible. To do so, you need to pay attention to style, punctuation, and syntax. (See pages 484–485.)

Use enough of the quotation to make your point without changing the meaning of the original. Use quotation marks around key phrases taken from the source.

> Ogden, Williams, and Larson also conclude that the hydrogen fuel-cell vehicle is "a strong candidate for becoming the Car of the Future," given the trend toward "tighter environmental constraints" and the "intense efforts underway" by automakers to develop commercially viable versions of such vehicles (25).

Integrate all sources thoughtfully. Fold source material into your discussion by relating it to your own thinking. Let your ideas guide the way, not your sources, by using this pattern:

1. **State and explain your idea,** creating a context for the source.
2. **Identify and introduce the source,** linking it to your discussion.
3. **Summarize, paraphrase, or quote the source,** providing a citation in an appropriate spot.
4. **Use the source by explaining, expanding, or refuting it.**
5. **When appropriate, refer back to a source** to further develop the ideas it contains.

Sample Passage: Note the integration of sources in the paragraph below.

Writer's ideas	The motivation and urgency to create and improve hybrid-electric technology comes from a range of complex forces. Some of these forces are economic, others
Attributive phrase	environmental, and still others social. In "Societal Lifestyle Costs of Cars with Alternative Fuels/Engines," Joan Ogden, Robert Williams, and Eric Larson argue
Paraphrase, quotation, or summary	that "[c]ontinued reliance on current transportation fuels and technologies poses serious oil supply insecurity, climate change, and urban air pollution risks" (7).
Citation	Because of the nonrenewable nature of fossil fuels as well as their negative side
Commentary	effects, the transportation industry is confronted with making the most radical changes since the introduction of the internal-combustion automobile more than
Conclusion	100 years ago. Hybrid-electric vehicles are one response to this pressure.

Fabio Berti/Shutterstock.com

Effectively Document Your Sources

Just as you need to integrate source material carefully into your writing, so you must also carefully document where that source material comes from. Readers should recognize which material is yours and which material is not.

Identify clearly where source material begins. Your discussion must offer a smooth transition to source material. Follow the guidelines below:

- For first reference to a source, use an attributive statement that indicates some of the following: author's name and credentials, title of the source, nature of the study or research, and helpful background.

  > **Joan Ogden, Robert Williams, and Eric Larson, members of the Princeton Environmental Institute, explain** that modest improvements in energy efficiency and emissions reductions will not be enough over the next century because of anticipated transportation increases (7).

- For subsequent references to a source, use a simplified attributive phrase, such as the author's last name or a shortened version of the title.

  > **Ogden, Williams, and Larson go on to argue** that "[e]ffectively addressing environmental and oil supply concerns will probably require radical changes in automotive engine/fuel technologies" (7).

- In some situations, such as providing straightforward facts, simply skip the attributive phrase. The parenthetical citation supplies sufficient attribution.

  > Various types of transportation are by far the main consumers of oil (three fourths of world oil imports); moreover, these same technologies are responsible for one fourth of all greenhouse gas sources (Ogden, Williams, and Larson 7).

- The verb you use to introduce source material is key. Use fitting verbs, such as those in the table below—verbs indicating that the source informs, analyzes, or argues. Normally, use the present tense. Use the past tense only to stress the "pastness" of a source.

  > In their 2004 study, "Societal Lifecycle Costs of Cars with Alternative Fuels/ Engines," Ogden, Williams, and Larson **present** a method for comparing and contrasting alternatives to internal-combustion engines. Earlier, these authors **made** preliminary steps . . .

Verbs for Signal Phrases

accepts	considers	explains	rejects	contrasts
contradicts	highlights	reminds	adds	insists
identifies	responds	affirms	criticizes	shows
shares	argues	declares	interprets	believes
asserts	defends	lists	states	describes
denies	maintains	stresses	cautions	points out
outlines	suggests	claims	disagrees	urges
supports	compares	discusses	praises	confirms
concludes	emphasizes	proposes	verifies	
enumerates	refutes	warns	acknowledges	

Indicate where source material ends. Closing quotation marks and a citation, as shown below, indicate the end of a source quotation. Generally, place the citation immediately after any quotation, paraphrase, or summary. However, you may also place the citation early in the sentence or at the end if the parenthetical note is obviously obtrusive. When you discuss several details from a page in a source, use an attributive phrase at the beginning of your discussion and a single citation at the end.

> As the "Lifestyle Costs" study concludes, when greenhouse gases, air pollution, and oil insecurity are factored into the analysis, alternative-fuel vehicles "offer lower LCCs than typical new cars" (Ogden, Williams, and Larson 25).

Set off longer quotations. If a quotation is longer than four typed lines, set it off from the main text. Generally, introduce the quotation with a complete sentence and a colon. Indent the quotation 2.5 cm (10 spaces) and double-space it, but don't put quotation marks around it. Put the citation outside the final punctuation mark.

> Toward the end of the study, Ogden, Williams, and Larson argue that changes to the fuel-delivery system must be factored into planning:
>
> > In charting a course to the Car of the Future, societal LCC comparisons should be complemented by considerations of fuel infrastructure requirements. Because fuel infrastructure changes are costly, the number of major changes made over time should be minimized. The bifurcated strategy advanced here—of focusing on the H2 FCV for the long term and advanced liquid hydrocarbon-fueled ICEVs and ICE/HEVs for the near term—would reduce the number of such infrastructure changes to one (an eventual shift to H2). (25)

Mark Changes to Quotations

You may shorten or change a quotation so that it fits smoothly into your sentence—but don't alter the original meaning. Use an ellipsis to indicate that you have omitted words from the original. An ellipsis is three periods with spaces between them.

> In their projections of where fuel-cell vehicles are heading, Ogden, Williams, and Larson discuss GM's AUTOnomy vehicle, with its "radical redesign of the entire car. . . . In these cars, steering, braking, and other vehicle systems are controlled electronically rather than mechanically" (24).

Use square brackets to indicate a clarification or to change a pronoun or verb tense or to switch around uppercase and lowercase.

> As Ogden, Williams, and Larson explain, "[e]ven if such barriers [the high cost of fuel cells and the lack of an H2 fuel infrastructure] can be overcome, decades would be required before this embryonic technology could make major contributions in reducing the major externalities that characterize today's cars" (25).

To indicate a spelling error or typographical error in the original source, add [sic] immediately after the error.

> **fyi** Part I of this text, especially Chapters 2–7, contains additional help on working through the writing process, including attention to working with sources.

Sample Research Paper

Good research writing demonstrates how the writer's curiosity has led to discoveries that are then shared with the reader in order to advance the dialogue on a topic. In the essay below, student writer Nancy Black does exactly that when she explores the cultural changes that Calgary has undergone. As you read Nancy's essay, explore how it is rooted in research and how she reasons with that research. Note: the sample essay shows source documentation according to MLA style. However, the paper does not show MLA format rules (heading, margins, spacing, etc.). Those details are addressed in Chapter 25.

The title and subtitle announce an intriguing focus and theme.

The essay starts with concrete details that illustrate one concept the paper will explore: isolationism.

The writer explores a contrasting concept, cosmopolitanism, by turning to and reflecting on two expert voices.

Dismantling the Scarecrow: An Exploration of Calgary's Cultural Coming of Age

A forty-five-minute drive south of Calgary on Highway 2 brings you to the edge of the Rocky Mountain foothills and the beginning of prime Alberta ranch country. On the side of the road, on the edge of a vast stretch of land, sits a well-maintained sign that proclaims in bold letters, "Less Ottawa, More Alberta." In a province where spare language is commonly employed to support peoples' passions ("Support Our Troops," "I ♥ Alberta Beef"), this slogan rings with a particularly brazen isolationist undertone. Most native Westerners can recognize the proclamation as yet another manifestation of decades-old western alienation born out of grudges over lost national contracts and oil revenues. The more self-conscious Albertan might wonder what, if any measure of comity, is expected to be elicited by the sign from newcomers or visitors passing by on their way to the next milepost of good fortune that dots a landscape so rich in blessings as to be convincingly branded "God's Country."

For every isolationist malcontent in the region, one wonders if there is an equal constituency that holds a more collectivist and universal view of the world and their place within it. Modern-day cosmopolitans, as Martha Nussbaum describes in her 1994 essay, "Patriotism and Cosmopolitanism," are those people who reject self-definition based on "morally irrelevant characteristics" such as nationhood or regional affiliation and hold out allegiance for "morally good" characteristics such as universal justice, reason, and mutual respect. Nussbaum's premise is that the "me/ my region first" ideology is not a sustainable foundation on which to build a society and that hyper-patriotism has the potential to turn subversive, as some would say occurred in American national security policy following the events of September 11, 2001. In this essay, we use Nussbaum's interpretations and those of her philosophical contemporaries as a guide to probe Calgary's social, political, and media institutions and to understand the extent to which the popular stereotype of Calgary as a predominantly isolationist culture continues to hold true.

1

2

As Kwame Anthony Appiah describes in *Examined Life: Excursions with Contemporary Thinkers*, cosmopolitanism is invoked not to denigrate parochial societies but to find a sustainable way forward. "We have to figure out how to live in a world in which our responsibilities are, not to just a hundred people with whom we can interact with [*sic*] and see, but to six or seven billion people whom we cannot see and whom we can affect only in indirect ways" (113). With so many eyes on Calgary for its significant influence on globally shared domains like the economy and the environment, this psychic and physical place is a worthy one in which to pull over, unpack our tools, and explore the competing forces of isolationism and cosmopolitanism in a real-world context.

A Culture in Context

The newly formed Calgary of the late 1800s did not hold the same broad appeal to immigrants as Canada's port cities or those with a more diverse or established economy. The city's first wave of newcomers, largely immigrants from Northern Europe, was drawn to its agricultural promise. The Leduc oil discovery of 1947 brought the second major wave, consisting largely of profit-seeking Americans responding to the burgeoning fossil fuel industry (Stamp 32). In Robert Stamp's *Suburban Modern: Postwar Dreams in Calgary*, historian Max Foran describes their influence: "By 1965, over 30,000 Americans lived in the city, with their numbers directed toward the higher income brackets. They figured prominently in the city's social and economic life, and in many ways Calgary had 'more in common with Tulsa or Houston than with Toronto, Montreal or Hamilton'" (qtd. in Stamp 33).

Modern-day Calgary is virtually unrecognizable from its postwar years. A visit downtown on Stampede Parade day reveals a diverse citizenry. Families of multiple ethnicities line the parade route to enjoy the cultural panorama. Here, a Caribbean steel band, there, the Ismaeli Muslim/Habitat for Humanity float, next the Stoney Indians, then the pioneer women. A recent article in *Maclean's* provides the numbers behind Calgary's changing face: "Its dynamic economy makes it home to more immigrants per capita than Montreal… Nearly a quarter of the population is a visible minority" ("Real Face"). But modern cosmopolitanism demands more from a society than ethnic diversity. In her commentary on North London, Ranji Devadason makes an important distinction between a city that happens to be culturally diverse and one that is truly cosmopolitan, defining the latter as "not something which can be inferred from diversity in itself; it requires transformation in 'structures of meaning' both for the individual and the political community." In what ways, if any then, might Calgary be building those structures of meaning to bridge over to its democratically cosmopolitan ideal?

3

4

5

Using a subheading to indicate a shift, the writer describes Calgary's current cultural landscape by first tracing its history. Evidence includes a quotation from a historian, personal observation, information from a respected news magazine, and commentary from a global thinker.

Ideology vs. Ideas

The writer refines her thinking about cosmopolitanism by distinguishing and critiquing different forms. She then contrasts an entrenched conservative political culture with the election of a cosmopolitan mayor.

While Calgary's politicians may endorse economic cosmopolitanism (i.e., free trade, foreign ownership), experts would say this is of little relevance to the moral cosmopolitan ("Cosmopolitanism"). Moral cosmopolitanism favours the free trade of ideas over commerce and, therefore, seldom do the two ideologies jibe. Calgary's political ideology could be safely characterized as entrenched. Its citizens have supported the provincial Progressive Conservative government's uninterrupted forty-year reign and the lengthy run of the even more traditional party that preceded it (Government of Alberta). The current regime's most viable rival is the even more conservative and isolationist Wild Rose Party. Calgary is the birthplace of the two right-wing parties that morphed into the current ruling federal Conservative party, the party that continues to support Member of Parliament Rob Anders despite his highly publicized 2001 accusation that Nobel Peace Prize winner Nelson Mandela was a "terrorist" ("PM Blasts MP"), the party that has publicly withdrawn from a 2011 United Nations conference on racism ("Canada Skipping"), and has cultivated a cavalier acceptance of that organization's decision to reject Canada's bid for a two-year seat on its Security Council (Parmar). If there were a contest to name the city whose historical voting practices support everything cosmopolitanism is not, Calgary would place prominently.   6

Conversely, if there were a poster child for everything cosmopolitanism personifies, Calgary Mayor Naheed Nenshi would be it. Elected in October 2010 to the non-partisan job of mayor, Nenshi is a visible minority person of Muslim faith. He is an intellectual. His election platform proposed progressive concepts like bike lanes and transit funding. The very fact of his being elected garnered poorly veiled amazement from other jurisdictions, raising deep questions as to what this signified about the city, still viewed in some corners as a "white-bread oil town" ("Real Face"). When asked to respond, Nenshi coolly commented, "issues of race and religion have not come up very much — except, frankly, by the media" ("Calgary Chooses").   7

An Emerging Commons

While traditional media ownership in Calgary is not as concentrated as in some Canadian cities (Raboy and Taras), the bias of its two major newspapers is skewed to the interests of business. *The Calgary Herald* and the *Calgary Sun*, though owned by separate entities, appear to present the same business-focused viewpoint albeit to slightly different audiences (white-collar versus blue-collar) and in different formats (broadsheet and tabloid). If, as Nussbaum believes "one of the greatest barriers to rational deliberation in politics is the unexamined feeling that one's own current preferences and ways are neutral and natural," then Calgary's talk radio station AM770 CHQR is doing its best to hold up the blinders. Notorious for its hosts' unceremonious silencing of dissenting voices and indulgence of anti-government   8 rants, the highest-rated radio station in Calgary ("Calgary CMA") provides the breeding ground for the inflammatory shorthand so appealing to folks like our griping landowner with the billboard. By luring the disenfranchised to its bully pulpit for their own forty-five seconds of fame, it perpetuates—among a sufficiently large proportion of the citizenry—the illusion of democratic dialogue.

After critiquing the media scene in Calgary, the writer turns to Twitter as an example of a counter voice.

The relatively recent adoption of Twitter has created a popular, unmediated commons that has allowed a grassroots discourse to develop in Calgary; one more in tune with people than lobbies. The defeat of two media and business-friendly candidates in the 2010 Calgary mayoral campaign attests to the phenomenon. Nenshi used social media to sustain a free-flowing, uncensored dialogue with Calgarians that propelled popular support of his campaign from 8 to 40 percent in four weeks (Braid). The intensive wave of public and media interest that followed is evidence that Calgary is no social media laggard. What this says about Calgary is that two-way, twenty-four-hour public conversation has the potential to usurp artificial discourse and awaken people to the possibility that the landowner's billboard, the irrelevant press, and the radio rants are straw men created to divert attention from meaningful debates about Calgary's true democratic fitness and its citizens' responsibilities to their wider family of brothers and sisters.

Hearts and Minds beyond Borders

The final section of the essay describes the changing face of Calgary, with a particular focus on young people. The writer draws on statistics and reports to support her conclusions about trends.

It may come as a surprise to many that Calgary lags behind only Toronto and Vancouver in its percentage of multiracial or "mixed" unions. According a Statistics Canada report by Anne Milan, Hélène Maheux, and Tina Chui, Calgary stands at 6.1 percent versus a national average of 3.9 percent. They go on to explain that this trend has the potential to significantly influence identity and attitudes over time: "The impact of mixed unions could be far-reaching in changing the dynamic and nature of Canada's ethnocultural diversity in future generations. These consequences may impact the language transfer that takes place within mixed union households, as well as the experiences of children in mixed families and the way in which children of mixed unions report their ethnocultural origins and identify with visible minority groups." This trend anticipates a future in which Calgarians find borders of the heart and mind less significant than now.

Calgary's young people are well-positioned to be the catalyst for the city's ultimate cosmopolitan breakthrough. Here is an excerpt from the report of the *Calgary's Youth, Canada's Future* conference, an event commemorating the province's centennial that involved seventy young people at the University of Calgary:

> When asked to describe their [the participants'] principal attachments…
>
> Alberta does not seem to be part of their psychic imagination. It has either been displaced or is overshadowed by other identities. . . . When asked if Albertans

9

10

11

should emphasize their regional identity less and their Canadian identity more, over 60 percent gave priority to Canada. There is little comfort in these results for those who argue that there is a distinct Alberta way of life, or who trumpet the need to erect "firewalls" to protect provincial institutions and promote the politics of western alienation, let alone separation. (Felske et al.)

The report suggests that immigration and information technology are providing unprecedented access to other cultures and ideologies, rendering the once popular concept of regionalism irrelevant to Calgary's youth. While it is possible passions will cool as Calgary's young citizens take their places as workers and leaders in contemporary life, there is an equal potential for passions to ignite and give rise to substantive ideological progress.

> The conclusion speculates on where Calgary's culture is going, calling for a more decisive move toward cosmopolitanism, backed up by reference again to one of the scholars of this concept.

Yet despite all progressive indicators, static provincial and federal voting patterns and a tacit acceptance of propagandist local media would indicate that Calgary has yet to confront an existential urgency to evolve toward its cosmopolitan potential. Despite its small steps toward fully integrated democracy, Calgary remains ideologically virgin territory with a sizeable constituency—like our griping landowner—still holding back from discovering "the other." Kwame Anthony Appiah prescribes a spree of ideological promiscuity to such societies: "great civilizations and great cultural moments are usually not the result of purity but of the contamination and combination of ideas to produce new things" (110). Calgary's intellectual history is built upon the fluke emergence of a singular industry with singular values that its power players and the cultural, educational, and media institutions they operate must perpetuate. While the elements of true cosmopolitanism are drifting into its cultural gulfstream, Calgary is ripe for that decisive catalystic gust that will propel its citizens toward a true understanding of their privilege and an openness to true representational and operational democracy. It could be catastrophe that ignites this change, but it could also be the collective power of individual human agency as witnessed in the historic 2010 mayoral race. Until that time, while the ideological scarecrows still stand, we see slow but promising evidence of decay as pieces lose their hold and blow off into a borderless wind.

12

Reading for Better Writing

Working by yourself or with a group, do the following:

1. Nancy Black's essay focuses on cultural allegiances. What does her writing suggest about your own cultural position?

2. What is Black's thesis? How does she organize her essay to explore and advance that thesis?

3. Study the range of resources that Black uses, as well as how she uses them in her writing. Does she demonstrate effective research-writing practices?

Works Cited

Appiah, Kwame Anthony. "Cosmopolitanism." *Examined Life: Excursions with Contemporary Thinkers.* Ed. Astra Taylor. New York: New Press, 2009. 87-114. Print.

Braid, Don. "Nenshi Capitalizing on Social Media Buzz." *Calgary Herald* 26 Sept. 2010. Web. 4 Jan. 2011.

"Calgary Chooses Nenshi as New Mayor." *CBC Online.* 19 Oct. 2010. Web. 4 Jan. 2011.

"Calgary CMA (August 30-November 28, 2010)." *Bureau of Broadcast Measurement.* N.d. Web. 4 Jan. 2011.

"Canada Skipping UN Racism 'Hatefest' Again, Ottawa Says." *Toronto Star. Thestar. com.* 25 Nov. 2010. Web. 6 Jan. 2011.

"Cosmopolitanism." *Stanford Encyclopedia of Philosophy.* N.d. Web. 5 Jan. 2011.

Devadason, Ranji. "Cosmopolitanism, Geographic Imaginaries and Belonging in North London." *Urban Studies* 47.14 (2010): 2945-63. *Humanities International Complete.* Web. 5 Jan. 2011.

Felske, Larry, et al. *Report: Calgary's Youth, Canada's Future.* 2005. Web. 4 Jan. 2011.

Government of Alberta. "Electoral Summary 1905-2004." *Web.archive.org.* N.d. Web. 4 Jan. 2011.

Gradon, Stuart. "The Real Face of Calgary—Young, Cosmopolitan, Confident." *Maclean's* 28 Oct. 2010. Web. 5 Jan. 2011.

Milan, Anne, Hélène Maheux, and Tina Chui. "A Portrait of Couples in Mixed Unions." *Statistics Canada.* 20 April 2010. Web. 6 Jan. 2011.

Nussbaum, Martha. "Patriotism and Cosmopolitanism." *Boston Review* 1 Oct. 1994. Web. 6 Jan. 2012.

Parmar, Parminder. "2010 'Crystallized' Canada's Changing Foreign Policy." *CTV News Online.* 2 Jan. 2011. Web. 6 Jan. 2011.

"PM Blasts MP for Blocking Mandela Honour." *CBC Online.* 8 June 2001. Web. 5 Jan. 2011.

Raboy, Marc and David Taras. "Transparency and Accountability in Canadian Media Policy." *Communications: The European Journal of Communication Research* 29.1 (2004): 59-76. Print.

Stamp, Robert. *Suburban Modern: Postwar Dreams in Calgary.* Calgary: TouchWood, 2004. Print.

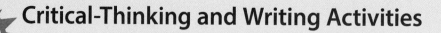

Critical-Thinking and Writing Activities

As directed by your instructor, complete the following critical-thinking and writing activities by yourself or with classmates.

1. According to Thorstein Veblen, "The outcome of any serious research can only be to make two questions grow where only one grew before." Consider the truth of this statement in light of the discussion of research writing in this chapter and your own experiences of doing such research and writing.

2. The first pages of this chapter focus on making the transition from research to writing, as well as on strategies for engaging your research findings, developing your research-based thinking, and drafting your research paper. What does this instruction suggest about the nature and purpose of research writing? How does it differ from other forms of writing?

3. Review a research paper that you wrote in the past. Does that paper follow the principles for using, integrating, and documenting source material, as outlined in this chapter? How might you improve the treatment of sources in your paper?

4. Compare and contrast the sample essay on pages 486–491 and a research-based essay or report that you wrote some time in the past. What similarities do they share with respect to research and research writing? What differences stand out? What conclusions do you reach about your own research-writing habits and practices?

5. Nancy Black's "Dismantling the Scarecrow" explores the cultural character of Calgary. Think about a town or city that is important to you—where you are from or where you are currently living. Research the city and write a paper in which you explore a specific dimension of the city's life, character, or history.

Learning-Objectives Checklist ✓

Have you achieved this chapter's learning objectives? Check your progress with the items below, revisiting topics in the chapter as needed. *I have . . .*

____ carefully examined my research findings so as to deepen my thinking on the topic and imagine my paper (476).

____ assessed my working thesis and strengthened it in light of my research (477).

____ organized my thinking by considering what I discovered through research, along with traditional methods of organization (478–479).

____ drafted my paper either systematically or freely, but have focused on respecting my sources and reasoning with the evidence (480–481).

____ smoothly integrated and carefully documented source material into my writing (482–485).

____ compared and contrasted research-writing practices in a sample essay with those shown in one of my own essays (486–491).

MLA Style

In writing research papers, it is commonly said, "You are commanded to borrow but forbidden to steal." To borrow ideas while avoiding plagiarism (see pages 465–474), you must not only mention the sources you borrow from but also document them completely and accurately. You must follow to the last dot the documentation conventions for papers written in your area of study.

If you are composing a research paper in the humanities, your instructor will most likely require you to follow the conventions established in the style manual of the Modern Language Association (MLA). This chapter provides you with explanations and examples for citing sources in MLA format.

Visually Speaking As suggested by the photo below, library shelves organize a vast amount of knowledge. In what sense does a system such as MLA style make sense of and order knowledge in research writing?

Learning **Objectives**

By working through this chapter, you will be able to

- explain and implement MLA guidelines for documenting sources.
- produce research writing that adheres to MLA guidelines for formatting.
- evaluate MLA practices at work in a sample student research-based essay.

Amy Johansson/Shutterstock.com

fig. 25.1

MLA Documentation: Quick Guide

The MLA system involves two parts: (1) an in-text citation within your paper when you use a source and (2) a matching bibliographic entry at the end of your paper. Note these features of the MLA system:

- **It's minimalist.** In your paper, you provide the least amount of information needed for your reader to identify the source in the works-cited list.
- **It uses signal phrases and parenthetical references** to set off source material from your own thinking and discussion.
  Note: A signal phrase names the author and places the material in context (e.g., "As Margaret Atwood argues in *Survival*").
- **It's smooth, unobtrusive, and orderly.** MLA in-text citations identify borrowed material while keeping the paper readable. Moreover, alphabetized entries in the works-cited list at the end of the paper make locating source details easy.

You can see these features at work in the example below. "Anna Hutchens" and "(449)" tell the reader the following things:

- The borrowed material came from a source written by Anna Hutchens.
- The specific material can be found on page 449 of the source.
- Full source details are in the works-cited list under the author's last name.

1. In-Text Citation in Body of Paper

> As Anna Hutchens puts it, there is an "absence of a policy framework and institutional mechanisms that promote women's empowerment as a rights-based rather than a culture-based issue" (449).

2. Matching Works-Cited Entry at End of Paper

> Hutchens, Anna. "Empowering Women Through Fair Trade? Lessons from Asia." *Third World Quarterly* 31.3 (2010): 449-67. *Academic Search Premier.* Web. 18 Jan. 2014.

In-Text Citation: The Basics

In MLA, in-text citations typically follow these guidelines:

1. Refer to the author (plus the work's title, if helpful) and a page number by using one of these methods:

Last name and page number in parentheses:

> — last name only in citation
> Fair trade is not necessary for consumers to "exercise a moral choice" with their money (Chandler 256). — no "p." for "page"
> — no comma between name and page number

Name cited in sentence, page number in parentheses:

> — full name in first reference
> As Paul Chandler admits, fair trade is not necessary for consumers to "exercise a moral choice" with their money (256). — page number only in citation

2. Present and punctuate citations according to these rules:
- Place the parenthetical reference after the source material.
- Within the parentheses, normally give the author's last name only.
- Do not put a comma between the author's last name and the page reference.
- Cite the page number as a numeral, not a word.
- Don't use *p.*, *pp.*, or *page(s)* before the page number(s).
- Place any sentence punctuation after the closed parenthesis.

 For many of these rules, exceptions exist. For example, classic literary texts could be cited by chapters, books, acts, scenes, or lines. Moreover, many electronic sources have no stated authors and/or no pagination. See pages 500–507 for complete coverage of in-text citation practices.

Works Cited: The Basics

Complete coverage of MLA works-cited issues (examples included) is offered on pages 508–524, rules for formatting the works-cited page are on page 496, and a sample works-cited page is shown on page 533. Here, however, are some templates for the most common entries:

Template for Book:

> Author's Last Name, First Name. *Title of Book*. Publication City: Publisher, year of publication. Medium. (Other publication details are integrated as needed.)
>
> Nichols, Alex, and Charlotte Opal. *Fair Trade: Market-Driven Ethical Consumption*. London: Sage, 2004. Print.

Template for Periodical Article in an Online Database:

> Author's Last Name, First Name. "Title of Article." *Journal Title* volume, issue, and/or date details: page numbers. *Title of Database*. Medium. Date of access.
>
> Chandler, Paul. "Fair Trade and Global Justice." *Globalizations* 3.2 (2006): 255-57. *Academic Search Premier*. Web. 19 Jan. 2014.

 If you read the print article, end the citation after the page numbers with "Print" as the medium.

Template for a Web Document:

> Author's or Editor's Last Name, First Name (if available). "Title of Page, Posting, or Document." *Title of Website* (if different from document title). Version or edition used. Publisher or sponsor of site (if known; if not, use *N.p.*), Date of publication, last update, or posting (if known; if not, use *n.d.*). Medium. Date of access.
>
> "What is Fairtrade?" *Fairtrade International*. Fairtrade Labelling Organizations Intl., n.d. Web. 10 Feb. 2014.

Web Link: For additional questions and answers about MLA format, see the MLA Q&A page at http://www.mla.org/handbook_faq.

MLA Format Guidelines

The MLA system offers guidelines not only for documentation but also for the paper's format—its parts and their presentation. Format guidelines are detailed in Figures 25.2–25.4 and on the following pages, as well as in the sample MLA paper on page 525.

MLA Format at a Glance

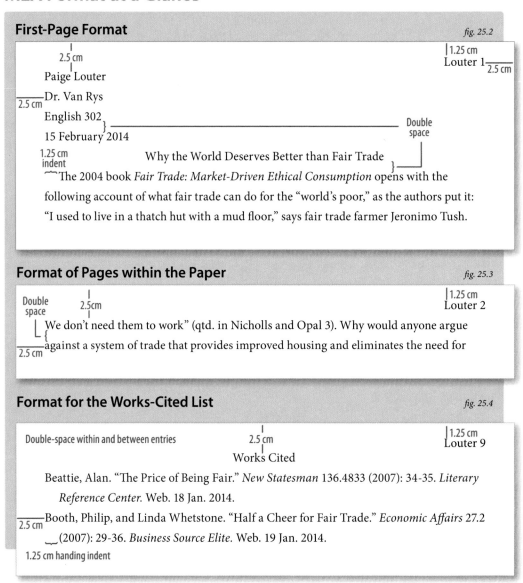

First-Page Format   *fig. 25.2*

| 2.5 cm |
| 1.25 cm Louter 1 ——— 2.5 cm |

Paige Louter

——— Dr. Van Rys
2.5 cm

English 302

15 February 2014   } ———————————————————— Double space

1.25 cm indent   Why the World Deserves Better than Fair Trade }———

The 2004 book *Fair Trade: Market-Driven Ethical Consumption* opens with the

following account of what fair trade can do for the "world's poor," as the authors put it:

"I used to live in a thatch hut with a mud floor," says fair trade farmer Jeronimo Tush.

Format of Pages within the Paper   *fig. 25.3*

Double space   2.5 cm
                              1.25 cm Louter 2

L We don't need them to work" (qtd. in Nicholls and Opal 3). Why would anyone argue

——— against a system of trade that provides improved housing and eliminates the need for
2.5 cm

Format for the Works-Cited List   *fig. 25.4*

Double-space within and between entries   2.5 cm
                                                          1.25 cm Louter 9

Works Cited

Beattie, Alan. "The Price of Being Fair." *New Statesman* 136.4833 (2007): 34-35. *Literary*

    Reference Center. Web. 18 Jan. 2014.

——— Booth, Philip, and Linda Whetstone. "Half a Cheer for Fair Trade." *Economic Affairs* 27.2
2.5 cm

__ (2007): 29-36. *Business Source Elite.* Web. 19 Jan. 2014.

1.25 cm handing indent

Whole-Paper Format and Printing Issues

The instruction below and on the next pages explain how to set up the parts of your paper and print it for submission. Page references are to the sample MLA paper later in this chapter.

Running Head and Pagination (page 525)

- Number pages consecutively in the upper-right corner, 1.25 cm from the top and flush with the right margin (2.5 cm from the edge of the page).
- Use numerals only—without *p., page, #,* or any other symbol.
- Include your last name on each page typed one space before the page number. (Your name identifies the page if it's misplaced.)

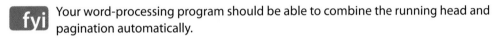 Your word-processing program should be able to combine the running head and pagination automatically.

Heading on First Page (page 525)

MLA does not require a separate title page. On the first page of your paper, include the following details flush left and double spaced, 2.5 cm from the top:

- Your name, both first and last in regular order
- Your professor's or instructor's name (presented as he or she prefers)
- The course name and number, plus the section number if appropriate (e.g., History 100-05). Follow your instructor's directions.
- The date that you are submitting the paper: use the international format (e.g., 11 November 2014).

Paper Title (page 525)

- Double-spaced below the heading, centre your paper's title.
- Do not italicize, underline, or boldface the title; do not show the title in quotation marks or all caps; and do not use a period (though a question mark may be acceptable if warranted).
- Follow standard capitalization practices for titles.

Works-Cited List (page 533)

- Start the list on a new page immediately after your paper's conclusion.
- Continue the running head and pagination.
- Centre the heading "Works Cited" 2.5 cm from the top of the page; don't use quotation marks, underlining, boldface, or any other typographical markers.
- Begin your list two spaces below the heading. Arrange all entries alphabetically by the authors' last names; for sources without identified authors, alphabetize using the work's title, ignoring *a, an,* or *the.*
- If you are listing two or more works by the same author, alphabetize them by the titles of the works. Use the author's name for the first entry; in later entries, replace the name with three hyphens.

(See more "Works-Cited List" formatting tips on the next page.)

- Start each entry flush left; indent second and subsequent lines for specific entries 1.25 cm. Use your word-processing program's hanging indent feature.
- Double-space within and between all entries, and follow standard rules for capitalization, italics, quotation marks, and punctuation.
- Do not repeat the "Works Cited" heading if your list runs longer than one page.
- Print on standard 216 mm × 279 mm paper.

Paper, Printing, and Binding

- Use quality 75 g/m² bond paper. Avoid both thin, erasable paper and heavy card stock. Similarly, stick with standard white or off-white paper—no neons, pastels, letterheads, or scents.
- Use a laser or inkjet printer to create a crisp, clean copy; avoid using nearly empty print cartridges.
- Avoid submitting a paper with handwritten corrections; however, if you must make a change, make a caret symbol (^), put a single clean line through words that must be dropped, and write additions above the line.
- As a first choice, use a paperclip. A single staple in the upper left corner may be acceptable. Avoid fancy covers or bindings, and never simply fold over the corners.
- Print your essay single-sided. Do double-sided printing only with your instructor's permission.

> **Electronic Submission or Posting:** If your instructor accepts or encourages electronic submission, follow his or her guidelines concerning these issues:
> - **Mode of submission:** email attachment, pdf posting, flash drive, and so on
> - **Pagination/reference markers:** If your document will not have stable page numbers, number the paragraphs. Place the paragraph number in brackets, follow with a space, and then begin the paragraph.
> - **Internet addresses:** If you have included URLs, reverse the MLA print practice of putting them in angle brackets; instead, make URLs live links.

Typographical Issues

Typeface: Choose a standard serif typeface like Times New Roman. (Serif type, for example, the type you're reading, has finishes on each letter, as opposed to sans serif, like this.) Avoid unusual, hard-to-read typefaces.

Type Size: Use a readable type size, preferably 12 points, throughout the paper.

Type Styles (underlining, italics, bold, etc.):

- Use italics (not underlining) for titles of resources and individual words requiring this feature. An exception may be an online publication or posting; consult your instructor.
- Avoid using boldface, yellow highlighting, all caps, and so on.

Page-Layout Issues

Spacing

- **Margins:** Set margins top and bottom, left and right at 2.5 cm, with the exception of the running head (1.25 cm from top).
- **Line Spacing:** Double-space the entire paper—including the heading and works-cited entries, as well as tables, captions, and inset quotations.
- **Line Justification:** Use left justified throughout, except for the running head (right justified) and the title and works-cited heading (both centred). Leave the right margin ragged.
- **Word Hyphenation:** Avoid hyphenating words at the end of lines; in your word processor, turn off this tool.
- **Spacing after Punctuation:** Use one space after most forms of punctuation, including end punctuation—but not before or after a dash or a hyphen.
- **Paragraph Indenting:** Indent all paragraphs 1.25 cm.

Longer (Inset) Quotations (see page 527)

- Indent 2.5 cm verse quotations longer than three lines and prose quotations longer than four typed lines.
- Use no quotation marks, and place the parenthetical citation after the closing punctuation.
- With a verse quotation, make each line of the poem or play a new line; do not run the lines together. Follow the indenting and spacing in the verse itself.
- To quote two or more paragraphs, indent the first line of each paragraph 0.6 cm in addition to the 2.5 cm for the whole passage. However, if the first sentence quoted does not begin a paragraph in the source, do not make the additional indent. Indent only the first lines of subsequent paragraphs.

Tables and Illustrations

Position tables, illustrations, and other visuals near your discussion of them—ideally, immediately after your first reference to the graphic, whether pasted in after a paragraph or positioned on a separate following page. Observe these rules:

- **Tables:** Identify all tables using "Table," an Arabic numeral, and a caption (descriptive title). Both the identifying headings and captions should be flush left, appropriately capitalized. Provide source information and explanatory notes below the table. Identify notes with superscript lowercase letters, not numerals. Double-space throughout the table.
- **Illustrations:** Number and label other visuals (graphs, charts, drawings, photos, maps, etc.) using "Figure" or "Fig.," an Arabic numeral (followed by a period), and a title or caption one space after the period—all flush left below the illustration, along with source information and notes.

Guidelines for In-Text Citations

The *MLA Handbook for Writers of Research Papers*, Seventh Edition (2009), suggests giving credit for your sources of information in the body of your research paper. One way to do so is by indicating the author and/or title in the text of your essay, and then putting a page reference in parentheses after the summary, paraphrase, or quotation, as needed. The simplest way to do so is to insert the appropriate information (usually the author and page number) in parentheses after the words or ideas taken from the source.

To avoid disrupting your writing, place citations where a pause would naturally occur (usually at the end of a sentence but sometimes within a sentence, before internal punctuation such as a comma or semicolon). These in-text citations (often called "parenthetical references") refer to sources listed on the "Works Cited" page at the end of your paper. (See page 533 for a sample works-cited list.) Essentially, each in-text citation must clearly point to a source in your works cited, and every source in the works-cited list must be referred to at least once within your paper.

Citations for Regular Sources

As you integrate citations into your paper, follow the guidelines below, referring to the sample citation as needed.

Sample In-Text Citation

> As James Cuno, director of the Harvard University Art Museums, points out, the public, which subsidizes museums either directly through donations or indirectly via museums' status as tax-free nonprofit organizations, expects them to "carry out their duties professionally on its behalf" (164).

- **Make sure each in-text citation clearly points to an entry in your list of works cited.** The identifying information provided (usually the author's last name) must be the word or words by which the entry is alphabetized in that list.

- **Keep citations brief, and integrate them smoothly** into your writing.

- **When paraphrasing or summarizing rather than quoting, make it clear where your borrowing begins and ends.** Use stylistic cues to distinguish the source's thoughts ("Kalmbach points out . . . ," "Some critics argue . . .") from your own ("I believe . . . ," "It seems obvious, however"). See pages 482–485 for more on integrating sources.

- **When using a shortened title of a work, begin with the word by which the work is alphabetized** in your list of works cited (e.g., "Egyptian, Classical," not "Middle Eastern Art," for "Egyptian, Classical, and Middle Eastern Art").

- **For inclusive page numbers larger than ninety-nine, give only the last two digits of the second number** (346–48, not 346–348).

- **When including a parenthetical citation at the end of a sentence, place it before the end punctuation.** (Citations for long, indented quotations are an exception. See page 485.)

Citations for Sources without Traditional Authorship and/or Pagination

Today many sources, especially electronic ones, have no stated authors and/or no pagination. For such sources, use these in-text citation strategies:

Source Without a Stated Author

In a signal phrase or in the parenthetical reference, identify the source as precisely as possible by indicating the sponsoring agency, the type of document, or the title (shortened in the parenthetical reference). See pages 502–503.

> While the Brooklyn Museum may be best known for the recent controversy over the Sensation exhibition, it does contain a strong collection of contemporary if less controversial art, "ranging from representational to abstract to conceptual" ("Contemporary Art").

Source with No Pagination

If no pagination exists within the document, use paragraph numbers (with the abbreviation *par.*), if the document provides them. If the document includes neither page nor paragraph numbers, cite the entire work. Do not create your own numbering system.

> The Museum's *Art of the Americas* collection includes extensive holdings of works by the Aboriginal peoples of North, Central, and South America, many of these gathered by archaeologist Herbert Spinden during at least seven expeditions between 1929 and 1950 (*Art of the Americas* par. 3).

Because parenthetical notations are used to signal the end of an attribution, sources with no pagination or paragraph numbers offer a special challenge. When no parenthetical notation is possible, signal a shift back to your own discussion with a source-reflective statement indicating your thinking about the source.

> ... indicated by his recording the audio tour of the exhibit, his supporting the show financially, and his promoting *Sensation* at his website. As Welland's discussion of David Bowie's participation suggests, the controversy over the Brooklyn Museum of Art's *Sensation* exhibit ...

`INSIGHT` Stable pagination for many electronic resources is available when you use the ".pdf" rather than the ".html" version of the source. For instruction on smoothly integrating source material into your paper, see pages 482–485. For cautions about sources without identified authors, see pages 502, 503, 510, and 516.

Ilin Sergey/Shutterstock.com

Sample In-Text Citations

The following entries illustrate the most common in-text citations.

One Author: A Complete Work

You do not need a parenthetical citation if you identify the author in your text. (See the first entry below.) However, you must give the author's last name in a parenthetical citation if it is not mentioned in the text. (See the second entry.) When a source is listed in your works-cited page with an editor, a translator, a speaker, or an artist instead of the author, use that person's name in your citation.

With Author in Text: (This is the preferred way of citing a complete work.)

> In *Payback*, Margaret Atwood explores the historical, cultural, and literary significance of indebtedness.

Without Author in Text:

> *Payback* explores the historical, cultural, and literary significance of indebtedness (Atwood).

Note: Do not offer page numbers when citing complete works, articles in alphabetized encyclopedias, one-page articles, and unpaginated sources.

One Author: Part of a Work

List the necessary page numbers in parentheses if you borrow words or ideas from a particular source. Leave a space between the author's last name and the page reference. No abbreviation or punctuation is needed.

With Author in Text:

> Bullough writes that genetic engineering was dubbed "eugenics" by a cousin of Darwin's, Sir Francis Galton, in 1885 (5).

Without Author in Text:

> Genetic engineering was dubbed "eugenics" by a cousin of Darwin's, Sir Francis Galton, in 1885 (Bullough 5).

A Work by Two or Three Authors

Give the last names of every author in the same order that they appear in the works-cited section. (The correct order of the authors' names can be found on the title page of the book.)

> Students learned more than a full year's Spanish in ten days using the complete supermemory method (Ostrander and Schroeder 51).

A Work by Four or More Authors

Give the first author's last name as it appears in the works-cited section followed by *et al.* (meaning "and others").

> Communication on the job is more than talking; it is "inseparable from your total behavior" (Culligan et al. 111).

Note: You may instead choose to list all of the authors' last names.

Two or More Works by the Same Author(s)

In addition to the author's last name(s) and page number(s), include a shortened version of the work's title when you cite two or more works by the same author(s).

With Author in Text:

> Wallerstein and Blakeslee claim that divorce creates an enduring identity for children of the marriage (*Unexpected Legacy* 62).

Without Author in Text:

> They are intensely lonely despite active social lives (Wallerstein and Blakeslee, *Second Chances* 51).

Note: When including both author(s) and title in a parenthetical reference, separate them with a comma, as shown above, but do not put a comma between the title and the page number.

Works by Authors with the Same Last Name

When citing different sources by authors with the same last name, it is best to use the authors' full names in the text to avoid confusion. However, if circumstances call for parenthetical references, add each author's first initial. If first initials are the same, use each author's full name.

> Some critics think *Titus Andronicus* too abysmally melodramatic to be a work of Shakespeare (A. Parker 73). Others suggest that Shakespeare meant it as black comedy (D. Parker 486).

A Work Authored by an Agency, a Committee, or an Organization

If a book or other work was written by an organization such as an agency, a committee, or a task force, it is said to have a corporate author. (See also page 510.) If the corporate name is long, include it in the text (rather than in parentheses) to avoid disrupting the flow of your writing. After the full name has been used at least once, use a shortened form of the name (common abbreviations are acceptable) in subsequent references. For example, Task Force may be used for Task Force on Education for Economic Growth.

> The thesis of the Task Force's report is that economic success depends on our ability to improve large-scale education and training as quickly as possible (113–14).

An Anonymous Work

When there is no author listed, give the title or a shortened version of the title as it appears in the works-cited section. (See page 510.)

> Statistics indicate that drinking water can make up 20 percent of a person's total exposure to lead (*Information* 572).

Two or More Works Included in One Citation

To cite multiple works within a single parenthetical reference, separate the references with a semicolon.

> In Medieval Europe, Latin translations of the works of Rhazes, a Persian scholar, were a primary source of medical knowledge (Albala 22; Lewis 266).

A Series of Citations from a Single Work

If no confusion is possible, it is not necessary to name a source repeatedly when making multiple parenthetical references to that source in a single paragraph. If all references are to the same page, identify that page in a parenthetical note after the last reference. If the references are to different pages within the same work, you need identify the work only once, and then use a parenthetical note with page number alone for the subsequent references.

> Domesticating science meant not only spreading scientific knowledge, but also promoting it as a topic of public conversation (Heilbron 2). One way to enhance its charm was by depicting cherubic putti as "angelic research assistants" in book illustrations (5).

A Work Referred to in Another Work

If you must cite an indirect source—that is, information from a source that is quoted from another source—use the abbreviation *qtd. in* (quoted in) before the indirect source in your reference.

> Paton improved the conditions in Diepkloof (a prison) by "removing all the more obvious aids to detention. The dormitories [were] open at night: the great barred gate [was] gone" (qtd. in Callan xviii).

A Work Without Page Numbers

If a work has no page numbers or paragraph numbers, treat it as you would a complete work. (See page 502.) This is commonly the case with electronic resources, for example. Do not count pages to create reference numbers of your own.

> Antibiotics become ineffective against such organisms through two natural processes: first, genetic mutation; and second, the subsequent transfer of this mutated genetic material to other organisms (Davies).

A Work in an Anthology or a Collection

When citing the entirety of a work that is part of an anthology or a collection, if it is identified by author in your list of works cited, treat the citation as you would for any other complete work. (See page 502.)

> In "The Canadian Postmodern," Linda Hutcheon offers a clear analysis of the self-reflexive nature of contemporary Canadian fiction.

Similarly, if you are citing particular pages of such a work, follow the directions for citing part of a work. (See page 502.)

> According to Hutcheon, "postmodernism seems to designate cultural practices that are fundamentally self-reflexive, in other words, art that is self-consciously artifice" (18).

(To format this sort of entry in your list of works cited, see pages 510–511.)

An Item from a Reference Work

An entry from a reference work such as an encyclopedia or a dictionary should be cited similarly to a work from an anthology or a collection (see above). For a dictionary definition, include the abbreviation *def.* followed by the particular entry designation.

> This message becomes a juggernaut in the truest sense, a belief that "elicits blind devotion or sacrifice" ("Juggernaut," def. 1).

Note: While many such entries are identified only by title (as above), some reference works include an author's name for each entry (as below). Others may identify the entry author by initials, with a list of full names elsewhere in the work.

> The decisions of the International Court of Justice are "based on principles of international law and cannot be appealed" (Pranger).

(See pages 512–513 for guidelines to formatting these entries in your works-cited list.)

A Part of a Multivolume Work

When citing only one volume of a multivolume work, if you identify the volume number in the works-cited list, there is no need to include it in your in-text citation. However, if you cite more than one volume of a work, each in-text reference must identify the appropriate volume. Give the volume number followed by page number, separated by a colon and a space.

> "A human being asleep," says Spengler, ". . . is leading only a plantlike existence" (2: 4).

When citing a whole volume, however, either identify the volume number in parentheses with the abbreviation *vol.* (using a comma to separate it from the author's name) or use the full word *volume* in your text.

> The land of northern British Columbia has shaped its inhabitants more significantly than they ever shaped that land (Trembley, vol. 1).

A One-Page Work

Cite a one-page work just as you would a complete work. (See page 502.)

> As Alice Renfrew argued in her recent editorial, "the Canadian Space Agency must capitalize on the popularizing work done by Chris Hadfield in his time commanding the International Space Station."

A Sacred Text or Famous Literary Work

Sacred texts and famous literary works are published in many different editions. For that reason, it is helpful to identify sections, parts, chapters, and such instead of or in addition to page numbers. If using page numbers, list them first, followed by an abbreviation for the type of division and the division number.

> The more important a person's role in society—the more apparent power an individual has—the more that person is a slave to the forces of history (Tolstoy 690; bk. 9, ch. 1).

Books of the Bible and other well-known literary works may be abbreviated, if no confusion is possible.

> "A generation goes, and a generation comes, but the earth remains forever" (*The New Oxford Annotated Bible*, Eccles. 1.4).

> As Shakespeare's famous Danish prince observes, "One may smile, and smile, and be a villain" (Ham. 1.5.104).

Quoting Prose

To cite prose from fiction (novels, short stories), list more than the page number if the work is available in several editions. Give the page reference first, and then add a chapter, section, or book number in abbreviated form after a semicolon.

> In *The House of the Spirits,* Isabel Allende describes Marcos, "dressed in mechanic's overalls, with huge racer's goggles" (13; ch. 1).

When you are quoting any sort of prose that takes more than four typed lines, indent each line of the quotation 2.5 cm (ten spaces) and double-space it; do not add quotation marks. In this case, you put the parenthetical citation (the pages and chapter numbers) outside the end punctuation mark of the quotation itself.

> Allende describes the flying machine that Marcos has assembled:
>
> > The contraption lay with its stomach on terra firma, heavy and sluggish and looking more like a wounded duck than like one of those newfangled airplanes they were starting to produce in the United States. There was nothing in its appearance to suggest that it could move, much less take flight across the snowy peaks. (12; ch. 1)
> >
> > —Allende, Isabel. *The House of the Spirits*. Trans. Magda Bogin. London: Jonathan Cape, 1985.

Quoting Verse

Do not use page numbers when referencing classic verse plays and poems. Instead, cite them by division (act, scene, canto, book, part) and line, using Arabic numerals for the various divisions unless your instructor prefers Roman numerals. Use periods to separate the various numbers.

> In the first act, Hamlet comments, "How weary, stale, flat and unprofitable, / Seem to me all the uses of this world" (1.2.133–34).

Note: A slash, with a space on each side, shows where each new line of verse begins.
If you are citing lines only, use the word *line* or *lines* in your first reference and numbers only in additional references.

> At the beginning of the sestet in Robert Frost's "Design," the speaker asks this pointed question: "What had that flower to do with being white, / The wayside blue and innocent heal-all?" (lines 9–10).

Verse quotations of more than three lines should be indented 2.5 cm and double-spaced. Do not add quotation marks. Each line of the poem or play begins a new line of the quotation; do not run the lines together. If a line or lines of poetry are dropped from the quotation, ellipses that extend the width of the stanza should be used to indicate the omission.

> In "Daily and Lifelong, Josephine," Margaret Avison envisages a winter scene filled with promise:
>
> > On the empty-handed earth
> > the snow stars blot and fur and dwell
> > > roughing eyelashes of winter grass
> > > and on the open gaze touching, muffling.
> > On the snow the slow, rich sun, in time
> > Seeds roots coolness
> > > through a new sundeep season. (12-18)
> > > > —Reprinted by permission of The Porcupine's Quill.

Listing an Internet Address

The current (seventh edition) *MLA Handbook* discourages use of Internet addresses, or URLs, as they can so easily change with time. Ideally, you should refer to an entire website by its title, or to a specific article on a site by its author; then, include full reference information in your works-cited list. A URL should be listed in your document or in your works-cited list only when the reader probably cannot locate the source without it, or if your instructor requires it. If that is the case, enclose the address in brackets:

> <www.pm.gc.ca>

Because most word-processing software will automatically convert the URL to a live hyperlink, you can either turn off the auto-formatting option on your computer or cancel the formatting as soon as it appears. If the instructor allows it, however, you may use live links in digital submissions.

Quick Guide

MLA Works Cited

The works-cited section lists only the sources you have cited in your text. Begin your list on the page after the text and continue numbering each page. Format your works-cited pages using these guidelines and page 533.

1. **Type the page number in the upper-right corner,** 1.25 cm from the top of the page, with your last name before it.

2. **Centre the title *Works Cited*** (not in italics, in quotation marks, or underlined) 2.5 cm from the top; then double-space before the first entry.

3. **Begin each entry flush with the left margin.** If the entry runs more than one line, indent additional lines 1.25 cm or use the hanging indent function on your computer.

4. **End each element of the entry with a period.** (Elements are separated by periods in most cases unless only a space is sufficient.) Use a single space after all punctuation.

5. **Double-space lines within each entry and between entries.**

6. **List each entry alphabetically by the author's last name.** If there is no author, use the first word of the title (disregard *A, An,* or *The* as the first word). If there are multiple authors, alphabetize them according to which author is listed first in the publication.

7. **The *MLA Handbook*, Seventh Edition, requires that each source be identified as print, Web, or other** (such as television or DVD). For print sources, this information is included after the publisher and date. For Web publications, include *Web.* after the date of publication or updating of the site, and before the date you accessed the site.

8. **A basic entry for a book would be as follows:**

   > Alt, Christina. *Virginia Woolf and the Study of Nature.* New York: Cambridge
   >   UP, 2010. Print.

9. **A basic entry for a journal or magazine would be as follows:**

   > Ferguson Smith, Martin. "Virginia Woolf's Second Visit to Greece." *English
   >   Studies* 92.1 (2011): 55-83. Print.

10. **A basic entry for an online source would be as follows.** Note that the URL is included only if the reader probably cannot locate the source without it, or when your instructor requires it. (See page 518.)

    > Clarke, S. N. "Virginia Woolf (1882-1941): A Short Biography." *Virginia Woolf
    >   Society of Great Britain.* N.p. 2000. Web. 12 March 2014.

Works-Cited Entries

Nonperiodical Print Publications

Components

The entries that follow illustrate the information needed to cite books, sections of a book, pamphlets, and government publications published in print format. The possible components of these entries are listed in order below:

1. Author's name
2. Title of a part of the book (an article in the book or a foreword)
3. Title of the book, italicized
4. Name of editor or translator
5. Edition
6. Number of volume
7. Name of series
8. Place of publication, publisher, year of publication
9. Page numbers, if citation is to only a part (For page spans, use a hyphen; if clarity is maintained, for pages above 100 you may also drop a digit from the second number—for example, 234-41, 234-332.)
10. Medium of publication (Print)

 In general, if any of these components do not apply, they are not included in the works-cited entry. However, in the rare instance that a book does not state publication information, use the following abbreviations in place of information you cannot supply:

> **N.p.** No place of publication given
> **N.p.** No publisher given
> **N.d.** No date of publication given
> **N. pag.** No pagination given

Additional Guidelines

- List only the city for the place of publication. Add an abbreviation for the country if necessary for clarity. If several cities are listed, give only the first.
- Publishers' names should be shortened by omitting articles *(a, an, the)*, business abbreviations *(Co., Inc.)*, and descriptive words *(Books, Press)*. For publishing houses that consist of the names of more than one person, cite only the first of the surnames. Abbreviate University Press as UP. Also use standard abbreviations whenever possible.

A Book by One Author

> Hiebert, Ted. *In Praise of Nonsense: Aesthetics, Uncertainty, and Postmodern Identity.*
>   Montreal: McGill-Queen's UP, 2012. Print.

Two or More Books by the Same Author

List the books alphabetically according to title. After the first entry, substitute three hyphens for the author's name.

> McCluhan, Marshall. *Counterblast.* New York: Harcourt, 1969. Print.
>   - - - . *The Gutenberg Galaxy: The Making of Typographic Man.* Toronto: U of
>   Toronto P, 1962. Print.

A Work by Two or Three Authors

> Shields, Carol, and Blanche Howard. *A Celibate Season.* Regina: Coteau, 1991.
>   Print.

Note: List authors in title-page order. Reverse only the first author's name.

A Work by Four or More Authors

> Schulte-Peevers, Andrea, et al. *Germany.* Victoria, Austral.: Lonely Planet, 2000. Print.

A Work Authored by an Agency, a Committee, or an Organization

> Exxon Mobil Corporation. *Great Plains 2000.* Lincolnwood: Publications Intl.,
>   2001. Print.

An Anonymous Book

> *Chase's Calendar of Events 2002.* Chicago: Contemporary, 2002. Print.

A Single Work from an Anthology

> Sugars, Cynthia. "Worlding the (Post-Colonial) Nation: Canada's Americas." *Canada
>   and Its Americas: Transnational Navigations.* Ed. Winfried Siemerling and Sarah
>   Phillips Casteel. Montreal: McGill-Queen's UP, 2010. 31–47. Print.

A Complete Anthology

If you cite a complete anthology, begin the entry with the editor(s).

> Henderson, Eric, and Geoff Hancock, eds. *Short Fiction & Critical Contexts: A Compact
>   Reader.* Toronto: Oxford UP, 2010. Print.

> Elledge, Jim, and Susan Swartwout, eds. *Real Things: An Anthology of Popular Culture
>   in American Poetry.* Bloomington: Indiana UP, 1999. Print.

Two or More Works from an Anthology or a Collection

To avoid unnecessary repetition when citing two or more entries from a larger collection, you may cite the collection once with complete publication information (see Dvořák and Jones, below). The individual entries (see Howells and Paillot, below) can then be cross-referenced by listing the author, title of the piece, editor of the collection, and page numbers.

> Dvořák, Marta, and Manina Jones, eds. *Carol Shields and the Extra-Ordinary*. Montreal: McGill-Queen's UP, 2007. Print.

> Howells, Coral Ann. "Larry's A/Mazing Spaces." Dvořák and Jones 115-35. Print.

> Paillot, Patricia-Léa. "Pioneering Interlaced Spaces: Shifting Perspectives and Self-Representation in *Larry's Party*." Dvořák and Jones 157-71. Print.

One Volume of a Multivolume Work

> Cooke, Jacob Ernest, and Milton M. Klein, eds. *North America in Colonial Times*. Vol. 2. New York: Scribner's, 1998. Print.

Note: If you cite two or more volumes in a multivolume work, give the total number of volumes after each title. Offer specific references to volume and page numbers in the parenthetical reference in your text, like this: (3: 112-14).

> Salzman, Jack, David Lionel Smith, and Cornel West, eds. *Encyclopedia of African-American Culture and History*. 5 vols. New York: Simon, 1996. Print.

An Introduction, a Preface, a Foreword, or an Afterword

To cite the introduction, preface, foreword, or afterword of a book, list the author of the part first. Then identify the part by type, with no quotation marks or italics, followed by the book title. Next, identify the author of the work, using the word *by*. (If the book's author and the part's author are the same person, give just the last name after *by*.) For a book that gives cover credit to an editor instead of an author, identify the editor as usual. List any page numbers for the part cited.

> Barry, Anne. Afterword. *Making Room for Students*. By Celia Oyler. New York: Teachers College, 1996. 139-40. Print.

> Proulx, Annie. Introduction. *Dance of the Happy Shades*. By Alice Munro. Toronto: Penguin Canada, 2005. ix-xvi. Print.

> Atwood, Margaret. Introduction. *Alice Munro's Best: Selected Stories*. By Alice Monro. Toronto: McClelland, 2006. vii-xviii. Print.

A Republished Book (Reprint)

Give the original publication date after the title.

▌ Atwood, Margaret. *Surfacing*. 1972. New York: Doubleday, 1998. Print.

Note: After the original publication facts, cite new material added: Introd. C. Becker.

A Book with Multiple Publishers

When a book lists more than one publisher (not just different offices of the same publisher), include all of them in the order given on the book's title page, separated by a semicolon.

▌ Wells, H. G. *The Complete Short Stories of H. G. Wells*. New York: St. Martin's; London: A. & C. Black, 1987. Print.

Second and Subsequent Editions

An edition refers to the particular publication you are citing, as in the third (3rd) edition.

▌ Joss, Molly W. *Looking Good in Presentations*. 3rd ed. Scottsdale: Coriolis, 1999. Print.

An Edition with Author and Editor

The abbreviation *ed.* also refers to the work of one or more persons that is prepared by another person, an editor.

▌ Shakespeare, William. *A Midsummer Night's Dream*. Ed. Jane Bachman. Lincolnwood: NTC, 1994. Print.

A Translation

▌ Lebert, Stephan, and Norbert Lebert. *My Father's Keeper*. Trans. Julian Evans. Boston: Little, 2001. Print.

An Article in a Familiar Reference Book

It is not necessary to give full publication information for familiar reference works (encyclopedias and dictionaries). For these titles, list only the edition (if available), the publication year, and the medium of publication you used. If an article is initialled, check the index of authors (in the opening section of each volume) for the author's full name.

▌ "Technical Education." *Encyclopedia Americana*. 2001 ed. Print.

▌ Lum, P. Andrea. "Computed Tomography." *World Book*. 2000 ed. Print.

When citing a single definition of several listed, add the abbreviation *Def.* and the particular number or letter for that definition.

▌ "Macaroni." Def. 2b. *The American Heritage College Dictionary*. 4th ed. 2002. Print.

An Article in an Unfamiliar Reference Book

For citations of lesser-known reference works, give full publication information, as for any other sort of book.

> "S Corporation." *The Portable MBA Desk Reference.* Ed. Paul A. Argenti. New York: Wiley, 1994. Print.

A Government Publication

State the name of the government (country, province or territory, and so on) followed by the name of the agency. Here is an example from Canada's federal government:

> Government of Canada. Environment Canada. Canadian Wildlife Service. *The Greater Sage-Grouse.* N.p.: Public Works and Government Services Canada, 2013. Print.

In the United States, most federal publications are published by the Government Printing Office (GPO).

> United States. Dept. of Labor. Bureau of Labor Statistics. *Occupational Outlook Handbook 2006-2007.* Indianapolis: Jist Works, 2006. Print.

A Book in a Series

Give the series name and number (if any), neither italicized nor in quotation marks, followed by a period, at the end of the listing, after the medium of publication.

> Cudworth, Erika. *Environment and Society.* London: Routledge, 2003. Print. Routledge Introductions to Environment Ser.

A Book with a Title Within Its Title

If the title contains a title normally in quotation marks, keep the quotation marks and italicize the entire title.

> Stuckey-French, Elizabeth. *"The First Paper Girl in Red Oak, Iowa" and Other Stories.* New York: Doubleday, 2000. Print.

Note: If the title contains a title that is normally italicized, do not italicize that title in your entry:

> Beckwith, Charles E. *Twentieth Century Interpretations of* A Tale of Two Cities: *A Collection of Critical Essays.* Upper Saddle River: Prentice, 1972. Print.

A Sacred Text

The Bible and other such sacred texts are treated as anonymous books. Documentation should read exactly as it is printed on the title page.

> *The Jerusalem Bible.* Garden City: Doubleday, 1966. Print.

The Published Proceedings of a Conference

The published proceedings of a conference should be treated as a book. However, if the title of the publication does not identify the conference by title, date, and location, add the appropriate information immediately after the title.

> Hildy, Franklin J., ed. *New Issues in the Reconstruction of Shakespeare's Theatre: Proceedings of the Conference Held at the University of Georgia, February 16–18, 1990.* New York: Peter Lang, 1990. Print.

To cite a particular presentation from the published proceedings of a conference, treat it as a work in an anthology.

> Beckerman, Bernard. "The Uses and Management of the Elizabethan Stage." *The Third Globe: Symposium for the Reconstruction of the Globe Playhouse, Wayne State University, 1979.* Ed. C. Walter Hodges, S. Schoenbaum, and Leonard Leone. Detroit: Wayne State UP, 1981. 151-63. Print.

A Published Dissertation

An entry for a published dissertation contains the same information as a book entry, with a few added details. Add the abbreviation *Diss.* and the degree-granting institution before the publication facts and medium.

> Jansen, James Richard. *Images of Dostoevsky in German Literary Expressionism.* Diss. U of Utah, 2003. Ann Arbor: UMI, 2003. Print.

An Unpublished Dissertation

The entry for an unpublished dissertation lists author, title in quotation marks, degree-granting institution, year of acceptance, and medium. (For a master's thesis, use MA thesis or MS thesis rather than Diss.)

> Hall, Norma. *The Significance of Seafarers of Hudson Bay, 1508–1920, to the History of Western Canadian Development.* Diss. Memorial University of Newfoundland, 2009. Print.

A Pamphlet, Manual, or Other Workplace Document

Treat any such publication as you would a book.

> Grayson, George W. *The North American Free Trade Agreement.* New York: Foreign Policy Assn., 1993. Print.

If publication information is missing, list the country of publication in brackets if known. Use n.p. (no place) if the country or the publisher is unknown and n.d. if the date is unknown, just as you would for a book.

> *Pedestrian Safety.* [Canada]: n.p., n.d. Print.

Print Periodical Articles

Possible Components, in Order

1. Author's name, last name first
2. Title of article, in quotation marks and headline-style capitalization
3. Name of periodical, italicized
4. Series number or name, if relevant (not preceded by period or comma)
5. Volume number (for a scholarly journal)
6. Issue number, separated from volume with a period but no space
7. Date of publication (abbreviate all months but May, June, July)
8. Page numbers, preceded by a colon, without "p." or "pp." (For articles continued nonconsecutively, add a plus sign after the first page number.)
9. Medium of publication (Print)
10. Supplementary information as needed

Note: Any components that do not apply are not listed.

An Article in a Weekly or Biweekly Magazine

List the author (if identified), article title (in quotation marks), publication title (italicized), full date of publication, and page numbers for the article. Do not include volume and issue numbers.

> Bethune, Brian. "Dystopia Now." *Maclean's* 16 Apr. 2012: 84-88. Print.

An Article in a Monthly or Bimonthly Magazine

For a monthly or bimonthly magazine, list the author (if identified), article title (in quotation marks), and publication title (italicized). Then identify the month(s) and year of the issue, followed by page numbers for the article. Do not give volume and issue numbers.

> Rubinstein, Dan. "The Walking Cure." *The Walrus* Sept. 2013: 32-39. Print.

An Article in a Scholarly Journal Paginated by Issue

List the volume number immediately after the journal title, followed by a period and the issue number, and then the year of publication (in parentheses). End with the page numbers of the article followed by the medium of publication (Print.).

> Go, Kenji. "Montaigne's 'Cannibals' and *The Tempest* Revisited." *Studies in Philology* 109.4 (2012): 455-73. Print.

An Article in a Scholarly Journal with Continuous Pagination

An article in a scholarly journal with continuous pagination uses the same citation format, with volume, issue, month or season, and inclusive page numbers.

> Frosch, Thomas R. "The Missing Child in *A Midsummer Night's Dream.*" *American Imago* 64.2 (2007): 485-511. Print.

An Unsigned Article in a Periodical

If no author is identified for an article, list the entry alphabetically by title among your works cited (ignoring any initial *A, An,* or *The*).

> "Feeding the Hungry." *Economist* 371.8374 (2004): 74. Print.

A Printed Interview

Begin with the name of the person interviewed if that's who you are quoting.

> Robinson, Marilynne. "Marilynne Robinson: The Art of Fiction No. 198." By Sarah Fay. *Paris Review* 186 (2008): 37–66. Print.

Note: If the interview is untitled, the word *Interview* (no italics) and a period follow the interviewee's name.

A Newspaper Article

> Barber, John. "Vincent Lam's First Novel, about Vietnam, Has Makings of a Masterpiece." *The Globe and Mail* 22 Apr. 2012: C1. Print.

Note: Cite the edition of a major daily newspaper (if given) after the date (1 May 1995, Midwest ed.: 1). If a local paper's name does not include the city of publication, add it in brackets (not italicized) after the name.

To cite an article in a lettered section of the newspaper, list the section and the page number. (For example, A4 would refer to page 4 in section A of the newspaper.) If the sections are numbered, however, use a comma after the year (or the edition); then indicate the section and follow it with a colon, the page number (sec. 1: 20), and the medium of publication you used.

An Unsigned Newspaper Article

An unsigned newspaper article follows the same format as citing a regular newspaper article:

> "Bombs—Real and Threatened—Keep Northern Ireland Edgy." *Chicago Tribune* 6 Dec. 2001, sec. 1: 20. Print.

A Newspaper Editorial or Letter to the Editor

If an article is an unsigned editorial, put *Editorial* (no italics) and a period after the title.

> "New Accord Hailed as Model for First Nations Negotiations." Editorial. *The Vancouver Sun* 2 Aug. 2012: A6. Print.

To identify a letter to the editor, put *Letter* (no italics) and a period after the author's name.

> Summers, Rory. Letter. *The Vancouver Sun* 9 June 2009: A3. Print.

A Review

Begin with the author (if identified) and title of the review. Use the notation *Rev. of* between the title of the review and that of the original work. Identify the author of the original work with the word *by*. Then follow with publication data for the review.

> Greer, Andrew Sean. "Final Showdown." Rev. of *MaddAddam*, by Margaret Atwood. *The New York Times* 8 Sept. 2013: BR11. Print.

Note: If you cite the review of a work by an editor, translator, or director, use *ed., trans.,* or *dir.,* instead of *by*.

An Abstract

An abstract is a summary of a work. To cite an abstract, first give the publication information for the original work (if any); then list the publication information for the abstract itself. Add the term *Abstract* and a period between these if the journal title does not include that word. If the journal identifies abstracts by item number, include the word *item* followed by the number. (Add the section identifier [A, B, or C] for those volumes of *Dissertation Abstracts* [DA] and *Dissertation Abstracts International* [DAI] that have one.) If no item number exists, list the page number(s).

> Faber, A. J. "Examining Remarried Couples Through a Bowenian Family System Lens." *Journal of Divorce and Remarriage* 40.4 (2004): 121-33. *Social Work Abstracts* 40 (2004): item 1298. Print.

An Article with a Title or Quotation Within Its Title

When an article title contains within it a title of a longer work (e.g., a novel or a film), italicize that title. If the article title contains within it a quotation or the title of a shorter work (e.g., a poem or a short story), then place that quotation or title within single quotation marks.

> Petit, Susan. "Field of Deferred Dreams: Baseball and Historical Amnesia in Marilynne Robinson's *Gilead* and *Home*." *MELUS* 37.4 (2012): 119-37. Print.

> Clark, Miriam Marty. "Allegories of Reading in Alice Munro's 'Carried Away.'" *Contemporary Literature* 37.1 (1996): 49-61. Print.

An Article Reprinted in a Loose-Leaf Collection

The entry begins with original publication information, including the medium of publication, and ends with the name of the loose-leaf volume *(Youth)*, editor, volume number, publication information including name of the information service (SIRS), and the article number. In the example below, the plus sign indicates continuing but nonconsecutive pages.

> O'Connell, Loraine. "Busy Teens Feel the Beep." *Orlando Sentinel* 7 Jan. 1993: E1+. Print. *Youth*. Ed. Eleanor Goldstein. Vol. 4. Boca Raton: SIRS, 1993. Art. 41.

Online Sources

Components

Citations for online sources generally follow the strategies used for print sources, including the medium of publication (Web). After the author's name and title of the work (either italicized or in quotes, depending on the type of work), include the title of the overall website in italics, and additional information as described below. Because URLs can change, the URL should be provided only if the reader probably cannot locate the source without it, or if your instructor requires it.

1. Author's name
2. Title of the article or work, italicized or in quotation marks
3. Title of the overall website, italicized (if different from item 2)
4. Version or edition used
5. Publisher or sponsor of the site; if not available, use *n.p.*
6. Date of publication, with day, month, and year if available; if nothing is available, use *n.d.*
7. Medium of publication *(Web)*
8. Date of access (day, month, and year)

Including a URL for a Site

If you must include a URL to provide guidance to a site (or because your instructor requires URLs), give it after the date of access, a period, and a space. Enclose it in angle brackets and follow it with a period.

> "Fort Walsh National Historic Site." *Cypress Hills Interprovincial Park*. Parks Canada, n.d. Web. 7 Aug. 2012. <http://www.cypresshills.com/index.php?id=228>.

If the URL must be divided between two lines, break it only after a single or double slash. Do not add a hyphen. If possible, include the complete address, including *http://* for the work you are citing.

> MacLeod, Donald. "Shake-Up for Academic Publishing." *Guardian Unlimited*. Guardian News and Media Ltd., 10 Nov. 2008. Web. 6 Jan. 2014. <http://www.guardian.co.uk/Archive/>.

A Nonperiodical Publication

Most items online are not posted on a regular schedule; they are nonperiodical. Business pages, blog entries, PDF documents, online books, audio or video posts, and a host of other postings are nonperiodical publications. This includes most websites sponsored by magazines and newspapers. Such items can be identified following the guidelines on the previous page. (For additional guidelines regarding scholarly journals or periodical publications in an online database, see page 521.)

Items Existing Only Online

Many publications exist only in online form. Because such publications can move unexpectedly, it is important to include enough information for your reader to locate them again regardless of their new location.

- **A Typical Online Item**

    > Booth, Philip. "Robert Frost's Prime Directive." *Poets.org.* Academy of American Poets, n.d. Web. 1 Oct. 2014.

- **An Online Item, No Author Identified**

    Begin with the title of the work, in quotation marks or italics, as appropriate. Alphabetize this entry by the first significant word of the title ("Calgary CMA" in this case).

    > "Calgary CMA (August 30-November 28, 2010)." *Bureau of Broadcast Measurement.* N.d. Web. 4 Jan. 2011.

- **A Home Page**

    If a nonperiodical publication has no title, identify it with a descriptor such as *Home page, Introduction,* or *Online posting* (using no italics or quotation marks). You may add the name of the publication's creator or editor after the overall site title, if appropriate.

    > Wheaton, Wil. Home page. *Wil Wheaton dot Net.* N.p., 31 May 2006. Web. 19 Mar. 2014.

- **An Online Item with a Compiler, an Editor, or a Translator**

    When alphabetizing an entry by its compiler, editor, or translator, treat that person's name as usual, followed by an abbreviation for her or his role. If an author is identified, however, the compiler, editor, or translator follows the item title, with the abbreviation for the role preceding the compiler, editor, or translator's name.

    > Webster, Michael, comp. "Books and Articles Cited in 'Notes on the Writings of E. E. Cummings.'" Spring. E. E. Cummings Society, n.d. Web. 4 Oct. 2014.

    > Lao-tzu. *Tao Te Ching.* Trans. J. Legge. *Internet Sacred Text Archive.* John Bruno Hare, n.d. Web. 14 Apr. 2014.

An Entry in an Online Reference Work

Unless the author of the entry is identified, begin with the entry name in quotation marks. Follow with the usual online publication information.

> "Eakins, Thomas." *Britannica Online Encyclopedia.* Encyclopedia Britannica, 2008. Web. 26 Sept. 2014.

An Online Poem

List the poet's name, the title of the poem, and any print publication information before the electronic publication details.

> Lane, Patrick. "The Last Farm." *Mortal Remains.* Toronto: Exile Editions, 1992. 37. *Books. google.ca.* Web. 30 Sept. 2013.

An Online Transcript of a Broadcast

Give the original publication information for the broadcast. Following the medium of publication, add *Transcript*, followed by a period.

> Lehrer, Jim. "Character Above All." *Online NewsHour.* Natl. Public Radio, 29 May 1996. PBS.org. Web. Transcript. 23 Apr. 2014.

An Online Government Publication

As with a governmental publication in print, begin with the name of the government (country, province or territory, and so on) followed by the name of the agency. After the publication title, add the electronic publication information.

> Government of Canada. Office of the Commissioner of Official Languages. *Challenges: The New Environment for Language Training in the Federal Public Service.* Sept. 2013. Web. 21 Feb. 2014.

Items Including Print Publication Information

In general, follow the format for printed books. Include publication information for the original print version if available. Follow the date of publication with the electronic information, including the title of the site or database, sponsor, date of electronic posting (or *n.d.* if not available), medium of publication *(Web.)*, and your date of access.

> Simon, Julian L. *The Ultimate Resource II: People, Materials, and Environment.* College Park: U of Maryland, 1996. *U of Maryland Libraries.* Web. 9 Apr. 2014.

When citing part of an online book (such as the foreword) follow the example on page 511, but end with the online source, the term *Web*, and the date of access.

> Taylor, Bayard. Preface. *Faust.* Trans. Bayard Taylor. Boston: Houghton, 1883. iii-xvii. *Google Book Search.* Web. 7 March 2014.

Items Including Nonprint Publication Information

For online postings of photographs, videos, sound recordings, works of art, and so on, follow the examples on pages 522–524. In place of the original medium of publication, however, include the title of the database or website (italicized), followed by the medium *(Web.)* and the date of access, as for other online entries.

- **An Artwork**

  Goya, Francisco de. *Saturn Devouring His Children.* 1819-1823. Museo Nacional del Prado, Madrid. *Museodelprado.es.* Web. 13 Dec. 2013.

- **A Photograph**

  Brumfield, William Craft. *Church of Saint Nicholas Mokryi.* 1996. Prints and Photographs Div., Lib. of Cong. *Brumfield Photograph Collection.* Web. 9 May 2014.

- **An Audio Recording**

  "Gildy Arrives in Summerfield." *The Great Gildersleeve.* NBC. 31 Aug. 1941. *EThomsen.com.* Web. 13 Apr. 2014.

- **A Video**

  Sita Sings the Blues. Prod. Nina Paley. 2008. *Internet Archive.* Web. 5 June 2014.

- **An Unpublished Manuscript**

  "The Work-for-All Plan." 1933. Mildred Hicks Papers. Manuscript, Archives, and Rare Book Lib., Emory U. *Online Manuscript Resources in Southern Women's History.* Web. 31 Jan. 2014.

Journal Published Only Online

Some journals are published only on the Web, with no print version. For such publications, follow the basic guidelines given for print periodicals, though conclude with *Web* instead of *Print*, followed by your date of access. Also, if no page numbers are given, or if each item in the journal is numbered separately, replace the normal page notation with *n. pag.*

Marsden, Steve. "Texts and Transformission: Teaching American Literature with Juxta." *Teaching American Literature: A Journal of Theory and Practice.* 2011. Web. 30 Sept. 2014.

A Periodical Publication in an Online Database

Articles from different sources may be incorporated into an online database. To cite an article from a database, begin your citation with the usual information for citing print periodicals, but drop the medium of original publication *(Print)*. Instead, include the title of the database (italicized), the medium of publication *(Web)*, and the date of access.

Trussler, Michael. "Pockets of Nothingness: 'Metaphysical Solitude' in Alice Munro's 'Passion.'" *Narrative* 20.2 (2012): 183-97. *Literary Reference Center.* Web. 2 Oct. 2014.

Other Sources: Primary, Personal, and Multimedia

The following examples of works-cited entries illustrate how to cite sources such as television or radio programs, films, live performances, works of art, and other miscellaneous nonprint sources.

A Periodically Published Database on CD-ROM or DVD-ROM

Citations for materials published on CD-ROM or DVD-ROM are similar to those for print sources, with these added considerations: (1) The contents of a work may vary from one medium to another; therefore, the citation should always identify the medium. (2) The publisher and vendor of the publication may be different, in which case both must be identified. (3) Because of periodic updates, multiple versions of the same database may exist, which calls for citation if possible of both the date of the document cited and the date of the database itself.

> Ackley, Patricia. "Jobs of the Twenty-First Century." *New Rochelle Informer* 15 Apr. 1994: A4. CD-ROM. *New Rochelle Informer Ondisc.* Oct. 1994.

> Baker, Anthony. *The New Earth Science.* Cincinnati: Freeman's P, 1991. DVD-ROM. *New Media Inc.*, 2004.

Reference Work on CD-ROM

If you use an encyclopedia or other reference book recorded on CD-ROM, use the form below. If available, include publication information for the printed source.

> *The American Heritage Dictionary of the English Language.* 3rd ed. Boston: Houghton, 1992. CD-ROM. Cambridge, MA: Softkey Intl., 1994.

A Television or Radio Program

Include the medium (*Television* or *Radio*) at the end of the citation, followed by a period.

> "The War of 1812: Been There, Won That." *Doc Zone.* CBC News Network. 4 Oct. 2012. Television.

A Film

The director, distributor, and year of release follow the title. Other information may be included if pertinent. End with the medium, in this case *Film*, followed by a period.

> *Take This Waltz.* Dir. Sarah Polley. Perf. Michelle Williams, Seth Rogen, Sarah Silverman, Luke Kirby. Mongrel Media, 2011. Film.

Serg64/Shutterstock.com

A Video Recording or an Audio Recording

Cite a filmstrip, slide program, videocassette, or DVD as you do a film; include the medium of publication last, followed by a period.

> *Monet: Shadow & Light.* Devine Productions, 1999. Videocassette.

If you are citing a specific song on a musical recording, place its title in quotation marks before the title of the recording.

> Bernstein, Leonard. "Maria." *West Side Story.* Columbia, 1995. CD.

A Performance

Treat this similarly to a film, adding the location and date of the performance.

> *Blithe Spirit.* By Noël Coward. Dir. Brian Bedford. The Stratford Shakespeare Festival.
> Avon Theatre, Stratford, ON. 18 Oct. 2013. Performance.

An Artwork on Display

> Titian. *The Entombment.* N.d. Painting. Louvre, Paris.

A Letter, Memo, or Email Received by the Author (You)

For an unpublished letter or memo, include the form of the material after the date: *TS* for a typescript or printout, and *MS* for a work written by hand.

> Thomas, Bob. "Re: Research Plan." Message to author. 10 Jan. 2014. Email.

An Interview by the Author (You)

> Brooks, Sarah. Personal interview. 15 Oct. 2014.

A Cartoon or Comic Strip (in Print)

> Chast, Roz. "Ed Revere, Spam Courier." Cartoon. *The New Yorker* 22 Apr. 2013: 67. Print.

An Advertisement (in Print)

List the subject of the advertisement (product, company, organization, or such), followed by *Advertisement* and a period. Then give the usual publication information.

> Mesopotamia Exhibit, Royal Ontario Museum. Advertisement. *The Walrus* Oct. 2013.
> Print.

A Lecture, a Speech, an Address, or a Reading

Provide the speaker's name, the title of the presentation (if known) in quotation marks, the meeting and the sponsoring organization, the location, and the date. End with an appropriate descriptive label such as *Address, Lecture,* or *Reading.*

> Gopnik, Adam. "Radical Winter." CBC Massey Lectures. Dalhousie Arts Centre, Halifax,
> Nova Scotia. 12 Oct. 2011. Lecture.

A Legal or Historical Document

If your paper requires a number of legal citations, the MLA advises consulting the most recent edition of *The Bluebook: A Uniform System of Citation* (Cambridge: Harvard Law Rev. Assn.: Print). If you are providing only a few such citations, the MLA provides that the titles of laws, acts, and similar documents should appear in regular type (not italicized or enclosed in quotation marks), both within the text and in the list of works cited. The titles are abbreviated, and works are cited by sections, with years included if relevant. End your citation with the medium of publication followed by a period.

> 7 USC. Sec. 308a. 1928. Print.

> Do-Not-Call Implementation Act. Pub. L. 108-10. Stat. 117-557. 11 Mar. 2003. Print.

Abbreviate the names of law cases (spelling out the first important word of each party's name). Do not italicize the name in your works-cited list (although it should be italicized within the body of your paper). Follow with the case number or volume, inclusive page or reference numbers, the name of the court, the date (or year) of the decision, the medium consulted, and the date of access for a Web site.

> Envision Credit Union v. Canada. 34619. Supreme Court of Canada. 26 Sept. 2013. Web. 11 March 2014.

A Map or Chart

Follow the format for an anonymous book, adding *Map* or *Chart* (without italics), followed by a period, the city and publisher, date, and the medium of publication.

> *Wisconsin Territory.* Map. Madison: Wisconsin Trails, 1988. Print.

Sample MLA Paper

Student writer Paige Louter wrote "Why the World Deserves Better than Fair Trade" as an argumentative research paper for her expository writing class. In her paper, she explores the limited success of the fair trade movement, documenting her research using MLA style. Strictly speaking, MLA format does not require or even recommend a title page or an outline. (For more on outlines, you can also see pages 49–55.) You can use Paige's paper in three ways:

1. To study how a well-written, major research paper develops careful thinking, builds a discussion, and orders supporting points and evidence.

2. To examine how source summaries, paraphrases, and quotations are carefully integrated into the writer's discussion to advance her thinking— a full-length example of the strategies addressed on pages 482–485.

3. To see in detail the format and documentation practices of MLA style, practices that allow the writer to share a professional-looking paper that fairly respects sources used.

Sample Paper: Format, In-Text Citation, and Works-Cited List

Note that MLA format requires that the paper be double-spaced throughout.

Louter 1

Paige Louter

Dr. Van Rys

English 302

15 February 2014

Why the World Deserves Better than Fair Trade

The 2004 book *Fair Trade: Market-Driven Ethical Consumption* opens with the following account of what fair trade can do for the "world's poor": "I used to live in a thatch hut with a mud floor," says fair trade farmer Jeronimo Tush. "Now I have two concrete houses. And . . . my children now only go to school. We don't need them to work" (qtd. in Nicholls and Opal 3). Why would anyone argue against a system of trade that provides improved housing and eliminates the need for child labor? Fair trade is admirable in its effort to address injustice, to promote human rights all over the world, to fight poverty, and to promote ethical food-production and consumption practices. However, there is a darker side to the fair trade movement: this seemingly just-trade model is in reality falling short of its idealistic claims, and is in fact creating new problems. Though the fair trade movement is perhaps not beyond saving, it must undergo radical change to survive. Additionally, in order to demand change and perhaps even offer solutions themselves, consumers—especially those who wish to call themselves socially conscious—must educate themselves as to the harmful effects for which fair trade is responsible.

To begin with, the term "fair trade" itself is a source of confusion among many consumers. "Fair trade," not capitalized and written as two words, is the general term for the concept. However, "fairtrade" written as one word is the official name of products labeled by the Fairtrade Labelling Organizations International (FLO)— thereby making the products eligible for the Fairtrade International certification mark. Here's where it gets more confusing: the American branch of fair trade product certification is called Fair Trade USA—two words, both capitalized (Figure 1 below). Anyone can claim that his or her product is fair trade, but without one of the logos, a product cannot be Fairtrade (or Fair Trade); however, companies themselves may

Louter 2

not fully realize this. As Amarjit Sahota, the director of Organic Monitor puts it, "Companies do not always distinguish between Fairtrade and fair trade. Only the first concept is independently audited and internationally recognized [. . .]. Firms that use the latter term aren't necessarily trying to deceive consumers. It's simply hard to distinguish [between the two]" (qtd. in Hodge 17-18). This essay will consistently use the terms "fair trade" and "Fairtrade."

Fig. 1. Fair Trade USA's Certification Label

Considering this difference in terminology, then, what guidelines are necessary for a product to achieve Fairtrade status? "Fair trade" as a general term could potentially be applied to any product that appears to empower disadvantaged producers. "Fairtrade" as a label, however, indicates certain guarantees for those supplying the products. These guarantees are, according to the Fairtrade International Web site, "Stable prices . . . a Fairtrade Premium . . . partnership. [. . . and] empowerment of farmers and workers" ("What is [sic] Fairtrade?"). Further unpacked, this means that Fairtrade producers have guaranteed minimum prices for their goods, an extra amount or Premium paid to the management of the producers, and a say in how their own goods are to be produced and sold. The Premium is a concept that consumers are often unfamiliar with, and in concept, it could indeed do much good for the communities of Fairtrade producers; the Premium is intended for investment in beneficial projects such as schools and healthcare facilities. None of these guarantees appear to be objectively wrong, and perhaps in a perfect world Fairtrade could operate under these principles in an entirely beneficial way. There is a shocking gap, however, between Fairtrade ideals and reality—a concept that will be more fully addressed later in the essay.

In the parenthetical citation, "qtd. in" indicates that the source was quoted in another source (an indirect quotation). Ellipses and brackets indicate omissions from and changes to the quotation.

A visual is properly referenced in the essay and labelled.

Because it has no author, a reliable website is clearly identified by sponsoring agency; without pagination, no parenthetical citation is needed.

The typeface is a traditional serif type, Times New Roman.

Courtesy of Fair Trade USA.

Louter 3

Before criticizing the fair trade movement, one should pay attention to the benefits that the movement provides. Paul Chandler, the Chief Executive of Traidcraft (a fair trade organization in the UK), offers a succinct summary of the positive effects of purchasing fair trade products:

> Fair trade activity has a positive impact on the livelihoods and welfare of those producers directly involved in fair trade supply chains [. . . .] Second, fair trade gives consumers an opportunity to exercise a moral choice in their own purchasing practices [. . . .] Third, fair trade offers an effective critique of business practices, showing there are practical alternative ways of trading that can be more beneficial for the poor. (Chandler 256)

Chandler is obviously not bias-free in his analysis of the fair trade industry, yet his points have merit. There are indeed many success stories generated by fair trade practices: families lifted out of poverty, farmers supported when they would have otherwise faced ruin, children freed from daily labor and allowed to go to school. In addition, fair trade does provide consumers with at least the awareness that their dollars can make a difference when it comes to social justice. Finally, the fair trade movement does deserve credit for demonstrating that the current global system of trade, which does not always have the concerns of the poor at heart, is not the only option.

After taking all these benefits into account, it seems that ethically-minded consumers should choose fair trade products whenever possible. These pros, however, are only a small piece of the bigger picture. In fact, each of Chandler's claims is only partially true: each declaration needs to be modified and qualified before it can accurately speak to the reality of fair trade. First, not every producer "directly involved in fair trade supply chains" benefits from the guaranteed minimum price that is a key tenant of Fairtrade products (Chandler 256). Next, as Philip Booth and Linda Whetstone argue, "those promoting fair trade should have the humility to accept that their way of doing business is not objectively better for the poor than other ways of doing business" (29). In other words, fair trade is not necessary for consumers to "exercise a moral choice" with their money (Chandler 256). Chandler's final claim is that fair trade shows that alternative ways of trading, ones that better address the needs of the poor around the world, can and do exist. Yet while most consumers would immediately agree that poverty must be addressed head-on, Chandler offers no objective reasons as to why fair trade practice is the best

---

Margin notes:

Louter acknowledges the benefits of fair trade before continuing her argument about its weaknesses.

A quotation longer than four typed lines is inset—indented 10 spaces (about 2.5 cm) and double-spaced throughout; ellipses indicate material left out of the quotation; end punctuation is placed before the parenthetical citation.

The writer transitions to arguments critiquing fair trade; she quotes from and debates a source.

Margins of 2.5 cm are used left and right, top and bottom, with the exception of the header, which is 1.25 cm from the top.

Louter 4

The text is double-spaced throughout, including inset quotations, tables, and visuals. No extra space or lines are added between paragraphs.

avenue through which to do this. Still, the fair trade movement has demonstrated that many consumers are willing to spend more in response to the promise that their dollars are helping those in need. In addition, perhaps future ethical consumption initiatives will gain more immediate legitimacy as a result. Later in this essay, each of these responses to Chandler's claims will be unpacked in further detail, and with more support. This initial set of responses is valuable, however, because it demonstrates a key problem with the claims of many who support fair trade: the claims are often only partially true, based on feel-good rhetoric and fair trade ideals rather than on hard evidence. Further, evidence, when cited, is often very selective. Nevertheless, many fair trade proponents have legitimate, well-supported arguments that will be addressed later in this paper.

Paige develops her critique by addressing issues of coffee quality and of gender inequity.

When the author of a source is not named in the sentence, his or her last name appears in the in-text citation.

Considering that the livelihoods (and lives) of many are at stake in the failure of the fair trade movement, perhaps a less dramatic—yet serious—problem is that the quality of certified Fairtrade coffee is often significantly poorer than coffee that is not Fairtrade. However, this problem is significant when one considers that some consumers will forgo Fairtrade coffee based on its inferior taste. If the WFTO wishes to avoid charges of providing charity rather than actual trade opportunities to its producers, the organization must have some way of ensuring that its products are purchased for their quality as well as for the economic aid they offer farmers. One critic of the Fairtrade industry asserted that it is "stuck in a charity-driven, charity-supported model . . . that smacks of colonialism" (Hutchens 458). In order to address this issue, one must ask why Fairtrade coffee would taste consistently poorer than other coffee. The answer essentially comes down to a lack of quality control. There are, shockingly, no Fairtrade standards regarding the quality of the product. Because quality-control is lacking, and because there is a maximum amount of coffee beans that the Fairtrade buyers will accept from any one cooperative, the farmers can sell only part of their produce at the Fairtrade price, and they sell the remainder on the open market. In other words, because the Fairtrade market does not monitor the quality of the beans that they receive, farmers consistently sell their higher quality beans on the open market. In addition, the coffee co-ops do not keep track of which beans come from which farmers. In fact, co-ops regularly mix all purchased beans together, thereby removing any incentive for farmers to sell only their best beans as fair trade produce. David Henderson calls this a "free-ride problem" (63). In contrast

6

When an author is named in an attributive phrase, the parenthetical citation includes only a page number.

Louter 5

to the "Organic Specialty" label which assures a consumer that a product is healthier, grown with less harmful chemicals and so on, the "Fairtrade" label offers no similar assurance of quality. Therefore, Fairtrade consumers are often purchasing products out of charity, a practice that is not a sustainable business model. Furthermore, when quality standards are not enforced, the implication is that the Fairtrade system believes that the producers are incapable of creating excellent product.

Unfortunately, Fairtrade has even bigger problems than quality control, one of which is its failure to promote women's rights, a principle ostensibly championed by the World Fair Trade Organization (WFTO). However, as Anna Hutchens puts it, there is an "absence of a policy framework and institutional mechanisms that promote women's empowerment as a rights-based rather than a culture-based issue" (449). In other words, the WFTO does not intentionally seek to universalize human rights when it comes to women. Consumers are told that women in the Fairtrade system are empowered and uplifted, but in practice, the WFTO does not seek to actively include them. The best that can be said is that they are not actively excluded. In order to achieve FLO certification, producer organizations are not required to meet any standards when it comes to working to empower women, and when it came to one coffee cooperative, "only seven of the 116 . . . members . . . were female and no women had served on the cooperative board or its managerial positions" (Hutchens 452). Sadly, this particular cooperative appears to be the rule rather than the exception. A further problem, stemming from the lack of universally applied empowerment of women, is that "women are not made exempt from their existing household duties" despite their increased workload of producing Fairtrade goods (452). And even those women who manage to find time to balance their domestic and fair trade producing roles may not benefit as they should: "Fairtrade payments typically go to the assumed male head of the household and cannot be assumed to 'trickle down' to benefit all the household members" (452).

Though gender-based disparity is bad enough, women are not the only ones who do not reap the full reward that the WFTO would like consumers to believe exists. Others denied these rewards are the farmers barred from entering the Fairtrade coffee business, as well as those workers who are employed under the Fairtrade label yet work in substandard conditions and receive substandard pay. Many agree that "there are . . . significant opportunities for corruption within the

A series of quotations from one source begins with a complete parenthetical citation but then follows with page numbers only, as the quotes are clearly from the same source. The last quotation is introduced with a complete sentence ending in a colon; words in quotation marks within the quotation are put in single quotation marks, not double.

7

8

Louter 6

fair trade co-operatives [sic]" (Booth and Whetstone 33). In other words, the idea that the payment for a cup of coffee purchased in Europe or North America goes directly to the hand of an impoverished coffee bean farmer is a myth.

> **The writer transitions to a critique based upon economic theory, summarizing and quoting from a source.**

Beyond all these problems, many economists such as those who work at the Adam Smith Institute say that fair trade simply does not make sense in terms of the market system by which it operates. These economic arguments are potentially devastating if it is found that fair trade ultimately increases, rather than alleviates, the economic hardships in which the producers work. Fair trade operates on the principle of guaranteeing a minimum price for a product, regardless of how low the real market value for that product drops. This minimum price is called a price floor, which, when set above the market price, creates a surplus, and which in turn creates a price drop in the market price. "If there were a free market," writes Jeremy Weber, "new entrants would increase supply and decrease price. The minimum price . . . by

> **The right margin is ragged, not justified.**

definition prevents that outcome" (113). The result? There is just too much Fairtrade coffee being produced. Farmers are often unable to sell more than a small percentage of their coffee beans to Fairtrade buyers, and new producers who wish to enter the Fairtrade business are finding it nearly impossible: "The increased difficulty of entering the Fair Trade market threatens to exclude the marginalized coffee growers

> **Paragraphs are indented 5 spaces, inset quotations 10 spaces.**

who Fair Trade supposedly supports" (Weber 113). For example, starting in 2004, Fair Trade certification cost $3200. In fact, dual-certification of Fairtrade and Organic is often now required, and the latter costs anywhere between $300 and $2000. But the difficulty doesn't end there—renewal fees too can cost thousands of dollars. As a result, even if a coffee cooperative desiring the Fairtrade mark can raise the necessary money, the waiting list is seemingly endless: thousands of co-ops await certification, hoping to get a chance to sell their products at artificially high Fairtrade prices.

> **After discussing economic theory and providing some statistics, the writer concludes her point with an authoritative and well-phrased quotation.**

Essentially, the economic principles on which Fairtrade operates are inevitably leading towards increased difficulties for any coffee farmer who did not achieve Fairtrade certification in the early days of the movement. "Fair trade may be fashionable and give people a nice warm feeling," say Philip Booth and Linda Whetstone, "but only free trade backed up by the rule of law and the protection of private property have actually lifted entire populations out of poverty for the long term" (35).

Perhaps of less concern to the world at large, but of more concern to the university and college community (and indeed most North American and European

9

10

Louter 7

In a series of paragraphs, the writer enumerates judgment traps created by fair trade, culminating in neo-colonialism.

consumers), is the illusion evoked by purchasing fair trade products. First, the purchase can lull consumers into a false sense of accomplishment, leaving them less likely to investigate the idealistic claims of the movement or to seek out alternate forms of spending ethically. "The fair trade movement . . . suggests that the production and purchase of fair trade produce somehow lies on a higher moral plane than other business activity," say Booth and Whetstone (30). However, consumers do have other options such as simply purchasing cheaper coffee and donating the difference in price between the regular and the fair trade product to a charity. Booth and Whetstone continue: "the fair trade movement may have found a successful marketing device for increasing philanthropy but that does not make their products ethical" (31).

Strong topic sentences offer transitions between paragraphs and move the discussion forward.

But Fairtrade customers are also subject to a second illusion: that their purchases make them more ethical than other consumers who do not actively pursue Fairtrade purchases. There are countless alternatives to certified Fairtrade in terms of ethical consumption, many of which are more sustainable in the long term and not as rife with complications and downsides. Fairtrade purchases, though, tend to have a public component; people can see and hear other consumers requesting Fairtrade coffee or chocolate at cafés or grocery stores, and these same militantly moral consumers can publically call attention to those who do not make the same choice.

11

Throughout the paper, authors' names, titles of works, and page references create clear, accurate citations for borrowed material—summaries, paraphrases, and quotations.

Finally, Fairtrade consumers can misjudge producers. Whereas Fairtrade has been rightly criticized for inadvertently spreading a sort of neo-colonial attitude, consider, for instance, the problem of quality control that was explored earlier: that Fairtrade does not press producers to develop high quality products. "Companies such as Green & Black's," on the other hand, "say they aid farmers more by helping them to improve quality and go organic rather than just guaranteeing a price" (Beattie 34). The Fairtrade model ensures that producers will never be able to grow beyond the need for a fixed minimum, while alternate models seek to empower producers. It is not hard to see which paradigm is rife with paternalistic, colonialist implications. Getting consumers in the right frame of mind is not an irrelevant need. As Ian Hussey puts it, "decolonization is not just a material process, but also a mental one" (17). Fair trade, he says, "serves to reinforce racist and colonial distinctions between the poor Global South farmer and the benevolent Global North

12

Louter 8

consumer" (15). In the long run, this mindset is destructive in that it denigrates Fairtrade producers as charity cases rather than potential partners.

It may at this point appear that fair trade and its proponents have not been given a fair voice. After all, as thinkers such as Andrew Walton have pointed out, fair trade needs to be understood as being an interim measure for seeking justice. The world is "non-ideal" and fair trade is only a second-best measure—not "global market justice" in and of itself (Walton 435). Indeed, critics of the movement do fair trade an injustice when they argue that it should be rejected simply because it is not a perfect and complete alternative to the current global economy. Ignoring for a moment all practical considerations, fair trade and movements such as the "Make Poverty History" campaign do the entire world a service in bringing issues of poverty and injustice to the forefront of the continuing global conversation. How consumers spend their money can make a serious difference. It is a shame that fair trade has not proven to be the solution that it originally aspired to be.   13

In this light, the future of fair trade, of ethical consuming at all, seems bleak. The claims of Fairtrade organizations do not match up with reality, and the best intentions of countless activists and socially concerned consumers appear to have ultimately done more damage than good. But it is not enough to tear down an existing structure such as fair trade. Alternatives or changes to fair trade must be sought; consumers and producers alike have a right and a responsibility to demand better. In the future, strong claims such as those of the fair trade movement must "be subject to strong tests" (Booth and Whetstone 29). Consumers must no longer praise a solution such as fair trade without being educated as to its implications and consequences. Luckily, the burden for change does not rest on the "Global North consumer" alone. By transcending the colonial mindset, North can work with South, and a united global force can share the challenges of addressing injustices from the personal to the economic. Fair trade may not have all the answers, but it has certainly taught us to ask the right questions.   14

In her closing paragraphs, the writer consolidates her critique while offering some balance, and then points forward to possible solutions.

Louter 9

Works Cited

Beattie, Alan. "The Price of Being Fair." *New Statesman* 136.4833 (2007): 34-35. *Literary Reference Center*. Web. 18 Jan. 2014.

Booth, Philip, and Linda Whetstone. "Half a Cheer for Fair Trade." *Economic Affairs* 27.2 (2007): 29-36. *Business Source Elite*. Web. 19 Jan. 2014.

Chandler, Paul. "Fair Trade and Global Justice." *Globalizations* 3.2 (2006): 255-57. *Academic Search Premier*. Web. 19 Jan. 2014.

Henderson, David R. "Fair Trade Is Counterproductive—And Unfair." *Economic Affairs* 28.3 (2008): 62-64. *Business Source Elite*. Web. 19 Jan. 2014.

Hodge, Neil. "Chocs Away." *Financial Management* (2010): 14-21. *Business Source Elite*. Web. 18 Jan. 2014.

Hussey, Ian. "Fair Trade and Empire: An Anti-Capitalist Critique of the Fair Trade Movement." *Briarpatch* 40.5 (2011): 15-18. *Canadian Reference Centre*. Web. 18 Jan. 2014.

Hutchens, Anna. "Empowering Women Through Fair Trade? Lessons from Asia." *Third World Quarterly* 31.3 (2010): 449-67. *Academic Search Premier*. Web. 18 Jan. 2014.

Nichols, Alex, and Charlotte Opal. *Fair Trade: Market-Driven Ethical Consumption*. London: Sage, 2004. Print.

Walton, Andrew. "What Is Fair Trade?" *Third World Quarterly* 31.3 (2010): 431-47. *Academic Search Premier*. Web. 19 Jan. 2014.

"What is [sic] Fairtrade?" *Fairtrade International*. Fairtrade Labelling Organizations International, n.d. Web. 10 Feb. 2014.

Weber, Jeremy. "Fair Trade Coffee Enthusiasts Should Confront Reality." *CATO Journal* 27.1 (2007): 109-17. *Academic Search Premier*. Web. 19 Jan. 2014.

The paper's bibliography lists a range of scholarly books, scholarly articles, and websites on the topic.

Sources are listed in alphabetical order by author (or by title if no author is given).

The list is double-spaced throughout—both between and within entries.

Second and subsequent lines of entries are indented 1.25 cm (hanging indent).

Titles are properly italicized or placed in quotation marks.

Correct abbreviations are used throughout.

Reading for Better Writing

Working by yourself or with a group, answer these questions:

1. How did Paige Louter's paper impact your understanding of global justice?
2. By reviewing topic sentences and skimming the paper, outline Paige's argument. How would you characterize her logic? How does her reasoning unfold?
3. What types of evidence does Paige use? Where has she gotten her evidence? Are her sources reliable? Does she have a balanced range of sources?
4. How does Paige distinguish her own thinking from source material? Why are these strategies necessary?

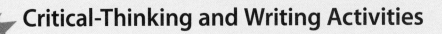

Critical-Thinking and Writing Activities

As directed by your instructor, complete the following critical-thinking and writing activities by yourself or with classmates.

1. Samuel Johnson once wrote, "Integrity without knowledge is weak and useless, and knowledge without integrity is dangerous and dreadful." Reflect on Johnson's statement as it relates to research writing and documentation. In what ways is such writing about both integrity and knowledge? If one is absent, what are the results?

2. The MLA style involves many rules about format and documentation. To make some sense of these rules, answer these questions: What is the essential logic of the MLA system? In other words, what does the MLA hope to accomplish with these rules?

3. Create MLA works-cited entries for the following publications:
   - An article by Laura Robinson in the Autumn 2005 issue (vol. 186) of *Canadian Literature*: "Remodeling *An Old-Fashioned Girl*: Troubling Girlhood in Ann-Marie MacDonald's *Fall on Your Knees*" (pages 30-45).
   - Lawrence Hill's novel *The Book of Negroes*, published in 2007 by HarperCollins Publishers, Ltd., located in Toronto.
   - The Web page "Haiti," part of the *Where We Work in International Development* section of the website for the Canadian federal government's department Foreign Affairs, Trade and Development Canada. No author or publication date is listed. The site was last accessed August 7, 2013, at http://www.acdi-cida.gc.ca/acdi-cida/ACDI-CIDA.nsf/eng/JUD-12912349-NLX.

Learning-Objectives Checklist ✓

Have you achieved this chapter's learning objectives? Check your progress with the items below, revisiting topics in the chapter as needed. *I have . . .*

____ gained an overview of the MLA system of documentation—the basic logic of in-text citations in relation to works-cited entries (494–495).

____ correctly implemented MLA format guidelines for whole-paper issues (e.g., header, heading on the first page, pagination), typography, and page layout (496–499).

____ applied rules of in-text citation, whether for regular sources or for sources without traditional authorship and/or pagination (500–507).

____ developed a works-cited list that is properly formatted and that correctly and fully identifies sources, whether books or journal articles or online documents (508–524).

____ examined MLA style at work in Paige Louter's "Why the World Deserves Better Than Fair Trade," learning how the system is practised concretely in a research-based argumentative essay (524–533).

APA Style

Those who write papers in the social sciences—psychology, sociology, political science, and education, for example—usually follow the research-writing guidelines of the American Psychological Association (APA). This chapter summarizes these guidelines and helps you use APA format and documentation.

APA format is similar to MLA format in two ways: Both require (1) parenthetical citations within the text and (2) a final listing of all references cited in the paper. But in the social sciences, the date of publication is often much more crucial than it is in the humanities, so the date is highlighted in in-text citations. APA format also requires a cover page and an abstract.

Visually Speaking   Figure 26.1 suggests something about humans and their societies. Consider the possibilities, and explore what social-science research and research writing in particular seek to contribute to an understanding of people and the societies they build.

Learning **Objectives**

By working through this chapter, you will be able to

- explain and implement APA guidelines for documenting sources.
- produce research writing that adheres to APA guidelines for format.
- identify and critique APA practices at work in a sample student research report.

Scott Norsworthy/Shutterstock.com

fig. 26.1

APA Documentation Guidelines

The APA system involves two parts: (1) an in-text citation within your paper when you use a source and (2) a matching bibliographic entry at the end of your paper. Note these features of the APA author-date system:

- **It uses signal phrases and parenthetical references** to set off source material from your own thinking and discussion. A signal phrase names the author and places the material in context (e.g., "As Jung described it, the collective unconscious. . .").
- **It's date-sensitive.** Because the publication dates of resources are especially important in social-science research, the publication year is included in the parenthetical reference and after the authors' names in the reference entry.
- **It's smooth, unobtrusive, and orderly.** APA in-text citations identify borrowed material while keeping the paper readable. Moreover, alphabetized reference entries at the end of the paper make locating source details easy.

You can see these features at work in the example below. The parenthetical material "Pascopella, 2011, p. 32" tells the reader these things:

- The borrowed material came from a source authored by Pascopella.
- The source was published in 2011.
- The specific material can be found on page 32 of the source.
- Full source details are in the reference list under the surname Pascopella.

1. In-Text Citation in Body of Paper

> In newcomer programs, "separate, relatively self-contained educational interventions" (Pascopella, 2011, p. 32) are implemented to meet the academic and transitional needs of recent immigrants before they enter a mainstream English Language Development.

2. Matching Reference Entry at End of Paper

> Pascopella, A. (2011). Successful strategies for English language learners. *District Administration, 47*(2), 29–44.

In-Text Citation: The Basics

See pages 539–542 for complete details on in-text citation.

1. Refer to the author(s) and date of publication by using one of these methods:

Last name(s), publication date in parentheses:

> ELLs normally spend just three years in 30-minute "pull-out" English language development programs (Calderón et al., 2011).

Last name(s) cited in text with publication date in parentheses:

> In "Key Issues for Teaching English Learners in Academic Classrooms," Carrier (2005) explained that it takes an average of one to three years to reach conversational proficiency in a second language, but five to seven years to reach academic proficiency.

2. Present and punctuate citations according to these rules:
- Keep authors and publication dates as close together as possible in the sentence.
- Separate the author's last name, the date, and any locating detail with commas.
- If referencing part of a source, use an appropriate abbreviation: *p.* (page), *para.* (paragraph)—but do not abbreviate *chapter*.

Note: When citing previous research, use past tense or present perfect tense—Smith (2003) found *or* Smith (2003) has found.

References: The Basics

Complete coverage of reference issues is offered on pages 543–553, and a sample references list is shown on page 562. Here, however, are templates for the most common entries:

Template for Book:

> Author's Last Name, Initials. (Publication Year). *Title of book*. Publication City, State, Province, Territory, or Country: Publisher. [Other publication details are integrated as needed.]

— authors' names, followed by period   publication year in parentheses, followed by period   — exact and full title in italics, first word and proper nouns capitalized, followed by period

Stanford, J., & Vosko, L. F. (2004). *Challenging the market: The struggle to regulate work and income*. Montreal, QC: McGill-Queen's University Press.

publication location from title page, followed by colon   publisher name from title page, followed by period

fig. 26.2

Template for Periodical Article:

> Author's Last Name, Initials. (Publication Year). Title of article. *Journal Title, volume*(issue), page numbers. [Other publication details are integrated as needed. For online periodical articles, add the digital object identifier (see page 549).]

— authors' names, followed by period   — article title, no quotation marks, first word and proper nouns capitalized

Campolieti, M., Gomez, R., & Gunderson, M. (2013). Managerial hostility and attitudes towards unions: A Canada-U.S. comparison. *Journal of Labor Research, 34*(1), 99–119. doi: 10.1007/s12122-012-9150-0

page numbers followed by period   journal title and volume number italicized

fig. 26.3

Template for Online Document:

> Author's Last Name, Initials. (Publication Date). *Title of work* OR Title of entry. DOI (digital object identifier) OR Retrieval statement including URL

— author's name, followed by period   publication date in parentheses, followed by period   document title

Government of Canada Department of Human Services. (2013, June). *Canada Labour Code*. Retrieved from http://laws-lois.justice.gc.ca/eng/acts/L-2/index.html/

retrieval statement

fig. 26.4

APA Format Guidelines

To submit a polished academic paper in APA format, follow the rules below and refer to the sample APA paper on pages 554–563.

- **Title Page:** On the first page, include your paper's title, your name, and your institution's name on three separate lines, double-spaced, centred, and positioned in the top half of the page. Flush left at the top, type *Running head:* (no italics) followed by your abbreviated title in all uppercase letters; and flush right at the top, type the page number 1.

- **Abstract:** On the second page, include an abstract—a 150- to 250-word paragraph summarizing your paper. Place the title *Abstract* (no italics) approximately 2.5 cm from the top of the page and centre it. Place the running head and page number 2 at the top of the page.

- **Body:** Format the body (which begins on the third page) as follows:

  - **Margins:** Leave a 2.5 cm margin on all four sides of each page (3.8 cm on the left if the paper will be bound). Do not justify lines, but rather leave a ragged right margin and do not break words at the ends of lines.

  - **Line Spacing:** Double-space your entire paper, unless your instructor allows single spacing for tables and figures.

  - **Page Numbers:** Place your running head and the page number flush left and flush right respectively, at the top of each page, beginning with the title page.

  - **Headings:** Like an outline, headings show the organization of your paper and the importance of each topic. All topics of equal importance should have headings of the same level, or style. Below are the various levels of headings used in APA papers.

  Level 1:   **Centred, Boldface, Uppercase and Lowercase Heading**
  Level 2: **Flush Left, Boldface, Uppercase and Lowercase Side Heading**
  Level 3:   **Indented, boldface, lowercase paragraph heading ending with a period.**
  Level 4:   ***Indented, boldface, italicized, lowercase paragraph heading with a period.***
  Level 5:   *Indented, italicized, lowercase paragraph heading with a period.*

  ## Example:

  Teaching K-12 English Language Learners in the Mainstream Classroom
  The English Language Learner Landscape
  Myths and misconceptions.
  Myth 1: Exposure will lead to learning.
  The need for explicit morphological instruction.

  - **Appendix:** Tables and figures (graphs, charts, maps, etc.) already appear on separate pages following the reference list. If necessary, one or more appendices may also supplement your text, following any tables or figures.

Guidelines for In-Text Citations

The Form of an Entry

The APA documentation style is sometimes called the "author–date" system because both the author and the date of the publication must be mentioned in the text when citing a source. Both might appear in the flow of the sentence, like this:

> Children in India are being trafficked for adoption, organ transplants, and labour such as prostitution, according to a 2007 article by Nilanjana Ray.

If either name or date does not appear in the text, it must be mentioned within parentheses at the most convenient place, like this:

> According to an article by Nilanjana Ray (2007), children in India . . .

> According to a recent article (Ray, 2007), children in India . . .

Points to Remember

1. When paraphrasing rather than quoting, make it clear where your borrowing begins and ends. Use stylistic cues to distinguish the source's thoughts ("Kalmbach points out . . . ," "Some critics argue . . .") from your own ("I believe . . . ," "It seems obvious, however . . .").
2. When using a shortened title of a work, begin with the word by which the work is alphabetized in your references list (for example, for "Measurement of Stress in Fasting Man," use "Measurement of Stress," not "Fasting Man").
3. When including a parenthetical citation at the end of a sentence, place it before the end punctuation: (Sacks, 1964).

Sample In-Text Citations

One Author: A Complete Work

The correct form for a parenthetical reference to a single source by a single author is parenthesis, last name, comma, space, year of publication, parenthesis. Also note that final punctuation should be placed outside the parentheses.

> . . . in this way, the public began to connect certain childhood vaccinations with an autism epidemic (Baker, 2008).

One Author: Part of a Work

When you cite a specific part of a source, give the page number, chapter, or section, using the appropriate abbreviations (p. or pp., para., or sec. For others, see page 543). Always give the page number for a direct quotation.

> . . . while a variety of political and scientific forces were at work in the developing crisis, it was parents who pressed the case "that autism had become epidemic and that vaccines were its cause" (Baker, 2008, p. 251).

One Author: Several Publications in the Same Year

If the same author has published two or more articles in the same year, avoid confusion by placing a small letter *a* after the first work listed in the references list, *b* after the next one, and so on. Determine the order alphabetically by title.

Parenthetical Citation:

▪ Reefs harbour life forms heretofore unknown (Milius, 2001a, 2001b).

References:

Milius, D. (2001a). Another world hides inside coral reefs. *Science News, 160*(16), 244.

Milius, D. (2001b). Unknown squids—with elbows—tease science. *Science News, 160*(24), 390.

Works by Authors with the Same Last Name

When citing different sources by authors with the same last name, add the authors' initials to avoid confusion, even if the publication dates are different.

While J. D. Wallace (2011) argued that eliminating the long-gun registry would hurt law-enforcement agencies, E. S. Wallace (2012) supported the Conservative Party's abolition of the registry based on his interpretation of the Charter of Rights and Freedoms.

Two to Five Authors

In APA style, all authors—up to as many as five—must be mentioned in the first text citation, like this:

Love changes not just who we are, but who we can become, as well (Lewis, Amini, & Lannon, 2000).

Note: The last two authors' names are always separated by a comma and an ampersand (&) when enclosed in parentheses.

For works with two authors, list both in every citation. For works with three to five authors, list all only the first time; after that, use only the name of the first author followed by "et al.," like this:

These discoveries lead to the hypothesis that love actually alters the brain's structure (Lewis et al., 2000).

Six or More Authors

If your source has six or more authors, refer to the work by the first author's name followed by "et al.," both for the first reference in the text and all references after that. However, be sure to list all the authors (up to seven) in your references list.

According to a recent study, post-traumatic stress disorder (PTSD) continues to dominate the lives of Vietnam veterans, though in modified forms (Trembley et al., 2012).

A Work Authored by an Agency, a Committee, or Other Organization

Treat the name of the group as if it were the last name of the author. If the name is long and easily abbreviated, provide the abbreviation in square brackets. Use the abbreviation without brackets in subsequent references, as follows:

First Text Citation:

> A problem for many veterans continues to be heightened sensitivity to noise (National Institute of Mental Health [NIMH], 2012).

Subsequent Citations:

> In addition, veterans suffering from PTSD continue to have difficulty discussing their experiences (NIMH, 2012).

A Work with No Author Indicated

If your source lists no author, treat the first few words of the title (capitalized normally) as you would an author's last name. A title of an article or a chapter belongs in quotation marks; the titles of books or reports should be italicized:

> . . . including a guide to low-stress postures ("How to Do It," 2013).

A Work Referred to in Another Work

If you need to cite a source that you have found referred to in another source (a "secondary" source), mention the original source in your text. Then, in your parenthetical citation, cite the secondary source, using the words "as cited in."

> . . . theorem given by Ullman (as cited in Hoffman, 2008).

Note: In your references list at the end of the paper, you would write out a full citation for Hoffman (not Ullman).

A Work in an Anthology

When citing an article or a chapter in an anthology or a collection, use the authors' names for the specific article, not the names of the anthology's editors. (Similarly, the article should be listed by its authors' names in the references section. See page 544.)

> Phonological changes can be understood from a variationist perspective (Guy, 2005).

An Electronic or Other Internet Source

As with print sources, cite an electronic source by the author (or by shortened title if the author is unknown) and the publication date (not the date you accessed the source).

> One study compared and contrasted the use of Web and touch screen transaction log files in a hospital setting (Nicholas, Huntington, & Williams, 2001).

A Website

Whenever possible, cite a website by its author and posting date. In addition, refer to a specific page or document rather than to a home page or a menu page. If you are referring to a specific part of a Web page that does not have page numbers, direct your reader, if possible, with a section heading and a paragraph number.

> According to the National Multiple Sclerosis Society (2009, "Complexities" section, para. 2), understanding of MS could not begin until scientists began to research nerve transmission in the 1920s.

Two or More Works in a Parenthetical Reference

Sometimes it is necessary to lump several citations into one parenthetical reference. In that case, cite the sources as you usually would, separating the citations with semicolons. Place the citations in alphabetical order, just as they would be ordered in the references list.

> Others report near-death experiences (Rommer, 2007; Sabom, 2010).

A Sacred Text or Famous Literary Work

Sacred texts and famous literary works are published in many different editions. For that reason, the original date of publication may be unavailable or not pertinent. In these cases, use your edition's year of translation (for example, *trans.* 2003) or indicate your edition's year of publication (2003 *version*). When you are referring to specific sections of the work, it is best to identify parts, chapters, or other divisions instead of your version's page numbers.

> An interesting literary case of such dysfunctional family behaviour can be found in Franz Kafka's *The Metamorphosis,* where it becomes the commandment of family duty for Gregor's parents and sister to swallow their disgust and endure him (trans. 1972, part 3).

Books of the Bible and other well-known literary works may be abbreviated, if no confusion is possible.

> "Generations come and generations go, but the earth remains forever" (*The New International Version Study Bible,* 1985 version, Eccles. 1.4).

Personal Communications

If you do the kind of personal research recommended elsewhere in *Writing Life*, you may have to cite personal communications that have provided you with some of your knowledge. Personal communications may include personal letters, phone calls, emails, and so forth. Because they are not published in a permanent form, APA style does not place them among the citations in your references list. Instead, cite them only in the text of your paper in parentheses, like this:

> . . . according to M. T. Cann (personal communication, April 1, 2014).

> . . . by today (M. T. Cann, personal communication, April 1, 2014).

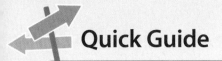

Quick Guide

APA References

The references section lists all the sources you have cited in your text (with the exception of personal communications such as phone calls and emails). Begin your references list on a new page after the last page of your paper. Number each references page, continuing the numbering from the text. Then format your references list by following the guidelines below.

1. Type the running head in the upper-left corner and the page number in the upper-right corner, approximately 1.25 cm from the top of the page.

2. Centre the title, *References,* approximately 2.5 cm from the top; then double-space before the first entry.

3. Begin each entry flush with the left margin. If the entry runs more than one line, indent additional lines approximately 1.25 cm (five to seven spaces) using a hanging indent.

4. Adhere to the following conventions about spacing, capitalization, and italics:
   - Double-space between all lines on the references page.
   - Use one space following each word and punctuation mark.
   - With book and article titles, capitalize only the first letter of the title (and subtitle) and proper nouns. (Note that this practice differs from the presentation of titles in the body of the essay.) ***Example:*** *The agricultural economy of Manitoba Hutterite colonies.*
   - Use italics for titles of books and periodicals, not underlining.

5. List each entry alphabetically by the last name of the author, or, if no author is given, by the title (disregarding *A*, *An*, or *The*). For works with multiple authors, use the first author listed in the publication.

6. Follow these conventions with respect to abbreviations:
   - With authors' names, generally shorten first and middle names to initials, leaving a space after the period. For a work with more than one author, use an ampersand (&) before the last author's name.
   - For publisher locations, use the full city name plus the two-letter Canada Post abbreviation for the province. For U.S. Publishers, use the two-letter U.S. Postal Service abbreviation for the state. For other international publishers, include a spelled-out province and country name.
   - Spell out "Press" or "Books" in full, but omit unnecessary terms like "Publishers," "Company," or "Inc."

7. With online sources, use the DOI (digital object identifier) whenever one exists to identify the sources (see page 549 for more details).

Reference Entries

Books and Other Documents

The general form for a book or brochure entry is this:

> ▌ Author, A. (year). *Title.* Location: Publisher.

The entries that follow illustrate the information needed to cite books, sections of a book, brochures, and government publications.

A Book by One Author

> ▌ DeVries, L. (2012). *Conflict in Caledonia: Aboriginal land rights and the rule of law.* Vancouver, BC: UBC Press.

A Book by Two or More Authors

List up to seven authors by last name and first initial, separating them by commas, with an ampersand (&) before the last.

> ▌ Crysdale, C., King, A. J. C., & Mandell, N. (1999). *On their own: Making the transition from school to work in the information age.* Montreal, QC: McGill-Queen's University Press.

For eight or more authors, list the first six followed by an ellipsis, and then the last.

An Anonymous Book

If an author is listed as "Anonymous," treat it as the author's name. Otherwise, follow this format:

> ▌ *Publication manual of the American Psychological Association* (6th ed.). (2010). Washington, DC: American Psychological Association.

A Chapter from a Book

List the chapter title after the date of publication, followed by a period or appropriate end punctuation. Use *In* before the book title, and follow the book title with the inclusive page numbers of the chapter.

> ▌ Tattersall, I. (2002). How did we achieve humanity? In *The monkey in the mirror: Essays on the science of what makes us human* (pp. 138–168). New York, NY: Harcourt.

A Single Work from an Anthology

Start with information about the individual work, followed by details about the collection in which it appears, including the page span. For editors' names in the middle of an entry, follow the usual order: initial first, surname last. Note the placement of Eds. in parentheses.

> ▌ Guy, G. R. (2005). Variationist approaches to phonological change. In B. D. Joseph & R. D. Janda (Eds.), *The handbook of historical linguistics* (pp. 369–400). Malden, MA: Blackwell.

One Volume of a Multivolume Edited Work

Indicate the volume in parentheses after the work's title.

> Salzman, J., Smith, D. L., & West, C. (Eds.). (1996). *Encyclopedia of African-American culture and history* (Vol. 4). New York, NY: Simon & Schuster Macmillan.

A Separately Titled Volume in a Multivolume Work

> The Associated Press. (1995). *Twentieth-century America: Vol. 8. The crisis of national confidence: 1974–1980.* Danbury, CT: Grolier Educational Corp.

Note: When a work is part of a larger series or collection, as with this example, make a two-part title with the series and the particular volume you are citing.

An Edited Work, One in a Series

Start the entry with the work's author, publication date, and title. Then follow with publication details about the series.

> Marshall, P. G. (2002). The impact of the cold war on Asia. In T. O'Neill (Ed.), *World history by era: Vol. 9. The nuclear age* (pp. 162–166). San Diego, CA: Greenhaven Press.

A Group Author as Publisher

When the author is also the publisher, simply put Author in the spot where you would list the publisher's name.

> Amnesty International. (2007). *Maze of injustice: The failure to protect indigenous women from sexual violence in the USA.* London, England: Author.

Note: If the publication is a brochure, identify it as such in brackets after the title.

An Edition Other Than the First

> Baylis, J., Smith, S., & Owens, P. (2011). *The globalization of world politics: An introduction to international relations* (5th ed.). Oxford, England: Oxford University Press.

Two or More Books by the Same Author

When you are listing multiple works by the same author, arrange them by the year of publication, earliest first.

> Sacks, O. (1995). *An anthropologist on Mars: Seven paradoxical tales.* New York, NY: Alfred A. Knopf.

> Sacks, O. (2007). *Musicophilia: Tales of music and the brain.* New York, NY: Alfred A. Knopf.

An English Translation

> Setha, R. (1998). *Unarmed* (R. Narasimhan, Trans.). Chennai, India: Macmillan. (Original work published 1995)

Note: If you use the original work, cite the original version; the non-English title is followed by its English translation, not italicized, in square brackets.

An Article in a Reference Book

Start the entry with the author of the article, if identified. If no author is listed, begin the entry with the title of the article.

> Lewer, N. (1999). Non-lethal weapons. In *World encyclopedia of peace* (pp. 279–280). Oxford, England: Pergamon Press.

A Reprint, Different Form

> Albanov, V. (2000). *In the land of white death: An epic story of survival in the Siberian Arctic.* New York, NY: Modern Library. (Original work published 1917)

Note: This work was originally published in Russia in 1917; the 2000 reprint is the first English version. If you are citing a reprint from another source, the parentheses would contain "Reprinted from Title, pp. xx–xx, by A. Author, year, Location: Publisher."

A Technical or Research Report

> Arthurs, H. W. (2006). *Fairness at work: Federal labour standards for the 21st century.* Gatineau, QC: Human Resources and Skills Development Canada.

A Government Publication

Generally, refer to the government agency as the author. When possible, provide an identification number for the document after the title in parentheses.

Example from a Canadian government agency:

> Human Resources and Skills Development Canada. (2012). *Wage earner protection program: A program to protect workers' wages!* (Cat. No. HS24-45/2011). Gatineau, QC: Public Works and Government Services Canada.

Example from a U.S. government agency:

> National Institute on Drug Abuse. (2000). *Inhalant abuse* (NIH Publication No. 00–3818). Rockville, MD: National Clearinghouse on Alcohol and Drug Information.

For reports obtained from the U.S. Government Printing Office, list location and publisher as "Washington, DC: Government Printing Office."

Print Periodical Articles

The general form for a periodical entry is this:

> Author, A. (year). Article title. *Periodical Title, volume number*(issue number), page numbers.

If the periodical does not use volume and issue numbers, include some other designation with the year, such as a date, a month, or a season. The entries that follow illustrate the information and arrangement needed to cite most types of print periodicals.

Note: Issue number is required only for journals that paginate each issue separately.

An Article in a Scholarly Journal

> Premdas, R. R. (2011). Identity, ethnicity, and the Caribbean homeland in an era of globalization. *Social Identities, 17*(6), 811–832.

 Pay attention to the features of this basic reference to a scholarly journal:

1. Provide the authors' last names and initials, as for a book reference.
2. Place the year of publication in parentheses, followed by a period.
3. Format the article's title in lowercase, except for the first word of the main title and of a subtitle and except for proper nouns, acronyms, or initialisms; do not italicize the article title or place it in quotation marks.
4. Capitalize the first and all main words in the journal title; italicize it.
5. Italicize the volume number but not the issue number; place the issue in parentheses, without a space after the volume number. No issue number is needed if the journal is paginated consecutively throughout a volume.
6. Provide inclusive page numbers, without "pp." or "pages."

An Abstract of a Scholarly Article (from a Secondary Source)

When referencing an abstract published separately from an article, provide publication details of the article followed by information about where the abstract was published.

> Shlipak, M. G., Simon, J. A., Grady, O., Lin, F., Wenger, N. K., & Furberg, C. D. (2001, September). Renal insufficiency and cardiovascular events in postmenopausal women with coronary heart disease. *Journal of the American College of Cardiology, 38*, 705–711. Abstract obtained from *Geriatrics, 2001, 56*(12). (Abstract No. 5645351.)

A Journal Article, More Than Seven Authors

Yamada, A., Suzuki, M., Kato, M., Suzuki, M., Tanaka, S., Shindo, . . . Furkawa, T. A. (2007). Emotional distress and its correlates among parents of children with persuasive developmental disorders. *Psychiatry & Clinical Neurosciences, 61*(6), 651–657.

Note: In the text, abbreviate the parenthetical citation: (Yamada et al., 2007).

A Review

To reference a book review or a review of another medium (film, exhibit, and so on), indicate the review and the medium in brackets, along with the title of the work being reviewed by the author listed.

Hutcheon, L., & Hutcheon, M. (2008). Turning into the mind. [Review of the book *Musicophilia: Tales of music and the brain,* by O. Sacks]. *Canadian Medical Association Journal, 178*(4), 441.

A Magazine Article

Weintraub, B. (2007, October). Unusual suspects. *Psychology Today, 40*(5), 80–87.

Note: If the article is unsigned, begin the entry with the title of the article.

Tomatoes target toughest cancer. (2002, February). *Prevention, 54*(2), 53.

A Newspaper Article

For newspaper articles, include the full publication date, year first followed by a comma, the month (spelled out) and the day. Identify the article's location in the newspaper using page numbers and section letters, as appropriate. If the article is a letter to the editor, identify it as such in brackets following the title. For newspapers, use *p.* or *pp.* before the page numbers; if the article is not on continuous pages, give all the page numbers, separated by commas.

Schmitt, E., & Shanker, T. (2008, March 18). U.S. adapts cold-war idea to fight terrorists. *The New York Times,* pp. 1A, 14A–15A.

Knaub, M. (2013, August 12). Area men recall their time as 'braceros.' *Yuma Times,* pp. 1A, 5A.

A Newsletter Article

Newsletter article entries are similar to newspaper article entries; only a volume number is added.

Teaching mainstreamed special education students. (2002, February). *The Council Chronicle,* 11, pp. 6–8.

Online Sources

When it comes to references for online sources, follow these guidelines:

1. **Whenever possible, use the final version of an electronic resource.** Typically, this is called the archival copy or the version of record, as opposed to a prepublished version. Right now, that final version is likely the same as the printed version of an article, though there is some movement toward the online publication being the final version (complete with additional data, graphics, and so on).

2. **In the reference entry for an electronic source, start with the same elements in the same order for print or other fixed-media resources** (author, title, and so on). Then add the most reliable electronic retrieval information that will (a) clarify what version of the source you used and (b) help your reader find the source him- or herself. Determine what you need to include based on these guidelines:

   - **Whenever possible, use the electronic document's Digital Object Identifier (DOI).** More and more, electronic publishers are using this registration code for the content of journal articles and other documents so that the document can be located on the Internet, even if the URL changes. The DOI will usually be published at the beginning of the article or be available in the article's citation.

     > Author, A. A. (year). Title of article. *Title of Periodical, volume number*(issue number), pages. doi: code

   - **If a DOI is not available for the electronic document,** give the URL (without a period at the end). Generally, a database name is no longer needed, except for hard-to-find documents and those accessed through subscription-only databases. Use the home- or menu-page URL for subscription-only databases and online reference works.

     > Author, A. A. (year). Title of article. *Title of Periodical, volume number*(issue number), pages. Retrieved from URL

   - **If the content of the document is stable** (e.g., archival copy or copy of record with DOI), do not include a retrieval date in your reference entry. However, if the content is likely to change or be updated, as is the case with a lot of the material on the free Web, then offer a retrieval date. This would be the case with open-Web material with no fixed publication date, edition, or version, or material that is prepublished (in preparation, in press).

     > Author, A. A. (year). *Title of document.* Retrieved date from website: URL

A Journal Article with DOI

> Knowles, F. E. (2012). Toward emancipatory education: An application of Habermasian theory to Native American educational policy. *International Journal of Qualitative Studies in Education 25*(7), 885–904. doi: 10.1080/09518398.2012.720735

Note: Because the DOI references the final version of the article, the retrieval date, URL, and database name are not needed. If the online article is a preprint version, add "Advance online publication" and your retrieval date before the DOI.

A Journal Article without DOI

> Bell, J. B., & Nye, E. C. (2007). Specific symptoms predict suicidal ideation in Vietnam combat veterans with Post-Traumatic Stress Disorder. *Military Medicine, 172*(11), 1144–1147. Retrieved from http://www.ebscohost.com

Note: Because this article has no DOI, the URL is provided for the subscription database search service. If you retrieved the article from the open Web, you would supply the exact URL. If the version of the article you access is in press and you have retrieved it from the author's personal or institutional website, place "in press" in parentheses after the author's name and add a retrieval date before the URL.

A Newspaper Article

> Clifford, S., & Rampell, C. (2013, April 13). Sometimes, we want prices to fool us. *The New York Times*. Retrieved from http://www.nytimes.com

An Article in an Online Magazine (Ezine) not Published in Print

> Morris, A. (2013, February). Hidden within ourselves: A psychoanalytic examination of the effects of repression in Michael Haneke's *Caché*. *Bright Lights Film Journal*. Retrieved April 27, 2013, from http://brightlightsfilm.com/79/79-cache-michael -haneke-psychoanalysis-interpretation_morris.php

A Book Review

> Shapiro, K. (2007). Mystic chords. [Review of the book *Musicophilia: Tales of music and the brain,* by O. Sacks]. *Commentary, 124*(5), 73–77. Retrieved from http://web.ebscohost.com

An Electronic Book

> Kafka, F. (2002). *Metamorphosis.* D. Wylie (Trans.). Available from http:// www.gutenberg.org/etext/5200

Note: If the URL goes directly to the ebook, use "Retrieved from."

Material from an Online Reference Work

▌ Agonism. (2008). *In Encyclopaedia Britannica.* Retrieved from http://search.eb.com

Note: See pages 458–459 for advice on using Wikipedia.

Online Course Material

▌ Roderiguez, N. Unit 3, *Lecture 3: Sociological Theories of Deviance.* Retrieved from University of Houston website: http://www.uh.edu/~nestor/lecturenotes /unit3lecture3.html

A Workplace Document or Other "Grey Literature"

"Grey Literature" refers to informative documents (e.g., brochures, fact sheets, white papers) produced by government agencies, corporations, and nonprofit groups. If possible, give a document number or identify the type of document in brackets.

▌ Foehr, U. G. (2006). *Media multitasking among American youth: Prevalance, predictors and pairings* (Publication No. 7592). Retrieved from the Kaiser Family Foundation: http://www.kff.org/entmedia/upload/7592.pdf

Undated Content on Website

▌ Canadian Mental Health Association. (n.d.). *Children and attention deficit disorders.* Retrieved from http://www.cmha.ca/mental_health/facts-about-attention-deficit-disorders/#.UkwUVxAqRoE

A Podcast

▌ Byrd, D., & Block, J. (Producers). (2008, February 5). Antonio Rangel: This is your brain on wine. *Earth & Sky: A Clear Voice for Science* [Audio podcast]. Retrieved from http://www.earthsky.org/clear-voices/52199

Message on a Newsgroup, an Online Forum, or a Discussion Group

▌ Avnish, J. (2008, March 18). Sex education especially vital to teens nowadays. [Online forum post]. Retrieved from http://groups.google.ca/group/AIDS-Beyond -Borders/topics

A Blog Post

▌ Sherren, R. (2013, March 27). King Kwong. [Web log post]. Retrieved from http://www. cbc.ca/thenational/blog/2013/03/larry-kwong.html

Note about URLs: When necessary, break a URL before a slash or other punctuation mark or after a double slash. Do not underline or italicize the URL, place it in angle brackets, or end it with a period.

Other Sources: Primary, Personal, and Multimedia

Cite audiovisual media sources and electronic sources as follows.

Specialized Computer Software with Limited Distribution

Standard nonspecialized computer software does not require a reference entry. Treat software as an unauthored work unless an individual has property rights to it.

> Carreau, S. (2001). Champfoot (Version 3.3) [Computer software]. Saint Mandé, France: Author.

Show the software version in parentheses after the title and the medium in brackets.

A Television or Radio Broadcast

Indicate the episode by writers, if possible. Then follow with the airing date, the episode title, and the type of series in brackets. Add the producer(s) as you would the editors(s) of a print medium, and complete the entry with details about the series itself.

> O'Reilly, T. (Writer). (2012, May 19). When brands apologize: Sorry seems to be the smartest word [Radio series program]. In *Under the Influence*. Toronto, ON: CBC Radio.

An Audio Recording

Begin the entry with the speaker's or writer's name, not the producer. Indicate the type of recording in brackets.

> Kim, E. (Author, speaker). (2000). *Ten thousand sorrows* [CD]. New York, NY: Random House.

A Music Recording

Give the name and function of the originators or primary contributors. Indicate the recording medium in brackets immediately following the title.

> ARS Femina Ensemble. (Performers). (1998). *Musica de la puebla de Los Angeles: Music by women of baroque Mexico, Cuba, & Europe* [CD]. Louisville, KY: Nannerl Recordings.

A Motion Picture

Give the name and function of the director, producer, or both.

> Lee, A. (Director). (2012). *Life of Pi* [Motion picture]. United States: Twentieth-Century Fox.

A Published Interview, Titled, No Author

Start the entry with the interview's title, followed by publication details.

> Stephen Harper: The Report interview. (2002, January 7). *The Report* (Alberta, BC), 29, 10–11.

A Published Interview, Titled, Single Author

Start the entry with the interviewee's name, followed by the date and the title. Place the interviewer's name in brackets before other publication details.

> Fussman, C. (2002, January). What I've learned. [Interview by Robert McNamara.] *Esquire, 137,* 85.

An Unpublished Paper Presented at a Meeting

Indicate when the paper was presented, at what meeting, in what location.

> Sifferd, K., & Hirstein, W. (2012, June). *On the criminal culpability of successful and unsuccessful psychopaths.* Paper presented at the meeting of the Society for Philosophy and Psychology, Boulder, CO.

An Unpublished Doctoral Dissertation

Place the dissertation's title in italics, even though the work is unpublished. Indicate the school at which the writer completed the dissertation.

> Paquette, S. (2008). *Knowledge management systems and customer knowledge use in organizations* (Unpublished doctoral dissertation). University of Toronto, Toronto, ON.

Sample APA Paper

Student writers Thomas DeJong and Adam Smit wrote the following research paper based on an experiment that they conducted in a psychology course. You can use the sample paper in three ways:

1. To study how a well-written research paper based in experimentation organizes and builds a discussion from start to finish. (See the online chapter on science writing for more on experimentation.)
2. To examine how sources are used and integrated into social-science research writing—a full-length example of the strategies addressed on pages 482–485.
3. To see in detail the format and documentation practices of APA style.

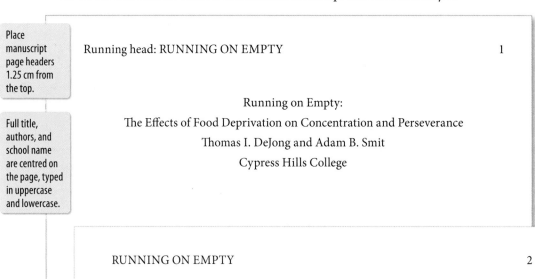

Place manuscript page headers 1.25 cm from the top.

Running head: RUNNING ON EMPTY   1

Running on Empty:

The Effects of Food Deprivation on Concentration and Perseverance

Thomas I. DeJong and Adam B. Smit

Cypress Hills College

Full title, authors, and school name are centred on the page, typed in uppercase and lowercase.

RUNNING ON EMPTY   2

Abstract

This study examined the effects of short-term food deprivation on two cognitive abilities—concentration and perseverance. Undergraduate students (N-51) were tested on both a concentration task and a perseverance task after one of three levels of food deprivation: none, 12 hours, or 24 hours. We predicted that food deprivation would impair both concentration scores and perseverance time. Food deprivation had no significant effect on concentration scores, which is consistent with recent research on the effects of food deprivation (Green, Elliman, & Rogers, 1995; Green, Elliman, & Rogers, 1997). However, participants in the 12-hour deprivation group spent significantly less time on the perseverance task than those in both the control and 24-hour deprivation groups, suggesting that short-term deprivation may affect some aspects of cognition and not others.

The abstract summarizes the problem, participants, hypotheses, methods used, results, and conclusions.

RUNNING ON EMPTY   3

Running on Empty: The Effects of Food Deprivation
on Concentration and Perseverance

Many things interrupt people's ability to focus on a task: distractions, *1*
headaches, noisy environments, and even psychological disorders. To some extent,
people can control the environmental factors that make it difficult to focus.
However, what about internal factors, such as an empty stomach? Can people
increase their ability to focus simply by eating regularly?

One theory that prompted research on how food intake affects the average *2*
person was the glucostatic theory. Several researchers in the 1940s and 1950s
suggested that the brain regulates food intake in order to maintain a blood-glucose
set point. The idea was that people become hungry when their blood-glucose levels
drop significantly below their set point and that they become satisfied after eating,
when their blood-glucose levels return to that set point. This theory seemed logical
because glucose is the brain's primary fuel (Pinel, 2000). The earliest investigation
of the general effects of food deprivation found that long-term food deprivation
(36 hours and longer) was associated with sluggishness, depression, irritability,
reduced heart rate, and inability to concentrate (Keys, Brozek, Henschel, Mickelsen,
& Taylor, 1950). Another study found that fasting for several days produced
muscular weakness, irritability, and apathy or depression (Kollar, Slater, Palmer,
Docter, & Mandell, 1964). Since that time, research has focused mainly on how
nutrition affects cognition. However, as Green, Elliman, and Rogers (1995) pointed
out, the effects of food deprivation on cognition have received comparatively less
attention in recent years.

The relatively sparse research on food deprivation has left room for further *3*
research. First, much of the research has focused either on chronic starvation at
one end of the continuum or on missing a single meal at the other end (Green et al.,
1995). Second, some of the findings have been contradictory. One study found that
skipping breakfast impairs certain aspects of cognition, such as problem-solving
abilities (Pollitt, Lewis, Garza, & Shulman, 1982–1983). However, other research
by M. W. Green, N. A. Elliman, and P. J. Rogers (1995, 1997) found that food

Centre the title 2.5 cm from the top. Double-space throughout.

The introduction states the topic and the main questions to be explored.

The researchers supply background information by discussing past research on the topic.

Extensive referencing establishes support for the discussion.

The researchers explain how their study will add to past research on the topic.	deprivation ranging from missing a single meal to 24 hours without eating does not significantly impair cognition. Third, not all groups of people have been sufficiently studied. Studies have been done on 9–11 year-olds (Pollitt et al., 1983), obese subjects (Crumpton, Wine, & Drenick, 1966), college-age men and women (Green et al., 1995, 1996, 1997), and middle-age males (Kollar et al., 1964). Fourth, not all cognitive aspects have been studied. In 1995 Green, Elliman, and Rogers studied

Clear transitions guide readers through the researchers' reasoning.

sustained attention, simple reaction time, and immediate memory; in 1996 they studied attentional bias; and in 1997 they studied simple reaction time, two-finger tapping, recognition memory, and free recall. In 1983, another study focused on reaction time and accuracy, intelligence quotient, and problem solving (Pollitt et al.).

According to some researchers, most of the results so far indicate that cognitive function is not affected significantly by short-term fasting (Green et al., 1995, p. 246). However, this conclusion seems premature due to the relative lack of research on cognitive functions such as concentration and perseverance. To date, no study has tested perseverance, despite its importance in cognitive functioning. In fact, perseverance may be a better indicator than achievement tests in assessing growth in learning and thinking abilities, as perseverance helps in solving complex problems (Costa, 1984). Another study also recognized that perseverance, better

The researchers support their decision to focus on concentration and perseverance.

learning techniques, and effort are cognitions worth studying (D'Agostino, 1996). Testing as many aspects of cognition as possible is key because the nature of the task is important when interpreting the link between food deprivation and cognitive performance (Smith & Kendrick, 1992). Therefore, the current study helps us understand how short-term food deprivation affects concentration on and perseverance with a difficult task. Specifically, participants deprived of food for 24 hours were expected to perform worse on a concentration test and a perseverance

The researchers state their initial hypotheses.

task than those deprived for 12 hours, who in turn were predicted to perform worse than those who were not deprived of food.

Method

Headings and subheadings show the paper's organization.

Participants

Participants included 51 undergraduate-student volunteers (32 females, 19 males), some of whom received a small amount of extra credit in a college course.

The mean college grade point average (GPA) was 3.19. Potential participants were excluded if they were dieting, menstruating, or taking special medication. Those who were struggling with or had struggled with an eating disorder were excluded, as were potential participants addicted to nicotine or caffeine.

Materials

Concentration speed and accuracy were measured using an online numbers-matching test (www.psychtests.com/tests/iq/concentration.html) that consisted of 26 lines of 25 numbers each. In 6 minutes, participants were required to find pairs of numbers in each line that added up to 10. Scores were calculated as the percentage of correctly identified pairs out of a possible 120. Perseverance was measured with a puzzle that contained five octagons—each of which included a stencil of a specific object (such as an animal or a flower). The octagons were to be placed on top of each other in a specific way to make the silhouette of a rabbit. However, three of the shapes were slightly altered so that the task was impossible. Perseverance scores were calculated as the number of minutes that a participant spent on the puzzle task before giving up.

Procedure

At an initial meeting, participants gave informed consent. Each consent form contained an assigned identification number and requested the participant's GPA. Students were then informed that they would be notified by email and telephone about their assignment to one of the three experimental groups. Next, students were given an instruction sheet. These written instructions, which we also read aloud, explained the experimental conditions, clarified guidelines for the food deprivation period, and specified the time and location of testing.

Participants were randomly assigned to one of these conditions using a matched-triplets design based on the GPAs collected at the initial meeting. This design was used to control individual differences in cognitive ability. Two days after the initial meeting, participants were informed of their group assignment and its condition and reminded that, if they were in a food-deprived group, they should not eat anything after 10 a.m. the next day. Participants from the control group were tested at 7:30 p.m. in a designated computer lab on the day the deprivation started.

Sidebar annotations:

The experiment's method is described, using the terms and acronyms of the discipline.

Passive voice is used to emphasize the experiment, not the researchers; otherwise, active voice is used.

The experiment is laid out step by step, with time transitions like "then" and "next."

Attention is shown to the control features.

Margin numbers: 6, 7, 8

Those in the 12-hour group were tested at 10 p.m. on that same day. Those in the 24-hour group were tested at 10:40 a.m. on the following day.

At their assigned time, participants arrived at a computer lab for testing. Each participant was given written testing instructions, which were also read aloud. The online concentration test had already been loaded on the computers for participants before they arrived for testing, so shortly after they arrived they proceeded to complete the test. Immediately after all participants had completed the test and their scores were recorded, participants were each given the silhouette puzzle and instructed how to proceed. In addition, they were told that (1) they would have an unlimited amount of time to complete the task, and (2) they were not to tell any other participant whether they had completed the puzzle or simply given up. This procedure was followed to prevent the group influence of some participants seeing others give up. Any participant still working on the puzzle after 40 minutes was stopped to keep the time of the study manageable. Immediately after each participant stopped working on the puzzle, he or she gave demographic information and completed a few manipulation-check items. We then debriefed and dismissed each participant outside of the lab.

Results

The writers summarize their findings, including problems encountered.

Perseverance data from one control-group participant were eliminated because she had to leave the session early. Concentration data from another control-group participant were dropped because he did not complete the test correctly. Three manipulation-check questions indicated that each participant correctly perceived his or her deprivation condition and had followed the rules for it. The average concentration score was 77.78 (SD = 14.21), which was very good considering that anything over 50 percent is labeled "good" or "above average." The average time spent on the puzzle was 24.00 minutes (SD = 10.16), with a maximum of 40 minutes allowed.

"See Figure 1" sends readers to a figure (graph, photograph, chart, or drawing) contained in the paper.

We predicted that participants in the 24-hour deprivation group would perform worse on the concentration test and the perseverance task than those in the 12-hour group, who in turn would perform worse than those in the control group. A one-way analysis of variance (ANOVA) showed no significant effect of deprivation

Chapter 26 | Sample APA Paper   559

condition on concentration, $F(2,46) = 1.06$, $p = .36$ (see Figure 1). Another one-way ANOVA indicated a significant effect of deprivation condition on perseverance time, $F(2,47) = 7.41$, $p < .05$. Post-hoc Tukey tests indicated that the 12-hour deprivation group ($M = 17.79$, $SD = 7.84$) spent significantly less time on the perseverance task than either the control group ($M = 26.80$, $SD = 6.20$) or the 24-hour group ($M = 28.75$, $SD = 12.11$), with no significant difference between the latter two groups (see Figure 2). No significant effect was found for gender either generally or with specific deprivation conditions, $Fs < 1.00$. Unexpectedly, food deprivation had no significant effect on concentration scores. Overall, we found support for our hypothesis that 12 hours of food deprivation would significantly impair perseverance when compared to no deprivation. Unexpectedly, 24 hours of food deprivation did not significantly affect perseverance relative to the control group. Also unexpectedly, food deprivation did not significantly affect concentration scores.

Figure 1

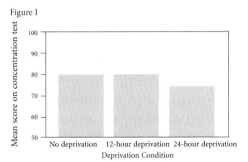

Figure 2

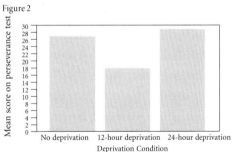

All figures and illustrations (other than tables) are numbered in the order that they are first mentioned in the text.

Both figures: Reprinted by permission of Thomas I. DeJong and Adam B. Smit.

Discussion

The purpose of this study was to test how different levels of food deprivation   *12*
affect concentration on and perseverance with difficult tasks. We predicted that
the longer people had been deprived of food, the lower they would score on the
concentration task, and the less time they would spend on the perseverance task.
In this study, those deprived of food did give up more quickly on the puzzle, but
only in the 12-hour group. Thus, the hypothesis was partially supported for the
perseverance task. However, concentration was found to be unaffected by food
deprivation, and thus the hypothesis was not supported for that task.

The researchers restate their hypotheses and the results, and go on to interpret those results.

The findings of this study are consistent with those of Green et al. (1995), where   *13*
short-term food deprivation did not affect some aspects of cognition, including
attentional focus. Taken together, these findings suggest that concentration is not
significantly impaired by short-term food deprivation. The findings on perseverance,
however, are not as easily explained. We surmise that the participants in the
12-hour group gave up more quickly on the perseverance task because of their
hunger produced by the food deprivation. But why, then, did those in the 24-hour
group fail to yield the same effect? We postulate that this result can be explained by
the concept of "learned industriousness," wherein participants who perform one
difficult task do better on a subsequent task than the participants who never took
the initial task (Eisenberger & Leonard, 1980; Hickman, Stromme, & Lippman,
1998). Because participants had successfully completed 24 hours of fasting already,
their tendency to persevere had already been increased, if only temporarily.
Another possible explanation is that the motivational state of a participant may be
a significant determinant of behaviour under testing (Saugstad, 1967). This idea
may also explain the short perseverance times in the 12-hour group: because these
participants took the tests at 10 p.m., a prime time of the night for conducting
business and socializing on a college campus, they may have been less motivated to
take the time to work on the puzzle.

The writers speculate on possible explanations for the unexpected results.

Research on food deprivation and cognition could continue in several   *14*
directions. First, other aspects of cognition may be affected by short-term food

deprivation, such as reading comprehension or motivation. With respect to this latter topic, some students in this study reported decreased motivation to complete the tasks because of a desire to eat immediately after the testing. In addition, the time of day when the respective groups took the tests may have influenced the results: those in the 24-hour group took the tests in the morning and may have been fresher and more relaxed than those in the 12-hour group, who took the tests at night. Perhaps, then, the motivation level of food-deprived participants could be effectively tested. Second, longer-term food deprivation periods, such as those experienced by people fasting for religious reasons, could be explored. It is possible that cognitive function fluctuates over the duration of deprivation. Studies could ask how long a person can remain focused despite a lack of nutrition. Third, and perhaps most fascinating, studies could explore how food deprivation affects learned industriousness. As stated above, one possible explanation for the better perseverance times in the 24-hour group could be that they spontaneously improved their perseverance faculties by simply forcing themselves not to eat for 24 hours. Therefore, research could study how food deprivation affects the acquisition of perseverance.

In conclusion, the results of this study provide some fascinating insights into the cognitive and physiological effects of skipping meals. Contrary to what we predicted, a person may indeed be very capable of concentrating after not eating for many hours. On the other hand, if one is taking a long test or working long hours at a tedious task that requires perseverance, one may be hindered by not eating for a short time, as shown by the 12-hour group's performance on the perseverance task. Many people—students, working mothers, and those interested in fasting, to mention a few—have to deal with short-term food deprivation, intentional or unintentional. This research and other research to follow will contribute to knowledge of the disadvantages—and possible advantages—of skipping meals. The mixed results of this study suggest that we have much more to learn about short-term food deprivation.

The writers suggest further research to address the questions left unanswered by their experiment.

The conclusion summarizes the outcomes, stresses the experiment's value, and anticipates further advances on the topic.

15

References

Costa, A. L. (1984). Thinking: How do we know students are getting better at it? *Roeper Review, 6*(4), 197–199.

Crumpton, E., Wine, D. B., & Drenick, E. J. (1966). Starvation: Stress or satisfaction? *Journal of the American Medical Association, 196*(5), 394–396.

D'Agostino, C. A. F. (1996). Testing a social-cognitive model of achievement motivation. *Dissertation Abstracts International: Section A. Humanities and Social Sciences, 57*, 1985.

Eisenberger, R., & Leonard, J. M. (1980). Effects of conceptual task difficulty on generalized persistence. *American Journal of Psychology, 93*(2), 285–298.

Green, M. W., Elliman, N. A., & Rogers, P. J. (1995). Lack of effect of short-term fasting on cognitive function. *Journal of Psychiatric Research, 29*(3), 245–253.

Green, M. W., Elliman, N. A., & Rogers, P. J. (1996). Hunger, caloric preloading, and the selective processing of food and body shape words. *British Journal of Clinical Psychology, 35*, 143–151.

Green, M. W., Elliman, N. A., & Rogers, P. J. (1997). The study effects of food deprivation and incentive motivation on blood glucose levels and cognitive function. *Psychopharmacology, 134*(1), 88–94.

Hickman, K. L., Stromme, C., & Lippman, L. G. (1998). Learned industriousness: Replication in principle. *Journal of General Psychology, 125*(3), 213–217.

Keys, A., Brozek, J., Henschel, A., Mickelsen, O., & Taylor, H. L. (1950). *The biology of human starvation* (Vol. 2). Minneapolis, MN: University of Minnesota Press.

Kollar, E. J., Slater, G. R., Palmer, J. O., Docter, R. F., & Mandell, A. J. (1964). Measurement of stress in fasting man. *Archives of General Psychology, 11*, 113–125.

Pinel, J. P. (2000). *Biopsychology* (4th ed.). Boston, MA: Allyn and Bacon.

Pollitt, E., Lewis, N. L., Garza, C., & Shulman, R. J. (1982–1983). Fasting and cognitive function. *Journal of Psychiatric Research, 17*(2), 169–174.

Saugstad, P. (1967). [Comments on the article "Effect of food deprivation on perception-cognition: A comment" by D. L. Wolitzky]. *Psychological Bulletin, 68*(5), 345–346.

All works referred to in the paper appear on the reference page, listed alphabetically by author (or title).

Each entry follows APA guidelines for listing authors, dates, titles, and publishing information.

Capitalization, punctuation, and hanging indentation are consistent with APA format.

Smith, A. P., & Kendrick, A. M. (1992). Meals and performance. In A. P. Smith & D. M. Jones (Eds.), *Handbook of human performance: Vol. 2. Health and performance* (pp. 1–23). San Diego, CA: Academic Press.

Smith, A. P., Kendrick, A. M., & Maben, A. L. (1992). Effects of breakfast and caffeine on performance and mood in the late morning and after lunch. *Neuropsychobiology, 26*(4), 198–204.

Reading for Better Writing

Working by yourself or with a group, answer these questions:

1. Before you read Thomas DeJong and Adam Smit's paper, what were your expectations about food deprivation's effects on concentration and perserverance? Did the paper confirm or confound your expectations?

2. Did you find the report interesting? Why or why not?

3. What types of evidence did Thomas and Adam use in their paper? Where did they obtain their evidence?

4. How did Thomas and Adam distinguish their own ideas from their sources' ideas? Was it necessary for them to do so, and if so, why?

5. Could the results of Thomas and Adam's research be applied to other situations? In other words, how might particular groups interpret these findings?

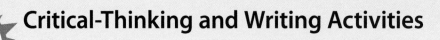

Critical-Thinking and Writing Activities

As directed by your instructor, complete the following critical-thinking and writing activities by yourself or with classmates.

1. "In looking for people to hire," explains well-known investor Warren Buffet, "you look for three qualities: integrity, intelligence, and energy. And if they don't have the first, the other two will kill you." Reflect on Buffet's statement. How does his thinking about employees relate to principles of research and writing?

2. To make sense of APA format rules, answer these questions: What is the essential logic of the APA system? How does this logic reflect research practices and values in the social sciences?

3. Create references list entries in correct APA style for the following sources:

   - An article in the summer 2009 issue (volume 34, no. 2) of the periodical *MELUS*, by Joni Adamson and Scott Slovic: "The Shoulders We Stand On: An Introduction to Ethnicity and Ecocriticism" (pages 5–24)

   - The book *The Playful World: How Technology Is Transforming Our Imagination,* by Mark Pesce, published in 2000 by Ballantine Books, located in New York City

   - The Web page "Vaccines for Children Program (VCP)," part of the Vaccines and Immunizations section of the Centers for Disease Control and Prevention (CDC) website, sponsored by the U.S. government's Department of Health and Human Services. No author or publication date is listed. The site was last accessed April 26, 2014, at http://www.cdc.gov/vaccines/programs/vfc/index.html.

Learning-Objectives Checklist ✓

Have you achieved this chapter's learning objectives? Check your progress with the items below, revisiting topics in the chapter as needed. *I have . . .*

_____ gained an overview of the APA system of documentation—the basic logic of in-text citations in relation to reference entries (536–537).

_____ correctly implemented APA format guidelines (e.g., title page, abstract, running head, pagination, heading system, references page) (538).

_____ applied rules of in-text citation for a whole range of sources (539–542).

_____ developed a references list that is properly formatted and that correctly and fully identifies sources, whether books or journal articles or online documents (543–553).

_____ examined APA style at work in "Running on Empty: The Effects of Food Deprivation on Concentration and Perseverance," learning how the system is practised effectively in an experiment report (554–563).

IV. Handbook

Chapter 27

Understanding Grammar

"The skill of writing is to create a context in which other people can think."

—Edwin Schlossberg

Grammar is the study of the structure and features of the language, consisting of rules and standards that are to be followed to produce acceptable writing and speaking. **Parts of speech** refers to the eight different categories that indicate how words are used in the English language—as *nouns, pronouns, verbs, adjectives, adverbs, prepositions, conjunctions,* or *interjections*.

Noun

567.1

A **noun** is a word that names something: a person, a place, a thing, or an idea.

Alice Munro/author	*Lone Star*/film	Renaissance/era
Acadia/university	*A Congress of Wonders*/book	

ell Note: See 655.1–656.1 for information on count and noncount nouns.

Classes of Nouns

All nouns are either proper nouns or common nouns. Nouns may also be classified as *individual* or *collective,* or *concrete* or *abstract*.

Proper Nouns

567.2

A **proper noun,** which is always capitalized, names a specific person, place, thing, or idea.

Rembrandt, Bertrand Russell (people)

Stratford-upon-Avon, Tower of London (places)

The Night Watch, **Rosetta stone** (things)

Renaissance, Christianity (ideas)

Common Nouns

567.3

A **common noun** is a general name for a person, a place, a thing, or an idea. Common nouns are not capitalized.

optimist, instructor (people)	**cafeteria, park** (places)
computer, chair (things)	**freedom, love** (ideas)

568.1 Collective Nouns

A **collective noun** names a group or a unit.

> family   audience   crowd   committee   team   class

568.2 Concrete Nouns

A **concrete noun** names a thing that is tangible (can be seen, touched, heard, smelled, or tasted).

> child   Arcade Fire   gym   village   microwave oven   pizza

568.3 Abstract Nouns

An **abstract noun** names an idea, a condition, or a feeling—in other words, something that cannot be seen, touched, heard, smelled, or tasted.

> beauty   Jungian psychology   anxiety   agoraphobia   trust

Forms of Nouns

Nouns are grouped according to their *number, gender,* and *case.*

568.4 Number of Nouns

Number indicates whether a noun is singular or plural.

A singular noun refers to one person, place, thing, or idea.

> student   laboratory   lecture   note   grade   result

A plural noun refers to more than one person, place, thing, or idea.

> students   laboratories   lectures   notes   grades   results

568.5 Gender of Nouns

Gender indicates whether a noun is masculine, feminine, neuter, or indefinite.

> **Masculine:**
> father   king   brother   men   colt   rooster
> **Feminine:**
> mother   queen   sister   women   filly   hen
> **Neuter** (without sex):
> notebook   monitor   car   printer
> **Indefinite or common** (masculine or feminine):
> professor   customer   children   doctor   people

Case of Nouns

The **case** of a noun tells what role the noun plays in a sentence. There are three cases: *nominative, possessive,* and *objective.*

A noun in the **nominative case** is used as a subject. The subject of a sentence tells who or what the sentence is about.

> **Dean Henning** manages the College of Arts and Communication.

> **Note:** A noun is also in the nominative case when it is used as a predicate noun (or predicate nominative). A predicate noun follows a linking verb, usually a form of the *be* verb (such as *am, is, are, was, were, be, being, been*), and repeats or renames the subject.
>
> Ms. Yokum is the **person** to talk to about the program's impact in our community.

A noun in the **possessive case** shows possession or ownership. In this form, it acts as an adjective.

> Our **president's** willingness to discuss concerns with students has boosted campus morale.

A noun in the **objective case** serves as an object of the preposition, a direct object, an indirect object, or an object complement.

> To survive, institutions of higher **learning** sometimes cut **budgets** in spite of **protests** from **students** and **instructors**. (*Learning* is the object of the preposition *of*, *protests* is the object of the preposition *in spite of*, *budgets* is the direct object of the verb *cut*, and *students* and *instructors* are the objects of the preposition *from*.)

A Closer Look
at Direct and Indirect Objects

A **direct object** is a noun (or pronoun) that identifies what or who receives the action of the verb.

> Budget cutbacks reduced class **choices.** (*Choices* is the direct object of the active verb *reduced.*)

An **indirect object** is a noun (or pronoun) that identifies the person *to whom* or *for whom* something is done, or the thing *to which or for which* something is done. An indirect object is always accompanied by a direct object.

> Recent budget cuts have given **students** fewer class choices. (*Choices* is the direct object of *have given; students* is the indirect object.)

> **ell Note:** Not every transitive verb is followed by *both* a direct object and an indirect object. Both can, however, follow *give, send, show, tell, teach, find, sell, ask, offer, pay, pass,* and *hand.*

570.1 Pronoun

A **pronoun** is a word that is used in place of a noun.

> Roger was the most interesting 10-year-old **I** ever taught. **He** was a good thinker and thus a good writer. **I** remember **his** paragraph about the cowboy hat **he** received from **his** grandparents. **It** was "too new looking." The brim was not rolled properly. But the hat's imperfections were not the main idea in Roger's writing. No, the main idea was how **he** was fixing the hat **himself** by wearing it when **he** showered.

570.2 Antecedents

An **antecedent** is the noun or pronoun that the pronoun refers to or replaces. Most pronouns have antecedents, but not all do. (See 571.4.)

> As the wellness **Counsellor** checked *her* chart, several **students** *who* were waiting *their* turns shifted uncomfortably. (*Counsellor* is the antecedent of *her*; *students* is the antecedent of *who* and *their*.)

> **Note:** Each pronoun must agree with its antecedent in number, person, and gender. (See pages 572–573 and 597.)

570.3

Classes of Pronouns

Personal

I, me, my, mine / we, us, our, ours / you, your, yours
they, them, their, theirs / he, him, his, she, her, hers, it, its

Reflexive and Intensive

myself, yourself, himself, herself, itself, ourselves, yourselves, themselves

Relative

who, whose, whom, which, that

Indefinite

all	anything	everybody	most	no one	some
another	both	everyone	much	nothing	somebody
any	each	everything	neither	one	someone
anybody	each one	few	nobody	other	something
anyone	either	many	none	several	such

Interrogative

who, whose, whom, which, what

Demonstrative

this, that, these, those

Reciprocal

each other, one another

Classes of Pronouns

There are several classes of pronouns: *personal, reflexive and intensive, relative, indefinite, interrogative,* and *demonstrative.*

Personal Pronouns   571.1

A **personal pronoun** refers to a specific person or thing.

> *Marge* started **her** car; **she** drove the antique *convertible* to Victoria, where **she** hoped to sell **it** at an auction.

Reflexive and Intensive Pronouns   571.2

A **reflexive pronoun** is formed by adding *-self* or *-selves* to a personal pronoun. A reflexive pronoun can act as a direct object or an indirect object of a verb, an object of a preposition, or a predicate nominative.

> Charles loves **himself**. (direct object of *loves*)
>
> Charles gives **himself** an A grade for fashion sense. (indirect object of *gives*)
>
> Charles smiles at **himself** in store windows. (object of preposition *at*)
>
> Charles can be **himself** anywhere. (predicate nominative)

An **intensive pronoun** intensifies, or emphasizes, the noun or pronoun it refers to.

> Leo **himself** taught his children to invest their lives in others.
>
> The lesson was sometimes painful—but they learned it **themselves**.

Relative Pronouns   571.3

A **relative pronoun** relates an adjective dependent (relative) clause to the noun or pronoun it modifies. (The noun is italicized in each example below; the relative pronoun is in bold.)

> *First-year students* **who** believe they have a lot to learn are absolutely right.
>
> Just navigating this *campus,* **which** is huge, can be challenging.

Make sure you know when to use the relative pronouns *who* or *whom* and *that* or *which*. (See 590.3, 610.3, 654.7, and 654.8.)

Indefinite Pronouns   571.4

An **indefinite pronoun** refers to unnamed or unknown people, places, or things.

> **Everyone** seemed amused when I was searching for my classroom in the student centre. (The antecedent of *everyone* is unnamed.)
>
> **Nothing** is more unnerving than rushing at the last minute into the wrong room for the wrong class. (The antecedent of *nothing* is unknown.)

Most indefinite pronouns are singular, so when they are used as subjects, they should have singular verbs. (See pages 593–596.)

572.1   **Interrogative Pronouns**

An **interrogative pronoun** asks a question.

So **which** will it be—highlighting and attaching a campus map to the inside of your backpack, or being lost and late for the first two weeks?

Note: When an interrogative pronoun modifies a noun, it functions as an adjective.

572.2   **Demonstrative Pronouns**

A **demonstrative pronoun** points out people, places, or things.

We advise **this:** Bring along as many maps and schedules as you need.
Those are useful tools. **That** is the solution.

Note: When a demonstrative pronoun modifies a noun, it functions as an adjective.

Forms of Personal Pronouns

The **form** of a personal pronoun indicates its *number* (singular or plural), its *person* (first, second, or third), its *case* (nominative, possessive, or objective), and its *gender* (masculine, feminine, neuter, or indefinite).

572.3   **Number of Pronouns**

A **personal pronoun** is either singular *(I, you, he, she, it)* or plural *(we, you, they).*

He should have a budget and stick to it. (singular)

We can help new students learn about budgeting. (plural)

572.4   **Person of Pronouns**

The **person** of a pronoun indicates whether the person is speaking (first person), is spoken to (second person), or is spoken about (third person).

First person is used to name the speaker(s).

I know **I** need to handle **my** stress in a healthful way, especially during exam week; **my** usual chips-and-doughnuts binge isn't helping. (singular)
We all decided to bike to the tennis court. (plural)

Second person is used to name the person(s) spoken to.

Maria, **you** grab the rackets, okay? (singular)
John and Tanya, can **you** find the water bottles? (plural)

Third person is used to name the person(s) or thing(s) spoken about.

Today's students are interested in wellness issues. **They** are concerned about **their** health, fitness, and nutrition. (plural)
Maria practices yoga and feels **she** is calmer for **her** choice. (singular)
One of the advantages of regular exercise is that **it** raises one's energy level. (singular)

Case of Pronouns

The **case** of each pronoun tells what role it plays in a sentence. There are three cases: *nominative, possessive,* and *objective.*

A pronoun in the **nominative case** is used as a subject. The following are nominative forms: *I, you, he, she, it, we, they.*

> **He** found an old map in the trunk.
>
> My friend and **I** went biking. (not *me*)

A pronoun is also in the nominative case when it is used as a predicate nominative, following a linking verb *(am, is, are, was, were, seems)* and renaming the subject.

> It was **he** who discovered electricity. (not *him*)

A pronoun in the **possessive case** shows possession or ownership: *my, mine, our, ours, his, her, hers, their, theirs, its, your, yours.* A possessive pronoun before a noun acts as an adjective: *your* coat.

> That coat is **hers**.   This coat is **mine**.   **Your** coat is lost.

A pronoun in the **objective case** can be used as the direct object, indirect object, object of a preposition, or object complement: *me, you, him, her, it, us, them.*

> Professor Adler hired **her**. (*Her* is the direct object of the verb *hired*.)
>
> He showed Mary and **me** the language lab. (*Me* is the indirect object of the verb *showed*.)
>
> He introduced the three of **us**—Mary, Shavonn, and **me**—to the faculty.
> (*Us* is the object of the preposition *of*; *me* is part of the appositive renaming *us*.)

Gender of Pronouns

The **gender** of a pronoun indicates whether the pronoun is masculine, feminine, neuter, or indefinite. (See page 108.)

Masculine:	**Neuter** (without sex):
he, him, his	it, its
Feminine:	**Indefinite** (masculine or feminine):
she, her, hers	they, them, their

Number, Person, and Case of Personal Pronouns

	Nominative Case	Possessive Case	Objective Case
First Person Singular	I	my, mine	me
Second Person Singular	you	your, yours	you
Third Person Singular	he, she, it	his, her, hers, its	him, her, it
First Person Plural	we	our, ours	us
Second Person Plural	you	your, yours	you
Third Person Plural	they	their, theirs	them

574.1

Verb

A **verb** shows action *(pondered, grins)*, links words *(is, seemed)*, or accompanies another action verb as an auxiliary or helping verb *(can, does)*.

> Harry **honked** the horn. (shows action)
>
> Harry **is** impatient. (links words)
>
> Harry **was** honking the truck's horn. (accompanies the verb *honking*)

Classes of Verbs

Verbs are classified as action, auxiliary (helping), or linking (state of being).

574.2

Action Verbs: Transitive and Intransitive

As its name implies, an **action verb** shows action. Some action verbs are *transitive*; others are *intransitive*. (The term *action* does not always refer to a physical activity.)

> Rain **splashed** the windshield. (transitive verb)
>
> Josie **drove** off the road. (intransitive verb)

Transitive verbs have direct objects that receive the action (587.5, 659.2).

> In 2010, skiers **spent** more than **$903 million** at Canadian ski slopes.
> (The words *$903 million* represent the direct object of the action verb *spent*.)

Intransitive verbs communicate action that is complete in itself. They do not need an object to receive the action.

> My new roommate **smiles** and **laughs** a lot.

> **Note:** Some verbs can be either transitive or intransitive.
>
> Dr. Hull **teaches** physiology and microbiology. (transitive)
>
> She **teaches** well. (intransitive)

574.3

Auxiliary (Helping) Verbs

Auxiliary verbs (helping verbs) help to form some of the *tenses* (576.1), the *mood* (577.2), and the *voice* (577.1) of the main verb. In the following example, the auxiliary verbs are in **bold**, and the main verbs are in *italics*.

> I **have** often *thought* that my whole political life—my whole life as a matter of fact—
> **could be** *summed* up in the words "printer, preacher, politician, premier—or the
> descent of man."
> —Tommy Douglas

Common Auxiliary Verbs

am	been	could	does	have	might	should	will
are	being	did	had	is	must	was	would
be	can	do	has	may	shall	were	

> **ell Note:** "Be" auxiliary verbs are always followed by either a verb ending in *ing* or a past participle. Also see "Common Modal Auxiliary Verbs" (660.2).

Linking (State of Being) Verbs

575.1

A **linking verb** is a special form of intransitive verb that links the subject of a sentence to a noun, a pronoun, or an adjective in the predicate. (See the chart below.)

The streets **are** flooded. (adjective)   The streets **are** rivers! (noun)

Common Linking Verbs

am   are   be   become   been   being   is   was   were

Additional Linking Verbs

appear   feel   look   seem   sound   grow   remain   smell   taste

Note: The verbs listed as "additional linking verbs" above function as linking verbs when they do not show actual action. An adjective usually follows these linking verbs.

The thunder **sounded** ominous. (adjective)

My little brother **grew** frightened. (adjective)

Note: When these same words are used as action verbs, an adverb or a direct object may follow them.

I **looked** carefully at him. (adverb)

My little brother **grew** corn for a science project. (direct object)

Forms of Verbs

A verb's **form** differs depending on its *number* (singular, plural), *person* (first, second, third), *tense* (present, past, future, present perfect, past perfect, future perfect), *voice* (active, passive), and *mood* (indicative, imperative, subjunctive).

Number of a Verb

575.2

Number indicates whether a verb is singular or plural. The verb and its subject both must be singular, or they both must be plural. (See "Subject–Verb Agreement," pages 593–596.)

The city **employs** many students during the summer. (singular)

Many cities **employ** a large number of students during the summer. (plural)

Person of a Verb

575.3

Person indicates whether the subject of the verb is *first, second,* or *third person.* The verb and its subject must be in the same person. Verbs usually have a different form only in **third person singular of the present tense.**

	First Person	Second Person	Third Person
Singular	I think	you think	he/she/it thinks
Plural	we think	you think	they think

576.1 Tense of a Verb

Tense indicates the time of an action or state of being. There are three basic tenses (*past, present,* and *future*) and three verbal aspects (*progressive, perfect,* and *perfect progressive*).

576.2 Present Tense

Present tense expresses action happening at the present time or regularly.

> In Canada, approximately 11 percent of workers **hold** jobs in healthcare and social assistance.

Present progressive tense also expresses action that is happening continually, in an ongoing fashion at the present time, but it is formed by combining *am, are,* or *is* and the present participle (ending in *ing*) of the main verb.

> More women than ever before **are working** outside the home.

Present perfect tense expresses action that began in the past and has recently been completed or that continues up to the present time.

> My sister **has taken** four years of swimming lessons.

Present perfect progressive tense also expresses an action that began in the past but stresses the continuing nature of the action. Like the present progressive tense, it is formed by combining auxiliary verbs (*have been* or *has been*) and present participles.

> She **has been taking** them since she was six years old.

576.3 Past Tense

Past tense expresses action that was completed at a particular time in the past.

> A hundred years ago, more than 75 percent of labourers **worked** in agriculture.

Past progressive tense expresses past action that continued over an interval of time. It is formed by combining *was* or *were* with the present participle of the main verb.

> A century ago, my great-grandparents **were farming**.

Past perfect tense expresses an action in the past that was completed at a specific time before another past action occurred.

> By the time we sat down for dinner, my cousins **had eaten** all the olives.

Past perfect progressive tense expresses a past action but stresses the continuing nature of the action. It is formed by using *had been* along with the present participle.

> They **had been eating** the olives all afternoon.

576.4 Future Tense

Future tense expresses action that will take place in the future.

> Next summer I **will work** as a lifeguard.

Future progressive tense expresses an action that will be continuous in the future.

> I **will be working** for the park district at North Beach.

Future perfect tense expresses future action that will be completed by a specific time.

> By 10:00 p.m., I **will have completed** my research project.

Future perfect progressive tense also expresses future action that will be completed by a specific time but (as with other perfect progressive tenses) stresses the action's continuous nature. It is formed using *will have been* along with the present participle.

> I **will have been researching** the project for three weeks by the time it's due.

Voice of a Verb

Voice indicates whether the subject is acting or being acted upon.

Active voice indicates that the subject of the verb is performing the action.

> People **update** their resumés on a regular basis. (The subject, *People,* is acting; *resumés* is the direct object.)

Passive voice indicates that the subject of the verb is being acted upon or is receiving the action. A passive verb is formed by combining a *be* verb with a past participle.

> Your resumé **should be updated** on a regular basis. (The subject, *resumé,* is receiving the action.)

Using Active Voice

Generally, use active voice rather than passive voice for more direct, energetic writing. To change your passive sentences to active ones, do the following: First, find the noun that is doing the action and make it the subject. Then find the word that had been the subject and use it as the direct object.

> **Passive:** The winning goal **was scored** by Eva. (The subject, *goal,* is not acting.)
> **Active:** Eva **scored** the winning goal. (The subject, *Eva,* is acting.)

Note: When you want to emphasize the receiver more than the doer—or when the doer is unknown—use the passive voice. (Much technical and scientific writing regularly uses the passive voice.)

Mood of a Verb

The mood of a verb indicates the tone or attitude with which a statement is made.

Indicative mood, the most common, is used to state a fact or to ask a question.

> **Can** any event **capture** the spirit of Canada in the early 1980s? Terry Fox's Marathon of Hope in 1980 and his death from cancer in 1981 **set** the tone for the decade.

Imperative mood is used to give a command. (The subject of an imperative sentence is *you,* which is usually understood and not stated in the sentence.)

> **Participate** in this year's Terry Fox Run and **help** raise funds for cancer research.

Subjunctive mood is used to express a wish, an impossibility or unlikely condition, or a necessity. The subjunctive mood is often used with *if* or *that.* The verb forms below create an atypical subject–verb agreement, forming the subjunctive mood.

> If I **were** rich, I would travel for the rest of my life. (a wish)
>
> If each of your brain cells **were** one person, there would be enough people to populate 25 planets. (an impossibility)
>
> The English Department requires that every student **pass** a proficiency test. (a necessity)

578.1 Verbals

A **verbal** is a word that is made from a verb, but it functions as a noun, an adjective, or an adverb. There are three types of verbals: *gerunds, infinitives,* and *participles.*

578.2 Gerunds

A **gerund** ends in *ing* and is used as a noun.

Waking each morning is the first challenge. (subject)

I start **moving** at about seven o'clock. (direct object)

I work at **jump-starting** my weary system. (object of the preposition)

As Woody Allen once said, "Eighty percent of life is **showing up**." (predicate nominative)

578.3 Infinitives

An infinitive is *to* and the base form of the verb. The infinitive may be used as a noun, an adjective, or an adverb.

To succeed is not easy. (noun)

That is the most important thing **to remember**. (adjective)

Students are wise **to work** hard. (adverb)

ell Note: It can be difficult to know whether a gerund or an infinitive should follow a verb. It's helpful to become familiar with lists of specific verbs that can be followed by one but not the other. (See 659.2–660.1.)

578.4 Participles

A **present participle** ends in *ing* and functions as an adjective. A **past participle** ends in *ed* (or another past tense form) and also functions as an adjective.

The **studying** students were annoyed by the **partying** ones.

The students **playing** loud music were **annoying**.
(These participles function as adjectives: *studying* students and *partying* students. Notice, however, that *playing* has a direct object: *music*. All three types of verbals may have direct objects. See 588.3.)

Using Verbals

Make sure that you use verbals correctly; look carefully at the examples below.

Verbal: **Diving** is a popular Olympic sport.
(*Diving* is a gerund used as a subject.)

Diving gracefully, the Olympian hoped to get high marks.
(*Diving* is a participle modifying *Olympian*.)

Verb: The next competitor was **diving** in the practice pool.
(Here, *diving* is a verb, not a verbal.)

Irregular Verbs

Irregular verbs can often be confusing. That's because the past tense and past participle of irregular verbs are formed by changing the word itself, not merely by adding *d* or *ed*. The following list contains the most troublesome irregular verbs.

Common Irregular Verbs and Their Principal Parts

Present Tense	Past Tense	Past Participle	Present Tense	Past Tense	Past Participle	Present Tense	Past Tense	Past Participle
am, be	was, were	been	fly	flew	flown	see	saw	seen
arise	arose	arisen	forget	forgot	forgotten,	set	set	set
awake	awoke,	awoken,			forgot	shake	shook	shaken
	awaked	awaked	freeze	froze	frozen	shine (light)	shone	shone
beat	beat	beaten	get	got	gotten	shine (polish)	shined	shined
become	became	become	give	gave	given	show	showed	shown
begin	began	begun	go	went	gone	shrink	shrank	shrunk
bite	bit	bitten, bit	grow	grew	grown	sing	sang	sung
blow	blew	blown	hang (execute)	hanged	hanged	sink	sank	sunk
break	broke	broken	hang (suspend)	hung	hung	sit	sat	sat
bring	brought	brought	have	had	had	sleep	slept	slept
build	built	built	hear	heard	heard	speak	spoke	spoken
burn	burnt,	burnt,	hide	hid	hidden	spend	spent	spent
	burned	burned	hit	hit	hit	spring	sprang	sprung
burst	burst	burst	keep	kept	kept	stand	stood	stood
buy	bought	bought	know	knew	known	steal	stole	stolen
catch	caught	caught	lay	laid	laid	strike	struck	struck,
choose	chose	chosen	lead	led	led			stricken
come	came	come	leave	left	left	strive	strove	striven
cost	cost	cost	lend	lent	lent	swear	swore	sworn
cut	cut	cut	let	let	let	swim	swam	swum
dig	dug	dug	lie (deceive)	lied	lied	swing	swung	swung
dive	dived, dove	dived	lie (recline)	lay	lain	take	took	taken
do	did	done	make	made	made	teach	taught	taught
draw	drew	drawn	mean	meant	meant	tear	tore	torn
dream	dreamed,	dreamed,	meet	met	met	tell	told	told
	dreamt	dreamt	pay	paid	paid	think	thought	thought
drink	drank	drunk	prove	proved	proved,	throw	threw	thrown
drive	drove	driven			proven	wake	woke,	woken,
eat	ate	eaten	put	put	put		waked	waked
fall	fell	fallen	read	read	read			
feel	felt	felt	ride	rode	ridden	wear	wore	worn
fight	fought	fought	ring	rang	rung	weave	wove	woven
find	found	found	rise	rose	risen	wind	wound	wound
flee	fled	fled	run	ran	run	wring	wrung	wrung
						write	wrote	written

580.1   Adjective

An **adjective** describes or modifies a noun or pronoun. The articles *a, an,* and *the* are adjectives.

> Advertising is **a big** and **powerful** industry. (*A, big,* and *powerful* modify the noun *industry.*)

Numbers are also adjectives.

> **Fifty-three** relatives came to my party.

580.2

> **Note:** Many demonstrative, indefinite, and interrogative forms may be used as either adjectives or pronouns (*that, these, many, some, whose,* and so on). These words are adjectives if they come before a noun and modify it; they are pronouns if they stand alone.

> **Some** advertisements are less than truthful. (*Some* modifies *advertisements* and is an adjective.)

> **Many** cause us to chuckle at their outrageous claims. (*Many* stands alone; it is a pronoun and replaces the noun *advertisements.*)

580.3   Proper Adjectives

Proper adjectives are created from proper nouns and are capitalized.

> **English** has been influenced by advertising slogans. (proper noun)
> The **English** language is constantly changing. (proper adjective)

580.4   Predicate Adjectives

A **predicate adjective** follows a form of the *be* verb (or other linking verb) and describes the subject. (See 575.1.)

> At its best, advertising is **useful**; at its worst, **deceptive**. (*Useful* and *deceptive* modify the noun *advertising.*)

580.5   Forms of Adjectives

Adjectives have three forms: *positive, comparative,* and *superlative.*

The **positive form** is the adjective in its regular form. It describes a noun or a pronoun without comparing it to anyone or anything else.

> Joysport walking shoes are **strong** and **comfortable**.

The **comparative form** (*-er, more,* or *less*) compares two things. (*More* and *less* are used generally with adjectives of two or more syllables.)

> Air soles make Mile Eaters **stronger** and **more comfortable** than Joysports.

The **superlative form** (*-est, most,* or *least*) compares three or more things. (*Most* and *least* are used most often with adjectives of two or more syllables.)

> My old Canvas Wonders are the **strongest**, **most comfortable** shoes of all!

> **ell Note:** Two or more adjectives before a noun should have a certain order when they do not modify the noun equally. (See 608.3.)

Adverb

An **adverb** describes or modifies a verb, an adjective, another adverb, or a whole sentence. An adverb answers questions such as *how, when, where, why, how often,* or *how much.*

> The temperature fell **sharply**. (*Sharply* modifies the verb *fell*.)
>
> The temperature was **quite** low. (*Quite* modifies the adjective *low*.)
>
> The temperature dropped **very quickly**. (*Very* modifies the adverb *quickly*, which modifies the verb *dropped*.)
>
> **Unfortunately**, the temperature stayed cool. (*Unfortunately* modifies the whole sentence.)

Note: When used to express affirmation or negation, *yes* and *no* function as adverbs. Example: Did I finish my essay on time? *Yes.* Did I have enough time to revise and edit it? *No.*

Types of Adverbs

Adverbs can be grouped in four ways: *time, place, manner,* and *degree.*

Time (These adverbs tell *when, how often,* and *how long.*)

> today, yesterday   daily, weekly   briefly, eternally

Place (These adverbs tell *where, to where,* and *from where.*)

> here, there   nearby, beyond   backward, forward

Manner (These adverbs often end in *ly* and tell *how* something is done.)

> precisely   regularly   regally   smoothly   well

Degree (These adverbs tell *how much* or *how little.*)

> substantially   greatly   entirely   partly   too

Forms of Adverbs

Adverbs have three forms: *positive, comparative,* and *superlative.*

The **positive form** is the adverb in its regular form. It describes a verb, an adjective, or another adverb without comparing it to anyone or anything else.

> With Joysport shoes, you'll walk **fast**. They support your feet **well**.

The **comparative form** (*-er, more,* or *less*) compares two things. (*More* and *less* are used generally with adverbs of two or more syllables.)

> Wear Jockos instead of Joysports, and you'll walk **faster**. Jockos' special soles support your feet **better** than the Joysports do.

The **superlative form** (*-est, most,* or *least*) compares three or more things. (*Most* and *least* are used most often with adverbs of two or more syllables.)

> Really, I walk **fastest** wearing my old Canvas Wonders. They seem to support my feet, my knees, and my pocketbook **best** of all.

Regular Adverbs			Irregular Adverbs		
positive	**comparative**	**superlative**	**positive**	**comparative**	**superlative**
fast	faster	fastest	well	better	best
effectively	more effectively	most effectively	badly	worse	worst

Preposition

A **preposition** is a word (or group of words) that shows the relationship between its object (a noun or pronoun following the preposition) and another word in the sentence.

Regarding your reasons **for** going **to** school, do they all hinge **on** getting a good job **after** graduation? (In this sentence, *reasons, going, school, getting,* and *graduation* are objects of their preceding prepositions *regarding, for, to, on,* and *after.*)

Prepositional Phrases

A **prepositional phrase** includes the preposition, the object of the preposition, and the modifiers of the object. A prepositional phrase may function as an adverb or an adjective.

A broader knowledge **of the world** is one benefit **of higher education.** (The two phrases function as adjectives modifying the nouns *knowledge* and *benefit* respectively.)

He placed the flower **in the window.** (The phrase functions as an adverb modifying the verb *placed.*)

Prepositions

aboard	back of	excepting	notwithstanding	save
about	because of	for	of	since
above	before	from	off	subsequent to
according to	behind	from among	on	through
across	below	from between	on account of	throughout
across from	beneath	from under	on behalf of	'til
after	beside	in	onto	to
against	besides	in addition to	on top of	together with
along	between	in behalf of	opposite	toward
alongside	beyond	in front of	out	under
alongside of	by	in place of	out of	underneath
along with	by means of	in regard to	outside	until
amid	concerning	inside	outside of	unto
among	considering	inside of	over	up
apart from	despite	in spite of	over to	upon
around	down	instead of	owing to	up to
as far as	down from	into	past	with
aside from	during	like	prior to	within
at	except	near	regarding	without
away from	except for	near to	round	

ell Note: Prepositions often pair up with a verb and become part of an idiom, a slang expression, or a two-word verb. (See pages 661 and 672–674.)

Conjunction

583.1

A **conjunction** connects individual words or groups of words.

> **When** we came back to Paris, it was clear **and** cold **and** lovely.
>
> —Ernest Hemingway

Coordinating Conjunctions

583.2

Coordinating conjunctions usually connect a word to a word, a phrase to a phrase, or a clause to a clause. The words, phrases, or clauses joined by a coordinating conjunction are equal in importance or are of the same type.

> Civilization is a race between education **and** catastrophe.
>
> —H. G. Wells

Correlative Conjunctions

583.3

Correlative conjunctions are a type of coordinating conjunction used in pairs.

> There are two inadvisable ways to think: **either** believe everything **or** doubt everything.

Subordinating Conjunctions

583.4

Subordinating conjunctions connect two clauses that are not equally important. A subordinating conjunction connects a dependent clause to an independent clause. The conjunction is part of the dependent clause.

> Experience is the worst teacher; it gives the test **before** it presents the lesson. (The clause *before it presents the lesson* is dependent. It connects to the independent clause *it gives the test*.)

Conjunctions

583.5

Coordinating:	and, but, or, nor, for, so, yet
Correlative:	either, or; neither, nor; not only, but (but also); both, and; whether, or
Subordinating:	after, although, as, as if, as long as, because, before, even though, if, in order that, provided that, since, so that, though, unless, until, when, whenever, where, while

Note: Relative pronouns (596.1) can also connect clauses.

Interjection

583.6

An **interjection** communicates strong emotion or surprise (*oh, ouch, hey,* and so on). Punctuation (often a comma or an exclamation point) is used to set off an interjection.

> **Hey! Wait! Well,** so much for catching the bus.

A Closer Look
at the Parts of Speech

Noun

A **noun** is a word that names something: a person, a place, a thing, or an idea.

Alice Munro/author	*Lone Star*/film
Acadia/university	Renaissance/era
A Congress of Wonders/book	

Pronoun

A **pronoun** is a word used in place of a noun.

I	my	that	themselves	which
it	ours	they	everybody	you

Verb

A **verb** is a word that expresses action, links words, or acts as an auxiliary verb to the main verb.

are	break	drag	fly	run	sit	was
bite	catch	eat	is	see	tear	were

Adjective

An **adjective** describes or modifies a noun or pronoun. (The articles *a, an,* and *the* are adjectives.)

The carbonated drink went down easy on **that hot, dry** day. (*The* and *carbonated* modify *drink; that, hot,* and *dry* modify *day.*)

Adverb

An **adverb** describes or modifies a verb, an adjective, another adverb, or a whole sentence. An adverb generally answers questions such as *how, when, where, how often,* or *how much.*

greatly	precisely	regularly	there
here	today	partly	quickly
slowly	yesterday	nearly	loudly

Preposition

A **preposition** is a word (or group of words) that shows the relationship between its object (a noun or pronoun that follows the preposition) and another word in the sentence. Prepositions introduce prepositional phrases, which are modifiers.

across   for   with   out   to   of

Conjunction

A **conjunction** connects individual words or groups of words.

and   because   but   for   or   since   so   yet

Interjection

An **interjection** is a word that communicates strong emotion or surprise. Punctuation (often a comma or an exclamation point) is used to set off an interjection from the rest of the sentence.

Stop! No! What, am I invisible?

Chapter 28

Constructing Sentences

585.1

"A writer is not someone who expresses his thoughts, his passions, or his imagination in sentences but someone who thinks sentences."

—Roland Barthes

As a group of words expressing a complete thought, a **sentence** is made up of at least a subject (sometimes understood) and a verb. Sentences can make statements, ask questions, give commands, or express feelings.

> The Web delivers the universe in a box.

Using Subjects and Predicates

585.2

Sentences have two main parts: a **subject** and a **predicate**.

> Technology frustrates many people.

> **Note:** In the sentence above, *technology* is the subject—the sentence talks about technology. *Frustrates many people* is the complete predicate—it tells what the subject is doing.

The Subject

585.3

The **subject** names the person or thing either performing the action, receiving the action, or being described or renamed. The subject is most often a noun or a pronoun.

> **Technology** is an integral part of almost every business.
> **Manufacturers** need technology to compete in the world market.
> **They** could not go far without it.

A verbal phrase or a noun dependent clause may also function as a subject.

> **To survive without technology** is difficult. (infinitive phrase)
> **Downloading information from the Web** is easy. (gerund phrase)
> **That the information age would arrive** was inevitable. (noun dependent clause)

> **Note:** To determine the subject of a sentence, ask yourself *who* or *what* performs or receives the action or is described. In most sentences, the subject comes before the verb; however, in some instances, that order is reversed. (See 591.2, 591.3, 594.1, and 667.)

> **ell Note:** Some languages permit the omission of a subject; English does not. A subject must be included in every sentence. (The only exception is an "understood subject," 586.4.)

586.1 Simple Subject

A **simple subject** is the subject without the words that describe or modify it.

Thirty years ago, reasonably well-trained **mechanics** could fix any car on the road.

586.2 Complete Subject

A **complete subject** is the simple subject *and* the words that describe or modify it.

Thirty years ago, **reasonably well-trained mechanics** could fix any car on the road.

586.3 Compound Subject

A **compound subject** is composed of two or more simple subjects joined by a conjunction and sharing the same predicate(s).

Today, **mechanics** and **technicians** would need to master a half million manual pages to fix every car on the road.

Dealerships and their service **departments** must sometimes explain that situation to the customers.

586.4 Understood Subject

Sometimes a subject is **understood**. This means it is not stated in the sentence, but a reader clearly understands what the subject is. An understood subject occurs in a command (imperative sentence). (See 591.3.)

(You) Park on this side of the street. (The subject *you* is understood.)

Put the CD player in the trunk.

586.5 Delayed Subject

In sentences that begin with *There is, There was,* or *Here is,* the subject follows the verb.

There are 70,000 **fans** in the stadium. (The subject is *fans; are* is the verb. *There* is an expletive, an empty word.)

Here is a **problem** for stadium security. (*Problem* is the subject. *Here* is an adverb.)

The subject is also delayed in questions.

Where was the **event**? (*Event* is the subject.)

Was **Neil Young** playing? (*Neil Young* is the subject.)

The Predicate (Verb)

The **predicate**, which contains the verb, is the part of the sentence that either tells what the subject is doing, tells what is being done to the subject, or describes or renames the subject.

Students **need technical skills as well as basic academic skills.**

Simple Predicate

A **simple predicate** is the complete verb without the words that describe or modify it. (The complete verb can consist of more that one word.)

Today's workplace **requires** employees to have a range of skills.

Complete Predicate

A **complete predicate** is the verb, all the words that modify or explain it, and any objects or complements.

Today's workplace **requires employees to have a range of skills.**

Compound Predicate

A **compound predicate** is composed of two or more verbs, all the words that modify or explain them, and any objects or complements.

Engineers **analyze problems** and **calculate solutions.**

Direct Object

A **direct object** is the part of the predicate that receives the action of an active transitive verb. A direct object makes the meaning of the verb complete.

Marcos visited several **campuses.** (The direct object *campuses* receives the action of the verb *visited* by answering the question "Marcos visited what?")

Note: A direct object may be compound.

A counsellor explained the academic **programs** and the application **process.**

Indirect Object

An **indirect object** is the word(s) that tells *to whom/to what* or *for whom/for what* something is done. A sentence must have a direct object before it can have an indirect object.

I showed our **children** my new school.

Use these questions to find an indirect object:

- What is the verb?   *showed*
- *Showed* what?   *school* (direct object)
- Showed *school* to whom?   *children* (indirect object)

I wrote **them** a note.

Note: An indirect object may be compound.

I gave the **instructor** and a few **classmates** my email address.

Using Phrases

A **phrase** is a group of related words that functions as a single part of speech. A phrase lacks a subject, a predicate, or both. There are three phrases in the following sentence:

> **Examples of technology can be found in ancient civilizations.**
>
> **of technology**
> (prepositional phrase that functions as an adjective; no subject or predicate)
>
> **can be found**
> (verb phrase—all of the words of the verb; no subject)
>
> **in ancient civilizations**
> (prepositional phrase that functions as an adverb; no subject or predicate)

Types of Phrases

There are several types of phrases: *verb, verbal, prepositional, appositive,* and *absolute.*

Verb Phrase

A **verb phrase** consists of a main verb and its helping verbs.

> Students, worried about exams, **have camped** at the library all week.

Verbal Phrase

A **verbal phrase** is a phrase that expands on one of the three types of verbals: *gerund, infinitive,* or *participle.* (See 578.)

A **gerund phrase** consists of a gerund and its modifiers and objects. The whole phrase functions as a noun. (See 578.2.)

> **Becoming a marine biologist** is Rashanda's dream. (The gerund phrase is used as the subject of the sentence.)
>
> She has acquainted herself with the various methods for **collecting sea-life samples**. (The gerund phrase is the object of the preposition *for.*)

An **infinitive phrase** consists of an infinitive and its modifiers and objects. The whole phrase functions as a noun, an adjective, or an adverb. (See 578.3.)

> **To dream** is the first step in any endeavour. (The infinitive phrase functions as a noun used as the subject.)
>
> Remember **to make a plan to realize your dream**. (The infinitive phrase *to make a plan* functions as a noun used as a direct object; *to realize your dream* functions as an adjective modifying plan.)
>
> Finally, apply all of your talents and skills **to achieve your goals**. (The infinitive phrase functions as an adverb modifying *apply.*)

A **participial phrase** consists of a present or past participle (a verb form ending in *ing* or *ed*) and its modifiers. The phrase functions as an adjective. (See 578.4.)

> **Doing poorly in biology**, Theo signed up for a tutor. (The participial phrase modifies the noun *Theo.*)
>
> Some students **frustrated by difficult course work** don't seek help. (The participial phrase modifies the noun *students.*)

fig. 28.1

589.1

Functions of Verbal Phrases

	Noun	Adjective	Adverb
Gerund	■		
Infinitive	■	■	■
Participial		■	

Prepositional Phrase

589.2

A **prepositional phrase** is a group of words beginning with a preposition and ending with its object, a noun or a pronoun. Prepositional phrases are used mainly as adjectives and adverbs. See 582.3 for a list of prepositions.

> Denying the existence **of exam week** hasn't worked **for anyone** yet.
> (The prepositional phrase *of exam week* is used as an adjective modifying the noun *existence; for anyone* is used as an adverb modifying the verb *has worked*.)

> Test days still dawn and GPAs still plummet **for the unprepared student**.
> (The prepositional phrase *for the unprepared student* is used as an adverb modifying the verbs *dawn* and *plummet*.)

ell Note: Do not mistake the following adverbs for nouns and incorrectly use them as objects of prepositions: *here, there, everywhere*.

Appositive Phrase

589.3

An **appositive phrase**, which follows a noun or a pronoun and renames it, consists of a noun and its modifiers. An appositive adds new information about the noun or pronoun it follows.

> The Olympic-size pool, **a prized addition to the physical education building,** gets plenty of use. (The appositive phrase renames *pool*.)

Absolute Phrase

589.4

An **absolute phrase** consists of a noun and a participle (plus the participle's object, if there is one, and any modifiers). It usually modifies the entire sentence.

> **Their enthusiasm sometimes waning,** the students who cannot swim are required to take lessons. (The noun *enthusiasm* is modified by the present participle *waning;* the entire phrase modifies *students*.)

fyi Phrases can add valuable information to sentences, but some phrases add nothing but "fat" to your writing. For a list of phrases to avoid, see page 102.

Using Clauses

A **clause** is a group of related words that has both a subject and a verb.

590.1   Independent/Dependent Clauses

An **independent clause** contains at least one subject and one verb, presents a complete thought, and can stand alone as a sentence; a **dependent clause** (also called a subordinate clause) does not present a complete thought and cannot stand alone (make sense) as a sentence.

> Though airplanes are twentieth-century inventions (dependent clause), people have always dreamed of flying (independent clause).

Types of Clauses

There are three basic types of dependent, or subordinate, clauses: *adverb, adjective,* and *noun.* These dependent clauses are combined with independent clauses to form complex and compound-complex sentences.

590.2   Adverb Clause

An **adverb clause** is used like an adverb to modify a verb, an adjective, or an adverb. All adverb clauses begin with subordinating conjunctions. (See 583.4.)

> **Because Orville won a coin toss**, he got to fly the power-driven air machine first. (The adverb clause modifies the verb *got.*)

590.3   Adjective Clause

An **adjective clause** is used like an adjective to modify a noun or a pronoun. Adjective clauses begin with relative pronouns *(which, that, who).* (See 571.3.)

> The men **who invented the first airplane** were brothers, Orville and Wilbur Wright. (The adjective clause modifies the noun *men. Who* is the subject of the adjective clause.)

> The first flight, **which took place December 17, 1903,** was made by Orville. (The adjective clause modifies the noun *flight. Which* is the subject of the adjective clause.)

590.4   Noun Clause

A **noun clause** is used in place of a noun. Noun clauses can appear as subjects, as direct or indirect objects, as predicate nominatives, or as objects of prepositions. Noun clauses can also play a role in the independent clause. They are introduced by subordinating words such as *what, that, when, why, how, whatever, who, whom, whoever,* and *whomever.*

> He wants to know **what made modern aviation possible.** (The noun clause functions as the object of the infinitive.)

> **Whoever invents an airplane with vertical takeoff ability** will be a hero. (The noun clause functions as the subject.)

Note: If you can replace a whole clause with the pronoun *something* or *someone,* it is a noun clause.

Using Sentence Variety

A sentence can be classified according to the kind of statement it makes and according to the way it is constructed.

Kinds of Sentences

Sentences can make five basic kinds of statements: *declarative, interrogative, imperative, exclamatory,* or *conditional.*

Declarative Sentence

591.1

Declarative sentences make statements. They tell us something about a person, a place, a thing, or an idea.

> Between April 9 and 12, 1917, the Canadian Corps fought and won the Battle of Vimy Ridge.

Interrogative Sentence

591.2

Interrogative sentences ask questions.

> How many casualties, dead and wounded, did Canadians suffer?

> What was the significance of the battle for World War I and for Canada as a nation?

Imperative Sentence

591.3

Imperative sentences give commands. They often contain an understood subject (*you*). (See 586.4.)

> For answers to these and other questions about Canada's participation in World War I, read pages 89–110 in your textbook.

ell Note: Imperative sentences with an understood subject are the only sentences in which it is acceptable to have no subjects stated.

Exclamatory Sentence

591.4

Exclamatory sentences communicate strong emotion or surprise. They are punctuated with exclamation points.

> I simply can't keep up with these long reading assignments!

> Oh my gosh, you scared me!

Conditional Sentence

591.5

Conditional sentences express two circumstances. One of the circumstances depends on the other circumstance. The words *if, when,* or *unless* are often used in the dependent clause in conditional sentences.

> **If** you practise a few study-reading techniques, course reading loads will be manageable.

> **When** I manage my time, it seems I have more of it.

> Don't ask me to help you **unless** you are willing to do the reading first.

Structure of Sentences

A sentence may be *simple, compound, complex,* or *compound-complex,* depending on how the independent and dependent clauses are combined.

592.1   Simple Sentence

A **simple sentence** contains one independent clause. The independent clause may have compound subjects and verbs, and it may also contain phrases.

> My **back aches**.
> (single subject: *back;* single verb: *aches*)

> My **teeth** and my **eyes hurt**.
> (compound subject: *teeth* and *eyes;* single verb: *hurt*)

> My **memory** and my **logic come** and **go**.
> (compound subject: *memory* and *logic;* compound verb: *come* and *go*)

> I **must need a vacation**.
> (single subject: *I;* single verb: *must need;* direct object: *vacation*)

592.2   Compound Sentence

A **compound sentence** consists of two independent clauses. The clauses must be joined by a semicolon, by a comma and a coordinating conjunction *(and, but, or, nor, so, for, yet),* or by a semicolon followed by a conjunctive adverb *(besides, however, instead, meanwhile, then, therefore)* and a comma.

> I had eight hours of sleep, **so** why am I so exhausted?

> I take good care of myself; I get enough sleep.

> I still feel fatigued; **therefore,** I must need more exercise.

592.3   Complex Sentence

A **complex sentence** contains one independent clause (in bold) and one or more dependent clauses (underlined).

> When I can, **I get eight hours of sleep**. (dependent clause; independent clause)

> When I get up on time, and if someone hasn't used up all the milk,
> **I eat breakfast**. (two dependent clauses; independent clause)

When the dependent clause comes before the independent clause, use a comma.

592.4   Compound-Complex Sentence

A **compound-complex sentence** contains two or more independent clauses (in bold type) and one or more dependent clauses (underlined).

> If I'm not in a hurry, **I take leisurely walks,** and **I try to spot some wildlife**.
> (dependent clause; two independent clauses)

> **I saw a hawk** when I was walking, and **other smaller birds were chasing it**.
> (dependent clause, independent clause; independent clause)

Chapter 29

Avoiding Sentence Errors

"If I can write a fine sentence in one day, I can be happy the whole day."

—Claire Mckay

Subject–Verb Agreement

593.1

The subject and verb of any clause must agree in both *person* and *number*. Person indicates whether the subject of the verb is *first, second,* or *third person. Number* indicates whether the subject and verb are *singular* or *plural*. (See 575.2 and 575.3.)

	Singular	**Plural**
First Person	I think	we think
Second Person	you think	you think
Third Person	he/she/it thinks	they think

Agreement in Number

593.2

A verb must agree in number (singular or plural) with its subject.

> The **student was** rewarded for her hard work. (Both the subject *student* and the verb *was* are singular; they agree in number.)

> **Note:** Do not be confused by phrases that come between the subject and the verb. Such phrases may begin with words like *in addition to, as well as,* or *together with.*

> The **instructor**, as well as the students, is expected to attend the orientation. (*Instructor,* not *students,* is the subject.)

Compound Subjects

593.3

Compound subjects connected with *and* usually require a plural verb.

> **Dedication and creativity are** trademarks of successful students.

> **Note:** If a compound subject joined by *and* is thought of as a unit, use a singular verb.

> **Macaroni and cheese is** always available in the cafeteria.

(Also see 594.3 and 594.4.)

594.1   Delayed Subjects

Delayed subjects occur when the verb comes *before* the subject in a sentence. In these inverted sentences, the true (delayed) subject must still agree with the verb.

> There **are** many nontraditional **students** on our campus.
> Here **is** the **syllabus** you need.
> (*Students* and *syllabus* are the subjects of these sentences, not the adverbs *there* and *here*.)

> **Note:** Using an inverted sentence, on occasion, will lend variety to your writing style. Simply remember to make the delayed subjects agree with the verbs.

> However, included among the list's topmost items **was "revise research paper."**
> (Because the true subject here is singular—one item—the singular verb *was* is correct.)

594.2   Titles as Subjects

When the subject of a sentence is the title of a work of art, literature, or music, the verb should be singular. This is also true of a word (or phrase) being used as a word (or phrase).

> *Lyrical Ballads* **was** published in 1798 by two of England's greatest poets, Wordsworth and Coleridge. (Even though the title of the book, *Lyrical Ballads,* is plural in form, it is still a single title being used as the subject, correctly taking the singular verb *was*.)

> **"Over-the-counter drugs" is** a phrase that means nonprescription medications. (Even though the phrase is plural in form, it is still a single phrase being used as the subject, correctly taking the singular verb *is*.)

594.3   Singular Subjects with *Or* or *Nor*

Singular subjects joined by *or* or *nor* take a singular verb.

> Neither a **textbook** nor a **notebook is required** for this class.

> **Note:** When the subject nearer a present-tense verb is the singular pronoun *I* or *you,* the correct singular verb does not end in *s*.

> Neither **Marcus** nor **I feel** (not *feels*) right about this.
> Either **Rosa** or **you have** (not *has*) to take notes for me.
> Either **you** or **Rosa has** to take notes for me.

594.4   Singular/Plural Subjects

When one of the subjects joined by *or* or *nor* is singular and one is plural, the verb must agree with the subject nearer the verb.

> Neither the **professor** nor her **students were** in the lab. (The plural subject *students* is nearer the verb; therefore, the plural verb *were* agrees with *students*.)

> Neither the **students** nor the **professor was** in the lab. (The singular subject *professor* is nearer the verb; therefore, the singular verb *was* is used to agree with *professor*.)

Collective Nouns 595.1

Generally, **collective nouns** (*faculty, pair, crew, assembly, congress, species, crowd, army, team, committee,* and so on) take a singular verb. However, if you want to emphasize differences among individuals in the group or are referring to the group as individuals, you can use a plural verb.

> My lab **team takes** its work very seriously. (*Team* refers to the group as a unit; it requires a singular verb, *takes*.)
>
> The **team assume** separate responsibilities for each study they undertake. (In this example, *team* refers to individuals within the group; it requires a plural verb, *assume*.)

Note: Collective nouns such as (the) *police, poor, elderly,* and *young* use plural verbs.
> The police direct traffic here between 7:00 and 9:00 a.m.

Plural Nouns with Singular Meaning 595.2

Some nouns that are plural in form but singular in meaning take a singular verb: *mumps, measles, news, mathematics, economics, robotics,* and so on.

> **Economics is** sometimes called "the dismal science."
>
> The economic **news is** not very good.

Note: The most common exceptions are *scissors, trousers, tidings,* and *pliers*.
> The **scissors are** missing again.
>
> **Are** these **trousers** prewashed?

With Linking Verbs 595.3

When a sentence contains a linking verb (usually a form of *be*)—and a noun or pronoun comes before and after that verb—the verb must agree with the subject, not the predicate nominative (the noun or pronoun coming after the verb).

> The cause of his problem **was** poor study habits. (*Cause* requires a singular verb, even though the predicate nominative, *habits*, is plural.)
>
> His poor study habits **were** the cause of his problem. (*Habits* requires a plural verb, even though the predicate nominative, *cause*, is singular.)

Nouns Showing Measurement, Time, and Money 595.4

Mathematical phrases and phrases that name a period of time, a unit of measurement, or an amount of money take a singular verb.

> Three and three **is** six.
>
> Eight pages **is** a long paper on this topic.
>
> In my opinion, two dollars **is** a high price for a cup of coffee.

596.1   Relative Pronouns

When a **relative pronoun** *(who, which, that)* is used as the subject of a dependent clause, the number of the verb is determined by that pronoun's antecedent. (The *antecedent* is the word to which the pronoun refers.)

> This is one of the **books that are** required for English class.
> (The relative pronoun *that* requires the plural verb *are* because its antecedent is *books*, not the word *one*. To test this type of sentence for agreement, read the *of* phrase first: *Of the books that are . . .*)

> **Note:** Generally, the antecedent is the nearest noun or pronoun to the relative pronoun and is often the object of a preposition. Sometimes, however, the antecedent is not the nearest noun or pronoun, especially in sentences with the phrase "the only one of."

> Dr. Graciosa wondered why Claire was the only **one** of her students **who was** not attending lectures regularly. (In this case, the addition of the modifiers *the only* changes the meaning of the sentence. The antecedent of *who* is *one*, not *students*. Only one student was not attending.)

596.2   Indefinite Pronoun with Singular Verb

Many indefinite pronouns *(someone, somebody, something; anyone, anybody, anything; no one, nobody, nothing; everyone, everybody, everything; each, either, neither, one, this)* serving as subjects require a singular verb.

> **Everybody is** welcome to attend the chancellor's reception.

> **No one was** sent an invitation.

> **Note:** Although it may seem to indicate more than one, *each* is a singular pronoun and requires a singular verb. Do not be confused by words or phrases that come between the indefinite pronoun and the verb.

> **Each** of the new students **is** (not *are*) **encouraged** to attend the reception.

596.3   Indefinite Pronoun with Plural Verb

Some indefinite pronouns *(both, few, many, most, and several)* are plural; they require a plural verb.

> **Few are** offered the opportunity to study abroad.

> **Most take** advantage of opportunities closer to home.

596.4   Indefinite Pronoun or Quantity Word with Singular/Plural Verb

Some indefinite pronouns or quantity words *(all, any, most, part, half, none, and some)* may be either singular or plural, depending on the nouns they refer to. Look inside the prepositional phrase to see what the antecedent is.

> **Some** of the students **were** missing. (*Students,* the noun that *some* refers to, is plural; therefore, the pronoun *some* is considered plural, and the plural verb *were* is used to agree with it.)

> **Most** of the lecture **was** over by the time we arrived. (Because *lecture* is singular, *most* is also singular, requiring the singular verb *was.*)

Pronoun–Antecedent Agreement

597.1

A pronoun must agree in number, person, and gender (sex) with its *antecedent*. The antecedent is the word to which the pronoun refers.

> **Yoshi** brought **his** laptop computer and ebook to school. (The pronoun *his* refers to the antecedent *Yoshi*. Both the pronoun and its antecedent are singular, third person, and masculine; therefore, the pronoun is said to agree with its antecedent.)

Singular Pronoun

597.2

Use a singular pronoun to refer to such antecedents as *each, either, neither, one, anyone, anybody, everyone, everybody, somebody, another, nobody,* and *a person.*

> **Each** of the maintenance vehicles has **their** doors locked at night. (Incorrect)
>
> **Each** of the maintenance vehicles has **its** doors locked at night. (Correct: Both *Each* and *its* are singular.)
>
> **Somebody** left **his or her** (not *their*) vehicle unlocked. (Correct)

> **Note:** The impersonal pronoun *one* is sometimes used in formal prose to mean "a person." Pronouns referring to *one* should be singular.
>
> If **one** wishes to avoid dents to **their** (or **your**) car, it is best to park in Siberia. (Incorrect)
>
> If **one** wishes to avoid dents to **one's** (or **his** or **her**) car, it is best to park in Siberia. (Correct)

Plural Pronoun

597.3

When a plural pronoun *(they, their)* is mistakenly used with a singular indefinite pronoun (such as *everyone* or *everybody*), you may correct the sentence by replacing *their* or *they* with optional pronouns *(her or his* or *he or she),* or make the antecedent plural.

> **Everyone** must learn to wait **their** turn. (Incorrect)
>
> **Everyone** must learn to wait **her or his** turn. (Correct: Optional pronouns *her* or *his* are used.)
>
> **People** must learn to wait **their** turns. (Correct: The singular antecedent, *Everyone,* is changed to the plural antecedent, *People.*)

Two or More Antecedents

597.4

When two or more antecedents are joined by *and,* they are considered plural.

> **Tomas** and **Jamal** are finishing **their** assignments.

When two or more singular antecedents are joined by *or* or *nor,* they are considered singular.

> **Connie** or **Shavonn** left **her** headset in the library.

> **Note:** If one of the antecedents is masculine and one feminine, the pronouns should likewise be masculine and feminine.
>
> Is **Ahmad** or **Phyllis** bringing **his or her** laptop computer?

> **Note:** If one of the antecedents joined by *or* or *nor* is singular and one is plural, the pronoun is made to agree with the nearer antecedent.
>
> Neither **Ravi** nor **his friends** want to spend **their** time studying.
>
> Neither **his friends** nor **Ravi** wants to spend **his** time studying.

Shifts in Sentence Construction

A shift is an improper change in structure midway through a sentence. The following examples will help you identify and fix several different kinds of shifts.

598.1

Unparallel Construction

Unparallel construction occurs when the kind of words or phrases being used shifts or changes in the middle of a sentence.

> ***Shift:*** In my hometown, people pass the time shooting pool, pitching horseshoes, and at hockey games. (Sentence shifts from a series of general phrases, *shooting pool* and *pitching horseshoes,* to the prepositional phrase *at hockey games.*)

> ***Parallel:*** In my hometown, people pass the time **shooting pool, pitching horseshoes, and playing hockey.** (Now all three activities are gerund phrases—they are consistent, or parallel.)

Mixed Construction

In a mixed construction, subjects and predicates don't match. Essentially, the writer starts the sentence with one syntactic pattern and then adds to it another syntactic pattern that doesn't fit. Two common errors involving mixed construction are *is because* and *is when*. In both these errors, an adverbial clause follows the linking verb *is*; what is required, however, is a noun or an adjective.

> ***Mixed:*** The reason that we couldn't find an apartment **is because** none of those we looked at allowed pets.

> ***Corrected:*** The reason that we couldn't find an apartment **is that** none of those we looked at allowed pets.

> ***Corrected:*** We couldn't find an apartment **because** none of those we looked at allowed pets.

598.2

Shift in Person

Shift in person is mixing first, second, or third person within a sentence. (See 572.4 and 575.3.)

> ***Shift:*** **One** may get spring fever unless **you** live in California or Florida. (The sentence shifts from third person, *one,* to second person, *you.*)

> ***Corrected:*** **You** may get spring fever unless **you** live in California or Florida. (Stays in second person.)

> ***Corrected:*** **People** may get spring fever unless **they** live in California or Florida. (*People,* a third person plural noun, requires a third person plural pronoun, *they.*)

598.3

Shift in Tense

Shift in tense is using more than one tense in a sentence when only one is needed.

> ***Shift:*** Sheila **looked** at nine apartments in one weekend before she **had chosen** one. (Tense shifts from past to past perfect for no reason.)

> ***Corrected:*** Sheila **looked** at nine apartments in one weekend before she **chose** one. (Tense stays in past.)

Shift in Voice

Shift in voice is mixing active with passive voice. Usually, a sentence beginning in active voice should remain so to the end.

> *Shift:* As you look (active voice) for just the right place, many interesting apartments **will probably be seen.** (passive voice)

> *Corrected:* As you look (active voice) for just the right place, **you will probably see** (active voice) many interesting apartments.

Fragments, Comma Splices, and Run-Ons

Except in a few special situations, you should use complete sentences when you write. By definition, a complete sentence expresses a complete thought. However, a sentence may actually contain several ideas, not just one. The trick is getting those ideas to work together to form a clear, interesting sentence that expresses your exact meaning. Among the most common sentence errors that writers make are fragments, comma splices, and run-ons.

Fragments

A **fragment** is a phrase or dependent clause used as a sentence. It is not a sentence, however, because a phrase lacks a subject, a verb, or some other essential part, and a dependent clause must be connected to an independent clause to complete its meaning.

> *Fragment:* Pete gunned the engine. Forgetting that the boat was hooked to the truck. (This is a sentence followed by a fragment. This error can be corrected by combining the fragment with the sentence.)

> *Corrected:* Pete gunned the engine, forgetting that the boat was hooked to the truck.

> *Fragment:* Even though my best friend had a little boy last year. (This clause does not convey a complete thought. We need to know what is happening despite the birth of the little boy.)

> *Corrected:* Even though my best friend had a little boy last year, **I do not comprehend the full meaning of "motherhood."**

Comma Splices

A **comma splice** is a mistake made when two independent clauses are connected ("spliced") with only a comma. The comma is not enough: A period, semicolon, or conjunction is needed.

> *Splice:* People say that being a stay-at-home mom or dad is an important job, their actions tell a different story.

> *Corrected:* People say that being a stay-at-home mom or dad is an important job, **but** their actions tell a different story. (The coordinating conjunction *but*, added after the comma, corrects the splice.)

> *Corrected:* People say that being a stay-at-home mom or dad is an important job**;** their actions tell a different story. (A semicolon—rather than just a comma—makes the sentence correct.)

> *Corrected:* People say that being a stay-at-home mom or dad is an important job. **Their** actions tell a different story. (A period creates two sentences and corrects the splice.)

600.1   Run-Ons

A run-on sentence is actually two sentences (two independent clauses) joined without adequate punctuation or a connecting word.

Run-on: Queenston Heights holds a special place in Canadian history it was the site of an important battle during the War of 1812 between the United States and Britain.

Corrected: Queenston Heights holds a special place in Canadian history **because** it was the site of an important battle during the War of 1812 between the United States and Britain.
(A subordinating conjunction is added to fix the run-on by making the second clause dependent.)

Run-on: The Battle of Queenston Heights was one of the first key battles of the war it took place on October 13, 1812, it resulted in a British victory it also came at a cost, namely the death of the British leader, Major General Isaac Brock. The battle took place near Queenston. Queenston is in the Niagara region of Ontario. The American forces were made up of 900 regulars and 2,650 New York militia 100 were killed, 170 wounded, and more than 800 captured. The British forces were made up of 1,300 British regulars, Canadian militia, and Mohawks they had 21 killed, 85 wounded, and 22 captured. The British victory prevented the Americans from gaining ground on the Canadian side of the Niagara River.

Corrected: The Battle of Queenston Heights was one of the first key battles of the **war. It** took place on October 13, 1812, **and** resulted in a British **victory, but** it also came at a cost, namely the death of the British leader, Major General Isaac Brock. The battle took place near Queenston. Queenston is in the Niagara region of Ontario. The American forces were made up of 900 regulars and 2,650 New York **militia, of which** 100 were killed, 170 wounded, and more than 800 captured. The British forces were made up of 1,300 British regulars, Canadian militia, and **Mohawks: they** had 21 killed, 85 wounded, and 22 captured. The British victory prevented the Americans from gaining ground on the Canadian side of the Niagara River.

600.2

The writer corrected the run-on sentences in the paragraph above by adding punctuation, by inserting conjunctions, and by turning some clauses into dependent clauses. Below, the writer makes further improvements in the paragraph by combining short sentences and strengthening transitions.

Improved: The Battle of Queenston Heights **(October 13, 1812)** was one of the first key battles of the war. **While it** resulted in a British **victory, it** also came at a cost, namely the death of the British leader, Major General Isaac Brock. The battle took place near **Queenston, located** in the Niagara region of Ontario. **Of** the 900 regulars and 2,650 New York militia **that made up the American forces**, 100 were killed, 170 wounded, and more than 800 captured. **By comparison**, the British **forces, made** up of 1,300 British regulars, Canadian militia, and Mohawks, **suffered far fewer casualties in the victory:** 21 killed, 85 wounded, and 22 captured. **As a result**, the British victory prevented the Americans from gaining ground on the Canadian side of the Niagara River.

Misplaced, Dangling, and Squinting Modifiers

Generally, modifiers (adjectives and adverbs) must be placed in the sentence so that it is clear what is being modified. The problems below involve a lack of clarity.

Misplaced Modifiers

601.1

Misplaced modifiers are descriptive words or phrases so separated from what they are describing that the reader is confused.

Misplaced: The neighbour's dog has nearly been barking nonstop for two hours. (*Nearly* been barking?)

Corrected: The neighbour's dog has been barking nonstop **for nearly two hours**. (Watch your placement of *only, just, nearly, barely,* and so on.)

Misplaced: The pool staff gave large beach towels to the students marked with chlorine-resistant ID numbers. (*Students* marked with chlorine-resistant ID numbers?)

Corrected: The pool staff gave large beach towels **marked with chlorine-resistant ID numbers to the students**. (*Towels* marked with chlorine-resistant ID numbers)

Dangling Modifiers

601.2

Dangling modifiers are descriptive phrases that tell about a subject that isn't stated in the sentence. These often occur as participial phrases containing *ing* or *ed* words.

Dangling: After standing in line all afternoon, the manager informed us that all the tickets had been sold. (It sounds as if the manager has been *standing in line all afternoon*.)

Corrected: **After we had stood in line all afternoon,** the manager informed us that all the tickets had been sold.

Dangling: After living in the house for one month, the electrician recommended we update all the wiring. (It sounds as if the electrician has been *living in the house*.)

Corrected: After living in the house for one month, **we hired an electrician, who recommended we update all the wiring**.

Squinting Modifiers

A **squinting modifier** is an adjective or adverb (either a word or a phrase) that stands between two elements in a sentence, either of which could be modified. Hence, the modifier "squints" in two directions, causing ambiguity.

Squinting: It was raining so hard **for the whole weekend** we played video games. (Does the modifying phrase modify *was raining or played*?)

Corrected: It was raining so hard **that** we played video games **for the whole weekend**. (Adding *that* and moving the modifying phrase removes the ambiguity.)

Ambiguous Wording

Ambiguity can create vagueness and confusion. Test your sentences for the kinds of ambiguous wording described below.

602.1

Indefinite and Broad Pronoun References

An **indefinite reference** is a problem caused by careless use of pronouns. There must always be a word or phrase nearby (its antecedent) that a pronoun clearly replaces.

Broad pronoun reference involves using a pronoun (typically *this*, *that*, or *it*) to refer not to a specific antecedent (a noun or another pronoun) but vaguely to an entire clause or sentence.

Indefinite: When Tonya attempted to put her dictionary on the shelf, it fell to the floor. (The pronoun *it* could refer to either the dictionary or the shelf since both are singular nouns.)

Corrected: When Tonya attempted to put her dictionary on the shelf, **the shelf** fell to the floor.

Indefinite: Juanita reminded Kerri that she needed to photocopy her resumé before going to her interview. (Who *needed to photocopy her resumé*—Juanita or Kerri?)

Corrected: Juanita reminded Kerri **to photocopy her resumé before going to her interview.**

Broad: We went to the library to research the Cypress Hills Massacre. **This** gave us a great start on the project.

Corrected: We went to the library to research the Cypress Hills Massacre. **This visit** gave us a great start on the project.

602.2

Incomplete Comparisons

Incomplete comparisons—leaving out words that show exactly what is being compared to what—can confuse readers.

Incomplete: After completing our lab experiment, we concluded that helium is lighter. (*Lighter* than what?)

Corrected: After completing our lab experiment, we concluded that helium is lighter **than oxygen.**

602.3

Unclear Wording

One type of ambiguous writing is wording that has two or more possible meanings due to an unclear reference to something elsewhere in the sentence. (See 602.1.)

Unclear: I couldn't believe that my sister bought a cat with all those allergy problems. (Who has the *allergy problems*—the cat or the sister?)

Corrected: I couldn't believe that my sister, **who is very allergic, bought a cat**.

Unclear: Dao intended to wash the car when he finished his homework, but he never did. (It is unclear which he *never did*—wash the car or finish his homework.)

Corrected: Dao intended to wash the car when he finished his homework, **but he never did manage to wash the car.**

Nonstandard Language

Nonstandard language is language that does not conform to the standards set by schools, media, and public institutions. It is often acceptable in everyday conversation and in fictional writing but seldom is used in formal speech or other forms of writing.

Colloquial Language   603.1

Colloquial language is wording used in informal conversation that is unacceptable in formal writing.

> *Colloquial:* Hey, wait up! Cal wants to go with.
>
> *Standard:* **Hey, wait!** Cal wants to go with **us.**

Double Preposition   603.2

The use of certain **double prepositions**—*off of, off to, from off*—is unacceptable.

> *Double Preposition:* Pick up the dirty clothes from off the floor.
>
> *Standard:* Pick up the dirty clothes **from the floor.**

Substitution   603.3

Avoid substituting *and* for *to.*

> *Substitution:* Try and get to class on time.
>
> *Standard:* **Try to** get to class on time.

Avoid substituting *of* for *have* when combining with *could, would, should,* or *might.*

> *Substitution:* I should of studied for that exam.
>
> *Standard:* **I should have** studied for that exam.

Double Negative   603.4

A **double negative** is a sentence that contains two negative words used to express a single negative idea. Double negatives are unacceptable in academic writing.

> *Double Negative:* After paying for essentials, I haven't got no money left.
>
> *Standard:* **I haven't got** any money left. / **I have no** money left.

Slang   603.5

Avoid the use of **slang** or any "in" words in formal writing.

> *Slang:* The way the stadium roof opened was way cool.
>
> *Standard:* The way the stadium roof opened **was remarkable.**

Quick Guide

Avoiding Sentence Problems

Does every subject agree with its verb? (See pages 593–596.)

- In person and number?
- When a word or phrase comes between the subject and the verb?
- When the subject is delayed?
- When the subject is a title?
- When a compound subject is connected with *or*?
- When the subject is a collective noun (*faculty, team,* or *crowd*)?
- When the subject is a relative pronoun *(who, which, that)*?
- When the subject is an indefinite pronoun (*everyone, anybody,* or *many*)?

Does every pronoun agree with its antecedent? (See page 597.)

- When the pronoun is a singular indefinite pronoun such as *each, either,* or *another*?
- When two antecedents are joined with *and*?
- When two antecedents are joined with *or*?

Did you unintentionally create inappropriate shifts? (See pages 598–599.)

- In person?
- In tense?
- From active voice to passive voice?
- In another unparallel construction?

Are all your sentences complete? (See pages 599–600.)

- Have you used sentence fragments?
- Are some sentences "spliced" or run together?

Did you use any misplaced modifiers or ambiguous wording? (See pages 601–602.)

- Have you used misplaced, dangling, or squinting modifiers?
- Have you used incomplete comparisons or indefinite references?

Did you use any nonstandard language? (See page 603.)

- Have you used slang or colloquial language?
- Have you used double negatives or double prepositions?

Chapter 30

Marking Punctuation

"You need only two tools: WD-40 and duct tape. If it doesn't move and it should, use WD-40. If it moves and it shouldn't, use the duct tape."

—Red Green

Period

After Sentences

605.1

Use a **period** to end a sentence that makes a statement, requests something, or gives a mild command.

Statement: By 2013, women made up 56 percent of undergraduate students and 59 percent of graduate students.

Request: Please read the instructions carefully.

Mild command: If your topic sentence isn't clear, rewrite it.

Indirect question: The professor asked if we had completed the test.

Note: It is not necessary to place a period after a statement that has parentheses around it and is part of another sentence.

Think about joining a club **(the student affairs office has a list of organizations)** for fun and for leadership experience.

After Initials and Abbreviations

605.2

Use a period after an initial and some abbreviations.

Mr.	Mrs.	B.C.E.	Ph.D.	M.P. Jack Lagton
Jr.	Sr.	D.D.S.	U.S.	Charles G. D. Roberts
Dr.	M.A.	p.m.	B.A.	A.A. Milne

Some abbreviations (such as *pm*) also can be written without periods. Use no spacing in abbreviations except when providing a person's initials. When an abbreviation is the last word in a sentence, use only one period at the end of the sentence.

Mikhail eyed each door until he found the name Rosa Lopez, **Ph.D.**

As Decimal Points

605.3

Use a period as a decimal point.

The municipal government spent approximately **$11.8** million last year to add bike lanes to city streets.

Ellipsis

606.1   To Show Omitted Words

Use an **ellipsis** (three periods) to show that one or more words have been omitted in a quotation. When typing, leave one space before and after each period.

> (Original) The English linguistic community and the French linguistic community in New Brunswick have equality of status and equal rights and privileges, including the right to distinct educational institutions and such distinct cultural institutions as are necessary for the preservation and promotion of those communities.
>
> *—Canadian Charter of Rights and Freedoms*

> (Quotation) "The English linguistic community and the French linguistic community in New Brunswick have . ▼ . the right to distinct educational institutions . ▼ . for the preservation and promotion of those communities."

> **Note:** Omit internal punctuation (a comma, a semicolon, a colon, or a dash) on either side of the ellipsis marks unless it is needed for clarity.

606.2   To Use After Sentences

If words from a quotation are omitted at the end of a sentence, place the ellipsis after the period or other end punctuation.

> (Quotation) "We are not anti-American. We do not dislike Americans though we abhor American imperialism. ▼ . But then, so do many Americans. Many of them have said that even more forthrightly than we have, and many of them have suffered more than any of us for their plain speaking."
>
> *—Tommy Douglas*

The first word of a sentence following a period and an ellipsis may be capitalized, even though it was not capitalized in the original.

> (Quotation) "We do not dislike Americans though we abhor American imperialism in all its manifestations. ▼ . So do many Americans. . ▼ . Many of them have suffered more than any of us for their plain speaking."

> **Note:** If the quoted material forms a complete sentence (even if it was not in the original), use a period, then an ellipsis.

> (Original) We do not dislike Americans though we abhor American imperialism in all its manifestations. But then, so do many Americans.

> (Quotation) "We do not dislike Americans though we abhor American imperialism. ▼ . But then, so do many Americans."

606.3   To Show Pauses

Use an ellipsis to indicate a pause or to show unfinished thoughts.

> Listen . . . did you hear that?

> I can't figure out . . . this number doesn't . . . just how do I apply the equation in this case?

Question Mark

After Direct Questions   607.1

Use a **question mark** at the end of a direct question.

> What can I know? What ought I to do? What may I hope?   —Immanuel Kant

> Since when do you have to agree with people to defend them from injustice?
> —Lillian Hellman

Not After Indirect Questions   607.2

No question mark is used after an indirect question.

> After listening to Edgar sing, Mr. Noteworthy asked him if he had ever had formal voice training.

> **Note:** When a single-word question like *how, when,* or *why* is woven into the flow of a sentence, capitalization and special punctuation are not usually required.

> The questions we need to address at our next board meeting are not *why* or *whether,* but *how* and *when.*

After Quotations That Are Questions   607.3

When a question ends with a quotation that is also a question, use only one question mark, and place it within the quotation marks. (Also see 618.4.)

> Do you often ask yourself, "What should I be?"

To Show Uncertainty   607.4

Use a question mark within parentheses to show uncertainty about a word or phrase within a sentence.

> This July will be the 34th (?) anniversary of the first moonwalk.

> **Note:** Do *not* use a question mark in this manner for formal writing.

For Questions in Parentheses or Dashes   607.5

A question within parentheses—or a question set off by dashes—is punctuated with a question mark unless the sentence ends with a question mark.

> You must consult your handbook **(what choice do you have?)** when you need to know a punctuation rule.

> Should I use your charge card (you have one, don't you), or should I pay cash?

> Maybe somewhere in the pasts of these humbled people, there were cases of bad mothering or absent fathering or emotional neglect—**what family surviving the '50s was exempt?**—but I couldn't believe these human errors brought the physical changes in Frank.
> —Mary Kay Blakely, *Wake Me When It's Over*

Comma

608.1

Between Independent Clauses

Use a **comma** between independent clauses that are joined by a coordinating conjunction (*and, but, or, nor, for, yet, so*). (See 592.2.)

> Heath Ledger completed his brilliant portrayal of the Joker in *The Dark Knight,* **but** he died before the film was released.

> **Note:** Do not confuse a compound verb with a compound sentence.

> Ledger's Joker became instantly iconic and won him the Oscar for best supporting actor. (compound verb)

> His death resulted from the abuse of prescription drugs, but it was ruled an accident. (compound sentence)

608.2

Between Items in a Series

Use commas to separate individual words, phrases, or clauses in a series. (A series contains at least three items.)

> Many students must balance studying with **taking care of a family, working a job, getting exercise, and finding time to relax.**

> **Note:** Do *not* use commas when all the items in a series are connected with *or, nor,* or *and.*

> Hmm . . . should I study **or** do laundry **or** go out?

> **Note:** You may omit the final comma before the conjunction, called an Oxford comma. However, we recommend including it to prevent potential confusion.

> This weekend, Roger and Lorraine plan to visit the farmers' market, Sunshine Festival with its hot-air balloons and the beach at Long Point Provincial Park.

> (Are the balloons and the beach both part of the Sunshine Festival? Is the festival being held at Long Point? Add the comma before the conjunction, and the series is clear.)

608.3

To Separate Adjectives

Use commas to separate adjectives that *equally* modify the same noun. Notice in the example below that no comma separates the last adjective from the noun.

> You should exercise regularly and follow a **sensible, healthful** diet.

To determine whether adjectives modify a noun *equally,* use these two tests.

1. Reverse the order of the adjectives; if the sentence is clear, the adjectives modify equally. (In the example below, *hot* and *crowded* can be reversed, and the sentence is still clear; *short* and *coffee* cannot.)

> Matt was tired of working in the **hot, crowded** lab and decided to take a **short coffee** break.

2. Insert *and* between the adjectives; if the sentence reads well, use a comma when *and* is omitted. (The word *and* can be inserted between *hot* and *crowded,* but *and* does not make sense between *short* and *coffee.*)

To Set Off Nonrestrictive Appositives 609.1

A specific kind of explanatory word or phrase called an **appositive** identifies or renames a preceding noun or pronoun.

> Albert Einstein, **the famous mathematician and physicist,** developed the theory of relativity.

Note: Do *not* use commas with *restrictive appositives*. A restrictive appositive is essential to the basic meaning of the sentence.

> The famous mathematician and physicist **Albert Einstein** developed the theory of relativity.

To Set Off Adverb Dependent Clauses 609.2

Use a comma after most introductory dependent clauses functioning as adverbs.

> **Although Charlemagne was a great patron of learning,** he never learned to write properly. (adverb dependent clause)

You may use a comma if the adverb dependent clause following the independent clause is not essential. Adverb clauses beginning with *even though, although, while,* or another conjunction expressing a contrast are usually not needed to complete the meaning of a sentence.

> Charlemagne never learned to write properly, **even though he continued to practise.**

Note: A comma is *not* used if the dependent clause following the independent clause is needed to complete the meaning of the sentence.

> Maybe Charlemagne didn't learn **because he had an empire to run.**

After Introductory Phrases 609.3

Use a comma after introductory phrases.

> **In spite of his practising,** Charlemagne's handwriting remained poor.

Note: A comma is usually omitted if the phrase follows an independent clause.

> Charlemagne's handwriting remained poor **in spite of his practising.**

Also Note: You may omit the comma after a short (four or fewer words) introductory phrase unless it is needed to ensure clarity.

> **At 6:00 a.m.** he would rise and practise his penmanship.

To Set Off Transitional Expressions 609.4

Use a comma to set off conjunctive adverbs and transitional phrases. (See 613.2–613.3.)

> Handwriting is not, **as a matter of fact,** easy to improve upon later in life; **however,** it can be done if you are determined enough.

Note: If a transitional expression blends smoothly with the rest of the sentence, it does not need to be set off. ***Example:*** If you are in fact coming, I'll see you there.

A Closer Look
Nonrestrictive and Restrictive Clauses and Phrases

610.1 | ### Use Commas with Nonrestrictive Clauses and Phrases

Use commas to enclose **nonrestrictive** (unnecessary) phrases or dependent (adjective) clauses. A nonrestrictive phrase or dependent clause adds information that is not necessary to the basic meaning of the sentence. For example, if the clause or phrase (in **boldface**) were left out of the two examples below, the meaning of the sentences would remain clear. Therefore, commas are used to set off the nonrestrictive information.

The locker rooms in Swain Hall, **which were painted and updated last summer**, give professors a place to shower. (nonrestrictive clause)

Work-study programs, **offered on many campuses,** give students the opportunity to earn tuition money. (nonrestrictive phrase)

610.2 | ### Don't Use Commas with Restrictive Clauses and Phrases

Do *not* use commas to set off **restrictive** (necessary) adjective clauses and phrases. A restrictive clause or phrase adds information that the reader needs to understand the sentence. For example, if the adjective clause and phrase (in **boldface**) were dropped from the examples below, the meaning would be unclear.

Only the professors **who run at noon** use the locker rooms in Swain Hall to shower. (restrictive clause)

Using tuition money **earned through work-study programs** is the only way some students can afford to go to college or university. (restrictive phrase)

610.3 | ### Using "That" or "Which"

Use *that* to introduce restrictive (necessary) adjective clauses; use *which* to introduce nonrestrictive (unnecessary) adjective clauses. When the two words are used in this way, the reader can quickly distinguish the necessary information from the unnecessary.

Campus jobs **that are funded by the university** are awarded to students only. (restrictive)

The cafeteria, **which is run by an independent contractor**, can hire nonstudents. (nonrestrictive)

Note: Clauses beginning with *who* can be either restrictive or nonrestrictive.

Students **who pay for their own education** are highly motivated. (restrictive)

The admissions counsellor, **who has studied student records,** said that many returning students earn high GPAs in spite of demanding family obligations. (nonrestrictive)

To Set Off Items in Addresses and Dates

Use commas to set off items in an address and the year in a date.

> Please send your request to 1120 Birchmount Road, Toronto, ON M1K 5G4, before January 1, 2014, or visit our website at www.nelson.com to submit your request online.

Note: No comma is placed between the province and the postal code. Also, no comma separates the items if only the month and year are given: January 2014.

To Set Off Dialogue

Use commas to set off the words of the speaker from the rest of the sentence.

> **"With the evidence that we now have,"** Professor Thom said, **"many scientists believe there is life on Mars."**

To Separate Nouns of Direct Address

Use a comma to separate a noun of direct address from the rest of the sentence.

> **Jamie,** would you please stop whistling while I'm trying to work?

To Separate Interjections

Use a comma to separate a mild interjection from the rest of the sentence.

> **Okay,** so now what do I do?

Note: Exclamation points are used after strong interjections: Wow! You're kidding!

To Set Off Interruptions

Use commas to set off a word, phrase, or clause that interrupts the movement of a sentence. Such expressions usually can be identified through the following tests: (1) They may be omitted without changing the meaning of a sentence; and (2) they may be placed nearly anywhere in the sentence without changing its meaning.

> For me, **well,** it was just a good job gone!   —Langston Hughes, "A Good Job Gone"

> Lela, **as a general rule,** always comes to class ready for a pop quiz.

To Separate Numbers

Use commas to separate a series of numbers to distinguish hundreds, thousands, millions, and so on.

> Do you know how to write the amount **$2,025** on a cheque?

> **25,000   973,240   18,620,197**

If you are following the metric system—also known as the International System of Units (abbreviated SI, after the French Système international)—as is common in science, separate groups of three numbers on either side of the decimal point with a space. If the number is a four-digit one, the space is optional. (Note: do not use this system for money and addresses.)

> **$390,000   39457 Queen Street   4560** or **4 560**

> **33 567 906   23.3468** or **23.346 8   78 564.328 56**

612.1 To Enclose Explanatory Words

Use commas to enclose an explanatory word or phrase.

> Time management, **according to many professionals,** is such an important skill that it should be taught in college.

612.2 To Separate Contrasted Elements

Use commas to separate contrasted elements within a sentence.

> We work to become, **not to acquire.** —Eugene Delacroix

> Where all think alike, **no one thinks very much.** —Walter Lippmann

612.3 Before Tags

Use a comma before tags, which are short statements or questions at the ends of sentences.

> You studied for the test, **right?**

612.4 To Enclose Titles or Initials

Use commas to enclose a title or initials and given names that follow a surname.

> Until Martin, **Sr.,** was 15, he never had more than three months of schooling in any one year.
>
> —Ed Clayton, *Martin Luther King: The Peaceful Warrior*

> The genealogical files included the names Sanders, **L. H.,** and Sanders, **Lucy Hale.**

Note: Some style manuals no longer require commas around titles.

612.5 For Clarity or Emphasis

Use a comma for clarity or for emphasis. There will be times when none of the traditional rules call for a comma, but one will be needed to prevent misreading or to emphasize an important idea.

> What she does, does matter to us. (clarity)

> It may be those who do most, dream most. (emphasis) —Stephen Leacock

Avoid Overusing Commas

The commas (in **red**) below are used incorrectly. Do *not* use a comma between the subject and its verb or the verb and its object.

> Current periodicals on the subject of psychology, are available at nearly all bookstores.

> I think she should read, *Psychology Today.*

Do *not* use a comma before an indirect quotation.

> My roommate said, that she doesn't understand the notes I took.

Semicolon

To Join Two Independent Clauses

Use a **semicolon** to join two or more closely related independent clauses that are not connected with a coordinating conjunction. In other words, each of the clauses could stand alone as a separate sentence.

> Below a certain point, if you keep too quiet, people no longer see you as thoughtful or deep; they simply forget you.
>
> —Douglas Coupland

Before Conjunctive Adverbs

Use a semicolon before a conjunctive adverb when the word clarifies the relationship between two independent clauses in a compound sentence. A comma often follows the conjunctive adverb. If you move the conjunctive adverb to another spot in the second clause, the semicolon must remain between the two independent clauses and the conjunctive adverb placed within commas. Common conjunctive adverbs include *also, besides, however, instead, meanwhile, then,* and *therefore.*

> Many university and college students are on their own for the first time; **however,** others are already independent and even have families.

> Many university and college students are on their own for the first time; others are already independent, **however,** and even have families.

Before Transitional Phrases

Use a semicolon before a transitional phrase when the phrase clarifies the relationship between two independent clauses in a compound sentence. A comma usually follows the transitional phrase.

> Pablo was born in the Andes; **as a result,** he loves mountains.

Transitional Phrases

after all	at the same time	in addition	in the first place
as a matter of fact	even so	in conclusion	on the contrary
as a result	for example	in fact	on the other hand

To Separate Independent Clauses Containing Commas

Use a semicolon to separate independent clauses that contain internal commas, even when the independent clauses are connected by a coordinating conjunction.

> Your MP3 player, computer, bike, and other valuables are expensive to replace; so include these items in your homeowner's insurance policy and remember to use the locks on your door, bike, and storage area.

To Separate Items in a Series That Contains Commas

Use a semicolon to separate items in a series that already contain commas.

> My favourite foods are pizza with pepperoni, onions, and olives; peanut butter and banana sandwiches; and liver with bacon, peppers, and onions.

Colon

614.1 After Salutations

Use a **colon** after the salutation of a business letter.

    Dear Ms. Polley: Dear Professor Higgins: Dear Members:

614.2 Between Numbers Indicating Time or Ratios

Use a colon between the hours, minutes, and seconds of a number indicating time.

    8:30 p.m.   9:45 a.m.   10:24:55

Use a colon between two numbers in a ratio.

    The ratio of computers to students is 1:20. (one to twenty)

614.3 For Emphasis

Use a colon to emphasize a word, a phrase, a clause, or a sentence that explains or adds impact to the main clause.

    I have one goal for myself: to become the first person in my family to graduate from college.

614.4 To Distinguish Parts of Publications

Use a colon between a title and a subtitle, volume and page, and chapter and verse.

    Canada and Its Americas: Transnational Navigations   *Britannica* 4: 211   Psalm 23:1–6

614.5 To Introduce Quotations

Use a colon to introduce a quotation following a complete sentence.

    John Locke is credited with this prescription for a good life: "A sound mind in a sound body."

    Lou Gottlieb, however, offered this version: "A sound mind or a sound body—take your pick."

614.6 To Introduce a List

Use a colon to introduce a list following a complete sentence.

    A student needs a number of things to succeed: basic skills, creativity, and determination.

Avoid Colon Errors

Do *not* use a colon between a verb and its object or complement.

    Dave likes: comfortable space and time to think. **(Incorrect)**

    Dave likes two things: comfortable space and time to think. **(Correct)**

Hyphen

In Compound Words   615.1

Use a **hyphen** to make some compound words.

great-great-grandfather (noun)   starry-eyed (adjective)

mother-in-law (noun)   three-year-old (adjective)

Writers sometimes combine words in new and unexpected ways. Such combinations are usually hyphenated.

> And they pried pieces of **baked-too-fast** sunshine cake from the roofs of their mouths and looked once more into the boy's eyes.
>
> —Toni Morrison, *Song of Solomon*

Note: Consult a dictionary to find how it lists a particular compound word. Some compound words (*living room*) do not use a hyphen and are written separately. Some are written solid (*bedroom*). Some do not use a hyphen when the word is a noun (*ice cream*) but do use a hyphen when it is a verb or an adjective (*ice-cream sundae*).

To Join Letters and Words   615.2

Use a hyphen to join a capital letter or a lowercase letter to a noun or a participle.

T-shirt   U-turn   V-shaped   X-ray   Y-axis

To Join Words in Compound Numbers   615.3

Use a hyphen to join the words in compound numbers from twenty-one to ninety-nine when it is necessary to write them out. (See 631.1.)

Forty-two people found seats in the cramped classroom.

Between Numbers in Fractions   615.4

Use a hyphen between the numerator and the denominator of a fraction, but not when one or both of these elements are already hyphenated.

four-tenths   five-sixteenths   seven thirty-seconds (7/32)

In a Special Series   615.5

Use a hyphen when two or more words have a common element that is omitted in all but the last term.

We have cedar posts in **four-**, **six-**, and **eight-**inch widths.

To Create New Words   615.6

Use a hyphen to form new words beginning with the prefixes *self, ex, all,* and *half.* Also use a hyphen to join any prefix to a proper noun, a proper adjective, or the official name of an office.

post-Depression   mid-May   ex-mayor

616.1

To Prevent Confusion

Use a hyphen with prefixes or suffixes to avoid confusion or awkward spelling.

re-cover (not *recover*) the sofa   **shell-like** (not *shelllike*) shape

616.2

To Join Numbers

Use a hyphen to join numbers indicating a range, a score, or a vote.

Students study **30-40** hours a week.   The final score was **84-82**.

616.3

To Divide Words

Use a hyphen to divide a word between syllables at the end of a line of print.

Guidelines for Word Division

1. Leave enough of the word at the end of the line to identify the word.
2. Never divide a one-syllable word: **rained, skills, through.**
3. Avoid dividing a word of five or fewer letters: **paper, study, July.**
4. Never divide a one-letter syllable from the rest of the word: **omit-ted,** not **o-mitted.**
5. Always divide a compound word between its basic units: **sister-in-law,** not **sis-ter-in-law.**
6. Never divide abbreviations or contractions: **shouldn't,** not **should-n't.**
7. When a vowel is a syllable by itself, divide the word after the vowel: **epi-sode,** not **ep-isode.**
8. Avoid dividing a numeral: **1,000,000,** not **1,000,-000.**
9. Avoid dividing the last word in a paragraph.
10. Never divide the last word in more than two lines in a row.
11. Check a dictionary for acceptable word divisions.

616.4

To Form Adjectives

Use a hyphen to join two or more words that serve as a single-thought adjective before a noun.

Case can see that **oil-painted** wonder now, a few hundred yards off at the end of the dusty buggy track down which he is tramping, a **two-storey** frame house with a long gallery porch running along its entire front.

—Guy Vanderhaeghe, *A Good Man*

Most single-thought adjectives are not hyphenated when they come after the noun. (Check the dictionary to be sure.)

The frame house was **oil painted** and **two storeyed**.

Note: When the first of these words is an adverb ending in *ly*, do not use a hyphen. Also, do not use a hyphen when a number or a letter is the final element in a single-thought adjective.

fresh**ly** painted barn   grade **A** milk (letter is the final element)

Dash

To Set Off Nonessential Elements

Use a **dash** to set off nonessential elements—explanations, examples, or definitions—when you want to emphasize them.

> Near the semester's end—**and this is not always due to poor planning**—some students may find themselves in academic trouble.

> The term *caveat emptor*—**let the buyer beware**—is especially appropriate to Internet shopping.

Note: A dash is indicated by two hyphens--with no spacing before or after--in typewriter-generated material. Don't use a single hyphen when a dash (two hyphens) is required.

To Set Off an Introductory Series

Use a dash to set off an introductory series from the clause that explains the series.

> **Cereal, coffee, and Facebook**—without these I can't get going in the morning.

To Show Missing Text

Use a dash to show that words or letters are missing.

> **Mr. —** won't let us marry.
>
> —Alice Walker, *The Color Purple*

To Show Interrupted Speech

Use a dash (or an ellipsis) to show interrupted or faltering speech in dialogue. (Also see 606.3.)

> Well, I—**ah**—**had** this terrible case of the flu, **and**—**then**—**ah**—**the** library closed because of that flash flood, **and**—**well**—**the** high humidity jammed my printer.
>
> —Excuse No. 101

> "If you *think* you can—"
> "Oh, I *know*—"
> "Don't interrupt!"

For Emphasis

Use a dash in place of a colon to introduce or to emphasize a word, a series, a phrase, or a clause.

> **Jogging**—that's what he lives for.

> **Life is like a grindstone**—whether it grinds you down or polishes you up depends on what you're made of.

> **This is how the world moves**—not like an arrow, but a boomerang.
>
> —Ralph Ellison

Quotation Marks

618.1

To Punctuate Titles

Use **quotation marks** to punctuate some titles, generally titles of shorter works. (Also see 620.2.)

"A Wilderness Station" (short story)
"Saving the Planet One Swamp at a Time" (newspaper article)
"Deeper Understanding" (song)
"In the Company of Whales" (magazine article)
"The Postmodern Challenge to Boundaries" (chapter in a book)
"Murdoch at the Opera" (television episode from *Murdoch Mysteries*)
"Said the Canoe" (short poem)

618.2

For Special Words

Use quotation marks (1) to show that a word is being discussed as a word, (2) to indicate that a word or phrase is directly quoted, (3) to indicate that a word is slang, or (4) to point out that a word is being used in a humorous or ironic way.

1. A commentary on the times is that the word **"honesty"** is now preceded by **"old-fashioned."**

2. She said she was **"incensed."**

3. I drank a Dixie and ate bar peanuts and asked the bartender where I could hear **"chanky-chank,"** as Cajuns call their music. —William Least Heat-Moon, *Blue Highways*

4. In an attempt to be popular, he works very hard at being **"cute."**

618.3

Placement of Periods or Commas

Generally, the North American practice is to place periods and commas inside quotation marks, with the exception of quotations followed by in-text citations (pages 494–495). The British practice, however, is the opposite. Whatever choice you make, be consistent.

He decided to fake a laugh. "I tell myself," he said loudly to her, to the earrings, to the wallpaper, "that I've been unlucky." —Carol Shields, *The Republic of Love*

618.4

Placement of Exclamation Points or Question Marks

Place an exclamation point or a question mark inside quotation marks when it punctuates both the main sentence and the quotation *or* just the quotation; place it outside when it punctuates the main sentence.

Do you often ask yourself, "What should I be?"

I almost croaked when he asked, "That won't be a problem, will it?"

Did he really say, "Finish this by tomorrow"?

618.5

Placement of Semicolons or Colons

Always place semicolons or colons outside quotation marks.

I just read "Computers and Creativity"; I now have some different ideas about the role of computers in the arts.

A Closer Look
Marking Quoted Material

For Direct Quotations

Use quotation marks before and after a direct quotation—a person's exact words.

Sitting in my one-room apartment, I remember Mom saying, **"Don't go to the party with him."**

Note: Do *not* use quotation marks for *indirect* quotations.

I remember Mom saying **that I should not date him.** (These are not the speaker's exact words.)

For Quoted Passages

Use quotation marks before and after a quoted passage. Any word that is not part of the original quotation must be placed inside brackets.

(Original) First of all, it must accept responsibility for providing shelter for the homeless.

(Quotation) "First of all, it **[the federal government]** must accept responsibility for providing shelter for the homeless."

Note: If you quote only part of the original passage, be sure to construct a sentence that is both accurate and grammatically correct.

The report goes on to say that the federal government **"must accept responsibility for providing shelter for the homeless."**

For Long Quotations

If more than one paragraph is quoted, quotation marks are placed before each paragraph and at the end of the last paragraph **(Example A).** Quotations that are five or more lines (MLA style) or forty words or more (APA style) are usually set off from the text by indenting ten spaces from the left margin (a style called "block form"). Do not use quotation marks before or after a block-form quotation **(Example B),** except in cases where quotation marks appear in the original passage **(Example C).**

Example A   *fig. 30.1*

Example B   *fig. 30.2*

Example C   *fig. 30.3*

For Quoting Quotations

Use single quotation marks to punctuate quoted material within a quotation.

"I was lucky," said Jane. **"The proctor announced, 'Put your pencils down,'** just as I was filling in the last answer."

Italics (Underlining)

620.1

In Handwritten and Printed Material

Italics is a printer's term for type that is slightly slanted. In material that is handwritten or typed on a machine that cannot print in italics, underline each word or letter that should be in italics.

> In <u>A Good Man</u>, Wesley Case navigates the complex politics of the Canada–U.S. border in the West after the American Civil War. (typed or handwritten)

> Guy Vanderhaeghe's *A Good Man* centres on the relationship between Ada Tarr and Wesley Case. (printed)

620.2

In Titles

Use italics to indicate the titles of magazines, newspapers, books, pamphlets, full-length plays, films, videos, radio and television programs, book-length poems, ballets, operas, lengthy musical compositions, CDs, paintings and sculptures, legal cases, websites, and the names of ships and aircraft. (Also see 618.1)

Maclean's (magazine)	*The National Post* (newspaper)
Three Day Road (book)	*Much Ado About Nothing* (play)
Silver Dart (airplane)	*The Suburbs* (album)
Away from Her (film)	*Billy the Kid* (ballet)
Murdoch Mysteries (TV program)	*The Thinker* (sculpture)
Financing Your Education (pamphlet)	*GeoCities* (website)

When one title appears within another title, punctuate as follows:

> **I read an article entitled "The Making of *Up*."** (title of movie in an article title)

> **She loves Jane Austen so much that she bought *The Making of* Pride and Prejudice, a book about the BBC miniseries starring Jennifer Ehle and Colin Firth.**
> (Title of TV miniseries in title of book)

620.3

For Key Terms

Italics are often used for a important or technical term, especially when it is followed by its definition. Italicize the term the first time it is used. Thereafter, put the term in roman type.

> This flower has a **zygomorphic** (bilateral symmetry) structure.

620.4

For Foreign Words and Scientific Names

Use italics for foreign words that have not been adopted into the English language; italics are also used to denote scientific names.

> Say **arrivederci** to your fears and try new activities. (foreign word)

> The voyageurs discovered the shy **Castor canadensis**, or North American beaver. (scientific name)

Parentheses

To Enclose Explanatory or Supplementary Material   621.1

Use **parentheses** to enclose explanatory or supplementary material that interrupts the normal sentence structure.

> DART (the Disaster Assistance Response Team) rushed to the earthquake zone immediately after the quake.

To Set Off Numbers in a List   621.2

Use parentheses to set off numbers used with a series of words or phrases.

> Dr. Beck told us **(1)** plan ahead, **(2)** stay flexible, and **(3)** follow through.

For Parenthetical Sentences   621.3

When using a full "sentence" within another sentence, do not capitalize it or use a period inside the parentheses.

> Your friend doesn't have the assignment **(he was just thinking about calling you)**, so you'll have to make a few more calls.

When the parenthetical sentence comes after the main sentence, capitalize and punctuate it the same way you would any other complete sentence.

> But Mom doesn't say boo to Dad; she's always sweet to him. **(Actually she's sort of sweet to everybody.)**
> —Norma Fox Mazer, *Up on Fong Mountain*

To Set Off References   621.4

Use parentheses to set off references to authors, titles, pages, and years.

> The statistics are alarming **(see page 9)** and demand action.

> **Note:** For unavoidable parentheses within parentheses (. . . [. . .] . . .), use brackets. Avoid overuse of parentheses by using commas instead.

Diagonal

To Form Fractions or Show Choices   621.5

Use a **diagonal** (also called a *slash*) to form a fraction. Also place a diagonal between two words to indicate that either is acceptable.

> My **walking/running** shoe size is **5 1/2**; my dress shoes are **6 1/2**.

When Quoting Poetry   621.6

When quoting poetry, use a diagonal (with one space before and after) to show where each line ends in the actual poem.

> We remember the time around scars, / they freeze irrelevant emotions / and divide us from present friends.
> —Michael Ondaatje, "The Time Around Scars"

Brackets

622.1 With Words That Clarify

Use **brackets** before and after words that are added to clarify what another person has said or written.

> "Somewhere out in the country they [**the horses**] would lose the sound of each other's bells."
> —Alice Munro, "Carried Away"

> **Note:** The brackets indicate that the words *the horses* are not part of the original quotation but were added for clarification. (See 619.2.)

622.2 Around Comments by Someone Other Than the Author

Place brackets around comments that have been added by someone other than the author or speaker.

> "In conclusion, *docendo discimus*. Let the school year begin!" [**Huh?**]

622.3 Around Editorial Corrections

Place brackets around an editorial correction or addition.

> "In the recent XL tainted beef scandal, Alberta had 25 percent of food poisoning [**victims**] nationwide," said the Health Canada spokesperson.

622.4 Around the Word *Sic*

Brackets should be placed around the word *sic* (Latin for "so" or "thus") in quoted material; the word indicates that an error appearing in the quoted material was made by the original speaker or writer.

> "There is a higher principal [**sic**] at stake here: Is the school administration aware of the situation?"

Exclamation Point

622.5 To Express Strong Feeling

Use an **exclamation point** to express strong feeling. It may be placed at the end of a sentence (or an elliptical expression that stands for a sentence). Use exclamation points sparingly.

> They're all chanting "Song! Song!" at the top of their lungs, and Celeste appears to be contemplating burying her face in Mother's skirts. "Gentleman! Gentleman! Please! Please, gentleman!" Gradually, the clamour dies down.
> —Guy Vanderhaeghe, *A Good Man*

> Su-su-something's crawling up the back of my neck!
> —Mark Twain, *Roughing It*

> She was on tiptoe, stretching for an orange, when they heard, "**HEY YOU!**"
> —Beverley Naidoo, *Journey to Jo'burg*

Apostrophe

In Contractions

623.1

Use an **apostrophe** to show that one or more letters have been left out of two words joined to form a contraction.

don't → **o** is left out   **she'd** → **woul** is left out   **it's** → **i** or **ha** is left out

> **Note:** An apostrophe is also used to show that one or more numerals or letters have been left out of numbers or words.
>
> class of '18 → **20** is left out   good **mornin'** → **g** is left out

To Form Singular Possessives

623.2

The possessive form of singular nouns is usually made by adding an apostrophe and an s.

Spock's ears   my **computer's** memory

> **Note:** When a singular noun of more than one syllable ends with an *s* or a *z* sound, the possessive may be formed by adding just an apostrophe—or an apostrophe and an *s*.

When the singular noun is a one-syllable word, however, the possessive is usually formed by adding both an apostrophe and an *s*.

Carlos' books *or* **Carlos's** books (two-syllable word)

Rush's next concert   my **boss's** generosity (one-syllable words)

To Form Plural Possessives

623.3

The possessive form of plural nouns ending in s is made by adding just an apostrophe.

the **Joneses'** great-grandfather   **bosses'** offices

> **Note:** For plural nouns not ending in *s*, add an apostrophe and *s*.
>
> **women's** health issues   **children's** program

To Determine Ownership

You will punctuate possessives correctly if you remember that the word that comes immediately before the apostrophe is the owner.

girl's guitar *(girl is the owner)*   **girls'** guitar *(girls are the owners)*

boss's office *(boss is the owner)*   **bosses'** office *(bosses are the owners)*

624.1 To Show Shared Possession

When possession is shared by more than one noun, use the possessive form for the last noun in the series.

> Jason, Kamil, and **Elana's** sound system
> (All three own the same system.)

> **Jason's, Kamil's, and Elana's** sound systems
> (Each owns a separate system.)

624.2 In Compound Nouns

The possessive of a compound noun is formed by placing the possessive ending after the last word.

> his **mother-in-law's** name (singular)
> the **governor general's duties** (singular)

> their **mothers-in-law's** names (plural)
> the **governors general's duties** (plural)

624.3 With Indefinite Pronouns

The possessive form of an indefinite pronoun is made by adding an apostrophe and an *s* to the pronoun. (See 571.4.)

> **everybody's** grades   **no one's** mistake   **one's** choice

In expressions using *else*, add the apostrophe and *s* after the last word.

> **anyone else's**   **somebody else's**

624.4 To Show Time or Amount

Use an apostrophe and an *s* with an adjective that is part of an expression indicating time or amount.

> **yesterday's** news   a **day's** wage   a **month's** pay

624.5

Punctuation Marks

´ (é)	Accent, acute	:	Colon	¶	Paragraph
` (è)	Accent, grave	,	Comma	( )	Parentheses
< >	Angle brackets	†	Dagger	.	Period
'	Apostrophe	—	Dash	?	Question mark
*	Asterisk	/	Diagonal/slash	" "	Quotation marks
{ }	Braces	(ä)	Dieresis	§	Section
[ ]	Brackets	...	Ellipsis	;	Semicolon
^	Caret	!	Exclamation point	˜ (ñ)	Tilde
ç	Cedilla	-	Hyphen	___	Underscore
^ (â)	Circumflex	.....	Leaders		

Chapter 31

Checking Mechanics

"There are few, if any, Canadian men that have never spelled their name in a snow bank."
—Douglas Coupland

Capitalization

Proper Nouns and Adjectives

625.1

Capitalize all proper nouns and all proper adjectives (adjectives derived from proper nouns). The chart below provides a quick overview of capitalization rules. The pages following explain specific or special uses of capitalization.

Capitalization at a Glance

Days of the week . . . . Sunday, Monday, Tuesday
Months . . . . June, July, August
Holidays, holy days . . . . .Thanksgiving, Easter, Hanukkah
Periods, events in history . . . . Middle Ages, World War I
Special events . . . . 2012 Olympics Closing Ceremony
Political parties . . . . Conservative Party, New Democratic Party
Official documents . . . . .Canadian Charter of Rights and Freedoms
Trade names . . . . Maple Leaf hot dogs, Honda Civic
Formal epithets . . . . .Alexander the Great
Official titles . . . . .Mayor Naheed Nenshi
Geographical names
 Planets, heavenly bodies . . . . Earth, Jupiter, the Milky Way
 Continents . . . . Australia, South America
 Countries . . . . Ireland, Grenada, Sri Lanka
 Provinces, states . . . . Nova Scotia, Ontario, Oregon
 Cities, towns, villages . . . . Winnipeg, Wolfville, Selkirk
 Streets, roads, highways . . . . Bay Street, Highway 5
 Sections of Canada
 and the world . . . . the North, the Far East
 Landforms . . . . the Rocky Mountains, the Boreal Forest
 Bodies of water . . . . the Nile River, Lake Superior, Dingman Creek
 Public areas . . . . Halifax Citadel, Banff National Park

626.1   First Words

Capitalize the first word in every sentence and the first word in a full-sentence direct quotation. (Also see 619.1.)

Attending the orientation for new students is a good idea.

Max suggested, "**Let's** take the guided tour of the campus first."

626.2   Sentences in Parentheses

Capitalize the first word in a sentence that is enclosed in parentheses if that sentence is not contained within another complete sentence.

The bookstore has the software. (**Now** all I need is the computer.)

Note: Do *not* capitalize a sentence that is enclosed in parentheses and is located in the middle of another sentence. (Also see 621.3.)

Your school will probably offer everything (**this** includes general access to a computer) that you'll need for a successful year.

626.3   Sentences Following Colons

Capitalize a complete sentence that follows a colon when that sentence is a formal statement, a quotation, or a sentence that you want to emphasize. (Also see 614.5.)

Sydney Harris had this to say about computers: "**The** real danger is not that computers will begin to think like people, but that people will begin to think like computers."

626.4   Salutation and Complimentary Closing

In a letter, capitalize the first and all major words of the salutation. Capitalize only the first word of the complimentary closing.

Dear Personnel Director: **Sincerely** yours,

626.5   Sections of the Country

Words that indicate sections of the country are proper nouns and should be capitalized; words that simply indicate direction are not proper nouns.

Many Newfoundlanders work in the **West.** (section of the country)

We headed **west** for our summer road trip. (direction)

626.6   Languages, Ethnic Groups, Nationalities, and Religions

Capitalize languages, ethnic groups, nationalities, and religions.

African Canadian   Latino   Mohawk   French   Islam

Nouns that refer to the Supreme Being and holy books are capitalized.

God   Allah   Jehovah   the Koran   Exodus   the Bible

Titles

Capitalize the first word of a title, the last word, and every word in between except articles (*a, an, the*), short prepositions, *to* in an infinitive, and coordinating conjunctions. Follow this rule for titles of books, newspapers, magazines, poems, plays, songs, articles, films, works of art, and stories.

Death Comes to Pemberley	*Vancouver Sun*
"The Cariboo Horses"	"It's 'Apartheid' Time Again. Pick Your Villain."
A Midsummer Night's Dream	*The Lord of the Rings*

Note: When citing titles in a bibliography, check the style manual you've been asked to follow. For example, in APA style, only the first word of a title is capitalized.

Organizations

Capitalize the name of an organization or a team and its members.

Assembly of First Nations	**Liberal Party**
Winnipeg Jets	**Beothuk Street Players**

Abbreviations

Capitalize abbreviations of titles and organizations. (Some other abbreviations are also capitalized. See pages 633–634.) (Also see 605.2.)

M.D.   Ph.D.   NATO   C.E.   B.C.E.   GPA

Letters

Capitalize letters used to indicate a form or shape.

U-turn   **I**-beam   **S**-curve   **V**-shaped   **T**-shirt

Words Used as Names

Capitalize words like *father, mother, uncle, senator,* and *professor* when they are parts of titles that include a personal name or when they are substituted for proper nouns (especially in direct address). (Also see 611.3.)

We submitted our request to **Senator** Marjorie LeBreton. (*Senator* is part of the name.)

We were hoping that the **senators** would allow us to make a presentation to their standing committee on Aboriginal peoples.

Who was your chemistry **professor** last quarter?
I had **Professor** Williams for Chemistry 101.

Note: To test whether a word is being substituted for a proper noun, simply read the sentence with a proper noun in place of the word. If the proper noun fits in the sentence, the word being tested should be capitalized. Usually the word is not capitalized if it follows a possessive—*my, his, our, your,* and so on.

Did **Dad (Brad)** pack the stereo in the trailer? (Brad works in this sentence.)

Did your **dad (Brad)** pack the stereo in the trailer? (*Brad* does not work in this sentence; the word *dad* follows the possessive *your.*)

628.1 Titles of Courses

Words such as *technology, history,* and *science* are proper nouns when they are included in the titles of specific courses; they are common nouns when they name a field of study.

> Who teaches **Art History 202?** (title of a specific course)
>
> Professor Bunker loves teaching **history.** (a field of study)

Note: The words *freshman, sophomore, junior,* and *senior* (used routinely in the United States) are not capitalized unless they are part of an official title.

> The **seniors** who maintained high GPAs were honoured at the **Mount Mary Senior Honours Banquet.**

628.2 Internet and Email

The words *Internet* and *World Wide Web* are always capitalized because they are considered proper nouns. When your writing includes a Web address (URL), capitalize any letters that the site's owner does (on printed materials or on the site itself). Not only is it respectful to reprint a Web address exactly as it appears elsewhere, but, in fact, some Web addresses are case-sensitive and must be entered into a browser's address bar exactly as presented.

> When doing research on the **Internet,** be sure to record each site's **Web** address **(URL)** and each contact's **email** address.

Note: Some people include capital letters in their email addresses to make certain features evident. Although email addresses are not case-sensitive, repeat each letter in print just as its owner uses it.

Avoid Capitalization Errors

Do not capitalize any of the following:

- A prefix attached to a proper noun
- Seasons of the year
- Words used to indicate direction or position
- Common nouns and titles that appear near, but are not part of, a proper noun

Capitalize	Do Not Capitalize
Canadian	un-Canadian
January, February	winter, spring
The West is quite conservative.	Turn west at the stop sign.
University of Toronto	a Toronto university
Chancellor John Bohm	John Bohm, our chancellor
Prime Minister Harper	the prime minister of Canada
Earth (the planet)	earthmover
Internet	email

Plurals

Nouns Ending in a Consonant 629.1

Some nouns remain unchanged when used as plurals (*species, moose, halibut,* and so on), but the plurals of most nouns are formed by adding an *s* to the singular form.

> dorm—**dorms**   credit—**credits**   midterm—**midterms**

The plurals of nouns ending in *sh, ch, x, s,* and *z* are made by adding *es* to the singular form.

> lunch—**lunches**   wish—**wishes**   class—**classes**

Nouns Ending in *y* 629.2

The plurals of common nouns that end in *y* (preceded by a consonant) are formed by changing the *y* to *i* and adding *es.*

> dormitory—**dormitories**   sorority—**sororities**   duty—**duties**

The plurals of common nouns that end in *y* (preceded by a vowel) are formed by adding only an s.

> attorney—**attorneys**   monkey—**monkeys**   toy—**toys**

The plurals of all proper nouns ending in *y* (whether preceded by a consonant or a vowel) are formed by adding an *s.*

> the three **Kathys**   the five **Faheys**

Nouns Ending in *o* 629.3

The plurals of words ending in *o* (preceded by a vowel) are formed by adding an *s.*

> radio—**radios**   cameo—**cameos**   studio—**studios**

The plurals of most nouns ending in *o* (preceded by a consonant) are formed by adding *es.*

> echo—**echoes**   hero—**heroes**   tomato—**tomatoes**

Musical terms always form plurals by adding an *s;* check a dictionary for other words of this type.

> alto—**altos**   banjo—**banjos**   solo—**solos**   piano—**pianos**

Nouns Ending in *f* or *fe* 629.4

The plurals of nouns that end in *f* or *fe* are formed in one of two ways: If the final *f* sound is still heard in the plural form of the word, simply add *s;* if the final sound is a *v* sound, change the *f* to *ve* and add an *s.*

> **Plural ends with *f* sound:** roof—**roofs**   chief—**chiefs**
> **Plural ends with *v* sound:** wife—**wives**   loaf—**loaves**

Note: The plurals of some nouns that end in *f* or *fe* can be formed by either adding *s* or changing the *f* to *ve* and adding an *s.*

> **Plural ends with either sound:** hoof—**hoofs, hooves**

630.1 Irregular Spelling

Many foreign words (as well as some of English origin) form a plural by taking on an irregular spelling; others are now acceptable with the commonly used *s* or *es* ending. Take time to check a dictionary.

child—**children**	alumnus—**alumni**	syllabus—**syllabi, syllabuses**
goose—**geese**	datum—**data**	radius—**radii, radiuses**

630.2 Words Discussed as Words

The plurals of symbols, letters, figures, and words discussed as words are formed by adding an *s*.

Many schools have now added **A/Bs** and **B/Cs** as standard grades.

630.3 Nouns Ending in *ful*

The plurals of nouns that end with *ful* are formed by adding an *s* at the end of the word.

three **teaspoonfuls**   two **tankfuls**   four **bagfuls**

630.4 Compound Nouns

The plurals of compound nouns are usually formed by adding an *s* or an *es* to the important word in the compound. (Also see 615.1.)

brothers-in-law   **maids** of honour   **secretaries** of state

630.5 Collective Nouns

Collective nouns do not change in form when they are used as plurals.

class (a unit—singular form)

class (individual members—plural form)

Because the spelling of the collective noun does not change, it is often the pronoun used in place of the collective noun that indicates whether the noun is singular or plural. Use a singular pronoun (**its**) to show that the collective noun is singular. Use a plural pronoun (**their**) to show that the collective noun is plural.

The class needs to change **its** motto.

(The writer is thinking of the group as a unit.)

The class brainstormed with **their** professor.

(The writer is thinking of the group as individuals.)

> **ell Note:** To determine whether a plural requires the article *the*, you must first determine whether it is definite or indefinite. Definite plurals use *the*, whereas indefinite plurals do not require any article. (See 656.3–657.1.)

Numbers

Numerals or Words

Numbers from one to one hundred are usually written as words; numbers 101 and greater are usually written as numerals. (APA style uses numerals for numbers 10 and higher.) Hyphenate numbers written as two words if less than one hundred.

two   seven   ten   twenty-five   106   1,079

The same rule applies to the use of ordinal numbers.

second   tenth   twenty-fifth   ninety-eighth   106th   333rd

If numbers greater than 101 are used infrequently in a piece of writing, you may spell out those that can be written in one or two words.

two hundred   fifty thousand   six billion

You may use a combination of numerals and words for very large numbers.

1.5 million   3 billion to 3.2 billion   6 trillion

Numbers being compared or contrasted should be kept in the same style.

8 to **11** years old *or* **eight** to **eleven** years old

Particular decades may be spelled out or written as numerals.

the **'80s** and **'90s** *or* the **eighties** and **nineties**

Numerals Only

Use numerals for the following forms: decimals, percentages, pages, chapters (and other parts of a book), addresses, dates, telephone numbers, identification numbers, and statistics.

26.2	**8** percent	Chapter **7**
pages **287–289**	Highway **36**	**(212) 555–1234**
398-555-001	a vote of **23** to **4**	May **8, 2007**

Note: Abbreviations and symbols are often used in charts, graphs, footnotes, and so forth, but typically they are not used in texts.

He weighs **forty-five kilograms** and is **ten years old.**

She walked **three kilometres** to work through **twelve centimetres** of snow.

However, abbreviations and symbols may be used in scientific, mathematical, statistical, and technical texts (APA style).

Between **20%** and **23%** of the cultures yielded positive results.

Your **245B** model requires **220V.**

Always use numerals with abbreviations and symbols.

5'4"   8%   10 cm   3 tbsp.   12.7 kg   32°C

Use numerals after the name of local branches of labour unions.

Canadian Union of Public Employees, Local **23**

632.1 Hyphenated Numbers

Hyphens are used to form compound modifiers indicating measurement. They are also used for inclusive numbers and written-out fractions.

a **three-kilometre** trip   the **2001–2005** presidential term

a **ten-kilogram** bag of flour   **one-sixth** of the pie

a **three-metre** clearance   **three-eighths** of the book

632.2 Time and Money

If time is expressed with an abbreviation, use numerals; if it is expressed in words, spell out the number.

4:00 a.m. *or* **four** o'clock (not 4 o'clock)

the **5:15** p.m. train

a **seven o'clock** wake-up call

If money is expressed with a symbol, use numerals; if the currency is expressed in words, spell out the number.

$20 or **twenty** dollars (not 20 dollars)

Abbreviations of time and of money may be used in text.

The concert begins at **7:00** p.m., and tickets cost **$30**.

632.3 Words Only

Use words to express numbers that begin a sentence.

Fourteen students "forgot" their assignments.

Three hundred contest entries were received.

Note: Change the sentence structure if this rule creates a clumsy construction.

Six hundred and **thirty-nine** students are new to the campus this fall. (Clumsy)

This fall, **639** students are new to the campus. (Better)

Use words for numbers that precede a compound modifier that includes a numeral. (If the compound modifier uses a spelled-out number, use numerals in front of it.)

She sold **twenty 35-millimetre** cameras in one day.

The chef prepared **24 thirty-gram** meatballs.

Use words for the names of numbered streets of one hundred or less.

Ninth Avenue

123 Forty-fourth Street

Use words for the names of buildings if that name is also its address.

One Thousand Queen Street   **Two Fifty Pearson Avenue**

Use words for references to particular centuries.

the twenty-first century   **the fourth century B.C.E.**

Abbreviations

An **abbreviation** is the shortened form of a word or a phrase. These abbreviations are always acceptable in both formal and informal writing:

Mr.   Mrs.   Ms.   Dr.   Jr.   a.m. (A.M.)   p.m. (P.M.)

Note: In formal writing, do not abbreviate the names of provinces or states, countries, months, days, units of measure, or courses of study. Do not abbreviate the words *Street, Road, Avenue, Company,* and similar words when they are part of a proper name. Also, do not use signs or symbols (%, &, #, @) in place of words. (The dollar sign, however, is appropriate when numerals are used to express an amount of money. See 632.2.)

Also Note: When abbreviations are called for (in charts, lists, bibliographies, notes, and indexes, for example), standard abbreviations are preferred. Reserve the postal abbreviations for postal code addresses.

Correspondence Abbreviations

Canadian Provinces

	Standard	Postal
Alberta	Alta.	AB
British	B.C.	BC
Columbia		
Manitoba	Man.	MB
New Brunswick	N.B.	NB
Newfoundland	N.F.	
and Labrador	Lab.	NL
Northwest		
Territories	N.W.T.	NT
Nova Scotia	N.S.	NS
Nunavut		NU
Ontario	Ont.	ON
Prince Edward		
Island	P.E.I.	PE
Quebec	Que.	QC
Saskatchewan	Sask.	SK
Yukon Territory	Y.T.	YT

Address Abbreviations

	Standard	Postal
Apartment	Apt.	APT
Avenue	Ave.	AVE
Boulevard	Blvd.	BLVD
Circle	Cir.	CIR
Court	Ct.	CT
Drive	Dr.	DR
East	E.	E
Expressway	Expy.	EXPY
Freeway	Frwy.	FWY
Heights	Hts.	HTS
Highway	Hwy.	HWY
Hospital	Hosp.	HOSP
Junction	Junc.	JCT
Lake	L.	LK
Lakes	Ls.	LKS
Lane	Ln.	LN
Meadows	Mdws.	MDWS
North	N.	N
Palms	Palms	PLMS
Park	Pk.	PK

	Standard	Postal
Parkway	Pky.	PKY
Place	Pl.	PL
Plaza	Plaza	PLZ
Post Office Box	P.O. Box	PO BOX
Ridge	Rdg.	RDG
River	R.	RV
Road	Rd.	RD
Room	Rm.	RM
Rural	R.	R
Rural Route	R.R.	RR
Shore	Sh.	SH
South	S.	S
Square	Sq.	SQ
Station	Sta.	STA
Street	St.	ST
Suite	Ste.	STE
Terrace	Ter.	TER
Turnpike	Tpke.	TPKE
Union	Un.	UN
View	View	VW
Village	Vil.	VLG
West	W.	W

U.S. States/Territories

	Standard	Postal
Alabama	Ala.	AL
Alaska	Alaska	AK
Arizona	Ariz.	AZ
Arkansas	Ark.	AR
California	Cal.	CA
Colorado	Colo.	CO
Connecticut	Conn.	CT
Delaware	Del.	DE
District of		
Columbia	D.C.	DC
Florida	Fla.	FL
Georgia	Ga.	GA
Guam	Guam	GU
Hawaii	Hawaii	HI

	Standard	Postal
Idaho	Idaho	ID
Illinois	Ill.	IL
Indiana	Ind.	IN
Iowa	Ia.	IA
Kansas	Kans.	KS
Kentucky	Ky.	KY
Louisiana	La.	LA
Maine	Me.	ME
Maryland	Md.	MD
Massachusetts	Mass.	MA
Michigan	Mich.	MI
Minnesota	Minn.	MN
Mississippi	Miss.	MS
Missouri	Mo.	MO
Montana	Mont.	MT
Nebraska	Neb.	NE
Nevada	Nev.	NV
New		
Hampshire	N.H.	NH
New Jersey	N.J.	NJ
New Mexico	N. Mex.	NM
New York	N.Y.	NY
North Carolina	N.C.	NC
North Dakota	N. Dak.	ND
Ohio	Ohio	OH
Oklahoma	Okla.	OK
Oregon	Ore.	OR
Pennsylvania	Pa.	PA
Puerto Rico	P.R.	PR
Rhode Island	R.I.	RI
South Carolina	S.C.	SC
South Dakota	S. Dak.	SD
Tennessee	Tenn.	TN
Texas	Tex.	TX
Utah	Utah	UT
Vermont	Vt.	VT
Virginia	Va.	VA
Virgin Islands	V.I.	VI
Washington	Wash.	WA
West Virginia	W. Va.	WV
Wisconsin	Wis.	WI
Wyoming	Wyo.	WY

Common Abbreviations

abr. abridged, abridgment
AC, ac alternating current, air-conditioning
ack. acknowledgment
ADT, A.D.T. Atlantic daylight time
AM amplitude modulation
A.M., a.m. before noon (Latin *ante meridiem*)
ASAP as soon as possible
AST, A.S.T. Atlantic standard time
avg., av. average
B.A. bachelor of arts degree
BBB Better Business Bureau
B.C.E. before common era
bibliog. bibliography
biog. biographer, biographical, biography
B.S. bachelor of science degree
C 1. Celsius **2.** centigrade **3.** coulomb
c. 1. circa (about) **2.** cup(s)
cc 1. cubic centimetre **2.** carbon copy **3.** community college
CAD Canadian dollar
CDT, C.D.T. central daylight time
C.E. common era
chap. chapter(s)
cm centimeter(s)
c/o care of
COD, c.o.d. 1. cash on delivery **2.** collect on delivery
co-op cooperative
CST, C.S.T. central standard time
cu 1. cubic **2.** cumulative
d.b.a., d/b/a doing business as
DC, dc direct current
dec. deceased
dept. department
disc. discount
DST, D.S.T. daylight saving time
dup. duplicate
ed. edition, editor
EDT, E.D.T. eastern daylight time
e.g. for example (Latin *exempli gratia*)
EST, E.S.T. eastern standard time
etc. and so forth (Latin *et cetera*)
F Fahrenheit, French, Friday
FM frequency modulation
F.O.B., f.o.b. free on board
FYI for your information
g 1. gravity **2.** gram(s)
gal. gallon(s)
gds. goods
gloss. glossary
GNP gross national product
GPA grade point average
hdqrs. headquarters
HIV human immunodeficiency virus

hp horsepower
Hz hertz
ibid. in the same place (Latin *ibidem*)
id. the same (Latin *idem*)
i.e. that is (Latin *id est*)
illus. illustration
inc. incorporated
IQ, I.Q. intelligence quotient
ISBN International Standard Book Number
JP, J.P. justice of the peace
K 1. kelvin (temperature unit) **2.** Kelvin (temperature scale)
kc kilocycle(s)
kg kilogram(s)
km kilometer(s)
kn knot(s)
kw kilowatt(s)
L litre(s), lake
lat. latitude
l.c. lowercase
lit. literary; literature
log logarithm, logic
long. longitude
Ltd., ltd. limited
m metre(s)
M.A. master of arts degree
man. manual
Mc, mc megacycle
MC master of ceremonies
M.D. doctor of medicine (Latin *medicinae doctor*)
mdse. merchandise
MDT, M.D.T. mountain daylight time
mfg. manufacture, manufacturing
mg milligram(s)
mi. 1. mile(s) **2.** mill(s) (monetary unit)
misc. miscellaneous
mL milliliter(s)
mm millimeter(s)
mpg, m.p.g. miles per gallon
mph, m.p.h. miles per hour
MS 1. manuscript **2.** multiple sclerosis
Ms. title of courtesy for a woman
M.S. master of science degree
MST, M.S.T. mountain standard time
NDT, N.D.T. Newfoundland daylight time
NE northeast
neg. negative
N.S.F., n.s.f. not sufficient funds
NST, N.S.T. Newfoundland standard time
NW northwest

oz, oz. ounce(s)
PA public-address system
pct. percent
pd. paid
PDT, P.D.T. Pacific daylight time
PFC, Pfc. private first class
pg., p. page
Ph.D. doctor of philosophy
PIN personal identification number
P.M., p.m. after noon (Latin *post meridiem*)
POW, P.O.W. prisoner of war
pp. pages
ppd. 1. postpaid **2.** prepaid
PR, P.R. public relations
PSAT Preliminary Scholastic Aptitude Test
psi, p.s.i. pounds per square inch
PST, P.S.T. Pacific standard time
PTA, P.T.A. Parent-Teacher Association
R.A. residence assistant, research assistant
RF radio frequency
R.P.M., rpm revolutions per minute
R.S.V.P., r.s.v.p. please reply (French *répondez s'il vous plaît*)
SAT Scholastic Aptitude Test
SE southeast
SOS 1. international distress signal **2.** any call for help
Sr. 1. senior (after surname) **2.** sister (religious)
SRO, S.R.O. standing room only
std. standard
SW southwest
syn. synonymous, synonym
tbs., tbsp. tablespoon(s)
TM trademark
UHF, uhf ultrahigh frequency
v 1. physics: velocity **2.** volume
V electricity: volt
VHF, vhf very high frequency
VIP informal: very important person
vol. 1. volume **2.** volunteer
vs. versus, verse
W 1. electricity: watt(s) **2.** physics: (also **w**) work **3.** west
whse., whs. warehouse
whsle. wholesale
wkly. weekly
w/o without
wt. weight
www World Wide Web

Acronyms and Initialisms

Acronyms

An **acronym** is a word formed from the first (or first few) letters of words in a set phrase. Even though acronyms are abbreviations, they require no periods.

radar	radio detecting and ranging
CANDU	Canada Deuterium Uranium
CUPE	Canadian Union of Public Employees (pronounced KEW-pee)
DART	Disaster Assistance Response Team
SIN	Social Insurance Number

Initialisms

An **initialism** is similar to an acronym except that the initials used to form this abbreviation are pronounced individually.

CBC	Canadian Broadcasting Corporation
EMT	emergency medical technician
RCMP	Royal Canadian Mounted Police

Common Acronyms and Initialisms

AI	artificial intelligence	**NATO**	North Atlantic Treaty Organization
AIDS	acquired immune deficiency syndrome	**NDP**	New Democratic Party
		NFB	National Film Board
APR	annual percentage rate	**NGO**	non-governmental organization
CAD	computer-aided design	**ORV**	off-road vehicle
CAM	computer-aided manufacturing	**PIN**	personal identification number
CFB	Canadian Forces Base	**POP**	point of purchase
CFCs	chlorofluorocarbons	**PM**	Prime Minister
CRA	Canada Revenue Agency	**PSA**	public service announcement
CSIS	Canadian Security Intelligence Service	**R&D**	research and development
EI	Employment Insurance	**SADD**	Students Against Destructive Decisions
EU	European Union	**SASE**	self-addressed stamped envelope
FAQ	frequently asked question	**SPOT**	satellite positioning and tracking
GHGs	greenhouse gases	**StatsCan**	Statistics Canada
GPS	Global Positioning System	**SUV**	sport-utility vehicle
GST	Goods and Services Tax	**SWAT**	Special Weapons and Tactics
HST	Harmonized Sales Tax	**TDD**	telecommunications device for the deaf
MADD	Mothers Against Drunk Driving	**TMJ**	temporomandibular joint
MP	Member of Parliament	**UPC**	Universal Product Code
NAFTA	North American Free Trade Agreement	**WHO**	World Health Organization

Basic Spelling Rules

As with many other cultural practices, Canadian spelling has been influenced by both British and U.S. conventions. Moreover, as time passes, what is considered acceptable and expected spelling also changes. An American spelling for a term may become typical, or a British spelling may continue to dominate. Consider these pairs, with the first the British spelling and the second American: *aluminium, aluminum; analyse, analyze; centre, center; colour, color; draught, draft; honour, honor; humour, humor; judgement, judgment; neighbour, neighbor; theatre, theater.* A Canadian dictionary (such as the *Oxford Canadian Dictionary*, 2nd edition) will tell you what alternatives are acceptable for a given word; the one listed first is usually the option that is currently preferred. You are encouraged to be consistent within a particular document about spelling words of the same form; for example, if you use *colour*, then use *honour, humour,* and *neighbour.*

636.1 Write *i* Before *e*

Write *i* before *e* except after *c,* or when sounded like *a* as in *neighbour* and *weigh.*

believe   relief   receive   eight

> **Note:** This sentence contains eight exceptions:
> **Neither sheik dared leisurely seize either weird species of financiers.**

636.2 Words with Consonant Endings

When a one-syllable word (*bat*) ends in a consonant (*t*) preceded by one vowel (*a*), double the final consonant before adding a suffix that begins with a vowel (*batting*).

sum—**summary**   god—**goddess**

> **Note:** When a multisyllable word (*control*) ends in a consonant (*l*) preceded by one vowel (*o*), the accent is on the last syllable (*con trol´*), and the suffix begins with a vowel (*ing*)—the same rule holds true: Double the final consonant (*controlling*).
>
> prefer—**preferred**   begin—**beginning**
> forget—**forgettable**   admit—**admittance**

636.3 Words with a Final Silent *e*

If a word ends with a silent *e,* drop the *e* before adding a suffix that begins with a vowel. Do *not* drop the *e* when the suffix begins with a consonant.

state—**stating**—**statement**   like—**liking**—**likeness**
use—**using**—**useful**   nine—**ninety**—**nineteen**

> **Note:** Exceptions are **truly, argument, ninth.**

636.4 Words Ending in *y*

When *y* is the last letter in a word and the *y* is preceded by a consonant, change the *y* to *i* before adding any suffix except those beginning with *i.*

fry—**fries, frying**   hurry—**hurried, hurrying**
lady—**ladies**   ply—**pliable**
happy—**happiness**   beauty—**beautiful**

Note: When forming the plural of a word that ends with a *y* that is preceded by a vowel, add *s*.

toy—**toys**   play—**plays**   monkey—**monkeys**

Tip: Never trust your spelling to even the best spell checker. Carefully proofread and use a dictionary for words you know your spell checker does not cover.

Steps to Becoming a Better Speller

1. **Be patient.** Becoming a good speller takes time.

2. **Check the correct pronunciation of each word you are attempting to spell.**
   Knowing the correct pronunciation of each word can help you to remember its spelling.

3. **Note the meaning and history of each word as you are checking the dictionary for the pronunciation.**
   Knowing the meaning and history of a word provides you with a better notion of how the word is properly used, and it can help you remember the word's spelling.

4. **Before you close the dictionary, practise spelling the word.**
   You can do so by looking away from the page and trying to "see" the word in your "mind's eye." Write the word on a piece of paper. Check the spelling in the dictionary and repeat the process until you are able to spell the word correctly.

5. **Learn some spelling rules.**
   The four rules in this handbook (page 636) are four of the most useful—although there are others.

6. **Make a list of the words that you misspell.**
   Select the first ten words and practise spelling them.
   First: Read each word carefully; then write it on a piece of paper. Look at the written word to see that it's spelled correctly. Repeat the process for those words that you misspelled.
   Then: Ask someone to read the words to you so you can write them again. Then check for misspellings. Repeat both steps with your next ten words.

7. **Write often.**
   As noted educator Frank Smith said,

> *"There is little point in learning to spell
> if you have little intention of writing."*

Commonly Misspelled Words

The commonly misspelled words that follow are hyphenated to show where they would logically be broken at the end of a line.

A

ab-bre-vi-ate
abrupt
ab-scess
ab-sence
ab-so-lute (-ly)
ab-sorb-ent
ab-surd
abun-dance
ac-a-dem-ic
ac-cede
ac-cel-er-ate
ac-cept (-ance)
ac-ces-si-ble
ac-ces-so-ry
ac-ci-den-tal-ly
ac-com-mo-date
ac-com-pa-ny
ac-com-plice
ac-com-plish
ac-cor-dance
ac-cord-ing
ac-count
ac-crued
ac-cu-mu-late
ac-cu-rate
ac-cus-tom (-ed)
ache
achieve (-ment)
ac-knowl-edge
ac-quaint-ance
ac-qui-esce
ac-quired
ac-tu-al
adapt
ad-di-tion (-al)
ad-dress
ad-e-quate
ad-journed
ad-just-ment
ad-mi-ra-ble
ad-mis-si-ble
ad-mit-tance
ad-van-ta-geous
ad-ver-tise-ment
ad-ver-tis-ing

ad-vice (n.)
ad-vis-able
ad-vise (v.)
ad-vis-er
ae-ri-al
af-fect
af-fi-da-vit
a-gainst
ag-gra-vate
ag-gres-sion
a-gree-able
a-gree-ment
aisle
al-co-hol
a-lign-ment
al-ley
al-lot-ted
al-low-ance
all right
al-most
al-ready
al-though
al-to-geth-er
a-lu-mi-num
al-um-nus
al-ways
am-a-teur
a-mend-ment
a-mong
a-mount
a-nal-y-sis
an-a-lyze
an-cient
an-ec-dote
an-es-thet-ic
an-gle
an-ni-hi-late
an-ni-ver-sa-ry
an-nounce
an-noy-ance
an-nu-al
a-noint
a-non-y-mous
an-swer
ant-arc-tic
an-tic-i-pate

anx-i-ety
anx-ious
a-part-ment
a-pol-o-gize
ap-pa-ra-tus
ap-par-ent (-ly)
ap-peal
ap-pear-ance
ap-pe-tite
ap-pli-ance
ap-pli-ca-ble
ap-pli-ca-tion
ap-point-ment
ap-prais-al
ap-pre-ci-ate
ap-proach
ap-pro-pri-ate
ap-prov-al
ap-prox-i-mate-ly
ap-ti-tude
ar-chi-tect
arc-tic
ar-gu-ment
a-rith-me-tic
a-rouse
ar-range-ment
ar-riv-al
ar-ti-cle
ar-ti-fi-cial
as-cend
as-cer-tain
as-i-nine
as-sas-sin
as-sess (-ment)
as-sign-ment
as-sist-ance
as-so-ci-ate
as-so-ci-a-tion
as-sume
as-sur-ance
as-ter-isk
ath-lete
ath-let-ic
at-tach
at-tack (-ed)
at-tempt

at-tend-ance
at-ten-tion
at-ti-tude
at-tor-ney
at-trac-tive
au-di-ble
au-di-ence
au-dit
au-thor-i-ty
au-to-mo-bile
au-tumn
aux-il-ia-ry
a-vail-a-ble
av-er-age
aw-ful
aw-ful-ly
awk-ward

B

bac-ca-lau-re-ate
bach-e-lor
bag-gage
bal-ance
bal-loon
bal-lot
ba-nan-a
ban-dage
bank-rupt
bar-gain
bar-rel
base-ment
ba-sis
bat-tery
beau-ti-ful
beau-ty
be-com-ing
beg-gar
be-gin-ning
be-hav-iour
be-ing
be-lief
be-lieve
ben-e-fi-cial
ben-e-fit (-ed)
be-tween
bi-cy-cle

bis-cuit
bliz-zard
book-keep-er
bought
bouil-lon
bound-a-ry
break-fast
breath (n.)
breathe (v.)
brief
bril-liant
Brit-ain
bro-chure
brought
bruise
bud-get
bul-le-tin
buoy-ant
bu-reau
bur-glar
bury
busi-ness
busy

C

caf-e-te-ria
caf-feine
cal-en-dar
cam-paign
can-celled
can-di-date
can-is-ter
ca-noe
ca-pac-i-ty
cap-i-tal
cap-i-tol
cap-tain
car-bu-ret-or
ca-reer
car-i-ca-ture
car-riage
cash-ier
cas-se-role
cas-u-al-ty
cat-a-logue
ca-tas-tro-phe

caught
cav-al-ry
cel-e-bra-tion
cem-e-ter-y
cen-sus
cen-tu-ry
cer-tain
cer-tif-i-cate
ces-sa-tion
chal-lenge
chan-cel-lor
change-a-ble
char-ac-ter (-is-tic)
chauf-feur
chief
chim-ney
choc-o-late
choice
choose
Chris-tian
cir-cuit
cir-cu-lar
cir-cum-stance
civ-i-li-za-tion
cli-en-tele
cli-mate
climb
clothes
coach
co-coa
co-er-cion
col-lar
col-lat-er-al
col-lege
col-le-giate
col-lo-qui-al
colo-nel
col-our
co-los-sal
col-umn
com-e-dy
com-ing
com-mence
com-mer-cial
com-mis-sion
com-mit
com-mit-ment
com-mit-ted
com-mit-tee
com-mu-ni-cate
com-mu-ni-ty
com-par-a-tive

com-par-i-son
com-pel
com-pe-tent
com-pe-ti-tion
com-pet-i-tive-ly
com-plain
com-ple-ment
com-plete-ly
com-plex-ion
com-pli-ment
com-pro-mise
con-cede
con-ceive
con-cern-ing
con-cert
con-ces-sion
con-clude
con-crete
con-curred
con-cur-rence
con-cur-rence
con-demn
con-de-scend
con-di-tion
con-fer-ence
con-ferred
con-fi-dence
con-fi-den-tial
con-grat-u-late
con-science
con-sci-en-tious
con-scious
con-sen-sus
con-se-quence
con-ser-va-tive
con-sid-er-ably
con-sign-ment
con-sis-tent
con-sti-tu-tion
con-tempt-ible
con-tin-u-al-ly
con-tin-ue
con-tin-u-ous
con-trol
con-tro-ver-sy
con-ven-ience
con-vince
cool-ly
co-op-er-ate
cor-dial
cor-po-ra-tion
cor-re-late
cor-re-spond

cor-re-spond-
  ence
cor-rob-o-rate
cough
coun-cil
coun-sel
coun-ter-feit
coun-try
cour-age
cou-ra-geous
cour-te-ous
cour-te-sy
cous-in
cov-er-age
cred-i-tor
cri-sis
crit-i-cism
crit-i-cize
cru-el
cu-ri-os-i-ty
cu-ri-ous
cur-rent
cur-ric-u-lum
cus-tom
cus-tom-ary
cus-tom-er
cyl-in-der

D

dai-ly
dair-y
dealt
debt-or
de-ceased
de-ceit-ful
de-ceive
de-cid-ed
de-ci-sion
dec-la-ra-tion
dec-o-rate
de-duct-i-ble
de-fend-ant
de-fence
de-ferred
def-i-cit
def-i-nite (-ly)
def-i-ni-tion
del-e-gate
de-li-cious
de-pend-ent
de-pos-i-tor
de-pot

de-scend
de-scribe
de-scrip-tion
de-sert
de-serve
de-sign
de-sir-able
de-sir-ous
de-spair
des-per-ate
de-spise
des-sert
de-te-ri-o-rate
de-ter-mine
de-vel-op
de-vel-op-ment
de-vice
de-vise
di-a-mond
di-a-phragm
di-ar-rhe-a
dic-tio-nary
dif-fer-ence
dif-fer-ent
dif-fi-cul-ty
di-lap-i-dat-ed
di-lem-ma
din-ing
di-plo-ma
di-rec-tor
dis-agree-able
dis-ap-pear
dis-ap-point
dis-ap-prove
dis-as-trous
dis-ci-pline
dis-cov-er
dis-crep-an-cy
dis-cuss
dis-cus-sion
dis-ease
dis-sat-is-fied
dis-si-pate
dis-tin-guish
dis-trib-ute
di-vide
di-vis-i-ble
di-vi-sion
doc-tor
doesn't
dom-i-nant
dor-mi-to-ry

doubt
drudg-ery
du-pli-cate
dye-ing
dy-ing

E

ea-ger-ly
ear-nest
eco-nom-i-cal
econ-o-my
ec-sta-sy
e-di-tion
ef-fer-ves-cent
ef-fi-ca-cy
ef-fi-cien-cy
eighth
ei-ther
e-lab-o-rate
e-lec-tric-i-ty
el-e-phant
el-i-gi-ble
e-lim-i-nate
el-lipse
em-bar-rass
e-mer-gen-cy
em-i-nent
em-pha-size
em-ploy-ee
em-ploy-ment
e-mul-sion
en-close
en-cour-age
en-deav-our
en-dorse-ment
en-gi-neer
En-glish
e-nor-mous
e-nough
en-ter-prise
en-ter-tain
en-thu-si-as-tic
en-tire-ly
en-trance
en-vel-op (v.)
en-ve-lope (n.)
en-vi-ron-ment
equip-ment
equipped
e-quiv-a-lent
es-pe-cial-ly
es-sen-tial

es-tab-lish
es-teemed
et-i-quette
ev-i-dence
ex-ag-ger-ate
ex-ceed
ex-cel-lent
ex-cept
ex-cep-tion-al-ly
ex-ces-sive
ex-cite
ex-ec-u-tive
ex-er-cise
ex-haust (-ed)
ex-hi-bi-tion
ex-hil-a-ra-tion
ex-is-tence
ex-or-bi-tant
ex-pect
ex-pe-di-tion
ex-pend-i-ture
ex-pen-sive
ex-pe-ri-ence
ex-plain
ex-pla-na-tion
ex-pres-sion
ex-qui-site
ex-ten-sion
ex-tinct
ex-traor-di-nar-y
ex-treme-ly

F

fa-cil-i-ties
fal-la-cy
fa-mil-iar
fa-mous
fas-ci-nate
fash-ion
fa-tigue (-d)
fau-cet
fa-vour-ite
fea-si-ble
fea-ture
Feb-ru-ar-y
fed-er-al
fem-i-nine
fer-tile
fic-ti-tious
field
fierce
fi-ery

fi-nal-ly
fi-nan-cial-ly
fo-li-age
for-ci-ble
for-eign
for-feit
for-go
for-mal-ly
for-mer-ly
for-tu-nate
for-ty
for-ward
foun-tain
fourth
frag-ile
fran-ti-cal-ly
freight
friend
ful-fill
fun-da-men-tal
fur-ther-more
fu-tile

G

gad-get
gan-grene
ga-rage
gas-o-line
gauge
ge-ne-al-o-gy
gen-er-al-ly
gen-er-ous
ge-nius
gen-u-ine
ge-og-ra-phy
ghet-to
ghost
glo-ri-ous
gnaw
go-ril-la
gov-ern-ment
gov-er-nor
gra-cious
grad-u-a-tion
gram-mar
grate-ful
grat-i-tude
grease
grief
griev-ous
gro-cery
grudge

grue-some
guar-an-tee
guard
guard-i-an
guer-ril-la
guess
guid-ance
guide
guilty
gym-na-si-um
gyp-sy
gy-ro-scope

H

hab-i-tat
ham-mer
hand-ker-chief
han-dle (-d)
hand-some
hap-haz-ard
hap-pen
hap-pi-ness
ha-rass
har-bour
hast-i-ly
hav-ing
haz-ard-ous
height
hem-or-rhage
hes-i-tate
hin-drance
his-to-ry
hoarse
hol-i-day
hon-our
hop-ing
hop-ping
horde
hor-ri-ble
hos-pi-tal
hu-mor-ous
hur-ried-ly
hy-drau-lic
hy-giene

I

i-am-bic
i-ci-cle
i-den-ti-cal
id-io-syn-cra-sy
il-leg-i-ble
il-lit-er-ate

il-lus-trate
im-ag-i-nary
im-ag-i-na-tive
im-ag-ine
im-i-ta-tion
im-me-di-ate-ly
im-mense
im-mi-grant
im-mor-tal
im-pa-tient
im-per-a-tive
im-por-tance
im-pos-si-ble
im-promp-tu
im-prove-ment
in-al-ien-able
in-ci-den-tal-ly
in-con-ve-nience
in-cred-i-ble
in-curred
in-def-i-nite-ly
in-del-ible
in-de-pend-ence
in-de-pend-ent
in-dict-ment
in-dis-pens-able
in-di-vid-u-al
in-duce-ment
in-dus-tri-al
in-dus-tri-ous
in-ev-i-ta-ble
in-fe-ri-or
in-ferred
in-fi-nite
in-flam-ma-ble
in-flu-en-tial
in-ge-nious
in-gen-u-ous
in-im-i-ta-ble
in-i-tial
ini-ti-a-tion
in-no-cence
in-no-cent
in-oc-u-la-tion
in-quir-y
in-stal-la-tion
in-stance
in-stead
in-sti-tute
in-struc-tor
in-sur-ance
in-tel-lec-tu-al

in-tel-li-gence
in-ten-tion
in-ter-cede
in-ter-est-ing
in-ter-fere
in-ter-mit-tent
in-ter-pret (-ed)
in-ter-rupt
in-ter-view
in-ti-mate
in-va-lid
in-ves-ti-gate
in-ves-tor
in-vi-ta-tion
ir-i-des-cent
ir-rel-e-vant
ir-re-sis-ti-ble
ir-rev-er-ent
ir-ri-gate
is-land
is-sue
i-tem-ized
i-tin-er-ar-y

J

jan-i-tor
jeal-ous (-y)
jeop-ar-dize
jew-el-lery
jour-nal
jour-ney
judg-ment
jus-tice
jus-ti-fi-able

K

kitch-en
knowl-edge
knuck-le

L

la-bel
lab-o-ra-to-ry
lac-quer
lan-guage
laugh
laun-dry
law-yer
league
lec-ture
le-gal
leg-i-ble

leg-is-la-ture
le-git-i-mate
lei-sure
length
let-ter-head
li-a-bil-i-ty
li-a-ble
li-ai-son
lib-er-al
li-brar-y
li-cence(n₁)
li-cense(v₁)
lieu-ten-ant
light-ning
lik-able
like-ly
lin-eage
liq-ue-fy
liq-uid
lis-ten
lit-er-ary
lit-er-a-ture
live-li-hood
log-a-rithm
lone-li-ness
loose
lose
los-ing
lov-able
love-ly
lun-cheon
lux-u-ry

M

ma-chine
mag-a-zine
mag-nif-i-cent
main-tain
main-te-nance
ma-jor-i-ty
mak-ing
man-age-ment
ma-noeu-vre
man-u-al
man-u-fac-ture
man-u-script
mar-riage
mar-shal
ma-te-ri-al
math-e-mat-ics
max-i-mum
may-or

mean-ness
meant
mea-sure
med-i-cine
me-di-eval
me-di-o-cre
me-di-um
mem-o-ran-dum
men-us
mer-chan-dise
mer-it
mes-sage
mile-age
mil-lion-aire
min-i-a-ture
min-i-mum
min-ute
mir-ror
mis-cel-la-neous
mis-chief
mis-chie-vous
mis-er-a-ble
mis-ery
mis-sile
mis-sion-ary
mis-spell
mois-ture
mol-e-cule
mo-men-tous
mo-not-o-nous
mon-u-ment
mort-gage
mu-nic-i-pal
mus-cle
mu-si-cian
mus-tache
mys-te-ri-ous

N

na-ive
nat-u-ral-ly
nec-es-sary
ne-ces-si-ty
neg-li-gi-ble
ne-go-ti-ate
neigh-bour-hood
nev-er-the-less
nick-el
niece
nine-teenth
nine-ty
no-tice-able

no-to-ri-ety
nu-cle-ar
nui-sance

O

o-be-di-ence
o-bey
o-blige
ob-sta-cle
oc-ca-sion
oc-ca-sion-al-ly
oc-cu-pant
oc-cur
oc-curred
oc-cur-rence
of-fence
of-fi-cial
of-ten
o-mis-sion
o-mit-ted
op-er-ate
o-pin-ion
op-po-nent
op-por-tu-ni-ty
op-po-site
op-ti-mism
or-di-nance
or-di-nar-i-ly
orig-i-nal
out-ra-geous

P

pag-eant
pam-phlet
par-a-dise
para-graph
par-al-lel
par-a-lyze
pa-ren-the-ses
pa-ren-the-sis
par-lia-ment
par-tial
par-tic-i-pant
par-tic-i-pate
par-tic-u-lar-ly
pas-time
pa-tience
pa-tron-age
pe-cu-liar
per-ceive
per-haps
per-il

per-ma-nent
per-mis-si-ble
per-pen-dic-u-lar
per-se-ver-ance
per-sis-tent
per-son-al (-ly)
per-son-nel
per-spi-ra-tion
per-suade
phase
phe-nom-e-non
phi-los-o-phy
phy-si-cian
piece
planned
pla-teau
plau-si-ble
play-wright
pleas-ant
plea-sure
pneu-mo-nia
pol-i-ti-cian
pos-sess
pos-ses-sion
pos-si-ble
prac-ti-cal-ly
prai-rie
pre-cede
pre-ce-dence
pre-ced-ing
pre-cious
pre-cise-ly
pre-ci-sion
pre-de-ces-sor
pref-er-a-ble
pref-er-ence
pre-ferred
prej-u-dice
pre-lim-i-nar-y
pre-mi-um
prep-a-ra-tion
pres-ence
prev-a-lent
pre-vi-ous
prim-i-tive
prin-ci-pal
prin-ci-ple
pri-or-i-ty
pris-on-er
priv-i-lege
prob-a-bly
pro-ce-dure

pro-ceed
pro-fes-sor
prom-i-nent
pro-nounce
pro-nun-ci-a-tion
pro-pa-gan-da
pros-e-cute
pro-tein
psy-chol-o-gy
pub-lic-ly
pump-kin
pur-chase
pur-sue
pur-su-ing
pur-suit

Q

qual-i-fied
qual-i-ty
quan-ti-ty
quar-ter
ques-tion-naire
quite
quo-tient

R

raise
rap-port
re-al-ize
re-al-ly
re-cede
re-ceipt
re-ceive
re-ceived
rec-i-pe
re-cip-i-ent
rec-og-ni-tion
rec-og-nize
rec-om-mend
re-cur-rence
ref-er-ence
re-ferred
reg-is-tra-tion
re-hearse
reign
re-im-burse
rel-e-vant
re-lieve
re-li-gious
re-mem-ber
re-mem-brance
rem-i-nisce

ren-dez-vous
re-new-al
rep-e-ti-tion
rep-re-sen-ta-tive
req-ui-si-tion
res-er-voir
re-sis-tance
re-spect-a-bly
re-spect-ful-ly
re-spec-tive-ly
re-spon-si-bil-i-ty
res-tau-rant
rheu-ma-tism
rhyme
rhythm
ri-dic-u-lous
route

S

sac-ri-le-gious
safe-ty
sal-a-ry
sand-wich
sat-is-fac-to-ry
Sat-ur-day
scarce-ly
scene
scen-er-y
sched-ule
schol-ar-ship
sci-ence
scis-sors
sec-re-tary
seize
sen-si-ble
sen-tence
sen-ti-nel
sep-a-rate
ser-geant
sev-er-al
se-vere-ly
shep-herd
sher-iff
shin-ing
siege
sig-nif-i-cance

sim-i-lar
si-mul-ta-ne-ous
since
sin-cere-ly
ski-ing
sol-dier
sol-emn
so-phis-ti-cat-ed
soph-o-more
so-ror-i-ty
source
sou-ve-nir
spa-ghet-ti
spe-cif-ic
spec-i-men
speech
sphere
spon-sor
spon-ta-ne-ous
sta-tion-ary
sta-tion-ery
sta-tis-tic
stat-ue
stat-ure
stat-ute
stom-ach
stopped
straight
strat-e-gy
strength
stretched
study-ing
sub-si-dize
sub-stan-tial
sub-sti-tute
sub-tle
suc-ceed
suc-cess
suf-fi-cient
sum-ma-rize
su-per-fi-cial
su-per-in-tend-
   ent
su-pe-ri-or-i-ty
su-per-sede
sup-ple-ment

sup-pose
sure-ly
sur-prise
sur-veil-lance
sur-vey
sus-cep-ti-ble
sus-pi-cious
sus-te-nance
syl-la-ble
sym-met-ri-cal
sym-pa-thy
sym-pho-ny
symp-tom
syn-chro-nous

T

tar-iff
tech-nique
tele-gram
tem-per-a-ment
tem-per-a-ture
tem-po-rary
ten-den-cy
ten-ta-tive
ter-res-tri-al
ter-ri-ble
ter-ri-to-ry
the-atre
their
there-fore
thief
thor-ough (-ly)
though
through-out
tired
to-bac-co
to-geth-er
to-mor-row
tongue
to-night
touch
tour-na-ment
tour-ni-quet
to-ward
trag-e-dy
trai-tor

tran-quil-iz-er
trans-ferred
trea-sur-er
tru-ly
Tues-day
tu-i-tion
typ-i-cal
typ-ing

U

unan-i-mous
un-con-scious
un-doubt-ed-ly
un-for-tu-nate-ly
unique
u-ni-son
uni-ver-si-ty
un-nec-es-sary
un-prec-e-dent-ed
un-til
up-per
ur-gent
us-able
use-ful
using
usu-al-ly
u-ten-sil
u-til-ize

V

va-can-cies
va-ca-tion
vac-u-um
vague
valu-able
va-ri-ety
var-i-ous
veg-e-ta-ble
ve-hi-cle
veil
ve-loc-i-ty
ven-geance
vi-cin-i-ty
view
vig-i-lance
vil-lain

vi-o-lence
vis-i-bil-i-ty
vis-i-ble
vis-i-tor
voice
vol-ume
vol-un-tary
vol-un-teer

W

wan-der
war-rant
weath-er
Wednes-day
weird
wel-come
wel-fare
where
wheth-er
which
whole
whol-ly
whose
width
wom-en
worth-while
wor-thy
wreck-age
wres-tler
writ-ing
writ-ten
wrought

Y

yel-low
yes-ter-day
yield

Chapter 32

Using the Right Word

"The difference between the right word and the almost right word is the difference between lightning and the lightning bug."

—Mark Twain

The following glossary contains words that are commonly confused.

a, an Use *a* as the article before words that begin with consonant sounds and before words that begin with the long vowel sound *u* (yü). Use *an* before words that begin with other vowel sounds.

An older student showed Kris **an** easier way to get to class.

A uniform is required attire for **a** cafeteria worker.

643.1

a lot, alot, allot *Alot* is not a word; *a lot* (two words) is a vague descriptive phrase that should be used sparingly, especially in formal writing. *Allot* means to give someone a share.

Prof Dubi **allots** each of us five spelling errors per semester, and he thinks that's **a lot**.

643.2

accept, except The verb *accept* means "to receive or believe"; the preposition *except* means "other than."

The instructor **accepted** the student's story about being late, but she wondered why no one **except** him had forgotten about the change to daylight-saving time.

643.3

adapt, adopt, adept *Adapt* means "to adjust or change to fit"; *adopt* means "to choose and treat as your own" (a child, an idea). *Adept* is an adjective meaning "proficient or well trained."

After much thought and deliberation, we agreed to **adopt** the black Lab from the shelter. Now we have to agree on how to **adapt** our lifestyle to fit our new roommate.

643.4

adverse, averse *Adverse* means "hostile, unfavourable, or harmful." *Averse* means "to have a definite feeling of distaste—disinclined."

Groans and other **adverse** reactions were noted as the new students, **averse** to strenuous exercise, were ushered past the X-5000 pump-and-crunch machine.

643.5

advice, advise *Advice* is a noun meaning "information or recommendation"; *advise* is a verb meaning "to recommend."

Successful people will often give you sound **advice**, so I **advise** you to listen.

643.6

affect, effect *Affect* means "to influence"; the noun *effect* means "the result."

The employment growth in a field will **affect** your chances of getting a job. The **effect** may be a new career choice.

643.7

644.1   **aid, aide** As a verb, *aid* means "to help"; as a noun, *aid* means "the help given." An *aide* is a person who acts as an assistant.

644.2   **all, of** *Of* is seldom needed after *all*.

> **All** the reports had an error in them.
> **All** the speakers spoke English.
> **All of** us voted to reschedule the meeting.
> (Here *of* is needed for the sentence to make sense.)

644.3   **all right, alright** *Alright* is the incorrect form of *all right*. (**Note:** The following are spelled correctly: *always, altogether, already, almost*.)

644.4   **allude, elude** *Allude* means "to indirectly refer to or hint at something"; *elude* means "to escape attention or understanding altogether."

> Ravi often **alluded** to wanting a supper invitation by mentioning the "awfully good" smells from the kitchen. These hints never **eluded** Ma's good heart.

644.5   **allusion, illusion** *Allusion* is an indirect reference to something or someone, especially in literature; *illusion* is a false picture or idea.

> Did you recognize the **allusion** to David in the reading assignment? Until I read that part, I was under the **illusion** that the young boy would run away from the bully.

644.6   **already, all ready** *Already* is an adverb meaning "before this time" or "by this time." *All ready* is an adjective form meaning "fully prepared." (**Note:** Use *all ready* if you can substitute *ready* alone in the sentence.)

> Jasmine had **already** finished reading "The Peace of Utrecht" when she sat down to watch *Lincoln* for her history class. That way, she was **all ready** for her in-class essay on Munro's short story the next morning.

644.7   **altogether, all together** *Altogether* means "entirely." *All together* means "in a group" or "all at once." (**Note:** Use *all together* if you can substitute *together* alone in the sentence.)

> **All together** there are 35,000 job titles to choose from. That's **altogether** too many to even think about.

644.8   **among, between** *Among* is used when emphasizing distribution throughout a body or a group of three or more; *between* is used when emphasizing distribution to two individuals.

> There was discontent **among** the relatives after learning that their aunt had divided her entire fortune **between** a canary and a favourite waitress at the local cafe.

644.9   **amoral, immoral** *Amoral* means "neither moral (right) nor immoral (wrong)"; *immoral* means "wrong, or in conflict with traditional values."

> Carnivores are **amoral** in their hunt; poachers are **immoral** in theirs.

644.10   **amount, number** *Amount* is used for bulk measurement. *Number* is used to count separate units. (See also fewer.)

> The **number** of new instructors hired next year will depend on the **amount** of revenue raised by the new sales tax.

and etc. Don't use *and* before *etc.* since *et cetera* means "and the rest."

> Did you remember your textbook, notebook, handout, **etc.**?

645.1

annual, biannual, semiannual, biennial, perennial An *annual* event happens once every year. A *biannual* event happens twice a year (*semiannual* is the same as *biannual*). A *biennial* event happens every two years. A *perennial* event happens throughout the year, every year.

645.2

anxious, eager Both words mean "looking forward to," but *anxious* also connotes fear or concern.

> The professor is **eager** to move into the new building, but she's a little **anxious** that students won't be able to find her new office.

645.3

anymore, any more *Anymore* (an adverb) means "any longer"; *any more* means "any additional."

> We won't use that textbook **anymore**; call if you have **any more** questions.

645.4

any one (of), anyone *Any one* means "any one of a number of people, places, or things"; *anyone* is a pronoun meaning "any person."

> Choose **any one** of the proposed weekend schedules. **Anyone** wishing to work on Saturday instead of Sunday may do so.

645.5

appraise, apprise *Appraise* means "to determine value." *Apprise* means "to inform."

> Because of the tax assessor's recent **appraisal** of our home, we were **apprised** of an increase in our property tax.

645.6

as Don't use *as* in place of *whether* or *if.*

> I don't know **as** I'll accept the offer. (Incorrect)
>
> I don't know **whether** I'll accept the offer. (Correct)

645.7

Don't use *as* when it is unclear whether it means *because* or *when.*

> We rowed toward shore **as** it started raining. (Unclear)
>
> We rowed toward shore **because** it started raining. (Correct)

assure, ensure, insure (See insure.)

bad, badly *Bad* is an adjective, used both before nouns and as a predicate adjective after linking verbs. *Badly* is an adverb.

645.8

> Christina felt **bad** about serving us **bad** food.
>
> Larisa played **badly** today.

beside, besides *Beside* means "by the side of." *Besides* means "in addition to."

645.9

> **Besides** the two suitcases you've already loaded into the trunk, remember the smaller one **beside** the van.

between, among (See among.)

bring, take *Bring* suggests the action is directed toward the speaker; *take* suggests the action is directed away from the speaker.

645.10

> If you're not going to **bring** the video to class, **take** it back to the resource centre.

646.1   **can, may** In formal contexts, *can* is used to mean "being able to do"; *may* is used to mean "having permission to do."

> **May** I borrow your bicycle to get to the library? Then I **can** start working on our group project.

646.2   **capital, capitol** The noun *capital* refers to a city or to money. The adjective *capital* means "major or important" or "seat of government." *Capitol* refers to a building.

> The **capitol** is in the **capital** city for a **capital** reason. The city government contributed **capital** for the building expense.

646.3   **cent, sent, scent** *Cent* is a coin; *sent* is the past tense of the verb "send"; *scent* is an odour or a smell.

> For forty-one **cents**, I **sent** my friend a love poem in a perfumed envelope. She adored the **scent** but hated the poem.

646.4   **chord, cord** *Chord* may mean "an emotion or a feeling," but it also may mean "the combination of three or more tones sounded at the same time," as with a guitar *chord*. A *cord* is a string or a rope.

> The guitar player strummed the opening **chord**, which struck a responsive **chord** with the audience.

646.5   **chose, choose** *Chose* (chōz) is the past tense of the verb *choose* (chüz). (See page 579.)

> For generations, people **chose** their careers based on their parents' careers; now people **choose** their careers based on the job market.

646.6   **climactic, climatic** *Climactic* refers to the climax, or high point, of an event; *climatic* refers to the climate, or weather conditions.

> Because we are using the open-air amphitheatre, **climatic** conditions will just about guarantee the wind gusts we need for the **climactic** third act.

646.7   **coarse, course** *Coarse* means "of inferior quality, rough, or crude"; *course* means "a direction or a path taken." *Course* also means "a class or a series of studies."

> A basic writing **course** is required of all students.
>
> Due to years of woodworking, the instructor's hands are rather **coarse**.

646.8   **compare with, compare to** Things in the same category are *compared with* each other; things in different categories are *compared to* each other.

> **Compare** Christopher Marlowe's plays **with** William Shakespeare's plays.
>
> My brother **compared** reading *The Tempest* **to** visiting another country.

646.9   **complement, compliment** *Complement* means "to complete or go well with." *Compliment* means "to offer an expression of admiration or praise."

> We wanted to **compliment** Zach on his decorating efforts; the bright yellow walls **complement** the purple carpet.

646.10   **comprehensible, comprehensive** *Comprehensible* means "capable of being understood"; *comprehensive* means "covering a broad range, or inclusive."

> The theory is **comprehensible** only to those who have a **comprehensive** knowledge of physics.

comprise, compose *Comprise* means "to contain or consist of"; *compose* means "to create or form by bringing parts together."   **647.1**

> Fruitcake **comprises** a variety of nuts, candied fruit, and spice.
>
> Fruitcake is **composed of** (not *comprised of*) a variety of ingredients.

conscience, conscious A *conscience* gives one the capacity to know right from wrong. *Conscious* means "awake or alert, not sleeping or comatose."   **647.2**

> Your **conscience** will guide you, but you have to be **conscious** to hear what it's "saying."

continual, continuous *Continual* often implies that something is happening often, recurring; *continuous* usually implies that something keeps happening, uninterrupted.   **647.3**

> The **continuous** loud music during the night gave the building manager not only a headache but also **continual** phone calls.

counsel, council, consul When used as a noun, *counsel* means "advice"; when used as a verb, *counsel* means "to advise." *Council* refers to a group that advises. A *consul* is a government official appointed to reside in a foreign country.   **647.4**

> The city **council** was asked to **counsel** our student **council** on running an efficient meeting. Their **counsel** was very helpful.

decent, descent, dissent *Decent* means "good." *Descent* is the process of going or stepping downward. *Dissent* means "disagreement."   **647.5**

> The food was **decent**.
>
> The elevator's fast **descent** clogged my ears.
>
> Their **dissent** over the decisions was obvious in their sullen expressions.

desert, dessert *Desert* is barren wilderness. *Dessert* is food served at the end of a meal. The verb *desert* means "to abandon."   **647.6**

different from, different than Use *different from* in formal writing; use either form in informal or colloquial settings.   **647.7**

> Rafael's interpretation was **different from** Andrea's.

discreet, discrete *Discreet* means "showing good judgment, unobtrusive, modest"; *discrete* means "distinct, separate."   **647.8**

> The essay question had three **discrete** parts.
>
> Her roommate had apparently never heard of quiet, **discreet** conversation.

disinterested, uninterested Both words mean "not interested." However, *disinterested* is also used to mean "unbiased or impartial."   **647.9**

> A person chosen as an arbitrator must be a **disinterested** party.
>
> Professor Eldridge was **uninterested** in our complaints about the assignment.

effect, affect (See affect.)

elicit, illicit *Elicit* is a verb meaning "to bring out." *Illicit* is an adjective meaning "unlawful."   **647.10**

> It took a hand signal to **elicit** the **illicit** exchange of cash for drugs.

648.1   **eminent, imminent** *Eminent* means "prominent, conspicuous, or famous"; *imminent* means "ready or threatening to happen."

> With the island's government about to collapse, assassination attempts on several **eminent** officials seemed **imminent**.

ensure, insure, assure (See insure.)

everyday, every day Functioning as an adjective, *everyday* means daily or ordinary. By contrast, *every day* is an adverb answering the question *when?* or *how often?*

> When you drink ten cups of coffee **every day**, the jitters become an **everyday** occurrence

except, accept (See accept.)

648.2   **explicit, implicit** *Explicit* means "expressed directly or clearly defined"; *implicit* means "implied or unstated."

> The professor **explicitly** asked that the experiment be wrapped up on Monday, **implicitly** demanding that her lab assistants work on the weekend.

648.3   **farther, further** *Farther* refers to a physical distance; *further* refers to additional time, quantity, or degree.

> **Further** research showed that walking **farther** rather than faster would improve his health.

648.4   **fewer, less** *Fewer* refers to the number of separate units; *less* refers to bulk quantity.

> Because of spell checkers, students can produce papers containing **fewer** errors in **less** time.

648.5   **figuratively, literally** *Figuratively* means "in a metaphorical or analogous way—describing something by comparing it to something else"; *literally* means "actually."

> The lab was **literally** filled with sulfurous gases—**figuratively** speaking, dragon's breath.

648.6   **first, firstly** Both words are adverbs meaning "before another in time" or "in the first place." However, do not use *firstly*, which is stiff and unnatural sounding.

> **Firstly** I want to see the manager. (Incorrect)

> **First** I want to see the manager. (Correct)

Note: When enumerating, use the forms *first, second, third, next, last*—without the *ly*.

648.7   **fiscal, physical** *Fiscal* means "related to financial matters"; *physical* means "related to material things."

> The school's **fiscal** work is handled by its accounting staff.

> The **physical** work is handled by its maintenance staff.

648.8   **for, fore, four** *For* is a conjunction meaning "because" or is a preposition used to indicate the object or recipient of something; *fore* means "earlier" or "the front"; *four* is the word for the number 4.

> The crew brought treats **for** the barge's **four** dogs, who always enjoy the breeze at the **fore** of the vessel.

648.9   **former, latter** When two things are being discussed, *former* refers to the first thing, and *latter* to the second.

> Our choices are going to a movie or eating at the Pizza Palace: The **former** is too expensive, and the **latter** too fattening.

good, well *Good* is an adjective; *well* is nearly always an adverb. (When used to indicate state of health, *well* is an adjective.)

649.1

> A **good** job offers opportunities for advancement, especially for those who do their jobs **well**.

heal, heel *Heal* (a verb) means "to mend or restore to health"; a *heel* (noun) is the back part of a human foot.

649.2

healthful, healthy *Healthful* means "causing or improving health"; *healthy* means "possessing health."

649.3

> **Healthful** foods and regular exercise build **healthy** bodies.

I, me *I* is a subject pronoun; *me* is used as an object of a preposition, a direct object, or an indirect object. (See 573.1.) (A good way to know if *I* or *me* should be used in a compound subject is to eliminate the other subject; the sentence should make sense with the pronoun—*I* or *me*—alone.)

649.4

> My roommate and **me** went to the library last night. (Incorrect)
>
> My roommate and **I** went to the library last night. (Correct: Eliminate "my roommate and"; the sentence still makes sense.)
>
> Rasheed gave the concert tickets to Erick and **I**. (Incorrect)
>
> Rasheed gave the concert tickets to Erick and **me**. (Correct: Eliminate "Erick and"; the sentence still makes sense.)

illusion, allusion (See allusion.)

immigrate (to), emigrate (from) *Immigrate* means "to come into a new country or environment." *Emigrate* means "to go out of one country to live in another."

649.5

> **Immigrating** to a new country is a challenging experience.
>
> People **emigrating** from their homelands face unknown challenges.

imminent, eminent (See eminent.)

imply, infer *Imply* means "to suggest without saying outright"; *infer* means "to draw a conclusion from facts." (A writer or a speaker *implies*; a reader or a listener *infers*.)

649.6

> Dr. Rufus **implied** I should study more; I **inferred** he meant my grades had to improve, or I'd be repeating the class.

ingenious, ingenuous *Ingenious* means "intelligent, discerning, clever"; *ingenuous* means "unassuming, natural, showing childlike innocence and candidness."

649.7

> Gretchen devised an **ingenious** plan to work and receive college credit for it.
>
> Ramón displays an **ingenuous** quality that attracts others.

insure, ensure, assure *Insure* means "to secure from financial harm or loss," *ensure* means "to make certain of something," and *assure* means "to put someone's mind at rest."

649.8

> Plenty of studying generally **ensures** academic success.
>
> Nicole **assured** her father that she had **insured** her new car.

interstate, intrastate *Interstate* means "existing between two or more states"; *intrastate* means "existing within a state."

649.9

650.1 **irregardless, regardless** *Irregardless* is a nonstandard synonym for *regardless*.

> **Irregardless** of his circumstance, José is cheerful. (Incorrect)
> **Regardless** of his circumstance, José is cheerful. (Correct)

650.2 **it's, its** *It's* is the contraction of "it is." *Its* is the possessive form of "it."

> **It's** not hard to see why my husband feeds that alley cat; **its** pitiful limp and mournful mewing would melt any heart.

650.3 **later, latter** *Later* means "after a period of time." *Latter* refers to the second of two things mentioned.

> The **latter** of the two restaurants you mentioned sounds good.
> Let's meet there **later**.

650.4 **lay, lie** *Lay* means "to place." *Lay* is a transitive verb. (See 574.2.) Its principal parts are *lay, laid, laid*. (See 579.)

> If you **lay** another book on my table, I won't have room for anything else.
> Yesterday, you **laid** two books on the table.
> Over the last few days, you must have **laid** at least 20 books there.

Lie means "to recline." *Lie* is an intransitive verb. (See 574.2.) Its principal parts are *lie, lay, lain*.

> The cat **lies** down anywhere it pleases.
> It **lay** down yesterday on my tax forms.
> It has **lain** down many times on the kitchen table.

650.5 **learn, teach** *Learn* means "to acquire information"; *teach* means "to give information."

> Sometimes it's easier to **teach** someone else a lesson than it is to **learn** one yourself.

650.6 **leave, let** *Leave* means "to allow something to remain behind." *Let* means "to permit."

> Please **let** me help you carry that chair; otherwise, **leave** it for the movers to pick up.

650.7 **lend, borrow** *Lend* means "to give for temporary use"; *borrow* means "to receive for temporary use."

> I asked Haddad to **lend** me $15 for a CD, but he said I'd have to find someone else to **borrow** the money from.

less, fewer (See **fewer**.)

650.8 **liable, libel** *Liable* is an adjective meaning "responsible according to the law" or "exposed to an adverse action"; the noun *libel* is a written defamatory statement about someone, and the verb *libel* means "to publish or make such a statement."

> Supermarket tabloids, **liable** for ruining many a reputation, make a practice of **libelling** the rich and the famous.

650.9 **liable, likely** *Liable* means "responsible according to the law" or "exposed to an adverse action"; *likely* means "in all probability."

> Rain seems **likely** today, but if we cancel the game, we are still **liable** for paying the referees.

like, as *Like* should not be used in place of *as*. *Like* is a preposition, which is followed by its object (a noun, a pronoun, or a noun phrase). *As* is a subordinating conjunction, which introduces a clause. Do not use *like* as a subordinating conjunction. Use *as* instead.

> You don't know her **like** I do. (Incorrect)
>
> You don't know her **as** I do. (Correct)
>
> **Like** the others in my study group, I do my work as any serious student would—carefully and thoroughly. (Correct)

651.1

literally, figuratively (See figuratively.)

loose, lose, loss The adjective *loose* (lüs) means "free, untied, unrestricted"; the verb *lose* (lüz) means "to misplace or fail to find or control"; the noun *loss* (los) means "something that is misplaced and cannot be found."

> Her sadness at the **loss** of her longtime companion caused her to **lose** weight, and her clothes felt uncomfortably **loose**.

651.2

may, can (See can.)

maybe, may be Use *maybe* as an adverb meaning "perhaps;" use *may be* as a verb phrase.

> She **may be** the computer technician we've been looking for. **Maybe** she will upgrade the software and memory.

651.3

miner, minor A *miner* digs in the ground for ore. A *minor* is a person who is not legally an adult. The adjective *minor* means "of no great importance."

> The use of **minors** as coal **miners** is no **minor** problem.

651.4

number, amount (See amount.)

OK, okay This expression, spelled either way, is appropriate in informal writing; however, avoid using it in papers, reports, or formal correspondence of any kind.

> Your proposal is satisfactory [not okay] on most levels.

651.5

oral, verbal *Oral* means "uttered with the mouth"; *verbal* means "relating to or consisting of words and the comprehension of words."

> The actor's **oral** abilities were outstanding, her pronunciation and intonation impeccable, but I doubted the playwright's **verbal** skills after trying to decipher the play's meaning.

651.6

passed, past *Passed* is a verb. *Past* can be used as a noun, an adjective, or a preposition.

> That little pickup truck **passed** my 'Vette! (verb)
>
> My stepchildren hold on dearly to the **past**. (noun)
>
> I'm sorry, but my **past** life is not your business. (adjective)
>
> The officer drove **past** us, not noticing our flat tire. (preposition)

651.7

peace, piece *Peace* means "tranquility or freedom from war." A *piece* is a part or fragment.

> Someone once observed that **peace** is not a condition, but a process—a process of building goodwill one **piece** at a time.

651.8

652.1 **people, person** Use *people* to refer to human populations, races, or groups; use *person* to refer to an individual or the physical body.

> Late in 2012, many of Canada's Aboriginal **people** joined together to create the "Idle No More" movement.

> The forest ranger recommends that we check our **persons** for wood ticks when we leave the woods.

652.2 **percent, percentage** *Percent* means "per hundred"; for example, 60 percent of 100 jelly beans would be 60 jelly beans. *Percentage* refers to a portion of the whole. Generally, use the word *percent* when it is preceded by a number. Use *percentage* when no number is used.

> Each person's **percentage** of the reward amounted to $125—25 **percent** of the $500 offered by Crime Stoppers.

652.3 **personal, personnel** *Personal* (an adjective) means "private." *Personnel* (a noun) are people working at a particular job.

> Although choosing a major is a **personal** decision, it can be helpful to consult with guidance **personnel**.

652.4 **perspective, prospective** *Perspective* (a noun) is a point of view or the capacity to view things realistically; *prospective* is an adjective meaning "expected in or related to the future."

> From my immigrant neighbour's **perspective**, any job is a good job.

> **Prospective** students wandered the campus on visitors' day.

652.5 **pore, pour, poor** The noun *pore* is an opening in the skin; the verb *pore* means "to gaze intently." *Pour* means "to move with a continuous flow." *Poor* means "needy or pitiable."

> **Pour** hot water into a bowl, put your face over it, and let the steam open your **pores**. Your **poor** skin will thank you.

652.6 **precede, proceed** To *precede* means "to go or come before"; *proceed* means "to move on after having stopped" or "go ahead."

> Our biology instructor often **preceded** his lecture with these words:

> "OK, sponges, **proceed** to soak up more fascinating facts!"

652.7 **principal, principle** As an adjective, *principal* means "primary." As a noun, it can mean "a school administrator" or "a sum of money." A *principle* (noun) is an idea or a doctrine.

> His **principal** gripe is lack of freedom. (adjective)

> My son's **principal** expressed his concerns to the teachers. (noun)

> After 20 years, the amount of interest was higher than the **principal**. (noun)

> The **principle** of *caveat emptor* guides most consumer groups. (noun)

652.8 **quiet, quit, quite** *Quiet* is the opposite of noisy. *Quit* means "to stop or give up." *Quite* (an adverb) means "completely" or "to a considerable extent."

> The meeting remained **quite quiet** when the boss told us he'd **quit**.

652.9 **quote, quotation** *Quote* is a verb; *quotation* is a noun.

> The **quotation** I used was from Woody Allen. You may **quote** me on that.

652.10 **real, very, really** Do not use the adjective *real* in place of the adverbs *very* or *really*.

> My friend's cake is usually **very** [not *real*] fresh, but this cake is **really** stale.

right, write, wright, rite *Right* means "correct or proper"; it also refers to that which a person has a legal claim to, as in *copyright*. *Write* means "to inscribe or record." A *wright* is a person who makes or builds something. *Rite* is a ritual or ceremonial act.

653.1

> Did you **write** that it is the **right** of the **shipwright** to perform the **rite** of christening—breaking a bottle of champagne on the bow of the ship?

scene, seen *Scene* refers to the setting or location where something happens; it also may mean "sight or spectacle." *Seen* is the past participle of the verb "see."

653.2

> An exhibitionist likes to be **seen** making a **scene**.

set, sit *Set* means "to place." *Sit* means "to put the body in a seated position." *Set* is a transitive verb; *sit* is an intransitive verb. (See 574.2.)

653.3

> How can you just **sit** there and watch as I **set** the table?

sight, cite, site *Sight* means "the act of seeing" (a verb) or "something that is seen" (a noun). *Cite* (a verb) means "to quote" or "to summon to court." *Site* means "a place or location" (noun) or "to place on a site" (verb).

653.4

> After **sighting** the faulty wiring, the inspector **cited** the building contractor for breaking two city codes at a downtown work **site**.

some, sum *Some* refers to an unknown thing, an unspecified number, or a part of something. *Sum* is a certain amount of money or the result of adding numbers together.

653.5

> **Some** of the students answered too quickly and came up with the wrong **sum**.

stationary, stationery *Stationary* means "not movable"; *stationery* refers to the paper and envelopes used to write letters.

653.6

> Odina uses **stationery** that she can feed through her portable printer. Then she drops the mail into a **stationary** mail receptacle at the mall.

take, bring (See bring.)

teach, learn (See learn.)

than, then *Than* is used in a comparison; *then* is an adverb that tells when.

653.7

> Study more **than** you think you need to. **Then** you will probably be satisfied with your grades.

their, there, they're *Their* is a possessive personal pronoun. *There* is an adverb used as a filler word or to point out location. *They're* is the contraction for "they are."

653.8

> Look over **there**. **There** is a comfortable place for students to study for **their** exams, so **they're** more likely to do a good job.

threw, through *Threw* is the past tense of "throw." *Through* (a preposition) means "from one side of something to the other."

653.9

> In a fit of frustration, Sachiko **threw** her cellphone right **through** the window.

to, too, two *To* is a preposition that can mean "in the direction of." *To* is also used to form an infinitive. *Too* (an adverb) means "also" or "very." *Two* is the number 2.

653.10

> **Two** causes of eye problems among students are lights that fail **to** illuminate properly and computer screens with **too** much glare.

654.1   **vain, vane, vein** *Vain* means "valueless or fruitless"; it may also mean "holding a high regard for oneself." *Vane* is a flat piece of material set up to show which way the wind blows. *Vein* refers to a blood vessel or a mineral deposit.

> The weather **vane** indicates the direction of the wind; the blood **vein** determines the direction of flowing blood; and the **vain** mind moves in no particular direction, content to think only about itself.

654.2   **vary, very** The verb *vary* means "to change"; the adverb *very* means "to a high degree."

> To ensure the **very** best employee relations, the workloads should not **vary** greatly from worker to worker.

verbal, oral (See oral.)

654.3   **waist, waste** The noun *waist* refers to the part of the body just above the hips. The verb *waste* means "to squander" or "to wear away, decay"; the noun *waste* refers to material that is unused or useless.

> His **waist** is small because he **wastes** no opportunity to exercise.

654.4   **wait, weight** *Wait* means "to stay somewhere expecting something." *Weight* refers to a degree or unit of heaviness.

> The **weight** of sadness eventually lessens; one must simply **wait** for the pain to dissipate.

654.5   **ware, wear, where** The noun *ware* refers to a product that is sold; the verb *wear* means "to have on or to carry on one's body"; the adverb *where* asks the question "In what place?" or "In what situation?"

> The designer boasted, "**Where** can one **wear** my **wares**? Anywhere."

654.6   **weather, whether** *Weather* refers to the condition of the atmosphere. *Whether* refers to a possibility.

> **Weather** conditions affect all of us, **whether** we are farmers or plumbers.

well, good (See good.)

which, that (See 610.3.)

654.7   **who, which, that** *Who* refers to people. *Which* refers to nonliving objects or to animals. (*Which* should never refer to people.) *That* may refer to animals, people, or nonliving objects. (See also 610.3.)

654.8   **who, whom** *Who* is used as the subject of a verb; *whom* is used as the object of a preposition or as a direct object.

> Captain Mather, to **whom** the survivors owe their lives, is the man **who** is being honoured today.

654.9   **who's, whose** *Who's* is the contraction for "who is." *Whose* is a possessive pronoun.

> **Whose** car are we using, and **who's** going to pay for the gas?

654.10   **your, you're** *Your* is a possessive pronoun. *You're* is the contraction for "you are."

> If **you're** like most Canadians, you will have held eight jobs by **your** fortieth birthday.

Chapter 33

Multilingual and ELL Guidelines

"Until I came to Canada I never knew 'snow' was a four letter word."

—Alberto Manguel

English may be your second, third, or fifth language. If it is, you are an English Language Learner (ELL). As a multilingual learner, you bring to your writing the culture and knowledge of the languages you use. This broader perspective enables you to draw on many experiences and greater knowledge as you write and speak. Whether you are an international student or someone who has lived in Canada a long time and is now learning more about English, this chapter provides you with important information about writing in English.

Five Parts of Speech

Noun

Count Nouns

655.1

Count nouns refer to things that can be counted. They can have *a, an, the,* or *one* in front of them. One or more adjectives can come between the articles *a, an, the,* or *one* and the singular count noun.

> **an apple, one orange, a plum, a purple plum**

Count nouns can be singular, as in the examples above, or plural, as in the examples below.

> **plums, apples, oranges**

> **Note:** When count nouns are plural, they can have the article *the,* a number, or a demonstrative adjective in front of them. (See 657.1 and 657.3.)
>
> I used **the** plums to make a pie.
>
> He placed **five** apples on my desk.
>
> **These** oranges are so juicy!

The *number* of a noun refers to whether it names a single thing (*book*), in which case its number is *singular,* or whether it names more than one thing (*books*), in which case the number of the noun is *plural.*

> **Note:** There are different ways in which the plural form of nouns is created. For more information, see pages 629–630.

656.1 Noncount Nouns

Noncount nouns refer to things that cannot be counted. Do not use *a, an,* or *one* in front of them. They have no plural form, so they always take a singular verb. Some nouns that end in *s* are not plural; they are noncount nouns.

fruit, furniture, rain, thunder, advice, mathematics, news

Abstract nouns name ideas or conditions rather than people, places, or objects. Many abstract nouns are noncount nouns.

The students had **fun** at the party. Good **health** is a wonderful gift.

Collective nouns name a whole category or group and are often noncount nouns.

homework, furniture, money

Note: The parts or components of a group or category named by a noncount noun are often count nouns. For example, *report* and *assignment* are count nouns that are parts of the collective, noncount noun *homework.*

656.2 Two-Way Nouns

Some nouns can be used as either count or noncount nouns, depending on what they refer to.

I would like a **glass** of water. (count noun)

Glass is used to make windows. (noncount noun)

Articles and Other Noun Markers

656.3 Specific Articles

Use articles and other noun markers or modifiers to give more information about nouns. The **specific** (or **definite**) **article** *the* is used to refer to a specific noun.

I found **the** book I misplaced yesterday.

656.4 Indefinite Articles and Indefinite Adjectives

Use the **indefinite article** *a* or *an* to refer to a nonspecific noun. Use *an* before singular nouns beginning with the vowels *a, e, i, o,* and *u.* Use *a* before nouns beginning with all other letters of the alphabet, the consonants. Exceptions do occur: *a* unit; *a* university.

I always take **an** apple to work.

It is good to have **a** book with you when you travel.

Indefinite adjectives can also mark nonspecific nouns—*all, any, each, either, every, few, many, more, most, neither, several, some* (for singular and plural count nouns); *all, any, more, most, much, some* (for noncount nouns).

Every student is encouraged to register early.

Most classes fill quickly.

Determining Whether to Use Articles

657.1

Listed below are a number of guidelines to help you determine whether to use an article and which one to use.

Use *a* or *an* with singular count nouns that do not refer to one specific item.

A zebra has black and white stripes. **An apple** is good for you.

Do not use *a* or *an* with plural count nouns.

Zebras have black and white stripes. **Apples** are good for you.

Do not use *a* or *an* with noncount nouns.

Homework needs to be done promptly.

Use *the* with singular count nouns that refer to one specific item.

The apple you gave me was delicious.

Use *the* with plural count nouns.

The zebras at Bowmanville Zoo were healthy.

Use *the* with noncount nouns.

The money from my uncle is a gift.

Do not use *the* with most singular proper nouns.

Mother Teresa loved the poor and downcast.

> **Note:** There are many exceptions: *the* Sahara Desert, *the* University of Alberta, *the* Atlantic Ocean

Use *the* with plural nouns.

the Joneses (both Mr. and Mrs. Jones), **the Rocky Mountains, the Maritimes**

Possessive Adjectives

657.2

The possessive case of nouns and pronouns can be used as adjectives to mark nouns.

possessive nouns: *Tanya's, father's, store's*

The car is **Tanya's,** not her **father's.**

possessive pronouns: *my, your, his, her, its, our*

My hat is purple.

Demonstrative Adjectives

657.3

Demonstrative pronouns can be used as adjectives to mark nouns.

Demonstrative adjectives: *this, that, these, those* (for singular and plural count nouns); *this, that* (for noncount nouns)

Those chairs are lovely. Where did you buy **that** furniture?

658.1 ## Quantifiers

Expressions of quantity and measure are often used with nouns. Below are some of these expressions and guidelines for using them.

The following expressions of quantity can be used with count nouns: *each, every, both, a couple of, a few, several, many, a number of.*

> We enjoyed **both** concerts we attended. **A couple of** songs performed were familiar to us.

Use a number to indicate a specific quantity of a continuum.

> I saw **fifteen** cardinals in the park.

To indicate a specific quantity of a noncount noun, use *a* + quantity (such as *bag, bottle, bowl, carton, glass,* or *piece*) + *of* + noun.

> I bought **a carton of milk, a head of lettuce, a piece of cheese,** and **a bag of flour** at the grocery store.

The following expressions can be used with noncount nouns: *a little, much, a great deal of.*

> We had **much** wind and **a little** rain as the storm passed through yesterday.

The following expressions of quantity can be used with both count and noncount nouns: *no/not any, some, a lot of, lots of, plenty of, most, all, this, that.*

> I would like **some** apples *(count noun)* and **some** rice *(noncount noun),* please.

Verb

As the main part of the predicate, a verb conveys much of a sentence's meaning. Using verb tenses and forms correctly ensures that your readers will understand your sentences as you intend them to. For a more thorough review of verbs, see pages 574–579.

658.2 ## Progressive (Continuous) Tenses

Progressive or continuous tense verbs express action in progress (see page 576).

To form the **present progressive** tense, use the helping verb *am, is,* or *are* with the *ing* form of the main verb.

> He **is washing** the car right now.
> Kent and Chen **are studying** for a test.

To form the **past progressive** tense, use the helping verb *was* or *were* with the *ing* form of the main verb.

> Yesterday he **was working** in the garden all day.
> Julia and Juan **were watching** a movie.

To form the future progressive tense, use *will* or a phrase that indicates the future, the helping verb *be,* and the *ing* form of the main verb.

> Next week he **will be painting** the house.
> He **plans to be painting** the house soon.

Note that some verbs are generally not used in the progressive tenses, such as the following groups of frequently used verbs:

- Verbs that express thoughts, attitudes, and desires: *know, understand, want, prefer*
- Verbs that describe appearances: *seem, resemble*
- Verbs that indicate possession: *belong, have, own, possess*
- Verbs that signify inclusion: *contain, hold*

Kala **knows** how to ride a motorcycle.

NOT THIS: Kala is **knowing** how to ride a motorcycle.

659.1

Objects and Complements of Verbs

659.2

Active transitive verbs take objects. These can be direct objects, indirect objects, or object complements. Linking verbs take subject complements—predicate nominatives or predicate adjectives—that rename or describe the subject.

Infinitives as Objects

659.3

Infinitives can follow many verbs, including these: *agree, appear, attempt, consent, decide, demand, deserve, endeavour, fail, hesitate, hope, intend, need, offer, plan, prepare, promise, refuse, seem, tend, volunteer, wish.* (See 578.3 for more on infinitives.)

He **promised to bring** some samples.

The following verbs are among those that can be followed by a noun or pronoun plus the infinitive: *ask, beg, choose, expect, intend, need, prepare, promise, want.*

I **expect you to be** there on time.

Note: Except in the passive voice, the following verbs must have a noun or pronoun before the infinitive: *advise, allow, appoint, authorize, cause, challenge, command, convince, encourage, forbid, force, hire, instruct, invite, order, permit, remind, require, select, teach, tell, tempt, trust.*

I will **authorize Emily to use** my credit card.

Unmarked infinitives (no *to*) can follow these verbs: *have, help, let, make.*

These glasses **help me see** the board.

Gerunds as Objects

659.4

Gerunds can follow these verbs: *admit, avoid, consider, deny, discuss, dislike, enjoy, finish, imagine, miss, postpone, quit, recall, recommend, regret.* (Also see 578.2.)

I **recommended hiring** Ian for the job.

Here *hiring* is the direct object of the active verb *recommended*, and *Ian* is the object of the gerund.

660.1

Infinitives or Gerunds as Objects

Either **gerunds** or **infinitives** can follow these verbs: *begin, continue, hate, like, love, prefer, remember, start, stop, try.*

> I **hate having** cold feet. I **hate to have** cold feet. (In either form, the verbal phrase is the direct object of the verb hate.)

> **Note:** Sometimes the meaning of a sentence will change depending on whether you use a gerund or an infinitive.
>
> I stopped to smoke. (I *stopped* weeding the garden *to smoke* a cigarette.)
> I stopped smoking. (I no longer smoke.)

660.2

Common Modal Auxiliary Verbs

Modal auxiliary verbs are a kind of auxiliary verb. (See 574.3.) They help the main verb express meaning. Modals are sometimes grouped with other helping or auxiliary verbs.

Modal verbs must be followed by the base form of a verb without *to* (not by a gerund or an infinitive). Also, modal verbs do not change form; they are always used as they appear in the following chart.

Modal	Expresses	Sample Sentence
can	ability	I *can* make tamales.
could	ability	I *could* babysit Tuesday.
	possibility	He *could* be sick.
might	possibility	I *might* be early.
may, might	possibility	I *may* sleep late Saturday.
	request	*May* I be excused?
must	strong need	I *must* study more.
have to	strong need	I *have to* (have got to) exercise.
ought to	feeling of duty	I *ought to* (should) help Dad.
should	advisability	She *should* retire.
	expectation	I *should* have caught that train.
shall	intent	*Shall* I stay longer?
will	intent	I *will* visit my grandma soon.
would	intent	I *would* live to regret my offer.
	repeated action	He *would* walk in the meadow.
would + you	polite request	*Would you* help me?
could + you	polite request	*Could you* type this letter?
will + you	polite request	*Will you* give me a ride?
can + you	polite request	*Can you* make supper tonight?

Common Two-Word Verbs

This chart lists some common verbs in which two words—a verb and a preposition—work together to express a specific action. A noun or pronoun is often inserted between the parts of the two-word verb when it is used in a sentence: *break it down, call it off.*

	break down	to take apart or fall apart
	call off	cancel
	call up	make a phone call
	clear out	leave a place quickly
	cross out	draw a line through
	do over	repeat
	figure out	find a solution
	fill in/out	complete a form or an application
	fill up	fill a container or tank
*	**find out**	discover
*	**get in**	enter a vehicle or building
*	**get out of**	leave a car, a house, or a situation
*	**get over**	recover from a sickness or a problem
	give back	return something
	give in/up	surrender or quit
	hand in	give homework to a teacher
	hand out	give someone something
	hang up	put down a phone receiver
	leave out	omit or don't use
	let in/out	allow someone or something to enter or go out
	look up	find information
	mix up	confuse
	pay back	return money or a favour
	pick out	choose
	point out	call attention to
	put away	return something to its proper place
	put down	place something on a table, the floor, and so on.
	put off	delay doing something
	shut off	turn off a machine or light
*	**take part**	participate
	talk over	discuss
	think over	consider carefully
	try on	put on clothing to see if it fits
	turn down	lower the volume
	turn up	raise the volume
	write down	write on a piece of paper

* These two-word verbs should not have a noun or pronoun inserted between their parts.

Spelling Guidelines for Verb Forms

The same spelling rules that apply when adding a suffix to other words apply to verbs as well. Most verbs need a suffix to indicate tense or form. The third-person singular form of a verb, for example, usually ends in *s*, but it can also end in *es*. Formation of *ing* and *ed* forms of verbs and verbals needs careful attention, too. Consult the rules below to determine which spelling is correct for each verb. (For general spelling guidelines, see page 636.)

 There may be exceptions to these rules when forming the past tense of irregular verbs because the verbs are formed by changing the word itself, not merely by adding *d* or *ed*. (See the chart of irregular verbs on page 579.)

662.1

Past Tense: Adding *ed*

Add *ed* . . .

- When a verb ends with two consonants:
  touch—**touched**   ask—**asked**   pass—**passed**

- When a verb ends with a consonant preceded by two vowels:
  heal—**healed**   gain—**gained**

- When a verb ends in *y* preceded by a vowel:
  annoy—**annoyed**   flay—**flayed**

- When a multisyllable verb's last syllable is not stressed (even when the last syllable ends with a consonant preceded by a vowel):
  budget—**budgeted**   enter—**entered**   interpret—**interpreted**

Change *y* to *i* and add *ed* when a verb ends in a consonant followed by *y*:
  liquefy—**liquefied**   worry—**worried**

Double the final consonant and add *ed* . . .

- When a verb has one syllable and ends with a consonant preceded by a vowel:
  wrap—**wrapped**   drop—**dropped**

- When a multisyllable verb's last syllable (ending in a consonant preceded by a vowel) is stressed:
  admit—**admitted**   confer—**conferred**   abut—**abutted**

662.2

Past Tense: Adding *d*

Add *d* . . .

- When a verb ends with *e*:
  chime—**chimed**   tape—**taped**

- When a verb ends with *ie*:
  tie—**tied**   die—**died**   lie—**lied**

Present Tense: Adding *s* or *es*   663.1

Add *es* . . .

- When a verb ends in *ch, sh, s, x,* or *z*:
  watch—**watches**   fix—**fixes**

- To *do* and *go*:
  do—**does**   go—**goes**

Change *y* to *i* and add *es* when the verb ends in a consonant followed by *y*:
  liquefy—**liquefies**   quantify—**quantifies**

Add *s* to most other verbs, including those already ending in *e* and those that end in a vowel followed by *y*:
  write—**writes**   buy—**buys**

Present Tense: Adding *ing*   663.2

Drop the *e* and add *ing* when the verb ends in *e*:
  drive—**driving**   rise—**rising**

Double the final consonant and add *ing* . . .

- When a verb has one syllable and ends with a consonant preceded by a single vowel:
  wrap—**wrapping**   sit—**sitting**

- When a multisyllable verb's last syllable (ending in a consonant preceded by a single vowel) is stressed:
  forget—**forgetting**   begin—**beginning**   abut—**abutting**

Change *ie* to *y* and add *ing* when a verb ends with *ie*:
  tie—**tying**   die—**dying**   lie—**lying**

Add *ing* . . .

- When a verb ends with two consonants:
  touch—**touching**   ask—**asking**   pass—**passing**

- When a verb ends with a consonant preceded by two vowels:
  heal—**healing**   gain—**gaining**

- When a verb ends in *y*:
  buy—**buying**   study—**studying**   cry—**crying**

- When a multisyllable verb's last syllable is not stressed (even when the last syllable ends with a consonant preceded by a vowel):
  budget—**budgeting**   enter—**entering**   interpret—**interpreting**

Note: Never trust your spelling to even the best computer spell checker. Carefully proofread. Use a dictionary for questionable words your spell checker may miss.

Adjective

664.1 ## Placing Adjectives

You probably know that an adjective often comes before the noun it modifies. When several adjectives are used in a row to modify a single noun, it is important to arrange the adjectives in the well-established sequence used in English writing and speaking. The following list shows the usual order of adjectives. (Also see 608.3.)

First, place . . .

1. articles . . . . **a, an, the**
   demonstrative adjectives . . . . **that, those**
   possessives. . . . . **my, her, Misha's**

Then place words that . . .

2. indicate time. . . . . **first, next, final**
3. tell how many. . . . .**one, few, some**
4. evaluate . . . . **beautiful, dignified, graceful**
5. tell what size. . . . .**big, small, short, tall**
6. tell what shape . . . . **round, square**
7. describe a condition . . . . **messy, clean, dark**
8. tell what age . . . . **old, young, new, antique**
9. tell what colour . . . .**blue, red, yellow**
10. tell what nationality . . . . **English, Chinese, Mexican**
11. tell what religion . . . . **Buddhist, Jewish, Protestant**
12. tell what material. . . . .**satin, velvet, wooden**

Finally, place nouns . . .

13. used as adjectives. . . . . **computer [monitor], spice [rack]**
    my second try (1 + 2 + noun)
    gorgeous young white swans (4 + 8 + 9 + noun)

664.2 ## Present and Past Participles as Adjectives

Both the **present participle** and the **past participle** can be used as adjectives. (Also see 578.4.) Exercise care in choosing whether to use the present participle or the past participle. A participle can come either before a noun or after a linking verb.

A **present participle** used as an adjective should describe a person or thing that is causing a feeling or situation.

His **annoying** comments made me angry.

A **past participle** should describe a person or thing that experiences a feeling or situation.

He was **annoyed** because he had to wait so long.

Note: Within each of the following pairs, the present (*ing* form) and past (*ed* form) participles have different meanings.

annoying/annoyed	depressing/depressed	fascinating/fascinated
boring/bored	exciting/excited	surprising/surprised
confusing/confused	exhausting/exhausted	

Nouns as Adjectives

665.1

Nouns sometimes function as adjectives by modifying another noun. When a noun is used as an adjective, it is always singular.

Many European cities have **rose** gardens.

Marta recently joined a **book** club.

TIP: Try to avoid using more than two nouns as adjectives for another noun. These "noun compounds" can get confusing. Prepositional phrases may get the meaning across better than long noun strings.

Correct: Omar is a **crew** member in the **restaurant** kitchen during **second** shift.

Not correct: Omar is a **second-shift restaurant kitchen crew** member.

Adverb

Placing Adverbs

665.2

Consider the following guidelines for placing adverbs correctly. See page 581 for more information about adverbs.

Place adverbs that tell how often (*frequently, seldom, never, always, sometimes*) after a helping (auxiliary) verb and before the main verb. In a sentence without a helping verb, adverbs that tell *how often* are placed before an action verb but after a linking verb.

The salesclerk will **usually** help me.

Place adverbs that tell when (*yesterday, now, at five o'clock*) at the end of a sentence.

Auntie El came home **yesterday.**

Adverbs that tell where (*upside-down, around, downstairs*) usually follow the verb they modify. Many prepositional phrases (*at the beach, under the stairs, below the water*) function as adverbs that tell where.

We waited **on the porch.**

Adverbs that tell how (*quickly, slowly, loudly*) can be placed either at the beginning, in the middle, or at the end of a sentence—but not between a verb and its direct object.

Softly he called my name. He **softly** called my name. He called my name **softly.**

Place adverbs that modify adjectives directly before the adjective.

That is a **most** unusual dress.

Adverbs that modify clauses are most often placed in front of the clause, but they can also go inside or at the end of the clause.

Fortunately, we were not involved in the accident.
We were not involved, **fortunately,** in the accident.
We were not involved in the accident, **fortunately.**

Note: Adverbs that are used with verbs that have direct objects must *not* be placed between the verb and its object.

Correct: Luis **usually** catches the most fish.   **Usually,** Luis catches the most fish.

Not correct: Luis catches **usually** the most fish.

Preposition

A **preposition** combines with a noun to form a prepositional phrase, which acts as a modifier—an adverb or an adjective. See pages 582 and 584 for a list of common prepositions and for more information about prepositions.

666.1   Using *in, on, at,* and *by*

In, on, at, and *by* are four common prepositions that refer to time and place. Here are some examples of how these prepositions are used in each case.

To show time

>**on** a specific day or date: ***on*** June 7, ***on*** Wednesday
>
>**in** part of a day: ***in*** the afternoon
>
>**in** a year or month: ***in*** 2015, ***in*** April
>
>**in** a period of time: completed ***in*** an hour
>
>**by** a specific time or date: ***by*** noon, ***by*** the fifth of May
>
>**at** a specific time of day or night: ***at*** 3:30 this afternoon

To show place

>**at** a meeting place or location: ***at*** school, ***at*** the park
>
>**at** the edge of something: standing ***at*** the bar
>
>**at** the corner of something: turning ***at*** the intersection
>
>**at** a target: throwing a dart ***at*** the target
>
>**on** a surface: left ***on*** the floor
>
>**on** an electronic medium: ***on*** the Internet, ***on*** television
>
>**in** an enclosed space: ***in*** the box, ***in*** the room
>
>**in** a geographic location: ***in*** Calgary, ***in*** Germany
>
>**in** a print medium: ***in*** a journal
>
>**by** a landmark: ***by*** the fountain

TIP: Do not insert a preposition between a transitive verb and its direct object. Intransitive verbs, however, are often followed by a prepositional phrase (a phrase that begins with a preposition).

>I **cooked** hot dogs on the grill. (transitive verb)
>
>I **ate** in the park. (intransitive verb)

666.2   Phrasal Prepositions

Some prepositional phrases begin with more than one preposition. These **phrasal prepositions** are commonly used in both written and spoken communication. A list of common phrasal prepositions follows:

according to	because of	in case of	on the side of
across from	by way of	in spite of	up to
along with	except for	instead of	with respect to

Understanding Sentence Basics

Simple sentences in the English language follow the five basic patterns shown below. (See pages 585–592 for more information.)

Subject + Verb

┌─S─┐┌─V─┐
Naomie winked.

Some verbs like *winked* are intransitive. Intransitive verbs do not need a direct object to express a complete thought. (See 574.2.)

Subject + Verb + Direct Object

┌S┐┌V┐┌DO┐
Harris grinds his teeth.

Some verbs like *grinds* are transitive. Transitive verbs *do* need a direct object to express a complete thought. (See 574.2.)

Subject + Verb + Indirect Object + Direct Object

┌S┐┌V┐┌IO┐┌DO┐
Elena offered her friend an anchovy.

The direct object names who or what receives the action; the indirect object names to whom or for whom the action was done.

Subject + Verb + Direct Object + Object Complement

┌─S─┐┌V┐ DO ┌─OC─┐
The chancellor named Ravi the outstanding student of 2014.

The object complement renames or describes the direct object.

Subject + Linking Verb + Predicate Nominative (or Predicate Adjective)

┌S┐LV┌─PN─┐   ┌S┐LV┌─PA─┐
Paula is a computer programmer.   **Paula is very intelligent.**

A linking verb connects the subject to the predicate noun or predicate adjective. The predicate noun renames the subject; the predicate adjective describes the subject.

Inverted Order

In the sentence patterns above, the subject comes before the verb. In a few types of sentences, such as those below, the subject comes *after* the verb.

LV┌S┐ ┌PN┐   LV ┌─S─┐
Is Larisa a poet?   **There was a meeting.**

(A question)   (A sentence beginning with "there")

Sentence Problems

This section looks at potential trouble spots and sentence problems. For more information about English sentences, their parts, and how to construct them, see pages 585–592 in the handbook. Pages 593–603 cover the types of problems and errors found in English writing. The guide to avoiding sentence problems found on page 604 is an excellent editing tool.

668.1   ## Double Negatives

When making a sentence negative, use *not* or another negative adverb (*never, rarely, hardly, seldom,* and so on), but not both. Using both results in a double negative (see 603.4).

668.2   ## Subject–Verb Agreement

Be sure the subject and verb in every clause agree in person and number. (See pages 593–596.)

The **student was** rewarded for her hard work.

The **students were** rewarded for their hard work.

The **instructor,** as well as the students, **is** expected to attend the orientation.

The **students,** as well as the instructor, **are** expected to attend the orientation.

668.3   ## Omitted Words

Do not omit subjects or the expletives *there* or *here*. In all English clauses and sentences (except imperatives in which the subject *you* is understood), there must be a subject.

Correct: Your mother was very quiet; **she** seemed to be upset.
Not correct: Your mother was very quiet; seemed to be upset.

Correct: **There** is not much time left.
Not correct: Not much time left.

668.4   ## Repeated Words

Do not repeat the subject of a clause or sentence.

Correct: The doctor prescribed an antibiotic.
Not correct: The doctor, **she** prescribed an antibiotic.

Do not repeat an object in an adjective dependent clause.

Correct: I forgot the flowers that I intended to give to my hosts.
Not correct: I forgot the flowers that I intended to give **them** to my hosts.

> **Note:** Sometimes the relative pronoun that begins the adjective dependent clause is omitted but understood.

I forgot the flowers I intended to give to my hosts.
(The relative pronoun *that* is omitted.)

Conditional Sentences   669.1

Conditional sentences express a situation requiring that a condition be met in order to be true. Selecting the correct verb tense for use in the two clauses of a conditional sentence can be problematic. Below you will find an explanation of the three types of conditional sentences and the verb tenses that are needed to form them.

1. **Factual conditionals:** The conditional clause begins with *if, when, whenever,* or a similar expression. Furthermore, the verbs in the conditional clause and the main clause should be in the same tense.

   Whenever we **had** time, we **took** a break and **went** for a swim.

2. **Predictive conditionals** express future conditions and possible results. The conditional clause begins with *if* or *unless* and has a present tense verb. The main clause uses a modal (*will, can, should, may, might*) plus the base form of the verb.

   Unless we **find** a better deal, we **will buy** this sound system.

3. **Hypothetical past conditionals** describe a situation that is unlikely to happen or that is contrary to fact. To describe situations in the past, the verb in the conditional clause is in the past perfect tense, and the verb in the main clause is formed from *would have, could have,* or *might have* plus the past participle.

   If we **had started out** earlier, we **would have arrived** on time.

Note: If the hypothetical situation is a present or future one, the verb in the conditional clause is in the past tense, and the verb in the main clause is formed from *would, could,* or *might* plus the base form of the verb.

   If we **bought** groceries once a week, we **would** not **have** to go to the store so often.

Quoted and Reported Speech   669.2

Quoted speech is the use of exact words from another source in your own writing; you must enclose these words in quotation marks. It is also possible to report nearly exact words without quotation marks. This is called **reported speech,** or indirect quotation. (See page 607 for a review of the use of quotation marks.)

   Direct quotation: Felicia said, "Don't worry about tomorrow."

   Indirect quotation: Felicia said that you don't have to worry about tomorrow.

In the case of a question, when a direct quotation is changed to an indirect quotation, the question mark is not needed.

   Direct quotation: Ahmad asked, "Which of you will give me a hand?"

   Indirect quotation: Ahmad asked which of us would give him a hand.

Notice how pronouns are often changed in indirect quotations.

   Direct quotation: My friends said, "**You**'re crazy."

   Indirect quotation: My friends said that **I** was crazy.

Note: In academic writing, the use of another source's spoken or written words in one's own writing without proper acknowledgment is called *plagiarism*. Plagiarism is severely penalized in academic situations. (See pages 468–471.)

Numbers, Word Parts, and Idioms

Numbers

As a multilingual/ELL learner, you may be accustomed to a way of writing numbers that is different than the way it is done in North America. Become familiar with the North American conventions for writing numbers. Pages 631–632 show you how numbers are written and punctuated in both word and numeral form.

670.1   Using Punctuation with Numerals

Note that the **period** is used to express percentages (5.5%, 75.9%) and the **comma** is used to organize large numbers into units (7,000; 23,100; 231,990,000). Commas are not used, however, in writing the year (2011). (Also see 611.1 and 611.6.)

670.2   Cardinal Numbers

Cardinal numbers are used when counting a number of parts or objects. Cardinal numbers can be used as nouns (she counted to **ten**), pronouns (I invited many guests, but only **three** came), or adjectives (there are **ten** boys here).

Write out in words the numbers one through one hundred. Numbers 101 and greater are often written as numerals. (See 631.1.)

670.3   Ordinal Numbers

Ordinal numbers show place or succession in a series: the fourth row, the twenty-first century, the tenth time, and so on. Ordinal numbers are used to talk about the parts into which a whole can be divided, such as a fourth or a tenth, and as the denominator in fractions, such as one-fourth or three-fifths. Written fractions can also be used as nouns (I gave him **four-fifths**) or as adjectives (a **four-fifths** majority).

> **Note:** See the list below for names and symbols of the first twenty-five ordinal numbers. Consult a dictionary for a complete list of cardinal and ordinal numbers.

First	1st	Tenth	10th	Nineteenth	19th
Second	2nd	Eleventh	11th	Twentieth	20th
Third	3rd	Twelfth	12th	Twenty-first	21st
Fourth	4th	Thirteenth	13th	Twenty-second	22nd
Fifth	5th	Fourteenth	14th	Twenty-third	23rd
Sixth	6th	Fifteenth	15th	Twenty-fourth	24th
Seventh	7th	Sixteenth	16th	Twenty-fifth	25th
Eighth	8th	Seventeenth	17th		
Ninth	9th	Eighteenth	18th		

Prefixes, Suffixes, and Roots

Following is a list of many common word parts and their meanings. Learning them can help you determine the meaning of unfamiliar words as you come across them in your reading. For instance, if you know that *hemi* means "half," you can conclude that *hemisphere* means "half of a sphere."

Prefixes	Meaning	Suffixes	Meaning
a, an	not, without	able, ible	able, can do
anti, ant	against	age	act of, state of
co, con, com	together, with	al	relating to
di	two, twice	ate	cause, make
dis, dif	apart, away	en	made of
ex, e, ec, ef	out	ence, ency	action, quality
hemi, semi	half	esis, osis	action, process
il, ir, in, im	not	ice	condition, quality
inter	between	ile	relating to
intra	within	ish	resembling
multi	many	ment	act of, state of
non	not	ology	study, theory
ob, of, op, oc	toward, against	ous	full of, having
per	throughout	sion, tion	act of, state of
post	after	some	like, tending to
super, supr	above, more	tude	state of
trans, tra	across, beyond	ward	in the direction of
tri	three		
uni	one		

Roots	Meaning	Roots	Meaning
acu	sharp	ject	throw
am, amor	love, liking	log, ology	word, study, speech
anthrop	man	man	hand
aster, astr	star	micro	small
auto	self	mit, miss	send
biblio	book	nom	law, order
bio	life	onym	name
capit, capt	head	path, pathy	feeling, suffering
chron	time	rupt	break
cit	to call, start	scrib, script	write
cred	believe	spec, spect, spic	look
dem	people	tele	far
dict	say, speak	tempo	time
erg	work	tox	poison
fid, feder	faith, trust	vac	empty
fract, frag	break	ver, veri	true
graph, gram	write, written	zo	animal

Idioms

Idioms are phrases that are used in a special way. An idiom can't be understood just by knowing the meaning of each word in the phrase. It must be learned as a whole. For example, the idiom to *bury the hatchet* means to "settle an argument," even though the individual words in the phrase mean something much different. These pages list some of the common idioms in Canadian English.

a bad apple	• One troublemaker on a team may be called **a bad apple.** (*a bad influence*)
an axe to grind	• Mom has **an axe to grind** with the owners of the dog that dug up her flower garden. (*a problem to settle*)
as the crow flies	• She lives only two kilometres from here **as the crow flies.** (*in a straight line*)
beat around the bush	• Dad said, "Where were you? Don't **beat around the bush.**" (*avoid getting to the point*)
benefit of the doubt	• Ms. Hy gave Henri the **benefit of the doubt** when he explained why he fell asleep in class. (*another chance*)
beyond the shadow of a doubt	• Salvatore won the fifty-metre dash **beyond the shadow of a doubt.** (*for certain*)
blew my top	• When my money got stolen, I **blew my top.** (*showed great anger*)
bone to pick	• Nick had a **bone to pick** with Adrian when he learned they both liked the same girl. (*problem to settle*)
break the ice	• Shanta was the first to **break the ice** in the room full of new students. (*start a conversation*)
burn the midnight oil	• Carmen had to **burn the midnight oil** the day before the big test. (*work late into the night*)
chomping at the bit	• Dwayne was **chomping at the bit** when it was his turn to bat. (*eager, excited*)
cold shoulder	• Alicia always gives me the **cold shoulder** after our disagreements. (*ignores me*)
cry wolf	• If you **cry wolf** too often, no one will come when you really need help. (*say you are in trouble when you aren't*)
drop in the bucket	• My donation was a **drop in the bucket.** (*a small amount compared with what's needed*)
face the music	• José had to **face the music** when he got caught cheating on the test. (*deal with the punishment*)
flew off the handle	• Tramayne **flew off the handle** when he saw his little brother playing with matches. (*became very angry*)
floating on air	• Teresa was **floating on air** when she read the letter. (*feeling very happy*)

food for thought	• The coach gave us some **food for thought** when she said that winning isn't everything. *(something to think about)*
get down to business	• In five minutes you need to **get down to business** on this assignment. *(start working)*
get the upper hand	• The other team will **get the upper hand** if we don't play better in the second half. *(probably win)*
go overboard	• The teacher told us not **to go overboard** with fancy lettering on our posters. *(do too much)*
hit the ceiling	• Rosa **hit the ceiling** when she saw her sister painting the television. *(was very angry)*
hit the hay	• Patrice **hit the hay** early because she was tired. *(went to bed)*
in a nutshell	• **In a nutshell,** Coach Roby told us to play our best. *(to summarize)*
in the nick of time	• Zong grabbed his little brother's hand **in the nick of time** before he touched the hot pan. *(just in time)*
in the same boat	• My friend and I are **in the same boat** when it comes to doing Saturday chores. *(have the same problem)*
iron out	• Jamil and his brother were told to **iron out** their differences about cleaning their room. *(solve, work out)*
it stands to reason	• **It stands to reason** that if you keep lifting weights, you will get stronger. *(it makes sense)*
knuckle down	• Grandpa told me to **knuckle down** at school if I want to be a doctor. *(work hard)*
learn the ropes	• Being new in school, I knew it would take some time to **learn the ropes.** *(get to know how things are done)*
let's face it	• "**Let's face it!**" said Mr. Sills. "You're a better long-distance runner than you are a sprinter." *(let's admit it)*
let the cat out of the bag	• Tia **let the cat out of the bag** and got her sister in trouble. *(told a secret)*
lose face	• If I strike out again, I will **lose face.** *(be embarrassed)*
nose to the grindstone	• If I keep my **nose to the grindstone,** I will finish my homework in one hour. *(working hard)*
on cloud nine	• Walking home from the party, I was **on cloud nine.** *(feeling very happy)*
on pins and needles	• I was **on pins and needles** as I waited to see the doctor. *(feeling nervous)*
over and above	• **Over and above** the assigned reading, I read two library books. *(in addition to)*

put his foot in his mouth	• Chivas **put his foot in his mouth** when he called his teacher by the wrong name. *(said something embarrassing)*
put your best foot forward	• Grandpa said that whenever you do something, you should **put your best foot forward.** *(do the best that you can do)*
rock the boat	• The coach said, "Don't **rock the boat** if you want to stay on the team." *(cause trouble)*
rude awakening	• I had a **rude awakening** when I saw the letter *F* at the top of my French quiz. *(sudden, unpleasant surprise)*
save face	• Grant tried to **save face** when he said he was sorry for making fun of me in class. *(fix an embarrassing situation)*
see eye to eye	• My sister and I finally **see eye to eye** about who gets to use the phone first after school. *(are in agreement)*
sight unseen	• Grandma bought the television **sight unseen.** *(without seeing it first)*
take a dim view	• My brother will **take a dim view** if I don't help him at the store. *(disapprove)*
take it with a grain of salt	• If my sister tells you she has no homework, **take it with a grain of salt.** *(don't believe everything you're told)*
take the bull by the horns	• This team needs to **take the bull by the horns** to win the game. *(take control)*
through thick and thin	• Max and I will be friends **through thick and thin.** *(in good times and in bad times)*
time flies	• When you're having fun, **time flies.** *(time passes quickly)*
time to kill	• We had **time to kill** before the stadium would open. *(extra time)*
under the weather	• I was feeling **under the weather,** so I didn't go to school. *(sick)*
word of mouth	• We found out who the new teacher was by **word of mouth.** *(talking to other people)*

Note: Like idioms, collocations are groups of words that often appear together. They may help you identify different senses of a word; for example, *old* means slightly different things in these collocations: *old man, old friends.* You will find sentence construction easier if you check for collocations.

Targeting Trouble Spots

A sentence that is perfectly acceptable in one language may be unacceptable when directly translated into English. For example, many East Asian languages do not use articles, so using these words can be a challenge to learners of English. The following pages will help you target trouble spots for your general language group.

Help for Speakers of Latin Languages

Advice	DO NOT Write . . .	DO Write . . .
Study the use of count and noncount nouns (655.1–656.2).	I have three homeworks.	I have three homework assignments. *or* I have three types of homework.
Do not omit the subject, *it* as subject, or *there* with delayed subjects (586.5, 668.3).	Is hot sitting in this room. Are going to the theatre.	It is hot sitting in this room. We are going to the theatre.
Place most subjects before the verb (667).	Gave I the tutor my thanks.	I gave the tutor my thanks.
Avoid using *the* with certain generalizations (657.1).	The business is a difficult major.	Business is a difficult major.
Avoid using *the* with singular proper nouns (657.1).	The April is the cruellest month.	April is the cruellest month.
Avoid double subjects (668.4).	My mother she is a nurse.	My mother is a nurse.
Learn whether to use a gerund or an infinitive after a verb (659.2–660.1).	The professor wants finishing the paperwork. She regrets to wait until the last minute.	The professor wants to finish the paperwork. She regrets waiting until the last minute.
Do not use *which* to refer to people (654.7).	The professors which teach English are here.	The professors who teach English are here. *or* The professors that teach English are here.
Avoid double negatives (668.1).	I never got no assignment.	I never got the assignment. *or* I got no assignment.

Help for Speakers of European Languages

Advice	DO NOT Write . . .	DO Write . . .
Do not omit the subject, *it* as a subject, or *there* with delayed subjects (586.5, 668.3).	Are thousands of books in the library. Is okay to talk.	There are thousands of books in the library. It is okay to talk.
Avoid using *the* with certain generalizations and singular proper nouns (657.1).	I excel at the physics. The Professor Smith marks grammar errors.	I excel at physics. Professor Smith marks grammar errors.
Learn to use progressive verb tenses (659.1).	I still work on my term paper.	I am working on my term paper.
Learn whether to use a gerund or an infinitive after a verb (659.2–660.1).	The students need finishing their projects. The professors finished to grade the papers.	The students need to finish their projects. The professors finished grading the papers.
Avoid placing adverbs between verbs and direct objects (665.2).	I wrote very quickly the first draft.	I wrote the first draft very quickly.
Do not use *which* to refer to people (654.7).	I am one of the students which sing in the choir.	I am one of the students who sing in the choir.

Help for Speakers of African and Caribbean Languages

Advice	DO NOT Write . . .	DO Write . . .
Avoid double subjects (668.4).	The professor she gave us an assignment.	The professor gave us an assignment.
Use plural nouns after plural numbers (658.1).	The class has two professor.	The class has two professors.
Use the correct form of the *be* verb (575.1).	The union be having a blood drive. We be going.	The union is having a blood drive. We are going.
Make subjects and verbs agree in number (593.2).	She have her own notes. They finishes on time.	She has her own notes. They finish on time.
Use past tense verbs correctly (576).	When the semester began, I study hard.	When the semester began, I studied hard.
Study the rules for article use (656.3–657.1).	I need to buy computer. Entrance exam is required.	I need to buy a computer. An entrance exam is required.

Help for Speakers of East Asian Languages

Advice	DO NOT Write ...	DO Write ...
Use plural forms of nouns (658.1).	I have three difficult class.	I have three difficult classes.
Learn to use adjectival forms (664.1–665.1).	He is a very intelligence professor.	He is a very intelligent professor.
Use the objective case of pronouns (571.1).	The tutor helps I with homework.	The tutor helps me with homework.
Include a subject (or *there*) (586.5, 668.3).	Is good to be here. Are many parts.	It is good to be here. There are many parts.
Study subject–verb agreement (593.2).	The course have a long reading list.	The course has a long reading list.
Study past tenses (576).	We study yesterday. At first, I don't get it.	We studied yesterday. At first, I didn't get it.
Use articles—*a, an,* and *the* (656.3–657.1).	I want to be nurse.	I want to be a nurse.
Study conjunction use (583.1–583.5).	Though she studies, but she struggles.	Though she studies, she struggles.
Learn whether to use a gerund or an infinitive (659.2–660.1).	The students need helping each other study.	The students need to help each other study.

Help for Speakers of Middle Eastern Languages

Advice	DO NOT Write ...	DO Write ...
Study pronoun gender and case (573.1–573.3).	My mother works hard at his job. Give she credit.	My mother works hard at her job. Give her credit.
Don't include a pronoun after a relative clause (590.3, 668.4).	The study space that I share with two others it is too small.	The study space that I share with two others is too small.
Place most subjects before the verb (667).	Received the students the assignment.	The students received the assignment.
Don't overuse progressive verb tenses (659.1).	I am needing a nap. I am wanting food.	I need a nap. I want food.
Use the definite article *the* correctly (657.1).	Union is closed during the July.	The union is closed during July.

Index